Lecture Notes in Computer Science 13202

More information about this series at https://link.springer.com/bookseries/558

Meikang Qiu · Keke Gai · Han Qiu (Eds.)

Smart Computing and Communication

6th International Conference, SmartCom 2021
New York City, NY, USA, December 29–31, 2021
Proceedings

Editors
Meikang Qiu (iD)
Texas A&M University-Commerce
Commerce, TX, USA

Keke Gai (iD)
Beijing Institute of Technology
Beijing, Beijing, China

Han Qiu (iD)
Tsinghua University
Beijing, China

ISSN 0302-9743   ISSN 1611-3349 (electronic)
Lecture Notes in Computer Science
ISBN 978-3-030-97773-3   ISBN 978-3-030-97774-0 (eBook)
https://doi.org/10.1007/978-3-030-97774-0

This Springer imprint is published by the registered company Springer Nature Switzerland AG
The registered company address is: Gewerbestrasse 11, 6330 Cham, Switzerland

Preface

This volume contains the papers presented at SmartCom 2021: the Sixth International Conference on Smart Computing and Communication held during December 29–31, 2021. Originally planned to take place in New York City, USA, the conference was held virtually owing to the outbreak of COVID-19.

There were 165 submissions. Each submission was reviewed by at least three reviewers, and on average three Program Committee members. The committee decided to accept 44 regular papers.

Recent booming developments in web-based technologies and mobile applications have facilitated a dramatic growth in the implementation of new techniques, such as cloud computing, big data, pervasive computing, the Internet of Things, security and blockchain, and social cyber-physical systems. Enabling a smart life has become a popular research topic with an urgent demand. Therefore, SmartCom 2021 focused on both smart computing and communications fields and aimed to collect recent academic work to improve the research and practical application in the field.

The scope of SmartCom 2021 was broad, from smart data to smart communications, and from smart cloud computing to smart security. The conference gathered all high-quality research/industrial papers related to smart computing and communications and aimed at proposing a reference guideline for further research. SmartCom 2021 was held online via New York City, USA, and the proceedings are published by Springer.

SmartCom 2021 continued in the series of successful academic get togethers, following SmartCom 2020 (New York, USA), SmartCom 2019 (Birmingham, UK), SmartCom 2018 (Tokyo, Japan), SmartCom 2017 (Shenzhen, China), and SmartCom 2016 (Shenzhen, China).

We would like to thank the conference sponsors: Springer LNCS, the North America Chinese Talents Association, and Longxiang High Tech Group Inc.

December 2021

Meikang Qiu
Keke Gai
Han Qiu

Organization

General Chairs

Zhihui Lv	Fudan University, China
Yongxin Zhu	Chinese Academy of Sciences, China
Cheng Zhang	Ibaraki University, Japan

Program Chairs

Meikang Qiu	Texas A&M University-Commerce, USA
Keke Gai	Beijing Institute of Technology, China
Han Qiu	Tsinghua University, China

Local Chairs

Yonghao Wang	Birmingham City University, UK
Xiangyu Gao	New York University, USA

Publicity Chairs

Yuanchao Shu	Microsoft Research Asia, China
Yu Huang	Peking University, China
Zhenyu Guan	Beihang University, China
Tao Ren	Beihang University, China

Program Committee

Yue Hu	Louisiana State University, USA
Aniello Castiglione	University of Salerno, Italy
Maribel Fernandez	King's College London, UK
Hao Hu	Nanjing University, China
Oluwaseyi Oginni	Birmingham City University, UK
Thomas Austin	San Jose State University, USA
Zhiyuan Tan	Edinburgh Napier University, Scotland
Xiang He	Birmingham City University, UK
Peter Bull	QA Ltd, UK
Hendri Murfi	Universitas Indonesia, Indonesia
Bo Du	ZF Friedrichshafen AG, Germany

Cefang Guo	Imperial College London, UK
Zengpeng Li	Lancaster University, UK
Paul Kearney	Birmingham City University, UK
Wenbo Shi	Inha University, South Korea
Pietro Ferrara	JuliaSoft, Italy
Ke Miao	Mitacs Inc., Canada
Xiaohu Zhou	Birmingham City University, UK
Guangxia Xu	Chongqing University of Posts and Telecommunications, China
Kui Zhang	Birmingham City University, UK
Matthew Roach	Swansea University, UK
Chunhua Deng	Wuhan University of Science and Technology, China
Katie Cover	Pennsylvania State University, USA
Jinguang Gu	Wuhan University of Science and Technology, China
Wei Cai	Chinese University of Hong Kong, China
Haikuo Zhang	China Internet Network Information Center, China
Junwei Zhang	Xidian University, China
Vitor Jesus	Birmingham City University, UK
Jue Wang	SCCAS, China
Hao Tang	City University of New York, USA
Md Ali	Rider University, USA
Li Bo	Beihang University, China
Zijian Zhang	Beijing Institute of Technology, China
Ian A. Williams	Birmingham City University, UK
Meng Ma	Peking University, China
Cheng Zhang	Waseda University, Japan
Fausto Spoto	Università degli Studi di, Verona, Italy
Song Yang	Beijing Institute of Technology, China
Lixin Tao	Pace University, USA
Alan Dolhasz	Birmingham City University, UK
Shaojing Fu	National University of Defense Technology, China
Agostino Cortesi	Università Ca' Foscari, Italy
Yunxia Liu	Huazhong University of Science and Technology, China
Yongxin Zhu	Chinese Academy of Sciences, China
Rehan Bhana	Birmingham City University, UK
Songmao Zhang	Chinese Academy of Sciences, China
Dawei Li	Beihang University, China

Jongpil Jeong	Sungkyunkwan University, South Korea
Shuangyin Ren	Chinese Academy of Military Science, China
Ding Wang	Peking University, China
Wenjia Li	New York Institute of Technology, USA
Peng Zhang	Stony Brook University, USA
Wayne Collymore	Birmingham City University, UK
Zehua Guo	Beijing Institute of Technology, China
Jeroen van den Bos	Netherlands Forensic Institute, The Netherlands
Haibo Zhang	University of Otago, New Zealand
Zhiqiang Lin	University of Texas at Dallas, USA
Xingfu Wu	Texas A&M University, USA
Dalei Wu	University of Tennessee at Chattanooga, USA
Jun Zheng	New Mexico Tech, USA
Minzhou Pan	Virginia Tech, USA
Suman Kumar	Troy University, USA
Shui Yu	Deakin University, Australia
Jeremy Foss	Birmingham City University, UK
Cham Athwal	Birmingham City University, UK
Petr Matousek	Brno University of Technology, Czech Republic
Javier Lopez	University of Malaga, Spain
Andrew Aftelak	Birmingham City University, UK
Yi Zheng	Virginia Tech, USA
Dong Dai	Texas Tech University, USA
Hiroyuki Sato	University of Tokyo, Japan
Bo Luo	University of Kansas, USA
Syed Rizvi	Pennsylvania State University, USA
Paul Rad	Rackspace, USA
Ruisheng Shi	Beijing University of Posts and Telecommunications, China
Fuji Ren	University of Tokushima, Japan
Jian Zhang	Institute of Software, Chinese Academy of Sciences, China
Chungsik Song	San Jose State University, USA
Sang-Yoon Chang	Advanced Digital Science Center, Singapore
Mohan Muppidi	University of Texas at San Antonio, USA
Kan Zhang	Tsinghua University, China
Malik Awan	Cardiff University, UK
Ming Xu	Hangzhou Dianzi University, China
Allan Tomlinson	Royal Holloway, University of London, UK
Long Fei	Google Inc., USA
Emmanuel Bernardez	IBM Research, USA

Contents

Short Papers

Regular Papers

Efficient Online Service Based on Go-Tensorflow in the Middle-Station Scenario of Grid Service

Peng Liu[1], Yiming Lu[1,2], Guoqing Wang[1], and Wang Zhou[2(✉)]

[1] State Grid Shanghai Energy Interconnection Research Institute, Beijing 100000, China
{liupeng1,luyiming,wangguoqing}@epri.sgcc.com.cn
[2] China Southern Power Grid Digital Grid Research Institute Co. Ltd.,
Guangzhou 510000, China

Abstract. The application of machine learning and deep learning is widely used in the business of the power grid. However, the business of the power grid is complicated, and the online service of deep learning faces greater performance challenges. In order to solve this problem, this paper proposes an online service EOSP based on go-tensorflow. EOSP service is divided into 3 modules, namely model configuration module, execution engine module and model management module. The model configuration module mainly includes functions such as online model configuration and model configuration information synchronization. The execution engine can execute graphical model calls, and has optimized performance based on the characteristics of golang language coroutines. The model management module is responsible for model registration, update, uninstallation and version management. Experiments show that the EOSP service is highly stable, which greatly reduces the time consumption of online services.

Keywords: Go-tensorflow · Go · Tf-servering · DAG · Online service · Grid

1 Introduction

With the rapid development of machine learning [1–3] and deep learning [4–6], a large number of machine learning and deep learning applications have begun to appear in the business of the power grid. Online service [7–9] is an unavoidable topic for machine learning and deep learning applications. With the surge in traffic, high-performance online services have become a topic of concern. Among them, the online model of the terminal [10] equipment [11–13] is a relatively novel issue. How to efficiently call machine learning and deep learning models for terminal devices will become an important research direction of edge computing [14–16]. Major Internet companies have recently launched a lot of related research, such as Alibaba, Tencent, Meituan, Megvii, and SenseTime.

The State Grid has a lot of terminal equipment, which provides a guarantee for high-performance and highly reliable grid services. High-performance online services are very important for terminal equipment. On the one hand, terminal devices are better, more stable and provide more services. On the other hand, a reasonable design can

M. Qiu et al. (Eds.): SmartCom 2021, LNCS 13202, pp. 3–13, 2022.
https://doi.org/10.1007/978-3-030-97774-0_1

provide the same service with a cheaper machine, saving costs. Some machine learning and deep learning models are usually run on terminal equipment, such as XGB [17–19], LightGbm [20–22], CNN [23–25], RNN [26–28], LSTM [29, 30]. In addition, online services are also particularly important for server-side services. High-performance online services can provide more stable services for the business. In response to these problems, this paper proposes to design and implement a high-performance online service EOSP service based on go-tensorflow [31–33].

2   Related Work

With the rapid development of cloud computing [34, 35], big data [36, 37], and machine learning [38], online problems of models have become more and more urgent. The online mode problem has attracted the attention of many large companies such as Alibaba, Meituan, Baidu, and State Grid. Ali's machine learning and deep learning calls use Ali PAI. Ali PAI was originally an internal machine learning platform. Not only supports ParameterServer, but also compatible with Caffe [39–41], PyTorch [42–44] and GPU-based large-scale clusters [45–47]. Meituan uses PMML (Predictive Model Markup Language) [48, 49] to call machine learning and deep learning models. In addition, Google open sourced tf-serving [32] to quickly deploy the model. The business scenario of the State Grid is more complicated. This article has launched a research on online services in the power grid scenario.

3   EOSP Service

3.1   EOSP Service Operation Framework

The EOSP service is mainly based on the business scenario of the power grid, and its design idea is to achieve high performance with the help of technologies such as Go-tensorflow and golang coroutines. EOSP will use algorithms such as BFS to traverse the model DAG, and then use the coroutine to execute. EOSP service is divided into 3 parts, namely online service configuration module, online service execution engine, and model management module (Fig. 1).

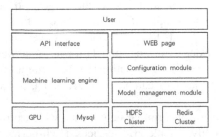

Fig. 1. EOSP overall architecture diagram.

Online Service Configuration Module. Service configuration is the first step in providing online services. Due to the complexity of the State Grid online service, multiple model files will be called for one request. Therefore, this article designs it as a model DAG. The user constructs the model DAG by dragging and dropping on the web page. Service configuration information will be synchronized to Redis, reducing the pressure on the database.

Execution Engine Module. The execution engine is the core module of EOSP, and the main core technologies are Go-tensorflow, coroutine and BFS algorithm. The execution engine traverses the nodes on the model DAG through the BFS algorithm, and uses the coroutine to execute the model call. When executing the next level node, the execution engine will wait for the node's upstream node to finish executing. In addition, the EOSP service uses the idea of the LRU algorithm to optimize the memory.

Model Management Module. The model management module is mainly responsible for functions such as model registration, update, uninstallation and model version management. In order to update the data in real time, the timing task in EOSP will periodically synchronize the model information to the Redis cluster. The execution engine detects the update and will retrieve the model file again.

3.2 EOSP Online Service Configuration Module

The online service configuration module is the foundation of EOSP service and provides online service configuration capabilities. The online service configuration module mainly has two aspects, namely the synchronization of the DAG of the online service model and the online service configuration.

How to Configure the Online Service Model DAG. There are two methods for constructing the online service model DAG, which are web pages and API interfaces. Users can choose the right way according to the needs of the business. The bottom layer of the Web page mode is also realized by calling the API interface. The following figure is an algorithm for processing the model DAG into JSON format data (Fig. 2).

```
1  flag ← True, father ← None , modellist ← [];
2  while flag do
3  |    model ← SelectModel() ;
4  |    model.addFateher(father);
5  |    father ← SetFather(father) ;
6  |    modellist.append(model);
7  |    flag ← SetDAGCondition(flag) ;
8  end
9  return modellist
```
Algorithm 1: An algorithm for gathering DAG model information

Fig. 2. A algorithm for gathering DAG model information overall architecture diagram.

Modellist is an array that stores data of Model type. An array of parents is maintained inside the Model. Parents hold the upstream Model of each Model. If the parents is empty, it means that the model does not depend on other models. The SelectModel function will select a model each time. The model calls the addFather function to specify the parent node for the model. After the model is configured, it will be added to the modellist. The SetDAGCondition function is used to set the build status. When the model DAG is built, the SetDAGCondition function will set the flag to false.

Synchronization of Online Service Configuration. The synchronization of online configuration information is particularly important. The model DAG configured by the user will be processed into JSON format and synchronized to the Redis cluster. The model DAG in the figure below contains 4 nodes, and Father and Name are used to identify the relationship between the nodes (Fig. 3).

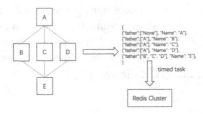

Fig. 3. Configure the synchronization model.

3.3 Execution Engine Module

The model execution engine is mainly divided into 3 sub-modules, namely the model building module, the model DAG execution module, and the execution engine memory optimization module.

Model Building Model. Model building is the basis of the execution engine, which contains 3 modules, which are divided into Model_Map, Syn_model and ModelLoading. Model_Map is mainly used to store the instances of Go-tensorflow after loading the model. Syn_model is a timed task, which regularly obtains the configuration information of the model from Redis, and then saves it in the memory. The ModelLoading module will obtain the latest model file from the HDFS cluster based on the information obtained by Syn_model. The figure below is a schematic diagram of the model building blocks (Fig. 4).

How to Perform DAG Model Configuration. Model execution is the core part of the execution engine. The model execution mainly relies on the BFS algorithm and Golang's coroutine. The execution engine will use the BFS algorithm to traverse the nodes of the model DAG. The model without a parent node is called first. A dependent node will wait for the dependent node to be executed before execution. When the execution engine executes a single-node model call, it will start a new coroutine to execute it. Therefore, the traversal of the model DAG does not block, and the performance is better (Fig. 5).

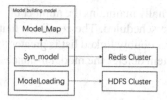

Fig. 4. Model building diagram.

```
input : modellist
1 runninglist ←[], finished ←[];
2 InitModelList(modellist, runninglist, finished);
3 if len (runninglist) == 0 then
4 |   return bool
5 end
6 while len(modellist) == 0 and len(runninglist) == 0 do
7 |   model ← CheckModelCondition(modellist, runninglist) ;
8 |   if modell =None then
9 |   |   finished.append(model);
10 |   |   CheckChildModel(model, runninglist) ;
11 |   end
12 end
```
Algorithm 2: An algorithm for building DAG model

Fig. 5. An algorithm for building DAG model.

Both runninglist and finished are arrays used to store instances of model nodes. The runninglist is used to store the running model node instances. Finished is used to store the completed model node instance. The InitModelList function will start the model nodes without parent nodes in the modellist and store them in the runninglist. If the runninglist is empty, the operation ends. The CheckModelCondition function is used to obtain the executed model nodes in the runninglist. If model is not None, it will be added to Finished. The CheckChildModel function detects the child nodes of the model, and if the self-node meets the operating requirements, it will be added to the runninglist. Repeated execution, until runninglist and modellist are empty, the function is executed.

Memory Optimization of Execution Engine. In order to allow EOSP service nodes to support more online access, it is necessary to optimize the memory of model instances. The execution of machine learning and deep learning models is relatively time-consuming. A certain number of models need to be maintained on a node, so as to ensure the stable operation of the system and maximize the resource utilization of the node. The implementation of the memory optimization of the execution engine refers to the memory optimization algorithm LRU. The system maintains a doubly linked list in the memory, as shown in the following figure (Fig. 6).

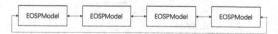

Fig. 6. Memory optimized doubly linked list.

In order to facilitate management and improve the efficiency of query modification, this article encapsulates the model instance into EOSPModel. EOSPModel is a node of a doubly linked list, which internally maintains the number of online services called by the model and the time it was last scheduled. The condition that the memory optimization triggers is that the length of the doubly linked list is greater than the threshold. After the threshold is triggered, the system deletes the model instance on the linked list and stores it on the disk.

3.4 Model Management Module

The model management module mainly includes model registration, model update, model uninstallation and model version management.

How to Perform DAG Model Configuration. When the user uses the model for the first time, he needs to register in the system, fill in the relevant information, and then he can use it after registration. After the configuration information of the model is changed, the configuration information will be synchronized to the Redis cluster, and the online model will take effect after the timing period. The following table shows some key fields of the model configuration (Table 1).

Table 1. Main parameters of model management.

Parameter	Font size and style
ModelName	Model name
Version	The version of the model
Path	Model file storage path
Condtion	The state of the model
Count	The number of online services that rely on the model

Model Files Synchronization Module. The main function of the model synchronization module is to detect whether there is a model file update. The model synchronization module exists in the system in the form of a scheduled task SynModel, which will monitor whether there is the latest version of the model in the specified file path of HDFS. When SynModel detects that HDFS has an updated model file, it will update the model information to the Mysql database (Fig. 7).

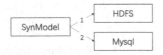

Fig. 7. Model file synchronization diagram.

4 EOSP Service

The experiment mainly includes functional test, accuracy test and performance test. Functional testing includes testing and unit testing of various basic functions of EOSP. The accuracy test mainly compares whether the output results of the traditional model call and the EOSP model call are consistent. The performance test mainly tests the QPS and average time consumption of a single node. The experimental data comes from the National Grid Service Center, and the data set size is about 7G. The experimental environment is a 16G, 8-core, 100G storage server. The service node uses Docker container to simulate. The Docker version is 18.09.

Experiment One. The function test of this article mainly starts from three aspects, namely the function test of the configuration module, the function test of the execution engine and the function test of the model management. Finally, a unit test will be performed. If the test passes, the EOSP service is operating normally (Table 2).

Table 2. Results of experiment one.

Function	Result	Function	Result
Model configuration function	Fit	Model loading function	Fit
Synchronization of model configuration	Fit	Model registration, uninstall and other functions	Fit
Execution engine synchronization function	Fit	Model synchronization function	Fit
Execution function of model DAG	Fit	Unit test	Fit

EOSP service functions are normal and meet the design requirements.

Experiment Two. The accuracy of EOSP is mainly tested from two aspects, namely the single-node test and the model DAG test. In order to test the simplicity of the test. Since the model DAG test is more accurate than the but node test, this article only tests the model DAG. If the input is the same as the traditional way and the output obtained is also the same, it indicates the accuracy of the EOSP service. The test cases for the accuracy test are 1000 inputs. The test results are shown in the table below (Table 3).

Table 3. Results of experiment two.

Tradition	EOSP	1000 same output number
2 nodes	2 nodes	1000
4 nodes	4 nodes	1000
5 nodes	5 nodes	1000

According to the input in the above table, the accuracy of the EOSP service is required by the load. The input that is the same as the traditional processing method of the power grid, the output obtained is 100% the same. The accuracy load requirements of EOSP service.

Experiment Three. The performance of EOSP service is mainly measured by two indicators, QPS and average Cost during allocation. In order to test the performance of EOSP service, this paper uses the services of two model nodes, three model nodes and four model nodes to verify the performance of EOSP. The EADP service is built in a Docker container. This article will separately perform stress testing on EOSP services and traditional services. The results of the test are shown in the table below (Table 4).

Table 4. Results of experiment three.

Tradition	QPS	Cost	Tradition	QPS	Cost
2 nodes	40	38.5 ms	2 nodes	180	13.1 ms
4 nodes	35	44.7 ms	4 nodes	130	15.8 ms
5 nodes	33	48.3 ms	5 nodes	126	16.2 ms

As shown in the above table, the performance of the EOS As shown in the above table, compared with the traditional online services of the power grid, the EOSP service has made great progress in both QPS and average time-consuming indicators. Therefore, the EOSP service meets the design requirements in terms of performance.

5 Conclusion

In order to improve the performance of online services, this paper proposes an online service EOSP based on go-tensorfow. EOSP is divided into online service configuration module, execution engine module and model management module. Considering the complexity of grid online services, the EOSP service supports DAG-type model access to improve the efficiency of model execution. At the same time, EOSP service also increases the reuse rate of the model. In summary, EOPS meets the business needs of the power grid and improves efficiency.

Acknowledgment. This work financially supported by Science and Technology Program of State Grid Corporation of China under Grant No.: 5700-202055183A-0-0-00, which named Research on Technology of Big Data Monitoring Analysis in Power Grid by Coordination of Data Middle platform & Edge Calculation. Without their help, it would be much harder to finish the program and this paper.

References

1. Witten, I.H., et al.: Data Mining: Practical Machine Learning Tools and Techniques, 4th edn. Morgan Kaufmann, Cambridge (2017)
2. Marsland, S.: Machine Learning: An Algorithmic Perspective, 2nd edn., p. 2014. CRC Press, Boca Raton (2015)
3. Anonymous: Machine learning. Machine Learning (1986)
4. Jianya, G., Shunping, J.: Photogrammetry and deep learning. Ce Hui Xue Bao **47**(6), 693–704 (2018)
5. Schmidhuber, J.: Deep learning in neural networks: an overview. Neural Netw. **61**, 85–117 (2015)
6. Shi, H., Xu, M., Li, R.: Deep learning for household load forecasting-a novel pooling deep RNN. IEEE Trans. Smart Grid **9**(5), 5271–5280 (2018)
7. Hsieh, J., et al.: Post-adoption switching behavior for online service substitutes: a perspective of the push–pull–mooring framework. Comput. Hum. Behav. **28**(5), 1912–1920 (2012)
8. Brenot, H., et al.: Support to Aviation Control Service (SACS): an online service for near-real-time satellite monitoring of volcanic plumes. Nat. Hazards Earth Syst. Sci. **14**(5), 1099–1123 (2014). https://doi.org/10.5194/nhess-14-1099-2014
9. Mothersbaugh, D.L., et al.: Disclosure antecedents in an online service context: the role of sensitivity of information. J. Serv. Res. **15**(1), 76–98 (2012)
10. Chung, Y.-L., Wu, S.: An effective toss-and-catch algorithm for fixed-rail mobile terminal equipment that ensures reliable transmission and non-interruptible handovers. Symmetry (Basel) **13**(4), 582 (2021). https://doi.org/10.3390/sym13040582
11. Hashemi, M.J., Masroor, A., Mosqueda, G.: Implementation of online model updating in hybrid simulation. Earthq. Eng. Struct. Dyn. **43**(3), 395–412 (2014)
12. Abouheaf, M., Gueaieb, W., Lewis, F.: Online model-free reinforcement learning for the automatic control of a flexible wing aircraft. IET Control Theory Appl. **14**(1), 73–84 (2021)
13. Aksoylar, C., Dogramaci Aksoylar, N.: Online model identification and updating in multi-platform pseudo-dynamic simulation of steel structures – experimental applications. J. Earthq. Eng.: JEE 1–25 (2021)
14. Yuying, G., Hui, S., Zhenming, L.: Exploration of OLT converged edge computing for Industrial Internet. Diànzǐ Jìshù Yīngyòng **47**(4), 5–8 (2021)
15. Li, Y., Song, T., Yang, Y.: Combinatorial auction-based mechanism for task offloading in edge computing. Jisuanji Kexue Yu Tansuo **15**(1), 73–83 (2021)
16. Arena, F., Pau, G.: When edge computing meets IoT systems: analysis of case studies. China Commun. **17**(10), 50–63 (2020)
17. Chen, T., Guestrin, C.: XGBoost: a scalable tree boosting system (2016). https://doi.org/10.1145/2939672.2939785
18. Li, H., et al.: XGBoost model and its application to personal credit evaluation. IEEE Intell. Syst. **35**(3), 52–61 (2020)
19. Li, Z., et al.: Application of XGBoost in P2P default prediction. In: Journal of Physics Conference Series, vol. 1871, no. 1 (2021)
20. Zhang, J., et al.: LightGBM: an effective and scalable algorithm for prediction of chemical toxicity–application to the Tox21 and mutagenicity data sets. J. Chem. Inf. Model. **59**(10), 4150–4158 (2019)
21. Al-kasassbeh, M., Abbadi, M., Al-Bustanji, A.: LightGBM algorithm for malware detection. In: Arai, K., Kapoor, S., Bhatia, R. (eds.) Intelligent Computing, pp. 391–403. Springer, Cham (2020). https://doi.org/10.1007/978-3-030-52243-8_28
22. Sun, X., Liu, M., Sima, Z.: A novel cryptocurrency price trend forecasting model based on LightGBM. Finan. Res. Lett. **32**, 101084 (2020)

23. Smirnov, E.A., et al.: Comparison of regularization methods for ImageNet classification with deep convolutional neural networks. AASRI Procedia **6**, 89–94 (2014)
24. Krizhevsky, A., Sutskever, I., Hinton, G.: ImageNet classification with deep convolutional neural networks. Commun. ACM **60**(6), 84–90 (2017)
25. Rastegari, M., et al.: XNOR-net: ImageNet classification using binary convolutional neural networks. In: Leibe, B., Matas, J., Sebe, N., Welling, M. (eds.) Computer Vision – ECCV 2016, pp. 525–542. Springer, Cham (2016). https://doi.org/10.1007/978-3-319-46493-0_32
26. Zaremba, W., Sutskever, I., Vinyals, O.: Recurrent Neural Network Regularization, arXiv: 1409.2329 (2014)
27. Chien, J., Lu, T.: Deep recurrent regularization neural network for speech recognition (2015). https://doi.org/10.1109/ICASSP.2015.7178834
28. Albahar, M.A.: Recurrent neural network model based on a new regularization technique for real-time intrusion detection in SDN environments. Secur. Commun. Netw. **2019**, 1–9 (2019)
29. Shi, X., et al.: Convolutional LSTM network: a machine learning approach for precipitation nowcasting (2015)
30. Zhao, R., et al.: Learning to monitor machine health with convolutional bi-directional LSTM networks. Sensors (Basel, Switzerland) **17**(2), 273 (2017). https://doi.org/10.3390/s17020273
31. Rampasek, L., Goldenberg, A.: TensorFlow: biology's gateway to deep learning? Cell Syst. **2**(1), 12–14 (2016)
32. Cabañas, R., Salmerón, A., Masegosa, A.R.: InferPy: probabilistic modeling with Tensorflow made easy. Knowl.-Based Syst. **168**, 25–27 (2019)
33. Hao, L., et al.: TensorD: a tensor decomposition library in TensorFlow. Neurocomput. (Amsterdam) **318**, 196–200 (2018)
34. Gai, K., Qiu, M., Elnagdy, S.: A novel secure big data cyber incident analytics framework for cloud-based cybersecurity insurance. In: IEEE BigDataSecurity (2016)
35. Lu, Z., Wang, N., Wu, J., Qiu, M.: IoTDeM: an IoT big data-oriented MapReduce performance prediction extended model in multiple edge clouds. JPDC **118**, 316–327 (2018)
36. Guo, Y., Zhuge, Q., Hu, J., et al.: Optimal data allocation for scratch-pad memory on embedded multi-core systems. In: IEEE ICPP Conference, pp. 464–471 (2011)
37. Lu, R., Jin, X., Zhang, S., Qiu, M., Wu, X.: A study on big knowledge and its engineering issues. IEEE Trans. Knowl. Data Eng. **31**(9), 1630–1644 (2018)
38. Qiu, H., Qiu, M., Lu, Z.: Selective encryption on ECG data in body sensor network based on supervised machine learning. Inf. Fusion **55**, 59–67 (2020)
39. Du, Y., et al.: A deep learning network-assisted bladder tumour recognition under cystoscopy based on Caffe deep learning framework and EasyDL platform. Int. J. Med. Robot. Comput. Assisted Surg. **17**(1), 1–8 (2021). https://doi.org/10.1002/rcs.2169
40. Roy, P., et al.: NUMA-Caffe: numa-aware deep learning neural networks. ACM Trans. Archit. Code Optim. **15**(2), 1–26 (2018)
41. Garea, A.S., Heras, D.B., Argüello, F.: Caffe CNN-based classification of hyperspectral images on GPU. J. Supercomput. **75**(3), 1065–1077 (2018). https://doi.org/10.1007/s11227-018-2300-2
42. Li, S., et al.: PyTorch distributed: experiences on accelerating data parallel training. Proc. VLDB Endow. **13**(12), 3005–3018 (2020)
43. Steppa, C., Holch, T.L.: HexagDLy—processing hexagonally sampled data with CNNs in PyTorch. Softwarex **9**, 193–198 (2019)
44. Gao, X., et al.: TorchANI: a free and open source PyTorch-based deep learning implementation of the ANI neural network potentials. J. Chem. Inf. Model. **60**(7), 3408–3415 (2020)
45. Le Grand, S., Götz, A.W., Walker, R.C.: SPFP: speed without compromise—a mixed precision model for GPU accelerated molecular dynamics simulations. Comput. Phys. Commun. **184**(2), 374–380 (2013)

46. Owens, J.D., et al.: GPU computing. Proc. IEEE **96**(5), 879–899 (2008)
47. Hong, C.-H., Spence, I., Nikolopoulos, D.S.: GPU virtualization and scheduling methods: a comprehensive survey. ACM Comput. Surv. **50**(3), 1–37 (2017). https://doi.org/10.1145/306 8281
48. Guazzelli, A., et al.: PMML: an open standard for sharing models. R J. **1**(1), 60 (2009). https://doi.org/10.32614/RJ-2009-010
49. Fernández, S., et al.: Using automated planning for improving data mining processes. Knowl. Eng. Rev. **28**(2), 157–173 (2013)

Resource Modeling of Power Communication Packet Optical Transport Network

ZhiXin Lu[✉], LianYu Fu, YiZhao Liu, and XiYang Yin

State Grid Tianjin Electric Power Company, Tianjin 300100, China
xiyang.yin@tj.sgcc.com.cn

Abstract. With the explosive growth of information, data traffic has gradually become the main body occupying the communication network, and the grouping of services and carriers is the current general trend. The industry has put forward a new power communication network POTN (Packet Optical Transmission Network), POTN can carry on the unified scheduling and management to different levels. After years of development, the POTN network has gradually matured, but there are still some problems such as weak communication network structure and insufficient transmission capacity. This paper mainly studies the POTN resource modeling, and develops the simulation system based on the POTN, realizes the mapping and reuse of client services, improves the protection mechanism of the POTN network, and completes the reasonable planning and optimization of the transmission network topology. Aiming at the convergence problem of multiple services based on POTN technology, the aggregation algorithm is designed to improve the bandwidth and port resource utilization of devices, Finally, the simulation analysis of the experiment provides important theoretical support for the construction of equipment model and network topology.

Keywords: Power communication network · Packet optical transmission network · Mapping and reuse · Protection mechanism · Aggregation algorithm

1 Introduction

In recent years, the trend of service types to multiple transformation, network traffic is no longer confined to the group service, makes it is hard to balance the large capacity of the existing transport network transmission and group service efficiently deal with these two aspects [1].

At present, the mainstream networking mode of backbone network is SDH (Synchronous Digital Hierarchy)/SMTP, OTN (Optical Transport Network), OTN+SDH/MSTP. As the mainstream IP bearer technology of transmission network, PTN (Packet Transport Network) has issued certain technical standards in aspects of OAM mechanism, network architecture and equipment specifications, among which MPLS-TP related technology is the most widely used [2, 3]. OTN's transmission network system is an improvement on the traditional transmission network technology system [4]. OTN adopts wave division on transmission lines, and introduces electrical

© The Author(s), under exclusive license to Springer Nature Switzerland AG 2022
M. Qiu et al. (Eds.): SmartCom 2021, LNCS 13202, pp. 14–25, 2022.
https://doi.org/10.1007/978-3-030-97774-0_2

layer. Provides technology for transmitting, multiplexing, exchanging and protecting customer signals at sub-wavelengths [5]. The existing backbone network communication network architecture cannot well balance the problem of unified carrying and transmission of services in the network [6]. For example, the service bandwidth that can be carried by PTN network is not large enough, so it can only play the advantages of packet transmission for small particle services. OTN is much less complex than SDH, and it provides large-particle cross-connection capability, has powerful networking protection capability and flexible network scheduling capability [7]. OTN cannot handle packet service transmission problems despite its large transmission capacity [8].

In the face of these problems with the development of power communication network, the POTN technology which has been studied more in recent years can solve these problems well [9]. POTN network inherits the advantages of PTN network and OTN network at the same time, which can not only solve the large capacity of service transmission but also realize the efficient processing of packet service; the POTN network provides high quality of service (QoS) and low delay guarantee, with higher network capacity scalability and networking flexibility; More accurate fault reporting for the entire network, better OAM transmission mechanism, improves fiber resource utilization and management capability [10]. In general, POTN can simultaneously possess many characteristics and advantages of traditional equipment, save the configuration cost of other equipment and facilitate the management of staff. It is an ideal way for the evolution of power backbone communication network [11]. However, there are still some problems that need to be solved urgently [12]. On the one hand, due to the unbalanced distribution of routing resources in the POTN network, the reliability of the network is low. On the other hand, the development of POTN network is seriously hindered by extensive network planning methods, over-reliance on experience in maintenance methods, and unreasonable resource allocation [13]. In order to better the POTN technology applied in the actual scenario of grid, based on the study of network architecture, network technology, also need to bearing, the network simulation technology in many business research and simulation work, including many business carrying problem, need to open small particles and large particles business group uniform bearing isolation, research methods and security; By developing POTN network simulation software, the adaptability of multi-service bearing is verified [14].

In order to solve the problems caused by the unbalanced distribution of POTN transmission network, we propose a method of POTN resource modeling. By using a better planning and optimization method, the POTN transmission network topology can be reasonably planned to improve the utilization rate of the existing network, and the problems of uneven distribution of POTN routing resources and low reliability of the network can be solved. The POTN network simulation system of power communication is developed, and the POTN network is planned. The aggregation algorithm is used to connect services to POTN ports and give full play to the technical advantages of POTN, minimize the total transmission bandwidth after aggregation. Finally, simulation analysis and comparison are carried out through experiments.

2 POTN Network Resource Model Construction

Based on the actual operation data of power grid, the slot resource model, node resource model, link resource model, network and protection resource model and service and channel resource model of power communication POTN optical transmission network are constructed from bottom to top (Fig. 1).

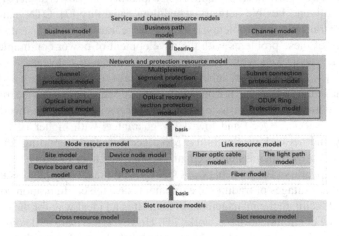

Fig. 1. Whole structure of POTN optical transmission network resource model.

2.1 Slot Resource Model

POTN transmission container resource model is divided into low-order transport containers and high-order transport containers (Fig. 2).

The customer signal is first mapped into the low-order transport container, and then from the low-order Optical channel data unit to the higher-order transport container. POTN devices support unified access and scheduling of packet service and OTN passthrough service in a configurable proportion within a single device, support unified package mapping of packet and OTN passthrough service to ODUK, and then through ODUK multiplexing to optical path frame structure interface, and then common wavelength mixed transmission, support point-to-point, point-to-multipoint, point-to-multipoint service.

2.2 Node and Link Resource Model

Node resource model includes site model, node model, device model and port model. The node model describes the attributes of the node, including the node name, node type, abscissa and ordinate of the node position, etc. The relationships of various models in the node resource model are shown in Fig. 3. Link resource model includes optical link group model, optical link model and optical fiber model. The relationship between optical fiber model, optical link model and optical link group model is shown in Fig. 4.

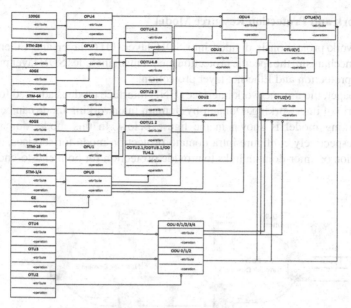

Fig. 2. POTN mapping and multiplexing graph.

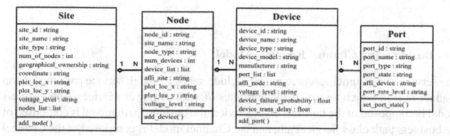

Fig. 3. Resource model relationship of each node.

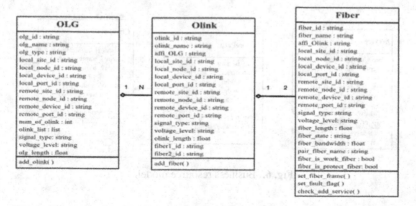

Fig. 4. Diagram of optical link group model, optical link and optical fiber model.

2.3 Network and Protection Resource Model

POTN network protection is divided into SDH layer, OTN layer and Ethernet layer protection mechanism, the specific protection mechanism includes SDH layer protection, OTN layer protection and Ethernet layer protection.

In this paper, the user network interface (UNI) interface mode is adopted for the network scenario of interworking. Domain-by-domain interworking mode can be adopted. The networking model is shown in the figure below. In this mode, domain 1 and domain 2 respectively configure intra-domain protection mode for services, and adopt link protection on inter-domain links to provide protection for both end-to-end services (Fig. 5).

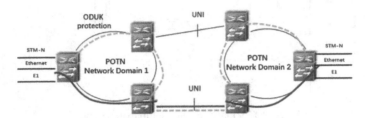

Fig. 5. POTN protection model.

2.4 Business and Channel Resource Model

The service and channel resource model include service model, service path model and channel model, which describes the attributes of various power services. The business model is composed of the business class Service, the business path model is composed of the business path class ServicePath, and the Channel model is composed of the Channel class Channel. The UML class diagrams for the business and channel resource models are shown (Fig. 6).

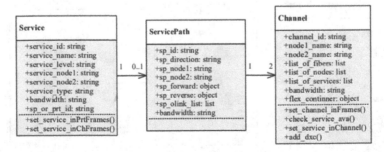

Fig. 6. Business resource model.

3 Development of POTN Network Simulation System

POTN network simulation system is composed of database module, resource simulation module, service function module, service protection module, network analysis module and control module. Among them, the database module is used to store the actual operation data and provide corresponding data interaction for the resource simulation module, the service function module and the service protection module. The control module sends instructions through the socket interface to control the corresponding operation of each module (Fig. 7).

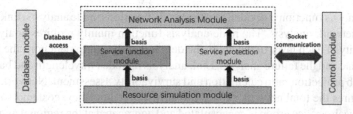

Fig. 7. The overall architecture diagram of simulation system.

3.1 Service Function Module

Service function modules are shown in the figure below. This module is mainly responsible for the management of the POTN service model, which mainly has two functions: service adaptation and service mapping. The main services considered in this system are FE/GE/ 10GE/40GE, STM-1/4/16/64, ODU0/1/2/3 and Optical Channel layer network (OCH). The service is directly mapped to the ODU pipeline for transmission. In this case, if and only if the service type is ODU0/1/2/3, it is possible to place multiple services into a larger ODU pipeline according to the multiplexing system of OTN, and other services need to be mapped to the ODU pipeline with appropriate bandwidth first. If the service is an OCH service, it can be regarded as a light path request directly. Finally, the result of routing selection is loaded into the network original service list (Fig. 8).

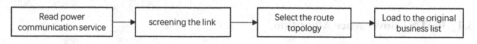

Fig. 8. Function diagram of service function module.

3.2 Service Protection Module

The protection attributes of the services in this system mainly have two kinds: linear network and ring network. For packet layer services with linear protection requirements, 1+1 protection or 1:1 protection of PTN can be adopted, or linear protection of lower layer can be adopted to protect the services according to the situation of business routing. For OTN layer services, linear protection based on ODUK or OCH can be adopted. For services requiring ring network protection, the system supports the transmission of non-ring network protection services over the ring network, which occupy time slots in the ring network in addition to the work and protection slots of normal ring network services. The internal conditions of different wavelengths in different directions between node A and node B in the ring network are shown in the figure. The arrow in the figure indicates the propagation direction.

3.3 Network Analysis Module

Network analysis function is divided into three sub-functions: node analysis, link analysis and entire network analysis. The node analysis function mainly requires analyzing the cross-capacity of each layer of the node, the demand of the equipment port, the load, the utilization rate and the failure analysis. Link analysis includes wavelength and bandwidth statistics, job protection ratio calculation and survivability assessment. Network analysis mainly requires the total network capacity, bandwidth redundancy, cost and so on.

Firstly, each service group is encapsulated and aggregated at the regional aggregation node with different particle sizes, and the bandwidth data of the same service group is read in descending order by bandwidth size. The cross granularity is determined according to the service bandwidth with the maximum bandwidth among the unprocessed services in the same group. Then read the services from large to small from the remaining unprocessed services and aggregate them into the cross granularity. If the bandwidth after aggregation is greater than the cross granularity, the next service with a smaller bandwidth will be skipped until all the services in the service group are traversed or the total bandwidth aggregated is equal to the cross granularity. Recirculation Starts to aggregate remaining services in the service group until all services in the service group are successfully aggregated and updated to the aggregation list (Fig. 9).

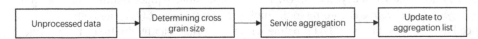

Fig. 9. Function diagram of network analysis module.

3.4 POTN Convergence Algorithm

(1) Description of convergence algorithm

In the electric power communication system, all kinds of grid services in different regions have different destination nodes, among which the source and destination nodes of some grid services belong to the same region. The source and destination nodes of other power grid services belong to different regions. Therefore, in the power grid system, such businesses with the same source and destination nodes can be aggregated by POTN devices and then transmitted, which can give full play to the advantages of POTN devices and reduce equipment costs [15]. The convergence algorithm proposed by us is shown in Fig. 10.

(2) Analysis of convergence algorithm

The simulation of the algorithm is carried out on POTN network simulation system. The original business list was obtained by collecting information through the service function module, and the aggregation list was obtained through the simulation of the algorithm through the network analysis module. The simulation data is mainly based on the sectional business flow of provincial companies, taking into account the dis-patching data network of provincial headquarters, terminals, directly regulated power plants and the business data of local companies. In the simulation, it is assumed that the attributes of aggregation service and the source and destination nodes are the same, and the aggregation results of different devices under different conditions are comprehensively compared.

We input the data of the original data without aggregation service and the data of the business group after aggregation into the POTN network simulation system, which can prove that the system can run normally. Meanwhile, according to the different convergence results of the two, and combined with the actual situation of the power grid business and POTN equipment, we analyze the reasons for the different routing results. It is further proved that the convergence algorithm transmission of power network service adapts to the general trend of the development of power communication.

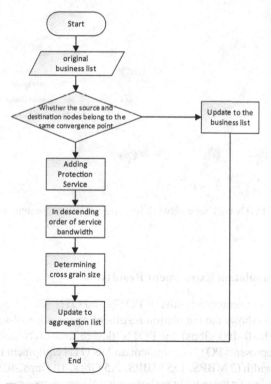

Fig. 10. Flow chart of POTN convergence algorithm.

We input the data of the original data without aggregation service and the data of the business group after aggregation into the POTN network simulation system, which can prove that the system can run normally. Meanwhile, according to the different convergence results of the two, and combined with the actual situation of the power grid business and POTN equipment, we analyze the reasons for the different routing results. It is further proved that the convergence algorithm transmission of power network service adapts to the general trend of the development of power communication.

4 Simulation Experiment

4.1 Experimental Environment

In order to apply the above model to the actual operation and maintenance of power communication POTN network, simulation experiments will be carried out in this chapter, and the resource model POTN transmission network researched and established is simulated, so as to verify the rationality and feasibility of the resource model of POTN transmission network studied in this paper. This paper adopts the topology diagram of a POTN backbone network of power communication as shown in the following figure. What we use is the data of business flow of a provincial section, which is abstracted into 15 points in total (Fig. 11).

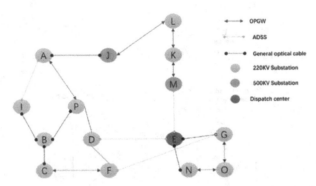

Fig. 11. POTN backbone network topology of power communication.

4.2 Analysis of Simulation Experiment Results

(1) Comparison of convergence results of POTN and OTN

Figure 12(a) shows the simulation results of aggregation of services with variable bandwidth (0–100 Gbps) by POTN device and OTN device respectively. Figure 12(b) represents POTN equipment and its OTN equipment respectively fixed size of a bandwidth (2 MBPS, 155 MBPS, 2.5 Gbps, 10 Gbps, 40 Gbps, 100 Gbps) simulation results of a business to gather figure; Services are aggregated in descending order by bandwidth size. The horizontal coordinate indicates the total bandwidth

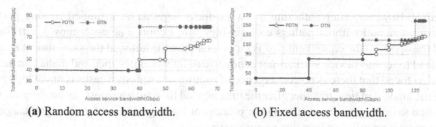

(a) Random access bandwidth.   **(b)** Fixed access bandwidth.

Fig. 12. Aggregation comparison diagram.

of services, and the vertical coordinate indicates the total bandwidth required by services.

As can be seen through the simulation experiment result, and whether the bandwidth of the fixed bandwidth is not fixed size case, POTN after mixing cross granularity gathering the required bandwidth than OTN single cross granularity gathering of bandwidth is smaller, It is proved that using POTN convergence algorithm can improve the carrying capacity of service and bandwidth utilization of equipment.

(2) Simulation results and analysis

The following table shows some data after route selection. We compare the route selection results of aggregated services with those of non-aggregated services (Tables 1 and 2).

Table 1. Service route selection results after aggregation.

id	Source	Goal	Result	Path
1	A	F	Success	A-P-D-F
3	A	D	Fail	
5	D	H	Fail	
6	C	J	Success	C-B-I-A-J

Table 2. Route selection results of non-aggregation routes.

id	Source	Goal	Result	Path
1	A	F	Success	A-P-D-F
6	A	F	Success	A-P-D-F
10	A	D	Success	A-P-D
12	C	H	Fail	

By observing the routing tables can be found: the proportion of the success of the business without gathering routing is larger than the scale of business success after together. However, after gathering a few business together in a unified routing port transmission, and without gathers each business must choose alone occupy a port for road transport, so the equipment cost is far greater than the latter, at the same time it also can lead to serious device stack, is not conducive to later maintenance and management. We also found that there is no convergence of routing transmission cases is much higher than the amount of time together after the time needed for road transport, so the algorithm also can save the amount of time in the process of routing, this is of great significance for some power grid services that require delay.

5 Conclusion

In this paper, a resource modeling method of power communication network POTN optical transmission network is proposed, and a simulation system of POTN is developed. Our proposed POTN convergence algorithm verifies the balanced scheduling of POTN equipment for the entire power communication network resources in the POTN simulation system.

Acknowledgment. This paper was supported by the science and technology project from State Grid Tianjin Electric Power Company (5203162000B1).

References

1. Shi, J.W., Wang, Y., Zhang, G., et al.: Distributed simulation system for power communication network. Comput. Eng. Appl. **55**(19), 246–252 (2019)
2. Shuai, L., Lu, Y., Ji, Y.: An enhanced IEEE 1588 time synchronization for asymmetric communication link in packet transport network. IEEE Commun. Lett. **14**(8), 764–766 (2010)
3. Zeng, L., Yuan, Y., Guo, B., et al.: Architecture of space-based packet transport network based on laser crosslinks. In: Sun, J., Yang, C., Xie, J. (eds.) China Satellite Navigation Conference (CSNC) 2020 Proceedings: Volume III. CSNC 2020. LNEE, vol. 652, pp. 154–163. Springer, Singapore (2020). https://doi.org/10.1007/978-981-15-3715-8_15
4. Winzer, P.J., Essiambre, R.J.: Advanced modulation formats for high-capacity optical transport networks. J. Lightwave Technol. **24**, 4711–4728 (2006)
5. Djordjevic, I.B., Arabaci, M., Minkov, L.L.: Next generation FEC for high-capacity communication in optical transport networks. J. Lightwave Technol. **27**(16), 3518–3530 (2009)
6. Kumar, P., Chen, J., Dezfouli, B.: QuicSDN: transitioning from TCP to QUIC for southbound communication in SDNs (2021)
7. Em, A., Dsa, B.: 100 Gbit/s AES-GCM cryptography engine for optical transport network systems: architecture, design and 40 nm silicon prototyping. Microelectron. J. (2021)
8. Zhao, Z., Zhao, Y., Wang, D., et al.: Reinforcement-learning-based multi-failure restoration in optical transport networks. In: 2019 Asia Communications and Photonics Conference (ACP). IEEE (2020)
9. Sauze, N.L., Chiaroni, D., Jourdan, A., et al.: Packet router for use in optical transmission networks. US (2006)
10. Maeda, K., Sakata, T.: Optical packet signal transmission device and WDM optical communication network. US (2014)

11. Ho, H.J.: Efficient multi-hop scheduling algorithms for packet transmissions in WDM optical star networks. AEU-Int. J. Electron. Commun. **64**(12), 1186–1191 (2010)
12. Lee, S.L.: The selection of logical rings for packet transmissions in WDM optical star networks. Medical Recapitulate (2013)
13. Zhou, Y.R., Smith, K.: Practical innovations enabling scalable optical transmission networks: real-world trials and experiences of advanced technologies in field deployed optical networks. J. Lightwave Technol. (2020)
14. Lun, H., Liu, X., Cai, M., et al.: Anomaly localization in optical transmissions based on receiver DSP and artificial neural network. In: Optical Fiber Communication Conference (2020)
15. Xiong, Y., Sampath, S.: A fast-convergence algorithm for reliability analysis based on the AK-MCS. Reliab. Eng. Syst. Saf. **213**, 107693 (2021)

Energy-Efficient Federated Learning in IoT Networks

Deyi Kong[1], Zehua You[1], Qimci Chen[1(✉)], Juanjuan Wang[2], Jiwei Hu[3], Yunfei Xiong[3], and Jing Wu[1]

[1] School of Electronic Information, Wuhan University, Wuhan 430072, China
{kongdeyi,youzehua,chenqimei,wujing}@whu.edu.cn
[2] School of Business Administration, Zhongnan University of Economics and Law, Wuhan 430072, China
Wangjj@zuel.edu.cn
[3] Wuhan Fiberhome Technical Services Co. Ltd., Wuhan 430072, China
{hujiwei,yfxiong}@fiberhome.com

Abstract. This paper investigated the problem of energy-efficient transmission resource allocation for Federated learning (FL). By processing data on the heterogeneous devices and uploading the model updates to the server, federated learning facilitates a large-scale model training with lower latency. Although FL has many promising advantages, the number of involved devices is limited by the communication and device battery resources. Therefore, it is rational to select devices due to its importance. This joint device selection and resource allocation problem is formulated to minimize the total energy cost and maximize the training accuracy. This optimization problem is a mixed integer nonlinear programming (MINLP), which is solved by a penalty dual decomposition (PDD) method. The closed-form expression solution shows that devices with more importance and less energy cost are more likely to be selected. The experiments show that the proposed algorithm has a desired performance and outperforms the random selection and full selection benchmarks.

Keywords: Federated learning · User selection · Resource management · Energy-efficiency

1 Introduction

With the development of Internet of Things (IoT), more devices will interact with each other. Thus, the data generated in their interaction will grow geometrically [1,2]. Due to the energy efficiency [3], storage [4], and privacy [5,6] concerns, it is often impractical for centralized machine learning and traditional communication framework to train and transmit the large scale of raw data. As the result, people proposed novel machine learning framework and energy-efficient communication strategies [7–9]. Federated learning (FL) is a variant of machine learning which has a lot of potentials [10,11]. However, due to the limitation of

M. Qiu et al. (Eds.): SmartCom 2021, LNCS 13202, pp. 26–36, 2022.
https://doi.org/10.1007/978-3-030-97774-0_3

wireless communication resources and battery resources of edge devices, latency and energy limitation issues still exists in FL.

To address these challenges, many works employed optimization algorithms to improve the accuracy of the model under limited resources situation. Specifically, the authors in [11] studied the tradeoff between wireless resource allocation and user selection via formulating an optimization problem. The authors in [12] analyzed the tradeoff between training accuracy and transmission latency under a Semi-asynchronous Hierarchical Federated Learning framework. Many resource allocation and user selection schemes are proposed to minimize the convergence time [13], total energy consumption [14] or computation latency [15].

In this paper, we propose a FL framework with user selection and resource allocation scheme. Inspired by [15], the model gradient-norm-value (GNV) is used to represent the importance of local data. We formulate the problem of joint device selection and resource allocation formulate as a constrained optimization problem, which is the mixed integer nonlinear programming (MINLP). To solve it, we propose a penalty dual decomposition (PDD) method with low computational complexity.

The rest of this paper is organized as follows. Section 2 introduces the system model and the FL learning mechanism. Section 3 formulates the tradeoff problem between data importance and power consumption. Section 4 solves the energy-efficient problem with the PDD algorithm. Section 5 verifies the performance of the proposed algorithm through numerical results, followed by the conclusions in Sect. 6.

2   System Model and FL Mechanism

In this section, we first introduce the FL model and its training procedure. Then we proposed its energy cost.

2.1   The FL Model

The FL model that is trained at local devices with the local dataset is called the local FL model. The FL model that is trained at the cloud server with the local updates is called the global FL model. Thus, under FL framework, the machine learning model can be distributed over all devices.

In FL, the local dataset $\mathcal{D} = \sum_k \mathcal{D}_k$ is distributed over a set $\mathcal{K}$ of k local devices. The updated model is aggregated at a cloud server, as shown in Fig. 1. Let $\mathcal{D}_k$ be the dataset of device k and $\mathcal{N}_k$ the number of its training data samples. Each data sample i in dataset $\mathcal{D}_k$ is defined as an input-output pair $(\boldsymbol{x}_{ik}, y_{ik})$. For simplicity, we assume the FL algorithm with a single output. Let the vector $\boldsymbol{w}$ be the parameters of global FL model. Furthermore, $f(\boldsymbol{w}, \boldsymbol{x}_{ik}, y_{ik})$ represents the loss function for data sample i with input $\boldsymbol{x}_{ik}$ and output y_{ik} on device k. The total loss function of local device k on dataset $\mathcal{D}_k$ can be written as

$$F_k(\boldsymbol{w}^t) = \frac{1}{N_k} \sum_{i=1}^{N_k} f(\boldsymbol{w}^t, \boldsymbol{x}_{ik}, y_{ik}), \ \forall k \in \mathcal{K}. \tag{1}$$

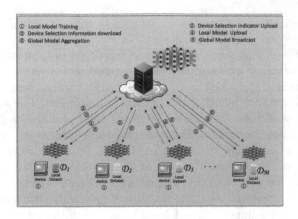

Fig. 1. Illustration of a federated learning process.

Due to the energy and communication limitation, we select the devices with higher importance which is represent by the gradient-norm-value (GNV) of the device [15,16]. The GNV of the device is calculated as

$$\vartheta_k^t = \|\hat{g}_k^t\|^2, \ \forall k \in \mathcal{K}, \tag{2}$$

where $\hat{g}_k^t$ is the loss function's gradient for device k with global model's parameter w^t, i.e.

$$\hat{g}_k^t = \nabla F_k(w^t). \tag{3}$$

The GNV will be transmitted to the cloud for selecting devices to complete the model upload task. Let Ω^t be the set of selected devices. Then, the selected local devices will upload their local gradients $g_k^t, \forall k \in \Omega^t$ to the cloud server. After receiving the selected device's parameters, the global model can be updated as

$$w^{t+1} = w^t - \frac{\iota^t}{\sum_{k \in \Omega^t} N_k} \sum_{k \in \Omega^t} N_k g_k^t. \tag{4}$$

The global loss function is calculated as

$$F(w) = \frac{1}{N} \sum_{k \in \Omega^t} N_k F_k(w), \tag{5}$$

where $N = \sum_{k \in \Omega^t} N_k$ is the total number of data samples for all devices, and ι^t is the learning rate at the t-th iteration. Thereafter, the cloud server will broadcast w^{t+1} to the devices for the next round of training.

2.2   Energy Cost Model Based on FL

We assumed that the orthogonal frequency-division multiple access (OFDMA) technique is used for uploading the data from local devices to the cloud server. Let B_k be the bandwidth assigned to local device k, and B the total bandwidth for the system. Thus, the communication limitation is formulated as $\sum_{k=1}^{K} B_k \le B$. Moreover, the achievable local update data rate is calculated as

$$r_k^{\mathrm{u}} = B_k \log_2 \left(1 + \frac{P_k g_k}{B_k N_0} \right), \tag{6}$$

where P_k is the transmission power of device k, and g_k is the channel gain between local device k and cloud server. Moreover, N_0 represents the noise power.

For the download stage, since the cloud server use the whole bandwidth for broadcasting, the download data rate can be expressed as

$$r_k^{\mathrm{d}} = B \log_2 \left(1 + \frac{P g_k}{B N_0} \right). \tag{7}$$

Since the global updating process will not change the size of the parameters, the size of the data transmitted on the download and upload link are the same. Let Z be the data size of model parameter for both upload and download. Thereafter, the transmission latency for upload and download can be respectively written as

$$T_k^{\mathrm{u}} = \frac{Z}{r_k^{\mathrm{u}}}, \ \forall k \in \Omega, \tag{8}$$

$$T_k^{\mathrm{d}} = \frac{Z}{r_k^{\mathrm{d}}}, \ \forall k \in \mathcal{K}. \tag{9}$$

Furthermore, the upload and download communication overhead can be calculated as

$$E_k^{\mathrm{u}} = P_k T_k^{\mathrm{u}} = \frac{P_k Z}{r_k^{\mathrm{u}}}, \ \forall k \in \Omega, \tag{10}$$

$$E_k^{\mathrm{d}} = P T_k^{\mathrm{d}} = \frac{P Z}{r_k^{\mathrm{d}}}, \ \forall k \in \mathcal{K}. \tag{11}$$

Here, the aggregation time of the cloud server is ignored due to its rich computing resources. In addition, since data size of the calculated GNV is much smaller than Z, the time for uploading the GNV can also be ignored. Thus, the energy cost in one training iteration is expressed as

$$E = \sum_{k=1}^{K} \left(E_k^{\mathrm{d}} + \alpha_k E_k^{\mathrm{u}} \right), \tag{12}$$

where $\alpha_k \in \{0, 1\}$, with $\alpha_k = 1$ indicating that device k performs model uploading and $\alpha_k = 0$, otherwise. For the device that is not selected, $E_k^{\mathrm{u}} = 0$.

3 Problem Formulation

In this section, we formulate the device selection and energy allocation problem as a constraint minimization.

Note that to achieve a higher training accuracy, more devices should be selected. However, the less devices are selected, the better communication quality each device will have. Thus, the optimization function is established as

$$\min_{\alpha, B} \left\{ (1 - \rho) \sum_{k=1}^{K} \alpha_k P_k T_k^{\mathrm{u}} - \rho \sum_{k=1}^{K} \alpha_k \vartheta_k \right\}, \tag{13}$$

s.t.

$$\sum_{k=1}^{K} B_k \leq B, \tag{13a}$$

$$\alpha_k \in \{0, 1\}, \ \forall k \in \mathcal{K}, \tag{13b}$$

where $\boldsymbol{\alpha} = [\alpha_1, \alpha_2, \cdots, \alpha_K]^{\mathrm{T}}$, $\boldsymbol{B} = [B_1, B_2, \cdots, B_K]^{\mathrm{T}}$. Besides, $\sum_{k=1}^{K} \alpha_k \vartheta_k$ represents the importance of selected data and $\sum_{k=1}^{K} \alpha_k P_k T_k^{\mathrm{u}}$ represents the power consumption. Here, $\rho \in [0, 1]$ is the weight factor that controls the tradeoff between GNV and energy cost. For simplicity, iteration t will be omitted in the following.

Obviously, the constraint minimization problem (13) is a mixed integer non-linear programming (MINLP), which is NP-hard. In the following section, we introduce a PDD method to solve this MINLP problem.

4 Joint Device Selection and Resource Allocation Scheme

We first solve the integer planning problem caused by binary vector $\boldsymbol{\alpha}$. After introducing an auxiliary variable $\tilde{\boldsymbol{\alpha}}$ [17], the equivalent problem for problem (13) is expressed as

$$\min_{\alpha, \tilde{\alpha}, B} (1 - \rho) \sum_{k=1}^{K} \alpha_k P_k T_k^{\mathrm{u}} - \rho \sum_{k=1}^{K} \alpha_k \vartheta_k, \tag{14}$$

s.t.

$$\sum_{k=1}^{K} B_k \leq B, \tag{14a}$$

$$\boldsymbol{\alpha} - \tilde{\boldsymbol{\alpha}} = \mathbf{0}, \tag{14b}$$

$$\alpha_k(1 - \tilde{\alpha}_k) = 0, \ \forall k \in \mathcal{K}, \tag{14c}$$

$$0 \leq \alpha_k \leq 1, \ \forall k \in \mathcal{K}. \tag{14d}$$

Then, to solve problem (14) we develop an algorithm based on the penalty dual decomposition (PDD) method [18]. PDD method solves the problem with double loop. In the inner loop, we use augmented Lagrangian (AL) algorithm to solve the block optimization subproblem. In the outer loop, constraint violation controls the update of dual variables and penalty parameter.

4.1   Inner Loop of PDD Method

In this part, we focus on applying augmented Lagrangian (AL) algorithm to block optimization subproblem. After penalizing and dualizing the equality constraints (14b) and (14c), problem (14) can be expressed as

$$\min_{\alpha, \tilde{\alpha}, \mathbf{B}} \quad [(1 - \rho) \sum_{k=1}^{K} \alpha_k P_k T_k^{\mathrm{u}} - \rho \sum_{k=1}^{K} \alpha_k \vartheta_k]$$

$$+ \frac{1}{2\nu} \sum_{k=1}^{K} [\alpha_k (1 - \tilde{\alpha}_k) + \nu \lambda_k]^2 + \frac{1}{2\nu} \sum_{k=1}^{K} \left(\alpha_k - \tilde{\alpha}_k + \nu \tilde{\lambda}_k \right)^2, \quad (15)$$

s.t.

$$\sum_{k=1}^{K} B_k \leq B, \tag{15a}$$

$$0 \leq \alpha_k \leq 1, \tag{15b}$$

where ν is the non-negative penalty parameter, $\boldsymbol{\lambda} = [\lambda_1, \lambda_2, ..., \lambda_K]$ and $\tilde{\boldsymbol{\lambda}} = [\tilde{\lambda}_1, \tilde{\lambda}_2, ..., \tilde{\lambda}_K]$ denote the dual variables associated with the equality constraints (14b) and (14c), respectively.

Next, variables $\boldsymbol{\alpha}$ and $\mathbf{B}$ can be solved by the distributed PDD algorithm. To optimize $(\boldsymbol{\alpha}, \tilde{\alpha}, \mathbf{B})$ in problem (15), we apply the alternating idea by dividing it into two subproblems. In the first subproblem, $\boldsymbol{\alpha}$ is optimized with a given $(\tilde{\alpha}, \mathbf{B})$. Then, $(\tilde{\alpha}, \mathbf{B})$ will be updated with $\boldsymbol{\alpha}$ obtained from the first subproblem. With the fixed $(\tilde{\alpha}, \mathbf{B})$, the first subproblem is expressed as

$$\min_{\alpha} \quad [(1 - \rho) \sum_{k=1}^{K} \alpha_k P_k T_k^{\mathrm{u}} - \rho \sum_{k=1}^{K} \alpha_k \vartheta_k]$$

$$+ \frac{1}{2\nu} \sum_{k=1}^{K} [\alpha_k (1 - \tilde{\alpha}_k) + \nu \lambda_k]^2 + \frac{1}{2\nu} \sum_{k=1}^{K} \left(\alpha_k - \tilde{\alpha}_k + \nu \tilde{\lambda}_k \right)^2, \quad (16)$$

s.t.

$$0 \leq \alpha_k \leq 1. \tag{16a}$$

Since (16) is a convex problem, we obtained its Lagrangian function with respect to $\boldsymbol{\alpha}$

$$
\begin{aligned}
L\left(\boldsymbol{\alpha}, \boldsymbol{\phi}, \boldsymbol{\zeta}\right) = & [(1-\rho)\sum_{k=1}^{K}\alpha_k P_k T_k^{\mathrm{u}} - \rho\sum_{k=1}^{K}\alpha_k \vartheta_k] \\
& +\frac{1}{2\nu}\sum_{k=1}^{K}[\alpha_k\left(1-\tilde{\alpha}_k\right)+\nu\lambda_k]^2 \\
& +\frac{1}{2\nu}\sum_{k=1}^{K}\left(\alpha_k - \tilde{\alpha}_k + \nu\tilde{\lambda}_k\right)^2 + \zeta_k\left(-\alpha_k\right) \\
& +\phi_k\left(\alpha_k - 1\right).
\end{aligned}
\tag{17}
$$

The first-order partial derivatives of (17) with respect to $\boldsymbol{\alpha}$ is

$$
\begin{aligned}
\frac{\partial L(\alpha_k, \phi_k, \zeta_k)}{\partial \alpha_k} = & \frac{1}{\nu}\left[\alpha_k\left(1-\tilde{\alpha}_k\right)^2 + \alpha_k - \tilde{\alpha}_k\right] \\
& +\lambda_k\left(1-\tilde{\alpha}_k\right) + \tilde{\lambda}_k + \phi_k - \zeta_k \\
& +(1-\rho)P_k T_k^{\mathrm{u}} - \rho\vartheta_k.
\end{aligned}
\tag{18}
$$

Optimal $\boldsymbol{\alpha}$ is obtained by setting (18) to 0, i.e.

$$
\alpha_k^* = \frac{\nu D_k + \nu\left[\rho\vartheta_k - (1-\rho)P_k T_k^{\mathrm{u}}\right]}{\left(1-\tilde{\alpha}_k\right)^2 + 1},
\tag{19}
$$

where $D_k = \zeta_k - \phi_k + \frac{1}{\nu}\tilde{\alpha}_k - \tilde{\lambda}_k - \lambda_k\left(1-\tilde{\alpha}_k\right)$. The Lagrangian multipliers ϕ and ζ can be found by one-dimensional search methods based on the complementary slackness conditions of (16). The result shows that device selection mainly depends on ϑ_k and $P_k T_k^{\mathrm{u}}$, which is associated with GNV and uplink energy cost. Intuitively, the cloud usually select local device with a larger GNV or smaller energy cost.

Using the $\boldsymbol{\alpha}$ obtained from problem (16), the second subproblem is

$$
\begin{aligned}
\min_{\tilde{\alpha}, \mathbf{B}} \quad & [(1-\rho)\sum_{k=1}^{K}\alpha_k P_k T_k^{\mathrm{u}} - \rho\sum_{k=1}^{K}\alpha_k \vartheta_k] \\
& +\frac{1}{2\nu}\sum_{k=1}^{K}[\alpha_k\left(1-\tilde{\alpha}_k\right)+\nu\lambda_k]^2 + \frac{1}{2\nu}\sum_{k=1}^{K}\left(\alpha_k - \tilde{\alpha}_k + \nu\tilde{\lambda}_k\right)^2,
\end{aligned}
\tag{20}
$$

s.t.

$$
\sum_{k=1}^{K} B_k \leq B.
\tag{20a}
$$

Obviously, problem (20) is convex, which can be solved similarly as problem (16) by Lagrangian method. Then we can obtain the optimal bandwidth B_k^* and auxiliary variable $\tilde{\alpha}_k^*$.

Thus, in the inner loop of PDD method, problem (15) can be solved by iteratively solving problem (16) and problem (20).

4.2   Outer Loop of PDD Method

The constraint violation h is defined as

$$h = \max_{\forall k \in \mathcal{S}}\{|\alpha_k\,(1 - \tilde{\alpha}_k)|, |\alpha_k - \tilde{\alpha}_k|\}. \tag{21}$$

If the constraint violation h is small enough, dual variables and penalty parameter are updated as

$$\boldsymbol{\lambda}^{(\ell)} = \boldsymbol{\lambda}^{(\ell-1)} + \frac{1}{\nu}\boldsymbol{\alpha}^{*(\ell-1)}\left(1 - \tilde{\boldsymbol{\alpha}}^{*(\ell-1)}\right), \tag{22}$$

$$\tilde{\boldsymbol{\lambda}}^{(\ell)} = \tilde{\boldsymbol{\lambda}}^{(\ell-1)} + \frac{1}{\nu}\left(\boldsymbol{\alpha}^{*(\ell-1)} - \tilde{\boldsymbol{\alpha}}^{*(\ell-1)}\right). \tag{23}$$

5   Simulation Results

In this section, we conduct numerical experiments to compare the proposed algorithm with full selection strategy and random selection strategy.

5.1   Experiment Settings

In our simulation, we consider a cloud server coverage area with a radius $r = 1000\,\text{m}$, and all local devices are uniformly distributed in the area. We adopt the path loss model as $128.1 + 37.6\log_{10}(d\,[\text{km}])$ dB.

We adopt the handwritten digit identification as the machine learning task on each local devices. Each device trains a convolutional neural network (CNN) with the MNIST database. To simulate the realistic situation, we split the training dataset in a non-iid way where local device has random data from part of the dataset categories.

5.2   Simulation Performance

In the simulation, we adopt two benchmark methods (*Random selection, Full selection*) to compare with the proposed FL method. In the benchmark methods, the bandwidth resources are equally allocated to the selected devices.

Figure 2 show the effectiveness of proposed FL method as identification accuracy increases with the number of iterations and converges around 1. Comparing with the baseline methods, the proposed algorithm converges faster, since both the accuracy and loss remain stable after 10 times of iterations. In contrast, the random selection method converges after 40 rounds. During the whole training process, the accuracy of the proposed algorithm is higher than the baseline methods and the loss is lower than the baseline methods.

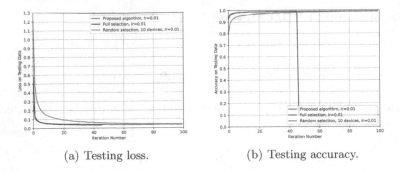

(a) Testing loss.   (b) Testing accuracy.

Fig. 2. Testing loss and accuracy of the proposed FL method and benchmark methods.

As in Fig. 3, as ρ increases, on average, more devices are selected. To know whether the added devices are worthy of more energy, we studied the energy efficiency. Here, the energy efficiency is defined as the total GNV of selected devices divided by the total energy consumption of selected devices, which means the data importance per unit energy. As in Fig. 4, the energy efficiency of the proposed algorithm decreases as ρ increases. As shown in problem (13), larger ρ means that the solution of the optimization problem will lead to a higher total GNV and relaxes the energy limit. The intuitive reason is that the device with higher data importance are more likely to be chosen despite the change of ρ. Thus, the data importance of the prior selection is higher than the added selection as ρ increases, which lead to the drop of the average data importance. Finally, with more energy consumed, the energy efficiency decreases. However, the overall energy efficiency of the proposed algorithm is higher than the benchmark methods, implying the advantage of the proposed algorithm.

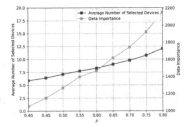

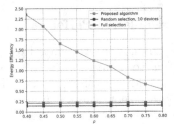

Fig. 3. The number of selected devices and data importance (total GNV) of the proposed FL method with different ρ.

Fig. 4. The energy efficiency of the proposed FL method and benchmark methods with different ρ.

6   Conclusion

In this paper, we consider a device selection and energy allocation problem, where the device selection is preformed according to GNV. This problem is formulated as a mixed integer nonlinear programming problem. Hence, to solve this problem we proposed a PDD algorithm with low computational complexity. Furthermore, the numerical results shows the proposed method can improve the FL learning accuracy with shorter training process.

References

1. Aazam, M., Zeadally, S., Harras, K.A.: Deploying fog computing in industrial Internet of things and Industry 4.0. IEEE Trans. Ind. Inform. **14**(10), 4674–4682 (2018)
2. Saad, W., Bennis, M., Chen, M.: A vision of 6G wireless systems: applications, trends, technologies, and open research problems. IEEE Netw. **34**(3), 134–142 (2020)
3. Gai, K., Qiu, M., Zhao, H., Sun, X.: Resource management in sustainable cyber-physical systems using heterogeneous cloud computing. IEEE Trans. Sustain. Comput. **3**(2), 60–72 (2018)
4. Jo, M., Maksymyuk, T., Strykhalyuk, B., Cho, C.-H.: Device-to-device-based heterogeneous radio access network architecture for mobile cloud computing. IEEE Wirel. Commun. **22**(3), 50–58 (2015)
5. Lu, Y., Huang, X., Dai, Y., Maharjan, S., Zhang, Y.: Differentially private asynchronous federated learning for mobile edge computing in urban informatics. IEEE Trans. Ind. Inform. **16**(3), 2134–2143 (2020)
6. Sun, Y., Liu, J., Wang, J., Cao, Y., Kato, N.: When machine learning meets privacy in 6G: a survey. IEEE Commun. Surv. Tuts. **22**(4), 2694–2724 (2020)
7. Chen, Q., Yu, G., Yin, R., Li, G.Y.: Energy-efficient user association and resource allocation for multistream carrier aggregation. IEEE Trans. Veh. Technol. **65**(8), 6366–6376 (2016)
8. Chen, Q., Yu, G., Yin, R., Maaref, A., Li, G.Y., Huang, A.: Energy-efficient resource block allocation for licensed-assisted access. In: 2015 IEEE 26th Annual International Symposium on Personal, Indoor, and Mobile Radio Communications, pp. 1018–1023 (2015)
9. Gai, K., Qiu, M.: Reinforcement learning-based content-centric services in mobile sensing. IEEE Netw. **32**(4), 34–39 (2018)
10. Wang, S., et al.: Adaptive federated learning in resource constrained edge computing systems. IEEE J. Sel. Areas Commun. **37**(6), 1205–1221 (2019)
11. Chen, M., Yang, Z., Saad, W., Yin, C., Poor, H.V., Cui, S.: A joint learning and communications framework for federated learning over wireless networks. IEEE Trans Wirel. Commun. **20**(1), 269–283 (2021)
12. Chen, Q., You, Z., Jiang, H.: Semi-asynchronous hierarchical federated learning for cooperative intelligent transportation systems, arXiv:2110.09073 (2021)
13. Chen, M., Poor, H.V., Saad, W., Cui, S.: Convergence time optimization for federated learning over wireless networks. IEEE Trans. Wirel. Commun. **20**(4), 2457–2471 (2021)
14. Yang, Z., Chen, M., Saad, W., Hong, C.S., Shikh-Bahaei, M.: Energy efficient federated learning over wireless communication networks. IEEE Trans. Wirel. Commun. **20**(3), 1935–1949 (2021)

15. He, Y., Ren, J., Yu, G., Yuan, J.: Importance-aware data selection and resource allocation in federated edge learning system. IEEE Trans. Veh. Tech. **69**(11), 13593–13605 (2020)
16. Katharopoulos, A., Fleuret, F.: Not all samples are created equal: deep learning with importance sampling, arXiv:1803.00942 (2018)
17. Guo, R., Cai, Y., Zhao, M., Shi, Q., Champagne, B.: Joint design of beam selection and precoding matrices for mmWave MU-MIMO systems relying on lens antenna arrays. IEEE J. Sel. Topics Signal Process. **12**(2), 313–325 (2018)
18. Shi, Q., Hong, M.: Penalty dual decomposition method for nonsmooth nonconvex optimization part I: algorithms and convergence analysis. IEEE Trans. Signal Process. **68**, 4108–4122 (2020)

Chinese Fine-Grained Sentiment Classification Based on Pre-trained Language Model and Attention Mechanism

Faguo Zhou, Jing Zhang, and Yanan Song[✉]

School of Mechanical Electronic and Information Engineering,
China University of Mining and Technology-Beijing, Beijing 100083, China
zhoufaguo@cumtb.edu.cn

Abstract. With the development of technology and the popularization of the Internet, the use of online platforms is gradually rising in all walks of life. People participate in the use of the platform and post comments, and the information interaction generated by this will affect other people's views on the matter in the future. It can be seen that the analysis of these subjective evaluation information is particularly important. Sentiment analysis research has gradually developed into specific aspects of sentiment judgment, which is called fine-grained sentiment classification. Nowadays, China has a large population of potential customers and Chinese fine-grained sentiment classification has become a current research hotspot. Aiming at the problem of low accuracy and poor classification effect of existing models in deep learning, this paper conducts experimental research based on the merchant review information data set of Dianping. The BERT-ftfl-SA model is proposed and integrate the attention mechanism to further strengthen the data characteristics. Compared with traditional models such as SVM and FastText, its classification effect is significantly improved. It is concluded that the improved BERT-ftfl-SA fine-grained sentiment classification model can achieve efficient sentiment classification of Chinese text.

Keywords: Chinese fine-grained sentiment classification · BERT · Word embedding · Attention mechanism

1 Introduction

With the rapid development of computer [1,2], software [3,4], and networks [5,6], Internet has become an important channel for people to express their views, opinions and exchange information [7]. Users comment on certain events or products when using platforms such as microblogs [8,9] and e-commerce [10], which produces a large amount of information that contains users' sentiment. In the face of large-scale comment information on the Internet [11,12], people cannot obtain all information and identify them one by one [13,14]. Therefore, the research work of sentiment analysis emerges as the times require. Now, people are no longer satisfied with sentiment analysis. *Aspect-Based Sentiment Analysis* (ABSA) came into being. Through fine-grained sentiment analysis, potential users' sentiment information can be analyzed to provide decision support for consumers and businesses. Even the analysis results can help the government and other relevant departments to formulate targeted policies to correctly guide the spread and development of public opinion in the information age [15]. In short, it has important application value.

In recent years, with the rapid development of deep learning [16,17], fine-grained sentiment analysis has made breakthrough progress, and research based on deep learning has become the main development area of sentiment analysis in the future. In order to further improve the effect of fine-grained sentiment classification, this paper will study and design a Chinese fine-grained sentiment classification model (BERT-ftfl-SA) based on a pre-trained language model and attention mechanism.

This paper briefly introduces BERT model and attention mechanism, and then optimizes BERT model and explains the framework of BERT-ftfl-SA model in detail. After that, the BERT-ftfl-SA model is compared with the commonly used feature representation models to verify and analyze the classification effect of the BERT-ftfl-SA model. Finally, the future research of fine-grained sentiment analysis is prospected.

2 Related Works

2.1 BERT

Google proposed BERT (Bidirectional Encoder Representations from Transformers) in 2018 [18]. In NLP tasks, people use it to transform word vectors to express features, and use it efficiently according to their own needs. Its characteristic is the use of transformer, which can better capture the bidirectional relationship in the sentence. In a specific NLP task, the feature representation of BERT can be directly used as the word embedding feature of the task. Therefore, BERT provides a model for migration learning of other tasks, which can be used as a feature extractor after being fine-tuned or fixed according to the task.

2.2 Self-attention

The existence of the attention mechanism has changed the problem of the length of the vector output by the encoder. It replaces the fixed single vector representation with the constantly changing middle layer, which highlights the relevance of the input content itself. With the development of deep learning, the establishment of a neural network with an attention mechanism has become more and more important. Attention mechanism has been widely used in a variety of neural networks to enhance their training performance. Self-attention is a kind of attention mechanism, and it fully considers the semantic and grammatical connections between different words in sentences.

3 Methodology Design

In order to further improve the effect of fine-grained sentiment classification, this paper proposes a Chinese fine-grained sentiment classification model (BERT-ftfl-SA) based on a pre-trained language model and attention mechanism. The main idea is to focus on the feature extraction effect of the vector transformation process of Chinese data, enhance the classification effect from the source, and then combine the attention mechanism to increase the weight description of the data to further improve the accuracy of fine-grained sentiment classification. Then, the classification effect of the BERT-ftfl-SA model is verified through a comparison experiment with the commonly used feature representation model.

3.1 Model Improvement

BERT Model Fine-Tuning. (1) Long text processing. The maximum sequence length that BERT can process is 512. In consideration of data exceeding, this paper makes improvements for data exceeding the upper limit of input. A truncation methods proposed in the reference [19], it uses the first 128 characters and the last 382 characters of the input text, which means that the input 510 characters are divided into four parts of 1:3, and the first part is taken from the beginning of the text. The last three parts are taken from the end of the text, in order to choose the content of the long text, and solve the problem of over-entry. (2) Adjust parameter. Fine-tuning is adjusted with reference to the single-sentence classification task. Most of the model parameters remain the pre-trained parameters, and only the batch size, epoch and learning rate of each batch are changed to fit the data set in this article. Batch Size adopts the maximum value 16 supported by the graphics card. Epoch through a comparative test, as shown in Fig. 1, it is concluded that when the value is 12, the effect is the best.

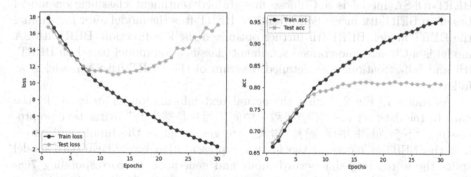

Fig. 1. Epoch comparative test results.

Optimizing Softmax Loss Function. In the classification task of Softmax classifier, there are two problems: the unbalanced sample distribution and the model does not pay attention to the samples with learning difficulties in the learning process. Therefore, this paper uses Focal Loss to alleviate the problems of class imbalance and difficulty sample imbalance when facing classification tasks [20].

The formula for Focal Loss function is expressed as follows:

$$\mathrm{L}_{fl} = \begin{cases} -(1-y')^{\gamma} \log y', y = 1 \\ -y'^{\gamma} \log (1-y'), y = 0 \end{cases} \tag{1}$$

In the formula, y' represents the probability that the sample is predicted to be 1, when $\gamma = 0$, focal loss function is cross entropy function. The 20 aspects of the data set in this paper differ greatly from the four categories. In order to balance the uneven sample categories, coefficient α is introduced on the basis of the above formula. In this experiment, the balance factor γ is set to 2 to reduce the contribution of simple samples to the loss value, and α is set to 0.25 to balance the imbalance of categories. Finally, the formula for the final loss function FL_20fc (Focal Loss_20 four categories) is as follows:

$$\mathrm{FL\_20fc} = \begin{cases} -0.25 (1-y')^2 \log (y'), y = 1 \\ -0.75 y'^2 \log (1-y'), \quad y \neq 1 \end{cases} \tag{2}$$

Therefore, the effect of FL_20fc function makes the model shift the focus to the samples that are difficult to distinguish. For simple samples, it greatly reduces the contribution of loss value, so that the proportion of samples that are difficult to distinguish will increase, and the imbalance of the contribution of positive and negative samples caused by uneven samples will also be alleviated.

3.2   BERT-ftfl-SA Model

BERT-ftfl-SA model is a Chinese fine-grained sentiment classification model based on BERT-ftfl fusion Self-attention. BERT-ft is the model after fine-tuning the BERT model. BERT-ftfl further optimized the loss function. BERT-ftfl-SA model is a Chinese fine-grained sentiment classification model based on BERT-ftfl and self-attention. The detailed diagram of the BERT-ftfl-SA model is as follows.

As shown in Fig. 2, taking the actual text information as an example, the data in the data set are "不会很甜，中间的照片是糯米的". After text preprocessing, "不会 很甜 中间 照片 糯米" are generated as the input, and enters into the BERT-ft model of the feature representation layer. BERT-ftfl model splits the words into single-word input and generates the corresponding 768-dimensional word vector, then reduces the dimension to 64 dimension through the full connection layer vector, and generates 4 dimension vector to output the classification results.

However, for BERT-ftfl-SA model, the maximum text input is 512 words. The generated 512 * 768 matrix enters the self-attention mechanism layer. After

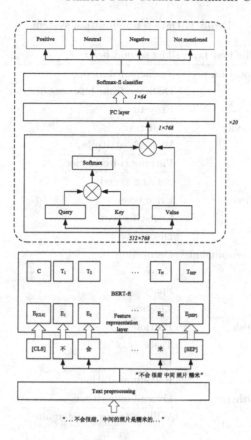

Fig. 2. Flow diagram of BERT-ftfl-SA.

further extracting the features, the vector dimension of the full connection layer is reduced to 64-dimensional. Through the improved Softmax-fl classifier, 4-dimensional vector output classification results are generated.

4 Experiments and Analysis

4.1 Data Set

The experimental data set in this paper uses the official data set of AI Challenger 2018 fine-grained sentiment analysis track. The data set is provided by the competition organizing committee. It is a massive data set of sentiment tendencies containing 6 categories and 20 fine-grained elements. Its main content is customer reviews of various businesses in public reviews. The data set consists of training, verification, test A and test B. There are 105000 data in the training set, 15000 data in the validation set and 15000 data in the test set. The specific description is shown in the following Table 1.

Table 1. Data set annotation system

The first layer	The second layer
Location	Traffic convenience
	Distance from business district
	Easy to find
Service	Wait time
	Waiter's attitude
	Parking convenience
	Serving speed
Price	Price level
	Cost-effective
	Discount
Environment	Decoration
	Noise
	Space
	Cleaness
Dish	Portion
	Taste
	Look
	Recommendation
Others	Overall experience
	Willing to consume again

Table 2. Four fine-grained element tags.

Sentimental labels	1	0	−1	−2
Meaning	Positive	Neutral	Negative	Not mentioned

There are four sentimental types for every fine-grained element: Positive, Neutral, Negative and Not mentioned, which are labelled as 1, 0, −1 and −2. The meaning of these four labels are listed in Table 2.

4.2   Experimental Evaluation Index

In order to verify the proposed model based on Bert-ftfl, the average values of precision (P), recall (R) and F1-Measure in 20 dimensions are used as the evaluation indexes of the experiment.

Accuracy, Precision, Recall and F1-Measure are commonly used as evaluation indicators in the study, which directly and comprehensively represent the classification effect. Based on the binary classification model to understand the above indicators, there will be four cases with confusion matrix representation.

Table 3. The classification under the two classification model.

	Forecast results: Positives	Forecast results: Negatives
True value: True	TP	TN
True value: False	FP	FN

The classification under the two classification model is shown in Table 3. The formulas of experimental evaluation index are as follows:

$$\text{Precision} = \frac{TP}{TP + FP} \tag{3}$$

$$\text{Recall} = \frac{TP}{TP + FN} \tag{4}$$

$$F_\beta = \left(1 + \beta^2\right) \cdot \frac{\text{precision} \cdot \text{recall}}{(\beta^2 \cdot \text{precision}) + \text{recall}} \tag{5}$$

$$F_1 = 2 \cdot \frac{\text{precision} \cdot \text{recall}}{\text{precision} + \text{recall}} \tag{6}$$

4.3 Design

The experiment compares the text classification model constructed by BERT-ftfl model with other seven mainstream classification models on AI Challenger 2018 fine-grained sentiment analysis trajectory data set. The 12 classification models are as follows:

(1) Word2Vec: The classic model of generating word vector by combining context and target word relationship [21].
(2) GloVe: Based on co-occurrence matrix, GloVe grasps the overall and local information, the model contains more comprehensive overall information than Word2Vec [22].
(3) ELMo: Two-stage training method is used to train the initial model based on bidirectional double LSTM, and then the model is adjusted according to subsequent specific tasks [23].
(4) GPT: It trains the initial model based on Transformer model's decoder variant structure. Compared with ELMo, GPT has faster speed and better feature extraction effect.
(5) SVM: SVM is a feature-based support vector machine classification model, which has achieved better classification effect than previous models, and it is the official baseline model.
(6) FastText: The core idea is to average the words and N-gram vector of the whole document to get the document vector, and then use the document vector to do Softmax multi-classification [24].
(7) CNN: The convolutional neural network model proposed in Reference is the most basic convolutional neural network [25].

(8) TextCNN: CNN is improved in uses multiple kernels of different sizes to extract key information in sentences, which can better capture local correlation than CNN [26].

(9) BERT-base-Chinese: Compared with GPT model, it combines MLM and NSP and uses target context information, so the effect is better.

(10) BERT-ft: Compared with BERT-base-Chinese model, BERT-ft solves the problem of long text input excess, adjusts the hyperparameters and introduces attenuation coefficients in the Adam optimizer using the layer by layer decreasing learning rate.

(11) BERT-ftfl: Based on the BERT-ft model, BERT-ftfl optimized the loss function in the classifier, so as to solve the problem of large loss ratio gap caused by unbalanced positive and negative samples and unbalanced simple and complex samples.

(12) BERT-ftfl-SA: BERT-ftfl-SA extracted features based on the BERT-ftfl model, then integrated the attention mechanism, combined with self-attention to further highlight the text features, and finally achieved more accurate training effects.

Table 4. Classification effect of each model.

No	Model	P	R	F1
1	Word2Vec	0.51	0.42	0.46
2	GloVe	0.53	0.44	0.48
3	ELMo	0.57	0.51	0.51
4	GPT	0.62	0.54	0.57
5	SVM	0.53	0.41	0.47
6	FastText	0.62	0.50	0.56
7	CNN	0.57	0.49	0.52
8	TextCNN	0.67	0.60	0.63
9	BERT-base-Chinese	0.63	0.58	0.61
10	BERT-ft	0.68	0.61	0.65
11	BERT-ftfl	0.71	0.63	0.67
12	BERT-ftfl-SA	0.74	0.68	0.71

4.4   Analysis of Results

The experimental results are shown in Table 4. Groups 1–4 and 9 analyze the learning effects of mainstream feature representation models in the target sentiment classification task. The Word2Vec model is relatively simple in structure, the polysemy problem cannot be solved and the learning effect based on the data set is not good. The learning effect of the GloVe model is not much different from that of Word2Vec. Even after the data set provided by the competition organizing committee is cleaned, there is still a problem of feature dispersion. Compared with Word2Vec, the GloVe model is more rapid. The ELMo model uses double-layer Bi-LSTM, which has a qualitative improvement compared with Word2Vec and GloVe. As a typical two-stage model, the GPT model achieves better training effect than the ELMo model, but it is limited to some extent because it adopts one-way modeling.

In groups 5–8, the SVM model has a simple structure, but the data set text is too complex, resulting in poor training results. The speed of FastText model is very fast, but the simple composition structure is easy to cause information omission in learning, and the complex information in the data set is not mastered, which affects the training results. CNN model has poor learning effect on text information. Valuable information is lost at the pooling layer, and the association between local and global information is ignored, leading to poor understanding of polarity analysis at different granularity. Compared with CNN model, TextCNN model achieves better classification effect, it uses the maximum timing pooling layer of one-dimensional convolution layer, but it is still 0.08 less than the mean F1 value of BERT-ftfl-SA model. The 9–12 groups are ablation experiments. According to the data in the table, the optimizations of BERT-ft and BERT-ftfl are effective and improve the classification level. The final results prove that the BERT-ftfl-SA model can complete the Chinese fine-grained sentiment classification task, and has a better classification effect than other models.

In future studies, more linguistic resources and other network models can be introduced to further improve the effect of fine-grained sentiment classification, such as linguistically regularized LSTMs and hierarchical attention networks (HAN). Compared with other neural network models, linguistically regularized LSTMs models do not rely on parsed trees, do not require phrase level notation and make full use of linguistic knowledge [27]. General network models (LSTM, CNN-word) don't make full use of hierarchical information in long text. HAN uses the word-level and sentence-level attention mechanism to better understand the semantic structure of the document. Compared with other methods, HAN fully considers the internal structure of the document. HAN is also widely used, for example, the time and space structure of videos and HAN can be used to complete video subtitle tasks [28].

5 Conclusion

In this paper, a Chinese fine-grained sentiment classification model based on pre-trained language model and attention mechanism was proposed. Through experiments, based on the official data set of AI Challenger 2018 fine-grained sentiment analysis track, and the experiment proved that the BERT-ftfl-SA model had a good classification effect, but the work of this paper still needs some improvement. Although the method proposed in this paper integrated attention mechanism, due to the complexity of the text, the upper limit of the effect of the model was limited.

References

1. Gao, Y., Iqbal, S., et al.: Performance and power analysis of high-density multi-GPGPU architectures: a preliminary case study. In: IEEE 17th HPCC (2015)
2. Qiu, M., Xue, C., et al.: Energy minimization with soft real-time and DVS for uniprocessor and multiprocessor embedded systems. In: IEEE DATE Conference, pp. 1–6 (2007)
3. Zhao, H., Chen, M., et al.: A novel pre-cache schema for high performance Android system. Futur. Gener. Comput. Syst. **56**, 766–772 (2016)
4. Liu, M., Zhang, S., et al.: H infinite state estimation for discrete-time chaotic systems based on a unified model. IEEE TSMC (B) (2012)
5. Qiu, L., Gai, K., Qiu, M.: Optimal big data sharing approach for tele-health in cloud computing. In: IEEE SmartCloud, pp. 184–189 (2016)
6. Zhang, Z., Wu, J., et al.: Jamming ACK attack to wireless networks and a mitigation approach. In: IEEE GLOBECOM Conference, pp. 1–5 (2008)
7. Li, H.Y., Li, Q., Zhou, P.F.: Sentiment analysis and mining for product review text. Inf. Sci. **35**(001), 51–55 (2017)
8. Ren, Z.J., Zhang, P., Li, S.C., et al.: Analysis on the emotional situation evolution of emergencies in emergencies based on Weibo data mining. J. Inf. **38**(02), 140–148 (2019)
9. Tian, W.G.: The mechanism and strategy of Netizens' emotion communication in Weibo comments. Contemp. Commun. (01), 66–69 (2019)
10. Yan, Q., Ma, L.Y., Wu, S.: The impact of electronic word-of-mouth publishing platform differences on consumers' perceived usefulness. Manag. Sci. **32**(03), 80–91 (2019)
11. Lu, R., Jin, X., Zhang, S., Qiu, M., Wu, X.: A study on big knowledge and its engineering issues. IEEE TKDE **31**(9), 1630–1644 (2018)
12. Qiu, M., Cao, D., et al.: Data transfer minimization for financial derivative pricing using Monte Carlo simulation with GPU in 5G. J. Commun. Syst. **29**(16), 2364–2374 (2016)
13. Thakur, K., Qiu, M., Gai, K., Ali, M.: An investigation on cyber security threats and security models. In: IEEE CSCloud (2015)
14. Gai, K., Qiu, M., Sun, X., Zhao, H.: Security and privacy issues: a survey on FinTech. In: SmartCom, pp. 236–247 (2016)
15. Li, R., Lin, Z., Lin, H.L., et al.: A review of text sentiment analysis. Comput. Res. Dev. **55**(001), 30–52 (2018)
16. Qiu, H., Qiu, M., Lu, Z.: Selective encryption on ECG data in body sensor network based on supervised machine learning. Inf. Fusion **55**, 59–67 (2020)
17. Qiu, H., Qiu, M., Memmi, G., Ming, Z., Liu, M.: A dynamic scalable blockchain based communication architecture for IoT. In: SmartBlock, pp. 159–166 (2018)
18. Devlin, J., Chang, M., Lee, K., et al.: BERT: pre-trained of deep bidirectional transformers for language understanding (2018)
19. Sun, C., Qiu, X., Xu, Y., Huang, X.: How to fine-tune BERT for text classification? In: Sun, M., Huang, X., Ji, H., Liu, Z., Liu, Y. (eds.) CCL 2019. LNCS (LNAI), vol. 11856, pp. 194–206. Springer, Cham (2019). https://doi.org/10.1007/978-3-030-32381-3_16
20. Lin, T.Y., Goyal, P., Girshick, R., et al.: Focal loss for dense object detection. IEEE Trans. Pattern Anal. Mach. Int. **PP**(99), 2999–3007 (2017)
21. Mikolov, T., Chen, K., Corrado, G., et al.: Efficient estimation of word representations in vector space. Computer Science (2013)

22. Pennington, J., Socher, R., Manning, C.: Glove: global vectors for word representation. In: Conference on Empirical Methods in NLP (2014)
23. Peters, M., Neumann, M., Iyyer, M., et al.: Deep contextualized word representations. North American Chapter of the Association for Computational Linguistics, vol. 1 (2018)
24. Joulin, A., Grave, E., Bojanowski, P., et al.: Bag of tricks for efficient text classification. European Chapter of the Association for Computational Linguistics, vol. 2 (2017)
25. Lecun, Y., Boser, B., Denker, J.S., et al.: Backpropagation applied to handwritten zip code recognition. Neural Comput. 1(4), 541–551 (1989)
26. Kim, Y.: Convolutional neural networks for sentence classification. In: Conference on Empirical Methods in NLP, Doha, Qatar, pp. 1746–1751 (2014)
27. Qian, Q., Huang, M., Lei, J., et al.: Linguistically regularized LSTMs for sentiment classification. arXiv preprint arXiv:1611.03949 (2016)
28. Li, X., Zhao, B., Lu, X.: MAM-RNN: multi-level attention model based RNN for video captioning. In: IJCAI, vol. 2017, pp. 2208–2214 (2017)

Link-Efficiency Multi-channel Transmission Protocol for Data Collection in UASNs

Xiaohui Wei, Xiaonan Wang, Haixiao Xu, Xingwang Wang$^{(\boxtimes)}$, and Hao Guo

College of Computer Science and Technology, Jilin University, Changchun, China
{weixh,haixiao,xww}@jlu.edu.cn, {wangxn21,guohao17}@mails.jlu.edu.cn

Abstract. With the burgeoning of underwater Internet of things, the amount of data generated by sensor nodes increases dramatically in UASNs, requiring efficient data collection schemes. The data collection process mainly considers MAC and routing design to ensure the link efficiency of sensing data to the sink, which refers to collision avoidance and high bandwidth utilization at low signaling overhead. In recent underwater MAC designs, multi-channel schemes have been adopted as an effective way to eliminate collisions. However, existing multi-channel schemes face the problem of low bandwidth utilization, resulting in a reduction in the performance of network throughput and end-to-end delay. Besides, in the routing design, the unbalanced transfer load may lead to partial transmission congestion, which also decreases the overall bandwidth utilization. To solve the above problems, in this paper, we propose a *Link-Efficiency Transmission Protocol* (LETP). In the routing layer, we propose a forwarding node probabilistic selection approach to solve the unbalanced transfer load problem at low signaling overhead. In the MAC layer, with the assistance of routing information, a *Link Efficiency Channel Allocation* (LECA) algorithm with low signaling overhead is applied on receiver sides to allocate dedicated communication channels to senders and optimize the allocation decision based on channel characteristics. Simulation results verify that LETP achieves a better network performance in comparison with existing protocols.

Keywords: Bandwidth utilization · Collision avoidance · Data collection · Multi-channel UASNs · Transmission protocol

1 Introduction

In the past decades, *Underwater Acoustic Sensor Networks* (UASNs) have emerged as a powerful tool to enable a wide range of applications, such as

This work is supported by the National Natural Science Foundation of China (NSFC) (Grants No. U19A2061, No. 61772228, No. 61902143), the Natural Science Foundation of Jilin Province, China under Grant No. YDZJ202101ZYTS191, Jilin Scientific and Technological Development Program (No. 2020122208JC), Research Project by the Education Department of Jilin Province (No. JJKH20211105KJ).

M. Qiu et al. (Eds.): SmartCom 2021, LNCS 13202, pp. 48–63, 2022.
https://doi.org/10.1007/978-3-030-97774-0_5

environmental monitoring, resource exploration, tactical surveillance, and early disaster warning [28]. With the advance of computer processor [16,18], network [7,17], and algorithm design [10,22], each node of UASNs will generate a large amount of data. Big data processing and transferring [5,13] had been studied in various applications [6,8]. Similarly, for UASNs, this poses the design of efficient data collection schemes a necessary problem [12]. In the data collection process, each node acts as the initiator or maybe the forwarder of information packets to transmit the sensing data hop by hop to the sink. The data collection process mainly considers MAC and routing design to ensure the *link efficiency* of sensing data to the sink, which refers to collision avoidance and high bandwidth utilization at low signaling overhead. Compared with the *Terrestrial Wireless Sensor Networks* (TWSNs) where the transmission is carried out through electromagnetic waves, acoustic communication faces problems of low signal-to-noise ratio, narrow bandwidth, and long propagation time. These fundamental differences make the protocols of TWSNs unfeasible in the underwater environment [23]. Thus conceiving transmission protocols especially tailored for UASNs is a demanding and challenging research work [1].

The MAC design in the protocol stack is mainly in charge of coordinating the channel access of each node to avoid collisions. Indeed, collisions are especially undesired in UASNs [1,9,28]. To avoid collisions in UASNs, multi-channel schemes which improve transmission parallelism have been used in recent studies [1,2,23]. According to the way that channel negotiation happens, existing multi-channel schemes can be classified into two categories: single rendezvous and multiple rendezvous [1]. However, existing multi-channel approaches face the problem of low bandwidth utilization, which reduces network performances on throughput and end-to-end delay. In multi-channel single rendezvous schemes, the common control channel will be a performance bottleneck in heavy-traffic networks, causing under-utilization of data channels [14,15]. Multi-channel multiple rendezvous schemes allow simultaneous handshaking on distinct channels through coordination among nodes, while these coordination mechanisms still fail to fully utilize multiple data channels [1,2]. Indeed, bandwidth utilization directly impacts throughput and end-to-end delay, especially in bandwidth-limited underwater acoustic scenarios.

The overall bandwidth utilization in multi-channel transmission can also be affected by the forwarder selection process in the routing design. Forwarder selection decisions among nodes are coupled, if too many nodes select a unique node (or a few nodes) as their forwarder, then the selected forwarders will undertake much more transfer load than others. In such a case, transmissions to these forwarders must share the insufficient channel bandwidth while other forwarders may have excess channel bandwidth, resulting in a decrease to the overall bandwidth utilization. Moreover, these selected forwarders may be exhausted prematurely, leading to the occurrence of void regions and a shorter network lifetime [26]. Thus, it would be beneficial to get a balanced transfer load through appropriate forwarder selection [27].

In this paper, we propose a *Link-Efficiency multi-channel Transmission Protocol* (LETP) for data collection in UASNs. To ensure link efficiency, the multi-channel MAC layer should guarantee collision avoidance and high bandwidth utilization in channel allocation. The routing layer should balance the transfer load by appropriate forwarding node selection. Note that only rough clock synchronization is required in LETP, which is practical to implement. The contributions of this paper can be summarized as follows:

- We propose a forwarding node probabilistic selection approach to balance the transfer load among nodes. In order to save the limited energy of underwater nodes, only a simple information exchange is needed. Then, by considering the estimated load conditions as well as the impact of each selection on load balancing, each node independently selects a forwarding node from the candidate set in different probabilities.
- We propose a *Link Efficiency Channel Allocation* (LECA) algorithm. Using the routing information from forwarder selection, the negotiation for the channel allocation of common neighbors can be reduced. In LECA, each node distributedly maintains an available channel set according to the channel allocation information from neighbors. Then, LECA allocates dedicated communication channels to each sender and optimize the allocation decision based on channel characteristics. Finally, the remaining available channels are further allocated to senders to improve bandwidth utilization.
- We evaluate the performance of LETP and compare it with existing transmission protocols in terms of throughput, packet delivery ratio, end-to-end delay, energy consumption, and network lifetime.

The remainder of this paper is organized as follows: Sect. 2 describes the system model and presents problem analysis. Two key components in LETP (forwarder selection and channel allocation) are discussed in Sect. 3. Simulation results are presented in Sect. 4. Section 5 reviews existing related works. Section 6 concludes the paper.

2   System Model and Problem Analysis

2.1   Network Model

We consider a multi-hop UASN where a sink node is placed on the water surface. Each node operates on mutually orthogonal frequency channels to conduct multi-channel communication, they may be the initiator as well as the forwarder of information packets. The data collection process is directional, that is, from the source node to the sink. Therefore, to facilitate data collection, we can virtually build the network into a layered structure according to the number of hops from underwater nodes to the sink. The layering algorithms have already been studied well in existing works such as *Gradient Field Establishment* (GFE) in [12,26,27], our work shed light on the data collection process based on the layered structure.

According to GFE, the sink first sends out a GFE packet and claims its layer to be $G(S) = 0$, nodes who have received this GFE packet set their layers to be $G(S) + 1$. Then, node n receives the GFE packet from a neighbor m within a back-off time will set its layer to be $G(n) = G(m) + 1$ until all nodes in the network obtain their layer. In this way, the network is constructed as a layered structure. During the GFE stage, each node n obtains its neighbor information and gets low-layer neighbor set as $Lower(n) = \{m : G(m) = G(n) - 1\}$ and high-layer neighbor set as $Higher(n) = \{m : G(m) = G(n) + 1\}$.

2.2 Overview of LETP

In our proposed protocol, all nodes in the network are labeled into layers through a GFE stage. By leveraging this layered structure, transmissions will take place between adjacent layers. The transmission process adopts a hierarchical slotted transmission scheme, which works in rounds, each round consists of several time slots of different lengths, the number of slots is equal to the number of layers in the network. At each time slot, a specific layer will transmit data to its adjacent lower layer. Only rough time synchronization is required in LETP. It is worth pointing out that the layers without transmission conflicts are able to transmit in parallel to boost spatial reuse.

LETP abandon the common control channel and operates on multiple data channels of total number $N_c = n_{max} - 1$ where n_{max} is the maximum neighborhood size in the network. Each channel is assigned for the transmissions between specific nodes within a neighborhood. In this way, a node will first receive data from its high-layer neighbor nodes, and then transmit its sensed data as well as the received data to a low-layer neighbor node. Thus, nodes are supposed to first select an appropriate forwarding node among low-layer neighbors, then allocate communication channels for high-layer neighbors.

2.3 Problem Analysis

In this subsection, we analyze the problems and considerations in the forwarder selection and channel allocation process.

Forwarder Selection. Sensing data of all nodes is forwarded to the sink hop-by-hop through relaying nodes. Use $FN(n)$ to represent the forwarding node decision of node n, $Data(n)$ to represent the sensing data of n, then the transfer load that a specific node n needs to forward is

$$W(n) = Data(n) + \sum_{m \in Higher(n)} W(m) \cdot I\{FN(m) == n\} \tag{1}$$

where $I\{A\}$ is an indicator function with $I\{A\} = 1$ if the event A is true and $I\{A\} = 0$ otherwise.

The problem of balancing transfer load among low-layer forwarders can be formulated as (2). For the convenience of description, we will use uppercase H and L to represent the set of higher and lower layer nodes between the adjacent two layers, respectively. Lowercase h_i and l_j refer to the high-layer and low-layer node, $h_i \in H$ and $l_j \in L$.

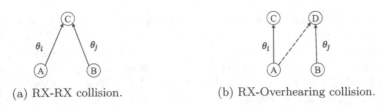

(a) RX-RX collision.   (b) RX-Overhearing collision.

Fig. 1. The possible collisions between two packets.

$$\min_{FN(h_i)} \sigma = \sqrt{\frac{1}{|L|}\sum_{l_j \in L}\left(\left(\sum_{h_i \in H}W(h_i)\cdot I\{FN(h_i)==l_j\}\right)-\mu\right)^2}$$

$$\text{s.t. }\forall h_i \in H, \quad \sum_{l_j \in L}(I\{FN(h_i)==l_j\})=1$$

(2)

Here $|L|$ is the cardinal number of L, μ is the average amount of transfer load of low-layer nodes. Due to the UASN characteristics, the forwarder selection should be performed at a low signaling overhead. We will introduce the forwarding node selection approach in detail at Sect. 3.1.

Channel Allocation. By leveraging the routing information from forwarder selection, the negotiation in the channel allocation process can be reduced, thereby reducing the signaling overhead. Therefore, between each adjacent layer, channel allocation process is carried out right after forwarder selection.

The primary requirement of channel allocation is **collision avoidance**. We avoid collisions by assigning dedicated channels for different transmission pairs within the two-hop collision domain. Collisions between two packets (denoted as θ_i and θ_j) are summarized as shown in Fig. 1. In RX-RX collision, two packets share a common node as the destination, at which the collision happens. In this case, with multiple data channels, the collision can be solved simply by providing θ_i and θ_j at different data channels as (3). Note that the hidden terminal problem in multi-hop transmission is essentially RX-RX collision.

$$\theta_i.channel \neq \theta_j.channel$$

(3)

In the RX-Overhearing collision in Fig. 1a, two packets are disjoint but within the two-hop collision domain, so that node D may overhear θ_i while receiving θ_j, leading to a collision. We avoid such kind of collision by guarantee:

$$\theta_{*\to D}.channel \neq \theta_i.channel$$

(4)

As expressed in (4), any packet destined to node D (a potential receiver within the communication range of sender of θ_i) can not use the channel used by θ_i.

Another requirement of channel allocation is **high bandwidth utilization**. When adopting the dedicated communication channel mechanism, each channel is assigned for the transmissions between specific nodes. As such, there may be several transmissions requiring a short time (e.g., small transfer load, sufficient bandwidth) while others requiring longer time(e.g., large transfer load, insufficient bandwidth). In this way, when the channels assigned for long transmissions are still busy, the channels assigned for short transmissions are already idle. However, duo to the dedicated communication channel mechanism, these idle channels can not be used for other transmissions, thereby causing the low bandwidth utilization problem. To alleviate this problem, we are suggested to make the duration of all data transmissions to be close to each other, so as to improve the bandwidth utilization. The channel allocation process satisfying the above two requirements will be introduced in detail at Sect. 3.2.

3   Two Key Components

This section introduces the two major components of LETP that achieve high link efficiency in detail.

3.1   Forwarder Selection

In this section, we consider the issue of selecting appropriate forwarding nodes between two adjacent layers to balance the transfer load. Specifically, for each high-layer node $h_i \in H$, an appropriate low-layer node $l_j \in L \cap Lower(h_i)$ is selected as its forwarder to jointly satisfy the objective in (2).

Intuitively, to meet the optimization goal in (2), a centralized solution can be used where a central node is responsible for global scheduling. However, the scalability of the centralized method is limited, frequent global re-scheduling is unrealistic in UASNs. Therefore, distributed solutions are tend to be used. In TWSNs, the distributed solution can be obtained through iterative negotiation, such as game theory-based methods [3]. However, the iterative negotiation process is computationally and communication intensive, which is not feasible in UASNs. The long latency, high transmission energy consumption of underwater acoustic communication, and limited battery energy of underwater nodes drive us to consider more practical solutions. A preferable solution is to minimize the control packets exchange. To this end, we consider (2) in an energy-efficient way with only a simple information exchange needed.

We propose the probabilistic selection approach, with a single information exchange, each high-layer node h_i selects its forwarding node from $Inner(h_i)$ with different probabilities. The basic idea of the derivation of the probability values is to consider the estimated load conditions as well as the impact of the selection on load balancing. By carefully manipulating the probabilities, load balancing can be obtained in a statistical sense.

To begin with, each high-layer node h_i transmits a report packet to all nodes in $Lower(h_i)$ to report its transfer load $W(h_i)$. At this point, if $|Lower(h_i)|$ ==1 (i.e. h_i has only one low-layer neighbor), then obviously h_i is only able to select this node as its forwarding node, in this case, the indicator bit in the report packet is set to 1. Otherwise, h_i has more than one low-layer neighbor (i.e. $|Lower(h_i)| > 1$), then the indicator bit in the report packet is set to 0 and h_i will select its forwarding node within $Lower(h_i)$ in different probabilities. Having received all report packets from high-layer neighbors, low-layer node l_j measures its load condition and partition it into static load $SL(l_j)$ and dynamic load $DL(l_j)$ according to the indicator bit.

$$SL(l_j) = \sum_{h_i \in Higher(l_j)} W(h_i) \cdot I\{|Lower(h_i)| == 1\} \qquad (5)$$

$$DL(l_j) = \sum_{h_i \in Higher(l_j)} W(h_i) \cdot I\{|Lower(h_i)| > 1\} \qquad (6)$$

The load condition information is then feedback to high-layer nodes to complete the information exchange. Next, high-layer nodes calculate the probability of selecting each node in $Lower(h_i)$ as their forwarding node based on the feedback load condition information.

To determine the probability value, high-layer node h_i first calculates a preference value for each node in $Lower(h_i)$, then normalizes these preference values to get the probability values. The calculation of preference value takes two aspects into consideration, the load condition of each candidate, and the impact of the selection on load balancing. Obviously, low-layer candidates with heavier load will get less preference value while lighter ones get more. In addition, all nodes comply with a unified rule, that is, for the same low-layer node l_j, a high-layer node with more load will select it with higher probability while nodes with relatively less load will incline not to select it. By doing so, a reasonable forwarder selection is achieved by first avoiding the occurrence of overloaded forwarders, then decentralizing the transfer load according to a uniform rule. A high-layer node h_i calculates its preference value for a low-layer neighbor l_j as

$$h_i.Q(l_j) = \left(\frac{\sum_{l_k \in Lower(h_i)} DL(l_k)}{DL(l_j) + 1} + \frac{\frac{W(h_i)}{Layer}}{SL(l_j) + 1} \right) \cdot \frac{W(h_i)}{AVG(l_j)} \qquad (7)$$

where $Layer$ is the layer number of node h_i. $AVG(l_j)$ denotes the average size of received dynamic loads at l_j. The former item of the multiplication is the load situation of node l_j, which considers both dynamic and static load. The latter item compares $W(h_i)$ with the average size of dynamic loads at l_j to get the tendency of h_i selecting l_j as its forwarding node under the unified rule. After getting the preference value for each candidate node, we use $Softmax\ function$ to finally calculate the probability of h_i selecting l_j as its forwarding node as follows where e is the exponential constant:

$$h_i.P(l_j) = \frac{e^{h_i.Q(l_j)}}{\sum_{l_k \in Lower(h_i)} e^{h_i.Q(l_k)}} \qquad (8)$$

Finally, h_i selects its forwarding node l_j according to the probability values and sends a selection packet to inform it and other neighbors.

3.2   Channel Allocation

After the forwarder selection, each low-layer node l_j gets to know its previous node set $PN(l_j)$ and will allocate communication channels for them. With the knowledge of routing information from forwarder selection, the negotiation for the channel allocation of common neighbors can be reduced. Specifically, a high-layer node h_i may be the common neighbor of multiple low-layer nodes, while only its forwarder will allocate channels for it.

Inspired by [1], with the use of multiple channels, we eliminate the collisions by guaranteeing that each node has a dedicated channel for data transmission to its forwarder. This dedicated channel is non-overlapping with all the other data channels both for transmissions to the same destination as analyzed in (3) and for transmissions in the neighborhood as analyzed in (4). As such, the RX-RX, RX-overhearing problems(including classic hidden terminal problems and missing receiver problems) is avoided during data transmission.

In LETP, we use multiple data channels of a total number $N_c = n_{max} - 1$ where n_{max} is the maximum neighborhood size in the network. The Shannon capacity formula computes the achievable data transmission rate when using a sufficiently long channel code for symbol transmission over a complex Gaussian channel of bandwidth W, under a power constraint P_t and background noise power N_0 as $C = W \log_2\left(1 + \frac{P_t |h_0|^2}{N_0 W}\right)$, where h_0 is the channel gain between the transmission pairs whose magnitude $|h_0|$ is the attenuation of acoustic signal. The attenuation of a signal is calculated as $A(l, f) = A_0 l^k a(f)^l$, where l, f are the signal transmission distance and frequency, A_0 is the unit-normalizing constant, k is the spreading factor and $a(f)$ is the absorption coefficient [20]. In multiple channels, each channel has a different frequency, environmental noise power, and other properties. On the other hand, the transmission distance of each sender node as well as their transfer load is also different form each other. Therefore, for each low-layer node l_j, when allocating channels to nodes in $PN(l_j)$, in addition to avoid collisions, we can further optimize the channel allocation decision by matching the *channels* of different inherent properties with *senders* of different transmission distance and transfer load to increase the bandwidth utilization, resulting in a reduction on the overall transmission time.

The objective function of the above matching problem is built to minimize the overall time for l_j to receive data transmissions from all nodes in $PN(l_j)$. Let T_{iu} be the time required for node h_i to transmit on the channel represented by u. S_{iu} is the allocation state of the channel represented by u to node h_i. The objective function is as follows

$$\min_{S_{iu} \in S} \left(findMax(S_{iu} \cdot T_{iu})\right) \tag{9}$$

$$\text{subject to } \forall u \in U, \sum_{i \in I} S_{iu} = \{0, 1\} \tag{10}$$

$$\forall i \in I, \sum_{u \in U} S_{iu} = 1 \tag{11}$$

Algorithm 1. LECA algorithm

1: each low-layer node l_j allocates channels for nodes in $PN(l_j)$ in parallel
2: add all channels to ACS_{l_j}
3: calculate $Upd(l_j) = Higher(l_j) - PN(l_j)$
/** Available Channel Set update **/
4: **while** $Upd(l_j) \neq \emptyset$ **do**
5:     **for each** h_i in $Upd(l_j)$ **do**
6:         receive the *selection packet* from h_i
7:         obtain the channel information used by h_i from its *selection packet*
8:         update ACS_{l_j} by subtract the channel used by h_i
9:         $Upd(l_j) = Upd(l_j) - \{h_i\}$
10:     **end for**
11: **end while**
/** channel allocation **/
12: solve the problem in (9) with $PN(l_j)$ and ACS_{l_j}
13: allocate the remaining channels in ACS_{l_j}
14: send out *allocating packet*

$$\{u| \sum_{i \in I} S_{iu} == 1\} \subseteq ACS \tag{12}$$

$$\sum_{i \in I} \sum_{u \in U} S_{iu} \leq |ACS| \tag{13}$$

The first constraint (10) indicates that each channel can only be allocated to at most one node. Constraint (11) states that each node in $PN(l_j)$ is allocated for one channel. In constraints (12–13), the allocated channels are specified to be within the available channel set (ACS). The overall time for node l_j to receive data from all nodes in $PN(l_j)$ is $findMax(S_{iu} \cdot T_{iu})$.

The channel allocation decision of node l_j is expressed by a matrix $S_{I \times U}$, the number of rows I is equal to the number of nodes in $PN(l_j)$, and the number of columns U is the number of multiple channels. Each element S_{iu} represents the allocation state of the channel represented by u to node h_i.

$$S_{iu} = \begin{cases} 1, & \text{Channel } u \text{ is allocated to node } h_i \\ 0, & \text{Otherwise} \end{cases} \tag{14}$$

The time required for node h_i to transmit its data on the channel represented by u consists of two parts, transmission time and propagation time, which can be formulated as:

$$T_{iu} = T_{trans} + T_{prop} = \frac{W(h_i)}{C_u} + \frac{D_i}{v_a} \tag{15}$$

where C_u is the transmission rate of the channel represented by u. v_a is the propagation speed of underwater acoustic signal. D_i is the Euclidean distance between h_i and l_j.

The LECA algorithm is shown in Algorithm 1. Each node first maintains an available channel set (ACS) which is initialized by adding all channels into it.

Table 1. Parameter settings

Simulation time	3600 s	Transmission range	200 m
Total bandwidth	50 kHz	Transmission power	10 W
Acoustic speed	1500 m/s	Reception power	80 mW
Data packet size	200 Bytes	Sleeping power	1 mW
Control packet size	20 Bytes	Number of nodes	50–100
Network region	2 km 2 km 2 km	Traffic rate	0.025–0.25

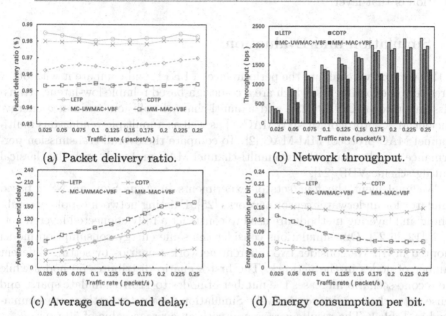

(a) Packet delivery ratio. (b) Network throughput.

(c) Average end-to-end delay. (d) Energy consumption per bit.

Fig. 2. Performance evaluation of four sets of experiments with $N = 50$.

Then, to eliminate RX-overhearing collision in (4), nodes calculate an updating set Upd by subtracting $PN(l_j)$ from $Higher(l_j)$ (lines 1–3). The channels used by nodes in Upd should be removed from ACS. The channel allocation information of nodes in Upd can be obtained in the forwarding node selection process. During the forwarding node selection process, low-layer nodes will use their $Higher(l_j)$ to act as $PN(l_j)$ to solve the optimization problem in (9) and add the obtained channel allocation decisions into their packet to high-layer neighbors. Then, the selection packets sent from high-layer nodes still contain these channel allocation decisions, which can be received by all low-layer neighbors so that they can update their respective ACS (lines 4–11). After clearing Upd, node l_j solves the problem in (9) with PN and ACS(line 12). Note that in order to avoid RX-overhearing collisions, for those nodes h_i satisfying $|Lower(h_i)| > 1$(i.e., h_i has more than one low-layer neighbor), the allocation decisions declared in their selection packets should be kept unchanged. This is because the allocation decisions declared by these nodes have already been used by their low-layer neighbors to update ACS. Finally, the remaining available channels are further allocated to those nodes with $|Lower(h_i)| == 1$ to increase their transmission rate as well as improve the bandwidth utilization in UASNs (lines 13–14).

In addition, each node estimates its *Maximum Receiving Time* (MRT) and add it into its allocating packet. This information will be inherited in the allocating packet of the forwarding node until it reaches the sink. Finally, the sink gets all MRTs and sets the largest MRT in each layer as the transmission slot duration of that layer.

4   Simulation and Evaluation

In this section, we evaluate the performance of LETP and compare it with other three sets of experiments, which are a co-design-based reliable low-latency transmission protocol CDTP [23], and a multi-channel collision avoidance energy-efficient MAC protocol MC-UWMAC [1] as well as a multiple-rendezvous multichannel MAC protocol MM-MAC [2]. To compare the overall transmission performance, we also equip the two multi-channel MAC protocols with the classical routing scheme VBF [24].

We implement the four sets of experiments in Aqua-Sim, an NS-2 based simulator for underwater sensor networks [25]. Existing network topology establishing and layering methods are used to construct a fully connected layered network [12,26,27]. Our simulations consider the same energy consumption model adopted in [1]. We consider two different network scenarios by setting different number of nodes in the network. The first scenario distributes 50 nodes while the second scenario increases the number of nodes to 120 to simulate sparse and dense network scenarios respectively. Simulation parameter settings are summarized in Table 1. The results correspond with an average value of 50 runs.

Figure 2a shows the packet delivery ratio as a function of the traffic rate for four sets of transmission protocols. All these protocols are designed to achieve reliable transmissions so all show a high PDR (more than 95%). LETP is able to achieve a high PDR. Indeed, after nodes negotiating their transmission paths and communication channels with each other, reliable transmission without collision can be guaranteed.

The evaluation of performance in terms of network throughput is shown in Fig. 2b. Observe that, LETP outperforms other protocols in terms of throughput, regardless of the generated traffic rate. LETP uses multiple channels for simultaneous transmissions so that the spatial reuse is better than CDTP. Compared with MC-UWMAC, LETP uses a more reasonable bandwidth for data transmission. In the case of the same total bandwidth B and maximum neighborhood size n, MC-UWMAC divides B into N_1 data channels where $N_1 = \frac{n(n-1)}{2}$, and data transmission between node pairs will use one of these N_1 channels. LETP only divides B into $N_2 = n - 1$ data channels, which is much less than that in MC-UWMAC, and node pairs may use multiple channels when communicating. As for MM-MAC, it divides time into control period and data period, each data

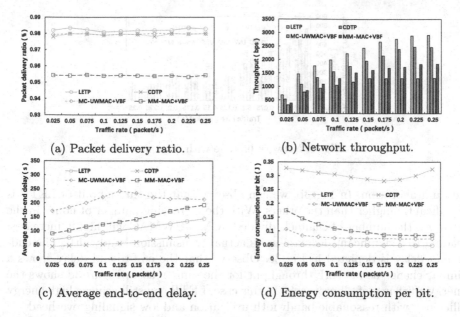

(a) Packet delivery ratio.   (b) Network throughput.

(c) Average end-to-end delay.   (d) Energy consumption per bit.

Fig. 3. Performance evaluation of four sets of experiments with $N = 120$.

period is performed after a control period, which increases the end-to-end delay of data transmission, thereby leading to degradation in throughput.

Figure 2c depicts the average end-to-end delay for all protocols as a function of the traffic rate. According to the hierarchical slotted transmission scheme, with the increasing traffic rate, the length of time slot will become longer, leading to a slowly and uniformly increase of average end-to-end delay in LETP. MC-UWMAC and MM-MAC +VBF have a higher average end-to-end delay mainly because the low bandwidth utilization. CDTP shortens the calculation time of holding time and leverages the hierarchical structure to find the nearest transmission path so it enables the shortest end-to-end delay.

The energy consumption per useful bit as a function of the traffic rate is shown in Fig. 2d. LETP achieves high energy efficiency with reasonable bandwidth utilization and low signaling overhead. It is worth noting that the curve of both MM-MAC and MC-UWMAC +VBF shows a downward trend. The reason is that under their burst mechanism, with the traffic rate increases, one successful handshake could responsible for more data transmission, which improves energy efficiency. In addition, all sets of protocol avoid collisions effectively which is beneficial to high energy efficiency.

Figure 3 shows the performance of the four sets of transmission protocols when the number of nodes is 120. As shown in Fig. 3a, in dense networks, LETP can still guarantee a high PDR. It is worth noting that the PDR of MC-UWMAC+VBF is improved compared with that when $N = 50$. This is because as the number of nodes increases, the probability that multiple nodes are located in the same small cell is greatly reduced, thus realizing a collision-free

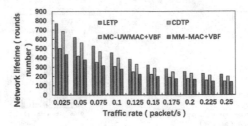

Fig. 4. Network lifetime with 50 nodes

quorum allocation. In Fig. 3b, we can observe that the throughput of LETP is significantly higher than the others. With the increasing number of nodes in the network, the number of channels divided by MC-UWMAC will highly increases, leading to a significant decrease in its actual transmission bandwidth. The end-to-end delay is depicted in Fig. 3c. Observe that the end-to-end delay shows a similar change as network throughput for the same reason. Figure 3d shows the energy efficiency of all protocols. In this case, LETP can still achieve high energy efficiency with reasonable bandwidth utilization and low signaling overhead.

Finally, we compared the network lifetimes under four sets of transmission protocols when the number of nodes $N = 50$. As shown in Fig. 4, LETP guarantees a long network lifetime duo to its high energy efficiency as well as balanced energy consumption.

5 Related Work

Multi-channel protocols have been widely studied to improve network performance and avoid collisions in UASNs during past years [1,2,4,19,21,28]. Different from the single-channel protocols such as [14,15] that use only one channel for communication, multi-channel protocols are able to let nodes within the communication range of each other simultaneously transmit packets on different data channels without collision. In [1], the main idea is to guarantee each pair of neighbor nodes use a unique data channel for their data transmission within the two-hop collision domain. By means of grid-based slot assignment on the control channel and quorum-based data channel allocation, a collision-free multi-channel scheme is proposed. Based on the investigation of the multi-channel MAC problem, [28] proposed the triple hidden terminal problem in UASNs, then designed CUMAC, which utilizes the cooperation of neighboring nodes to detect collisions before data transmissions to avoid collisions. Another multi-channel scheme MM-MAC is proposed in [2]. It assigns each node a default channel, then divides control slots into default and switching slots. By utilizing cyclic quorum systems, nodes are guaranteed to meet their destinations at a specific time slot, thus multiple-rendezvous communication is achieved without collisions.

As the sensor nodes in UASNs are battery-powered and hard to be recharged, designing energy-efficient protocols is also a paramount issue. Also, [11] proposed a Q-learning-based routing protocol QL-EEBDG to avoid immutable forwarder selection and the occurrence of void holes. Through the co-design of routing and MAC layer, CDTP [23] reduced the number of control packet exchange and data-packet copies to perform low latency and energy-efficient transmissions. In [27], with the implementation of multimodal communication, an energy efficiency multi-level transmission strategy is suggested, which considers three aspects, transmission latency, residual energy, and transfer load at the receiver.

This paper utilizes multiple channels as the basic tool to tackle the collision problem. After that, we improve the link efficiency by means of channel allocation and forwarder selection in both MAC and routing layers to balance energy consumption and improve network performance.

6 Conclusion

In this paper, to enable collision avoidance and high bandwidth utilization at low signaling overhead, we proposed a Link-Efficiency multi-channel Transmission Protocol for data collection in UASNs. In the routing layer, we proposed a forwarding node probabilistic selection approach to solve the unbalanced transfer load problem with low signaling overhead. In the MAC layer, a link efficiency channel allocation algorithm is applied on the receiver side to allocate dedicated communication channels to avoid collisions and optimize the allocation decision based on channel characteristics. Finally, transmissions take place on negotiated channels and transmission paths in a high link efficiency. Moreover, LETP can be further applied to all layered networks with a single sink or multiple sinks.

References

1. Bouabdallah, F., Zidi, C., Boutaba, R., Mehaoua, A.: Collision avoidance energy efficient multi-channel MAC protocol for underwater acoustic sensor networks. IEEE Trans. Mob. Comput. **18**(10), 2298–2314 (2019). https://doi.org/10.1109/TMC.2018.2871686
2. Chao, C.M., Wang, Y.Z., Lu, M.W.: Multiple-rendezvous multichannel MAC protocol design for underwater sensor networks. IEEE Trans. Syst. Man Cybern.: Syst **43**(1), 128–138 (2012)
3. Chen, X., Jiao, L., Li, W., Fu, X.: Efficient multi-user computation offloading for mobile-edge cloud computing. IEEE/ACM Trans. Netw. **24**(5), 2795–2808 (2016). https://doi.org/10.1109/TNET.2015.2487344
4. Cho, J., Cho, H.S.: A multi-channel MAC protocol in underwater acoustic sensor networks. In: Proceedings of the 11th ACM International Conference on Underwater Networks & Systems, pp. 1–2 (2016)
5. Gai, K., Qiu, M., Chen, L., Liu, M.: Electronic health record error prevention approach using ontology in big data. In: IEEE 17th HPCC Conference (2015)
6. Gai, K., Qiu, M., Elnagdy, S.: A novel secure big data cyber incident analytics framework for cloud-based cybersecurity insurance. In: IEEE BigDataSecurity Conference (2016)
7. Gai, K., Qiu, M., Zhao, H., Xiong, J.: Privacy-aware adaptive data encryption strategy of big data in cloud computing. In: IEEE 3rd CSCloud Conference (2016)

8. Gai, K., Qiu, M., Sun, X., Zhao, H.: Security and privacy issues: a survey on FinTech. In: SmartCom, pp. 236–247 (2016)

9. Gao, M., Chen, Z., Yao, X., Xu, N.: JM-MAC: a JSW-based multi-channel MAC protocol in underwater acoustic sensor networks. In: 2016 10th International Conference on Signal Processing and Communication Systems (ICSPCS), pp. 1–6 (2016). https://doi.org/10.1109/ICSPCS.2016.7843373

10. Guo, Y., Zhuge, Q., Hu, J., et al.: Data placement and duplication for embedded multicore systems with scratch pad memory. IEEE Trans. CAD (2013)

11. Javaid, N., Karim, O.A., Sher, A., Imran, M., Yasar, A.U.H., Guizani, M.: Q-learning for energy balancing and avoiding the void hole routing protocol in underwater sensor networks. In: 2018 14th International Wireless Communications & Mobile Computing Conference (IWCMC), pp. 702–706. IEEE (2018)

12. Khan, M.T.R., Ahmed, S.H., Kim, D.: AUV-aided energy-efficient clustering in the internet of underwater things. IEEE Trans. Green Commun. Netw. 3(4), 1132–1141 (2019). https://doi.org/10.1109/TGCN.2019.2922278

13. Lu, R., Jin, X., Zhang, S., Qiu, M., Wu, X.: A study on big knowledge and its engineering issues. IEEE Trans. Knowl. Data Eng. 31(9), 1630–1644 (2018)

14. Molins, M., Stojanovic, M.: Slotted FAMA: a MAC protocol for underwater acoustic networks. In: OCEANS 2006-Asia Pacific, pp. 1–7. IEEE (2006)

15. Noh, Y., et al.: Dots: a propagation delay-aware opportunistic MAC protocol for mobile underwater networks. IEEE Trans. Mob. Comput. 13(4), 766–782 (2014)

16. Qiu, M., Khisamutdinov, E., et al.: RNA nanotechnology for computer design and in vivo computation (2013)

17. Qiu, M., Ming, Z., Li, J., Liu, J., Quan, G., Zhu, Y.: Informer homed routing fault tolerance mechanism for wireless sensor networks. J. Syst. Arch. 59(4–5), 260–270 (2013)

18. Qiu, M., Ming, Z., Li, J., Liu, S., Wang, B., Lu, Z.: Three-phase time-aware energy minimization with DVFS and unrolling for chip multiprocessors. J. Syst. Archit. 58(10), 439–445 (2012)

19. Rahmati, M., Pompili, D.: Probabilistic spatially-divided multiple access in underwater acoustic sparse networks. IEEE Trans. Mob. Comput. 19(2), 405–418 (2020)

20. Stojanovic, M., Preisig, J.: Underwater acoustic communication channels: propagation models and statistical characterization. IEEE Commun. Mag. 47(1), 84–89 (2009). https://doi.org/10.1109/MCOM.2009.4752682

21. Su, Y., Jin, Z.: UMMAC: a multi-channel MAC protocol for underwater acoustic networks. J. Commun. Netw. 18(1), 75–83 (2016)

22. Tang, X., Li, K., et al.: A hierarchical reliability-driven scheduling algorithm in grid systems. J. Parallel Distrib. Comput. 72(4), 525–535 (2012)

23. Wei, X., et al.: A co-design-based reliable low-latency and energy-efficient transmission protocol for UWSNS. Sensors 20(21), 6370 (2020)

24. Xie, P., Cui, J.-H., Lao, L.: VBF: vector-based forwarding protocol for underwater sensor networks. In: Boavida, F., Plagemann, T., Stiller, B., Westphal, C., Monteiro, E. (eds.) NETWORKING 2006. LNCS, vol. 3976, pp. 1216–1221. Springer, Heidelberg (2006). https://doi.org/10.1007/11753810_111

25. Xie, P., et al.: Aqua-sim: an NS-2 based simulator for underwater sensor networks. In: OCEANS 2009, pp. 1–7. IEEE (2009)

26. Xu, Z., Chen, L., Chen, C., Guan, X.: Joint clustering and routing design for reliable and efficient data collection in large-scale wireless sensor networks. IEEE Internet Things J. 3(4), 520–532 (2016). https://doi.org/10.1109/JIOT.2015.2482363

27. Zhao, Z., Liu, C., Qu, W., Yu, T.: An energy efficiency multi-level transmission strategy based on underwater multimodal communication in UWSNS. In: IEEE INFOCOM 2020-IEEE Conference on Computer Communications, pp. 1579–1587. IEEE (2020)
28. Zhou, Z., Peng, Z., Cui, J., Jiang, Z.: Handling triple hidden terminal problems for multichannel MAC in long-delay underwater sensor networks. IEEE Trans. Mob. Comput. 11(1), 139–154 (2012). https://doi.org/10.1109/TMC.2011.28

A Multi-attribute Decision Handover Strategy for Giant LEO Mobile Satellite Networks

TingTing Zhang[1](✉), LinTao Yang[2], Tao Dong[1], Jie Yin[1], ZhiHui Liu[1], and ZhanWei Wang[1]

[1] State Key Laboratory of Space-Ground Integrated Information Technology, Beijing Institute of Satellite Information Engineering, Beijing 100095, China
[2] College of Physical Science and Technology, Central China Normal University, Wuhan 430079, China
ltaoyang@mail.ccnu.edu.cn

Abstract. Due to the characteristics of low orbital height and large number of satellites, the giant *Low Earth Orbit* (LEO) satellite network has more frequent handovers than ordinary LEO satellite communication systems. There are a large number of satellites available for handover, and the handover problem is more prominent. In this study, a handover strategy suitable for all users is designed for the inter-satellite handover in the giant LEO satellite network. This strategy designs two different handover methods for different handover users and new callers. For users who can predict the handover time, a multi-attribute decision handover strategy based on a directed graph is adopted. It uses the satellite service timetable (including satellite coverage at each time and each index value) to construct a satellite handover directed graph, and combine the handover path to reserve channel resources for users. For handover users and new callers who cannot predict the handover time, a multi-attribute decision handover strategy based on combined weights is adopted. The best candidate satellites are obtained by weighting each index combination, distinguishing user types and service types, and using channel queuing strategies to access satellites according to different priorities. The simulation results prove that this strategy can reduce the number of handovers while taking into account the signal strength and system load balance, and can effectively reduce the handover blocking rate.

Keywords: LEO satellite network · Inter-satellite handover · Multi-attribute decision

1 Introduction

Big data processing [1–3] had greatly changed the style of human life due to the fast advance in computer technology [4–6], software [7, 8], and Internet [9, 10]. Although communication technology is highly developed, there are more than 3.5 billion people in the world who do not enjoy Internet services. Some countries and companies propose to deploy a large number of satellites around the world to form a giant constellation to provide satellite Internet air interfaces, enabling users at any place and any time

© The Author(s), under exclusive license to Springer Nature Switzerland AG 2022
M. Qiu et al. (Eds.): SmartCom 2021, LNCS 13202, pp. 64–73, 2022.
https://doi.org/10.1007/978-3-030-97774-0_6

[11]. Compared with the traditional LEO satellite communication system, the giant LEO satellite communication system has the following advantages: more users can use the satellite communication service, the information transmission speed is fast, and the anti-interference ability is better. Because of these characteristics, countries have been vigorously developing their own giant LEO satellite communication systems in recent years, and the giant LEO satellite communication systems have relatively good and broad industry development prospects. However, in the giant LEO satellite network, there are a large number of satellites that can provide services to users at any time, and it is a problem that the user terminal chooses which satellite to access during handover. Therefore, it is very necessary to study the handover strategy for the giant LEO satellite network.

This paper used the mega constellation as the handover scenario to study the handover strategy applicable to the mega constellation to ensure user communication quality, handover success rate, and channel load balance. In view of the handover problem in the giant LEO satellite network, the method to obtain signal strength, satellite elevation angle, service duration, and number of idle channels is studied, and the gray model is used to predict the signal strength and idle channels in the next period of time. Then a multi-attribute decision-making inter-satellite handover strategy based on indicators such as signal strength, satellite elevation angle, service duration, and number of idle channels is proposed. And it distinguish the handover users and new call users in different handover trigger scenarios, and adopt the multi-attribute decision handover strategy based on the directed graph and the combination weight respectively.

The rest of this paper is organized as follows; in Sect. 2, we present related work. Section 3, we present our work in multi-attribute decision handover strategy. Section 4, we present our simulation environment and results. At last, in Sect. 5 we conclude the paper.

2 Related Work

In the LEO satellite communication system, during the continuous communication process of satellite motion, it is inevitably impossible to only be within the coverage of one star. In order to maintain the continuity of communication, the two parties must frequently handover between different satellites [12]. The quality of the handover strategy largely affects the entire LEO satellite network system performance, so the choice of handover strategy is very important in the whole handover process.

The inter-satellite handover strategy based on the maximum signal strength [13] is currently the most studied strategy. This handover strategy is the simplest and easy to implement, but the effect is not very good in practical applications and a high probability of erroneous handover. In order to further improve the handover performance of the strategy, Zhao W, Tafazolli R [14] and others proposed to combine the maximum signal strength strategy with user terminal position prediction, using the communication transmission delay and doppler shift between the user terminal and the satellite. It calculates the moment of handover between the user terminal and the satellite, reserve handover channel resources for the user in advance, and reduce the probability of call termination.

The inter-satellite handover strategy based on the remaining maximum service duration proposed by FN Pavlidou et al. [15] can minimize the number of handovers. However, this strategy always considers the remaining service duration and ignores the impact of other factors on handover. Wu Z, Jin F [16] et al. proposed a satellite handover model based on a directed graph according to the satellite service time, this model can only solve users who can predict the hand-over time in advance. Based on the shortest path inter-satellite handover strategy [17], the communication delay can be reduced, but when there are a large number of satellites in the constellation, the inter-satellite routing calculation is too complicated, which will lead to a longer handover delay. Based on the minimum load inter-satellite handover strategy [18] can reduce the handover blocking rate to the greatest extent, but the effect is not very obvious when the distribution of communication services in a certain area is extreme. The inter-satellite handover strategy based on the maximum elevation angle is to select the satellite with the largest elevation angle visible to the user terminal for each handover. The same strategy and the maximum signal strength strategy do not take into account the shadow effect and channel fading, and the shortcomings are also obvious.

All of the above handover strategies are basically studied with lightweight constellations as handover scenarios. Few handover strategies have been proposed for giant constellations. The current LEO satellite constellations are developing towards giant constellations, and there are a large number of constellation satellites. These strategies Not necessarily applicable in mega constellations.

3   Method

3.1   General Framework

There are generally three conditions for triggering satellite handover: the elevation angle between the user terminal and the satellite is less than the minimum communicable belief angle, and the satellite cannot continue to provide services for users; the communication link between the user terminal and the satellite is affected by environmental factors, and the satellite signal strength is not enough to provide good services for users; Load is too heavy, trigger load balancing to switch to other satellites with lighter load. This article designs a multi-attribute decision handover strategy for the handover users and new call users in the above-mentioned different handover trigger scenarios to choose to handover satellites.

The multi-attribute decision handover strategy selects different types of handover strategies according to the type of user after the user makes a handover call (see Fig. 1). First, a multi-attribute decision handover strategy based on a directed graph is adopted for the normal handover users at each handover moment. According to the main decision indicators, this model creates a weighted directed graph of the satellite's coverage of the user terminal at each time. By solving the shortest path of the directed graph, the optimal handover path for handover satellites in the entire communication process is obtained.

Secondly, for abnormal handover users (new call users) who cannot predict the handover time (access time) in advance, a multi-attribute decision handover strategy

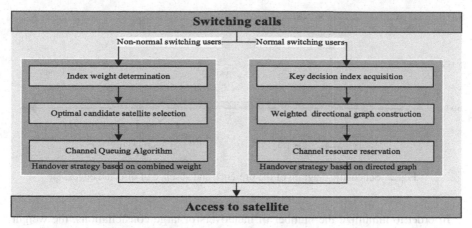

Fig. 1. The multi-attribute decision handover strategy.

based on combined weights is adopted. It creates a list of candidate service satellites for each user terminal connected to the satellite communication system, determines the weight of each index, then selected the best handover satellite, and finally uses the channel queuing strategy to handover the satellite.

3.2 Handover Strategy Based on Directed Graph

The handover scenario studied in this paper is the handover between different satellites under the coverage of the same gateway. The satellites only have the function of transparent forwarding. The multi-attribute decision handover strategy based on the directed graph used in the study include key decision index acquisition, weighted directed graph construction, and channel resource reservation [19].

The key decision indicators acquired by the switching strategy based on directional graphics are satellite inclination, service time and the number of free channels. Satellite inclination is defined as the angle between the horizon where the user terminal is located and the satellite [20]. In order to reduce the number of handovers, the service time of the satellite to be visited is a key indicator for the user terminal to switch satellites. The largest service time is the relevant constant in the same satellite network, the relevant constant in the same satellite network, and the arc between the user terminal and the satellite subsatellites. The number of free channels is the number of idle satellite channels obtained from the satellite broadcast information when the user terminal regularly measures the signal strength.

When T_{end_1} is greater than T_{start_2}, it means that there is a handover path from Sat_1 to Sat_2 (see Fig. 2). At this time, add a directed edge from the vertex of Sat_1 to the vertex of Sat_2 in the directed graph, and then continue to compare with Sat_3's T_{start3}, repeat the above steps until if T_{end_1} is smaller than a satellite Sat_x's T_{start}, it means that there is no directed edge between Sat_1 and Sat_x. At this time, the comparison process of Sat_1 is stopped, otherwise the comparison will continue to the last satellite. After the Sat_1 comparison is over, start the Sat_2 comparison and repeat the above steps. When all the satellites are compared, the whole satellite directed graph construction ends [16].

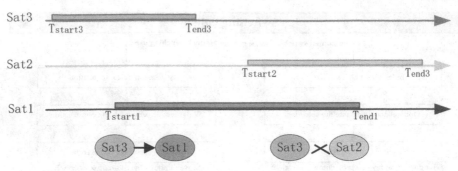

Fig. 2. Schematic diagram of the presence and absence of directed edges.

In order to minimize the number of handovers of large constellations, the weight of the service period is set to 1. Due to environmental factors and the lack of channel resources, elevation angle and air flow channels are nonlinearly weighted. To build a weight-based directional graph, the weight of each directional edge must be obtained based on the number of idle channels of the candidate satellite at mating and the weight of each directional edge.

After obtaining the optimal handover path through the satellite directed graph, based on the location information of each user and the location information of the satellite at each time, the satellite can calculate which users at which time the satellite serves, and channel resources are reserved for the corresponding users [21].

3.3 Handover Strategy Based on Combined Weight

Handover under the influence of environmental factors, the current serving satellite is overloaded to trigger load balancing. The handover trigger method of the two handover scenarios is unpredictable. When a new user calls to access the LEO satellite communication system, it is necessary to select a satellite for connection. Entry does not apply to the previous method. Therefore, this paper designs a multi-attribute decision satellite handover strategy based on combined weight for the above situation, including index weight determination, optimal candidate satellite selection, and channel queuing algorithm.

The evaluation criteria for each index obtained during the satellite handover process are different, and different standardized methods must be used for processing. In this paper, the signal strength prediction value and the remaining service time are standardized by the trigonometric function transformation method, and the idle channel prediction value is standardized by the range transformation method.

This paper uses the combination weighting method to determine the weights in the multi-attribute decision. Combination weighting method combines subjective weighting method and objective weighting method, comprehensively considering the influence of objective factors to consider the different importance of decision makers to each attribute. The subjective weighting method for the indicators obtained during the handover process is the AHP method [22], the objective weights are determined by the entropy method [23], and the weights are determined according to the amount of information of each indicator. Finally, the obtained subjective weights and objective weights are combined to obtain the combined weights. After obtaining the combined weight of each indicator, the TOPSIS method is used to select optimal candidate satellites.

The user terminal is divided into new calling users and handover users according to the type of call. When the user terminal uses the satellite network to communicate, the sudden disconnection of the call is more difficult for the user to accept than the unsuccessful call. Therefore, the priority of the handover is to Larger than the new call. The channel queuing algorithm, in addition to the determination of user priority, has a very important value for the queuing time of user calls, the value of which depends on the superimposed coverage duration between two adjacent satellites on the same orbital plane in the LEO satellite network.

4 Experiment and Result

4.1 Simulation Setup

To verify the effectiveness of the handover strategy proposed in this paper, we use simulation tools STK and simulation software Qualnet to simulate the handover scenarios of user terminals in the giant low-orbit satellite network. The simulation compares our handover strategy with other classic handover strategies.

This paper selects the representative giant constellation as SpaceX's Starlink constellation as a simulation scenario to verify the proposed handover strategy. The specific parameters of the core constellation are shown in Table 1. The experimental simulation scenario selected in this paper is that users in the New York area randomly access the Starlink low-orbit satellite communication system from nine to ten in the morning.

Table 1. Starlink constellation parameters.

Parameters	Values
Track surface number	70
Number of satellites per orbital surface	30
Satellite orbit height	500 km
Orbital inclination	57°
RAAN Spread	150°

4.2 Evaluation Metrics

To verify the effectiveness and superiority of the handover strategy proposed in this article, the paper mainly counts the following performance indicators in the simulation:

(1) Handover times: It refers to the number of the user terminal handover satellites from the start of communication to the end of the communication in the LEO satellite network.

(2) Blocking rate of new calls:

$$P_c = \frac{Number\ of\ failed\ new\ calls}{Total\ number\ of\ calls}$$

(3) Handover blocking rate:

$$P_s = \frac{Number\ of\ failed\ handovers}{Total\ number\ of\ handover}$$

(4) User Service Index:

$$\text{Gos} = (P_c + kP_s)/(k+1)$$

(5) The average signal strength of the satellite received by the user terminal during handover. The greater the signal strength received by the user, the better the stability of the satellite-to-earth link and the better the communication quality.

(6) Satellite load fairness: The load fairness of the satellite is defined by using the Jain fairness index as shown below.

4.3 Comparison to Existing Method

To verify the effectiveness of the satellite handover strategy based on multi-attribute decision proposed in this article, MAHS (Multi attribute handover strategy) handover strategy proposed in this paper is compared with the aforementioned handover strategy of maximum satellite elevation angle H1, maximum signal strength H2, maximum idle channel H3 and maximum remaining service duration H4. Then evaluation metrics are used to analyze the performance of different strategies.

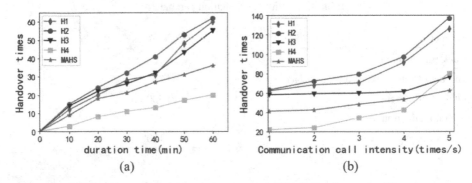

(a)   (b)

Fig. 3. Comparison of handover times of different handover strategies.

The H4 handover strategy has the least number of handovers during the entire communication process. The MAHS handover strategy considers the impact of various indicators, so the number of handovers experienced lies in the middle (see Fig. 3(a)). The

MAHS handover strategy is greater than the H4 handover strategy only when the communication call intensity is low. When the call intensity is high, it is similar to the H4 handover strategy, which basically achieves the purpose of reducing the number of handovers (see Fig. 3(b)).

Table 2. Performance evaluation index of various methods when the communication call intensity is 2 times/s.

Metrics	Handover strategy				
	H1	H2	H3	H4	MAHS
Handover blocking rate (%)	0.65	0.72	0.73	0.75	0.65
Blocking rate of new calls (%)	1.2	1.2	0.7	1.3	0.8
User service index	0.45	0.5	0.6	0.7	0.46
Load fairness	0.74	0.73	0.81	0.73	0.77
Average signal strength (−dBm)	64.8	64.7	67.5	68.7	65.4

Table 3. Performance evaluation index of various methods when the communication call intensity is 4 times/s.

Metrics	Handover strategy				
	H1	H2	H3	H4	MAHS
Handover blocking rate (%)	3.1	3.0	3.1	6.2	2.8
Blocking rate of new calls (%)	6.85	6.95	5.1	10.3	11.8
User service index	6.5	6.4	3.2	6.7	3.6
Load fairness	0.68	0.67	0.855	0.675	0.82
Average signal strength (−dBm)	65.4	65.1	67.8	67.4	66.3

The MAHS handover strategy always has the lowest handover blocking rate (see Tables 2, 3, 4). When the call intensity is too high, the new call blocking rate is the highest. Because when the number of users is too large, the allocated channel resources will be large, and the channel queuing strategy is used to first allocate channel resources for the exchange users. The user service index is not much different from the H3 handover strategy with low handover blocking rate and new call blocking rate. The MAHS handover strategy takes into account the influence of some channel resources when selecting a handover satellite, as well as the influence of satellite signal strength and service duration. Therefore, the satellite load fairness is lower than the H3 handover strategy that only considers the satellite load situation, and has a longer handover time than other handover strategies. The signal strength is affected by environmental factors to a certain extent, so the overall signal strength of the MAHS handover strategy during the handover process is not as good as the H1 and H2 handover strategies, but higher than other strategies.

Table 4. Performance evaluation index of various methods when the communication call intensity is 6 times/s.

Metrics	Handover strategy				
	H1	H2	H3	H4	MAHS
Handover blocking rate (%)	9.0	8.9	4.2	9.1	3.8
Blocking rate of new calls (%)	14.4	15	9.2	15.9	19.8
User service index	9.5	9.4	4.8	9.8	5.1
Load fairness	0.63	0.625	0.845	0.62	0.8
Average signal strength ($-$dBm)	65.3	65.3	68.5	68.3	66.7

Based on the above results, the MAHS handover strategy combines the advantages of the H1, H2, H3, and H4 handover strategies. The handover blocking rate of the MAHS handover strategy is the smallest, and the user service index is not much different from the best performance H3 handover strategy. The handover times, load fairness, and signal strength of the MAHS handover strategy are also at a good level among all strategies, which can provide users with better handover services.

5   Conclusion

Aiming at handover problems such as frequent handovers of giant LEO satellite networks, this paper studied handover strategies applicable to giant constellations. Considering the impact of various indicators on handover, for handover users and new call users in different handover trigger scenarios, a multi-attribute decision-making giant inter-satellite handover strategy based on directed graphs and a multi-attribute decision giant constellation based on combined weights were designed. The simulation proved that the handover strategy proposed in this paper can minimize the number of handovers while taking into account the signal strength and system load balance, and at the same time effectively reduced the handover blocking rate.

Acknowledgement. This work was supported by the Open Research Fund of State Key Laboratory of SpaceGround Integrated Information Technology under grant NO. 2018_SGIIT_KFJJ_TX_01.

References

1. Lu, R., Jin, X., Zhang, S., Qiu, M., Wu, X.: A study on big knowledge and its engineering issues. IEEE Trans. Knowl. Data Eng. **31**(9), 1630–1644 (2018)
2. Qiu, M., Cao, D., et al.: Data transfer minimization for financial derivative pricing using Monte Carlo simulation with GPU in 5G. J. Commun. Syst. **29**(16), 2364–2374 (2016)
3. Guo, Y., Zhuge, Q., Hu, J., et al.: Optimal data allocation for scratch-pad memory on embedded multi-core systems. In: IEEE ICPP Conference, pp. 464–471 (2011)

4. Zhang, L., Qiu, M., et al.: Variable partitioning and scheduling for MPSoC with virtually shared scratch pad memory. J. Signal Process. Syst. **58**(2), 247–265 (2010)
5. Qiu, M., Chen, Z., Liu, M.: Low-power low-latency data allocation for hybrid scratch-pad memory. IEEE Embed. Syst. Lett. **6**(4), 69–72 (2014)
6. Qiu, M., Khisamutdinov, E., et al.: RNA nanotechnology for computer design and in vivo computation. Philos. Trans. R. Soc. A (2013)
7. Gai, K., Qiu, M., Elnagdy, S.: A novel secure big data cyber incident analytics framework for cloud-based cybersecurity insurance. In: IEEE BigDataSecurity (2016)
8. Liu, M., Zhang, S., et al.: H infinite state estimation for discrete-time chaotic systems based on a unified model. IEEE Trans. Syst. Man Cybern. (B) (2012)
9. Lu, Z., Wang, N., Wu, J., Qiu, M.: IoTDeM: an IoT big data-oriented MapReduce performance prediction extended model in multiple edge clouds. JPDC **118**, 316–327 (2018)
10. Qiu, L., Gai, K., Qiu, M.: Optimal big data sharing approach for tele-health in cloud computing. In: IEEE SmartCloud, pp. 184–189 (2016)
11. Wu, Y., et al.: A satellite handover strategy based on the potential game in LEO satellite networks. IEEE Access **7**, 133641–133652 (2019)
12. Jin, J., Linling, K., Jian, Y., et al.: Smart Communication Satellite, Project Overview (2015)
13. Karapantazis, S., Pavlidou, F.N.: QoS handover management for multimedia LEO satellite networks. Telecommun. Syst. **32**(4), 225–245 (2006)
14. Zhao, W., Tafazolli, R., Evans, B.G.: Combined handover algorithm for dynamic satellite constellations. Electron. Lett. **32**(7), 622–624 (1996)
15. Pavlidou, F.-N., Papapetrou, E.: QoS handover management in LEO/MEO satellite systems. Wirel. Pers. Commun. Int. J. **24**(2), 189–204 (2003)
16. Wu, Z., Jin, F., Luo, J., et al.: A graph-based satellite handover framework for LEO satellite communication networks. IEEE Commun. Lett. **20**(8), 1547–1550 (2016)
17. Cho, S., Akyildiz, I.F., et al.: A new connection admission control for spotbeam handover in LEO satellite networks. Springer J. **8**(4), 403–415 (2002)
18. Papapetrou, E., Pavlidou, F.N.: QoS handover management in LEO/MEO satellite systems. Wirel. Pers. Commun. **24**(2), 189–204 (2003)
19. Bottcher, A., Werner, R.: Strategies for handover control in low Earth orbit satellite systems. In: Proceedings of IEEE Vehicular Technology Conference (VTC). IEEE (2002)
20. Miao, J., Wang, P., Yin, H., Chen, N., Wang, X.: A multi-attribute decision handover scheme for LEO mobile satellite networks. In: IEEE 5th ICCC, pp. 938–942 (2019)
21. Zhang, S., Liu, A., Liang, X.: A multi-objective satellite handover strategy based on entropy in LEO satellite communications. In: IEEE 6th ICCC, pp. 723–728 (2020)
22. Saaty, T.L.: Decision making - the analytic hierarchy and network processes (AHP/ANP). J. Syst. Sci. Syst. Eng. (01), 1–35 (2004)
23. Chen, S., Hong, J.: Fuzzy multiple attributes group decision-making based on ranking interval type-2 fuzzy sets and TOPSIS method. IEEE TSMC **44**(12), 1665–1673 (2014)

ML-ECN: Multilayer Emergency Communication Network Based on the Combination of Space and Earth

Liang Zhou[1,2], Hao Li[2(✉)], Jianguo Zhou[2], Changjia Zhou[2], and Tianzhu Shi[2]

[1] Wuhan University, Wuhan 430072, China
[2] Information and Communication Company of State Grid Hubei Electric Power Co., Wuhan 430077, China
{eehaoli,zjg,jj_zhou,2021282120185}@whu.edu.cn

Abstract. In recent years, major geological disasters have occurred, often accompanied by the massive destruction of infrastructure communication facilities. Therefore, quickly building an *Emergency Communication Network* (ECN) after a disaster is a key problem. At present, there are a variety of emergency communication network solutions, including *Unmanned Aerial Vehicle* (UAV) networks, satellite networks, wireless sensor networks, ground MESH networks, and so on. However, this kind of research rarely considers the comprehensive application of the abovementioned networks and the collaborative work between them. In this paper, an emergency communication network is proposed, which includes a wireless sensor network, ground MESH network, UAV MESH network, and satellite network. The multilayer network works together to ensure the smooth development of post-disaster rescue work. We also propose a location algorithm based on reverse verification, which relies mainly on wireless sensor networks. For network service quality, we propose an improved scheduling algorithm based on *Weighted Deficit Round Robin* (WDRR) and. Multiple measures are taken to ensure network *Quality of Service* (QoS). Numerical results show the superiority of our scheme.

Keywords: Geological disasters · Emergency Communication Network (ECN) · Location · Scheduling · Deployment

1 Introduction

Many geological disasters and severe weather may destroy existing basic communication facilities [1], and as a result, the disaster-affected area is unable to contact the outside world in a timely manner, introducing great difficulties during post-disaster rescue work. For example, in the 2011 Japan earthquake, more than 6000 base stations were damaged, and during Hurricane Harvey, only one of the 19 cell towers in Aransas County, Texas, was able to operate normally during the storm [2]. On the other hand, the 72 h following a disaster is generally called the golden 72 h [3], which is particularly important for the development of rescue work. Therefore, it is necessary to study a disaster response communication network that can achieve rapid deployment while

© The Author(s), under exclusive license to Springer Nature Switzerland AG 2022
M. Qiu et al. (Eds.): SmartCom 2021, LNCS 13202, pp. 74–89, 2022.
https://doi.org/10.1007/978-3-030-97774-0_7

considering the complexity of the disaster area environment [4]. The disaster response communication network should be able to adapt to the needs of complex environments and ensure that it can provide stable services. In addition, the bandwidth resources of emergency communication networks are usually relatively limited, and the network should be able to distinguish the priorities of services and provide higher network service quality guarantees for high-priority services.

In emergency and disaster response communication networks, satellite communication with high coverage is usually a reliable choice [5], and highly flexible UAV networks are also a common choice [6, 7]. In addition, common technologies for emergency communication include tethered balloon technology [8], device-to-device communication technology [9], wireless mesh network technology [10], etc. However, a single satellite portable station cannot achieve large-scale signal coverage in the disaster area; the energy of the *Unmanned Aerial Vehicle* (UAV) node is usually limited and cannot achieve long-term work; and the ground mesh network node has poor adaptability to the complex disaster area environment and cannot meet the needs of actual applications.

For the above reasons, we propose a *MultiLayer Emergency Communication Network* (ML-ECN) solution based on the combination of space and earth, which combines the advantages of satellite communications, UAV base stations and MESH networks. Our scheme also integrates the wireless sensor network at the bottom layer to realize the positioning of equipment or personnel and the collection of environmental data. Specifically, we divide ML-ECN into a perception layer and a transmission layer. The perception layer is a wireless sensor network. The transmission layer includes a ground MESH network, a UAV MESH network and a satellite network. The main challenges in implementing the ML-ECN described in this paper are how to realize the effective integration of multi-layer networks, the priority service guarantee of emergency and disaster relief business, the efficient deployment of UAV nodes and the accurate positioning of equipment.

The main contributions of this paper are as follows.

- We propose a positioning algorithm based on reverse verification. The direction of error reduction of the equation solution is obtained by iteration, and the acceptability of the solution is evaluated by reverse verification, which can effectively improve the positioning accuracy.
- We propose an improved scheduling algorithm based on weighted deficit round robin (WDRR) [11]. Based on the WDRR algorithm, we assign dynamic queue weights according to the relevant characteristics of the current flow, thereby realizing the network service quality guarantee for the high-priority business and ensuring the fairness of the service.
- Related experiments are carried out to evaluate the effectiveness of the method proposed in this paper. The experimental results show that the algorithms proposed in this paper can effectively improve the positioning accuracy and network service quality.

The rest of the article is arranged as follows. Section 2 introduces the related research work of emergency communication networks. The overall model architecture of the system is given in Sect. 3. Section 4 introduces the composition and realization of each part of the system in detail. The relevant performance evaluation results are given in Sect. 5. Finally, the related summary and future work are provided in Sect. 6.

2 Related Work

Research on emergency communications after disasters has been in a state of continuous development, and with the continuous advancement of technology, new solutions have also emerged. In the early days, the radio station was a main method of emergency communication, and this method still has certain applicability to this day. In [12], the authors studied the emergency communication network based on radio stations and mainly carried out research and analysis on the polling MAC protocol. However, radio station communication has greater limitations, and the communication range is relatively limited.

Later, emergency communications based on satellite networks gradually appeared [13], and these emergency communications can achieve signal coverage in the global area. In emergency communication based on satellite networks, mainly portable satellite communication station equipment is integrated into the flight platform [14] or the vehicle. In addition, there are also plans to directly use a portable satellite antenna [15] to interconnect the ground network with the satellite network. However, a single portable satellite communication device can only cover a limited area and has certain application limitations. In this plan, we take advantage of the satellite network and combine it with the MESH network to construct an emergency communication network.

Further, paper [16] introduced the on-board cognitive radio emergency communication network. Paper [17] conducted research on airborne communication networks that can be used for emergency communications and conducted research and analysis on high-altitude platform airborne networks, low-altitude platform airborne networks, and hybrid model airborne networks. In [18], the authors introduced a technical solution to applying *mobile ad hoc network* (MANET) to emergency communications. The authors in [19] applied a *wireless sensor network* (WSN) to personnel and equipment positioning in emergency situations and introduced a positioning algorithm based on *impulse radio ultra-wideband* (IR-UWB), but the positioning algorithm ignores the possible impact of IR-UWB on the existing narrowband communication system. In [20], Qiu et al. proposed a novel informer homed routing fault tolerance mechanism for WSN, which can be widely applied to various applications, such as smart grid [21, 22] and IoT [23]. The group of Qiu et al. [24] also used supervised machine learning to implement selective encryption on ECG data in body sensor network in order to improve the security and privacy of the data in transmission and storage [25–27].

The bandwidth resources of emergency communication networks are usually relatively limited. Therefore, improving the service quality of networks is an important task under the condition of limited bandwidth, especially to improve the network service quality of special services. In [6], a D2D emergency communication scheme with a QoS guarantee was discussed. Reference [28] introduced the location deployment and resource allocation scheme of UAV under QoS constraints. In addition, [29] discussed the queue scheduling problem in an emergency communication network and proposed a routing scheme based on business priority. These approaches are critical in the scenario of a large amounts of data need to be transferred with limited energy supply [31, 32] and bandwidth [33].

In this paper, we have constructed an emergency communication network model that combines space and earth. We propose a new WSN-based positioning algorithm, a queue scheduling algorithm based on priority and data flow characteristics. Through multiparty linkage, we jointly ensure the service quality of the emergency communication network.

3 Hierarchical Model of the ML-ECN System

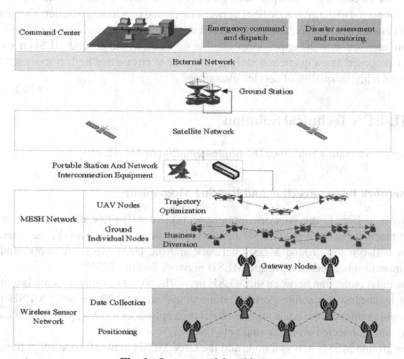

Fig. 1. System model architecture

The emergency communication network model architecture proposed in this article can be divided into wireless sensor networks, MESH networks and satellite networks from bottom to top. The wireless sensor network has the functions of data collection and positioning and is connected to the MESH network through the gateway node, and the communication between the nodes complies with the ZigBee protocol. In addition, the positioning of the node is based mainly on the received signal strength indicator (RSSI), and the data collection is realized by carrying the corresponding sensor for the node. In addition, data communication is realized through the serial port.

The main purpose of integrating the wireless sensor network into the emergency communication network is to realize the real-time positioning of emergency personnel and related equipment. The integration can also achieve high-precision positioning at a low cost and provide real-time personnel and equipment location information for emergency personnel dispatch. The environmental data collection function of the wireless sensor network can also provide necessary reference data for disaster assessment.

The MESH network includes the ground MESH network and the UAV MESH network. Among these networks, the UAV MESH network is used mainly as a relay network to provide communication relays for isolated nodes and give priority to important business. To achieve this goal, this paper proposes a UAV location deployment algorithm oriented to the location of ground nodes. The ground MESH network provides service support for all businesses and provides user access functions. The terminal equipment can be connected to the ground MESH network in a wired or wireless manner. The ground MESH network also provides a fusion interface with the lower-level sensor network and a fusion interface with the upper-level satellite network. In the ground MESH network, we have proposed a new queue scheduling algorithm to ensure that high-priority services can obtain a higher quality of service guarantee.

4 ML-ECN Technical Solution

In this part, we mainly introduce the implementation of ML-ECN.

4.1 Network Interconnection and Routing Mechanism

As shown in Fig. 1, the network interconnection of ML-ECN includes mainly the interconnection between the MESH network and the satellite network, the interconnection between the ground MESH network and the UAV MESH network, and the interconnection between the ground MESH network and the WSN.

The interconnection between the MESH network and the satellite network is realized mainly by means of satellite portable stations and routers. The ground MESH node equipment in this scheme has a wireless local area network (WLAN) port, which can be directly interconnected with external networks.

The ground MESH network node and the UAV MESH network node adopt the same communication protocol specification and have a common communication frequency band, so they can communicate directly to realize the interconnection of the two networks. In addition, the ground MESH network node uses a dual-band design, and the other frequency band is for end users to access.

The interconnection between the ground MESH network and the WSN is realized through the sink node of the WSN, which is equipped with a Wi-Fi module and can be connected directly to the ground MESH network.

The ground MESH network and the UAV MESH network can be regarded as a network, which generally uses the shortest path as its routing mechanism. The WSN network has a routing mechanism different from the mechanism of the ground MESH network. The data on the WSN that need to be transmitted to the upper network are aggregated to the sink node according to the WSN routing mechanism, then connected to the MESH network and then transmitted to the destination node according to the routing mechanism of the MESH network.

4.2 ML-ECN Perception Layer

The ML-ECN perception layer is a wireless sensor network. The network model is shown in Fig. 2, which contains two types of nodes: sensor nodes and sink nodes. The sink node can connect data to the upper network for transmission.

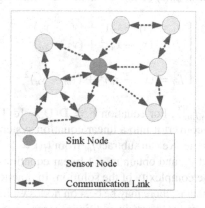

Fig. 2. Wireless sensor network model.

Data Collection. In ML-ECN, the wireless sensor network can be used to collect environmental data, such as the air temperature and humidity of the disaster site and the soil temperature and humidity.

The data acquisition node can be regarded as an embedded system composed of a microcontroller and several peripheral modules. In the actual design of the data acquisition node, you can choose the CC2430 or CC2530 series chips to design the corresponding embedded system and run the ZigBee protocol on the chip to realize data communication.

Environmental data collection is realized by integrating corresponding environmental sensors for each sensor node. The collected data are gathered to the sink node through data routing, connected to the upper transmission network and transmitted to the destination address. Cluster-Tree or AODVjr can be selected as the routing algorithm between WSN nodes.

Node Positioning. In the perception layer of ML-ECN, the RSSI between WSN links is used to locate unknown nodes. Every unknown node has a group of beacon nodes adjacent to it. These nodes can receive the wireless signal of the unknown node and predict the distance to the unknown node based on RSSI. The distance estimation based on RSSI is shown in (1) [30]:

$$PL(d) = PL(d_0) - 10\alpha\log\left(\frac{d}{d_0}\right) + \varepsilon \tag{1}$$

where, α is the path loss constant, ε is Gaussian random noise, $PL(d_0)$ is the received signal strength at the reference position d_0, and $PL(d)$ is the received signal strength at the unknown distance d. An unknown node n_u has a group of adjacent beacon nodes $n_{bea}(i)(i = 1, 2, 3, \ldots, m)$, and the distance between the unknown node n_u and the beacon node $n_{bea}(i)$ is $d(i)(i = 1, 2, 3 \ldots, m)$. Let the coordinates of node n_u be (x_u, y_u) and the coordinates of node $n_{bea}(i)$ be (x_i, y_i); then, the following expressions are given:

$$\begin{cases} f_1 = (x_1 - x_u)^2 + (y_1 - y_u)^2 \\ f_2 = (x_2 - x_u)^2 + (y_2 - y_u)^2 \\ \quad\quad\quad \ldots \\ f_m = (x_m - x_u)^2 + (y_m - y_u)^2 \end{cases} \tag{2}$$

Let $\mathbf{F} = [f_1, f_2, f_3, \ldots, f_m]^T$. For equation $\mathbf{F} = \mathbf{D}(\mathbf{D} = [d(1)^2, d(2)^2, \ldots, d(m)^2]^T)$, one of the solutions is to convert it into a linear equation system and then use the least squares method. For example, we can subtract f_m from $f_i(i = 1, 2, 3, ..m - 1)$, eliminate the square terms of x_u and y_u, and obtain m $-$ 1 linear equations [31]. This method can effectively reduce the time complexity of the solution. In practice, there may be several interference items in (2); that is, there may be beacon nodes with large distance measurement deviations, which introduces certain additional errors to the node position estimation. Therefore, such errors should be avoided as much as possible. We also convert (2) into a linear equation $\mathbf{F}' - \mathbf{D}' = \mathbf{0}$ to solve, where $\mathbf{F}' = [f_1 - f_m, f_2 - f_m, \ldots, f_{m-1} - f_m]^T$, $\mathbf{D}' = [d(1)^2 - d(m)^2, d(2)^2 - d(m)^2, \ldots, d(m - 1)^2 - d(m)^2]^T$. The error of the solution of the equation is defined as shown in (3):

$$E_s = \frac{1}{m}\sum_{i=1}^{m}\left(f_i(x_t, y_t)^{1/2} - d(i)\right)^2 \tag{3}$$

where (x_t, y_t) is the numerical solution of the equation. In addition, the prediction error is defined as the square of the distance between the predicted point and the actual point, as shown in (4):

$$E_p = (x_p - x_r)^2 + (y_p - y_r)^2 \tag{4}$$

ML-ECN Transport Layer. The ML-ECN transport layer includes the MESH network and satellite network. The MESH network nodes include ground nodes and air nodes, where the air nodes are composed mainly of UAVs carrying communication node equipment. Considering the complexity of various services in disaster areas and the priorities between services, we have integrated a new queue scheduling algorithm into the ground MESH network and proposed a location- and service-oriented UAV location deployment algorithm to ensure that high-priority business can obtain higher quality of service (QoS).

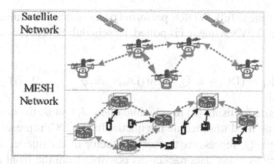

Fig. 3. ML-ECN transport layer model.

The ML-ECN transmission layer model is shown in Fig. 3. The ground MESH node provides user access functions and supports two access methods: wired access and wireless access. When a specific terminal service generates a data stream, a service type label is added to the service stream. The network node device selects an appropriate data processing method to process and forward the data packet according to the service type label of the service stream and the current network conditions. At the same time, the UAV node dynamically adjusts its position according to the current business conditions in the network. For business flows without a specific service type label, ML-ECN processes data packets according to its default service priority.

Queue Scheduling Mechanism. Considering the diversity of user services in disaster areas and the large differences in QoS requirements for services, this paper incorporates differentiated services technology in ECNs [32]. Specifically, the type of server (TOS) field in the IP packet header is used to distinguish service levels. In the newer standard, this field is also called differ server code point (DSCP). The difference is that the former uses 3 bits for service-level marking, and the latter uses 6 bits for service-level distinction. When the relevant service data packet in the network is generated, the TOS segment is assigned according to the priority of the service. The TOS field can be assigned a value between 0 and 7, where 0 has the lowest priority and 7 has the highest priority.

In the queue scheduling mechanism proposed in this article, router nodes in the network perform queue scheduling according to the value of the TOS field in the IP data packet and the characteristics of the data flow itself, thereby realizing the QoS guarantee of the service flow. In our solution, we perform a dynamic weight assignment based on the priority of the current queue and the characteristics of the data flow in the queue. Among these assignments, the characteristics of the flow we consider include the destination IP d of the data flow and the protocol number p_{id} of the corresponding data packet. WDRR is a byte-based round-robin scheduling algorithm that assigns a certain weight (bandwidth ratio) to each queue, and each queue has a difference counter (the maximum number of bytes allowed to be transmitted during each scheduling). The difference counter increases by a service factor proportional to the weight each time before the start of queue scheduling. In each queue, the first input first output (FIFO) mechanism is used for queue scheduling, and the tail drop mechanism is used to drop packets when the queue is full. WDRR performs round-robin scheduling for each queue (according to priority). When queue i is polled, its scheduling process can be represented by (5).

$$\text{WDRR}_i = (DC_i+ = Q_i)\text{then}((DC_i- = \sum\nolimits_{j=1}^{\max(m)} P(i)) \geq 0) \qquad (5)$$

There is a prerequisite for using (5) to schedule queue i, that is, the queue is not empty; otherwise, there is no need to schedule the queue. In (5), DC_i represents the difference counter of the queue, Q_i represents the service factor of the queue, and the part after "then" means taking as many data packets as possible from the front of the queue and ensuring that the total number of bytes in the data packets does not exceed DC_i. They are dequeued and forwarded in turn, and finally, the value of DC_i is subtracted from the total number of bytes of these data packets. In actual implementation, by comparing the number of bytes at the front of the queue with the current value of DC_i, you can determine whether the packet can be dequeued and further update the value of DC_i. The process is terminated when there is no data packet to dequeue.

WDRR is based on the premise that data packets are classified according to priority, and data packets with the same priority are assigned to the same queue. WDRR can solve the scheduling problem between different priority queues and can avoid the phenomenon that low priority queues are not served for a long time. Generally, WDRR considers only the priority of the business rather than the characteristics of the flow itself, which makes WDRR not well adapted to networks with complex and variable traffic. On the other hand, if the characteristics of the flow are directly used as the WDRR queue classification standard, there may be more queues. Moreover, some of the queues may have higher similarities, which may lead to more waste of resources and lower scheduling efficiency.

In our solution, we dynamically assign weights according to the characteristics of the data flow in the current queue and the priority of the queue. First, we define the mapping function shown in (6):

$$\Phi(p_{id}) = \begin{cases} 1.0, & p_{id} \in Control\ Prot \\ 0.8, & p_{id} \in Real - Time\ Trans\ Prot \\ 0.6, & others \end{cases} \qquad (6)$$

In (6), the protocols represented by the protocol number p_{id} are divided into three categories: control protocols, real-time transmission protocols, and other protocols. $\Phi(\cdot)$ maps it to a floating point.

For each packet dequeued from the queue, we count its protocol number p_{id} and destination address d (to estimate the remaining path length, which can be obtained from the network layer). Then, we use p_{id} and d as classification standards, classify the data packets in the data stream and count their rate υ.

To update the weight, we first define the concept of the expected transmission rate of the data stream, as shown in (7):

$$\upsilon_e(k_j) = Pri(k) * \Phi(p(k_j)) * \upsilon(k_j)/(1 - \alpha)^{h(k_j)} \qquad (7)$$

In (7), $Pri(k)$ is the priority parameter of the queue, and its value set is $\{1, 0.85, 0.75, 0.65, 0.55, 0.45, 0.35, 0.2\}$. The value of $Pri(k)$ is selected from high to low according to the priority. For example, priority 7 takes the value 1.0, and priority 0 takes the value 0.3. In addition, k_j represents the data stream j with specific p_{id} and d under the queue with priority k, and $\upsilon_e(k_j)$ represents its expected transmission rate. $p(k_j)$ is the protocol number of stream j, and $\upsilon(k_j)$ is the actual arrival rate of stream j. In addition, α is the average packet loss rate of single-hop transmission, and $h(k_j)$ is the number of forwarding times required for the corresponding data stream to reach the destination node.

The weight update method is shown in (8), and a normalized weight can be obtained through (8).

$$W(k) = \frac{\sum_j \upsilon_e(k_j)}{\sum_i \sum_j \upsilon_e(i_j)} \tag{8}$$

In (8), the meaning of related symbols is consistent with (7). In addition, to prevent a high-speed flow from monopolizing network resources, we set a weight upper limit $TH_i(i = 0, 1, 2, ..., 7)$ for each priority queue and set the queue according to the priority in descending order. If the normalized weight of queue m (m is the priority) obtained according to (8) exceeds the upper limit of weight, and the weight of the queue with priority higher than that queue does not exceed the upper limit of weight, we redistribute the weight of the queue with priority no less than queue m and the queue with priority lower than m. The allocation policy is referred to (9):

$$W(k)_{re} = \begin{cases} W_1 * W(k)_m^7, & k \geq m \\ (1 - W_1)W(k)_0^{m-1}, & k < m \end{cases} \tag{9}$$

In (9), $W(k)_{re}$ represents the reallocated weight of the queue with priority k, and W_1 is the average value of the upper limit of the weight of the queue whose priority is not lower than m. $W(k)_m^7$ represents the weight ratio of priority queue k in queues with priority not lower than m. The calculation of $W(k)_m^7$ can refer to (8), and the difference is that the value of i in (8) is limited to not less than m. The calculation method of $W(k)_0^{m-1}$ is similar.

If m is equal to 0 or there are no packets in the queues with priority lower than m, the weight of queue m is set to the upper limit. The normalized weight of the queue with priority higher than m is recalculated according to (8), and the new weight is obtained by multiplying by the remaining allocable weight. The above process can be iterated until all queues have no weight greater than the upper limit.

5   Performance Evaluation

In this part, we conduct a performance analysis test on the emergency communication network solution we proposed. The test content includes a positioning algorithm, queue scheduling algorithm, UAV deployment algorithm and their comprehensive test.

5.1   Positioning Algorithm Performance

We conducted the performance test of our proposed positioning algorithm under MATLAB and compared the performance with some existing algorithms.

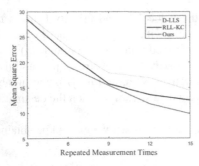

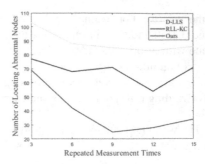

Fig. 4. Result of the MSE test.   **Fig. 5.** Result of the NoLAN test.

Figure 4 and Fig. 5 show the test results of the mean square error (MSE) and the number of locating abnormal nodes (NoLAN). The abnormal positioning node is the node where the specified position error exceeds a certain threshold (in this test, the specified position error is set to 10 m). The size of the simulation scene is set to 1000 m × 1000 m. The total number of nodes is 500, of which 100 nodes are beacon nodes, and the node communication radius is 150 m. In addition, the beacon nodes are approximately evenly distributed in the area, and the positions of all beacon nodes are preset. In the process of measuring the distance between the unknown node and the beacon node, an error value is randomly added to simulate an invalid beacon node. The path loss value is estimated through multiple measurements to simulate the complex disaster site environment.

In Fig. 4 and Fig. 5, D-LLS represents the linear equation system $\mathbf{F}' - \mathbf{D}' = \mathbf{0}$ directly solved by the least squares method, and the abscissa represents the number of RSSI measurements of each group. RLL-KC was introduced in [33], which selects a subset of several beacon nodes and then uses the subset to predict the position of nodes. Finally, the K-means method is used to perform cluster analysis on the prediction results using multiple different subsets, and a bad beacon node is found. After removing the bad node, the position is predicted again, and the final prediction result is obtained. In our test, the number of beacon nodes in the subset is set to the median of the optional number and rounded down. The test considers all the subsets with this number of elements. In addition, we set the cluster type to 3.

Figure 4 shows that as the number of measurements increases, the MSE shows a downward trend in the three schemes because with the increase in repeated measurement times, the average value of RSSI is closer to the theoretical value, thus reducing the impact of random error. Specifically, compared with D-LLS, the MSE of our scheme decreased by 20.54% on average, and compared with RLL-KC, the MSE decreased by 10.92% on average. In addition, the prediction data of abnormal positioning are not considered in Fig. 4.

For NoLAN, Fig. 5 shows that there is a certain fluctuation with an increase in the number of repeated measurements. In our scheme, when the number of repeated measurements is less than 9, NoLAN shows a downward trend and then has a small increase. In D-LLS, when the number of measurements is less than 12, NoLAN shows a downward trend, but the decline is relatively low, and then there is still a small increase. In RLL-KC, NoLAN fluctuates irregularly. Specifically, compared with D-LLS, NOLAN dropped by 56.52% on average in our scheme and dropped by 42.73% on average when compared with RLL-KC.

In addition, when the number of repeated measurements is 15, we calculated the distribution of positioning errors, as shown in Fig. 6. Figure 6 shows that in our scheme, the distribution density of the positioning error in the range of $[0, 4)$ is higher than the distribution density of D-LLS and RLL-KC, while the distribution density in the range of $[4, \infty)$ is lower than the distribution density of D-LLS and RLL-KC, which indicates that our scheme has higher positioning accuracy and can achieve more accurate positioning.

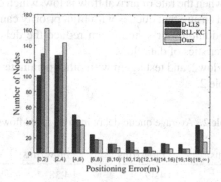

Fig. 6. Error distribution when the number of re-peated measurements is 15.

5.2   Queue Scheduling Algorithm Performance

For the queue scheduling algorithm, we analyze mainly its queue delay, that is, the time interval of a packet from entering the queue to leaving the queue. The experiment was carried out under MATLAB. We analyze and compare our scheme with the WDRR queue scheduling mechanism. We simulate the queue scheduling process of a node in the network. In our test, we assume that the queue buffer area is large enough; that is, no data packets are discarded. There are four groups of data streams with different priorities at the input of the queue. Their packet size, packet destination and protocol number are generated randomly, and each group of data streams meets the Poisson distribution of specific parameters. In different tests, the nodes have the same processing bandwidth (the amount of data that can be forwarded per second).

In the standard WDRR mechanism, each group of queues has a fixed weight and service factor (proportional to the weight). Data forwarding is performed according to the current DC value, and polling operations are performed in different queues. When there are no data to be processed, the DC value is set to 0. In our solution, queue scheduling is determined according to the destination of the data, the priority of the queue, and the flow rate of the data stream, and the queue weight in WDRR is dynamically updated.

We set the priority field of the four groups of test flows to [7, 5, 4, 2]. First, we test the queue delay in the case of a low rate. In this case, the node can process the data packet in time. The test results are shown in Table 1.

Table 1. Average queue delay in low-speed flows.

Scheme	Flow1/ms	Flow1/ms	Flow1/ms	Flow1/ms
WDRR	2.90	3.93	4.16	10.44
Ours	2.83	4.01	4.10	7.52

Table 1 shows that our scheme has a performance similar to the standard WDRR scheduling mechanism when the rate of arrival flow is low, which can realize scheduling according to priority and ensure that queues with high priority can obtain higher quality service guarantees. In addition, our scheme can reduce the delay of high-speed flow according to the characteristics of data flow.

Increase the rate of Flow2, and test again with other parameters unchanged. The test results are shown in Table 2.

Table 2. Average queue delay in high-speed flows.

Scheme	Flow1/ms	Flow1/ms	Flow1/ms	Flow1/ms
WDRR	2.89	4.49	4.38	739.61
Ours	3.04	3.45	5.63	376.83

Table 2 shows that when the flow rate of Flow2 increases, the queuing delay also increases. In standard WDRR, due to the use of fixed queue weights, the queue delay of Flow2 increases significantly, even higher than the queue delay of Flow3 with lower priority, and an increase in the Flow2 rate greatly affects the queue delay of low-priority traffic (such as the delay of Flow4). In our solution, due to the adoption of a dynamic weight strategy, the delay of Flow2 can be reduced, and the queuing delay of other queues can also meet the expectation. By comparing the queuing delay of Flow 4, we find that our scheme can effectively reduce the impact of high priority traffic flow on low priority traffic flow and ensure the quality of service and fairness at the same time.

5.3 Comprehensive Performance of ML-ECN

We tested the overall performance of ML-ECN through network simulation tools and made a comparative test. In the simulation, the network layer selects the OLSR routing protocol for routing addressing. In the test, the network delays of different queue scheduling mechanisms and whether there are UAV nodes involved are compared. In the test, the available number of UAV nodes is set to 10, and the number of ground nodes is set to 50. Since the wireless sensor network in ML-ECN is used only for data collection and positioning, the wireless sensor network is not considered in the comprehensive test, and other methods are used to obtain the location of the network node. The relevant test results are shown in Table 3. The value of the TOS field in the table represents the value of the corresponding field in the IP data packet, and different values represent data streams with different priorities.

Table 3. Simulation results of network transmission delay.

Scheme	TOS = 7 (ms)	TOS = 5 (ms)	TOS = 4 (ms)	TOS = 2 (ms)
Only-WDRR	49.89	63.39	71.22	85.74
Ours Queue Scheduling	48.58	62.76	67.05	87.21
Our Queue Scheduling & UAV Deployment	37.5	56.55	64.23	84.15

Table 3 shows that our scheme can effectively improve the service quality of the network and reduce the end-to-end delay of the network. By reasonably deploying UAVs at the location, a better path can be provided for data forwarding. Therefore, after adding UAV nodes, the end-to-end delay of data packets is significantly improved, especially for high-priority business flows.

6   Conclusion and Future Work

In this paper, we introduced a multilayer emergency communication network scheme based on the combination of space and earth: ML-ECN. This ECN could effectively improve the service quality of the network and give priority to high-priority services under the condition of limited bandwidth resources, which was suitable for the actual needs of emergency communication networks. The simulation test results showed that the positioning algorithm and the queue scheduling algorithm of our scheme were significantly improved compared to the basic algorithm model. In the network simulation test, the transmission delay of the data packet was significantly reduced. In future work, we will further study methods to improve the network service quality at the network layer and consider the lifetime of the network.

Acknowledgment. This work was supported in part by the National Key Research and Development Project of China under Grants No. 2017YFB0504103.

References

1. Masaracchia, A., Nguyen, L.D., Duong, T.Q., Nguyen, M.N.: An energy-efficient clustering and routing framework for disaster relief network. IEEE Access 7, 56520–56532 (2019)
2. Deepak, G.C., Ladas, A., Sambo, Y., Pervaiz, H., Politis, C., Imran, M.: An overview of post-disaster emergency communication systems in the future networks. IEEE Wirel. Commun. 26(6), 132–139 (2019). https://doi.org/10.1109/MWC.2019.1800467
3. Zhang, S., Liu, J.: Analysis and optimization of multiple unmanned aerial vehicle-assisted communications in post-disaster areas. IEEE Trans. Veh. Technol. 67(12), 12049–12060 (2018)

4. Rohman, B.P.A., Andra, M.B., Putra, H.F., Fandiantoro, D.H., Nishimoto, M.: Multisensory surveillance UAV for survivor detection and geolocalization in complex post-disaster environment. In: Proceedings of the IGARSS, Yokohama, Japan, pp. 9368–9371 (2019)
5. Asuquo, P., Cruickshank, H., Ogah, C.P.A., Lei, A., Sun, Z.: A distributed trust management scheme for data forwarding in satellite DTN emergency communications. IEEE J. Sel. Areas Commun. **36**(2), 246–256 (2018)
6. Wang, J., Cheng, W., Zhang, H.: Caching and D2D assisted wireless emergency communications networks with statistical QoS provisioning. J. Commun. Inf. Netw. **5**(3), 282–293 (2020)
7. Zhang, C., Dong, M., Ota, K.: Heterogeneous mobile networking for lightweight UAV assisted emergency communication. IEEE Trans. Green Commun. Netw **5**(3), 1345–1356 (2021)
8. Alsamhi, S.H., Almalki, F.A., Ma, O., Ansari, M.S., Angelides, M.C.: Performance optimization of tethered balloon technology for public safety and emergency communications. Telecommun. Syst. **75**(2), 235–244 (2020)
9. Ali, K., Nguyen, H.X., Vien, Q., Shah, P., Chu, Z.: Disaster management using D2D communication with power transfer and clustering techniques. IEEE Access **6**, 14643–14654 (2018)
10. Nishiyama, H., Rodrigues, T.G., Liu, J.: A Probabilistic approach to deploying disaster response network. IEEE Trans. Veh. Technol. **67**(12), 12086–12094 (2018)
11. Grilo, A., Macedo, M.M., Nunes, M.S.: IP QoS support in IEEE 802.11b WLANs. Comput. Commun. **26**(17), 1918–1930 (2003)
12. Cai, Q., Liu, Q.L., Ding, H.W., Zhou, J.: Polling MAC protocol implementation and performance analysis for emergency communication networks based on wireless radio stations. In: Proceedings of the 2nd WCSN, Chang Sha, China, pp. 216–226 (2016)
13. Pecorella, T., Ronga, L.S., Chiti, F., Jayousi, S., Franck, L.: Emergency satellite communications: research and standardization activities. IEEE Commun. Mag. **53**(5), 170–177 (2015)
14. Gomez, K., et al.: Aerial base stations with opportunistic links for next generation emergency communications. IEEE Commun. Mag. **54**(4), 31–39 (2016)
15. Zhao, Y., Liu, Z., Fan, X., Gao, P., Liu, T.: Design of a Ka broadband satellite communication antenna for low-earth-orbit constellation. In: Proceedings of the 12th ISAPE, Hangzhou, China, pp. 1–4 (2018)
16. Sun, Y., Chowdhury, K.R.: Enabling emergency communication through a cognitive radio vehicular network. IEEE Commun. Mag. **52**(10), 68–75 (2014)
17. Cao, X., Yang, P., Alzenad, M., Xi, X., Wu, D., Yanikomeroglu, H.: Airborne communication networks: a survey. IEEE J. Sel. Areas Commun. **36**(9), 1907–1926 (2018)
18. Verma, H., Chauhan, N.: MANET based emergency communication system for natural disasters. In: Proceedings of the 2015 ICCCA, Noida, India, pp. 480–485 (2015)
19. Mogale, T.H., Silva, B.J., Hancke, G.P.: A portable IR-UWB based WSN for personnel tracking in emergency scenarios. In: Proceeding of the 14th INDIN, Poitiers, France, pp. 961–965 (2016)
20. Qiu, M., Ming, Z., Li, J., Liu, J., Quan, G., Zhu, Y.: Informer homed routing fault tolerance mechanism for wireless sensor networks. J. Syst. Archit. **59**(4–5), 260–270 (2013)
21. Su, H., Qiu, M., Wang, H.: Secure wireless communication system for smart grid with rechargeable electric vehicles. IEEE Commun. Mag. **50**(8), 62–68 (2012)
22. Tang, X., Li, K., et al.: A hierarchical reliability-driven scheduling algorithm in grid systems. J. Parallel Distrib. Comput. **72**(4), 525–535 (2012)
23. Lu, Z., Wang, N., Wu, J., Qiu, M.: IoTDeM: an IoT big data-oriented MapReduce performance prediction extended model in multiple edge clouds. JPDC **118**, 316–327 (2018)
24. Qiu, H., Qiu, M., Lu, Z.: Selective encryption on ECG data in body sensor network based on supervised machine learning. Inf. Fusion **55**, 59–67 (2020)

25. Zhang, Z., Wu, J., et al.: Jamming ACK attack to wireless networks and a mitigation approach. IEEE GLOBECOM Conference, pp. 1–5 (2008)
26. Qiu, L., Gai, K., Qiu, M.: Optimal big data sharing approach for tele-health in cloud computing. In: IEEE SmartCloud, pp. 184–189 (2016)
27. Thakur, K., Qiu, M., Gai, K., Ali, M.: An investigation on cyber security threats and security models. In: IEEE CSCloud (2015)
28. Niu, H., Zhao, X., Li, J.: 3D location and resource allocation optimization for UAV-enabled emergency networks under statistical QoS constraint. IEEE Access 9, 41566–41576 (2021)
29. Khan, A., Aftab, F., Zhang, Z.: UAPM: an urgency-aware packet management for disaster management using flying ad-hoc networks. China Commun. 16(11), 167–182 (2019)
30. Yang, B., Guo, L., Guo, R., Zhao, M., Zhao, T.: A novel trilateration algorithm for RSSI-based indoor localization. IEEE Sens. J. 20(14), 8164–8172 (2020)
31. Qiu, M., Chen, Z., Liu, M.: Low-power low-latency data allocation for hybrid scratch-pad memory. IEEE Embed. Syst. Lett. 6(4), 69–72 (2014)
32. Qiu, M., Xue, C., Shao, Z., Sha, E.: Energy minimization with soft real-time and DVS for uniprocessor and multiprocessor embedded systems. In: IEEE DATE Conference, pp. 1–6 (2007)
33. Liu, M., Zhang, S., et al.: H infinite state estimation for discrete-time chaotic systems based on a unified model. IEEE Trans. Syst. Man Cybern. (B) (2012)

Multi-attribute Authentication Method Based on Continuous Trust Evaluation

Jing Guo[1(✉)], Bingsen Li[2], Ping Du[1], Ziyi Xin[1], Jianjun Zhang[1], and Jiawei Chen[3]

[1] Aostar Information Technologies Co., Ltd., Chengdu 610041, China
{guojing,duping,xinziyi,zhangjianjun}@sgitg.sgcc.com.cn
[2] State Grid Information and Communication Industry Group, Beijing 102211, China
libingsen@sgitg.sgcc.com.cn
[3] Engineering Research Center of Post Big Data Technology and Application of Jiangsu Province, Research and Development Center of Post Industry Technology of the State Posts Bureau (Internet of Things Technology), Nanjing University of Posts and Telecommunications, Nanjing 210000, China

Abstract. In order to solve the data security problems faced by the power Internet of Things, this article combines the trust evaluation technology and the token authentication method to propose a multi-attribute identity authentication method based on continuous trust evaluation. This method embeds the trust evaluation value into the token, and authenticate the user's identity through the real-time update of the token, thereby granting the corresponding authority. At the same time, the authentication process is encrypted and decrypted by mixing the random generation matrix encryption algorithm based on chaotic mapping and the RSA digital signature algorithm to improve the security of authentication. The experimental results show that the trust evaluation value obtained by the continuous trust evaluation algorithm for users with different identities are different, so the resource permissions obtained are also different. Therefore, the multi-attribute authentication method combined with trust evaluation in this paper has higher security and confidentiality than previous authentication methods.

Keywords: Multi-attribute authentication · Continuous trust assessment · Power Internet of Things · Mobile Internet

1 Introduction

Since the epidemic, the power mobile Internet business has become the company's internal and external interaction Important window. It connects the users, terminals, and applications of the power system, and shares the generated data, which facilitates users, power grids and society [1, 2]. In order to prevent the danger of the key being stolen, identification technology becomes particularly important. Identity authentication is at the forefront of access control, and it is the first identification defense line of network application systems [3, 4]. Identity authentication can be divided into static authentication and dynamic authentication. In the initial stage of the development of identity authentication, the computer uses static parameters to perform the most basic identity authentication. Before authentication, authentication information that characterizes the legal identity of the user is set in advance. Among them, static identity authentication mainly includes user password authentication, face secret-free recognition authentication, smart card authentication and other authentication methods [5]. Dynamic identity authentication is mainly based on the real-time changes of users or terminals to perform different authorizations [6].

The identity authentication technology based on static authentication. In 1981, Lamport [7] first proposed a password-based identity authentication protocol, but because in this protocol users always choose simple weak passwords for easy memory and use them repeatedly, so they are vulnerable to attacks. In order to improve the security of authentication and at the same time solve the problem that the software password is too simple and easy to be attacked and leaked, people consider that the security of authentication is ensured by hardware, and thus have smart card-based identity authentication [8, 9]. In the identity authentication technology based on dynamic authentication, researchers have found that static authentication has the disadvantage of using authentication information, which is fundamentally a security risk. Therefore, authentication methods based on dynamic passwords and dynamic passwords have been proposed [10, 11]. As network security requirements become more and more stringent, single-factor authentication methods are no longer sufficient to protect security. Therefore, multi-factor authentication has gradually become a more widely used identity authentication method in addition to static authentication and dynamic authentication [12].

Therefore, this paper proposed a multi-attribute identity authentication method based on trust evaluation. The trust evaluation method divided the mobile application into three levels, uses QoS indicators to collect data, and then completed the overall trust evaluation of the mobile application based on the four aspects of index weight calculation and comprehensive evaluation of application services. Among them, the interval number was used to represent the collected QoS index data; the fuzzy analytic hierarchy process was used to establish the weight system of the model; based on the established standardized decision matrix and weight system, the overall trust of the service provided and the user in the mobile application was evaluated [13, 14].

The main structure of this paper is as follows: Sect. 2 introduces related work. Section 3 designs multi-attribute authentication process based on continuous trust evaluation. Section 4 provides continuous trust evaluation algorithm. Section 5 verifies and analyzes the proposed scheme. Section 6 gives a conclusion.

2 Related Work

The multi-factor authentication method improves the overall security of authentication through the superposition of different authentication methods. At present, the mainstream multi-factor authentication scheme includes two schemes: digital certificate + static factor and static factor + dynamic factor. Atiewi et al. [15] use multi-factor authentication to access data stored in the cloud. They provide three levels of authentication to access stored data, namely reading files, downloading files, and downloading files from the hybrid cloud. Maciej et al. [16] use three authentication factors to enable user authentication: possession, knowledge, and immanence. The described authentication scheme refers to the possibility of performing the process in a mobile environment of the Android platform that guarantees authentication support.

Adopting the Token-based identity authentication mechanism can better solve the identity authentication problem in the current Internet of Things application system. The token is a kind of credential stored in the IoT application system to verify the identity of the user. When the IoT client initiates a login or connection request, the server will generate a string of strings for the user's access credentials according to the registration information of the user or the IoT terminal device, and feed it back to the client as a Token [17]. Yang et al. [18–20] applied the token identity authentication mechanism to the resource management system, which improved the network security level of the system and made up for the shortcomings of the traditional Session identity authentication mechanism. Qiu et al. had investigated on various cyber security threats and security models [21–23] and proposed several novel approaches to improve authentications and enhance trust evaluation, such as mitigation approach [24], machine learning approach [25], and block chain approach [26].

Based on the above-mentioned related technologies, this article combined trust evaluation technology and token authentication method to propose a multi-attribute identity authentication method based on trust evaluation. This method embedded the trust evaluation value into the token, and authenticated the user's identity through the real-time update of the token, thereby granting the corresponding authority.

3   Multi-attribute Authentication Progress Based on Continuous Trust Evaluation

3.1   Authenticated Encryption Algorithm Combining Chaotic Matrix Encryption and RSA Signature Algorithm

The matrix is used as the encryption and decryption key, that is, if the matrix is used as the encryption key, the inverse matrix is the decryption key. Therefore, the key to generating the encryption key matrix through the chaotic function is to construct the invertible matrix with the random number generated by the chaotic function. This paper selects logistic mapping chaotic function to generate encryption matrix.

The main definition form of logistic mapping is as follows:

$$x_{n+1} = x_n \mu (1 - x_n), \ \mu \in [0, 4], x_n \in (0, 1) \tag{1}$$

Where, μ It is called a branch parameter. The specific steps of the random generation matrix encryption algorithm based on the chaotic mapping are as follows:

(1) First, organize and arrange the data to be encrypted according to the dimensions of the encryption key matrix, and cut them into $(N \times N)$ data blocks.
(2) Suppose the data length is D, there may be $D\%(N \times N)$ remaining data, the remaining data needs to be filled into the last data block, the filling number is $N \times N - D\%(N \times N)$, and finally reused The logistic chaotic function generates data for filling.

(3) Encrypt the divided and filled data blocks in turn, and then send <D, e1, e2, e3, ..., en> as the final encryption result to the receiver, where D is the length of the original data, and e_i is the encryption The completed data block.

(4) After receiving the ciphertext, the receiver uses the decryption matrix to sequentially decrypt the encrypted data blocks, and then according to the original length of the received data, the original data can be restored.

Suppose the generated chaotic invertible matrix is Q, then its inverse matrix is Q^{-1}, and the original data matrix is P. The encryption and decryption process is as follows: First, the original data matrix P is encrypted using the chaotic reversible encryption matrix Q, and the ciphertext matrix G is generated after the matrix Q is encrypted. Decryption is the inverse process of encryption. Matrix G is right-multiplied by matrix Q^{-1}, and finally, the decrypted data matrix P is obtained.

The RSA digital signature algorithm is derived from the RSA public key cryptographic algorithm. The RSA digital signature algorithm encrypts data with a private key and decrypts the data with a public key. The cooperative work diagram based on the chaotic matrix encryption algorithm and the RSA digital signature algorithm is shown below (Fig. 1):

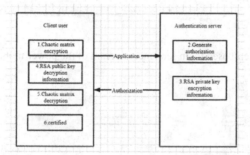

Fig. 1. Working diagram of hybrid matrix encryption algorithm and RSA signature algorithm

3.2 Certification Process

The token-based login process of the power mobile system is shown in Fig. 2: When logging in for the first time, the client user initiates a login request, enters the user name and password, and sends the request to the login server; Log in to the server to call the authentication service. The authentication service obtains user information through the user information database and verifies the accuracy of the user name and password. If the verification is passed, the token is produced in the authentication server; Then the authentication server calls the trust evaluation algorithm to calculate the trust evaluation value of the current user and inserts the value into the token. The authentication service returns the verification result to the login server, and the login server returns the token to the client; Finally, the client stores the token so that it can be used when requesting resources from the server.

The specific process of power mobile system requesting resources based on the token is shown in Fig. 3: When the client user requests any resource, the request is first submitted to the corresponding resource controller, and then the identity authentication service is called for identity authentication; When the authentication service finds the token information in the request object through the request object, it verifies the legitimacy of the token and performs role judgment to determine whether the role level matches the level of the requested resource; After confirming the validity of the token and the corresponding role, request the corresponding resource service to obtain the resources required by the user, and return the result to the resource controller, and then respond to the client user.

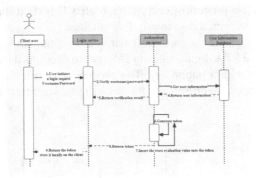

Fig. 2. Token-based login sequence diagram of the power mobile system

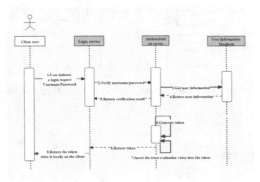

Fig. 3. Token-based resource request sequence diagram of the power mobile system

4   Continuous Trust Evaluation Algorithm

4.1   Trust Evaluation Algorithm Model and Data Processing

To objectively evaluate the subject and object of power mobile applications, monitor and collect QoS index data during application operation. The multi-attribute decision-making method [13] can effectively solve the problem of multiple targets to be evaluated and multiple evaluation indicators. To reasonably express the subordination relationship between the user layer and the service layer and the service layer and the index layer in the hierarchical model, the fuzzy analytic hierarchy process is used to calculate the weight system of trust evaluation according to the degree of influence of the lower layer on the upper layer in the hierarchical structure.

Suppose q^l, q^h are two real numbers, q^l, $q^h \in R$, and $q^l \leq q^h$, then $q = [q^l, q^h]$ is the interval number, where q^l is the lower bound of the interval number and q^h is the upper bound of the interval number. In particular, when q^l and q^h are equal in size, the interval number becomes a real number. q_{ij}^k represents the j-th QoS index of the i-th application operation for the k-th user. $q_{ij}^{k,l}$ represents the lower bound of the indicator's operating data during the detection process, $q_{ij}^{k,h}$ represents the upper bound of the indicator's operating data during the detection process. The interval number form of q_{ij}^k is $q_{ij} = [q_{ij}^{k,l}, q_{ij}^{k,h}]$. Based on the collected index data reflecting QoS, the data is classified according to different index attributes, and a decision matrix X reflecting the multiple attributes of QoS interval numbers is constructed as follows:

$$X = (q_{ij})_{m \times sn} = \begin{bmatrix} q_{11} & \cdots & q_{1n} \\ \cdots & \cdots & \cdots \\ q_{i1} & \cdots & q_{in} \\ \cdots & \cdots & \cdots \\ q_{m \times s1} & \cdots & q_{m \times sn} \end{bmatrix} \tag{2}$$

According to the interval number algorithm, normalization is based on the principle of vector normalization.

For the benefit index and the cost-type indicators in the decision matrix X, their standardized formulas are as follows:

$$\begin{cases} \left(q_{ij}^{k,l}\right)' = \dfrac{q_{ij}^{k,l}}{\sum\limits_{k=1}^{s} \sum\limits_{i=1}^{m} q_{ij}^{k,h}} \\[3ex] \left(q_{ij}^{k,h}\right)' = \dfrac{q_{ij}^{k,h}}{\sum\limits_{k=1}^{s} \sum\limits_{i=1}^{m} q_{ij}^{k,l}} \end{cases} \tag{3}$$

$$\begin{cases} \left(q_{ij}^{k,l}\right)' = \dfrac{\frac{1}{q_{ij}^{k,h}}}{\sum\limits_{k=1}^{s} \sum\limits_{i=1}^{m} \frac{1}{q_{ij}^{k,l}}} \\[3ex] \left(q_{ij}^{k,h}\right)' = \dfrac{\frac{1}{q_{ij}^{k,l}}}{\sum\limits_{k=1}^{s} \sum\limits_{i=1}^{m} \frac{1}{q_{ij}^{k,h}}} \end{cases} \tag{4}$$

After normalizing the decision matrix X, the decision matrix X' is as follows:

$$X' = (q_{ij})'_{m \times sn} \tag{5}$$

4.2 Hierarchical Model Weight System

The Fuzzy Analytic Hierarchy Process (FAHP) in the index weight method and the multi-attribute decision-making problem [14] is based on the analytic hierarchy process. Provides effective solutions to vague and difficult to quantify problems. In this paper, FAHP is used to establish the weight system of the hierarchical structure model.

According to the "0.1–0.9" scaling method [20], the various indicators of the service are compared, the membership degree between each indicator is obtained, and the fuzzy judgment matrix R of the indicator layer is established. For the i-th service in the service layer, the fuzzy judgment matrix R_i established by the degree of membership between its indicators is as follows:

$$R_i = \left(r_{kj}\right)_{n \times n} \tag{6}$$

The membership degree of the fuzzy judgment matrix quantifies the relationship between different indicators based on the actual collected data and is suitable for the calculation of the weight of multi-attribute uncertainty. In the same way, the fuzzy judgment matrix $R_1, R_2, \ldots, R_m$ of the service layer is established. Establish fuzzy judgment matrices E_1, $E_2, \ldots, E_k$ for different user types according to different user types. Then the consistency test is performed on each fuzzy judgment matrix to ensure the consistency between the importance of the elements in the matrix, and make the calculation result scientific and reliable.

4.3 Weight Calculation Method and Trust Assessment Method

The fuzzy judgment matrix weight formula is used to calculate the weight of the applied attribute index. Let ω_{ij} represent the weight of the j-th QoS index of the i-th application attribute, and its calculation formula is as follows:

$$\omega_{ij} = \frac{1}{n} - \frac{1}{2a} + \frac{1}{n \times a} \sum_{j=1}^{n} \left(r_{ij}\right)' \tag{7}$$

n is the number of indicators of the i-th cloud service, a = (n − 1)/2.

Finally, calculate the weight set of all indicators of all cloud services in the service layer, and obtain the weight matrix ω. The index weight matrix ω provides weights for trust evaluation.

Using the linear weighting method, T_i is used to represent the comprehensive evaluation value of the i-th application attribute, and the calculation formula is as follows:

$$T_i = \sum_{j=1}^{n} \left(\left(q_{ij}\right)' \times \omega_{ij}\right) \tag{8}$$

Among them, $(q_{ij})'$ is the QoS index data of the i-th row and j-th column in X'; ω_{ij} is the j-th index weight value of the i-th attribute in the index weight matrix ω.

Use F_i to represent the comprehensive evaluation value of the i-th user type, and the calculation formula is as follows:

$$F_i = \sum_{j=1}^{m} \left((T_{ij})' \times v_{ij} \right) \tag{9}$$

Among them, $(T_{ij})'$ is the comprehensive evaluation value of the j-th service of the user type i; v_{ij} is the j-th service weight value of the i-th user type in the matrix v. Similarly, the comprehensive evaluation value of different power mobile application user types can be calculated.

5 Verification and Analysis

This paper uses MATLAB and EXCEL to realize the standardization of the decision matrix in the model, weight calculation based on fuzzy analytic hierarchy process, comprehensive evaluation calculation and other functions, and process and evaluate the QoS index data of a service provided by an application software collected from the CloudHarmony website to verify the effectiveness of the method.

Process the original data obtained from the CloudHarmony website, list the corresponding decision matrix, and standardize it to obtain X' as follows:

$$X' = (q_{ij})'_{7\times3} = \begin{bmatrix} [0.0023, 0.0065] & [0.0016, 0.0092] & [0.0203, 0.0356] \\ [0.0003, 0.0051] & [0.0008, 0.0020] & [0.0089, 0.0159] \\ [0.0012, 0.0076] & [0.0003, 0.0090] & [0.0011, 0.0051] \\ [0.0005, 0.0021] & [0.0075, 0.0098] & [0.0008, 0.0060] \\ [0.0014, 0.0077] & [0.0033, 0.0115] & [0.0010, 0.0082] \\ [0.0228, 0.0425] & [0.0019, 0.0067] & [0.0011, 0.0053] \\ [0.0001, 0.0009] & [0.0047, 0.0057] & [0.0032, 0.0073] \end{bmatrix} \tag{10}$$

According to the indicator data corresponding to the application software, the different indicators obtained by different user types are calculated, and the weight matrix ω of the indicators is obtained as follows:

$$\omega = \begin{bmatrix} 0.1 & 0.5 & 0.6 \\ 0.39 & 0.25 & 0.4 \\ 0.1 & 0.57 & 0.4 \\ 0.3 & 0.4 & 0.77 \\ 0.2 & 0.2 & 0.4 \\ 0.6 & 0.2 & 0.6 \\ 0.2 & 0.1 & 0.4 \end{bmatrix} \tag{11}$$

According to the service data provided by the application, a fuzzy judgment matrix and a fuzzy consistency judgment matrix are established and the service weight vectors of three different customer types (ordinary user $U1$, employee $U2$, manager $U3$) are obtained as follows:

$$U1 = [0.31, 0.10, 0.32], \quad U2 = [0.33, 0.24, 0.40], \quad U3 = [0.56, 0.22, 0.81]$$

According to formula (8) and formula (9), the comprehensive trust evaluation values of three types of users are finally obtained:

$$F_{U1} = [0.0487, 0.0824], \; F_{U2} = [0.0433, 0.1074], \; F_{U3} = [0.0704, 0.1381]$$

Sort $F_{U3} > F_{U2} > F_{U1}$. The results show that, in this application software, the trust evaluation value of the management personnel service is the best, and that of the ordinary user service is the worst. The above results show that the method proposed in this paper can effectively evaluate the trust of the services provided by different types of users in the application software based on the indicator data collected by actual monitoring.

To reflect the accuracy of the method in this paper for trust evaluation, this experiment uses the same service trust evaluation value for different users to affect the situation and ultimately affects the comprehensive trust evaluation results of different user types under the same function. Based on the above experimental data, three user types (ordinary user $U1$, employee $U2$, manager $U3$) are set up, and the services provided to users will remain the same, and further trust evaluation will be carried out. The comprehensive evaluation results are as follows:

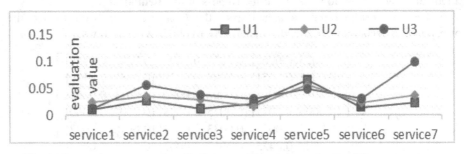

Fig. 4. Comparison test results of indicators of the same service for different user types

Figure 4 shows that for the three user types, the results of the trust evaluation will change accordingly when the application services are kept the same. Compared with the comprehensive trust evaluation values in different user types and different services, the overall comprehensive trust evaluation value order remains unchanged, still being $FU3 > FU2 > FU1$. The trust values of different types of users in most services are similar, indicating that the comprehensive trust evaluation value takes into account the impact of each type of user's unique service or operation, which shows that this method can correctly apply the trust changes in providing services according to different types of users, reflecting trust the accuracy of the assessment method.

Based on the same QoS index information and corresponding user data, the proposed method is compared with the approximate ideal point method, and the trust evaluation results are obtained. The results show that the sorting results of the two methods are consistent, but the algorithm complexity of the proposed method is $O(n)$, while the algorithm complexity of the ideal point approximation method is $O(n^2)$, which reflects the superiority and efficiency of the proposed method.

6 Conclusion

At present, data security has become crucial. Combining trust evaluation technology and token authentication method, this paper proposed a multi-attribute identity authentication method based on trust evaluation. Embedded the trust evaluation value into the token, and authenticated the user's identity through the real-time update of the token, thereby giving the corresponding authority. At the same time, the authentication process was encrypted and decrypted by mixing the random generation matrix encryption algorithm based on chaotic mapping and the RSA digital signature algorithm to improve the security of authentication. The experiment has calculated three different types of user trust evaluation and found that the resources obtained through this authentication method are different when the user's level is different. At the same time, when the user's level changes, the token will be updated to reduce or increase user permissions. Therefore, the multi-attribute authentication method combined with trust evaluation in this paper has higher security and confidentiality than previous authentication methods.

Acknowledgement. Supported by the science and technology project of State Grid Corporation of China: "Research on Dynamic Access Authentication and Trust Evaluation Technology of Power Mobile Internet Services Based on Zero Trust" (Grand No. 5700-202158183A-0-0-00).

References

1. Gong, Y., Chen, C., Liu, B.: Research on the ubiquitous electric power Internet of Things security management based on edge-cloud computing collaboration technology. In: IEEE Sustainable Power and Energy Conference (ISPEC), pp. 1997–2002 (2019)
2. Bedi, G., Singh, R.: Review of Internet of Things (IOT) in electric power and energy systems. IEEE Internet of Things J. **5**(2), 847–870 (2018)
3. Dalkılıç, H., Özcanhan, M.H.: Strong authentication protocol for identity verification in Internet of Things (IOT). In: 6th International Conference on Computer Science and Engineering (UBMK), pp. 199–203. IEEE (2021)
4. Huang, H., Chen, X.: Power mobile terminal identity authentication mechanism based on blockchain. In: International Wireless Communications and Mobile Computing (IWCMC), pp. 195–198 (2020)
5. Alashik, K.M., Yildirim, R.: Human identity verification from biometric dorsal hand vein images using the DL-GAN method. IEEE Access **9**, 74194–74208 (2021)
6. Aliev, H., Kim, H.-W.: Matrix-based dynamic authentication with conditional privacy-preservation for vehicular network security. IEEE Access **8**, 200883–200896 (2020)
7. Lamport, L.: Password authentication with insecure communication. Commun. ACM **24**(11), 770–772 (1981)
8. Chen, Y., Kong, W., Jiang, X.: Anti-synchronization and robust authentication for noisy PUF-based smart card. IEEE Access **7**, 142214–142223 (2019)
9. Carretero, J., Izquierdo-Moreno, G., Vasile-Cabezas, M., Garcia-Blas, J.: Federated identity architecture of the European eID system. IEEE Access **6**, 75302–75326 (2018)
10. Ahmed, A.A., Wendy, K., Kabir, M.N., Sadiq, A.S.: Dynamic reciprocal authentication protocol for mobile cloud computing. IEEE Syst. J. **15**(1), 727–737 (2020)
11. Mao, D., Liu, H., Zhang, W.: An enhanced three-factor authentication scheme with dynamic verification for medical multimedia information systems. IEEE Access **7**, 167683–167695 (2019)

12. Vinoth, R., Deborah, L., Vijayakumar, P., Kumar, N.: Secure multifactor authenticated key agreement scheme for industrial IoT. IEEE Internet of Things J. **8**(5), 3801–3811 (2021). https://doi.org/10.1109/JIOT.2020.3024703
13. Qu, C., Buyya, R.: A cloud trust evaluation system using hierarchical fuzzy inference system for service selection. In: International Conference on Advanced Information Networking and Applications, pp. 850–857. IEEE (2014)
14. Panigrahi, R., Srivastava, P.R.: Evaluation of travel websites a fuzzy analytical hierarchy process approach. In: IEEE UPCON Conference, Allahabad, pp. 1–6 (2015)
15. Atiewi, S.: Scalable and secure big data IoT system based on multifactor authentication and lightweight cryptography. IEEE Access **8**, 113498–113511 (2020)
16. Maciej, B., Imed, E.F., Kurkowski, M.: Multifactor authentication protocol in a mobile environment. IEEE Access **7**, 157185–157199 (2019)
17. Yang, Y.S., Lee, S.H., Chen, W.C., Yang, C.S., Huang, Y.M., Hou, T.W.: TTAS: trusted token authentication service of securing SCADA network in energy management system for industrial Internet of Things. Sensors **21**, 2685 (2021)
18. Qi, R., Zhou, J., Liu, Y.: Research on the network security system of water resources management decision support system based on token. Hydropower, pp. 1–7 (2021)
19. Zou, J.: Application research of token-based identity authentication in university training interactive platform. In: Wireless Internet Technology (2018)
20. Xu, Z., Liao, H.: Intuitionistic fuzzy analytic hierarchy process. IEEE Trans. Fuzzy Syst. **22**(4), 749–761 (2014). https://doi.org/10.1109/TFUZZ.2013.2272585
21. Thakur, K., Qiu, M., Gai, K., Ali, M.: An investigation on cyber security threats and security models. In: IEEE CSCloud (2015)
22. Gai, K., Qiu, M., Sun, X., Zhao, H.: Security and privacy issues: a survey on FinTech. In: Qiu, M. (ed.) SmartCom 2016. LNCS, vol. 10135, pp. 236–247. Springer, Cham (2017). https://doi.org/10.1007/978-3-319-52015-5_24
23. Gai, K., Qiu, M., Elnagdy, S.: A novel secure big data cyber incident analytics framework for cloud-based cybersecurity insurance. In: IEEE BigDataSecurity (2016)
24. Zhang, Z., Wu, J., et al.: Jamming ACK attack to wireless networks and a mitigation approach. In: IEEE GLOBECOM Conference, pp. 1–5 (2008)
25. Qiu, H., Qiu, M., Lu, Z.: Selective encryption on ECG data in body sensor network based on supervised machine learning. Inf. Fusion **55**, 59–67 (2020)
26. Qiu, H., Qiu, M., Memmi, G., Ming, Z., Liu, M.: A dynamic scalable blockchain based communication architecture for IoT. In: Qiu, M. (ed.) Smart Blockchain: First International Conference, SmartBlock 2018, pp. 159–166. Springer, Cham (2018). https://doi.org/10.1007/978-3-030-05764-0_17

Defects Detection System of Medical Gloves Based on Deep Learning

Jing Wang[1,2], Meng Wan[1](✉), Jue Wang[1,3], Xiaoguang Wang[1],
Yangang Wang[1,3], Fang Liu[1], Weixiao Min[2], He Lei[2], and Lihua Wang[2]

[1] Computer Network Information Center, Chinese Academy of Sciences,
Beijing 100083, China
{wanmengdamo,wangxg}@cnic.cn, {wangjue,wangyg,liufang}@sccas.cn
[2] Beihang University, Beijing 100191, China
{zf1921127,wanglihua}@buaa.edu.cn
[3] University of Chinese Academy of Sciences, Beijing 100049, China

Abstract. In industrial production, medical gloves with tear, stain and other defects will be produced. In traditional manual mode, the efficiency and accuracy of defect detection depend on the proficiency of spot-check workers, which results in uneven glove product quality. In this paper, a surface defect detection system of medical gloves based on deep learning is designed for the automatic detection with high efficiency and accuracy. According to the industrial requirements of high real-time, the system adopts a cache scheme to improve the data reading and writing speed, and an *Open Neural Network Exchange* (ONNX) to effectively improve the speed of model reasoning. For the demands of high detection accuracy, the system designs a dual model detection strategy, which divides texture detection and edge detection into two steps. The advantage of this strategy is to remove most useless information while ensuring the effective information of the image. Furthermore, two auxiliary models are used to promote the accuracy of detection based on classification methods. Finally, experiments are proposed to verify the functional indicators of the system. After the on-site test of the production line in the medical glove factory, the system has the ability to detect the gloves of two production lines with high real-time. The product missed detection rate is less than 2%, and the product mistakenly picked rate is less than 5/10000. Verified by the industry of gloves, the system can be put into production line.

Keywords: Medical gloves · Deep learning · Surface defect · Detection system · Image recognition · Auxiliary model

1 Introduction

Under the influence of COVID-19, the awareness of global health protection has been raised, and the demand for medical gloves has increased greatly. At present, the production of medical gloves is mainly in Southeast Asian countries and China, and most of the detection methods are manual testing [1]. The manual detection will produce a high cost, the accuracy of which is also affected by workers' subjective judgment and detection standards in different regions. Machine vision detection is a non-contact automatic detection technology, which has the advantages of high detection accuracy and long-time operation in a complex production environment. It is an effective solution for factory to implement automatic production and intelligent detection.

For the requirements of industry, it is necessary to detect 16 gloves per second on each production line. Therefore, the glove detection system has a high standard for detection speed and accuracy. Technically, the challenges of the system are as follows:

- The detection target has the problem of different defect sizes, in which small defects have always been the difficulty in the field of defect detection.
- The system should optimize the time-consuming of each module and achieve high real-time performance.
- The detection model of the system should achieve high accuracy to adapt to industrial automation scenarios.

To optimize the problems above, the high-accuracy detection model and lightweight architecture of the system are designed. The time delay of the system can be reduced by optimizing the data transmission time [2] between software and hardware and reducing the reasoning time of the detection model. We mainly put forward the following contributions:

- The dual model mode is designed to divide the edge detection and texture detection into two steps, aiming at the defects of tear and stain respectively.
- Cache queue based on Redis is used for real-time data access to improve data reading/Writing (RW) speed and model environment optimization is used to improve the reasoning efficiency.
- The classification model is combined as the auxiliary model of the detection model, and the reasoning results of the two models are weighted as the final results.

The introduction section introduces the background and contributions of this article. The related work section introduces several existing systems for glove detection. The architecture section introduces the overall architecture, and the Mysql+redis data storage strategy. Finally, a series of experiments were carried out to prove the accuracy of the glove model.

2   Related Work

With the development of computer and network technologies [3,4], big data processing and transferring [5–7] become a critical issue for various applications. Currently, there are few researches on the surface defect detection system of medical gloves. Li et al. [8] used multiple thresholds to improve the Canny algorithm for broken finger defect detection. The detection effect is reduced when the defect type is complicated. Zhang et al. [9] used a multi-feature SVM defect recognition classification method to identify and classify the defect types according to the difference in the types of glove surface defects. The defect recognition accuracy of this method was 93.46%, which could not meet the accuracy requirements of this system.

Traditional machine vision detection algorithms have low detection accuracy, and manual selection of features is subjective, and robustness is low when defects are complex. With the development of deep learning technology, the use of CNN [10] for feature extraction has become a hot topic in machine vision research. One-stage and two-stage are two typical target detection algorithms based on deep learning. The Two-stage algorithm divides detection into two steps: generating candidate regions and classifying candidate regions [11]. Common Two-stage algorithms include R-CNN [12], SPP-net [13], Fast R-CNN [14], Faster R-CNN [15]. The One-stage algorithm directly obtains the location information of the detection target and the probability value of the category to which it belongs, and has a higher detection speed. Typical one-stage algorithms include SSD [16] series algorithms and YOLO [17] series algorithms. In this paper, based on the system's real-time and accuracy requirements, yolov5 is selected as the medical glove defect detection algorithm.

3   System Architecture

3.1   Overall Process

The system uses Mako g-503b Poe camera of German AVT (Allied vision) company, fl-cc614a-2m lens of Japanese Ricoh company and LED white stroboscopic light source to build an optical imaging environment. In the optical imaging environment, the photoelectric sensor is used as the switch to automatically shoot when gloves pass by. The glove image will be stored in the Redis based task cache queue, and the Redis cache will be monitored through the reasoning model. Once there is data, the queue operation will be completed and reasoning will be carried out. The reasoning results will be stored in the result cache queue based on Redis. The main control program monitors and reads the reasoning results, and transmits the control signal to PLC according to the results. The PLC control device will remove the defective glove products. The detection flow chart is shown in Fig. 1.

3.2   Data Management

This paper uses the combination of MySQL + Redis as the way of data storage [18]. MySQL has the characteristics of small volume, high speed, the low overall cost of ownership and open source code. The lightweight development and deployment mode is suitable for the persistent storage of system running state, camera running state, glove image and result data. As a memory-based and high-performance key-value database, Redis is the fastest nonrelational database

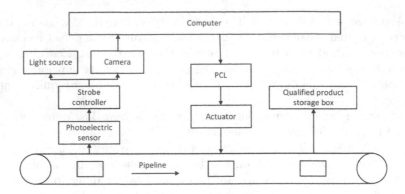

Fig. 1. The process of the detect system.

today. Sina Microblog is based on redis distributed cache implementation, supporting more than 200 million daily active users. As a real-time queue of the system, Redis can effectively reduce the delay caused by too slow disk data access.

This paper implements task and result message queues based on the Redis *blocking pull message command* (brpop). The interaction process diagram of producers and consumers is shown in Fig. 2. In this message queue mode, the producer stores the data in the Redis database, and the consumer pulls the data from the database. If the queue is empty, the consumer will enter the blocking state when pulling messages and will no longer read data. Once a new message comes, Redis will notify the consumer to process the new message immediately. It is worth noting that when using brpop to pull messages in a blocking way, it supports the incoming timeout. If the timeout is set to 0, it means that it is blocked until there is a new message. Otherwise, it will return null after the specified timeout. The timeout in this article is set to 0. Redis also provides queue size settings. The length of both queues in the system is 20.

Fig. 2. Message queues based on the Redis

3.3   Model Deployment Environment

This training is based on the PyTorch framework. To accelerate the system performance, this paper uses onnx (open neural network exchange) as the middle layer to convert the weight file of the trained Yolo model into onnx format first, and finally into tensorrt format reasoning accelerated detection system.

Tensorrt is a high-performance deep learning reasoning optimization engine. On the one hand, tensorrt reduces the calculation accuracy, on the other hand, it reconstructs the network structure, combines some operations that can be combined, optimizes according to the characteristics of GPU, and improves the reasoning speed. Xiangdong [19] uses tensorrt to accelerate the CNN inference model. On the TX2 embedded platform, the accelerated model infers the video frame time by 64.5%.

4 Method

4.1 Dual Model Strategy

It is difficult to improve the detection accuracy by using a detection model, this paper trains the detection network for different defect types. The overall process of the detection model is shown in Fig. 3. The glove image data is input to the data enhancement module for data enhancement, and the enhanced image data enters the shape real-time detection model. If the strict standard mode is opened for auxiliary detection, the enhanced image data also enters the shape auxiliary detection model. Judge the test results. If the shape is judged to be unqualified, deal with the equipment with unqualified shape; If the shape is judged to be qualified, the detected glove part is cut, and then the cut image is input into the

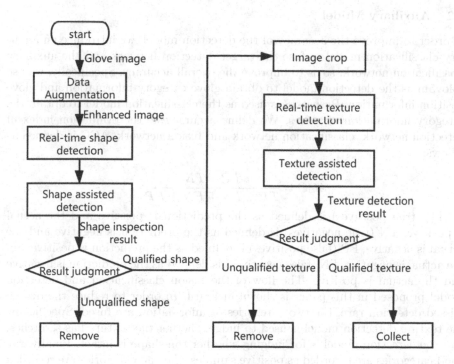

Fig. 3. Flow chart of detection model

texture real-time detection model for texture detection of glove surface. If the strict standard mode is opened for auxiliary detection, the cut image data is also entered into the texture auxiliary detection model. Judge the test results. If the texture is judged to be unqualified, deal with the texture unqualified equipment; If it is judged that the texture is qualified, the gloves meet both the shape requirements and the texture requirements, and it is judged as qualified gloves.

In the detection process, due to the different sizes of actual tear defects and stain defects, the accuracy of simultaneous detection is not high enough. Therefore, a two-stage model is introduced, namely, the shape real-time detection model and texture real-time detection model. The two-stage models detect shape defects and texture defects respectively, which improves the overall detection accuracy.

Data enhancement can improve the accuracy of the model and improve the generalization ability of the model [20]. We have introduced some common data enhancement methods in model training, including image scaling, flipping, clipping, brightness change, contrast transformation, chroma transformation, mixup and mosaic. Among them, the mosaic method is the most important and improves accuracy the most. We also use *Test time augmentation* (TTA) method in the reasoning stage of the model. Aiming at the imbalance of training samples, we adopt the improved loss function which based on the standard cross-entropy loss.

4.2   Auxiliary Model

In order to improve the accuracy of the detection model, we introduce an auxiliary classification model to fuse the target detection network and the auxiliary classification network, so as to improve the overall accuracy. Specifically, we use yolov5m as the detection model to obtain glove category information and glove position information. Resnet-18 is used as the classification model to obtain the category information of gloves. We define accuracy as the evaluation index of detection network, classification network and fusion network. ACC is defined as follows:

$$ACC = \frac{TP + TN}{TP + TN + FN + FP}$$

TP (true positives) is defined as the prediction is positive and the actual is positive, TN (true negatives) is defined as the prediction is negative and the actual is negative, FP (false positives) is defined as the prediction is positive and the actual is negative, FN (false negatives) is defined as the prediction is negative and the actual is positive. The flow of the fusion classification and detection model proposed in this paper is shown in Fig. 4. In order to reduce the overall missed detection rate, the two categories of information are fused. Specifically, the texture detection model is used to judge whether the texture has scratches, and the detection model is for judging whether the shape is intact. Finally, the good categories are recorded as positive samples, the bad categories are recorded as negative samples, and the two results are combined and calculated, which is the final result.

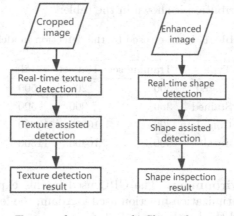

a. Texture detection   b. Shape detection

Fig. 4. Fusion classification and detection model process

To improve the accuracy of the model, we introduce an auxiliary classification model resnet18. Simply increasing the number of network layers will lead to the loss of information in the transmission process between network layers. RESNET model is to suppress overfitting and introduce the classification network with residual network structure. Resnet18 network structure includes input part, intermediate convolution part and output part.

5 Results

5.1 Training

Dataset. The data set used in this experiment is the defective glove images collected in the actual factory production. There are 11300 glove gray images with 2464 * 2056 pixels and their annotation information. The type of test gloves is shown in Fig. 5. A is intact gloves, B and C are tear and stain defect gloves respectively:

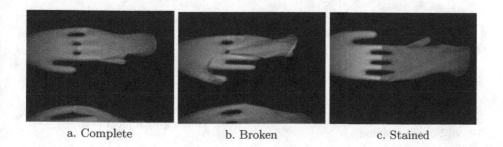

a. Complete   b. Broken   c. Stained

Fig. 5. Glove image comparison

The data set distribution is shown in the table:

Table 1. Dataset used by the detection model

Type	Training set	Test set	Total
Teared	300	200	500
Stained	300	200	500
Complete	300	10000	10300
Total	900	10400	11300

Experimental Environment. The GPU used in this experiment is geforce GTX 2080 Ti, the optimization function used is Adam, the learning rate is 0.01, the epoch is 200, and the batch size is 4.

Experimental Result. According to the requirements of the factory, this paper defines the detection indicators: missing rate and false picking rate. The missing rate refers to the proportion of defective products not detected in the inspection process in all defective products. The false picking rate refers to the proportion of good products removed by mistake in all products. The production line requires that the missed inspection rate shall not be higher than 2%, and the false picking rate shall not be higher than 5/10000.

Focal loss is modified based on the standard cross entropy loss. The cross entropy loss is corrected by using a coefficient inversely proportional to the target existence probability. In this way, the weight coefficient of a small number of positive samples is larger, and its contribution to the model will increase. The weight coefficient of a large number of negative samples is smaller, and its contribution to the model will be relatively weakened. Therefore, the model will learn more useful information. The validation results of focal loss method are shown in Fig. 6.

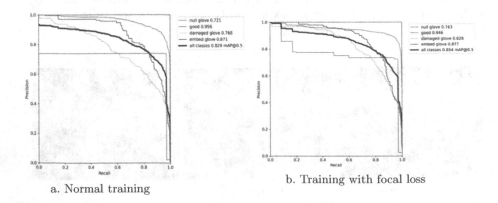

a. Normal training

b. Training with focal loss

Fig. 6. Variation of precision with recall rate

In this paper, experiments are designed to test Canny, HOG + SVM and fast R-CNN respectively with missed detection rate, false picking rate and FPS as detection indicators. The statistics of reasoning results are shown in Table 2.

Table 2. Results of different model test

Model	False picking rate	Missing rate	FPS
Canny	0.15%	4.5%	108
HOG+SVM	0.18%	4%	95
Faster R-CNN	0.03%	3%	1.3
YOLOV5+Alex	0.016%	1.2%	20

In order to verify the influence of auxiliary model on detection accuracy, three groups of comparative experiments are designed in this paper. The first group only adds shape auxiliary model, the second group only adds texture auxiliary model, and the third group adds both auxiliary models. The detection results are shown in Table 3. This system adopts the high-speed data access method based on redis cache, and the operating efficiency of the system is increased from 13.5FPS to 20FPS, which is 48% higher than that of the file system-based data access method. The system adopts the onnx+tensorrt model acceleration strategy, and the operating efficiency is increased from 11.3FPS to 20FPS.

Table 3. Add test results of different auxiliary models

Model	False picking rate	Missing rate	ACC
Add texture assist model only	0.035%	2.3%	97.67%
Add shape assist model	0.021%	1.7%	98.28%
Add both texture assist model and shape assist model	0.016%	1.21%	98.77%

5.2   System Test

The field test adopts Mako g-503b Poe camera and fl-cc614a-2m lens. The light source is set as white LED stroboscopic light source, placed on the same side as the camera. The GPU is used. The experiment is carried out every three hours: The statistical results after manual re inspection are shown in the table below. After calculation, the final false picking rate of the system is 1.6 per 10000, and the missed detection rate is 1.21%. The detection accuracy meets the requirements of the manufacturer. The system can run smoothly when about 16 gloves are detected per second on site.

Table 4. Add test results of different auxiliary models

Index	Test numbers	Defective numbers (detected)	False detection	Unidentified products	False picking rate	Missing rate
1	172522	422	21	5	1.2‰	1.21%
2	169732	313	24	3	1.4‰	1.01%
3	174990	415	37	5	2.1‰	1.31%
Sum	517244	1150	87	13	1.6‰	1.21%

6 Conclusion

The system realizes the real-time detection of medical glove defects based on deep learning technology, and the false picking rate is lower than 0.05%. Based on the real-time requirements of the system, this paper selects the high-speed data access mode based on Redis cache, and adopts the model deployment scheme of ONNX + tensorrt; Based on the requirements of model accuracy, we design the mode of double model and auxiliary model. The experiments show that the system can meet the production requirements.

Acknowledgment. This work was partially supported by the Beijing Natural Science Foundation-Haidian Original Innovation Joint Foundation (Grant No. L182053), the Network and Information Project of 14th five-year's plan in Chinese Academy of Sciences under the contact number WX145XQ09 and the Pilot Project in Chinese Academy of Sciences under the contact number XDB38050200.

References

1. Yangfeng, W.: Design of automatic grabbing device for medical latex gloves. Master's thesis, Shenyang University of Technology (2019)
2. Zhang, Z., Wu, J., Deng, J., Qiu, M.: Jamming ack attack to wireless networks and a mitigation approach. In: IEEE GlobalCom, pp. 1–5 (2008)
3. Zhao, H., Chen, M., et al.: A novel pre-cache schema for high performance android system. FGCS **56**, 766–772 (2016)
4. Gao, Y., et al.: Performance and power analysis of high-density multi-GPGPU architectures: a preliminary case study. In: IEEE 17th HPCC, pp. 29–35 (2015)
5. Qiu, H., Qiu, M., et al.: A dynamic scalable blockchain based communication architecture for IoT. In: SmartBlock, pp. 159–166 (2018)
6. Gai, K., Qiu, M., Sun, X., Zhao, H.: Security and privacy issues: a survey on fintech. In: Qiu, M. (ed.) SmartCom 2016. LNCS, vol. 10135, pp. 236–247. Springer, Cham (2017). https://doi.org/10.1007/978-3-319-52015-5_24
7. Thakur, K., Qiu, M., et al.: An investigation on cyber security threats and security models. In: CSCloud 2015, pp. 307–311 (2015)
8. Wenwen, L.: Research on Key Technologies and Testing Devices of Visual Inspection of Plastic Gloves. Master's thesis, Shandong University of Technology (2018)
9. Zhongkai, Z.: Research on size measurement and defect detection of latex gloves based on machine vision. Master's thesis, Shenyang University of Technology (2020)
10. Hong, M., Rim, B., Lee, H.C., et al.: Multi-class classification of lung diseases using CNN models. Appl. Sci. **11**(19), 9289 (2021)

11. Yongqiang, Z., Yuan, R., Shipeng, D., Junyi, Z.: Summary of deep learning target detection methods (2020)
12. Girshick, R., Donahue, J., Darrell, T., Malik, J.: Rich feature hierarchies for accurate object detection and semantic segmentation. In: Proceedings of the IEEE Conference on Computer Vision and Pattern Recognition, pp. 580–587 (2014)
13. He, K., Zhang, X., Ren, S., Sun, J.: Spatial pyramid pooling in deep convolutional networks for visual recognition. IEEE Trans. Pattern Anal. Mach. Intell. **37**(9), 1904–1916 (2015)
14. Li, J., Liang, X., Shen, S., et al.: Scale-aware fast R-CNN for pedestrian detection. IEEE Trans. Multimedia **20**(4), 985–996 (2017)
15. Ren, S., He, K., Girshick, R., Sun, J.: Faster R-CNN: towards real-time object detection with region proposal networks. Adv. Neural. Inf. Process. Syst. **28**, 91–99 (2015)
16. Pan, H., Li, Y., Zhao, D.: Recognizing human behaviors from surveillance videos using the SSD algorithm. J. Supercomput. 1–19 (2021)
17. Zhao, J., Zhang, X., Yan, J., et al.: A wheat spike detection method in UAV images based on improved yolov5. Remote Sens. **13**(16), 3095 (2021)
18. Qiu, H., Qiu, M., Lu, Z.: Selective encryption on ECG data in body sensor network based on supervised machine learning. Inf. Fusion **55**, 59–67 (2020)
19. Dong, X., Qin, H.X.L., Xiaohong, W.: Video crowd counting system based on deep learning (2020)
20. Qiu, M., Gai, K., Xiong, Z.: Privacy-preserving wireless communications using bipartite matching in social big data. FGCS **87**, 772–781 (2018)

Mobile Terminal Identity Authentication Method Based on IBC

Xuqiu Chen[1], Wei Wang[1(✉)], Wei Gan[2], Yi Yang[1], Su Yuan[1], and Meng Li[1]

[1] State Grid Chengdu Electric Power Supply Company, Chengdu 610000, China
[2] State Grid Sichuan Electric Power Company, Chengdu 610000, China

Abstract. With the rapid development of the power mobile Internet, traditional identity authentication and authentication modes still have identity information theft, are unable to prevent illegal behaviors of internal users, etc., which can no longer meet the security requirements of identity authentication in mobile Internet services. In response to this problem, this paper proposes a mobile terminal identity authentication method on the *Identity-Based Cryptography* (IBC). During registration, the user's voice is collected through the mobile terminal to establish an identity vector (i-vector) voiceprint model, and features are extracted and added to the identity mark to generate a user ID and a corresponding identity password system; during authentication, the legitimacy of the user is judged based on voice recognition to prevent illegal user intrusion, And then based on the identity password combined with the symmetric encryption algorithm AES to encrypt and decrypt data to achieve terminal identity authentication to resist common attacks in the mobile Internet. Finally, the experimental analysis shows that the method effectively improves the security of the power mobile Internet identity authentication process and has the advantages of low cost and high efficiency. In the power mobile Internet business scenario, this method greatly improves the identification ability of illegal users and the resistance to network malicious attacks.

Keywords: IBC · Identity authentication · AES algorithm · I-vector

1 Introduction

With the rapid development of power mobile Internet and the widespread use of mobile devices, people's traditional lifestyles in terms of food, clothing, housing, and transportation have undergone great changes. However, the popularity of mobile devices is also accompanied by problems such as the complexity of user and device identities, and the prominent features of scale and sea. Therefore, identity authentication is the most basic thing. Zero trust is a new concept of network security protection. Compared with traditional single identity authentication, identity authentication based on the concept of zero trust is characterized by continuous verification and never trust. It means that systems and devices remain untrusted, regardless of whether they are outside the network or inside the network. When they need to access related resources, they are authenticated and trusted by the identity authentication system to ensure user identity, application and The credibility of mobile terminals greatly improves the security of network protection,

© The Author(s), under exclusive license to Springer Nature Switzerland AG 2022
M. Qiu et al. (Eds.): SmartCom 2021, LNCS 13202, pp. 112–122, 2022.
https://doi.org/10.1007/978-3-030-97774-0_10

while the traditional single identity authentication and authentication mode still face hidden dangers such as identity information theft, vulnerability to network attacks, and inability to prevent illegal behaviors of internal users. Therefore, the traditional single authentication method will gradually be eliminated in the future.

As one of the main functions of cryptography, identity authentication is the process of authenticating real users, computer systems, network hosts, and other subjects. Identity identification cryptography is a cryptographic system based on identification, which is a traditional PKI certificate system. The latest developments. Compared with the traditional PKI certificate system, the ID password technology does not require a CA to issue a digital certificate. It can directly use user-specific IDs to generate public and private key pairs. These IDs can be email addresses, names, mobile phone numbers, etc., which are easy to obtain and reduce extra The cost of maintaining a complete set of user keys and certificate systems has greatly reduced costs and improved flexibility and applicability. In recent years, identification and encryption technology has developed vigorously and has been successfully used in certain government administrative fields and private fields. However, like the identity authentication mechanism of the PKI system, the identity authentication based on the identity identification password system still cannot avoid the common attacks in the mobile Internet, and there are security problems in key management.

At the same time, in recent decades, machine learning methods represented by neural networks have been rapidly developed and applied in many fields such as identity recognition and machine vision. At present, research based on neural networks mainly focuses on the authentication between real users such as passwords, biometric passwords, and computer systems. Therefore, the combination of neural networks and cryptography has a large research space in the field of identity authentication.

To solve the existing problems, this paper proposes a mobile terminal identity authentication method on IBC. Finally, the experimental analysis shows that the scheme effectively improves the security of the power mobile Internet identity authentication process, has the advantages of low cost, high efficiency, etc., and improves the identification ability of illegal users in the power mobile Internet business scenario and the malicious network. Resistance to attack.

Section 2 of this article is the research and development of related fields; Sect. 3 is the system design of this method; Sect. 4 of this article carries out simulation experiments and analysis of this method; Sect. 5 is a summary of this method.

2   Related Work

This section will discuss the development of the identity identification cryptosystem and the research of cryptography and neural networks in identity authentication. The following introduces domestic and foreign research related to this article.

In the literature [1], Shamir proposed the concept of identity identification cryptosystem in 1985. There is a key center (KGC) in the system to generate keys, manage keys, and update keys. Compared with the traditional PKI certification system has greatly improved its efficiency in all aspects. In literature [2] Boneh proposed a distributed key generation method to optimize key escrow in 2001. This method is based on Shamir(t,n) and designed n key center threshold passwords to protect The user's private key and the reasonable allocation of resources have solved the problem of over-concentration of rights in the key center. Literature [3] proposed a method of using an identity identification algorithm to realize the remote authentication between the internal end of the power grid system and the two-way authentication between mobile terminals. Literature [4] proposed a cross-domain authentication protocol, which is based on the identity identification algorithm by combining the PKI-based inter-chain trust transfer with the IBC domain-based intra-chain authentication to solve the traditional IBC system secret The problem of key revocation is difficult.

At the same time, some researchers thought of applying the emerging neural network technology to cryptography to optimize the management of keys. For example, in the literature [5], Jin et al. proposed a 3D CUBE hybrid algorithm based on artificial neural networks. This method can learn to generate keys and minimize shared information. A common problem in symmetric cryptosystems is the key problem. Exchange, this method can effectively solve this kind of problem, so that the safety is improved. In [6], for the first time, a combination of neural networks and genetic algorithms is used to generate keys for public-key cryptography. This method uses a mixture of different rounds to generate public and private keys. This ensures that the generated private key cannot be derived from the public key, which greatly improves the security during the key generation process. Literature [7] proposed a method to prevent key generation errors. This method uses the Hopfield neural network to identify the noise and regenerate the accuracy. The key and its error correction rate are also faster than other methods. Literature [8] proposed an identity authentication method based on Hopfield neural network, which removes the verification table and also has a more accurate recognition rate and faster processing time. Literature [9] introduced the use of password authentication based on the Hopfield network. This method obtains identity verification by converting text and graphic passwords into probability values. Compared with existing hierarchical neural networks, the proposed method provides better accuracy for registration and password changes.

Literature [10] proposed a multi-step fingerprint authentication system based on a neural network. This method uses a three-layer neural network of backpropagation learning algorithms. The authentication rate will increase as the number of steps increases. Therefore, this method can control the authentication rate by the number of steps. Literature [11] proposed a multi-biological feature recognition technology, which uses artificial neural networks and support vector machines to extract and recognize biometrics, and effectively improves the security and authenticity of system identification and authentication through multiple features. Literature [12] proposed a neural network system based on face recognition. This method uses a Fourier filter to extract feature vectors as the input vector of the neural network and uses random projection to reduce the dimensionality of the input vector. Therefore, this system has more advantages. Good robustness and accuracy.

In terms of data protection, literature [13] proposed an extended network allocation vector scheme, which can recover most of the lost throughput between nodes and reduce the energy flow of the attacked node. Qiu et al. [14] proposed a novel method of using the two-part matching method to achieve privacy-protected channel scheduling and improve privacy protection from adversary attack in big data environment [20, 21]. Literature [15, 22] proposed a data classification model based on supervised learning to protect healthcare data from illegal classification by attackers and further protect patient data privacy with new data allocation approaches [23, 24].

From the above research content, it can be seen that the current identity authentication function based on neural networks mainly focuses on the identity authentication between real people and computer systems such as biometric passwords, but lacks the exploration of identity authentication based on public-key cryptosystems in the mobile Internet environment. Therefore, this article will study identity authentication based on neural networks and cryptography.

3 System

3.1 Overall Framework

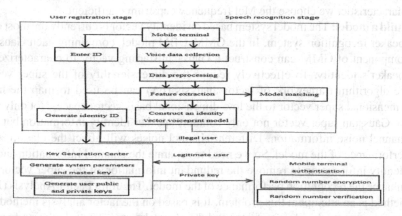

Fig. 1. System framework

As shown in Fig. 1, the realization of the mobile terminal identity authentication system on IBC proposed in this paper involves two aspects of neural network and cryptography, including two stages: the identity vector is established by collecting the user's voice through the mobile terminal during registration. Voiceprint model, extracting features and adding identity identification to generate a user ID and generate the corresponding identity password system; During authentication, first, judge the legitimacy of the user based on voice recognition, and then encrypt and decrypt data based on the identity password combined with the symmetric encryption algorithm AES to achieve terminal identity authentication.

3.2 User

(1) **Data preprocessing:** The collected voice signal contains a lot of interfering noise, and the system needs to preprocess the voice to obtain "clean" voice data that is

conducive to voiceprint feature extraction and pattern matching. In addition to the processing of noise, the voice signal is a long-term non-stationary signal, which is not conducive to feature extraction and analysis. Therefore, the voice signal needs to be pre-emphasized, framed, windowed and endpoint detection processed. When the quality of the collected voice is relatively poor, it is also necessary to perform processing such as noise reduction filtering or voice enhancement compensation on the voice.

(2) **Feature extraction:** After the speech signal is preprocessed, extracting effective feature parameters is the key to establishing a speaker model. The extracted feature parameters need to be able to characterize the personal characteristics of the speaker differently from others and be able to be processed by a mathematical model. At the same time, to improve the processing efficiency of the back-end model, it is necessary to consider the dimension of the feature parameters and the degree of contribution to the information and remove interference information that is not related to the speaker as much as possible to improve the performance of the system. The human ear's ability to perceive sound rate does not vary linearly. Based on this characteristic, we choose the Mel frequency cepstrum coefficient.

(3) **Build a model:** The model system based on identity vector is currently the most used speaker recognition system. In the GMM-UBM model, combining each Gaussian component of GMM can construct a Gaussian starting vector to characterize the speaker's identity. To effectively reduce the dimensionality of the super vector, the algorithm framework of factor analysis (FA) can be used to map the high-dimensional super vector to the low-dimensional basis vector space. Not only that, the Gaussian super vector not only contains speaker identity information but also channel noise information. Different channel noises will affect the classification performance of the model. So we need to separate the channel information and the identity information to remove the redundant information of the super vector and enhance the recognition performance of the model. The Joint Factor Analysis (JFA) method is an attempt at this problem. It is based on the factor analysis method and tries to separate the identity factor and the channel factor. The calculation formula is:

$$M = s + c \tag{1}$$

$$S = m + Vy + Dz \tag{2}$$

$$C = Ux \tag{3}$$

Among them, M is the mean super vector of GMM, which is composed of the super vector s related to the identity and the super vector c related to the channel. In the vector S, m is a factor irrelevant to the speaker, y is a factor related to the speaker, z is a residual factor related to the speaker, V is an eigentone matrix, and D is a diagonal residual matrix. In the vector c, U is the eigenchannel matrix, and x is a factor related to the channel. JFA can improve the performance of the GMM-UBM model. However, the lost channel factor still contains useful speaker information. Voiceprint information and channel information cannot be completely independent, a super vector subspace is used to simultaneously model these two kinds of different information, and an identity vector model is proposed. As shown in the formula:

$$M = m + Tw \tag{4}$$

Where M represents the GMM mean super vector of a piece of speech, which is related to the speaker and channel; m represents the UBM mean super vector, which is independent of the speaker and channel; T represents a variable subspace matrix; w Represents a vector related to the speaker and the channel, w is the i-vector containing the speaker information. In the i-vector model, each speech will be encoded as an identity vector, even if it is a different speech of the same person. The voice image is converted into a low-dimensional fixed-length vector through the i-vector model, and then the phase distance measurement algorithm is used to classify the identity to which the vector belongs [16].

(4) **User key generation:** The user enters relevant identification information through the client, such as name, IP address, email address, mobile phone number, etc. Select one of them and the extracted user's voiceprint features to form a new user ID. System initialization (Setup): Given the safety parameter λ, select the N-order additive cyclic groups G_1 and G_2 and the multiplicative cyclic group G_T respectively. P_1 and P_2 are the generators of the additive cyclic groups G_1 and G_2, respectively. The key generation center KGC selects the bilinear pair e: $G_1 \times G_2 \rightarrow G_T$, and selects two secure Hash functions H_1: $\{0, 1\} * \rightarrow Z * q$, H_2: $\{0, 1\} * \rightarrow Z* q$, randomly select $s \in [1, N - 1]$ as the system parameter master key, and calculate $P_{pub} = sP_2$ as the master key. KGC announces the system parameters params $= <\lambda, G_1, G_2,$ e, N, $P_{pub}, H_1, H_2>$ and keeps s secret. Key generation algorithm (KeyEx): For the user ID, KGC selects and publicly uses a private key to generate the function identifier hid, and calculates $t_1 = H_1(IDA\|hid, N) + s$ on the elliptic curve finite field FN, if $t_1 = 0$, the master private key 0 needs to be regenerated, otherwise $t_2 = s \cdot t_1^{-1}$, the private key $d = t_2 P_1 = s \cdot P_1/[H_1(ID\|hid, N + s)]$ and the public key $Q = H_1(ID\|hid, N)P_1 + P_{pub}$ [17].

3.3 Mobile Terminal

Identity authentication includes two stages, physical authentication and virtual authentication. The physical authentication uses voice recognition to confirm the legitimacy of the visiting user; the virtual authentication is based on the identity identification algorithm and the symmetric encryption algorithm AES to encrypt and verify the random number generated by the random number generator.

In the physical authentication phase, the user reads the randomly generated text on the device side, and the device side collects the voice for processing. The identity vector voiceprint model generated during registration is used for matching processing to identify whether the current user is legal. If the user is illegal, the device is locked. Corresponding treatment.

The user's voice data must also be processed to extract its features. The extracted features are used as the input of the model. The minimum distance between the feature values is calculated by comparing it with the feature library. A threshold value needs to be set in the voice confirmation. The threshold can be adjusted according to actual results. According to the calculated similarity, identity matching verification is performed to determine whether the user is legitimate, and the system responds according to the result.

Obtaining whether the user is legal from model matching is divided into two response mechanisms:

1) If the user is legal, the key generation center will send the user's private key to the client;
2) If the user is illegal, classify the illegal user. If it is an unregistered user, the server will lock the client device; if it is a registered user, input the newly collected voice data into the model for training, at the same time update the user ID, the key generation center regenerates the user key and deletes the original data.

Virtual identity authentication after physical identity authentication, for public-key encryption and private key decryption, because public-key encryption is used, it is difficult to prove that the encrypted ciphertext comes from the real sender, that is, it is difficult to prove the authenticity of the information. It is difficult to verify the true identity of the information publisher. The use of public keys for decryption undoubtedly reduces the degree of confidentiality of information. Encryption and decryption of random numbers based on identity identification algorithm and symmetric encryption algorithm AES is used as the second protection of identity authentication to improve the security of user identity authentication. The specific process is as follows:

When the user initiates a request for access on the device side, the random number generator generates a random number and synchronizes the random number to the device and the server; the server uses the symmetric AES algorithm to encrypt the random number and temporarily stores it on the server; when the user completes the voice on the device side After authentication, the server uses the public key to encrypt the AES key and sends it to the device; if the voice authentication fails, the random number is deleted. The device uses the obtained private key to decrypt the AES key, and then the server sends the encrypted random number to the device, and the device decrypts and verifies it. When the match is successful, the mobile terminal identity authentication is successful, otherwise, the mobile terminal is considered Identity authentication failed.

4   Experimental Results and Analysis

4.1   Experimental Results

To test the security and space overhead performance of the mobile terminal identity authentication method based on the i-vector identity password proposed in this paper, this experiment uses Matlab R2014a to conduct simulation experiments on the Windows10 64-bit operating system hardware platform. In this environment, it is compared with the fingerprint authentication system design based on PKI (literature [18]) and the biometric authentication based on PKI (literature [19]) to verify the safety and efficiency of the method in this paper.

4.2 Security Test

To verify the security of the solution in this paper, we have selected four common attack modes shown in Table 1 to conduct 50 simulation attacks based on the design of a fingerprint authentication system based on PKI and biometric authentication based on the use of PKI, as shown in Table 1. The number of times that the three kinds of attacks cannot be resisted.

Table 1. Attack mode

RA	Replay Attacks
SCA	Side Channel Attack
U2L	Remote illegal user access attack
DDoS	Distributed Denial of Service Attack

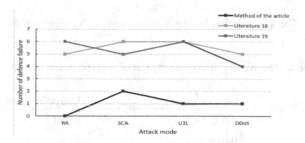

Fig. 2. Three methods to defend against attacks

The results of the above three authentication methods after simulating the attack are shown in Fig. 2. It can be seen from the figure that the method in this paper has been subjected to 50 attacks from anti-replay attacks, side-channel attacks, remote illegal user access attacks, and distributed denial of service attacks. The fingerprint authentication system design and biometric authentication based on the use of PKI are less than 3 times, mainly because this paper uses a neural network to extract the user's unique voiceprint feature and combine it with the identity to generate the user's public and private keys. Update according to the user's voiceprint dynamic changes. It can be shown that compared with the traditional single identity authentication, the method in this paper greatly improves the security of mobile terminal identity authentication.

4.3 Complexity

For the space cost, we choose to use the number of users as a variable to test the system space cost. The efficiency of the method in this paper is verified by comparing the two methods of literature [18] and literature [19]. The test result is shown in Fig. 3. From the analysis of the above figure, it can be seen that the space overhead of the method in this paper is significantly lower than that of the fingerprint authentication system design based on PKI and the biometric authentication based on the use of PKI. as the number of users increases, the space overhead of the method in this paper increases slowly, while the latter two increase at a relatively high rate. The comparison shows that the space overhead of the method in this paper is significantly reduced compared with the traditional identity authentication based on the PKI system, and the efficiency of identity authentication is improved. For the time complexity, the average time consumption shown in Table 2 is obtained by encrypting and decrypting information of different lengths 20 times.

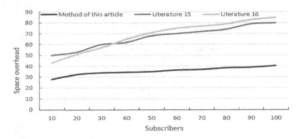

Fig. 3. The space overhead of the three methods with the number of users

Table 2. The average time consumption of encryption and decryption

Lm/B	t_{encry}/s	t_{decry}/s
64	0.062	0.350
128	0.073	0.582
256	0.090	0.638
512	0.136	0.794

L_m represents the length of information in Bytes, t_{encry} represents the average time consumption of encryption, and t_{decry} represents the average time consumption of decryption verification. It can be seen from the experimental data that the method in this paper is more efficient.

5   Conclusion

This paper mainly studied a mobile terminal identity authentication method based on ID passwords. It used a mobile terminal to collect user voice to establish an identity vector voiceprint model, extract features and add identity to generate a user ID, and generate a corresponding identity password system to complete user Registration; firstly judge user legitimacy based on voice recognition to prevent illegal user intrusion during authentication, and then encrypt and decrypt data based on identity password combined with symmetric encryption algorithm AES to achieve terminal identity authentication. Compared with other methods of the same type, the method effectively improved the security of the power mobile Internet identity authentication process and had the advantages of low cost and high efficiency.

Acknowledgment. This work is supported by the State Grid Sichuan Company Science and Technology Project: "Research and Application of Key Technologies of Network Security Protection System Based on Zero Trust Model" (No. SGSCCD00XTJS2101279).

References

1. Shamir, A.: Identity-based cryptosystems and signature schemes. In: Blakley, G.R., Chaum, D. (eds.) CRYPTO 1984. LNCS, vol. 196, pp. 47–53. Springer, Heidelberg (1985). https://doi.org/10.1007/3-540-39568-7_5
2. Boneh, D., Franklin, M.: Identity-based encryption from the weil pairing. In: Kilian, J. (ed.) CRYPTO 2001. LNCS, vol. 2139, pp. 213–229. Springer, Heidelberg (2001). https://doi.org/10.1007/3-540-44647-8_13
3. Xu, A., Liu, G., Xu, Y.: Security protection technology of smart substation based on SM9 identification code. Autom. Expo **35**(S2), 65–71 (2018)
4. Ma, X., Ma, W., Liu, X.: Cross-domain authentication scheme based on blockchain technology. Acta Electron. Sin. **46**(11), 9 (2018)
5. Jin, J., Kim, K.: 3D CUBE algorithm for the key generation method: applying deep neural network learning-based. IEEE Access **8**, 33689–33702 (2020)
6. Jhajharia, S., Mishra, S., Bali, S.: Public key cryptography using neural networks and genetic algorithms. In: International Conference on Contemporary Computing. IEEE (2013)
7. Alimohammadi, N., Shokouhi, B.: Secure hardware key based on Physically Unclonable Functions and artificial Neural Network. In: 2016 8th International Symposium on Telecommunications (IST). IEEE (2016)
8. Wei, H.: Password Authentication Using Hopfield Neural Networks (2012)
9. Chakravarthy, A.S.N., Avadhani, P.S., Krishna Prasad, P.E.S.N., et al.: A novel approach for authenticating textual or graphical passwords using hopfield neural network. Adv. Comput.: Int. J. **2**(4), 33–42 (2011). https://doi.org/10.5121/acij.2011.2404
10. Tanaka, A., Kinoshita, K., Kishida, S.: Construction and performance of authentication systems for fingerprint with neural networks. J. Signal Process. **17**(1), 1–9 (2013)
11. Debnath, S., Roy, P.: User authentication system based on speech and cascade hybrid facial feature. Int. J. Image Graph. **20**(3), 2050022 (2020)
12. Bouzalmat, A., Belghini, N., Zarghili, A., et al.: Face recognition using neural network based fourier gabor filters & random projection. Int. J. Comput. Sci. Secur. (IJCSS) **5**, 376–386 (2011)
13. Zhang, Z., Wu, J., Jing, D., et al.:Jamming ACK attack to wireless networks and a mitigation approach. In: Global Telecommunications Conference (2008)
14. Qiu, M., Gai, K., Xiong, Z.: Privacy-preserving wireless communications using bipartite matching in social big data. Future Gener. Comput. Syst. **87**, 772–781 (2018). https://doi.org/10.1016/j.future.2017.08.004
15. Qiu, H., Qiu, M., Lu, Z.: Selective encryption on ECG data in body sensor network based on supervised machine learning. Inf. Fusion **55**, 59–67 (2020)
16. Lin, S., Xi, S., Lin, et al.: Speaker recognition based on i-vector and deep learning. Comput. Technol. Dev. (2017)
17. Qiu, F., Hu, K., et al.: Distributed control identity authentication technology of distribution network based on national secret SM9. Comput. App. Softw. **37**(09), 291–295 (2020)

18. Zhu, X., Xu, H.: A fingerprinting authentication system design based on PKI (2006)
19. Ohkubo, C., Muraoka, Y.: Biometric authentication using PKI. DBLP (2003)
20. Qiu, H., Dong, T., et al.: Adversarial attacks against network intrusion detection in IoT systems. IEEE Internet of Things J. **8**, 10327–10335 (2020)
21. Qiu, M., Zhang, L., et al.: Security-aware optimization for ubiquitous computing systems with SEAT graph approach. J. Comput. Syst. Sci. **79**(5), 518–529 (2013)
22. Qiu, H., Qiu, M., Liu, M., Memmi, G.: Secure health data sharing for medical cyber-physical systems for the healthcare 4.0. IEEE J. Biomed. Health **24**, 2499–2505 (2020)
23. Wu, G., Zhang, H., Qiu, M., et al.: A decentralized approach for mining event correlations in distributed system monitoring. JPDC **73**(3), 330–340 (2013)
24. Guo, Y., Zhuge, Q., Hu, J., et al.: Optimal data allocation for scratch-pad memory on embedded multi-core systems. In: IEEE ICPP Conference, pp. 464–471 (2011)

Secure Shell Remote Access for Virtualized Computing Environment

He Li[1,2], Rongqiang Cao[1,2(✉)], Hanwen Xiu[1,2], Meng Wan[1], Kai Li[1], Xiaoguang Wang[1], Yangang Wang[1,2], and Jue Wang[1,2]

[1] Computer Network Information Center, Chinese Academy of Sciences, Beijing, China
{lihe,caorq,wanmengdamon,kai.li,wangxg}@cnic.cn
[2] University of Chinese Academy of Sciences, Beijing, China
xiuhanwen21@mails.ucas.ac.cn, {wangyg,wangjue}@sccas.cn

Abstract. Information processing in the era of big data is inseparable from the effective support of scientific computing. Complex scientific computing requires cloud computing to provide computing resources. One of the core foundations of Cloud computing is secure and reliable remote access technology. Users often log in to the remote server for scientific calculation. However, when users log in with public key, the steps are cumbersome. Therefore, this project develops a secure shell remote access information system for virtualized computing environment, which is called SSHRA for short. The system enables users to log in to the remote server more conveniently. The system can generate the corresponding certificate according to the public key provided by the user. Users use certificates for remote login. Users can obtain certificates through web or email. In addition, this system also designs an intelligent connection between multi hop servers. The system improves the security of remote login by limiting the IP, validity and available commands of the certificate. After users log in to the remote server with the certificate provided by the system, they can use commands to perform related operations. The system is developed based on open source software, so it has good scalability.

Keywords: Cloud computing · Scientific computing · Secure shell · Remote access · SSH certificate

1 Introduction

Scientific computing plays an important role in complex numerical calculation. In the era of big data, with the improvement of computing complexity, ordinary computing resources are difficult to meet the needs of complex computing. Whether it is high-performance computing based on bottom optimization or supercomputing based on remote services, it is inseparable from the support of scientific computing.

Cloud computing provides large-scale computing resources [1–3] for scientific computing. The rapid development of cloud computing reflects the increasing change of the information age. Mining valuable information from massive data has become more challenging. In order to give full play to the ability of cloud computing, more and more institutions begin to vigorously build the infrastructure of cloud services. However, the information security and privacy becomes a challenge problem [4–6].

Remote login using secure shell [7] technology is one of the important ways for users to access cloud computing resources. Most users log in directly with a password when connecting to a remote server. When setting passwords, users tend to use simple passwords. Simple passwords are easy to crack. In addition, some users use public key to log in, but when too many remote servers need to be connected, it is difficult for users to effectively manage the public key.

In view of the above problems, this project develops a *Secure SHell Remote Access* (SSHRA) information system for virtualized computing environment. Users log in by means of certificates in this system. Certificates are easy to manage and secure. On the one hand, the validity period of the certificate is limited, so the certificate is easy to manage. On the other hand, the certificate only takes effect for a specific IP, so the data of the remote server will not be disclosed. The system designs two ways for users to obtain certificates. One is to apply for certificates by web and the other is to apply for certificates by email. The system designs two kinds of certificates, one is the certificate that people perform relevant operations, and the other is the certificate that machines perform relevant operations.

In addition, the system creatively solves the problem of remote login of Internet users by means of multi hop login. In this system, network users can access the remote server by multi hop login. When network users log in with certificates, they first log in to the intermediate proxy server locally, and then log in to the target server from the intermediate proxy server.

The remainder of this paper is organized as follows. In Sect. 2, we introduce the work related to this paper. In Sect. 3, we introduce the overall architecture of SSHRA system. In Sect. 4, we introduce the core services of certificate signing. In Sect. 5, we introduce the certificate application service based on web. In Sect. 6, we introduce the certificate application service based on email. In Sect. 7, we introduce the system deployment and application. In Sect. 8,we conclude this paper.

2   Related Work

Aiming at the defect in SSH authentication process, Wendlandt et al. proposed a method to realize server authentication through time and space redundancy [8]. Oauth supports native restful style APIs [9] and JWT (JSON web token) [10] tokens. Proctor et al. proposed *time-based one-time password* (TOTP) [11] by combining one-time password and centralized public key authentication. OpenSSH certificate and LDAP based centralized public key management [12] are some solutions to the above problems. *Extended Network Allocation Vector* (ENAV) scheme recovers a significant portion of the lost throughput [13]. Qiu et al. proposed the selective encryption approach on ECG [14] data in body sensor network. Furthermore, they had studied the privacy-preserving wireless communications problem through bipartite matching to support applications with real-time constraints [15].

Andrew et al. found that more than 65% of SSH servers allow password authentication [16]. Gao et al. realized the token authentication function of SSH through a plug-in, and the token can be signed and issued by multiple authentication centers [17]. As part of the grid security infrastructure (GSI) [18], X.509 proxy certificates [19] can also be used for identity authentication. GLOBUS AUTH [20] secure shell provides a pluggable authentication module (PAM), which uses SCITOKEN-CPP library [21] for authentication. For many organizations, they can use GLOBUS AUTH Service [22] for identity authentication.

The above methods mainly focus on the login process between client and server, and do not discuss the jump login between multiple servers. In the authentication process, these articles focus on password or public key authentication. Therefore, this paper discusses the secure login of multiple springboard machines and certificates.

3 Overall Architecture

The overall architecture is illustrated in Fig. 1. The overall architecture of the system is divided into three layers: client layer, server layer and infrastructure layer.

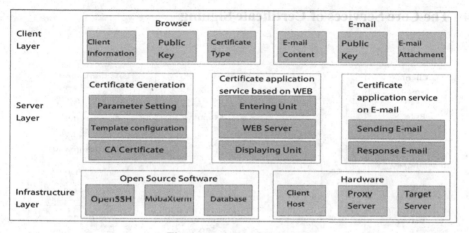

Fig. 1. Overall architecture

The introduction of the client layer is as follows. In the client layer, there are two main parts. The first part is the browser module, and the second part is the email module. The main function of the browser module is to obtain client information, public key and certificate type. The purpose of obtaining client information is to obtain a unique IP address, which can prevent a third party from maliciously stealing a certificate. Public key is obtained to generate corresponding certificate. The certificate type is obtained to distinguish whether certificate serves people or machines. The email module includes email content, public key and email attachment. E-mail content limits the body format of the message. Public key is used to generate the corresponding certificate. Email attachment contains other information such as IP address.

The server layer is described below. In the server layer, there are three main services: certificate generation, certificate application service based on web and certificate application service based on email. Parameter setting is required before certificate generation.

After the certificate is generated, template configuration files will be generated. The certificate application service based on web includes input unit, web server and displaying unit. Users enter their own IP address and public key in input unit. Web server will obtain the certificate after a series of operations. Displaying unit responds the obtained certificate information to the user. The certificate application service based on email includes sending email module and response email module. The sending email module obtains the certificate by calling the relevant script. The response email module returns the obtained certificate to the user.

The infrastructure layer is described below. The infrastructure layer consists of two parts: open source software and hardware. Open source software includes OpenSSH, MobaXterm and Database. Hardware includes client host, proxy server and target server. Client host is the user's local computer. Proxy server is used to act as a springboard during the login process of network users. Target server is the server that the user will eventually log in to. These open source software and hardware make the system easier to develop and maintain.

4   The Core Services of Certificate Signing

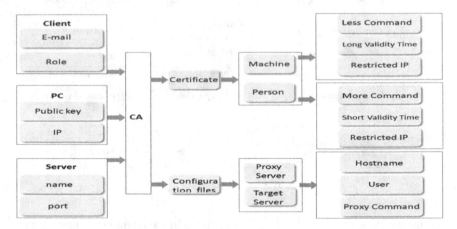

Fig. 2. The core services of certificate signing

The core services of certificate signing are illustrated in Fig. 2. Before generating a certificate, the certificate authority (CA) needs to obtain some input information, including client, PC and sever. After obtaining the input information, the certificate authority (CA) will generate certificate and configuration files.

The input information is described in detail below. The email information of the client module can be used to uniquely identify a specific user, so as to avoid the problem of user name duplication. The role of the client module is used to distinguish different identities of different users, and users with different identities have different management permissions. The public key information and IP information of the PC module are important components of the certificate. Different public keys will generate different certificates. Different IP will generate different certificates accordingly. The server module contains the name and port number of the server. It is essential for user to login in the server.

The generation of certificates by a certification authority (CA) is described below. Certificate Authority (CA) generates certificates according to certain rules. The generated certificates are divided into two types: one is the certificate serving the machine, and the other is the certificate serving the human. The certificate serving the machine has fewer available commands, which is to reduce the risk of errors in the running process of the code robot. Certificates serving machines have a longer validity period because code robots generally do not need to replace certificates over a long period of time. The certificate serving the machine has a restricted IP. Only a specific IP can use the certificate for remote login. The certificate serving people has more available commands, which is to facilitate users to perform a variety of operations on the remote server. Certificates serving people have shorter validity, which is to reduce the number of certificates that are idle for a long time. The certificate serving people has a restricted IP. Only a specific IP can use the certificate for remote login.

The available commands for certificates are described below. After successfully logging in to the remote server with a certificate, not all commands can be used, and some unauthorized commands cannot be used. Because when the certificate is generated, it specifies that some commands can be used after login, and other commands cannot be used after login.

The validity period of the certificate is described below. The validity period of a certificate refers to the time range from generation to destruction. Within the validity period of the certificate, users can use the certificate for remote login. Beyond the validity range of the certificate, users cannot log in using the certificate.

The restricted IP addresses of certificates are described below. Each certificate can only be used by a unique IP address. Only this unique IP can use this certificate for remote login. If other IP can log in remotely using this certificate, then when this certificate is stolen by a third party, the third party can log in using this certificate. At this time, the third party has the opportunity to tamper with the data of the remote server and steal the computing resources of the remote server.

The configuration file generated by the *certificate authority* (CA) is described below. The configuration file mainly includes the configuration file of the intermediate proxy server and the configuration file of the target server. Various parameters of multi hop forwarding login mode are set in the configuration file of the intermediate proxy server. In the configuration file of the target server, various parameters of the target server that the user needs to log in are set.

The configuration file of intermediate proxy server is described below. The configuration file of intermediate proxy server contains information such as host name, port number and proxy command. The system uses an intermediate proxy server to act as a springboard machine, and network users realize multi hop forwarding login through springboard machine. The number of springboard machines can be one or more.

The configuration file of the target server is described below. The configuration file of the target server contains information such as host name and user list. The host name is the name of the target server. The user list records the mailbox of the user who has permission to log in to the target server.

5 Certificate Application Service Based on Web

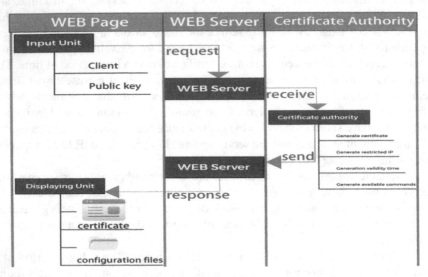

Fig. 3. Certificate application service based on web

The certificate application service based on web is illustrated in Fig. 3. Web based certificate application services include web page, web server and certificate authority. Web page contains two units, one is input unit and the other is displaying unit. Web server plays a connecting role. The function of certificate authority is to generate certificates and configuration files.

Input unit of web page is described as follows. In the input unit of the web page, the user first clicks the fill in button at the input page, and then the input box will pop up. The user enters public key and validity time in the input box, and then clicks the upload button. At this time, if a dialog box for successful submission appears on the web page, it means that the web server has successfully received the request. After the above series of operations, the page will refresh automatically.

The request phase of web server is described below. After the web server receives the input unit information, the web server will process the information. Then, the web server sends requests such as public key and validity time to the CA. The data format is JSON.

The phase of certificate authority is described below. After the certificate authority receives the information from the web server, the CA will call the relevant script to generate the corresponding certificate and configuration files. Then, the certificate authority will respond the generated certificate and configuration file to web server.

The response phase of web server is described below. Web server responds received certificate and configuration file to displaying unit of web page. At the same time, certificate and its restriction information will be stored in the MYSQL database. This will not only help the system maintenance personnel to manage certificate, but also facilitate the web page to display the certificate and its restriction information.

The phase of displaying unit of web page is described as follows. After the displaying unit of the web page receives the certificate and configuration file responded by the web server, the relevant information of the certificate will be displayed on the web page, including the certificate, the restricted IP of the certificate, the validity period of the certificate and the available commands of the certificate.

6   Certificate Application Service Based on Email

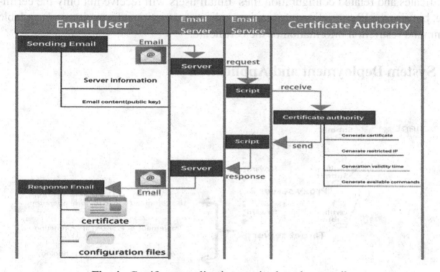

Fig. 4. Certificate application service based on email

In addition to applying for certificates based on web, users can also apply for certificates based on email. The certificate application service based on email is illustrated in Fig. 4. The email based certificate application service includes email user, email server, email service and certificate authority. Email user will involve two emails, one is to send the requested email and the other is to receive the response email. Email server plays the role of forwarding email in the middle. Email service plays the role of forwarding request and response in the middle. The certificate authority is used to generate certificates and related configuration files.

The phase of sending email of user is described as follows. The email user first sends a request email to the email server. In sending email, the format of email is fixed. The request message includes server information and body content. Server information refers to the information of the target server that the user needs to log in. The text includes public key information, the validity period of the certificate required by the user and the available commands.

The phase of email server is described below. After receiving the request email from the user, the email server will forward the request email to the email service. The email is sent in the form of SMTP, which has high security.

The phase of email service is described below. After receiving the request from the email server, the email service will forward the request to the certificate authority. Email service is not only fully functional, but also easy to operate.

The phase of certificate authority is described below. After receiving the request from email service, certificate authority will generate the certificate and related configuration files. The certificate authority will respond the generated certificate and configuration file to email service. Then, the email service will respond the certificate and configuration file to the email server.

The phase of response email of user is described below. Response email contains certificates and related configuration files. Email users will receive not only the certificate, but also the IP restriction information, validity restriction information and available command restriction information of the certificate.

7   System Deployment and Application

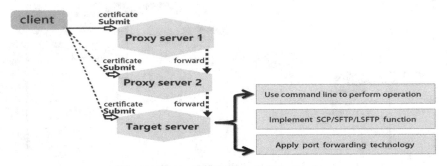

Fig. 5. System deployment and application

System deployment and application are illustrated in Fig. 5. This part includes two modules: system deployment and application. The system deployment module introduces the deployment of web system and proxy server. The application module includes certificate login, command line operation, port forwarding and file transfer. The deployment process is a prerequisite for the normal use of the system. After logging in with a certificate, users can implement many applications.

The deployment of web system is as follows. The system uses JQuery and BootStrap to design the front-end page. The system uses Ajax to send requests. The sending type is post and the data format is JSON. The system is developed by means of micro service. The database of this system is implemented by MySQL.

The proxy server is deployed as follows. A configuration file will be generated during deployment, which records the connection relationship between previous proxy server and next proxy server. Users only need to fill in the user name and password when logging in to the first proxy server. Each account in the proxy server corresponds to a unique principal, which can prevent users from having duplicate names.

The phase of using certificate to login is as follows. Users can log in to the remote server using a certificate. At first, the certificate is submitted to the first proxy server. After the certificate is verified by the first proxy server, the certificate will be submitted to the next proxy server. Until the certificate is verified by the target server, it means that the user successfully logs in to the target server.

The user can use commands to perform related operations. After the user successfully logs in to the target server, a series of command line related operations can be performed. User can view the CPU and memory usage of the remote server. The user can execute the PING command to check whether the network connection between the virtual machine and the server is smooth.

The user can implement the file transfer function. After the user successfully logs in to the target server, the user can use SCP command to copy files. This process is safe and reliable. Users can transfer SFTP files, and the data will not be leaked in the process of file transfer. For lightweight files, users can use LSFTP to transfer them, and the process also has good confidentiality.

The user can apply port forwarding technology. After the user successfully logs in to the target server, port forwarding technology can be applied. When host1 and host3 are not directly connected but need to communicate, host2 can be selected as a transfer station for communication.

8 Conclusion

This project develops a secure shell remote access information system (SSHRA) for virtualized computing environment. Through this system, users can obtain certificates in two ways: one is to apply for certificates based on web, and the other is to apply for certificates based on email. And this system supports the mode of multi hop login. Users can log in to one or more proxy servers with certificates, and then log in to the target server. The system not only facilitates users to obtain certificates, but also facilitates system maintenance personnel to manage certificates. Because the certificate generated by the system has the double restrictions of IP and validity, the system makes the process of users logging in to the remote server more secure and reliable. The system works well in our small-scale experimental environment. In the future, the system will further enhance the operation ability under large-scale server clusters, making the performance of the system more excellent under greater load.

Acknowledgement. This work was partially supported by the Beijing Natural Science Foundation-Haidian Original Innovation Joint Foundation (Grant No. L182053), the National Natural Science Foundation of China (Grant No. 61702476).

References

1. Gao, Y., Iqbal, S., et al.: Performance and power analysis of high-density multi-GPGPU architectures: a preliminary case study. In: IEEE 17th HPCC (2015)

2. Zhao, H., Chen, M., et al.: A novel pre-cache schema for high performance Android system. Futur. Gener. Comput. Syst. **56**, 766–772 (2016)

3. Qiu, H., Qiu, M., Memmi, G., Ming, Z., Liu, M.: A dynamic scalable blockchain based communication architecture for IoT. In: Qiu, M. (ed.) SmartBlock 2018. LNCS, vol. 11373, pp. 159–166. Springer, Cham (2018). https://doi.org/10.1007/978-3-030-05764-0_17

4. Thakur, K., Qiu, M., Gai, K., Ali, M.: An investigation on cyber security threats and security models. In: IEEE CSCloud (2015)

5. Gai, K., Qiu, M., Sun, X., Zhao, H.: Security and privacy issues: a survey on FinTech. In: Qiu, M. (ed.) SmartCom 2016. LNCS, vol. 10135, pp. 236–247. Springer, Cham (2017). https://doi.org/10.1007/978-3-319-52015-5_24

6. Gai, K., Qiu, M., Elnagdy, S.: A novel secure big data cyber incident analytics framework for cloud-based cybersecurity insurance. In: IEEE BigDataSecurity (2016)

7. Ylonen, T., Lonvick, C. (ed.): The Secure Shell (SSH) authentication protocol. RFC 4252 (2006). https://doi.org/10.17487/RFC4252

8. Wendlandt, D., Andersen, D., Perspectives, A.P.: Improving SSH-style host authentication with multi-path network probing. In: USENIX Annual Technical Conference (2008)

9. Hardt, D.: The OAuth 2.0 authorization framework. RFC 6749 (2012). https://doi.org/10.17487/RFC6749

10. Jones, M., Bradley, J., Sakimura, N.: JSON web token (JWT). RFC 7519 (2015). https://doi.org/10.17487/RFC7519

11. Proctor, W.C., Storm, P., Hanlon, M.R., Mendoza, N.: Securing HPC: development of a low cost, open source multi-factor authentication infrastructure. In: International Conference for High Performance Computing, Networking, Storage and Analysis, pp. 1–11 (2017)

12. Ylonen, T.: SSH Key management challenges and requirements. In: 10th IFIP International Conference on New Technologies, Mobility and Security (NTMS), pp. 1–5 (2019)

13. Zhang, Z., Wu, J., et al.: Jamming ACK attack to wireless networks and a mitigation approach. In: IEEE GLOBECOM, pp. 1–5 (2008)

14. Qiu, H., Qiu, M., Lu, Z.: Selective encryption on ECG data in body sensor network based on supervised machine learning. Inf. Fusion **55**, 59–67 (2020)

15. Qiu, M., Gai, K., Xiong, Z.: Privacy-preserving wireless communications using bipartite matching in social big data. Futur. Gener. Comput. Syst. **87**, 772–781 (2018)

16. Andrews, R., Hahn, D.A., Bardas, A.G.: Measuring the prevalence of the password authentication vulnerability in SSH. In: IEEE ICC, pp. 1–7 (2020)

17. Gao, Y.A., Basney, J., Withers, A.: SciTokens SSH: token-based authentication for remote login to scientific computing environments. In: Practice and Experience in Advanced Research Computing, pp. 465–468 (2020)

18. Welch, V., Siebenlist, F., Foster, I., Bresnahan, J., et al.: Security for grid services. In: 12th IEEE International Symposium on High Performance Distributed Computing, pp. 48–57 (2003)

19. Tuecke, S., Welch, V., Engert, D., Pearlman, L., Thompson, M.: Internet X.509 public key infrastructure (PKI) proxy certificate profile. RFC 3820 (2004)

20. Alt, J., Ananthakrishnan, R., Chard, K., et al.: OAuth SSH with globus auth. In: ACM Conference on Practice and Experience in Advanced Research Computing (PEARC 2020), NY, USA, p. 12 (2020). https://doi.org/10.1145/3311790.3396658

21. Bockelman, B., Weitzel, D.: Scitokens/scitokens-CPP (Version v0.3.0) (2019). https://doi.org/10.5281/zenodo.265667

22. Tuecke, S., et al.: Globus auth: a research identity and access management platform. In: 2016 IEEE 12th International Conference on e-Science, pp. 203–212 (2016). https://doi.org/10.1109/eScience.2016.7870901

A Survey of Machine Learning and Deep Learning Based DGA Detection Techniques

Amr M. H. Saeed[1], Danghui Wang[1,4(✉)], Hamas A. M. Alnedhari[2], Kuizhi Mei[3], and Jihe Wang[1,5]

[1] School of Computer Science, Northwestern Polytechnical University, Xi'an, China
wangdh@nwpu.edu.cn
[2] School of Artificial Intelligence, Xidian University, Xi'an, China
[3] Institute of Artificial Intelligence and Robotics, Xi'an Jiaotong University, Xi'an, China
[4] Engineering Research Center of Embedded System Integration, MOE, Beijing, China
[5] National Engineering Laboratory for Integrated Aero-Space-Ground-Ocean Big Data Application Technology, Xi'an, China

Abstract. Botnets are the most commonly used mechanisms for current cyberattacks such as DDoS, ransomware, email spamming, phishing data, etc. Botnets deploy the *Domain Generation Algorithm* (DGA) to conceal domain names of *Command & Control* (C&C) servers by generating several fake domain names. A sophisticated DGA can circumvent the traditional detection methods and successfully communicate with the C&C. Several detection methods like DNS sinkhole, DNS filtering and DNS logs analysis have been intensively studied to neutralize DGA. However, these methods have a high noise rate and require a massive amount of computational resources. To tackle this issue, several researchers leveraged *Machine learning* (ML) and *Deep Learning* (DL) algorithms to develop lightweight and cost-effective detection methods. The purpose of this paper is to investigate and evaluate the DGA detection methods based on ML/DL published in the last three years. After analyzing the relevant literature strengths and limitations, we conclude that low detection speed, encrypted DNS sensitivity, data imbalance sensitivity, and low detection accuracy with variant or unknown DGA are most likely the current research trends and opportunities. As far as we know, this survey is the first of its kind to discuss DGA detection techniques based on ML/DL in-depth, as well as analysis of their limitations and future trends.

Keywords: Domain generation algorithm · Botnet detection · DGA detection · Cybersecurity challenges

1   Introduction

Current consumer devices are equipped with the ability to connect to the Internet, which influences an increased use of the Internet in all spheres of modern life [1,2], making the world more productive and interactive [3,4]. However, it also increases its fragility by reinforcing reliance on internet-based technologies that might not be entirely secure or safe. Malware and botnets are modern cybersecurity concepts that have recently gained a lot of attention [5,6]. A botnet is a network of malware-infected devices known as bots, remotely controlled by a botmaster to carry out a variety of harmful activities, such as sending spam, launching *Distributed Denial of Service* (DDoS) attacks, and so on.

Botnet infrastructures are distinct from any other types of present-day cyberattacks in that they rely on setting up communication channels to get updates and send feed-backs to their botmasters. According to McAfee Enterprise Research [7], the United States, India, Australia, were the countries' most vulnerable to cyber-attacks in the second quarter of 2021. The most targeted industries are financial services, healthcare, manufacturing, and retail. According to PurpleSec's statistical report [8], cyber-attacks are estimated to cost $6 trillion annually by 2021 raising the challenge to find more robust and secure security solutions. Furthermore, typical security solutions that identify bot-malware based on pattern matching, hash matching, heuristic analysis, or behavior analysis are unable to detect around 45% of current malware [9].

The *Domain Name System* (DNS) assigns IP addresses to domain names and vise versa. Dynamic DNS is a technique of automatically updating a name server in the DNS with a domain name and ever-changing IP addresses. Cybercriminals, on the other hand, use this service to keep the communication channels between *Command and Control* (C&C) and the botnet running by using randomly generated domain names in the bot malware [10].

Domain Generation Algorithm (DGA) is a covert communication mechanism used by botnet to hide C&C domain names and communicate with them by generating numerous *Algorithmically Generated Domains* (AGD) based on a specific seed value. Bots then use AGDs to resolve C&C domain names by sending multiple DNS traffic until it finds the IP address of the matching C&C server. To ensure a successful communication, the bot-master legitimately registers a few C&C domains upfront using the same seed value embedded in the bot malware [11].

Network-based botnet detection methods are mainly categorized into four types namely, signature-based detection, network-based detection, DNS-based detection, and mining-based detection [12]. Since DGA is a DNS-based technique, this paper proposes a botnet detection systematic study with a focus on DGA-based detection methods and corresponding mitigation mechanisms based on the recent proposed *Machine Learning* (ML) and *Deep Learning* (DL) algorithms and analyzes their strengths, limitations, and research opportunities. An overview of botnet architectures, life cycle, and communication channels are also discussed.

The layout of this survey is organized as follows: Sect. 2 provides the relevant literature and botnet mechanism. Section 2.2 illustrates DGA detection approaches based on ML and DL algorithms. Section 3 presents the challenges and opportunities. Finally, Sect. 4 concludes this survey.

2   Background and Botnet Mechanism

2.1   Botnet Mechanism

A botnet is a collection of infected end-hosts known as bots controlled by attackers or botmasters that triggers via the spread of malware to unknown victims using any propagation methods, such as removable devices, phishing emails and malicious websites, etc. Botnets range in size from few thousand to millions of bots. In this section, we go over the botnet life-cycle, architectures, and communication channels.

Botnet Life-Cycle. Botnets typically follow a five-stage life-cycle, including propagation, rally, *Command & Control* (C&C), execution, and maintenance [12–14]. Propagation refers to the dissemination of bot malware via the network [4]. The behavior of bots in resolving the C&C locations and resources is referred as Rally. The botmaster issues commands or instructions to the bot army at C&C stage, allowing them to carry out malicious tasks in the execution stage. Finally, in the maintenance stage, bots are periodically upgraded to evade the latest detection techniques and keep active all the time.

Botnet Architectures. Based on communication topology, botnet architectures are categorized into centralized, decentralized, or hybrid [15] Centralized architecture is a client-server approach, which includes a C&C central control over the bots using the *Internet Relay Chat* (IRC) or *Hypertext Transfer Protocol* (HTTP). Distributed architecture is a decentralized P2P (peer-to-peer) scheme [16]. Any node may simultaneously operate as a client and a server where the connection process is preserved independently. With this architecture, botnet activities are difficult to detect since there is no central point in the network. A botnet with a hybrid architecture has both a centralized and decentralized architecture [17,18]. This concept is more challenging and often consists of an overall centralized architecture with a partial P2P.

Botnet Command and Control Channels. Communication channels are usually categorized into classical and modern C&C channels [14]. Classic C&C channels are primarily implemented through IRC, HTTP, and P2P protocols [19]. Modern C&C channels are divided into diversified platforms and covert communications. Cloud platforms, social networking sites, and block-chains are examples of diverse platforms. Covert communication means that the communication between C&C and botnets is concealed utilizing encryption, compression, obfuscation, and information stenography. Figure 1 shows the entire botnet mechanism.

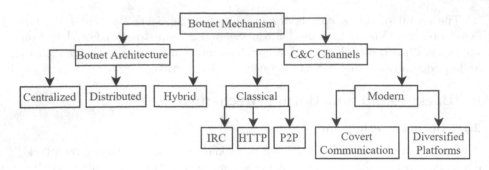

Fig. 1. Botnet mechanism.

2.2 DGA Classification Methods

In DGA detection, classical methods like DNS sinkhole, DNS filtering and DNS logs analysis are computationally expensive and inelastic in detecting malicious activities. Here is where machine learning (ML) techniques can show their value, improving higher detection rates and accuracy [17]. In this section, we discuss the recent proposed Machine/Deep Learning based DGA detection approaches.

Traditional Machine Learning Based Approaches. ML predicts the outcomes accurately without explicit programming. ML is based on human-defined features such as entropy, side information, linguistic and lexical attributes. N.F Ghalati et al. [20] proposed a static domain and URLs semantic features based Random Forest (RF) to identify malicious domains. The authors utilized blacklist features, lexical features and host-based features with N-gram technique. R. Sivaguru et al. [21] proposed a B-RF and LSTM feature extraction DGA detection method using side information and lexical features instead of domain names. The results showed that the utilization of such features improved the robustness of adversarial attacks detection as well. However, side information and B-RF are computationally expensive in the real-time.

KSDom [22] is a DGA detection approach based on k-means and SMOTE for imbalanced data processing, and CatBoost algorithm to classify domain names as benign or malicious. KSDom achieved a good accuracy with imbalanced dataset. Sun et al. [23] created DeepDom based on *Graph Convolutional Network* (GCN). DeepDom utilizes a *Heterogeneous Information Network* (HIN) model to automatically extracts complex semantics created in DNS, which makes it difficult for attackers to evade. Then, design SHetGCN classifier to inductively classify domain nodes in the HIN. DeepDom can detect malicious domains with only direct or indirect relations with others.

Almashhdani et al. [11] proposed a ML detection system for early detection of malicious domains by using easy-to-compute and language-independent features. The results showed a high accuracy and low False rate. A. Soleymani et al. [24] proposed a DGA detection model based on various ML classifiers. This model uses N-gram and PCA to extract statistical features from the network traffic based on a text-mining. J. Zhu et al. [25] combined the traditional SVM algorithm with self-feedback learning called F-SVM to solve the high-cost problem when updating models keeping high detection accuracy and precision and making it suitable for real time detection. However, true negative rates were not counted in the real time (Table 1).

Table 1. Summary of Binary DGA detection Methods based on ML: Model Complexity (Mod.C), Expensive Computations (Exp.C), Data Imbalance Sensitivity (D.I.S), Encrypted DNS Sensitivity (DNS.S), overfitting (O.F), language dependent features (L.D.F), Network Traffic Features (N.T.F), run in Real Time (R.T). supported ($\checkmark$), not supported ($\times$).

Paper	Algorithm	Mod.C	Exp.C	Performance (Acc = Accuracy)	D.I.S	DNS.S	O.F	L.D.F	N.T.F	R.T
[11]	DT, NB, SVM, KNN	$\times$	$\times$	Acc = 98.0%	$\times$	$\times$	$\checkmark$	$\checkmark$	$\times$	$\times$
[20]	RF, NB, LR	$\times$	$\checkmark$	AccRF = 96.78% AccLR = 92.32% AccNB = 87.63%	$\times$	$\times$	$\checkmark$	$\checkmark$	$\times$	$\times$
[21]	B-RF and LSTM, n-gram	$\checkmark$	$\checkmark$	AccAUC = 99.17%	$\times$	$\times$	$\checkmark$	$\checkmark$	$\checkmark$	$\checkmark$
[22]	K-means, Smote and CatBoost	$\checkmark$	$\checkmark$	Acc = 98.42%	$\checkmark$	$\times$	$\checkmark$	$\checkmark$	$\checkmark$	$\times$
[23]	GCN	$\checkmark$	$\times$	Acc = 97.91%	$\times$	$\times$	$\checkmark$	$\times$	$\checkmark$	$\times$
[24]	DT, SVM, RF and LR	$\times$	$\checkmark$	AccDT = 98.0% AccSVM = 96.0% AccRF = 99.0% AccLR = 93.0%	$\times$	$\times$	$\checkmark$	$\checkmark$	$\checkmark$	$\times$
[25]	Feedback SVM	$\checkmark$	$\checkmark$	AccPrecision = 99.2% AccRecall = 98.1%	$\times$	$\times$	$\checkmark$	$\checkmark$	$\checkmark$	$\checkmark$

Deep Learning Based Approaches. Deep learning is a subset of machine learning. Unlike ML, DL uses multiple layers to implicitly extract higher-level features from raw inputs without human intervention or feature engineering. DL algorithms has surpassed the traditional machine learning algorithms in various fields, including cyber-security and natural language processing (NLP) [26].

Convolution Neural Networks (CNN). CNN extracts local and positional information from the domain name string using filters and pooling layers. C. Xu et al. [27] developed a combined N-gram and CNN DGA classifier. This classifier was trained on DGArchive dataset [28] and evaluated on self-collected samples in the real-time. Experiments showed high accuracy and TPR. R. Vinayakumar et al. [29] proposed a binary DGA classifier to classify domain names by the implicitly extracted statistical features using a CNN-LSTM hybrid model on a self-collected dataset. The results showed high accuracy and low FPR compared to classical ML algorithms. Highnam et al. [30] introduced 'Bilbo', a CNN and LSTM hybrid architecture used for DGA detection. Bilbo was first trained and evaluated on DGArchive [28] and Alexa [31] using three DGA families before being deployed in real time. Bilbo was able to efficiently classify DGAs used by ad networks and other applications with good accuracy and a low FPR.

Recurrent Neural Networks (RNN). Since RNN can remember its last input, so it is an ideal solution to handle sequential data issues. H. Shahzad et al. [32] proposed a DGA classifier based on RNN architectures: LSTM, BiLSTM, and GRU. These architectures were applied at the same level to learn the important combination of letters that differentiate DGA from non-DGA domains. This model was trained on Alexa [31], CISCO [33] and OSINT [34]. Although results showed a good performance, the model is still suffering from time-consuming, data imbalance, and high FPR. R. Vinayakumar et al. [35] proposed a tow-level botnet detection system at the DNS application layer. The former level was the Siamese network that was applied to estimate the similarity measures of DNS queries. The latter level was constructed using LSTM and RNN for categorizing benign and malicious domain names. This framework achieved a slice of improvement in terms of F1 and speed. J. Namgung et al. [36] developed a DGA detection model based on bidirectional LSTM (BiLSTM) and CNN. As opposed to LSTM, BiLSTM learns bidirectional information. The results showed that the ensemble BiLSTM and CNN model outperformed single LSTM or single CNN. However, BiLSTM is slower than either LSTM or CNN (Table 2).

Table 2. Summary of DGA detection based on DL: Parallel Processing (P.Proc), Expensive Computation (Exp.C), Multi-classification (Multi. C), Binary Classification (Bin.C), max domain name length (Nmax), Data Imbalance Sensitivity (D.I.S), Encrypted DNS Sensitivity (DNS.S), Real Time (R.T), supporting ($\checkmark$), not supporting ($\times$), not available ($\otimes$).

Paper	Algorithm	P.Pro.	Iter.	Exp.C	Bin.C	Multi.C	Accuracy (Acc)	D.I.S	DNS.S	R.T	N(max)
[27]	CNN	$\times$	20	$\checkmark$	$\checkmark$	$\times$	Acc = 96.23%	$\otimes$	$\times$	$\checkmark$	64
[29]	CNN and LSTM	$\times$	30	$\checkmark$	$\checkmark$	$\times$	Acc = 97.60%	$\times$	$\times$	$\times$	$\otimes$
[30]	LSTM and CNN	$\checkmark$	10×3	$\checkmark$	$\checkmark$	$\checkmark$	Accbinary = 96% Accmulti = 65%	$\otimes$	$\times$	$\times$	$\otimes$
[32]	RNN, LSTM, GRU	$\times$	15	$\times$	$\checkmark$	$\times$	Acc = 87%	$\times$	$\times$	$\times$	$\otimes$
[35]	LSTM and RNN	$\times$	$\otimes$	$\times$	$\checkmark$	$\checkmark$	Acc = 78.80%	$\otimes$	$\times$	$\checkmark$	50
[36]	BiLSTM, At-tention and CNN	$\times$	10	$\checkmark$	$\checkmark$	$\checkmark$	Acc = 96.84%	$\times$	$\times$	$\checkmark$	$\otimes$

3 Research Challenges and Opportunities

3.1 Low Speed Rates

High-speed rates are required for real-time applications. The various proposed detection methods frequently yield to high performance in the offline; however, it is still too computationally expensive in real-time due to the use of either sequential processing algorithms like RNN and LSTM or feature extraction techniques like n-grams and sandbox. Furthermore, botnets typically generate a huge number of pseudo-random domain names before connecting to the corresponding server, making analyzing these domain names a time-consuming job [29]. For later real-time enhancement, employing specific hardware accelerators and paralleling or distributing the input sequence over the available GPUs might improve cost-effective detection methods. Additionally, using byte-level representations techniques instead of characters pairing techniques will reduce computations and enhance the model's real-time performance [37].

3.2 Data Imbalance Sensitivity

Data imbalance occurs when one or more classes in the data have unusually low proportions in comparison to the other classes. ML-based DGA detection methods usually derive a decision on the input based on the data provided during the training phase, where this data is roughly balanced between benign and malicious domains. However, in the real-world internet, the number of benign domains far outnumbers malicious domains, resulting in a severe data imbalance problem that often increases the false positives and causes a huge drop in the prediction performance especially in real time environments [38]. There are several proven data imbalance techniques for handling text-related data imbalance issues including oversampling, under sampling, SMOTE, WEMOTE, and cost sensitive learning. Thus, addressing data imbalance problems when designing later DGA detection methods would probably maintain the high performance of classifiers in real time environments, making them more stable and robust [39].

3.3 Low Detection Accuracy

DGA detection is challenging due to the number of new developed DGA algorithms, constantly evolving malware families, and the increasing complexity of existing algorithms. Most of proposed detection methods are built upon the known DGA properties and these methods usually perform well on their various testing sets but their performance suffers when attempting to generalize to new DGA families or new versions of previously seen families when deployed to the real-time environment [30]. Future improvements will include the continued reduction of false positive rates and application the advanced NLP techniques such as transformers, and byte-level tokenization [37,40]. One method to reduce FPR would be to add a generative model layer to determine if the input domain has seen before or not. Applicable NLP techniques evaluate the chance of words being collocated to identify anomalous sub-word occurrences in domains. This might be effective for DGA detection; however, it is strongly reliant on the corpus for parsing out words and accumulating preliminary collocation information in order to grasp what is normal.

3.4 Encrypted DNS Sensitivity

The DNS traffic is unencrypted and thus does not protect user's privacy and authentication. This feature has been negatively used by adversaries to trigger and covert different types of attacks, and by considering the same feature, the methods of detecting these attacks are designed assuming transparency of DNS traffic in real time [41]. Different DNS encryption protocols, such as DNSCrypt and DNS over HTTP/TLS/DTLS, have recently been implemented by major DNS servers, including Google and Mozilla, to provide end-users with confidentiality and privacy. Implementing such encrypted protocols will improve security, but will also reduce the performance of current detection methods based on the DNS transparency assumption, opening new research opportunities for analyzing the encrypted DNS traffic. Several studies have started to focus on this issue and propose novel privacy disclosure detection methods [41–43]. However, they are not effective enough for detection malicious domains. As far as we know, investigating issues caused by encrypted DNS is a point of focus for more robust applications in the future.

4   Conclusion

Domain Generation Algorithms (DGA) have played an essential role in most cyber attacks in recent years, facilitating the interaction between attackers and hijacked devices. Attackers have applied the DGA to mask communication channels in DNS traffic and circumvent detection. Traditional DGA detection techniques such as DNS sinkhole, DNS filtering and DNS logs analysis require a huge amount of computational resources in the real-time context. To address this issue, security experts have utilized ML/DL algorithms to detect malicious domains created by DGA using statistical and lexical features of domain name strings. In this survey, we analyzed several proposed ML/DL DGA detection solutions during the past three years to understand their strengths and limitations, as well as highlighted current challenges and promising research directions.

Acknowledgement. This work is supported by National NSF of China (No. 61802312), Natural Science Basic Research Plan in Shaanxi Province of China (No. 2019JQ-618), and open fund of Integrated Aero-Space-Ground-Ocean Big Data Application Technology (No. 20200105).

References

1. Gao, Y., Iqbal, S., et al.: Performance and power analysis of high-density multi-GPGPU architectures: a preliminary case study. In: IEEE HPCC 2015, pp. 29–35 (2015)

2. Zhao, H., Chen, M., et al.: A novel pre-cache schema for high performance android system. FGCS **56**, 766–772 (2016)
3. Zhang, Z., Wu, J., Deng, J., Qiu, M.: Jamming ack attack to wireless networks and a mitigation approach. In: IEEE GLOBECOM, pp. 1–5 (2008)
4. Qiu, H., Qiu, M., Memmi, G., Ming, Z., Liu, M.: A dynamic scalable blockchain based communication architecture for IoT. In: Qiu, M. (ed.) SmartBlock 2018. LNCS, vol. 11373, pp. 159–166. Springer, Cham (2018). https://doi.org/10.1007/978-3-030-05764-0_17
5. Thakur, K., Qiu, M., Gai, K., Ali, M.L.: An investigation on cyber security threats and security models. In: CSCloud 2015, pp. 307–311 (2015)
6. Gai, K., Qiu, M., Sun, X., Zhao, H.: Security and privacy issues: a survey on fintech. In: Qiu, M. (ed.) SmartCom 2016. LNCS, vol. 10135, pp. 236–247. Springer, Cham (2017). https://doi.org/10.1007/978-3-319-52015-5_24
7. Cyber security statistics. https://www.mcafee.com/enterprise/en-us/lp/threats-reports/oct-2021.html. Accessed 07 Oct 2021
8. Advanced threat research report 2021. https://purplesec.us/resources/cyber-security-statistics/. Accessed 09 Oct 2021
9. Mid-year update sonicwall cyber threat report. https://purplesec.us/resources/cyber-security-statistics/. Accessed 25 Sept 2021
10. Kumar, A.D., et al.: Enhanced domain generating algorithm detection based on deep neural networks. In: Alazab, M., Tang, M.J. (eds.) Deep Learning Applications for Cyber Security. ASTSA, pp. 151–173. Springer, Cham (2019). https://doi.org/10.1007/978-3-030-13057-2_7
11. Almashhadani, A.O., Kaiiali, M., Carlin, D., Sezer, S.: MaldomDetector: a system for detecting algorithmically generated domain names with machine learning. Comput. Secur. **93**, 101787 (2020)
12. Shetu, S.F., Saifuzzaman, M., Moon, N.N., Nur, F.N.: A survey of botnet in cyber security. In: 2019 2nd ICCT, pp. 174–177. IEEE (2019)
13. Maikudi, U., Abisoye, O., Ganiyu, S., Bashir, S.A.: A literature survey on IoT botnet detection techniques (2021)
14. Xing, Y., Shu, H., Zhao, H., Li, D., Guo, L.: Survey on botnet detection techniques: Classification, methods, and evaluation. Math. Probl. Eng. (2021)
15. Anagnostopoulos, M., Kambourakis, G., Drakatos, P., Karavolos, M., Kotsilitis, S., Yau, D.K.Y.: Botnet command and control architectures revisited: tor hidden services and fluxing. In: Bouguettaya, A., et al. (eds.) WISE 2017. LNCS, vol. 10570, pp. 517–527. Springer, Cham (2017). https://doi.org/10.1007/978-3-319-68786-5_41
16. Grizzard, J.B., Sharma, V., Nunnery, C., Kang, B.B., Dagon, D.: Peer-to-peer botnets: overview and case study. HotBots **7**(2007) (2007)
17. Wang, P., Sparks, S., Zou, C.C.: An advanced hybrid peer-to-peer botnet. IEEE Trans. Dependable Secure Comput. **7**(2), 113–127 (2008)
18. Gai, K., Wu, Y., Zhu, L., Zhang, Z., Qiu, M.: Differential privacy-based blockchain for industrial internet-of-things. IEEE Trans. Industr. Inf. **16**(6), 4156–4165 (2019)
19. Karim, A., Salleh, R.B., Shiraz, M., Shah, S.A.A., Awan, I., Anuar, N.B.: Botnet detection techniques: review, future trends, and issues. J. Zhejiang Univ. Sci. C **15**(11), 943–983 (2014). https://doi.org/10.1631/jzus.C1300242
20. Ghalati, N.F., Ghalaty, N.F., Barata, J.: Towards the detection of malicious URL and domain names using machine learning. In: Camarinha-Matos, L.M., Farhadi, N., Lopes, F., Pereira, H. (eds.) DoCEIS 2020. IAICT, vol. 577, pp. 109–117. Springer, Cham (2020). https://doi.org/10.1007/978-3-030-45124-0_10

21. Sivaguru, R., Peck, J., Olumofin, F., Nascimento, A., De Cock, M.: Inline detection of DGA domains using side information. IEEE Access **8**, 141910–141922 (2020)
22. Wang, Q., Li, L., Jiang, B., Lu, Z., Liu, J., Jian, S.: Malicious domain detection based on K-means and SMOTE. In: Krzhizhanovskaya, V.V., et al. (eds.) ICCS 2020. LNCS, vol. 12138, pp. 468–481. Springer, Cham (2020). https://doi.org/10.1007/978-3-030-50417-5_35
23. Sun, X., Wang, Z., Yang, J., Liu, X.: Deepdom: malicious domain detection with scalable and heterogeneous graph convolutional networks. Comput. Secur. **99**, 102057 (2020)
24. Soleymani, A., Arabgol, F.: A novel approach for detecting DGA-based botnets in DNS queries using machine learning techniques. J. Comput. Netw. Comm. (2021)
25. Zhu, J., Zou, F.: Detecting malicious domains using modified SVM model. In: IEEE 21st HPCC, pp. 492–499 (2019)
26. Kim, K., Tanuwidjaja, H.C.: Privacy-preserving deep learning a comprehensive survey (2021)
27. Xu, C., Shen, J., Du, X.: Detection method of domain names generated by DGAs based on semantic representation and deep neural network. Comput. Secur. **85**, 77–88 (2019)
28. Plohmann, D., Yakdan, K., Klatt, M., Bader, J., Gerhards-Padilla, E.: A comprehensive measurement study of domain generating malware. In: 25th {USENIX} Security Symposium ({USENIX} Security 16), pp. 263–278 (2016)
29. Vinayakumar, R., Soman, K.P., Poornachandran, P., Alazab, M., Jolfaei, A.: DBD: deep learning DGA-based botnet detection. In: Alazab, M., Tang, M.J. (eds.) Deep Learning Applications for Cyber Security. ASTSA, pp. 127–149. Springer, Cham (2019). https://doi.org/10.1007/978-3-030-13057-2_6
30. Highnam, K., Puzio, D., Luo, S., Jennings, N.R.: Real-time detection of dictionary DGA network traffic using deep learning. SN Comput. Sci. **2**(2), 1–17 (2021)
31. Alexa top 1 m. http://s3.amazonaws.com/alexa-static/top-1m.csv.zip. Accessed 05 Oct 2021
32. Shahzad, H., Sattar, A.R., Skandaraniyam, J.: DGA domain detection using deep learning. In: IEEE 5th International Conference on Cryptography, Security and Privacy (CSP), pp. 139–143 (2021)
33. Cisco umbrella popularity list. http://s3-us-west-1.amazonaws.com/umbrella-static/top-1m.csv.zip. Accessed 05 Oct 2021
34. Osint feeds from bambenek. http://osint.bambenekconsulting.com/feeds/. Accessed 05 Oct 2021
35. Vinayakumar, R., Alazab, M., Srinivasan, S., et al.: A visualized botnet detection system based deep learning for the internet of things networks of smart cities. IEEE Trans. Ind. Appl. **56**, 4436–4456 (2020)
36. Namgung, J., Son, S., Moon, Y.S.: Efficient deep learning models for dga domain detection. Secur. Commun. Netw. (2021)
37. Wang, C., Cho, K., Gu, J.: Neural machine translation with byte-level subwords. In: AAAI Conference, vol. 34, pp. 9154–9160 (2020)
38. Drichel, A., Meyer, U., Schüppen, S., Teubert, D.: Making use of NXt to nothing: the effect of class imbalances on DGA detection classifiers. In: 15th International Conference on Availability, Reliability and Security, pp. 1–9 (2020)
39. Padurariu, C., Breaban, M.E.: Dealing with data imbalance in text classification. Proc. Comput. Sci. **159**, 736–745 (2019)
40. Vaswani, A., et al.: Attention is all you need. In: Advances in Neural Information Processing Systems, pp. 5998–6008 (2017)

41. Patsakis, C., Casino, F., Katos, V.: Encrypted and covert DNS queries for botnets: challenges and countermeasures. Comput. Secur. **88**, 101614 (2020)
42. Bushart, J., Rossow, C.: Padding ain't enough: assessing the privacy guarantees of encrypted DNS. In: 10th USENIX Workshop FOCI (2020)
43. Siby, S., Juarez, M., Diaz, C., Vallina-Rodriguez, N., Troncoso, C.: Encrypted DNS privacy. In: NDSS (2020)

Sci-Base: A Resource Aggregation and Sharing Ecology for Software on Discovery Science

Meng Wan[1], Jiaheng Wang[1(✉)], Jue Wang[1,2], Rongqiang Cao[1,2],
Yangang Wang[1,2], and He Li[1,2]

[1] Computer Network Information Center, Chinese Academy of Sciences,
Beijing, China
{wanmengdamo,jhwang,lihe}@cnic.cn, {wangjue,caorq,wangyg}@sccas.cn
[2] University of Chinese Academy of Sciences, Beijing, China

Abstract. In the process of open science and Open research, scientific software affects all aspects of scientific research. Open-source scientific software is a cost-effective solution for many universities and research institutions. By exploring the ecological model of scientific software, this paper puts forward a design scheme of a safe and controllable support platform of open-source scientific software through putting the core mechanism of "sharing" and "continuous evaluation" into effect. China Science and technology has made breakthroughs from the four levels of theory and technology, support platform, ecosystem and operation system, and created a proven scientific software ecosystem based on the design scheme, including the service mode of "four platforms and one competition". The progress of research transparency in scientific research and gradual maturity of scientific software promote the cooperation between community developers. In the course of constructing the scientific open-source ecology, open-source culture has been integrated into scientific researches, continuously gathering excellent open-source scientific software, and gradually creating a favorable environment for scientific research talents. It can not only actively promote the breakthrough of technological monopoly and improve the talent training strategy of independent innovation, but also benefit the public and promote the progress of innovation ability of the whole society.

Keywords: Open research · Open science · Software platform · Open source · Software ecology

1 Introduction

Recent years have witness a spurt of progress in the dissemination of open-source software. The sharing and popularization of open-source software could benefit the progress of scientific research. For researchers who code, open-source software is available to become the cornerstone of further customizable and flexible secondary developments with visible source code. However, the discovery

M. Qiu et al. (Eds.): SmartCom 2021, LNCS 13202, pp. 144–153, 2022.
https://doi.org/10.1007/978-3-030-97774-0_13

of scientific software often faces challenges, and even becomes a time-consuming progress for researchers. Specifically, a valuable code repository which not results in the authorship of a research paper and accompanying citations, there is little way to measure its impact [1]. Therefore, software platforms rapidly emerge and become a common solution so as to achieve cost reduction and efficiency optimization, which also impels the iteration of open-source software [2]. A functional software platform could enable developers in the same field to acquire desirable open-source software or toolkit based on similar demands, which has a natural advantage to develop a matching ecosystem for Co-Development around available resources. At present, many open source communities are established by the internet enterprise, such as GitHub and Gitee, but there are few open source communities and ecosystems for researchers and scientists to promote discovery science. Aforementioned communities allow all kinds of code work could be published, however, software under different levels of quality are intermingled, which exacerbates the degree of confusion while searching.

As a scientific methodology which emphasizes analysis of large volumes of experimental data with the goal of finding new patterns or correlations, research projects of discovery science are leading formations of new hypotheses and promoting the technological advancement [3]. Scientific software and tools are widely used in discovery science, with applications ranging from modeling, scientific computing and numerical simulation [4]. The continuing development of novel software has huge potential to assist researchers polish their work and outcomes. These advances require ever aggregation and management of emerging but reliable resources. Therefore, we create the Sci-Base ecology, which consists of multiple sub-platforms for scientific software and a series of events. Researchers are able to acquire resources with different dimensions: scientific software, cutting-edge methods and even code snippets. Sci-Base is a secure software sharing platform that facilitates and simplifies the process of accessing reliable software and tools for research towards discover science. We mainly make the following contributions. Sci-Base has been established as a combination of four sub-platforms, including the Software Aggregation Platform, Open-source Community, a multi-institution collaboration tool: CSThub Code Hosting Platform, and the Expert Platform.

- Open-source Community: Build a systematic scientific software community and open source ecology for scientific discovery.
- Software Aggregation Platform: The Scientific Software Fusion Platform provides researchers with a way to quickly retrieve software in various fields, including commercial software, open source software and self-developed software.
- CSThub Code Hosting Platform: Provide users with code management and hosting mode under scientific research process, which helps efficient scientific research.
- Expert Platform: The Scientific Software Open-Source Community provides scientists with the source code of various scientific software, which can quickly obtain inspiration on the basis of other research groups.

The Sci-Base platform has general applicability for various of popular areas of discovery science including material science, protein science, astronomy, oceanography, etc., and could be adapted to benefit interdisciplinary research projects.

In this article, we present the overall architecture of Sci-Base, followed by a detailed description of each sub-platform and how they are connected in a unified ecology. Next, we record one Open-source Software Competition as a typical use case. Finally, conclusions are given as well as our future prospects.

2   Architecture

The Sci-Base focuses on solving the construction and development of scientific software application and sharing ecosystem, and provides shared software resource cloud services in public and discipline fields. It has made breakthroughs from four aspects: theory, platform, ecosystem and operation mode, helping to form a complete scientific software ecology. Generally speaking, researchers enter the Sci-Base from the Software Aggregation Platform and login with the science cloud pass check. The standard interface specification will provide RESTFul APIs for the capability output of software resources. Better yet, if the software is published according to the steps in guidelines, the software will automatically run on the docker based cluster and provide cloud services for other users. The upper service establishes a full pedigree and multi link scientific open ecosystem through "four platforms and one competition".The construction of Sci-Base is implemented from three aspects: infrastructure and operating environment, community content control and technical kernel at PasS level, as shown in Fig. 1.

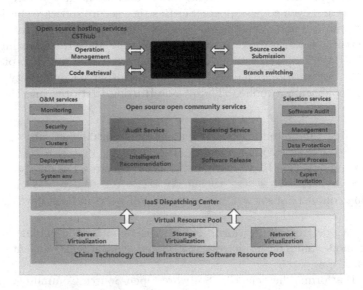

Fig. 1. The interaction model of community ecology.

The bottom layer of the Sci-Base relies on the virtual resource pool, including computing server, storage, network and other basic hardware resource to provide the upper application with virtualization run-time environment. The service layer consists of three different service modules to support the development of common software in the discipline field and the online use of software resources. The operation and management (O&M) services provide the uniform interface for each platform to monitor the capacity of virtual resources. The open source community services provide the audit service, indexing service, intelligent recommendation and software release to establishes a full pedigree and multi-link scientific research platform. The selection services enable the platform to undertake the screening and standardization of software submission. The CSThub uses the code managed kernel to implement warehouse related services, and provides users with choices through SSH and web.

2.1   Scientific Software Aggregation Platform

The scientific software aggregation platform is a general portal of the Sci-Base ecology which supports international version with English[1]. After passing the authority certification of "Science and Technology Cloud" passport, it can provide cross-platform software resource retrieval service and software convergence service for researchers. The platform includes three categories of software: open source software, commercial software and self-developed software. Through the cloud service empowerment of Science and Technology Cloud, the software deployed on the science and technology cloud server supports the function of running the cloud service online.

As a scientific researcher with software retrieval needs, the open source software retrieved on the platform can be directly linked to the open source community of scientific software, cooperating with the CSThub code hosting and collaboration platform, which is convenient for scientific researchers to develop in one stop and view and modify the source code; For non-open source software, you can directly download the installation package and view the relevant use documents;

Fast Retrieval Optimization. For most of disciplines in recent years, the development of *Interdisciplinary Scientific Research* (IDR) approaches is increasingly necessary, contributing to further knowledge discovery [5]. IDR emphasises the integration of expertise, theory or method from at least two different disciplines of research, which results in new collaborations and published outputs that reflect new insights into science [6]. However, interdisciplinarity leaves higher hurdles for researchers, which requires not only the knowledge of multidisciplinary fusion but also the skillful use of professional software in relevant fields. In the interests of researchers who just enter a new field to quickly participate in using tools of such field but they know not before, we created the Scientific Software Aggregation Platform as the collection of software which meets the

---

[1] http://www.scihub.cstcloud.cn/#/.

need of reliability and usefulness. In Scientific Software Aggregation Platform, there have been similar efforts along two directions for help. So far, researchers focus on integration of software as an essential factor distinguishing interdisciplinary research. A consensus is forming that science is structured around a problem, fact or methodology, which are generally labeled as research specialty, discipline or knowledge domain [7]. The platform is implemented with a tagging system that could push available software and resources in accordance with the classification.

Technology. Despite the tagging system as a procedure to facilitate software search, users of Scientific Software Aggregation Platform could benefit from another mechanism: *Instant Environment* (IE). Due to that platform is deployed on a *High Performance Computing* (HPC) cluster, the online deployments of large-scale applications or environments thus become possible [8–10]. User experience has been taken into consideration by conducting the service within the B/S structure. Therefore, IE utilizes virtualization technology, offering a real-time rendering graphical interface in the browser.

The Scientific Software Aggregation Platform is integrated with "Science and Technology Cloud" infrastructure based on the scalability and flexibility of container and cloud computing technology support platform. In the aspect of upper application, by providing a comprehensive WEB service interface, users can realize complex and diverse operation requests. Using container-based virtual technology to create multiple safe and isolated containers on a physical machine with the aid of Scratch-Pad Memory can make better use of hardware resources and ensure mutual isolation between software tools and applications [11–13]. The software convergence platform uses containers to provide the running environment for each running software tool session. The container is lightweight and can meet the application requirements of on-demand software services.

2.2 Scientific Software Open-Source Community

The Scientific Software Open-Source Community is built in response to the researchers' demand of open-source software retrieval[2]. In some scientific research fields, such as scientific computing and material science, the research work relies on commercial software, which has greatly hindered the development of scientific informatization. The open source software adopts the practice of parallel debugging and parallel development, bringing potential developers on the network to the software project, and effectively improving the quality and release rate of source code. The construction of the platform promotes the development of open source software in scientific research field, liberates the traditional monopoly of knowledge, encourages more researchers participate in open source projects, and gathers the strength of the majority of scientific software developers.

---

[2] http://cstsai.cstcloud.cn/#/.

Classification Standard of Software. In addition to providing open source services commonly used by researchers, we have innovatively added search labels by discipline and research area. This classification allows researchers to quickly find their field-related software. Our scheme is grounded on current software collections, serving for the long-term development of open-source software classification. To keep the category remain universal as facing the addition of new software, we formulated four principles:

- Integrity: We recognize the Open-source Community as a whole, which shall ensure that any software must belongs to a specific topic.
- Logicality: All categories must comply with logical partition rules. It implies that each partition must adopt a unique standard where two or more standards are not allowed to coexist;
- Stability: On the premise of flexibility, generalized categories should not be frequently changed. It can not only establish a classification platform for existing software according to the realms of application and the properties of content, but also open for new categories in the future due to potential software.
- Practicality: The classification hierarchy should remain simple, and over-detailed categories is abandoned, which enable users to query in a convenient way.

Technology. As shown in Fig. 2, the scientific software open-source community is flexibly expanded according to the access status of users. The infrastructure layer is mainly supported by Resource service model, which provides software running environment through software and hardware resources and application framework. MySQL database is selected as persistent storage and Redis is used as cache middleware to avoid performance bottleneck or even downtime caused by a large number of requests falling directly to the database. At the service interface layer, the platform abstracts different functional service modules, combining them in the form of micro-service mode, in which the authority verification module integrates the scientific unified certification alliance. Researcher can access various services and platforms through WEB pages without duplicate entries.

In summary, the scientific software open-source community bear following characteristics: integrity, logicality, stability and practicality, which provides researchers easy-to-use services to share and explore field-based software.

2.3   Code Hosting Platform: CSThub

CSThub[3], a code hosting and collaboration platform based on the dedicated kernel, is committed to creating a "Github" with independent property rights in the field of scientific research. On the basis of the dedicated version control kernel and localized language, it is an indispensable part in the research and development process of software platforms, which can effectively and quickly solve the

---

[3] http://www.cstos.cstcloud.cn/#/.

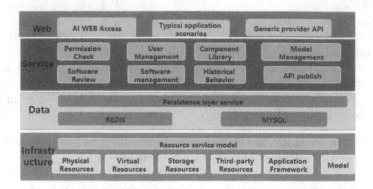

Fig. 2. The architecture of open-source community.

version management of projects from very small to very large, host the source code to the cloud, empower the cloud to collaborate and realize rapid iteration. In addition to the design of code warehouse hosting and Web management page, the platform also adds functions such as scientific research project management, authority verification, code review and project contribution statistics, etc. It also enhances the one-stop experience of developers when used in cooperation with the open-source community of scientific research, and avoids the risk of using traditional code hosting kernel. On the whole, CSThub mainly solves the pain points of four researchers:

– Scientific research process: It is in line with the current design of scientific research process by setting up functions such as multiple warehouses for a single project, direct hanging of code warehouses, and hierarchical management of personnel in different code warehouses under the same project.
– Fine-grained code hosting: code hosting can set different permissions, and participants in different roles are controlled by permissions, so it is not necessary to show all participants the whole code.
– Distributed code version control: The most important function of version control is to track the Software expert evaluation platform.
– Cross-platform compatibility: Scientific researchers can manage source code under any operating platform, the web page and mobile terminal can manage code through browsers, and under Linux and Windows, version control and team cooperation can be carried out through clients, which are compatible with the commands of git code hosting tools.

As shown in Fig. 3, the platform service of CSThub code hosting platform is mainly built by Spring Cloud, the back-end code hosting kernel function is mainly provided by Coding domestic kernel, and the client mainly uses ssh protocol for transmission and access. Redis database provides cache service. In the persistent service, developer data, project data, warehouse data, code fragments and public keys are stored and managed by MySQL.

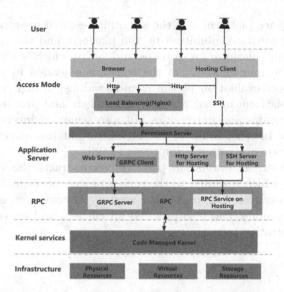

Fig. 3. The flowchart of the CSThub platform.

The platform provides a networked and graphical environment for code hosting and collaboration. Compared with previous command-line code management, it is more intuitive and convenient. Networking means that the platform adopts B/S architecture, and users do not need to download and install client software or install browser plug-in, thus eliminating the inconvenience caused by program maintenance and upgrade. Convert the version control in command line mode into corresponding functional points that users can see and click. The project manager can set the second-level subprojects according to the project architecture, and then divide the permissions of the members in detail, so that the members of each subproject can carry out collaborative development according to their own permissions, and all the modifications made by the project personnel to the project code files can be submitted to the platform. On the one hand, other developers can pull and get the latest code fragments in time. On the other hand, project managers can also grasp the progress of the project and the development contribution of each person. The graphical structure definition of the project is finally stored in MySQL relational database. This graphical way of project management and code hosting makes the operation more convenient and natural, and the user experience is better. Code hosting cloud is highly available and data security is guaranteed.

2.4 Software Expert Evaluation Platform

In order to select the demonstration software for personalized application tools and disciplines, a software expert evaluation platform is established. The software evaluation platform provides a strong support for the scientific research software convergence platform and the scientific research open source software community. Any software submitted by the platform and the community will enter the evaluation platform for examine and verify, which is not open to ordinary users. For further exposure of the software uploaded by users, examining through expert evaluation platform and grading through various aspects is needed. The platform invited not only researchers and professors from various scientific institutes and universities but also senior engineers and technical experts from the Internet industry as software evaluation experts. Thus, the accuracy of software evaluation is improved rapidly.

The software expert evaluation platform reconstructs the whole software examine process, which is similar to the review process of scientific papers. This newly built process greatly improves the security of convergence platform and open source community, and also provides an efficient and convenient way for selecting demonstration software.

3 Results

Sci-Base has promoted the formation of a shared ecosystem of scientific software and applications, which is gradually developing vigorously on the road of standardization and maturity. The open sharing of scientific software is an important way to promote the high cooperation and transparency of scientific research. Researchers can share the software tools used and developed in research, and conduct scientific research work such as data analysis and simulation through direct online use of software resources, so as to avoid repeated deployment.

At present, the Sci-Base has gathered more than 1100 funds of various scientific software. More than 300 teams from research institutes and universities participated in the delivery, with a total of more than 150000 visits. In addition, to expand the influence of Sci-Base and encourage open source culture into scientific research, our team created the Open Source Scientific Software Creativity Competition. With the theme of "Talent Innovation and Technology Open Source" and the purpose of "Developing Scientific Software Ecology", the competition mobilized the enthusiasm of scientific researchers, college students and social developers to participate in the construction of scientific software ecology.

The competition has been successfully held twice and sponsored by Internet companies. Our platform has also withstood the test of high concurrent access in the competition. Finally, more than 40 demonstration software were selected. Relying on the computing resources of the technology cloud and the stable architecture ability of the platform, researchers can run the demonstration software by click operation online. The demonstration open source projects have established warehouses in the CSThub. Typical application cases include:

- Xiaomi Mobile AI Compute Engine (MACE) is a neural network computing framework optimized for heterogeneous computing platforms on the mobile side (supporting Android, iOS, Linux, Windows).
- Data Hall (Beijing) Technology Co., Ltd., Data Hall interactive intelligent image segmentation and labeling client has been open source, developed to

meet the needs of hairline labeling of images in real scenes, and has high practicability.

- PiFlow, developed by Computer Network Information Center of Chinese Academy of Sciences, is an easy-to-use and powerful big data pipeline system.

4   Conclusion

Scientific ecological construction of software is a long-term and arduous task. Through the construction and operation of the Sci-Base, it has greatly solved the project code hosting and team development under scientific research process. The "platform + competition" mode built by Sci-Base is developing towards standardization and maturity. In the future, we will continue to optimize the platform architecture and add international and multilingual modules to improve the influence of the whole scientific ecosystem.

Acknowledgments. This work was partially supported by the Pilot Project in Chinese Academy of Sciences under the contact number XDB38050200, the Beijing Natural Science Foundation-Haidian Original Innovation Joint Foundation (Grant No. L182053), and the Network and Information Project of 14th five-year's plan in Chinese Academy of Sciences under the contact number WX145XQ09.

References

1. Chawla, D.S.: The unsung heroes of scientific software. Nature **529**(7584), 115–116 (2016)
2. David, W., Medvidovic, N., et al.: Scientific software as workflows: from discovery to distribution. IEEE Softw. **25**(4), 37–43 (2008)
3. Biswal, B.B., Mennes, M., et al.: Toward discovery science of human brain function. Proc. Natl. Acad. Sci. **107**(10), 4734–4739 (2010)
4. Segal, J., Morris, C.: Developing scientific software. IEEE Softw. **25**(4), 18–20 (2008)
5. Raimbault, J.: Exploration of an interdisciplinary scientific landscape. Scientometrics **119**(2), 617–641 (2019). https://doi.org/10.1007/s11192-019-03090-3
6. Research, C.: Facilitating interdisciplinary research, May 2005
7. Wagner, C.S., Roessner, J.D., et al.: Approaches to understanding and measuring interdisciplinary scientific research (IDR): a review of the literature. J. Informet. **5**(1), 14–26 (2011)
8. Gao, Y., et al.: Performance and power analysis of high-density multi-GPGPU architectures: a preliminary case study. In: IEEE 17th HPCC, pp. 29–35 (2015)
9. Zhao, H., Chen, M., et al.: A novel pre-cache schema for high performance Android system. FGCS **56**, 766–772 (2016)
10. Lu, Z., et al.: IoTDeM: an IoT big data-oriented MapReduce performance prediction extended model in multiple edge clouds. JPDC **118**, 316–327 (2018)
11. Guo, Y., Zhuge, Q., et al.: Optimal data allocation for scratch-pad memory on embedded multi-core systems. In: IEEE ICPP, pp. 464–471 (2011)
12. Zhang, L., Qiu, M., et al.: Variable partitioning and scheduling for MPSoC with virtually shared scratch pad memory. JSPS **58**(2), 247–265 (2010)
13. Qiu, M., Chen, Z., Liu, M.: Low-power low-latency data allocation for hybrid scratch-pad memory. IEEE Embed. Syst. Lett. **6**(4), 69–72 (2014)

Joint Accuracy and Resource Allocation for Green Federated Learning Networks

Xu Chu[1], Xiaoyang Liu[1], Qimei Chen[1(✉)], Yunfei Xiong[2], Juanjuan Wang[3], Han Yu[2], and Xiang Hu[2]

[1] School of Electronic Information, Wuhan University, Wuhan 430072, China
{chu_xu,liuxiaoyang,chenqimei}@whu.edu.cn
[2] Wuhan Fiberhome Technical Services Co. Ltd., Wuhan 433072, China
{yfxiong,yuhan,huxiang}@fiberhome.com
[3] School of Business Administration, Zhongnan University of Economics and Law,
Wuhan 430072, China
Wangjj@zuel.edu.cn

Abstract. This paper studies the energy and time resource optimization of federated learning (FL) in wireless communication networks. In the considered network model, each client uses local data for model training, and then sends the trained FL model to the central server. However, the energy budget of the local computing and transmission process is limited. Therefore, reducing energy consumption should be given priority when we consider the FL efficiency and accuracy. We invest a green communication joint learning issue and expressed as an optimization problem. To minimize the energy consumption under the condition that the overall FL time is constrained, we propose an iterative algorithm based on Lyapunov optimization. Our algorithm selects the clients participating in each round and allocates the different bandwidth to each client. At the same time, the connection between local training and communication process is considered so that we can get the optimal client local calculation force.

Keywords: Client selection · Resource allocation · Green communication

1 Introduction

In the era of big data, AI, and deep learning [1–3] continue to develop. Related technologies use massive amounts of data for training, so as to achieve the purpose of intelligence. The increasing requirements for storage space, computer capabilities, and privacy requirements have become urgent issues. The goal of federated learning is to enable mobile devices to collaboratively learn a shared machine learning model. Instead of sharing the entire training data to the central server, Federated learning only uploads the partial learning model to it [4]. Due to limited wireless resources, this process may affect the performance of FL.

M. Qiu et al. (Eds.): SmartCom 2021, LNCS 13202, pp. 154–163, 2022.
https://doi.org/10.1007/978-3-030-97774-0_14

In recent years, many studies have done a lot of work to optimize FL. [5–8] introduced several new designs of the FL algorithm and various problems as well as solutions to improve the FL effect. However, they mainly focused on the delay or accuracy of FL. As the focus on energy issues gradually increasing, the topic of Green Communication on how to reduce FL energy consumption continued to attract people's attention. In [8], the author proposed a new FL algorithm that can minimize the communication cost. [10–12] studied the scheme of reducing FL energy consumption or time consuming. However, the optimization problem of [9–12] is formed by treating each learning round equally, so equal network resources are allocated between learning rounds. In [13], the author found a phenomenon called "later is better" in the representative machine learning tasks such as image classification and text generation. They explicitly considered the different significance of each FL round for the final result, and studied the bandwidth allocation as well as customer selection under the conditions of long-term energy constraints and uncertain wireless channel information. However, paper [13] did not consider the efficiency and accuracy of FL. It also ignored the energy distribution between local and communication.

Our paper aims to describe the problem of client selection and bandwidth allocation in FL, while considering the optimization of the client's local energy consumption and transmission energy consumption in the presence of total time constraints. We have made better use of the phenomenon in [13] to reduce FL energy consumption and formulated a problem of minimizing FL energy under a time consuming limit. This work aims to minimizes the total energy consumption of local computing and wireless transmission without decreasing the FL efficiency and accuracy. We propose an algorithm based on Lyapunov optimization to solve the above optimization problem. The simulation results show that compared with the traditional FL method, the proposed scheme can achieve about 56.5% energy saving.

2 System Model

We now build a wireless joint learning network, which consists of K clients and a central server. Each client k has a local data set D_k. For each data set $D_k = \{x_{ki}, y_{ki}\}_{i=1}^{D_k}$, $x_{ki} \in R^d$ is the input vector of client k, y_{ki} is its output. For conveniently describing the relationship, the FL model trained by the data set of each client is called the local FL model. The FL model generated by the central server using the input of the local FL model of all clients is called the global FL model.

The FL process between the client and the central server includes three steps in each iteration: First, each client participates in the FL round is updated locally. Afterwards, the client transmits the local FL model to the central server. Finally, the results are aggregated and broadcast globally on the central server. Each iteration is called a learning round. The wireless joint learning network needs to select the appropriate client to upload the updated local model in each round. It depends on the channel state of each client in the current round, the previous accumulated time consuming and bandwidth allocation. The method will optimize the learning performance at the same time minimize the energy consumption. Therefore, we use $a_k^t = \{0,1\}$ to indicate whether client k is selected in round t and $a_k^t = 1$ indicates that the client k is selected.

2.1 Resource Consumption Model

Local Training Process. The local training time can be defined by the following formula:

$$\tau_k^{t,l} = \frac{I_k C_k D_k}{f_k^t}, \tag{1}$$

where f_k^t represents the computing power of client k, which is determined by the number of CPU cycles per second. I_k is the number of local iterations, and C_k is the number of CPU cycles required to process a piece of data. According to [10], the total local energy consumption of client k is

$$E_k^{t,l} = I_k \kappa C_k D_k (f_k^t)^2, \tag{2}$$

where κ is the effective switched capacitance that depends on the chip architecture.

Transmission Process. Use b_k^t as the bandwidth allocated by client k in round t. Since the bandwidth of the system has an upper limit, we have $\sum_{k=1}^K b_k^t \leq B^t$, where B^t is the upper limit of the total bandwidth in round t. According to Shannon's formula, for the achievable transmission rate of client k participating in round t, we have

$$r_k^{t,c} = b_k^t \log_2(1 + \frac{g_k^t p_k^t}{N_0 b_k^t}), \tag{3}$$

where p_k^t is the average transmit power of client k, g_k^t is the channel gain between client k and the central server, and N_0 is the power spectral density of Gaussian noise. According to (3) we can define the time consuming of upload process as $\tau_k^{t,c}$. It should be noted that the transmission efficiency defined by Shannon's formula is the upper limit of the transmission rate. In order to transmit the data completely, the inequation $r_k^t \tau_k^{t,c} \geq L$ should be satisfied, where L represents the data size of the machine learning model used. In order to reduce the time consuming, we order $\tau_k^{t,c} = \frac{L}{r_k^t}$. Therefore, we derive the average transmission power according to Eq. (3) and $\tau_k^{t,c}$ as

$$p_k^t = \frac{b_k^t N_0}{g_k^t} (2^{\frac{L}{b_k^t \tau_k^{t,c}}} - 1). \tag{4}$$

Then, the transmission energy consumption of client k in round t can be obtained as

$$E_k^{t,c} = \frac{b_k^t N_0 \tau_k^{t,c}}{g_k^t} (2^{\frac{L}{b_k^t \tau_k^{t,c}}} - 1). \tag{5}$$

Therefore, in round t, the total time consuming of client k is

$$\tau_k^t = \tau_k^{t,l} + \tau_k^{t,c}. \tag{6}$$

The total energy consumption of client k in round t is

$$E_k^t = E^{t,l} + E^{t,c}. \tag{7}$$

2.2 Packet Error Rates

In the process of transmission, there may be errors in the data. These errors will affect the accuracy of FL. To simplify the problem, we assume that each local FL model will be transmitted as a single packet in the uplink. The packet error rate when the client k transmits the local model to the central server is given by [14]:

$$w_k^t = 1 - e^{-\frac{m b_k^t N_0}{p_k^t g_k^t}}, \tag{8}$$

where m being a waterfall threshold [15].

The packet error rate helps us filter the client. If the central server determines that there is an error in the received local FL model, the local model will be refused to participate in this round of global aggregation process, and the client will be rejected to participate in the next FL process. We define $c_k^t = \{0, 1\}$, and $c_k^t = 0$ means that client k does not participate in the subsequent FL process.

2.3 Problem Formulation

For general high-accuracy, high-robust machine learning problems, fewer clients are selected in the early learning rounds, while more clients are selected in the later learning rounds. This distribution method will behave better than the average distribution. We call this phenomenon "later is better". Therefore, time weight λ^l is introduced to reflect the impact of choosing different numbers of clients in different learning stages on FL energy and performance.

To decrease the energy consumption of FL while avoiding the side effect, we propose an optimization problem. Its goal is to minimize the energy consumption of the client in the presence of a time consuming limit:

$$\text{P1:} \quad \min_{a^0, b^0, f^0, \dots, a^{T-1}, b^{T-1}, f^{T-1}} \sum_{t=0}^{T-1} E^t(a^t, b^t, f^t), \tag{9}$$

$$\text{s.t.} \sum_{t=0}^{T-1} \left(\frac{I_k C_k D_k}{f_k} + \frac{L}{b_k^t \log_2\left(1 + \frac{p_k^t g_k^t}{N_0 b_k^t}\right)} \right) \le T_k, \forall k, \tag{9a}$$

$$b_{\min} \le b_k^t \le b_{\max}, \forall k, \forall t, \sum_{k=1}^{K} b_k^t \le B^t, \forall t, \tag{9b}$$

$$f_{\min} \le f_k^t \le f_{\max}, \forall k, \forall t, \tag{9c}$$

$$a_k^t = \{0, 1\}, c_k^t = \{0, 1\}, \forall k, \forall t, \tag{9d}$$

where $E^t(a^t, b^t, f^t) = \lambda^t \sum_{k=1}^{K} E_k^t a_k^t c_k^{t-1}$. It should be noted that c_k^{t-1} represents the impact of the previous round of packet error rate on the current round of client selection decisions. Constraint (9a) requires that the total time consuming for the client k in T rounds to complete the FL task does not exceed the time consuming limit T_k. Constraint (9b) is the range of bandwidth allocation. Constraint (9c) limits the user's CPU computing power. Constraint (9d) jointly determine the decision of client selection.

3 Resource Allocation For Energy Minimization

In this section, we propose a low-complexity algorithm to solve P1 on a basis of the Lyapunov optimization. We assume that in terms of measuring energy and time consuming, the client's local update and upload processes are independent of each other. Therefore, we consider the optimization problems of these two processes separately.

3.1 Local Iterative Optimization Algorithm

For the selected client, the optimization problem of the local iteration is

$$\text{P2:} \quad \min_{f^0, \dots, f^{T-1}} \sum_{t=0}^{T-1} I_k \kappa C_k D_k \left(f_k^t\right)^2, \tag{10}$$

According to (10), using minimum f_k^t is always effective. If each task has a time-consuming threshold $\tilde{\tau}$, then we have $\frac{I_k C_k D_k}{f_k} \leq \tilde{\tau}$. So in order to minimize (10), the optimal solution of f_k^t is $f^* = \frac{I_k C_k D_k}{\tilde{\tau}}$. Therefore, the local time consuming satisfies $T_k^l = \sum_{t=0}^{T-1} \tilde{\tau}$. According to the total time consuming limit, it can be deduced that the time consuming limit of the upload process is $T_k^c = T_k - T_k^l$.

3.2 Optimization Algorithm for Uploading Process

Under the time consuming limit, the client's reasonable selection and assignment of tasks will reduce the overall time-consuming of FL. The time consumed in each round will cause the client to gradually approach the time-consuming limit T_k^c, which will be a dynamic problem. To solve this problem, we construct a time deviation queue $q_k(t)$ based on Lyapunov optimization, which is used to represent the deviation between the total time consuming of the current transmission process of client k and the time limit T_k^c. Client selection and bandwidth allocation decisions should be guided under the conditions of satisfying time constraints. We define the update of the queue as

$$q_k(t+1) = \left[\tau_k^{t,c} - \frac{T_k^c}{T} + q_k(t)\right]^+, \tag{11}$$

where $[\cdot]^+ = \max\{\cdot, 0\}$.

With $q_k(t)$, the constraint (9a) in P1 can be connected with the minimization problem (9). In this way the infinite time domain minimum average cost problem that is difficult to solve is transformed into the minimum value problem in each round. Now we are about to solve the following problem:

$$\text{P3:} \quad \min_{a^0,b^0,\ldots,a^{T-1},b^{T-1}} \left(V\lambda^t E^{t,c} + \sum_{k=1}^{K} q_k(t)\,\tau_k^{t,c} \right) a^t c^t, \quad (12)$$

$$\text{s.t. } (11),(13),(14). \quad (12a)$$

Among them, V is a set of penalty factors. The purpose is to make a trade-off between minimizing energy loss and satisfying time consuming limit. It is used to adjust the weight relationship between Lyapunov drift and penalty in each round t. The additional term $\sum_{k=1}^{K} q_k(t) \cdot \tau_k^{t,c}$ in Eq. (13) helps us to transform constraint (9a) into each round of problems, which appears in the form of penalty terms. P3 takes into account the deviation between the previous accumulated time of the client in the current round and the upper limit of the evenly allocated time, which can be called a time deficit. If $q_k(t)$ is larger, the client will be more inclined to invest in the round that suits it (always in the later rounds) to ensure that the total time consuming of communication process does not exceed the time consuming limit T_k^c. In this way, we have avoided meeting the time constraints while predicting future channel conditions, at the same time reduced energy consumption as much as possible.

Note that P3 still contains a_k^t and c_k^t. It is still a mixed integer problem. In order to solve P3, we need to strip a_k^t and c_k^t from the equation solving. Therefore, metric $\rho_k^t = \frac{V\lambda^t \tilde{p} + q_k(t)}{g_k^t}$ is introduced, where $\tilde{p}$ is the upper limit of the client's target transmit power. Based on the metric ρ_k^t, the client is gradually added to the selection set S in ascending order of ρ_k^t. The smaller ρ_k^t is, the higher the priority. This selection set will assist us in bandwidth allocation and client selection. For every selection set, bandwidth allocation is transformed into the following optimization problem:

$$\text{P4:} \quad \min_{\{b_k^t\}_{k \in S}} \sum_{k \in S} \left[V\lambda^t \tilde{p} + q_k(t) \right] \cdot \frac{L}{b_k^t \log_2\left(1 + \frac{\tilde{p} \cdot g_k^t}{N_0 b_k^t}\right)}, \quad (13)$$

$$\text{s.t. } b_{\min} \le b_k^t \le b_{\max}, \forall k \in S, \quad (13a)$$

$$\sum_{k \in S} b_k^t \le B^t, \forall t. \quad (13b)$$

For each selection set S, the corresponding client optimal bandwidth allocation result is $b^*(S)$. For the initial data set (i.e., a data set with only one client), we make the optimal bandwidth allocation of the first client to be $b^*(S_0) = b_{\max}$. As the client is continuously added to S, its termination condition is $B^t - \sum_{m=0}^{M-1} b^*(S_m) < b^*(S_M)$, which can control the choice of the client.

Algorithm 1. GFL (Green Federated Learning) Algorithm

Require: $q_k(0) = 0, \forall k$
1: Rank the clients according to ρ. Therefore we have $\rho_1 \leq \rho_2 \leq \dots \rho_K$
2: Let $S_0 = \{k : \rho_k = \rho_1\}, S = S_0, b^*(S_0) = b_{\max}$
3: **for** $k = |S_0| + 1, \dots, K - 1$ **do**
4:     Set $S = S + \{k\}$
5:     Solve **P5** and gain $\eta^*(S)$ and $b^*(S)$
6:     **if** $w > \tilde{w}$ **then**
7:         Refuse client k
8:     **end if**
9:     **if** $B - \sum_{m=1}^{k} b_m^* < b_k^*$ **then**
10:         $S = S - \{k\}$
11:         Let $S = S^*$
12:         Stop the iteration
13:     **end if**
14: **end for**
15: Obtain a^* where $a_k^* = \mathbf{1}\{k \in S^*\}, \forall k$ and $b^* = b^*(S^*)$

To find the optimal solution of P4 more intuitively, the variable $\eta_k^t = \frac{b_k^t}{g_k^t}$ is introduced. It represents the bandwidth under unit channel gain. Then P4 is transformed into P5. The pseudo code of this process is given in Algorithm 1.

$$\text{P5:} \quad \min_{\{b_k^t\}_{k \in S}} \sum_{k \in S} \frac{V\lambda^t \tilde{p} + q_k(t)}{g_k^t} \cdot \frac{L}{\eta_k^t \log_2\left(1 + \frac{\tilde{p}}{N_0 \eta_k^t}\right)}. \tag{14}$$

$$\text{s.t.} \quad b_{\min} \leq b_k^t \leq b_{\max}, \forall k \in S, \tag{14a}$$

$$\sum_{k \in S} b_k^t \leq B^t, \forall t. \tag{14b}$$

With regards to the complexity of GFL algorithm, we divide it into two parts. The first part is to sort the client with bubble sorting. The complexity in the worst case is $\mathcal{O}(k^2)$ and the best case is $\mathcal{O}(k)$. In the second part, we solve the minimum problem in cyclic iteration. We only consider the worst case, and the time complexity is $\mathcal{O}(k)$.

3.3   Overall Energy Optimization

In this subsection, we summarize the energy in the local and transmission process to describe and analyze the rationality of Algorithm 1. How the selection set assists us in selecting clients and allocating the bandwidth is also outlined. We make the following analysis to prove the optimality of Algorithm 1.

Proposition 1: In any FL round t, the allocated bandwidth of the client added to the S set will not be greater than the allocated bandwidth of the current existing client in the S set.

Proposition 1 shows that, according to the definition of the metric ρ_k^t, with smaller ρ_k^t, the client has better channel condition and less time consuming. Therefore, according to Proposition 1, we will allocate more bandwidth to clients with smaller ρ_k^t. According to constraint (13a), there are upper and lower limits for the bandwidth allocation of client k. The lower limit $b_{\min}$ is the minimum bandwidth that maintains the client's normal transmission of the local model, and is limited by the packet error rate. The relationship can be expressed as $b_{\min} = \frac{\tilde{p} \cdot g_k^t}{mN_0} \ln\left(\frac{1}{1-\tilde{w}}\right)$, where $\tilde{w}$ is the error rate threshold. As bandwidth is limited and the termination condition $B^t - \sum_{m=0}^{M-1} b^*(S_m) < b^*(S_M)$ is met, in round t, we select the first M clients by bandwidth.

Corollary 1: Assume that the size of the local data of all clients is the same, i.e., $D_{k_1} = D_{k_2}, \forall k_1 \neq k_2$. The number of local iterations of all clients and the number of CPU cycles required to process one data are also the same. In this way f^* only depends on the time-consuming threshold $\tilde{\tau}$. Therefore, it can be proved that the local energy minimization and the transmission energy minimization cooperate to solve the overall energy minimization problem.

4 Simulation Results And Analyze

We use the CIFAR10 data set to simulate the FL process. The total number of clients is set to 20, each client is allocated 500 training samples. The number of local iterations $I_k = 50$ and the number of CPU cycles required to process one data is set as $C_k = 2 \times 10^4$ cycles/sample. The total bandwidth of the wireless network during transmission is $B = 20$ MHz, and the power spectral density of Gaussian white noise is set as $N_0 = -174$ dBm/Hz. To limit the energy consumption of the client, we set the upload power as $\tilde{p} = 30$ dBm. The maximum allocated bandwidth $b_{\max} = 2$ MHz. For each client, FL runs a total of 150 rounds and the time consuming limit $T_k = 100$ s. We named our algorithm GFL (Green Federated Learning) and compared the performance with the Select-All FL model. We make all 20 clients selected by Select-All in each round. GFL dynamically selects clients based on "later is better" throughout the FL process.

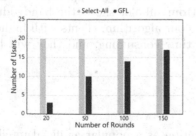

Fig. 1. Clients selection in each round

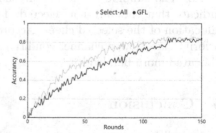

Fig. 2. Comparison of accuracy

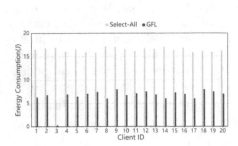

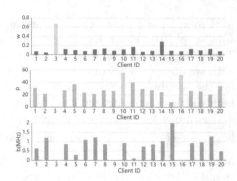

Fig. 3. Comparison of energy consumption

Fig. 4. Client selection and bandwidth allocation strategy

Figure 1 shows the number of clients selected by GFL and Select-All in each round. Select-All uses all 20 clients in each round, while GFL selects fewer clients in the early rounds and more clients in the later rounds. The distribution of client choices with rounds can be flexibly adjusted by time weights λ^t.

Figure 2 shows the accuracy of GFL and Select-All. Considering that Select-All has used all clients, it has good convergence efficiency and accuracy. Although the accuracy of GFL falls behind Select-All in the previous rounds, at the end of the FL round, its accuracy is close to Select-All.

Compared with GFL, Select-All generates a considerable amount of energy consumption. Figure 3 compares the energy consumption of the two methods for a single client. Since Select-All used all clients, its energy consumption was significantly higher than GFL at all stages. GFL saves a lot of energy consumption while ensuring the overall accuracy. It can be seen that the client 3 consumes very little energy. But it is not because it takes an advantage over other clients. We will introduce the specific reasons below.

Figure 4 shows our client selection and bandwidth allocation strategy. The top subplot shows that if the packet error rate w^t is higher than the threshold, the client will be refused to participate in the subsequent FL process. The packet error rate of client 3 exceeds the threshold, so it will not be selected. Therefore, although it consumes very little energy, it makes no contribution to the result of FL. The subplot in the middle shows the selection metric ρ_k^t. Gray clients indicate that they are not selected. The bottom subplot shows the bandwidth allocation of the selected client. According to our algorithm, clients with higher priority have lower channel conditions and time consuming, and they will be allocated more bandwidth.

5   Conclusion

Federated learning has attracted much attention as a popular artificial intelligence technology that can protect data privacy and solve the problem of data islands. The allocation of wireless network resources is one of the important and commonplace topics. This paper studied the client selection and bandwidth allocation issues in wireless communication networks. Based on the time dependence of different learning rounds, we formulated a joint accuracy and resource allocation problem to minimize the energy consumed in the training and transmission process with a total time consuming limit. We used Lyapunov optimization to find the solution of the problem. The results showed that our scheme is superior to the classic algorithm in terms of total energy consumption. It can achieve about 56.5% energy saving.

References

1. Qiu, H., Qiu, M., Lu, Z.: Selective encryption on ECG data in body sensor network based on supervised machine learning. Inf. Fusion **55**, 59–67 (2020)
2. Qiu, L., Gai, K., Qiu, M.: Optimal big data sharing approach for tele-health in cloud computing. In: IEEE SmartCloud, pp. 184–189 (2016)
3. Lu, R., Jin, X., Zhang, S., Qiu, M., Wu, X.: A study on big knowledge and its engineering issues. IEEE Trans. Knowl. Data Eng. **31**(9), 1630–1644 (2018)
4. Zhu, G., Liu, D., Du, Y., You, C., Zhang, J., Huang, K.: Towards an intelligent edge: wireless communication meets machine learning (2018). arXiv:1809.00343
5. Bonawitz, K., et al.: Towards federated learning at scale: system design. In: Proceedings of Systems and Machine Learning Conference, Stanford, CA, USA, pp. 1–15 (2019)
6. McMahan, H.B., Moore, E., et al.: Communication-efficient learning of deep networks from decentralized data. arXiv preprint arXiv:1602.05629 (2016)
7. Zhao, X., Yang, K., Chen, Q., et al.: Deep learning based mobile data offloading in mobile edge computing systems. Future Gener. Comput. Syst. **99**, 346–355 (2019)
8. Yang, Y., Chen, Q.: Distributed resource allocation under mobile edge computing networks: invited paper. In: 17th ISWCS, pp. 1–6 (2021)
9. Konečný, J., McMahan, B., Ramage, D.: Federated optimization: distributed optimization beyond the datacenter, November 2015. arXiv:1511.03575
10. Yang, Z., Chen, M., Saad, W., Hong, C.S., Shikh-Bahaei, M.: Energy efficient federated learning over wireless communication networks. IEEE Trans. Wirel. Comm. **20**(3), 1935–1949 (2021)
11. Hu, Y., Huang, H., Yu, N.: Device scheduling for energy-efficient federated learning over wireless network based on TDMA mode. In: International Conference on WCSP, pp. 286–291 (2020)
12. Tran, N.H., Bao, W., Zomaya, A., Nguyen, M., Hong, C.S.: Federated learning over wireless networks: optimization model design and analysis. In: IEEE INFOCOM 2019, pp. 1387–1395 (2019)
13. Xu, J., Wang, H.: Client selection and bandwidth allocation in wireless federated learning networks: a long-term perspective. IEEE Trans. Wirel. Comm. **20**(2), 1188–1200 (2021)
14. Zeng, Q., Du, Y., Huang, K., Leung, K.K.: Energy-efficient radio resource allocation for federated edge learning. In: Proceedings of IEEE International Conference on Communications Workshops (ICC Workshops), pp. 1–6, June 2020
15. Xi, Y., Burr, A., Wei, J., Grace, D.: A general upper bound to evaluate packet error rate over quasi-static fading channels. IEEE Trans. Wirel. Commun. **10**(5), 1373–1377 (2011)

Trust Evaluation Method Based on the Degree of Code Obfuscation

Lu Chen[1,2]($\boxtimes$), Zaojian Dai[1,2], Nige Li[1,2], and Yong Li[1,2]

[1] Institute of Information and Communication, Global Energy Interconnection Research Institute, Nanjing 210003, China
chenluchina@aliyun.com, {daizaojian,linige,
liyong}@geiri.sgcc.com.cn
[2] State Grid Key Laboratory of Information and Network Security, Nanjing 210003, China

Abstract. In the power grid environment, equipment certification is the key practice of zero trust security. Through the trust evaluation of equipment, the power grid environment can be effectively protected. This paper introduces identity authentication and behavior authentication to evaluate the security of devices from many aspects, and proposes a trust evaluation scheme based on code confusion for terminal devices. Through the identification and password technology and digital signature mechanism, the identity of terminal equipment is verified to prevent incomplete files caused by virus infection, Trojan horse/back door/man-made tampering, transmission failure and other reasons, and complete identity authentication. Through the improved trust evaluation model based on supervised learning to evaluate the effectiveness of code confusion, we can determine the ability of the code to resist malicious attacks, analyze whether the device will bring threatening behavior, indirectly verify the device behavior trust, and then prove the security of the terminal or software to complete behavior authentication.

Keywords: Trust assessment · Identification · Zero trust · Code obfuscation

1 Introduction

Information security and privacy protection are critical for various applications, such as computer [1, 2], networks [3, 4], data centers [5, 6], transportations [7], and healthcare [8]. How to protect software code is super important. Code obfuscation is a software protection technology that transforms the process structure and data relationship of the code to increase the attacker's reverse analysis and attack cost. Code obfuscation technology does not change the syntax and semantic rules of the original code [9]. Code obfuscation technology is first proposed. The main purpose of the software is to protect the safety of the software code, hinder the code understanding, and ultimately delay the malicious behavior to change the code. Although this technique does not completely hinder code understanding, code obfuscation makes reverse analysis more laborious and troublesome, thereby preventing or delaying attackers from tampering with the code [10].

© The Author(s), under exclusive license to Springer Nature Switzerland AG 2022
M. Qiu et al. (Eds.): SmartCom 2021, LNCS 13202, pp. 164–174, 2022.
https://doi.org/10.1007/978-3-030-97774-0_15

The trust evaluation model [11] can be used to build the security level of terminal equipment, help entities choose real and reliable equipment, and screen out equipment with security risks. The model dynamically collects changes in related subjective and objective factors [12]. Comprehensive considerations produce credibility a variety of factors that affect the trust relationship. Modeling is based on the evaluation attribute set of the trust relationship. The calculation of the trust degree and the authorization decision are realized.

In the open network environment [12], the trust relationship between entities is divided into two types: identity trust and behavior trust. Identity trust focuses on the verification of entity identity and entity authority, which is mainly achieved through encryption, digital signatures, and authentication protocols. Therefore, we have introduced a digital signature mechanism based on identification password technology, which is a digital signature system based on identification password technology. By verifying the identity of the terminal device, it prevents infection of viruses, implantation of Trojan horses/backdoors/manual tampering, transmission failures, etc. The resulting file is incomplete. This method achieves the effect of identity trust through identity verification. Behavioral trust dynamically updates the trust relationship between entities based on the interaction experience between entities. We evaluate the effectiveness of code obfuscation through the trust evaluation model, which can determine the code's ability to resist malicious attacks and analyze whether the device will carry The threatening behavior indirectly verifies the trustworthiness of the device behavior. In turn, the security of the terminal or software can be proved.

In the power grid environment, equipment certification is a key practice of zero-trust security. so the trust model in this article [13] is only for equipment users, and does not study the trust evaluation of individual users. For the four types of states of terminal devices in the zero-trust architecture: uncontrolled terminals, controlled terminals, trusted terminals and untrusted terminals. This paper proposes a trust evaluation scheme for terminal equipment based on the degree of code obfuscation [14].

The second chapter introduces the existing code obfuscation methods and trust evaluation models. The third chapter puts forward the specific trust evaluation scheme and overall framework, including identity authentication module and code obfuscation trust evaluation module. Section 4 carired out a comparative analysis experiment. Theproposed xgboost algorithm is compared with random forest and decision tree. Experiment shows that xgboost algorithm can maintain high accuracy and be more stable.

2 Related Work

The identity authentication method proposed in [15] aims at the problem of identity forgery in the process of network interaction and uses individual characteristics and behavior patterns to describe the user's identity.

Code obfuscation is a code protection technology that can help the device protect its own code security and reduce the possibility of code tampering by attackers. By analyzing the characteristics of the obfuscated code, the effectiveness of the code obfuscation can be evaluated. Y Zhao proposes a reverse engineering-oriented code obfuscation algorithm effectiveness evaluation idea [16], which evaluates the obfuscation algorithm through the attack effect in the reverse process. Su Qing proposes a code obfuscation effectiveness evaluation model based on a nonlinear fuzzy matrix [17], which evaluates the obfuscation effect of different obfuscation algorithms on the original code by comparing the comprehensive complexity between the obfuscated codes.

The main function of the trust model is to help the system screen out safe and reliable devices and avoid malicious devices from intruding. The general trust evaluation model often monitors all interactions between network entities, obtains and analyzes contextual information, quantifies the trust relationship, and uses the mutual trust evaluation of the entities in the network as the basis for trust evaluation. Z Chen and Y Liu proposed a behavior-based trust evaluation model [18, 19]. In [18], historical behaviors will be used to construct a set of trusted behaviors of users. On this basis, direct trust of user behaviors can be obtained. At the same time, suspicious thresholds and abnormal thresholds are defined to punish historical trust. The trust evaluation model in [19] calculates the comprehensive trust value through three trust factors: direct trust value, statistical trust value, and recommended trust value. Jiang W analyzes and compares the security mechanisms and security technologies of existing mobile agent systems from the perspective of blocking attacks [20]. On this basis, the host protection mobile agent protection technology is selected, and a method to enhance the security protection of the mobile agent is proposed. Shi L proposes a trust system based on dynamic and continuous authentication of identity, which restricts access to terminals with specified loopholes or insecure by identifying mobile terminals [21]. T Wang proposed a trust model based on mobile edge nodes [22], which collects the trust information of sensor nodes by collecting mobile edge nodes to ensure the reliability of nodes in the Internet of Things and prevent malicious attacks.

The above method is to directly identify the user's identity, or indirectly evaluate the credibility through the user's behavior. However, it is not enough to only evaluate the user's identity, and the equipment used by the user is still at risk of being attacked. In this paper, a trust evaluation method is proposed, which combines user identification with device security analysis. After the user passes the identification, the security of his device is evaluated, which increases the evaluation scope and improves the security The accuracy is also improved by dividing the trust level with xgboost.

3 Trust Assessment Method

3.1 Overall Framework

In the zero-trust architecture, terminal devices include four types of states: uncontrolled terminals, controlled terminals, trusted terminals, and untrusted terminals. By default, all terminal devices are marked as uncontrolled terminals. Through device initialization and registration, and device identity authentication, the state of the terminal device can be migrated.

In this paper, a digital signature system based on identification password technology is used to authenticate the terminal, and through code feature value extraction, an evaluation model is constructed to evaluate the degree of code confusion, obtain the terminal threat level, and confirm the trust level. The specific process is shown in Fig. 1. First, the terminal or related software needs to access the system. The terminal accessed for the first time uses the registration agent module to register the device, pass in the identity id, and obtain the key. The terminal changes from an uncontrollable state to a controllable state. The terminal that visits again passes the identity authentication module to carry on the identity verification, determine whether the terminal can visit the system. If the identity authentication is passed, the terminal device is converted from an untrusted terminal to a trusted terminal and enters the code obfuscation trust evaluation module. By extracting characteristic values, the established trust evaluation model is used to evaluate the level of code obfuscation in the terminal to obtain the trust level, According to the trust level, the range that can be accessed is given (Fig. 1).

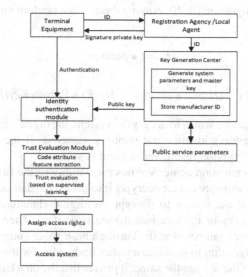

Fig. 1. Overall flow chart

3.2 Identity Authentication Module

After initialization and registration, the device can change from an uncontrollable state to a controllable state. The device authentication can be realized through the identity authentication method. Passing the authentication can make the terminal device change from an untrusted terminal to a trusted terminal.

The non-controlled terminal device is initialized and registered by submitting the ID to Ra or LA to change the non-controlled terminal device into the controlled one. The registration organization is responsible for the user registration and user management functions. The main functions are the acceptance and examination of the user registration application, the download of the user private key and the security management of the user registration. The local agent LA registers the remote user agent and requests the key to send the user information to RA, it can register and apply the key for local users, release the key and download the initial information in the carrier.

However, the device is still untrusted at this time, and the terminal device needs to pass the device ID to the key generation center, and in the key generation center, params and MasterKey are generated.

The public key Q is obtained by hashing the issuer's identity ID through the key generation center, and the public key is transmitted to the software center. The key generation center uses params, MasterKey and ID to return PrivateKeyID, and passes params and PrivateKeyID to the terminal device. The signature algorithm is as in formula (1), where ID is a string of arbitrary length. The terminal device directly or through the registration agent applies to the key generation center for the key to realize the storage and use of its own private key. Use a hash algorithm for encryption, such as formula (2), to generate a digital signature (R, S). Among them, r is a random number, and H(*) is a hash algorithm.

$$R = r \bullet params \tag{1}$$

$$S = r^{-1}(H(M) \bullet params + H_3(R) \bullet \mathrm{Pr}\ ivateKeyID) \tag{2}$$

When a terminal device wants to access the system, the digital signature is decrypted using the terminal device's identity and public parameters. If the digital signature is consistent with the decryption result, verification is achieved.

The identity authentication center verifies the identity of the firmware sender [15]. After receiving it, the software center decrypts it to obtain the data and digital signature. Use the public key of the sender to decrypt the digital signature. If the decryption is successful, the identity of the terminal device is verified. Then verify whether the terminal device has been tampered with. Through hash value comparison, the receiver uses the same hash algorithm to generate another hash value for the data, and compares the two hash values. If the two are the same, it proves that the data has not been tampered with during transmission. The terminal device can be converted from an untrusted state to a trusted state to perform firmware installation, and the verification algorithm is formula (3).

Enter the digital signature (R, S), system public parameters params and the issuer's identity ID, and output the verification result. That is, it is verified whether formula (3) is established, where Q is the public key calculated from the identity of the issuer.

$$e(params, params)^{H_2(M)} \bullet e(Q, H_1(ID))^{H_3(R)} = e(R, S) \tag{3}$$

3.3   Trust Evaluation Based on the Degree of Code Obfuscation

The device trust assessment can analyze the threat risk of the device, and evaluate the degree of code obfuscation by extracting the relevant attributes of the code complexity through reverse analysis. The threat degree of the device can be analyzed, and then the trust level of the trusted terminal device can be more detailed Divide.

This solution uses an integrated learning method to evaluate the code obfuscation model and applies the XGBoost algorithm. The XGBoost model is a learning model based on tree integration. Its basic idea is to build decision trees one by one, and gradually accumulate multiple decision trees after multiple iterations. Every time a decision tree is generated, its training results are evaluated, so that the next time it builds a decision tree model with a relatively higher accuracy rate, the model will continue to iteratively improve, and each iteration generates a new tree to fit the previous one The residual of the tree, this process is called gradient boosting. As the number of trees increases, the complexity of the ensemble model gradually increases until it approaches the complexity of the data itself, and the training reaches the optimal level.

The model representation based on the XGBoost algorithm is shown in formula (4), Where, $f \in F$, K is the number of cart trees.

$$y_i = \sum_{K=1}^{K} f_K(x_i) \quad f_K \in F \tag{4}$$

The XGBoost algorithm keeps the previous $i - 1$ rounds of prediction unchanged during each model training and adds a new function to the model [16]. Through continuous iteration, different individual learners are generated. As the accuracy of individual learners becomes higher and higher, the prediction effect will be better and better.

The key steps are described as follows:

(1) Determine the characteristics of trust evaluation

This paper mainly analyzes the indicators of code obfuscation strength and adopts the effectiveness evaluation indicators of the code obfuscation algorithm proposed in [8], including instruction execution rate, control flow loop complexity, fan-in/fan-out complexity, through disassembly The tool extracts the relevant attributes of the code and calculates the required feature values. The calculation method is as follows:

① Instruction execution rate (IE)

The ratio of the number of instructions actually executed when the program is dynamically executed to all the assembly instructions generated after the assembly instruction is disassembled and analyzed when the program is not executed, expressed as the instruction execution rate.

② Cyclomatic complexity (CC)

Control flow can reflect the order of execution of instructions. Through the construction of the program control flow graph, the execution order of the statements in the program and the number of edges e and the number of nodes n in the control flow graph can be determined. The calculation formula of the control flow loop complexity is:

$$CC = e - n + 2 \tag{5}$$

③ Fan-in/fan-out complexity (DC)

Data flow analysis is an important stage in retrograde analysis. Attackers analyze the specific algorithm and dependency of the program by analyzing the relationship of data objects in the program. The calculation formula of fan in/fan out complexity is:

$$DC = (Fan - in \times Fan - out)^2 \tag{6}$$

(2) Determine the trust evaluation level

The terminal is divided into three levels: low credibility, medium credibility, and high credibility. The terminal is assigned a trust level based on the evaluation of the degree of code confusion [25].

(3) Feature data preprocessing

The XGBoost algorithm uses the CART model, which is highly adaptable to data, so there is no need to normalize, standardize, and delete missing data. However, it is necessary to delete or modify some data that is far beyond the normal value.

(4) Model training

Step 1: Initialize the model and enter the data set.

The input is a given training set $\{(x_i, y_i)\}_{i=1}^{n}$, n represents the total number of training data samples, xi represents the characteristics of the data samples, and yi represents the label of the data sample, which is the trust value. For multi-classification tasks, the category label set is denoted as $\{y_0, y_1, y_2\}$.

Step 2: Grid tuning.

Using the grid method to adjust the parameters can make the model find a balance between accuracy and complexity, prevent overfitting of the model and improve robustness. The relevant parameters are as follows:

① eta: It can be understood as the learning rate. The larger the value, the faster the iteration speed, which may cause the algorithm to fail to converge to the optimal loss value, that is, to miss the optimal point.

$$F_m(x) = F_{m-1}(x) + v\gamma_m h_m(x) \ 0 < v \leq 1 \tag{7}$$

② Subsample: Use the parameter subsample to control the random sampling ratio of each tree. In xgb, this parameter defaults to 1 and cannot be set to 0. Decrease the value of this parameter, the algorithm will be more conservative and avoid overfitting. However, if this value is set too small, it may cause underfitting.

③ n estimators: It is the value of k in formula (1), which determines how many decision trees we need to build. The larger the value of k, the better the effect of the model. But correspondingly, any model has a decision boundary. After the k value reaches a certain level, the accuracy often does not rise or begin to fluctuate.

④ max depth: This value is also used to avoid overfitting. The larger the value, the more specific and local samples will be learned by the model.

⑤ min child weight: Determine the minimum leaf node sample weight sum to avoid over-fitting. When the value is large, it can prevent the model from learning local special samples.

Step 3: Train the model.

① Data set extraction: Random sampling of training set samples to generate multiple sampling sets.

② Using the greedy algorithm to recursively select features with higher corre-lation. According to these features, the data set is classified and divided until the maximum depth of the tree is reached. All samples are allocated to the leaf nodes of the tree, and a CART tree is generated.

③ Repeat step ② to build multiple CART decision trees in sequence in the direction of the gradient of the loss function. Then start training the next tree with the new predicted value. Gradient boosting tree accumulates the predicted values of all trees. As the final predicted value $y_i = \sum_{t=1}^{T} \eta f_t(x_i)$. Among them, T is the number of trees (n estimators), $f_t(x_i)$ is the prediction result of the t tree, and η is the eta.

④ Repeat the above steps, the model gradually tends to the direction of difficult samples, and obtaining a training data set $S = \{T_1, \ldots \ldots T_N\}$, T_N is a better decision tree model.

(5) Validation model

Use the test data to view the classification results of the model, and judge the classification effect through the mean square error and accuracy rate. The accuracy rate refers to the proportion of the correctly classified samples to the total samples. The higher the accuracy rate, the better the training results, and the smaller the mean square error training. The better the effect, the higher the accuracy. The performance of the training model using ensemble learning gradient algorithm is better than that of the general algorithm because the training framework of ensemble learning gradient algorithm can focus on overcoming the wrong data of previous decision tree classification, with the training of the model, the effect of the model will gradually improve [26].

4 Experimental Results and Analysis

4.1 Experimental Test Environment

The test environment uses the Python language's SKLearn module package, for code obfuscation before and after the change of the relevant property indicators we generated 600 simulated data using Python, the characteristic attributes are instruction execution rate, control flow cycle complexity and fan-in/fan-out complexity. The target attribute is divided into three levels: Low Trust, Medium Trust and High Trust.

4.2 Parameter Optimization

The XGBoost algorithm uses dozens of parameters. In order to improve the performance of the model, it is necessary to adjust the parameters. We mainly adjust the grid parameters of learning rate (eta), sampling ratio (Subsample), Maximum height of the tree(max_depth), and the number of trees (n estimators). The parameter range is: learning rate (0.05, 1), the best sampling ratio (0.05, 1), The number of optimal trees (0, 10), the running time of the comparison model during the grid search, the classification error rate and other indicators. The finally selected model parameters are shown in Table 1.

Table 1. Xgboost parameter optimal value.

Serial number	Example	The optimal value
1	eta	0.2
2	subsample	0.4
3	n estimators	8
4	Max_depth	[2, 4]
5	Max_leaf_nodes	2 × max_depth

4.3 Comparative Analysis

Use random forest, decision tree and xgboost to train the data set separately and perform cross-validation. As shown in Fig. 2. In the same experimental environment and based on the grid search method to select the most suitable hyperparameters, the accuracy of different models is compared as shown in the figure. It can be seen that the accuracy of the Decision Tree and Random Forest is greater when different cross-validation times are performed. Changes, the accuracy of xgboost has been high and very stable.

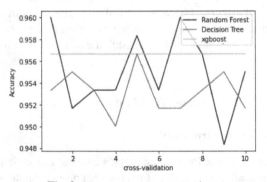

Fig. 2. Accuracy curve comparison

5 Conclusion

The combination of identity authentication and behavior authentication took into account the security of the device from many aspects. Using the XGBoost algorithm to evaluate the degree of code confusion can effectively analyze the security level of the device. At the same time, compare the performance of the XGBoost algorithm in the classification prediction through experiments A good effect is obtained, which proves the effectiveness of the method. The next step is to have a more in-depth understanding of the code attribute changes after the code is obfuscated, and the trust level will be more detailedly divided to further verify the effectiveness of the scheme.

Acknowledgment. This work is supported by the science and technology project of State Grid Corporation of China Funding Item: "Research on Dynamic Access Authentication and Trust Evaluation Technology of Power Mobile Internet Services Based on Zero Trust" (Grand No. 5700-202158183A-0-0-00) .

References

1. Thakur, K., Qiu, M., Gai, K., Ali, M.: An investigation on cyber security threats and security models. In: IEEE CSCloud (2015)
2. Gai, K., Qiu, M., Sun, X., Zhao, H.: Security and privacy issues: a survey on FinTech. In: Qiu, M. (ed.) SmartCom 2016. LNCS, vol. 10135, pp. 236–247. Springer, Cham (2016). https://doi.org/10.1007/978-3-319-52015-5_24
3. Zhang, Z., Wu, J., et al.: Jamming ACK attack to wireless networks and a mitigation approach. In: IEEE GLOBECOM Conference, pp. 1–5 (2008)
4. Qiu, H., Qiu, M., Memmi, G., Ming, Z., Liu, M.: A dynamic scalable blockchain based communication architecture for IoT. In: Qiu, M. (ed.) SmartBlock 2018. LNCS, vol. 11373, pp. 159–166. Springer, Cham (2018). https://doi.org/10.1007/978-3-030-05764-0_17
5. Gai, K., Qiu, M., Elnagdy, S.: A novel secure big data cyber incident analytics framework for cloud-based cybersecurity insurance. In: IEEE BigDataSecurity (2016)
6. Qiu, H., Qiu, M., Lu, Z.: Selective encryption on ECG data in body sensor network based on supervised machine learning. Inf. Fusion **55**, 59–67 (2020)
7. Qiu, M., Liu, J., et al.: A novel energy-aware fault tolerance mechanism for wireless sensor networks. In: IEEE/ACM Conference on Green Computing and Communications (2011)
8. Qiu, L., Gai, K., Qiu, M.: Optimal big data sharing approach for tele-health in cloud computing. In: IEEE SmartCloud, pp. 184–189 (2016)
9. Martinelli, F., Mercaldo, F., Nardone, V., et al.: Evaluating model checking for cyber threats code obfuscation identification. J. Parallel Dist. Comput. **119**, 203–218 (2018)
10. Cho, T., Kim, H., Yi, J.H.: Security assessment of code obfuscation based on dynamic monitoring in android things. IEEE Access **5**, 6361–6371 (2017)
11. Zhao, B., Xiao, C., Zhang, Y., et al.: Assessment of recommendation trust for access control in open networks. Clust. Comput. **22**(1), 565–571 (2019)
12. Chrysikos, A., McGuire, S.: A predictive model for risk and trust assessment in cloud computing: taxonomy and analysis for attack pattern detection. In: Parkinson, S., Crampton, A., Hill, R. (eds.) Guide to Vulnerability Analysis for Computer Networks and Systems. Computer Communications and Networks, pp. 81–99. Springer, Cham (2018). https://doi.org/10.1007/978-3-319-92624-7_4
13. Rose, S.W., Borchert, O., Mitchell, S., Connelly, S.: Zero trust architecture (2020)
14. Samaniego, M., Deters, R.: Zero-trust hierarchical management in IoT. In: 2018 IEEE International Congress on Internet of Things (ICIOT), pp. 88–95. IEEE (2018)
15. Tan, F.: Research on continuous identity authentication based on user behavior. Chongqing University of Posts and Telecommunications(2019)
16. Zhao, Y., Tang, Z., Wang, N., Fang, D.Y., Yuan-Xiang, G.U.: Evaluation of code obfuscating transformation. J. Softw. **23**(3), 700–711 (2012)
17. Qing, S., Lin, Z., Lin, Z., Huang, J.: Code obfuscation effectiveness assessment model based on nonlinear fuzzy matrices. Comput. Sci. **46**(4), 197–202 (2019)
18. Chen, Z., Tian, L., Lin, C.: Trust evaluation model of cloud user based on behavior data. Int. J. Distrib. Sens. Netw. **14**(5), 1550147718776924 (2018)
19. Liu, Y., Gong, X., Feng, Y.: Trust system based on node behavior detection in internet of things. J. Commun. **35**(05), 8–15 (2014)

20. Jiang, W., Wang, Y., Jiang, Y., et al.: Research on mobile Internet mobile agent system dynamic trust model for cloud computing. China Commun. **16**(7), 174–194 (2019)
21. Shi, L., Chen, N., Zhang, J.: Research on access trust technology of big data platform based on dynamic and continuous authentication of identity. Cyberspace Security **10**(7), 12 (2020)
22. Wang, T., et al.: Mobile edge-enabled trust evaluation for the internet of things. Inf. Fusion **75**, 90–100 (2021)
23. Aagaard, M., AlTawy, R., Gong, G.: ACE: An authenticated encryption and hash algorithm. Submission to NIST-LWC, p. 8 (2019)
24. Chen, T., He, T., Benesty, M.: Xgboost: extreme gradient boosting. R Package Version 0.4-2 **1**(4), 1–4 (2015)
25. Wang, J., Wang, H., Zhang H.: Trust and attribute-based dynamic access control model for internet of things, pp. 342–345. IEEE (2017)
26. Misra, I., Maaten, L.: Self-supervised learning of pretext-invariant representations. In: Proceedings of the IEEE/CVF Conference on Computer Vision and Pattern Recognition, pp. 6707–6717 (2020)

An SG-CIM Model Table Classification Method Based on Multi Feature Semantic Recognition Technology

Pengyu Zhang[1], Chunmei Wang[1], Baocong Hao[1], Wenhui Hu[2(✉)], Xueyang Liu[2], and Lizhuang Sun[3]

[1] Big Data Center of State Grid Corporation of China, Beijing, China
[2] National Engineering Research Center for Software Engineering, Peking University, Beijing, China
{huwenhui,liuxueyang}@pku.edu.cn
[3] School of Software and Microelectronics, Peking University, Beijing, China
sunlizhuang@stu.pku.edu.cn

Abstract. In this paper, based on the SG-CIM model Knowledge Graph, we introduce the semantic recognition technology in Natural Language Processing to model the information contained in the graph and mine the semantic information with multiple features according to the characteristics of the data itself. For the problem of graph domain name-related attribute complementation, this paper adopts a multi-feature semantic recognition approach to classify the given SG-CIM model table by domain name. We propose an ATT-ALE-TextRNN model for the descriptive features of the table, adding N times second-level domain name embeddings to the basic TextRNN and calculating the attention score together to capture the tendency of different contextual information for a given category. In this paper, with reference to the multidimensional discrete feature classification problem of the recommender system, an improved DeepFM model is proposed for the table discrete, class-forming features. It facilitates the discovery of semantic dependencies between class features, makes the feature distribution more diverse, and avoids the problems of low repetition between multidimensional features and low performance of combined computation. By combining the above two models, this paper achieves more accurate mining of multi-feature semantics and accurate classification of topic domains.

Keywords: Semantic recognition · Classification · Attention network · Deep learning

1 Introduction

In 2018, based on the construction of a full-service unified data center, State Grid carried out a comprehensive demonstration of the whole domain, completed the design of a data model covering 10 subject domains, and formed a unified data model (SG-CIM4.0) standard [1]. The big data [2–4] generated due to the fast advance in networks [5–7], machine learning [8, 9], and computer technologies [10, 11] provides both opportunities and challenges. The unified date model contains hundreds of information classes abstracted from problem domains as topics and sub-topic domains, such as security, finance, grid, customer, personnel, market, material, project, asset, and comprehensive domains. Nearly one thousand related entities and ten thousand attributes are covered under the domain at the same time [12], which is used as the uniform coding specification of the State Grid to provide a uniform data model for business applications.

In the SG-CIM table model, data processing of relevant features and so on is required, and semantic source data is intelligently extracted to serve as input for intelligent analysis. We need to take the domain name of the entity table as an important attribute value for building the graph, and intelligently extract the semantics related to the domain name from the descriptive features or other features of the table, and use them to classify different domains and other attributes under the domain, and complete the semantic attribute information.

The semantic recognition and classification complementation of domain-related attributes is done with different domains of a given table among the physical model for segmentation [13]. The entities or attributes under the domain are used as features of the domain. They can be used in a representation learning task for that domain to do domain classification of newly introduced knowledge. The application of a semantic recognition model based on deep learning or NLP in the automated mapping scenario of grid domain labels is relatively rare. It belongs to a prominent breakthrough explored in this field in this thesis.

2 Related Work

The semantic recognition can be divided into the application layer, NLP technology layer, and underlying data layer. Among them, the application layer is mainly implemented in the technical application of intelligent speech interaction systems [14]. The NLP technology layer includes the parsing and extraction of words, syntactic parsing and understanding [15], and the generation of natural language utterance information streams [16]. The underlying data layer includes lexicons, datasets, corpus, Knowledge Graph for semantic recognition models, and external commonsense knowledge [17]. Information retrieval techniques based on semantic analysis, text classification techniques, intelligent question and answer systems, conversational bots, etc. [18].

Each word is mapped into a dimension in a large text corpus by training a neural network. For example, the more commonly used word2vec model, which becomes significantly more effective in terms of efficiency and grammatical-semantic representation, represents each word by training a large corpus with vectors [20].

FastText is the method proposed by Mikolov et al. It is to average all the word vectors in a sentence and then normalize them and to obtain local sequence information with the help of the n-gram trick, but without considering word order information [19–21]. TextCNN was proposed by N-Kalchbrenner et al. It utilizes the structure of CNN itself and focuses more on local sequence classification information based on the trick of fasttext, thus achieving better prediction accuracy. But also because of the introduction of one-dimensional convolution, it is necessary to specify several convolution kernels of different sizes to obtain different widths of the field of view [22]. TextRNN is mainly proposed by Pengfei Liu et al. It solves the problem of specifying the filter-size size of CNN itself, and CNN mainly does the feature expression of the text. The introduction of RNN can better express to the information of text context in addition to feature expression. Its variants Bi-reactional RNN and Bi-LSTM can be understood in a sense as capturing variable-length and bidirectional n-gram information [23]. TextRNN + attention was proposed by Zichao Yang et al. The introduction of an attention mechanism can analyze which word is more influenced by the information related to text classification, thus improving the network effect [24]. However, *Hierarchical Attention* is still mainly based on text embedding, which weights the information of each vocabulary in the original sentence. Considering the category bias of the vocabulary itself, it may not be applicable to certain words with ambiguous bias and greater importance, which can easily trigger category confusion [25]. Attention mechanism for semantic recognition of emotional polarity was proposed by Yequan Wang et al., and it introduces the attention mechanism to recognize the semantics of emotional polarity and is able to capture important information about the response to a given polarity by adding N-times aspect embedding to the hidden layer of the basic LSTM [26].

3   Model Design of ATT-ALE-TextRNN Based on Table Description Features

As can be seen from the previous introduction, the task orientation of this paper dictates that what is to be learned is not all about the content understanding of the corpus itself but rather the aspects that the corpus is concerned with. As in this sentence in Fig. 1.

It is used to record the basic parameter information of the customer's circuit breaker. Circuit breaker files include rated voltage, operating mechanism model, rated current, rated breaking current, test cycle and other attributes

Fig. 1. Schematic diagram of a corpus containing aspect-specific semantics

The table name is "Circuit Breaker File", the corresponding domain name is "Customer Domain", and the secondary domain name is "Metering". From the corpus intuition, the only term that reflects the semantic meaning of "customer" is "record customer". Still, it may be easily misunderstood because of "circuit breaker", "rated voltage", "operation type", "rated current", and "grid domain" are easily misjudged as "grid domain".

Therefore, it is valuable to explore the connection between an aspect and the content of a sentence. Both of them can work together for the semantic understanding of the sentence. The inclusion of second-level domain information directly related to the domain name is considered as a complement to the corpus concern aspect, i.e., the second-level domain is defined as label-aspect embedding. In this paper, we propose a new way of attention weighting: the topic to be reinforced, or label-aspect embedding, is concatenated with textual information as input. The polarity information of the topic is then added to the hidden layer N times, and then the attention score is calculated together.

When different aspects are used as input, the attention mechanism will focus on different parts of the sentence. The long and short-term memory network is used to facilitate serialized feature extraction, which can better exploit the polarity information and key information of the text.

In terms of the overall architecture of the model, the fused second-level domain name features and deep attention-based TextRNN model constructed in this paper need to first use the second-level domain name information and text (table description) information together as input. Then, the two-way RNN network is used to train and share the weight information, and then the obtained domain name features and text features are fused. Finally, by processing these fused features with a deep attention mechanism, the tendency of polarity division of different domain names in the text can be effectively identified [27–30], thus improving the recognition ability of the whole model for domain name-related semantics.

The architecture of the model is shown in Fig. 2 below:

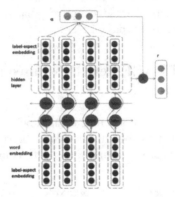

Fig. 2. Schematic diagram of ATT-ALE-TextRNN model architecture

Next, the main modules in the model are presented in separate blocks.

3.1 Text Embedded in ALE Layer

Because the standard TextRNN is unable to detect fine-grained polarity classification, this paper introduces the ALE module, which is attention aspect-level embedding. The main benefits of incorporating not only the original corpus code but also the second-level domain code at the input side are as follows:

(1) By training aspect-level embeddings into another vector space, the information from aspect can be more fully exploited further to strengthen the domain-related semantics in the original corpus.
(2) The problem of inconsistent word vector and aspect-level embeddings is solved, and the most important information of the response to a given aspect-level is captured. It can be guaranteed that the model can capture the most important part of the sentence at the moment when different second-level domains are given and the part that is distinguished when different aspect levels are given.

The experimental effect of the ablation if the aspect-level embedding is not introduced at the input side but made to appear directly in the ATTENTION calculation is also carried out in order to distinguish it from the ATT-TextRNN of the previous improved scheme. The module can be referred to as the ATT module. The effectiveness of fusing second-level domain names as input can be demonstrated to be significant in further experiments, as detailed in Sect. 4.

3.2 ATT Layer

Specifically, the attention mechanism is used to calculate the weights between the secondary domain name and the output vector of the original features processed by the deep network so as to calculate the attention level of the content of the original corpus with respect to the given aspects, i.e., the semantics related to the domain name that we focus on, enabling the model to pay attention to different parts of the sentence and thus capture the potential relevance of the content and the domain name [31]. As shown in the model architecture diagram, a matrix of hidden layer vectors [h1, h2, h3, ..., hN], where the size of the hidden layer is d, the length of a given sentence is N, and v_{la} is defined as the embedding of label-aspect, the attention mechanism generates an attention weight vector α and a weighted hidden layer vector r for characterizing the weighting of sentences with a given categorical polarity.

$$M = \tanh\left(\begin{bmatrix} W_h H \\ W_v v_a \otimes e_N \end{bmatrix}\right) \tag{1}$$

$$\alpha = soft\max\left(w^T M\right) \tag{2}$$

$$r = H\alpha^T \tag{3}$$

The $v_a \otimes e_N = [v, v, \ldots v]$ in Eq. (2) characterizes the process of joining v_{la} repetitions on v_{la}, which is the process of performing N linear transformations on v_{la} repetitions, the number of times being the length of the sentence.

The final sentence can be characterized in the following form:

$$h^* = \tanh(W_P r + W_x h_N) \tag{4}$$

h* can be considered as a new feature representation of the original sentence after adding a given second-level domain name. Next, a linear layer is added to transform the sentence vector into a vector e of length equal to the number of categories. Finally, e is transformed into a conditional probability distribution by a softmax layer. The loss function is also defined as a cross-entropy function.

$$y = soft\max(W_s h^* + b_s) \tag{5}$$

3.3 TextRNN Layer

Recurrent neural network (RNN) is one of the most commonly used structures to deal with Natural Language Processing problems due to its recursive structure, which is well suited for processing variable-length texts. It can recursively perform state transitions for the hidden internal states of the input sequence based on the activation of the input sequence and the previously hidden state vector at different time steps [23, 32].

There is a problem with using this form of RNN. There is a lack of learning of long-range correlations in a sequence during training, so gradient explosion or disappearance occurs. This is manifested by the gradient vector growing or decaying exponentially over a long period of time and is addressed by the introduction of LSTM networks [33]. There are many variants of the LSTM internal independent memory unit.

4 Model Design of DeepFM Based on Discrete Features of Table Fields and Source Systems

4.1 DeepFM Model Application and Improvement

In order to simultaneously take into account the higher-order feature representation and computational parallelism of the model, and according to our data needs, considering the cross-representation of domain-related semantic and feature fields and the tediousness of manually constructing features for numerous fields under the domain, a model combining FM and DNN, that is, DeepFM, was established; at the same time, some strategic modifications were made to the embedding side for better applicability to our data [25].

For example, in the task of this paper, the number of fields under the domain is not fixed, and therefore corresponding to each field dimension is not the same. At the same time, the number of fields in each table (sample) is also not fixed, and the variable number of features may result in each sample not getting a fixed size or an embedding representation with independent semantics. Therefore, each sample can be embedded by continuous text after first splitting into several independent features by field and then stitching by dimension. This can ensure that the embedding dimension of each sample is fixed. Then the fields that originally belong to the same field are merged, and to avoid the arbitrary length of the fields used as feature words, the model input x = [xfield1, xfield2, $\cdots$, xfieldm], which is a d-dimensional vector, where xfieldi is the feature field representation of the i-th field, and here it is discretized according to the commonly used fields, and its one-hot encoded category vector is taken. Then, by embedding each field separately, we can ensure that they are all of length k after embedding and ignore the problem that the dimensionality of each field is different. Thus, the above two problems are solved separately. In the FM layer, it is then possible to introduce the semantic field embedding and the feature field category embedding under the field as above for the secondary cross-terms, respectively, and to perform cross-learning of domain-related semantics and feature fields. This is also an improvement of this paper on the original DeepFM from a multilingual approach to use [35].

4.2 Discrete Processing of Data Features

As described in Sect. 3.2.1, the features summarized by fields need to be processed into separate fields for semantic embedding and discrete one-hot vector representation by domain, and embedding of fixed dimension size is learned by domain. Therefore, it is necessary to build a full-field lexicon of the corpus with good cleaning and de-duplication. Total 56508 fields. Also, consider fusing source system and source table features. According to the introduction of features above, it can be seen that the source system is mainly distributed in 30 categories, which is roughly three times the number of first-level domain names, and it is easy to do discrete representation.

And for example, "financial control system" and "e-commerce platform system" and the domain name "financial domain", "safety equipment (machine) control system" and the domain name "security domain", "human resources management system" and "science and technology work management system" and the domain name "Personnel Domain" is highly relevant. Therefore, it is necessary to incorporate this feature.

As for the source table feature, although it also carries semantics related to domain names, too many categories do not facilitate discretization. There is a high degree of overlap with the content of table description information. Even most of it is included in the table description information, so it is unnecessary to consider this feature again.

In summary, the field summary features and source system features can be discretized separately, taking two forms of one-hot encoding by class and direct discrete value encoding, respectively. The field features are represented by dense embedding separately.

4.3 DeepFM Model Design

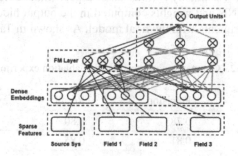

Fig. 3. DeepFM model structure diagram

The model structure is designed as shown in Fig. 3. The domain discrete features and the source system discrete features are introduced into the FM layer separately, while the domain continuous features are added to the FM for second-order cross-calculation with the discrete features. And combined with the high-dimensional embedding of the continuous features on the depth side, the logistic score and softmax normalized output is finally computed together and jointly influence the prediction results.

5   Model Design Based on Full Feature Fusion

Finally, two models, ATT-ALE-TextRNN and DeepFM, are combined to mine the semantics of recognizing multiform features. And the evaluation is redefined in such a way that the final result is decided based on the side with the high score by the two parts of the prediction regression. The overall results are shown in the next section of the experiments.

6   Experiments

(1)   Table description-based continuous feature modeling experiments (Table 1):

Table 1. Comparison of experimental effects of continuous features based on table description

Model	Precision	Recall	F1-Score
Baseline (TextCNN)	0.69	0.73	0.71
TextRNN	0.73	0.77	0.75
ATT-TextRNN	0.79	0.81	0.80
ATT-ALE-TextRNN	0.81	0.85	0.83

(2)   ATT-ALE-TextRNN ablation experiment:
An ablation experiment scheme is adopted here to verify the effectiveness of adding label-aspect embedding (secondary domain embedding) on the input side of the model. A model with only N times label-aspect embedding added to the output side of the TextRNN and weights computed in the output hidden layer is used for comparison experiments with the final model. As shown in Table 2:

Table 2. Comparison of the effects of ablation experiments

Model	Precision	Recall	F1-Score
ATT-TextRNN (2)	0.78	0.80	0.79
ATT-ALE-TextRNN	0.81	0.85	0.83

Note: The ATT-TextRNN here still uses label-aspect embedding (secondary domain embedding). In order to distinguish it from the ATT-TextRNN model that directly does hierarchical ATTENTION on the original corpus, it is labeled as ATT-TextRNN (2)

(3)   Modeling experiments based on discrete features such as table fields and source systems (Table 3):
As shown by the experimental results, DeepFM has the best results. It utilizes a combined modeling approach of FM and DNN, which has the advantages of both. Also, this paper practices the FNN model using FM pre-trained implicit vector as the input of a fully connected network.

Table 3. Comparison of experimental effects based on discrete features such as table fields and source systems

Model	Precision	Recall	F1-score
FM	0.62	0.66	0.64
DNN	0.78	0.74	0.76
FNN	0.75	0.73	0.73
DeepFM	0.84	0.81	0.82

(4) Confidence score selection of the fusion model and the final various effects:

Finally, two models, ATT-ALE-TextRNN and DeepFM, are combined to mine the semantics of recognizing multiform features. And the evaluation is redefined in such a way that the final result is decided based on the side with the high score by the two parts of the prediction regression. The final prediction results on the top ten domains are shown in Table 4:

Table 4. Comparison of the final types of experimental effects of the fusion model

Overall precision: 0.84 Recall: 0.89 F1-score: 0.86									
Domain name	Security	Finance	Electricity grid	Customer	Personnel	Market	Supplies	Item	Asset	Comprehensive
P	0.50	0.90	0.56	0.88	0.55	0.55	0.87	0.93	0.65	0.67
R	0.52	0.79	0.26	1.00	0.80	0.99	1.00	0.91	0.68	0.71
F1	0.51	0.84	0.35	0.94	0.65	0.71	0.93	0.92	0.66	0.69

The final Precision and Recall values are calculated to be roughly maintained around 0.84 and 0.89. It indicates that the fusion model can indeed play a better effect.

7 Conclusion

Based on the exploration and transformation of the common algorithms of Natural Language Processing, this paper focused on the key technology of semantic recognition to break through the problems of domain name related attribute classification and complementation, intelligent matching, and mapping of the relationship of SG-CIM model of the State Grid, The text polarity classification problem is referenced for table description features for the recognition classification task of domain name related semantic attributes for SG-CIM tables. The ATT-ALE-TextRNN model was proposed, which can capture the importance of different contextual information for a given category tendency, facilitate the discrimination of subtle category differences in a multi-category task, and reduce category confusion. For the field of the table, source system features, with reference to the recommender system multidimensional sparse feature classification problem, a solution using an improved DeepFM model is proposed to facilitate the discovery of semantic dependencies among discrete, class-forming features.

Acknowledgment. This work financially supported by Science and Technology Program of State Grid Corporation of China under Grant No.: SGSJ0000SJJS2100074.

References

1. Wan, Q., Wang, S., He, X.: Application method of Taiwan SG-CIM model in data. Telecommun. Sci. **36**(03), 140–147 (2020)
2. Lu, R., Jin, X., Zhang, S., Qiu, M., Wu, X.: A study on big knowledge and its engineering issues. IEEE Trans. Knowl. Data Eng. **31**(9), 1630–1644 (2018)
3. Qiu, L., Gai, K., Qiu, M.: Optimal big data sharing approach for tele-health in cloud computing. In: IEEE SmartCloud, pp. 184–189 (2016)
4. Qiu, M., Cao, D., et al.: Data transfer minimization for financial derivative pricing using Monte Carlo simulation with GPU in 5G. J. Commun. Syst. **29**(16), 2364–2374 (2016)
5. Lu, Z., Wang, N., Wu, J., Qiu, M.: IoTDeM: An IoT big data-oriented MapReduce performance prediction extended model in multiple edge clouds. JPDC **118**, 316–327 (2018)
6. Liu, M., Zhang, S., et al.: H infinite state estimation for discrete-time chaotic systems based on a unified model. IEEE Trans. Syst. Man Cybern. (B) (2012)
7. Qiu, H., Qiu, M., Lu, Z.: Selective encryption on ECG data in body sensor network based on supervised machine learning. Inform. Fusion **55**, 59–67 (2020)
8. Guo, Y., Zhuge, Q., Hu, J., et al.: Optimal data allocation for scratch-pad memory on embedded multi-core systems. In: IEEE ICPP Conference, pp. 464–471 (2011)
9. Qiu, M., Khisamutdinov, E., et al.: RNA nanotechnology for computer design and in vivo computation. Philos. Trans. Roy. Soc. A **371**, 20120310 (2013)
10. Qiu, M., Chen, Z., Liu, M.: Low-power low-latency data allocation for hybrid scratch-pad memory. IEEE Embed. Syst. Lett. **6**(4), 69–72 (2014)
11. Qiu, M., Xue, C., Shao, Z., Sha, E.: Energy minimization with soft real-time and DVS for uniprocessor and multiprocessor embedded systems. In: IEEE DATE Conference, pp. 1–6 (2007)
12. Wang, J., Wang, J.: Design and implementation of public data model for electric power enterprises based on IEC standard. China Electr. Power **44**(2), 87–90 (2011)
13. Yao, Q.: Network intelligent office management system based on SIP protocol. Doctoral dissertation, Shanghai Jiaotong University
14. Liu, B.: Analysis of intelligent technology of computer search engine. Mod. Inf. Technol. **003**(005), 102–104 (2019)
15. Wang, Y.: Study on the application of natural language processing in collaborative office software. Financ. Electron. (12), 61–63 (2019)
16. Nam, H.: Research on automatic scoring technology of subjective questions based on sentence similarity calculation. Doctoral dissertation, Yanbian University
17. Chen, F.: The evolution analysis of the knowledge map of the "belt and road" research–a survey of core journals at home and abroad. Ningxia Soc. Sci. (1), 156–164 (2018)
18. Li, L.: Bad image detection algorithm based on semantic sparse representation. Doctoral dissertation, Xidian University
19. Li, Z.: Research on fast and accurate classification algorithm for long text based on FastText. Doctoral dissertation, Zhejiang University (2018)

20. Liu, D., Fu, Q., Wei, Y., et al.: Social short text retrieval method based on multiple augmented graphs and topic analysis. Chin. J. Inf. **32**(3), 10 (2018)
21. Joulin, A., Grave, E., Bojanowski, P., Mikolov, T.: Bag of tricks for efficient text classification. arXiv preprint arXiv:1607.01759 (2016)
22. Kalchbrenner, N., Grefenstette, E., Blunsom, P.: A convolutional neural network for modelling sentences. arXiv preprint arXiv:1404.2188 (2014)
23. Liu, P., Qiu, X., Huang, X.: Recurrent neural network for text classification with multi-task learning. arXiv preprint arXiv:1605.05101 (2016)
24. Yang, Z., Yang, D., Dyer, C., He, X., Smola, A., Hovy, E.: Hierarchical attention networks for document classification. In: 2016 Conference of the North American Chapter of the Association for Computational Linguistics: Human Language Technologies, pp. 1480–1489, June 2016
25. Sun, J.: Research on expert recommendation method in community question answering system. Doctoral dissertation, Dalian University of Technology
26. Wang, Y., Huang, M., Zhu, X., Zhao, L.: Attention-based LSTM for aspect-level sentiment classification. In: 2016 Conference on Empirical Methods in Natural Language Processing, pp. 606–615, November 2016
27. Fan, K.: Research on the method of discriminating the tendency of Internet text based on multiple emotional characteristics. Comput. Knowl. Tech. **11**(22), 18–21 (2015)
28. Yan, C., Huang, Y., Xu, G., Huang, Y.: Field perception decomposition machine model based on time dynamics. Control Decis. (1), 5 (2020)
29. Song, R.: Cross-device identification of users and their behavior research. Doctoral dissertation, Southwest University
30. Hu, C., Liang, N.: Subject-specific sentiment analysis of LSTM based on deep attention. Comput. Appl. Res. **36**(4), 5 (2019)
31. Cheng, Y., Yao, L., Xiang, G., Zhang, G., Tang, T., Zhong, L.: Text sentiment orientation analysis based on multi-channel CNN and bidirectional GRU with attention mechanism. IEEE Access **8**, 134964–134975 (2020)
32. Lee, J.Y., Dernoncourt, F.: Sequential short-text classification with recurrent and convolutional neural networks. arXiv preprint arXiv:1603.03827 (2016)
33. Bai, X.: Text classification based on LSTM and attention. In: 2018 Thirteenth International Conference on Digital Information Management (ICDIM), pp. 29–32. IEEE, September 2018
34. Lu, C., Huang, L., Liu, J.: Research on diabetes prediction based on IG-DNN hybrid decision algorithm. Softw. Guide **18**(8), 5 (2019)
35. Liu, H., Lin, N., Chen, Z., Li, K., Jiang, S.: Learning deep matching-aware network for text recommendation using clickthrough data. In: 2019 Conference on IALP, pp. 96–101. IEEE (2019)

BBCT: A Smart Blockchain-Based Bulk Commodity Trade System

Jian Yang[1]([⊠]), Yawen Lu[1], Zhihui Lu[1,2], Jie Wu[1,3], and Hui Zhao[4]

[1] School of Computer Science, Fudan University, Shanghai 200433, China
{jyang18,18210240136,lzh,jwu}@fudan.edu.cn
[2] Shanghai Blockchain Engineering Research Center, Shanghai 200433, China
[3] Peng Cheng Laboratory, Shenzhen 518055, China
[4] Educational Information Technology Laboratory, Henan University, Kaifeng, China
zhh@henu.edu.cn

Abstract. The bulk commodity is a major strategic resource of the country, and related trade markets are booming. However, due to channel isolation and information barriers, the trade platforms also have risks and industry chaos, which make the bulk commodity trade process suffer from information asymmetry, difficulty in choosing a suitable commodity, difficulty in commodity pricing, and lack of trust in the trade platform. To cope with these challenges, we propose BBCT, a *Blockchain-based Bulk Commodity Trade* system, to achieve credible and fair bulk commodity trade. The process of multi-party trade is divided into four stages: matching, negotiation based on time-constrained Bayesian learning, decision-making based on the technique for order preference by similarity to ideal solution and signing. We design a "negotiation-signing" dual-channel blockchain architecture, so that buyers and sellers can complete the negotiation and signing process coordination on the blockchain. We finally verify the efficiency and reliability of BBCT through experiments.

Keywords: Blockchain · Bulk commodity · Hyperledger fabric · Smart contract · Trade negotiation

1 Introduction

The bulk commodity trade market involves national strategic materials such as energy, minerals, cotton, grain, and oil. Bulk commodities have the characteristics of large trade volume, large price fluctuations, large trade risks, and large impact radiation. Participants in bulk commodity trade mainly include buyers, sellers, and trade platforms. Since a single enterprise is like an "information island", it is difficult to find a suitable trade partner. Therefore, some trade platforms that gather resources from different bulk commodity industries appear on the market, and more and more buyers and sellers are attracted to join.

However, the current traditional bulk commodity trade platforms generally have the following problems. (1) Information asymmetry. Buyers and sellers negotiate indirectly through the platform and lack direct communication. (2) There are so many products on the platform that it is difficult for buyers to compare and choose. (3) It is difficult to price products and achieve win-win pricing. There is no theoretical pricing model or formula for bulk commodities. (4) Trade participants lack trust in centralized trade platforms. In recent years, a series of risk events and industry chaos in the bulk commodity market have reflected the severe problems of difficult market supervision and poor platform services.

To solve the above four problems, improve trade efficiency, and build trust between the trade parties and the trade platform, we propose BBCT: a *Blockchain-based Bulk Commodity Trade* system. The main contributions of this paper are as follows:

(1) We have established a blockchain-based agency trade consultation service model, which is divided into four stages: matching, negotiation, decision-making, and signing.
(2) In the negotiation stage, we adopt the Rubinstein bargaining model of game theory and propose a time-constrained Bayesian quotation strategy. In the decision-making stage, we use the technique for order preference by similarity to ideal solution to realize the buyer's personalized multi-attribute decision-making.
(3) We propose a "negotiation-signing" dual-channel blockchain architecture with private data sets. Finally, we verify the efficiency of the BBCT proposed in this paper through experiments.

The remaining contents of this paper are as follows. Section 2 introduces the relevant technology and background. Section 3 analyzes the BBCT model and architecture. Section 4 describes the algorithms in BBCT. Section 5 details the experiments. Finally, Sect. 6 summarizes the paper and shows the future work.

2 Background and Related Work

2.1 Blockchain Technology and Hyperledger Fabric

Blockchain has some excellent applications and research in many fields, such as IoT [1, 2], privacy [3, 4] and digital evidence [5]. In the field of bulk commodity trade, although there are some studies on the application of blockchain in specific commodity scenarios, such as trading electricity [6], the innovation of this paper is to solve the general commodity trade negotiation problem through blockchain. In both negotiation and signing phases of BBCT system in this paper, blockchain technology is adopted to ensure the privacy and safety of the transaction between the buyers and the sellers. Hyperledger Fabric [7] provides an enterprise-level distributed ledger solution based on blockchain. We use Fabric to build our BBCT system. In previous work, we proposed a smart-toy-edge-computing-oriented data exchange prototype [8] that also used Hyperledger Fabric. Fabric uses channel and private data set to protect the data privacy of different nodes. The channel contains several organizational nodes selected and divided by the sorting node, which are different subsets of the sorting node broadcasting on the blockchain. Only some members authorized by the private data set in the channel can obtain the specific content of the data in the private data set.

2.2 Bayesian Learning Model

In the Bayesian view, probability can express all uncertain forms, so the learning process is realized through continuous correction of probability [9]. Bayesian learning was originally a typical example of Bayes' theorem proved by mathematician Thomas Bayes in 1963. In the bilateral price game in this paper, the learner first obtains the prior probability of the learning object, and then uses the Bayesian learning formula to modify the prior probability according to the information obtained in the game process, and finally obtains the posterior probability.

2.3 Multi-attribute Decision Making and TOPSIS

The multi-attribute decision-making problem is a problem of selecting the optimal solution or ranking these solutions among the limited solutions with multiple attributes. Commonly used multi-attribute decision-making methods include Analytic Hierarchy Process [10, 11], TOPSIS (Technique for Order Preference by Similarity to Ideal Solution), RSR (Rank-Sum Ratio) and so on. TOPSIS is very effective and has low requirements for the number of data samples [12], so we choose it. It ranks the quality of the solutions by the "distance" between each attribute of each solution and the corresponding attribute of the ideal optimal solution [13].

3 BBCT Model

3.1 Overall Architecture

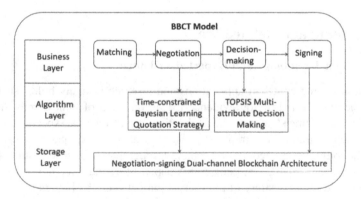

Fig. 1. The architecture of BBCT model.

As shown in Fig. 1, the trade process of the BBCT model is divided into four stages in order—matching, negotiation, decision-making, and signing. In the negotiation phase, buyers and sellers negotiate the price of commodities through automated agents. Participants only need to preset parameters, and the system can negotiate price according to the time-constrained Bayesian learning quotation strategy. The price-based negotiation process is like the Rubinstein model [14], as shown in Fig. 2. The Rubinstein model is a one-to-one bargaining model. Generally, one party proposes a price first, and the other party responds according to its own quotation strategy. If the other party accepts the price, the negotiation will end successfully. Otherwise, the rejecting party will propose a new price in the next round. The round continues until the negotiation succeeds or meets the conditions of failure [15]. In the decision-making stage, the buyer only needs to input its own preference for commodity attributes, and then the TOPSIS method can be used to automatically determine the most suitable commodity.

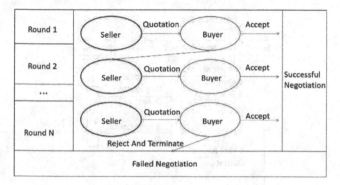

Fig. 2. Negotiation process based on Rubinstein model.

3.2 Blockchain Implementation

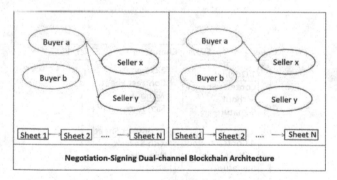

Fig. 3. Dual-channel architecture of BBCT blockchain.

To ensure that the negotiation stage between buyers and sellers is open and transparent, and the final trade contract is recognized by both buyers and sellers, we design a "negotiation-signing" dual-channel blockchain architecture. Buyers and sellers obtain and send information by monitoring and calling the blockchain API. As shown in Fig. 3, the participants joining on these two channels are buyers, sellers, and the trade platform. Such an architecture has the advantages of parallel business, isolated data storage, and

190   J. Yang et al.

strong scalability. In addition, for the purpose of data privacy, each participant only stores information related to itself through the private data set mechanism. The blockchain interaction mechanism of the negotiation channel is shown in Fig. 4. If the negotiation ends successfully, the negotiation sheet information will be generated into the final negotiation sheet. In the negotiation between a buyer and multiple sellers, the buyer will record the transaction ID of each seller's final negotiation sheet and initiate the signing process after the seller is decided according to TOPSIS. The blockchain interaction mechanism of the signing channel is shown in Fig. 5. The fairness of electronic contract signing is to ensure that both parties are in a balance of power during contract exchange and signing [16].

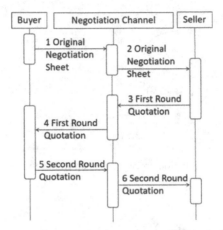

Fig. 4. The interaction sequence diagram of the buyer and the seller in the blockchain negotiation channel.

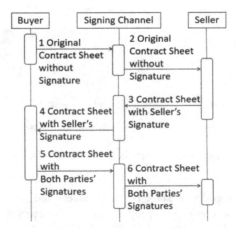

Fig. 5. The interaction sequence diagram of the buyer and the seller in the blockchain signing channel.

4 BBCT Algorithm

4.1 Time-Constrained Bayesian Negotiation Model

Before the buyer and seller start bilateral negotiations on the price, both parties have an expected price and a reserve price for the trade price. The expected price refers to the ideal price that the buyer or seller wants before the negotiation begins. The reserve price refers to the highest price that the buyer can accept or the lowest price that the seller can accept. Only when the buyer's reserve price is not less than the seller's reserve price, can both parties reach a negotiated price. Next, we model the negotiation process between buyers and sellers.

1) Obtain the initial prior probability. At the beginning, the buyer and seller have no record of each other's quotation. Therefore, before the negotiation, the buyer and seller should estimate the reserve price range of the other party based on the historical trade prices and quotations of the other party. Suppose the seller has n estimated values in the estimated buyer's reserve price range $[x_b, y_b]$, which are described by a set of discrete data $V_b (V_{b_i} \in [x_b, y_b], i = 1, 2, \cdots, n)$. Event A_i is used to describe "the seller estimates that the buyer's reserve price is V_{b_i}", and its corresponding probability is $P(A_i)$. It is also assumed that the buyer has m estimated values in the estimated seller reserve price range $[x_s, y_s]$, which are described by a set of discrete data $V_s (V_{s_j} \in [x_s, y_s], j = 1, 2, \cdots, m)$. Event B_j is used to describe "the buyer estimates that the seller's reserve price is V_{s_j}", and its corresponding probability is $P(B_j)$.

2) Assume that in the first round of quotation, the seller proposes a price w_s^1, as shown in formula (1).

$$w_s^1 = E(V_b) = \sum_{i=1}^{n} V_{b_i} P(A_i) \tag{1}$$

x_b^{max} means the buyer's actual reserve price. If $w_s^1 \leq x_b^{max}$, the buyer will accept the seller's price, and the negotiation will end successfully. Otherwise, the buyer will reject the seller's price, the negotiation will continue, and the buyer will propose a new price in the next round of quotation.

3) Quotation in round k (k > 1). After the k − 1 round of quotation, they reach the k round of quotation.

   a) If the buyer in the k − 1 round proposes a price w_b^{k-1}, the seller in the k round will propose a price w_s^k, as shown in formula (2).

$$w_s^k = E(V_b) = \sum_{i=1}^{n} V_{b_i} P\left(A_i | w_b^{k-1}\right) \tag{2}$$

   Where $P\left(A_i | w_b^{k-1}\right)$ is the posterior distribution of the estimated buyer's reserve price calculated by the seller based on the price proposed by the buyer in the k − 1 round, as shown in formula (3).

$$P\left(A_i | w_b^{k-1}\right) = \frac{P(w_b^{k-1} | A_i) P(A_i)}{\sum_{i=1}^{n} P(w_b^{k-1} | A_i) P(A_i)} \tag{3}$$

b) If the seller proposes the price w_s^{k-1} for the $k - 1$ round, the buyer will propose the price w_b^k for the k round, as shown in formula (4) .

$$w_b^k = E(V_s) = \sum_{j=1}^{m} V_{sj} P\left(B_j | w_s^{k-1}\right) \tag{4}$$

Where $P(B_j | w_s^{k-1})$ is the posterior distribution of the estimated seller's reserve price calculated by the buyer based on the price proposed by the seller in round $k - 1$, as shown in formula (5).

$$P\left(B_j | w_s^{k-1}\right) = \frac{P\left(w_s^{k-1} | B_j\right) P(B_j)}{\sum_{j=1}^{m} P\left(w_s^{k-1} | B_j\right) P(B_j)} \tag{5}$$

4) The end of the negotiation. When $w_s^k \leq x_b^{max}$ or $w_b^k \geq x_s^{min}$, the price proposed by one party will be accepted by the other party and the negotiation ends successfully. If the price quoted by one party is equal to its reserve price, but the other party still does not accept the price, the negotiation will fail.

Negotiations have costs. Both buyers and sellers involved in the trade hope to reach a deal within a limited time, and do not want multiple rounds of invalid negotiations. Therefore, based on Bayesian learning, we propose a time-constrained quotation strategy to improve the efficiency of negotiation. We set a time function $f(t)$, as shown in formula (6). T is the estimated total time of this bilateral negotiation, and t represents the time that the current negotiation has been conducted. We can also use negotiation rounds instead of time. In this case, T is the total negotiation round number, and t is the current round number. λ is the time impact factor [17], and its value reflects the urgency of the buyer and seller for the time of this negotiation.

$$f(t) = \left(\frac{t}{T}\right)^{\lambda}, (\lambda > 1, 0 < f(t) < 1) \tag{6}$$

$$w_b = E(V_s) + f_b(t)\left(X_b^{max} - E(V_s)\right) \tag{7}$$

$$w_s = E(V_b) - f_s(t)\left(E(V_b) - X_s^{min}\right) \tag{8}$$

The buyer's quotation is shown in formula (7), where $E(V_s)$ is the buyer's original quotation without time constraint, and $f_b(t)$ is the buyer's time constraint. The seller's quotation is shown in formula (8), where $E(V_b)$ is the seller's original quotation without time constraint, and $f_s(t)$ is the seller's time constraint.

4.2 Personalized Decision Based on TOPSIS

The problem to be solved in the decision-making stage is how to help the buyer select the most suitable product from a batch of candidate products with various attributes. We solve the buyer-oriented multi-attribute decision-making problem by combining the

TOPSIS method with the buyer's designated preference weight. The attribute vector of the product $v = (v_1, v_2, v_3, v_4, v_5)$ represents the five attribute values of product price, delivery speed, product score, seller reputation score, and historical trade quantity respectively.

The buyer presets a vector $w = (w_1, w_2, w_3, w_4, w_5)$ to reflect the buyer's importance and preference for each attribute of the product. It will be used as the weight vector of the attributes in the decision.

Assuming there are n commodities, we first homogenize v to construct an initial matrix $v_{ij}(i = 1, 2, \ldots, n; j = 1, 2, \ldots, 5)$ of n * 5. Then we normalize it to get the normalized vector z_{ij}. Then, we can calculate the weight normalized vector $r_{ij} = w_j z_{ij}$, where w_j is the weight of the j-th attribute input by the buyer. Thus, we can get the weight normalization matrix R, as shown in formula (9).

$$R = \begin{bmatrix} r_{11} & r_{12} & r_{13} & r_{14} & r_{15} \\ r_{21} & r_{22} & r_{23} & r_{24} & r_{25} \\ \cdots & \cdots & \cdots & \cdots & \cdots \\ r_{n1} & r_{n2} & r_{n3} & r_{n4} & r_{n5} \end{bmatrix} \tag{9}$$

$$R^+ = (\max\{r_{11}, r_{21}, \cdots, r_{n1}\}, \cdots, \max\{r_{15}, r_{25}, \cdots, r_{n5}\}) \tag{10}$$

$$R^- = (\min\{r_{11}, r_{21}, \cdots, r_{n1}\}, \cdots, \min\{r_{15}, r_{25}, \cdots, r_{n5}\}) \tag{11}$$

$$D_i^+ = \sqrt{\sum_{j=1}^{5} \left(R_j^+ - r_{ij}\right)^2}, D_i^- = \sqrt{\sum_{j=1}^{5} \left(R_j^- - r_{ij}\right)^2} (i = 1, 2, \cdots, n) \tag{12}$$

$$C_i^+ = \frac{D_i^-}{D_i^+ + D_i^-}(i = 1, 2, \cdots, n) \tag{13}$$

The optimal solution R^+ is composed of the maximum value of each column of R, as shown in formula (10). The worst solution R^- is composed of the minimum value of each column of R, as shown in formula (11). D_i^+/D_i^- respectively represents the closeness of each product to R^+/R^-, which can be calculated by the Euclidean distance calculation method [18], as shown in formula (12). Finally, we calculate the fit degree C_i^+ of each product with the optimal solution as shown in formula (13), where $0 \leq C_i^+ \leq 1$. Buyers pick the products with the highest fit degree.

5 Experiment

We use a test data set to simulate price games between buyers and sellers. Each item in this set contains the price of the first round of quotation and the historical trade prices of both buyers and sellers. By adjusting the negotiation price range between buyers and sellers, we set the overall negotiation success rate of the dataset to 75%.

We use two indicators to measure the quality of the quotation strategy. One is the number of quotation rounds, which represents the efficiency of the negotiation. The other is the joint utility function which is used to measure the gains of the negotiation, as shown in formula (14). U represents the joint utility obtained by both negotiating parties from this price game. P is the final trade price, x_s^{min} is the reserve price for the seller, and x_b^{max} is the reserve price for the buyer. We respectively calculate the average of the two indicators after each case was tested on the data set.

$$U = \frac{\left(P - x_s^{min}\right) * \left(x_b^{max} - P\right)}{\left(x_b^{max} - x_s^{min}\right)^2} \tag{14}$$

Experiment 1 compares the cases of whether the Bayesian learning model is used or not. The quotation strategy of the non-Bayesian learner is based on the expected price, and the price is reduced/increased by 5% in each round. The Bayesian learner's quotation strategy is based on the estimated reserve price of the other party.

We use three types of quotation cases. The first is that both buyers and sellers use a quotation strategy without Bayesian learning. The second is the quotation strategy that only buyers or sellers use Bayesian learning, that is, we use half of the data set to run cases where buyers use Bayesian learning, and the other half are used to run cases where sellers use Bayesian learning. The third is that both buyers and sellers use Bayesian learning quotation strategy. No time function was added in this experiment.

Table 1. The results of cases of whether the Bayesian learning model is used or not.

Case	Average number of quotation rounds	Average joint utility
Both parties without Bayesian learning	8.4	0.140
Only one party with Bayesian learning	6.3	0.108
Both parties with Bayesian learning	4.1	0.227

As shown in Table 1, the experimental results show that the average number of quotation rounds of the strategy based on Bayesian learning is less than that of the strategy without Bayesian learning, and the average utility is higher than that of the strategy without Bayesian learning. When only one party uses Bayesian learning, the average utility is the lowest. Although the number of quotation rounds can be reduced by changing the quotation strategy without Bayesian learning, the quotation strategy cannot be changed once it is set, and it cannot be self-adjusted with the quotation process during the negotiation like a Bayesian learning strategy. Therefore, compared to the case without Bayesian learning, the quotation strategy of Bayesian learning is more effective, which can reduce the average number of quotation rounds and increase the joint utility of both parties.

Experiment 2 compares the case of whether there is time constraint in Bayesian learning. T is the total round of bilateral negotiations, and t represents the current round of negotiations. According to the results of experiment 1, the average number of quotation rounds is above 4. So, we set T to 4.

Table 2. The results of different time factors used by the Bayesian learning model.

Time factor λ	Average number of quotation rounds	Average joint utility
2	2.2	0.110
4	3.2	0.221
6	3.8	0.219
Null	4.1	0.227

As shown in Table 2, the experimental results show that the choice of time factor has an impact on negotiation. When the value of the time factor is set properly, whether the time constraint is included has little effect on the average utility value of the Bayesian learning model but adding the time constraint can reduce the number of negotiation rounds and improve the efficiency of the negotiation.

Table 3. Attribute values of sample products in TOPSIS validation experiment.

Product	Price	Delivery speed	Score	Reputation	Historical trade quantity
A	0.75	0.5	4	5	31000
B	0.8	0.6	4.3	5	8000

Experiment 3 verifies TOPSIS method. The attribute values are shown in Table 3. We set the attribute weight vector $w = (0.5, 0.3, 0.1, 0.08, 0.02)$. Through TOPSIS algorithm, we can calculate that the fit degrees of A and B are 0.9407 and 0.8761 respectively. Therefore, the buyer will choose product A to enter the signing stage.

6 Conclusion

Based on the existing problems exposed in the actual bulk commodity trade scenario, in this paper, we focused on the negotiation and signing stage in the trade process and proposed BBCT—a smart blockchain-based bulk commodity trade system. In BBCT, we decomposed and modeled the trade process, which was divided into four stages: matching, negotiation, decision-making, and signing. In the negotiation stage, the Bayesian learning model was used to update and learn the quotation strategy and propose a more favorable quotation. We also added time constraints to the negotiation model to improve the efficiency of the negotiation phase and save time. In the decision-making stage, the TOPSIS multi-attribute decision-making model was used to allow the buyer to pick the most suitable product among multiple products to improve efficiency and trade experience. Through BBCT's "negotiation-signing" dual-channel blockchain structure, combined with private data collection, buyers and sellers could communicate, coordinate, and store information such as quotations and contracts in the blockchain, ensuring the anti-tampering of transaction data and privacy. Finally, we verified the usability and effectiveness of BBCT through experiments.

In the future, we will consider improvements in the following areas. (1) In the Bayesian learning model, considering the actual situation, the prior probability of the first round of negotiation can be obtained in a more scientific way. (2) In the decision-making process, the decision-maker can flexibly add or delete new decision-making attributes. (3) We can add a conversation-based negotiation method to the current negotiation model and combine natural language processing technology to obtain a more efficient and flexible negotiation method.

Acknowledgment. The work of this paper is supported by the National Key Research and Development Program of China (2019YFB1405000), National Natural Science Foundation of China under Grant (No. 92046024, 61873309), and Shanghai Science and Technology Innovation Action Plan Project under Grant (No. 19510710500, and No. 18510732000).

References

1. Qiu, H., Qiu, M., Memmi, G., Ming, Z., Liu, M.: A dynamic scalable blockchain based communication architecture for IoT. In: Qiu, M. (ed.) SmartBlock 2018. Lecture Notes in Computer Science, vol. 11373, pp. 159–166. Springer, Cham (2018). https://doi.org/10.1007/978-3-030-05764-0_17
2. Gai, K., et al.: Differential privacy-based blockchain for industrial Internet-of-Things. IEEE Trans. Industr. Inf. **16**(6), 4156–4165 (2019)
3. Qiu, M., Liu, X., Qi, Y., Zhao, H., Liu, M.: AI enhanced blockchain (II). In: The 3rd International Conference on Smart BlockChain (SmartBlock), pp. 147–152 (2020)
4. Pan, W., et al.: Application of blockchain in asset-backed securitization. In: IEEE 6th International Conference on Big Data Security (BigDataSecurity) (2020)
5. Tian, Z., et al.: Block-DEF: a secure digital evidence framework using blockchain. Inf. Sci. **491**, 151–165 (2019)
6. Dekker, P., Andrikopoulos, V.: Automating bulk commodity trading using smart contracts. In: IEEE International Conference on Decentralized Applications and Infrastructures (DAPPS) (2020)
7. hyperledger-fabricdocs main documentation. https://hyperledger-fabric.readthedocs.io/en/latest/. Accessed 30 Oct 2021
8. Yang, J., Lu, Z., Wu, J.: Smart-toy-edge-computing-oriented data exchange based on blockchain. J. Syst. Archit. **87**, 36–48 (2018)
9. Eshragh, F., Shahbazi, M., Far, B.: Real-time opponent learning in automated negotiation using recursive Bayesian filtering. Expert Syst. Appl. **128**, 28–53 (2019)
10. Gabriel, S., Riyanarto, S.: AHP-TOPSIS for analyzing job performance with factor evaluation system and process mining. Telkomnika (Telecom. Com. Elec. Cont.) **17**(3), 1344–1351 (2019)
11. Saaty, T.L.: The Analytic Hierarchy Process. Mc Graw-Hill Company, New York (1980)
12. Bapi, D., Duy, D.S., Luis, M., Mark, G.: An evolutionary strategic weight manipulation approach for multi-attribute decision making: TOPSIS method. Int. J. Approx. Reason. **129**, 64–83 (2021)
13. Vavrek, R.: Evaluation of the Impact of selected weighting methods on the results of the TOPSIS technique. Int. J. Inform. Tech. Decis. Making **18**(06), 1821–1843 (2019)
14. Rubinstein, A.: Perfect equilibrium in a bargaining model. Econometrica **50**(1), 97–109 (1982)

15. Torstensson, P.: An n-person Rubinstein bargaining game. Int. Game Theory Rev. 11(1), 111–115 (2009)
16. Al-Saggaf, A., Ghouti, L.: Efficient abuse-free fair contract-signing protocol based on an ordinary crisp commitment scheme. IET Inf. Secur. 9(1), 50–58 (2015)
17. Peyman, F.: Negotiation decision functions for autonomous agents. Robot. Auton. Syst. 24(3–4), 159–182 (1998)
18. Wang, Y., Chardonnet, J., Merienne, F.: Enhanced cognitive workload evaluation in 3D immersive environments with TOPSIS model. Int. J. Hum. Comput. Stud. 147, 102572 (2021)

Research on Data Fault-Tolerance Method Based on Disk Bad Track Isolation

Xu Zhang[✉], Li Zheng, and Sujuan Zhang

College of Software Engineering, Xiamen University of Technology, Xiamen 361024, China
lzhangxu@xmut.edu.cn

Abstract. Disk is not only an important carrier to save data, but also a key component of storage system. It is of great significance to improve the reliability and data availability of disk. In the big data environment, the number of disks in the storage system is huge and distributed, so the maintenance for disk failure is inefficient and costly. Disk bad track is one of the most common disk faults. To solve this problem, this paper proposes a disk bad track isolation algorithm. This approach uses a data fault-tolerance mechanism to isolate physical bad tracks, effectively reducing the disk failure rate, improving service stability, and reducing system maintenance costs. The results show that the bad track isolation method can reduce the Disk IO exception by 47%, and significantly reduce the disk failure rate. It is effective in improving system stability and reducing maintenance cost.

Keywords: Data fault-tolerance · Hard disk · Disk bad track · Cloud storage · Data center · S.M.A.R.T

1 Introduction

With the development of mobile internet, IOT [1], Blockchain [2, 3], artificial intelligence [4], big data and other fields, the daily data volume of enterprises and individuals is growing exponentially. The world is entering the era of data explosion, traditional storage systems have encountered bottlenecks. As a new IT resource ecology, cloud storage has emerged as powerful platforms in the era of big data. At present, in some large-scale distributed application environments, the number of disks is large and scattered so the disk failure rate is high and difficult to maintain [5]. For example, in a large data center or IDC edge node, when a disk fails, engineers are usually arranged to replace the failed disk after the disk drops or seriously affects the business service quality. This maintenance mode is inefficient and often cannot meet the business needs. Moreover, bad disk track is one of the most common faults of disk. If a new disk is used to replace a disk with only a few bad tracks, it will cause a large cost waste.

Traditional disk fault definition and maintenance methods have some disadvantages. Disk reuse through disk bad track isolation technology can improve disk availability and reduce the frequency and cost for on-site maintenance.

According to statistics, hard disk is the main fault source in the current data center, and the proportion of Microsoft data center is 78% [6]. One of the main reasons for hard

M. Qiu et al. (Eds.): SmartCom 2021, LNCS 13202, pp. 198–207, 2022.
https://doi.org/10.1007/978-3-030-97774-0_18

disk failures is the bad track. According to the software or hardware failure, the disk bad track can be divided into logical and physical. Logical bad track is generally caused by the data verification error and it can be repaired as long as the logical bad track is written [7]. Physical bad track is a real physical damage, which is generally irreparable [8–10]. The disk has some reserved areas for remapping the physical bad track (G-List), but the reserved area space is limited. When the disk reads the bad track area, it will repeatedly try to read until I/O times out, then the disk performance will decline sharply [11, 12]. When there are few bad tracks, the load of disk is temporarily high. In addition, if there are many bad tracks on the disk, it will cause the disk to slow down seriously [13–15].

The research to date has tended to focus on logical bad track rather than physical bad track. The main contribution of this research is to improve the reliability and stability of storage system based on the technology of physical bad track isolation.

2 Related Work

In recent years, most research on disk storage reliability can be divided into two categories. One is based on the hardware layer, mainly through *Redundant Arrays of Inexpensive Disks* (RAID) [16–18]. RAID5 with redundant single disk failure and RAID6 with dual disks failure are the most commonly used. Some hardware manufacturers have also studied relevant technologies. Xiotech company proposed intelligent storage element technology (ISE) [19], which realizes fault prevention and repair by enclosing preventive and repair parts in the storage capacity module, improving the disk working environment and disk repair processes.

In 1995, Compaq company invented S.M.A.R.T. (Self Monitoring Analysis and Reporting Technology), which has become a standard hard disk drive condition monitoring and fault early warning technology in the industrial field [20–22]. Then there are many researches based on S.M.A.R.T. technology, mainly using different algorithms to build hard disk fault prediction model, which has also achieved certain results. Yang Hongzhang of PKU proposes a whole process proactive fault tolerant on "Collection-Prediction-Migration-Feedback" mechanism which predict hard disk failures and migrate data ahead of time [23]. Jia runying and Li Jing of Nankai University realized the hard prediction model based on adaboost and genetic algorithm, which can improve the accuracy [24]. Hu Wei of NUDT studied the self-recovery storage system based on intelligent early warning, which can use the machine learning method to predict the disk failure. For the warning disk, through the data migration protection strategy, the storage reliability and availability is significantly improved [25]. Other researches use machine learning algorithms, including reverse neural network, decision tree, support vector machine and simple Bayes, which are verified and analyzed based on S.M.A.R.T. information. These studies focus on the prediction accuracy and the universality of applicable scenarios [26–28].

Although these studies have made in-depth research on system reliability and data fault-tolerance from the hardware layer and software layer, they have not effectively solved the fundamental problem of disk failure and data loss. Once disk failure occurs, the risk of data loss still exists. Moreover, from the perspective of disk failure rate, those studies cannot reduce the disk failure rate and do not improve the system maintenance.

In order to solve the above problems, we attempt to realize the algorithm of disk bad track isolation to improve the storage reliability and stability, based on the S.M.A.R.T. technology and the principle of bad track of disk. This method can be used alone or as a supplement to the above research and it will be very useful for the big data center with large-scale disks.

3 System Design and Implementation

In order to achieve the above purpose, the research implements a program of disks with bad track. The program obtains the target disk to be processed through monitoring, and detects the bad track in the target disk. By combining the bad track area, the available area in the target disk other than the bad track area can be obtained. If the target disk is judged to be available by the detection model, it will be reconstructed and set to online. In this study, the monitoring model can automatically identify whether the target disk needs bad track test. The health status information of the target disk can be obtained regularly, and used to determine whether the target disk needs test. When the bad track test is required, the bad track areas will be merged and isolated. So we can obtain the available areas excluding the bad track areas of the target disk. Due to the existence of bad track area, the available area may show discrete distribution in the target disk. Specifically, the target disk can be divided into multiple partitions according to the available area, and these partitions can be combined into one volume. After formatting the merged volume, the target disk can be reused.

This method does not need to replace the disk in case of a small number of bad tracks, but can make full use of the available area. Therefore, it can improve the processing efficiency of failed disks while saving disk resources.

3.1 System Architecture

The system implemented in this study mainly includes three modules.

Disk Monitoring Module (DMM)
In the actual business, especially in the big data environment, the number of disks is huge and the operation status is diverse. It is necessary to monitor and predict the status of disks. For a model being used online, it is very important to control the stability and utility of the model in real time. So our research needs a perfect monitoring module to help us fully master the status of the disk and locate it in time. The disk health model is defined in the DMM, which defines and obtains the sub-health target disk according to the S.M.A.R.T. information, and the bad track data of the target disk is detected and recorded.

Bad Track Isolation Module (BTIM)
After collecting the data of the target disk and its bad channel, the bad track isolation of the disk is realized in this module. The module first performs a bad track test on the target disk. It needs to stop the service in the target disk or the in the server where the target disk is located, and then isolate the bad track of the target disk. In this module, a

minimum area coverage algorithm based on linear bisection is implemented to isolate the bad track of the target disk. By merging the bad track area of the target disk and eliminating it, it can be used as an available area.

Disk Reconstruction Module (DRCM)

This module retests the target disk to determine whether the it can continue to be used. It is mainly measured by three indicators, including the number of bad tracks, the capacity of available areas and the number of partitions of available areas. After the disk is judged to be available, the disk can be divided into multiple partitions according to the obtained available area. Then the multiple partitions can be combined into a volume, which can be used as the reconstructed storage space. The storage directory will be reconstructed according to the recorded target disk access parameters. After the reconstruction, the disk can continue to be used, and the service can be resumed.

3.2 System Implementation

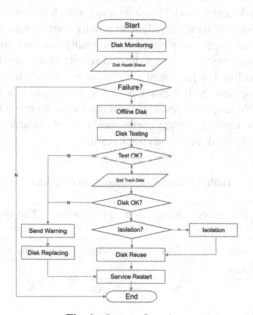

Fig. 1. System flowchart

In this study, the health status of the target disk is obtained through DMM, mainly including the self-checking information of the target disk, the log information of the operating system where the target disk is located and the input and output load information of the target disk (Fig. 1).

Disk Self-checking Information
Disk Self-checking Information mainly comes from the S.M.A.R.T. information retained in the service area of the disk. S.M.A.R.T. instructions can be divided into main commands and subcommands. The main commands provide information on whether the disk supports S.M.A.R.T. or ignores the characteristics of a certain instruction. The subcommands provide detection information supporting S.M.A.R.T. disk. In the S.M.A.R.T. information, you can display whether the target hard disk fails and whether the target disk has errors during operation. You can judge whether there are a large number of errors on the target disk according to the number of errors.

System Log Information
System log information can refer to the message information of the operating system, which can indicate whether there are read-write errors on the target disk and whether there are file system errors.

I/O Load Information
I/O load information can indicate whether the target disk is running under high load.

    In this study, a disk health model is established, which preset the multiple running status of the target disk. and then the judgment results corresponding to each operation state can be determined respectively based on the health state information of the target disk, so as to obtain the combination of judgment results of the target disk. Then, based on the health information, the judgment results corresponding to each running status can be determined respectively. For example, Table 1 lists multiple running states, and illustrates each possible judgment results. When the judgment result of the target disk is obtained, the preset processing strategy corresponding to the health model can be called to determine whether the disk needs bad track testing.

Table 1. Hard disk failure analysis model

Failed	High load	Few errors	Many errors	Disk errors	File system errors	Processing strategy
Y	Any	Any	Any	Any	Any	Replacing
N	Y	Any	Y	Any	Any	Replacing
N	Y	Y	N	Any	Any	Bad track testing
N	Y	Any	N	Y	Any	Bad track testing
N	Y	N	N	N	Y	Formating
N	N	Any	Any	Any	Any	/

    When it is necessary to perform a bad track test on the target disk, it is necessary to suspend the service in the target disk. Generally, common applications support temporarily removing the target disk from the server. When performing a bad track test on the target disk, first repair the logical bad track in the target disk, and then save the irreparable bad track data to a specified file, which can be preset in the operating system. After that, when analyzing the bad track data, we can read the bad track data through the access path of the specified file. After the bad track test is completed, the bad track data in the specified file can be analyzed. This method stores the bad track data into an one-dimensional array of nonnegative integers. Each element in the array can represent a bad track with a capacity of 4 KB and the value represent the location of the bad track on the target disk. For example, the element value N can represent the $(N + 1)$th area with a capacity of 4 KB in the target disk.

Considering the space utilization, this study adopts the linear bisection minimum area coverage algorithm to cover the area where the bad track is located. By isolating the area covering the bad track from the target disk, the available area in the target disk can be obtained. Then we can find the sub regions with bad tracks. As shown in Fig. 2, the shadow filled sub region can be used as the target sub region with bad tracks.

After determining the target sub region of each bad track, in order to avoid the region of bad channel being too discrete, adjacent target sub regions whose interval meets the specified conditions can be merged to obtain multiple merged regions.

When merging the target sub regions, the adaptive region can be used to cover multiple target sub regions whose intervals meet the specified conditions. The condition can mean that the number of sub regions separated between two adjacent target sub regions is less than or equal to the specified number threshold. For example, we set the threshold to 2, which means taking 2% of the total capacity of the target disk. Then, as long as the interval between two adjacent target sub regions does not exceed 2 sub regions, the two adjacent target sub regions can be merged. As shown in Fig. 2, the regions merge result is as follows:

- The first and second target sub regions are separated by one sub region, so the two target sub regions can be merged. When merging the two target sub regions, the sub regions contained between the two target sub regions need to be merged together. Therefore, the merged region after preliminary merging can include three sub regions.
- Since there are 4 sub regions between the second target sub region and the third target sub region, which do not meet the merging conditions, the second target sub region and the third target sub region will not be merged.
- The third, fourth and fifth target sub regions meet the merging conditions, so the three target sub regions can be merged together with the sub regions separated between them, and the merged region can include four sub regions.

After merging the target sub regions into merged regions, an isolation region may be determined at the head and or tail of each merged region. As shown in Fig. 2, because the first merge area is at the head of the target disk, only one sub area is used as the isolation area at the tail of the merge area. In this way, the four sub areas in the dotted box can be used as the bad track area. Since the second merge area is in the middle of the target disk, one sub area can be determined at the head and tail as the isolation area, so that the six sub areas in the dotted box can be used as the bad track area. After the bad track is isolated to obtain the bad track area, the area other than the bad track area can be used as the available area in the target disk.

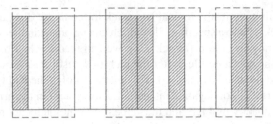

Fig. 2. Disk bad track isolation

After detecting and isolating the bad track, we can judge whether the target disk can continue to be used according to the detection results. In this study, the number of bad tracks, the capacity of available areas and the number of partitions of available areas are comprehensively considered. The conditions for determining that the target disk is unavailable mainly include the following three:

- The number of detected bad tracks is greater than the specified threshold number of bad tracks.
- The space capacity of the available area obtained is less than the specified capacity threshold.
- The number of partitions after partitioning according to the available area is greater than the threshold value of the specified number of partitions.

For the available target disk, a continuous plurality of available areas can be divided into one partition, so as to divide the target disk into multiple partitions. In Fig. 2, the empty white sub areas outside the dotted box are available areas. The remaining available areas are divided into two zones. The first zone contains two sub areas and the second zone contains only one sub area. After dividing the available area into multiple partitions, the multiple partitions can be merged into one volume through the LVM (logical volume manager) function, and the merged volume can be used as the reconstructed storage space. Then, these partitions can be merged into one volume through the LVM, and the merged volume can be used as the rebuilt storage space.

According to the volume label and mount point of the target disk recorded before, the access parameters are set after the reconstructed storage space is obtained. The target disk after bad track isolation and reconstruction can continue to be used. Here, we can resume the business and complete this work.

4 Experiment

We did the experiment in a real big data application environment which the running time of the system is more than 3 years, and the average power on time of the disks have exceeded 25000 h. The specific test environment is as follows (Table 2).

In order to verify the impact of this scheme on disk performance, we found two disks on the same server according to the log, which are enabled bad channel isolation and not. In the same server, it can be considered that the load of two disks is equal, which

Table 2. Testing environment

Hardware	Software
Per Cpu: 32cores	OS: CentOS 6.5
Per memory: 128G	App: Cloudera 5.13.2
Per disks: 8192G*12	Storage system: Hadoop 2.6.0

can be proved from the trend of the two curves in Fig. 3. As shown in Fig. 3, sdf is the disk with bad track isolation enabled and sde is the normal disk. The right side of the red vertical bar is the load of the sdf disk after enabling bad track isolation. Through the curve, it is found that the I/O Util of disk SDE is greater than 50%, which is 47% lower than that of SDF. This indicates a significant improvement in disk performance.

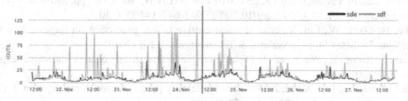

Fig. 3. Single disk performance testing

5 Conclusion

In this study, the disk bad track isolation was used to improve the performance of disk and reduce the failure rate, so as to improve the system reliability and cost performance of large-scale disk applications. From the test results of the actual system, it could be seen that this research can significantly improve the I/O performance of the disk and greatly reduce the failure rate of the disk. Today, with the continuous development of big data, the volume of data is still growing rapidly, and there will be more and more application scenarios of large-scale disks. This research will also play an increasingly important role.

References

1. Liang, W., Ning, Z., Xie, S., Hu, Yu., Lu, S., Zhang, D.: Secure fusion approach for the internet of things in smart autonomous multi-robot systems. Inf. Sci.1–20 (2021). https://doi.org/10.1016/j.ins.2021.08.035
2. Liang, W., Zhang, D., Lei, X., Tang, M., Li, K., Zomaya, A.: Circuit copyright blockchain: blockchain-based homomorphic encryption for IP circuit protection. IEEE Trans. Emerg. Top. Comput. 1 (2020). https://doi.org/10.1109/TETC.2020.2993032

3. Liang, W., Xiao, L., Zhang, K., Tang, M., He, D., Li, K.C.: Data fusion approach for collaborative anomaly intrusion detection in blockchain-based systems. IEEE Internet Things J. 1 (2021). https://doi.org/10.1109/JIOT.2021.3053842

4. Liang, W., et al.: Deep neural network security collaborative filtering scheme for service recommendation in intelligent cyber-physical systems. IEEE Internet Things J. (2021). https://doi.org/10.1109/JIOT.2021.3086845

5. Hughes, G.F., Murray, J.F., Kreutz-Delgado, K., et al.: Improved disk-drive failure warnings. IEEE Trans. Reliab. 51(3), 350–357 (2002)

6. Li, J., Wang, G., Liu, X., Li, Z.: Overview of storage system reliability prediction. J. Front. Comput. Sci. Technol. 11(03), 341–354 (2017)

7. Xu, C.: Research and design of disaster data recovery system. Chongqing University of technology (2010)

8. Xie, Y., Dan, F., Fang, W., et al.: OME: an optimized modeling engine for disk failure prediction in heterogeneous datacentre. In: 2018 IEEE 36th International Conference on Computer Design (ICCD). IEEE Computer Society (2018)

9. Zhao, Y., Liu, X., Gan, S., Zheng, W.: Predicting disk failures with HMM- and HSMM-based approaches. In: Perner, P. (ed.) ICDM 2010. LNCS (LNAI), vol. 6171, pp. 390–404. Springer, Heidelberg (2010). https://doi.org/10.1007/978-3-642-14400-4_30

10. Zhu, B., Gang, W., Liu, X., et al.: Proactive drive failure prediction for large scale storage systems. In: Mass Storage Systems & Technologies. IEEE (2013)

11. Xiao, J., Xiong, Z., Wu, S., et al.: Disk failure prediction in data centers via online learning, pp. 1–10 (2018)

12. Li, J., Wang, G., Liu, X., Li, Z.: Review of reliability prediction for storage system. J. Front. Comput. Sci. Technol. 11(03), 341–354 (2017)

13. Jia, Y., Li, J., Jia, R., et al.: Hard disk failure prediction model validation in large data center environment. J. Comput. Res. Dev. 52(S2), 54–61 (2015)

14. Jiang, S., Du, C., Chen, H., Li, J., Wu, J.: An unsupervised adversarial learning method for hard disk fault prediction. J. Xidian Univ. 47(02), 118–125 (2020)

15. Tan, Y., Gu, X.: On predictability of system anomalies in real world. In: 2010 IEEE International Symposium on Modeling, Analysis and Simulation of Computer and Telecommunication Systems, pp. 133–140 (2010). https://doi.org/10.1109/MASCOTS.2010.22

16. Patterson, D.A., Gibson, G.A., Katz, R.H.: A case for redundant arrays of inexpensive disks (RAID). In: Proceedings of the International Conference on Management of Data (SIGMOD), 109–116. ACM, New York (1988)

17. Hamerly, G., Elkan, C.: Bayesian approaches to failure prediction for disk drives (2003)

18. Agarwal, V., Bhattacharyya, C., Niranjan, T., et al.: Discovering rules from disk events for predicting hard drive failures. In: International Conference on Machine Learning & Applications. IEEE Computer Society (2009)

19. Xiotech: ISE-The new foundation of data storage, 08 May 2008. http://www.xiotech.com/ise-technoloty.php

20. Lei, Z., Qiu, M., Tseng, W.C., et al.: Variable partitioning and scheduling for MPSoC with virtually shared scratch pad memory. J. Signal Process. Syst. 58(2), 247–265 (2010)

21. Guo, Y., Zhuge, Q., Hu, J., et al.: Optimal data allocation for scratch-pad memory on embedded multi-core systems. In: International Conference on Parallel Processing. IEEE (2011)

22. Vishwanath, K.V., Nagappan, N.: Characterizing cloud computing hardware reliability. In: Proceedings of the 1st ACM symposium on Cloud computing (SoCC 2010), pp. 193–204. Association for Computing Machinery, New York (2010)

23. Yang, H., Yang, Y., Tu, Y., Sun, G., Wu, Z.: Proactive fault tolerance based on "collection—prediction—migration—feedback" mechanism. J. Comput. Res. Dev. 57(02), 306–317 (2020)

24. Jia, R., Li, J., Wang, G., Li, Z., Liu, X.: Optimization and choice of hard disk fault prediction model based on AdaBoost and genetic algorithm. J. Comput. Res. Dev. **51**(S1), 148–154 (2014)
25. Hu, W., Liu, G., Li, Q., Liu, X.: Research on intelligent failure prediction based self-healing storage system. J. Comput. Res. Dev. **48**(S1), 7–11 (2011)
26. Qiu, M., Chen, Z., Liu, M.: Low-power low-latency data allocation for hybrid scratch-pad memory. IEEE Embed. Syst. Lett. **6**(4), 69–72 (2014)
27. Murray, J.F., Hughers, G., Kreutz-Delgado, K.: Hard drive failure prediction using non-parametric statistical methods. In: Procof the ICANN/ICONIP, p. 1 (2003)
28. Murray, J.F., Hughes, G.F., et al.: Machine learning methods for predicting failures in hard drives: a multiple-instance application. J. Mach. Learn. Res. (2005)

Charge Prediction for Criminal Law with Semantic Attributes

Cong Zhou, Weipeng Cao$^{(\boxtimes)}$, and Zhiwu Xu$^{(\boxtimes)}$

College of Computer Science and Software Engineering, Shenzhen University,
Shenzhen, China
{caoweipeng,xuzhiwu}@szu.edu.cn

Abstract. Most of the existing machine learning methods for charge prediction adopt the training mechanism of supervised learning. These algorithms have high requirements for the number of training samples corresponding to each crime. However, few or no cases are corresponding to some crimes in real scenarios, which leads to the poor performance of these models in practice. To alleviate this problem, we propose a novel Zero-Shot Learning (ZSL) based method for legal charge prediction tasks. Specifically, we define a set of semantic attributes to represent the domain knowledge of charges, which enables the model to migrate knowledge from seen charges to unseen charges. In this way, with the help of the ZSL mechanism, unseen charges and charges with a small number of training samples could be relatively predicted accurately. We evaluate the performance of the proposed method on a dataset collected from China Judgements Online, and the experimental results show that our method obtains 32.4% accuracy for the unseen charges and can largely retain the predictive power for the seen charges.

1 Introduction

In recent years, driven by emerging technologies such as big data, cloud computing, and the Internet-of-Things (IoT), application areas such as intelligent prediction of legal charges, Body Sensor Networks (BSNs) [1], tel-health systems [2], and real-time embedded systems [3] have all been rapidly developed. Among them, the intelligent prediction of legal charges can be considered as a classification problem based on case description and factual text data. A popular way to solve this type of problem is to use neural network algorithms, especially deep learning. For example, in 2017, Luo et al. [4] provided an attention-based neural network to predict legal charges. Although neural network-based models have achieved promising accuracy on many benchmarks, there is a problem that cannot be ignored: most models need to collect a large number of cases corresponding to each crime during training. In other words, each criminal charge to be predicted requires enough training samples. However, in the real world, this premise is difficult to meet. For example, for some criminal charges such as "treason", there are very few public cases. Even for many criminal charges, one cannot collect any public cases. This problem leads to the poor performance of

M. Qiu et al. (Eds.): SmartCom 2021, LNCS 13202, pp. 208–217, 2022.
https://doi.org/10.1007/978-3-030-97774-0_19

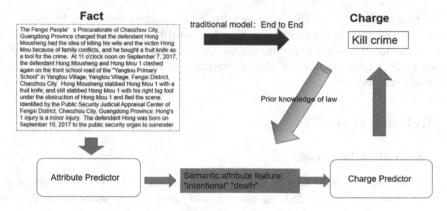

Fig. 1. An illustration of attribute-based charge prediction

many existing charge prediction models in practice. To solve the few-shot learning problem in the criminal charge prediction problem, Hu et al. [5] applied the less-sample learning and provided a charge attribute based method to assist in charge prediction. However, this method still cannot effectively deal with the zero-shot learning problem.

To alleviate the above problem, we propose to employ Zero-Shot Learning (ZSL) technique [6] to improve the prediction accuracy of the model on those charges with limited training samples. The premise of using ZSL is that a reasonable connection can be established between the unseen classes and the seen classes so that the model can transfer the reasoning ability learned from the seen classes to the prediction of the unseen classes [7,8]. For the problem studied in this paper, the first issue we have to solve is how to construct a semantic association among the majority criminal charges, minority criminal charges, and the criminal charges without any cases.

Therefore, according to the description of the provisions of the articles in the official documents and combined with the knowledge of the legal field, we define 19 semantic attributes (e.g., the manner of committing the crime, related objects, violence, and personal rights) for the criminal articles. These semantic attributes serve as a bridge between charges. With the help of the semantic attributes, we can use the ZSL technique to build an intelligent prediction model for legal charges. Specifically, using a large number of training samples for the seen classes, an intrinsic mapping model from the case fact text to attribute features can be obtained, which enables us to transfer the legal charge prediction from the text level to the attribute level, as shown in Fig. 1. As there is still a data imbalance problem at the attribute level, we also introduce the synthetic minority over-sampling technique (SMOTE) [9] to improve the performance of the attribute predictor. Our main contributions are summarized as follows:

– We defined a set of semantic attributes for the charges of Criminal Law and constructed a ZSL-oriented dataset for criminal charge prediction.

- We proposed a ZSL/GZSL approach for legal charge prediction, focusing on the charges with fewer or even no training samples.
- We conducted several experiments on the self-constructed dataset, and the experimental results confirm the effectiveness of our semantic attributes and our charge prediction.

2 Related Work

2.1 Zero-Shot Learning

The concept of ZSL was first proposed as a problem in 2008 by Larochelle et al. [10]. They formulated ZSL in general and used experiments to verify the feasibility and significance of ZSL in character recognition and multi-task sorting problems. In 2009, Lampert et al. [11] first proposed to solve the problem of unseen class recognition by introducing attribute based classification - direct attribute prediction model (DAP) [12] and Indirect attribute prediction model (IAP) [13], and also proposed the "Animals with Attributes" dataset, which is nowadays the most common ZSL dataset in computer vision. In the same year, Farhadi et al. [14] first transformed the class identification problem into an attribute description problem by generalizing attributes across classes and using the semantic information of attributes as a bridge between seen classes and unseen classes, thus enabling knowledge migration from seen classes to unseen classes. We recommend that readers refer to the review on ZSL for more progress in this field [6].

2.2 Charge Prediction

Although researchers in the legal field have always wanted to achieve intelligent legal judgments by machines, the methods proposed in the early years were quite limited due to technical limitations. It was only after the rapid development of machine learning and its successful application in several fields that legal charge prediction was gradually improved and made possible. In 2012, Lin et al. [15] extracted 21 feature labels for this purpose and designed a machine learning model for classification. In recent years, researchers have suggested combining neural networks with natural language processing. In 2017, Luo et al. [16] provided an attention-based neural network approach to train a charge prediction model. However, the above modes are built on charges with sufficient training data, which is ineffective in the charges with fewer samples. In 2018, to improve the performance on the charges with fewer samples, Hu et al. [5] provide a method based on the attributes of the charges for charge prediction. The method selected 10 representative attribute characteristics, including violence, profitable purpose, buying, and selling. But this method is still limited to focusing attention on supervised learning and almost ineffective in unseen charges.

3   Approach

In this section, we present our approach for charge prediction. We first define a set of semantic attributes to represent charge classes, and then propose a charge prediction method based on the semantic attributes.

3.1   Semantic Attributes of Offence

In ZSL, the classes that appear in the training phase are called seen classes while the ones that do not appear in the training phase are called unseen classes. To predict the unseen classes, one needs to express information of the unseen classes in terms of the one of seen class. Semantic Attributes are one of the effective way to bridge between seen and unseen classes as well as achieve knowledge migration. In this section, we define a set of semantic attributes, according to the description of the offences of criminal law.

To start with, we introduce the principles for defining of the semantic attributes:

1. Semantic attributes should be derived from the descriptions of each charge.
2. Semantic attributes should be able to distinguish different charges.
3. Most of semantic attributes should be common (*i.e.*, involved to a good number of charges, including the seen and unseen charges).

Clearly, these principles enable the knowledge migration between charges.

Guided by these principles, we carefully study the Criminal Law of the People's Republic of China, which consists of ten chapters and four hundred and fifty-one legal provisions in total. Then we find out the legal provisions related to the crime, and represent them as crime-provision pairs (crime, provision description). For example, one of the pair is (kill crime, intentional homicide), representing that the conditions for forming the Kill crime are *intentional* and causing *death* of the victim. Another example is (negligent homicide crime, negligence causing death), whose crime is quite closed to kill crime but its description emphasizes the condition of *negligence*, instead of *intentional*. This demonstrates our semantic attributes could help us to distinguish different (but similar) crimes. Some of these attributes are common to most crimes, such as *death* appear in both kill crime and negligent homicide crime. Moreover, some common attributes can be used as a necessary condition for the crime, such as the kill crime must satisfy the *death* condition. In addition, some (values of the) attributes are very representative so that then can be used as a sufficient condition. For example, if the location for crime is an ancient tomb, then clearly the crime is the one of excavation of ancient cultural sites. Such attributes can clearly distinguish the corresponding crimes from other ones.

Finally, according to logical perceptions, we grouped the extracted attributes into several classes, which contributes to making the attribute more general. For example, *intentional* and *negligence* can be grouped into *intent*. And both *death* and *detention* involve personal rights, so we group them into *personal rights*.

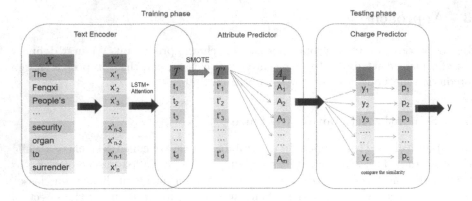

Fig. 2. Framework of charge prediction

Other attribute categories include, for example, consequences, location, violence, etc. In total, we define 19 semantic attributes and 153 features (*i.e.*, attribute values) in total.

3.2 Charge Prediction

In this section, we present our approach for charge prediction, based on semantic attributes we defined for the criminal law. The key idea of our approach is to reduce the task of charge prediction into the one of attribute prediction. Figure 2 shows the framework of our approach, which consists of three components, namely, *text encoder*, *attribute predictor*, and *charge predictor*. *Text encoder* encodes the factual text of the case into a multi-dimensional vector word by word, according to a pre-trained corpus; fed by the multidimensional vector from *text encoder*, *attribute predictor* predicts the semantic attributes for the case, and finally, *charge predictor* output a charge according to the predicted semantic attributes.

To start with, we give a formal definition of charge prediction. The charge prediction task is defined as a function (or model) $M : X \to Y$, where X denotes the set of the given cases and Y denotes the set of charges. Let Y_s denote the set of seen charges and Y_u denote the set of unseen charges. Thus, we have $Y = Y_u$ and $Y = Y_u \cup Y_s$ for ZSL and GZSL, respectively. Moreover, a sample data in charge prediction is represented as (x, y), where $x \in X$ is the factual text of a case and represented as its word sequence $x = [x_1, x_2, \ldots, x_n]$, n is the length of the factual text, and $y \in Y$ is the true charge of the case. Let W denote the set of words appearing in X. We assume there is a pre-trained corpus for W.

Text Encoder. According to the pre-trained corpus of W, each word x_i of a case x is first converted into a multi-Dimensional word vector x_i', where $x_i' \in R^{wd}$ and wd is dimension of the word vector. Then the resulting word vector sequence $x' = [x_1', x_2', \ldots, x_n']$ is fed into a neural network to extract semantic information from the text, wherein Long Short-Term Memory (LSTM) and Self-Attention Mechanism are used. The result is a vector $T = [t_1, t_2, \ldots, t_d]$ representing the semantic information of the text, where d is the text vector dimension. Let $E : X \rightarrow R^d$ denote the text encoder.

Attribute Predictor. To achieve knowledge migration between seen charges and unseen charges, we define a set of semantic attributes for charges in Sect. 3.1. Based on this set, we represent each charge y_i as a vector of semantic attributes, that is, $y_i = [a_1, a_2, \ldots, a_m]$, where $y_i \in Y$, a_i is a semantic attribute, and m is the number of semantic attributes. According to Principle 2, the vector of each charge is different. As mentioned before, we reduce the original text-to-crime prediction task into the text-to-attribute prediction one. Formally, the attribute prediction task is defined as a function $F : T \rightarrow [A_1, A_2, \ldots, A_m]$, where T is the set of possible text vectors and A_i is the set of features for the i-th semantic attribute.

Given a text vector T, the attribute predictor for each attribute is trained by sampling the true charges $\hat{y}$. However, although we consider the attributes that are as common as possible, there are still some attributes that only appear in several similar charges, due to that they are critical to these similar charges. This could yield the problem that the distribution of samples for different attributes is extremely unbalanced, resulting in a model tending to favor the charge with more attribute samples. Therefore, we have to consider the attributes with fewer samples. For that, we introduce the SMOTE algorithm to expand the original training set T to a set T' containing the original and generated samples, such that the distribution of samples for each attributes is relatively balanced. The basic idea of the SMOTE algorithm is to analyze the samples of the minority classes and artificially synthesize new samples and add them to the dataset.

Once the attribute predictors are trained, we are able to predict the semantic attributes for the factual text for a given case. In detail, given a case x, the predict attribute vector for x is $A_x = F(E(x)) = [a_1, a_2, \ldots, a_m]$, where $a_i \in A_i$ is predicted by the i-attribute predictor.

Charge Predictor. Our goal is to predict a charge. Thus, after predicting an attribute vector $A_x = [a_1, a_2, \ldots, a_m]$ for a given case x, we compare the attribute vector A_x with the predefined attribute vector A_i of each charge y_i, and take the most similar one as the predicted result. Here we use the cosine similarity, which is computed as follows:

$$p_x = \frac{A_x \cdot A_i}{\sqrt{|A_x| * |A_i|}} \tag{1}$$

where p_x denotes the similarity between the predicted attribute vector A_x and the i-attribute vector A_i. And the final predicted charge

$$y_x = y_{h(max(p_1, p_2, \ldots, p_c))} \tag{2}$$

where $h(max(p_1, p_2, \ldots, p_c))$ is a function that returns the index for the maximum value and c denotes the number of charges.

Finally, as a notice, the time complexities of our approach in the training phase and the prediction phase are respectively $O(m \times |X|)$ and $O(m + |Y|)$, where m is the number of attributes.

4   Experiments

We construct a ZSL-oriented dataset from *China Judgements Online*[1] (Sect. 4.1), following the way in Sect. 3.1. With this dataset, we evaluate the performance of our proposed ZSL charge prediction model (Sect. 4.2). We also perform ablation analysis experiments on the attention mechanism and the SMOTE technique (Sect. 4.3).

4.1   Dataset and Criteria

In our experiments, we collected 559,830 samples of the Criminal Law of the People's Republic of China from *China Judgements Online*, covering 91 charge classes. The charge classes with less than 100 samples are considered as unseen classes, which have 31 in total. All the samples of unseen classes are used as the testing samples for both ZSL and GZSL. On the contrary, the remaining charges are treated as seen classes. Most of their samples are used as the training samples for ZSL and GZSL, and the remaining samples are used as the testing samples for GZSL, so the testing set of GZSL contains the remaining samples from seen classes and the samples from the unseen classes. As mentioned in Sect. 3.1, the attribute vector is composed of 19 attributes and 153 features. The statistics of the dataset are given in Table 1.

Table 1. Statistics of the dataset.

Dataset	ZSL	GZSL
Charge	31 (unseen classes)/91	
Attribute	19	
Train samples	485142	
Test samples	1328	74688

In our experiment, we use the accuracy Acc to evaluate the prediction results. In particular, we use Acc_s and Acc_u to denote the accuracy of seen classes and the accuracy of unseen classes, respectively. As our dataset is an extremely unevenly distributed one, we also use the harmonic average Acc_h of Acc_s and Acc_u

$$Acc_h = \frac{2 * Acc_s * Acc_u}{Acc_s + Acc_u} \tag{3}$$

---

[1] https://wenshu.court.gov.cn/.

4.2   Charge Prediction Experiment

The charge prediction results of our model are given in Table 2. For comparison, Table 2 also includes the results of the traditional supervised learning, that is, SVM, KNN, CNN, and LSTM. Although there are no relevant unseen class samples during the training process, the accuracy of our model on the test set containing the samples of 31 unseen classes (*i.e.*, the test set for ZSL) is 32.4%, which is much larger than the random distribution probability 3.2% (1/31). This indicates that our proposed semantic attribute set is effective in knowledge migration from seen to unseen classes.

Table 2. The accuracies of charge prediction for various models.

Model	Acc_u	Acc_s	Acc	Acc_h
SVM	–	82.8	81.3 (−1.5)	–
KNN	–	86.9	85.4 (−1.5)	–
CNN	–	88.2	86.6 (−1.6)	–
LSTM	–	**89.3**	87.7 (−1.6)	–
Our model	**32.4**	79.8	**79.0** (−0.8)	**46.1**

On the testing set for GZSL, our model achieves an accuracy of 79.0%, wherein the accuracy for the samples from seen classes is 79.8%. Compared to traditional supervised learning, although our result is a little degraded, our model has the smallest reduction in overall accuracy. In other words, our model not only achieves performance on charge prediction closed to the traditional supervised learning but also guarantees a good accuracy (over 30% in our experiment) for the unseen charges. Moreover, the harmonic average of Acc_u and Acc_s for our model is 46.1%. Note that our GZSL test set contains 74,688 test samples, wherein less than 1.7% (1,328/74,688) samples are from 34.1% (31/91) unseen classes. This indicates that, unlike traditional supervised learning, our model would not focus on the classes with a large number of samples to get higher overall performance. The above results demonstrate that our semantic attributes are suitable for expressing charges, that is, they are not only logically helpful for better understanding but also able to achieve a closed expressiveness to the one of the abstract features extracted by machine learning itself.

4.3   Ablation Experiments

To evaluate the effectiveness of the attention mechanism and the SMOTE algorithm, we design separate ablation experiments. In detail, we remove the attention mechanism and the SMOTE algorithm from the text encoder and the attribute predictor, respectively. The results of ablation experiments are presented in Table 3.

Table 3. Results of ablation experiments

Model	Acc_u	Acc_s	Acc	Acc_h
Our model	**32.4**	**79.8**	**79.0**	**46.1**
W/o attention	30.5	75.1	74.3	43.4
W/o smote	25.8	77.3	76.4	38.7

As shown in Table 3, we can observe that all the accuracies decrease if either the attention mechanism or the SMOTE algorithm is removed. Moreover, we also found that the performance impact of the attention mechanism on charge prediction is smaller than the one of the SMOTE algorithm. This is because the attention mechanism is only helpful to filter the semantic information in the text embedding process, while the SMOTE algorithm is effective to solve the model over-fitting problem caused by data imbalance, which is the key to our model.

5 Conclusion

In this work, we have defined a set of semantic attributes for Criminal Law, which can achieve knowledge migration from seen charges to unseen charges. We have also proposed a ZSL/GZSL approach for charge prediction, based on the semantic attributes, which provides a feasible solution for the data-driven model to predict crimes that are difficult to collect precedents. Experimental results on our ZSL-oriented dataset have shown that our approach not only achieves comparable accuracy to the traditional supervised learning on seen charges but also achieves a prediction accuracy of over 30% for the unseen charges.

Acknowledgements. This work was partially supported by the National Natural Science Foundation of China (61836005 and 62106150), Guangdong Basic and Applied Basic Research Foundation (2019A1515011577), Stable Support Programs of Shenzhen City (20200810150421002), CCF-NSFOCUS (2021001), and CAAC Key Laboratory of Civil Aviation Wide Survellence and Safety Operation Management & Control Technology (202102).

References

1. Qiu, L., Gai, K., Qiu, M.: Optimal big data sharing approach for tele-health in cloud computing. In: 2016 IEEE International Conference on Smart Cloud, Smart-Cloud 2016, New York, NY, USA, 18–20 November 2016, pp. 184–189. IEEE Computer Society (2016)
2. Qiu, H., Qiu, M., Lu, Z.: Selective encryption on ECG data in body sensor network based on supervised machine learning. Inf. Fusion **55**, 59–67 (2020)
3. Qiu, M., Xue, C., Shao, Z., Sha, E.H.-M.: Energy minimization with soft real-time and DVS for uniprocessor and multiprocessor embedded systems. In: Lauwereins, R., Madsen, J. (eds.) 2007 Design, Automation and Test in Europe Conference and Exposition, DATE 2007, Nice, France, 16–20 April 2007, pp. 1641–1646. EDA Consortium, San Jose (2007)

4. Luo, B., Feng, Y., Xu, J., Zhang, X., Zhao, D.: Learning to predict charges for criminal cases with legal basis. CoRR, abs/1707.09168 (2017)
5. Hu, Z., Li, X., Tu, C., Liu, Z., Sun, M.: Few-shot charge prediction with discriminative legal attributes. In: Proceedings of the 27th International Conference on Computational Linguistics (COLING 2018), pp. 487–498 (2018)
6. Cao, W., Zhou, C., Wu, Y., Ming, Z., Xu, Z., Zhang, J.: Research progress of zero-shot learning beyond computer vision. In: Qiu, M. (ed.) ICA3PP 2020. LNCS, vol. 12453, pp. 538–551. Springer, Cham (2020). https://doi.org/10.1007/978-3-030-60239-0_36
7. Xie, Z., Cao, W., Ming, Z.: A further study on biologically inspired feature enhancement in zero-shot learning. Int. J. Mach. Learn. Cybern. **12**(1), 257–269 (2020). https://doi.org/10.1007/s13042-020-01170-y
8. Luo, Y., Wang, X., Cao, W.: A novel dataset-specific feature extractor for zero-shot learning. Neurocomputing **391**, 74–82 (2020)
9. Chawla, N.V., Bowyer, K.W., Hall, L.O., Philip Kegelmeyer, W.: SMOTE: synthetic minority over-sampling technique. J. Artif. Intell. Res. **16**, 321–357 (2002)
10. Larochelle, H., Erhan, D., Bengio, Y.: Zero-data learning of new tasks. In: Proceedings of the Twenty-Third AAAI Conference on Artificial Intelligence (AAAI 2008), pp. 646–651 (2008)
11. Lampert, C.H., Nickisch, H., Harmeling, S.: Learning to detect unseen object classes by between-class attribute transfer. In: IEEE Computer Society Conference on Computer Vision and Pattern Recognition (CVPR 2009), pp. 951–958 (2009)
12. Liang, K., Chang, H., Shan, S., Chen, X.: A unified multiplicative framework for attribute learning. In: IEEE International Conference on Computer Vision (ICCV 2015), pp. 2506–2514 (2015)
13. Lampert, C.H., Nickisch, H., Harmeling, S.: Attribute-based classification for zero-shot visual object categorization. IEEE Trans. Pattern Anal. Mach. Intell. **36**(3), 453–465 (2014)
14. Farhadi, A., Endres, I., Hoiem, D., Forsyth, D.A.: Describing objects by their attributes. In: IEEE Computer Society Conference on Computer Vision and Pattern Recognition (CVPR 2009), pp. 1778–1785. IEEE Computer Society (2009)
15. Lin, W.-C., Kuo, T.-T., Chang, T.-J., Yen, C.-A., Chen, C.-J., Lin, S.: Exploiting machine learning models for Chinese legal documents labeling, case classification, and sentencing prediction. Int. J. Comput. Linguist. Chin. Lang. Process. **17**(4), 140 (2012). (in Chinese)
16. Luo, B., Feng, Y., Xu, J., Zhang, X., Zhao, D.: Learning to predict charges for criminal cases with legal basis. In: Proceedings of the 2017 Conference on Empirical Methods in Natural Language Processing (EMNLP 2017), pp. 2727–2736 (2017)

Research on Enterprise Financial Accounting Based on Modern Information Technology

Jie Wan[✉]

Shanghai Publishing and Printing College, Shanghai 200093, China
wj20202@sppc.edu.cn

Abstract. In the process of the continuous development of market economy, the market has brought development opportunities for enterprises. If an enterprise wants to maximize its own economic benefits, it requires the enterprise to continuously optimize and reform its financial accounting work, so as to promote its rapid and steady development. For modern enterprises, information technology has become the main factor of competition among enterprises, which promotes the wide application of modern information technology by enterprises to a great extent. Modern information technology is highly integrated with enterprise financial management, which improves the efficiency and quality of financial accounting. As an indispensable and important department in the process of enterprise development, enterprise financial accounting must keep up with the trend of big data era and apply information technology to enterprise financial accounting to improve enterprise management. This paper analyzes the impact of modern information technology on enterprise financial accounting, and puts forward corresponding actions to promote the positive impact of modern information technology on enterprise financial accounting.

Keywords: Information technology · Accounting · Efficiency · Enterprise · Data

1 Introduction

In the era of big data, if enterprises want to seek greater development, they need to use modern information technology, such as cloud computing, *Artificial Intelligence* (AI), and *Machine Learning* (ML) [1–3]. Modern information technology has important practical significance for the development of enterprises. Its application in enterprise financial accounting will greatly change the enterprise financial accounting model [4, 5]. With the development of market economy, driven by Internet technology [6, 7] and computer technology [8–10], the market competition is becoming more and more fierce. The internal information level of enterprises has become a key factor affecting the quality of accounting information and improving the competitiveness of enterprises [11].

The application of modern information technology has effectively improved the work quality of enterprise financial accounting [12]. The current era is the information age. Information technology is applied in all walks of life, and the world economy is also developing under the promotion of information technology. Therefore, it is the general trend to carry out information management for enterprises [13]. In order to make the development of enterprises meet the needs of the information society, enterprises must change their ideas, choose the road of reform and innovation, form relevant systems for the application of information technology, and improve the degree of enterprise financial informatization.

This paper analyzes the impact of modern information technology on enterprise financial accounting, study the feature of enterprise financial accounting under modern information technology, analyze the actual needs of digital transformation of corporate finance, and puts forward relevant measures to promote the positive impact of modern information technology on enterprise financial accounting.

2 The Value of Modern Information Technology to Enterprise Financial Accounting

2.1 Improve the Work Efficiency and Quality of Enterprise Accounting

In the traditional business model, the financial management efficiency of enterprises is not high, a large number of personnel are required to analyze and classify a large number of data, and there are many errors in financial reports. When enterprise leaders use the wrong financial report as reference data, it may lead to wrong decision-making and bring huge losses to the company. The full application of modern information technology in enterprise financial accounting can provide scientific and accurate data support for enterprise leaders' decision-making, and improve the scientificity and accuracy of decision-making. The application of modern information technology in enterprise financial accounting management not only ensures the accuracy and timeliness of financial reports, but also greatly improves the efficiency of accounting management [13]. Accounting information management can improve the management of funds, enhance the effective utilization rate of funds, and ensure the rationality of the use of funds. The financial department of an enterprise can plan and use the funds in a unified way, so that the flexibility of dispatching funds is improved, and the operation of financial funds is more efficient and safe.

2.2 Provide Financial Reference for the Development of Enterprises

The full application of modern information technology in enterprise financial accounting can help enterprises maintain strong competitiveness in the fierce market competition environment, promote the optimization of enterprise management mode and obtain more economic benefits. A large number of financial data will be generated in the process of enterprise development. Dealing with this information in the traditional way requires a lot of human and material resources. The advantage of modern information technology is that it can process a large amount of information and data to ensure the efficiency of processing and the accuracy of processing results. The data mining process in financial analysis is shown in Fig. 1.

Under the traditional mode, the financial accounting management of enterprises can't supervise the use of funds in various departments of enterprises in real time, and can't find out the illegal use of funds by relevant personnel in time, which leads to a substantial waste of enterprises themselves. Under the influence of modern information technology, workers can quickly analyze and search data. To a great extent, it also improves the quality of enterprise financial management and makes it more scientific.

Fig. 1. Data mining process in financial analysis and management

3   Feature of Enterprise Financial Accounting Under Modern Information Technology

3.1   The Formation of a New Thinking Model

The new thinking mode is changing from flow driven to data driven, user driven and value driven. Traditional financial management pattern is to analyze enterprise's core business and management, comprehensive budget management, management, dynamic performance indicators, the financial statements are based on the balanced scorecard and strategy evaluation system of management, the enterprise will be in accordance with the functions divided into research and development, production, logistics, sales and after-sales, human administrative, financial, etc., Through the coordination between functions to complete complex business processes, as long as the internal and external processes are smooth, the enterprise can be in a good state of operation. This management approach treats the enterprise as an isolated machine that will operate normally as long as all its components follow established rules. But in order to reduce the transaction cost is the nature of enterprise and existing entity, rather than individual existence can be separated from the outside world, continually need to information, capital and value stream interaction with the outside world, behind this contains the supply and demand of data, embodies the concept of user-driven, deeper exchange and realize the value. Therefore, in the realization of financial digital transformation, we should not only consider how the new technology shapes and supports the management of enterprises, but also look at the management ideas reflected behind the new technology and the degree of change before. Especially with the integration of business and finance, financial management thinking has long gone from tradition to excellence, along the value chain data flow and value exchange, has become the focus of financial research and evaluation of the object [14].

3.2 Business Empowerment with Technology Support

The management mode in the digital era is from data control to value empowerment. Value empowerment first refers to financial empowerment to business, financial personnel to provide more real-time intelligent decision support for business departments; Followed by finance function itself can give financial personnel and business personnel, financial personnel is engaged in a lot of work, such as accounting, financial statements, financial analysis and management forecast and so on, the future can be directly through UNICOM intelligent management system by the business department, the business personnel directly to the processing of initial data, when undertaking business operations, All related business activities, contracts, income, customer records to achieve automatic entry, financial can be embedded through the interface management system, automatic number and management to achieve more and more integration of finance and business at the work level. The development direction of the future financial can match the autopilot in the field of automotive technology, with the development of enterprise financial intelligence, digital technology mature, industry degree of fusion of wealth will be further deepened, financial personnel proficient in business, familiar with finance business personnel, more financial knowledge will be assigned to the business personnel, management personnel, finance will become the universal knowledge of all personnel.

3.3 Organizational Iteration and Improvement of Organizational Efficiency

The future organization of finance will shift from the traditional pyramid to the multi-layer matrix system. The traditional financial management mode is linear and vertical, including the strategic decision-making of the leader, the business management of the middle layer and the execution of basic financial work at the grassroots level. However, this mode actually forms certain information barriers and information attenuation will occur in the transmission process. The core problem is that finance has been artificially sliced into modules with other functions, and the relevant work content has been sliced into slices, while the actual financial work is a relatively comprehensive management activity. In addition, internal finance functions are relatively independent of the business, which is kept outside. Regional finance or business finance will appear in the future financial management mode in the digital era, which plays an enabling service role and interacts most with the market and customers, including internal employees.

Financial functions are more intelligent functions and intelligent services. Platform finance will complete a large number of traditional financial work, which is the business center established by most enterprises at present. At the platform level, financial center, human resources center and supply chain center will carry out a series of integration, providing more data support to regional finance or group finance. Group finance (or decision-making background) no longer belongs to the original pyramid structure, the functions after reorganizing will be to enable regional finance and platform finance, complete the formulation of rules and coordination with other functions [15]. Therefore, with the deepening of financial digital transformation and the change of new financial management ideas, the new financial control mode will be an open structure, which can realize real-time interaction with customers, suppliers, partners and other upstream and downstream supply chains, automatic data exchange and analysis and collection. The specific structure is shown in Fig. 2.

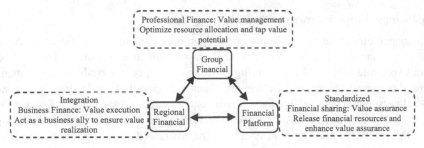

Fig. 2. New financial organization model after digital transformation

4 The Actual Needs of Digital Transformation of Corporate Finance

4.1 Changes in the External Business Environment

Digital technology impact, uncertainty and risk overlay. With the impact of multiple rounds of industrial revolution led by new technologies such as Internet technology, industry 4.0 and Internet of Things technology, the previously mature business model has undergone drastic changes, New business models are constantly being shaped. Figure 3 is Ernst & Young Public Accounting Firm of the investigation, the use of the emerging digital technology tools in the present, the definition of business model is becoming more difficult, the efficiency of the technology is becoming more and more short, the business model of steady state is broken, for the discovery of the "value" in the business also appear increasingly difficult, business conduction of key financial information, In particular, the transaction data gradually presents the characteristics of more and more complex content, larger and larger scale, and faster and faster.

However, under the new business model and operation system, the management mode of traditional financial functions has been unable to adapt to the development trend of new business in terms of the means and efficiency of obtaining effective business information, and even affected the time limit of disclosure of financial information. At present, more timely acquisition of business data, rapid processing and formation of valuable output information is the realistic demand for financial work in the new era. Traditional finance has been unable to support the integration of industry and finance under the new business model, which not only affects the efficiency and quality of financial basic work. At the same time, it cannot realize the financial control, risk management, decision support, resource allocation and strategic evaluation required by the big financial view. In addition, because don't match the digital technology and tools to build and finance function requires more resources to deal with data acquisition, check, sorting, such as low value-added work, resulting in financial organization bloated, employees generally work load and working value perception, in the era of digital economy pursuit of high efficiency, high quality, high yield, the request of the rapid response, Financial functions are in urgent need of transformation. It is particularly important to build a digitalized and intelligent financial system to promote the digitalized and intelligent transformation of finance [16].

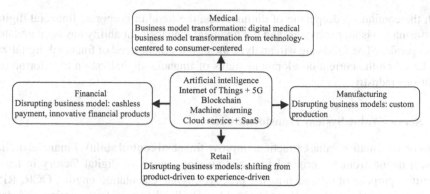

Fig. 3. New technology to business model subversion and value mining

4.2 Continuous Upgrading of Internal Management: Two-Wheel Drive of Lean Analysis and Strategic Evaluation

Compared with the past, the current internal management of enterprises emphasizes more on quick insight and agile adjustment, so enterprise managers need more, better and faster information support. As an important department at the core of enterprise information gathering, the financial function will be endowed with or require more management functions and information output in this process. According to a survey by Ernst & Young Public Accounting Firm, in addition to the traditional basic accounting functions, most of the financial sharing services of leading enterprises in various industries need to be improved or supplemented with analytical functions such as "optimizing revenue", "optimizing production efficiency" and "improving customer experience" or are required to provide relevant data. And finance is the core of digital transformation of earnings just can face to face with the internal and external challenges, on the one hand, help enterprise quickly enhance the level of informatization and greatly improve efficiency of financial work, on the other hand, the realization of digital and intelligent of financial management, improve financial management ability, from the underlying financial or business evolved to value financial and business integration. Therefore, sorting out the contents of financial functions and creating digital finance is an inevitable demand reflected in the intrinsic value of current enterprises. Financial intelligent systems in different scenarios can be designed according to the expected goals of internal management.

5 Digital Transformation Trend of Corporate Finance

In the context of the digital economy era, the digital transformation of finance basically starts from adjusting the organizational structure system of finance and setting up the financial sharing center. The financial sharing center can effectively strip the routine accounting and analysis business of finance and realize the financial control mode of big, middle and small background. With the construction and development of financial sharing center in all walks of life in recent years, the financial sharing center has gradually developed from an early accounting factory to an enterprise value operation center integrating data aggregation - information extraction-value analysis-process reengineering.

With the continuous deepening of digital tools, the trend of corporate financial digital transformation is more obvious, and the financial management ability has been updated and expanded. The following will analyze the development trend of financial digitalization based on the current development status of financial digitalization transformation in various industries.

5.1 Service Value System Transformation

Focus on information value extraction, improve financial control ability. Financial digital transformation from the original financial sharing center for digital factory in hand, the initial purpose of use, such as the process engine, calculation engine, OCR, RPA technologies such as convenience, to build centralized financial accounting and data processing workshops, by a new architecture, organization of standardized treatment of routine business, cost savings, Improving manual efficiency. So far, the domestic part of the industry's head enterprises, such as the Internet industry and real estate and other capital intensive enterprises sharing financial center construction has reached a high level of automation level, make full use of the information and digital technology, has realized the accounting service efficiency of the business, also greatly improve the service quality. As the growing demand for the external business environment and internal management, digital is in constant pursuit of financial accounting quality of excellence, in the process, financial sharing center brings together a large number of data, by means of building the analysis system, and began to extract value from multifarious data information, timely output to management, each assigned to the company's operating decisions. In addition, compared with traditional financial controls on offline control system and financial personnel, financial digital can through the process after the completion of the permissions automatically matching and automatic classification of financial information transmission, the system's compliance with financial information accessibility, and the maneuverability of the business level, implement financial control pattern change, Help to improve the ability of financial management.

5.2 Standardization of Data and Interfaces, Online Implementation

Opening up cross-functional data islands and realizing the sharing of business information. Benefited by the application of a series of digital tools brought by new technologies, the current enterprise interface in the transmission and use of information is constantly expanding and enriching. In addition to the original organizational structure setting, process efficiency, personnel performance evaluation and other aspects, in order to adapt to the implementation and promotion of new digital tools, data-related management has increasingly highlighted its importance and management value, including the formulation and maintenance of data standards, the extraction of rules and other standard management.

Due to different functions, requirements, or the needs of a large amount of data interaction between system platform, often the results of the data management is not only applied to sharing center range, also may make a lot of promotion within large groups, so the operation of the financial Shared development content can help enterprise management essentially better, carrying out the control requirements in the data level, Realize corresponding control requirements.

5.3 Enterprise System Functions and Construction Tend to Be Integrated, Simplified and Modular

When enterprises built financial sharing service centers, due to the lack of peripheral systems or functional limitations, they often set a large number of requirements on the financial sharing platform to achieve, resulting in a variety of functions of the financial sharing platform, and a large number of input and output interfaces. In recent years, with a large enterprise in informatization and intelligent investment increasing, and the digital transformation of management dividend appear ceaselessly, different scale enterprise all business functions to choose business support system architecture related to, for digital financial development, the most core is no longer to build huge data processing factory, but to undertake the relevant data of the surrounding professional systems, and get through the data flow channel, realize the automatic exchange and intelligent analysis of data, which puts forward new requirements for the enterprise's financial digital transformation and financial system integration ability.

In addition, due to the change of the external business environment and a new business model and financial management needs emerge in endlessly, financial digital transformation will abandon the past fragmentation or high load mode, more towards simplification and modularization, on the one hand, through the local adjustment or not can quickly response to a change in demand, on the other hand with modular can realize the function of flexible separation and combination, Reduce the change and technical difficulty caused by system change.

6 Development Measures of Modern Information Technology in Enterprise Financial Accounting

6.1 Improving Quality of Enterprise Financial Accounting Practitioners

In order to improve the quality of enterprise financial accounting staff, the key is to select professionals who can adapt to the information age. Only by ensuring the professional qualifications of the staff can the quality of the candidates be guaranteed from the source. Enterprises need to strengthen the propaganda of information concepts, let relevant staff improve their understanding of information technology, strengthen the transformation of enterprise financial accounting management methods, and improve the learning ability and professional skills of financial accountants. To apply modern information technology to the development of enterprises, first of all, the staff should change their working ideas, use new working ideas to guide their own work, combine the advantages of modern information technology, and at the same time, constantly strengthen their working ability, and make better use of information technology to carry out financial accounting work. In the learning process, the staff should first change the traditional ideas, update new technologies and ideas, upgrade their professional skills, actively learn new technologies, and realize their professional accomplishment. Enterprises should also help relevant personnel to improve their understanding of the importance of the in-depth application of modern information technology in enterprise financial accounting through training and learning activities, to enhance the professional work of financial accounting personnel.

6.2 Improve the Efficiency of Enterprise Financial Work

With the development of the information age, the traditional financial accounting function is no longer suitable for the development of modern enterprises. Many transactions between enterprises are carried out through online banking. This era mainly relies on virtual transaction mode to create enterprise financial accounting content related to modern information technology. When building a modern information accounting system, enterprises must pay full attention to historical cost data, provide an important basis for building an accounting system, and constantly optimize, reform and innovate on the basis of traditional accounting. In the financial accounting management method of modern information company, it effectively protects the internal financial accounting data information of the company and ensures the market competitiveness of the company. Therefore, enterprises must actively build a systematic and complete accounting platform and use modern information technology to generate confidential information data from the company's sensitive information in the shortest time. Enterprises should pay more attention to the management of their own information and data, strengthen the application of information technology, do a good job in security protection, prevent the leakage of enterprise information and data, and improve the competitiveness of enterprises. Continuously optimizing the company's financial and accounting operations plays an important role in the company's development. Therefore, in order to realize the sustainable development of enterprises, it is necessary to continuously optimize the financial accounting work of enterprises and establish a complete accounting system. When building the financial accounting platform, enterprises can query information and data in real time through the sharing function. In economic activities, enterprises can quickly obtain data and information in the shortest time, which is the basis for the formation and improvement of enterprise financial accounting system.

7 Conclusions

Using information technology to support and optimize enterprise financial accounting in the information society is in line with the general trend of the times. The in-depth application of information technology in financial accounting improves the company's economic interests and provides a strong guarantee for the company's daily orderly operation and future sustainable development. Modern electronic information technology is the product of social development and is widely used in daily life and enterprise production. The future development of enterprises must use modern electronic information technology to meet the growing needs of enterprises.

References

1. Liu, M., Zhang, S., et al.: H infinite state estimation for discrete-time chaotic systems based on a unified model. IEEE Trans. Syst. Man Cybern. (B) (2012)

2. Lu, Z., Wang, N., Wu, J., Qiu, M.: IoTDeM: an IoT big data-oriented MapReduce performance prediction extended model in multiple edge clouds. JPDC **118**, 316–327 (2018)
3. Qiu, H., Qiu, M., Lu, Z.: Selective encryption on ECG data in body sensor network based on supervised machine learning. Inform. Fusion **55**, 59–67 (2020)
4. Liu, M., Huang, H., Tong, C., Liu, K.: Research on the basic framework and construction idea of intelligent finance. Account. Res. **409**(12), 194–194 (2020)
5. Qiu, M., Cao, D., et al.: Data transfer minimization for financial derivative pricing using Monte Carlo simulation with GPU in 5G. J. Commun. Syst. **29**(16), 2364–2374 (2016)
6. Qiu, L., Gai, K., Qiu, M.: Optimal big data sharing approach for tele-health in cloud computing. In: IEEE International Conference on Smart Cloud (SmartCloud), pp. 184–189 (2016)
7. Guo, Y., Zhuge, Q., Hu, J., et al. Optimal data allocation for scratch-pad memory on embedded multi-core systems. In: IEEE ICPP Conference, pp. 464–471 (2011)
8. Qiu, M., Xue, C., Shao, Z., Sha, E.: Energy minimization with soft real-time and DVS for uniprocessor and multiprocessor embedded systems. IEEE DATE Conference, pp. 1–6 (2007)
9. Qiu, M., Chen, Z., Liu, M.: Low-power low-latency data allocation for hybrid scratch-pad memory. IEEE Embed. Syst. Lett. **6**(4), 69–72 (2014)
10. Qiu, M., Khisamutdinov, E., et al.: RNA nanotechnology for computer design and in vivo computation. Philos. Trans. Roy. Soc. A **371**, 20120310 (2013)
11. Lu, R., Jin, X., Zhang, S., Qiu, M., Wu, X.: A study on big knowledge and its engineering issues. IEEE Trans. Knowl. Data Eng. **31**(9), 1630–1644 (2018)
12. Zhang, W.: The impact of modern information technology on corporate financial accounting. Taxation **219**(03), 148 (2019)
13. Fan, Y.: On the influence of accounting informationization on traditional financial accounting functions. Sci. Tech. Innov. Appl. **190**(06), 273–274 (2017)
14. Tang, Y., Hu, X.: Digital transfer of enterprise finance under shared service mode. Friends Account. (8), 122–125 (2019)
15. Liu, Q., Yang, Y.: The architecture, realization path and application of intelligent finance. Manag. Account. Res. (1), 84–90 (2018)
16. Qin, R.: Artificial intelligence and intelligent accounting application research. Friends Account. (18), 11–13 (2020)

Financial Information Management Under the Background of Big Data

Dansheng Rao[1] and Jie Wan[2(✉)]

[1] COMAC Shanghai Aircraft and Research Institute, Shanghai 201210, China
raodansheng@comac.cc
[2] Shanghai Publishing and Printing College, Shanghai 200093, China
wj20202@sppc.edu.cn

Abstract. With the constant renewal of the knowledge age, economic global-ization is intensifying. Big data is the inevitable outcome of the development of information technology to a certain extent, which integrates various Internet tech-nologies and brings many conveniences to people's lives and work. Massive data not only brings difficulties to management and maintenance, but also provides great potential value. As an important development field of social and economic construction, it plays an important role in promoting the progress of Chinese soci-ety and the improvement of people's material level. The application of big data technology in financial management is an inevitable trend and need of the devel-opment of modern society, which makes new development and breakthrough in the financial field. Based on big data and its characteristics, this paper provides an important way to solve big data in financial industry. With the application of science and technology, financial information management based on big data has been realized, which is helpful to promote the continuous progress of financial industry.

Keywords: Big data · Finance · Informatization · Management · Knowledge

1 Introduction

With the development of computers [1, 2], software [3, 4], and new algorithms [5, 6], various sensors and mobile devices [7, 8] continue to create a huge amount of informa-tion. Due to the exponential growth under the leadership of emerging technologies such as the Internet of things, cloud computing and mobile Internet [9–11], Big data has an impact on every field [12, 13]. In business, economy and other fields [14, 15], decision-making behavior will be increasingly based on data analysis [16, 17]. At present, the rapid development of big data has impacted the business model and socio-economic development of all walks of life, and also changed people's daily life [18]. With the advent of the era of big data, enterprises need to closely combine big data with their own operation and management, so as to promote the continuous improvement of overall comprehensive strength.

At present, big data is developing rapidly, impacting the business model and socio-economic development of all walks of life, and changing people's daily life [19]. Under

M. Qiu et al. (Eds.): SmartCom 2021, LNCS 13202, pp. 228–237, 2022.
https://doi.org/10.1007/978-3-030-97774-0_21

the background of big data, new requirements are also made for the development direction of financial accounting. In the process of developing financial accounting, only by innovating financial accounting management mode can enterprises improve their core competitiveness. In the current informatization construction process of enterprise financial management, there are many problems, which have caused no small obstacles to the smooth construction of informatization. Targeted control measures need to be taken to remove the obstacles in the informatization construction process of financial management and promote the continuous improvement of the informatization management level of enterprise financial management.

As an important part of enterprise operation and management, financial management has very important practical significance for the orderly development of various businesses of enterprises, which should be paid full attention in the actual work process [20]. In the context of big data, the use of big data resources can better analyze customer information for enterprises and promote the reform and development of enterprises. In the process of the development of enterprise financial accounting, we should use big data management thinking to innovate management mode, which is also a problem that enterprises generally pay attention to [21]. In the era of big data, the financial industry has a good development momentum. In the process of the rapid development of the financial industry, financial management has attracted more and more attention. The traditional financial work mainly takes accounting as the work core, the work mode is relatively single, the work intensity is high, the innovation is insufficient, and the requirements for the comprehensive quality of financial personnel are not high, so it is difficult to meet the needs of financial development under the background of informatization [22]. Strengthening the information construction of financial management and building a perfect system can promote the more stable and sustainable development of the financial industry. At the same time, it is also an inevitable development trend in the era of big data [23].

Based on big data and its characteristics, this paper analyses financial information management system risk estimation methods, provides an important way to solve big data in the financial industry. Under the application of science and technology, it realizes financial information management based on big data, which helps to promote the continuous progress of financial industry.

2 Problems Faced by Financial Management Informatization Construction

2.1 Information Construction Lacks Unified Planning in Financial Management

The development of financial industry has virtually promoted economic development. The joining of information construction has played a major role in the development of financial industry. At the same time, financial institutions are actively establishing their own financial systems. Many enterprises lack sufficient demonstration in the process of informatization construction, thinking that introducing informatization tools can enhance the competitiveness of enterprises, while ignoring the preliminary research work of informatization system on-line, and ignoring how to effectively convert the characteristics of each link of their own operation and internal control requirements into informatization language. Under the background of big data, in the process of promoting financial accounting management, enterprises can start from the perspective of management mode. Although enterprises are still affected by the macro-control of the country in the process of development, if enterprises want to obtain social and economic benefits, they should formulate corresponding management mechanisms [24]. However, the system is independent, unable to share and exchange information systems, and the state's financial information management system is not perfect, which leads to the uneven degree of financial information construction, and there is no unified construction management standard, which has a negative impact on the development of financial information construction.

Some enterprises pay too much attention to the whole construction process, while ignoring the later application and maintenance work, which weakens the connectivity between them, resulting in the inability to share and exchange various data and information effectively. Under the background of big data, in the process of financial accounting management, enterprises should make it clear that this is the responsibility of financial management departments. In the construction of enterprise financial management informatization, the relevant departments only carry out informatization processing on financial data according to individual rules and regulations, ignoring the information exchange and communication with the financial departments, resulting in poor data exchange and transmission among departments and poor data circulation.

2.2 There Are Certain Risks in the Financial Information System

For most institutions, the financial informatization work under big data is seriously inadequate. It only uses informatization to assist related businesses, and still puts the traditional counter business in the main position. In this case, the innovation of financial products is even more difficult, and the process of information construction directly affects the development of financial institutions. In the actual financial management work, there are very few talents with professional knowledge of financial informatization, which virtually increases the probability of risks. The financial industry concentration leads to the explosion of big data. As the financial industry has been committed to system integration and data concentration, it has gradually completed centralized data management in the process of continuously improving the level of data integration. During the development of financial information system, it has brought many conveniences to financial management, and at the same time, risks have followed. In the financial information system, due to the centralization of business processing, the corresponding problems will be concentrated. At present, the construction of financial management informatization in some enterprises is mainly undertaken by specialized information technology personnel. Although they have rich experience in information technology, they often lack corresponding professional support for the construction involving a large number of financial management issues. With the increasing number of business types and products in the financial industry, the number of stored data types is also increasing. Some data types, such as video and audio, have the characteristics of continuity, which makes the data capacity surge and their own storage requirements are relatively high.

3 Financial Information Management System Risk Estimation Methods in Context of Big Data

3.1 Build a Risk Estimation Model for Financial Information Management System

The risk estimation method of the traditional financial information management system has less data throughput when it is used to assess the system risk, and only the method of sampling survey is used to assess data risk, ignoring the information association between data. Therefore, in the context of big data, fully consider the influence of system hardware, software and human factors, integrate all data information, refer to the description of system functions and devices of previous estimation models, build a financial information management system risk estimation model. Financial information management system each module to complete a common task, and the data through the communication module interconnection, to achieve a series of comprehensive tasks or a single sub-task function set,as shown in Fig. 1.

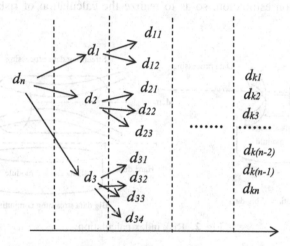

Fig. 1. Functional structure tree of risk assessment model

As can be seen from Fig. 1, the established evaluation model takes into account the logical node d of the financial system, which is used to abstractly understand the behavior characteristics of system hardware, software and operators when exchanging data or executing instructions to the system, and the communication link between nodes is the way of financial information interaction, so as to illustrate the interactive relationship between data. Aiming at the above structure, the risk assessment model of financial system is as follows:

$$\varepsilon = \prod_{k=1}^{k} k_i \bullet n \bullet \frac{A_d}{B_d} = e^{\sum_{i=1}^{n} k_i \bullet ln\left(\frac{a_x - a_y}{c_n}\right)} \tag{1}$$

Where: k_i represents the i-th function of function k_i of the management system; A_d represents the logical set of node D under function k_i; B_d represents the set of logical relations between nodes d under function k_i; n indicates the number of logical nodes. a_x and a_y represent the coordinates of any two logical nodes on the x and y axes; c_n represents c associations among n nodes.

When the calculated results exceed the given safety range, it indicates that the system has risks, so far the estimation model has been built.

3.2 Calculate Risk Indicators Based on Big Data

On the basis of the completion of the estimation model, when the evaluation results exceed the specified standard safety range, the risk index is calculated by using the big data analysis method for the massive financial information data. Risk index is to investigate all kinds of faults that may occur in the information management system, as well as the causes and results of the faults. The evaluation method in this paper adopts this concept to calculate the quantitative consequences under the severity function based on the estimation model of the system running time and the quantified possibility of the fault characteristics of the system running program through utility theory and risk preference function estimation, so as to realize the calculation of risk indicators, as shown in Fig. 2.

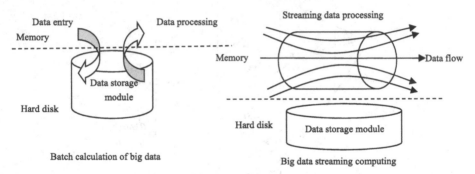

Fig. 2. Risk index calculation

As can be seen from Fig. 2, batch calculation and streaming calculation methods should be used to process financial data when calculating risk indicators, so as to improve the throughput of this risk estimation method for data processing. Among them, batch processing is carried out for the data that basically does not change, and streaming computing method is adopted for the data that changes dynamically in real time. The overcrossing risk index of the system running program reflects that under different management modules, the amount of data information in each control unit running exceeds the specified value that the system can bear. The trust-breaking risk index represents the risk that each data node will lose relevant data information when the operation of the management system fails. At this time, the calculation expressions of the two risk indexes are as follows:

$$\begin{cases} \omega_1 = \sum_{i=1}^{s} \lambda p_s \int_{-\infty}^{0} f(x_{si}) g(x_{si}) + \sum_{i=1}^{s} \lambda p_s \int_{0}^{\infty} f(x_{si}) g(x_{si}) \\ \omega_2 = \sum_{i=1}^{s} m\mu p_s q_{si} \end{cases} \tag{2}$$

Where: ω_1 represents system program risk index; λ represents risk data throughput; s represents the system management mode. i represents the data node where the system runs programs. p_s represents the probability of risk formation under s management mode; $f(x_{Si})$ represents the program operation data x, and the risk probability density function of data node i in the s-th network management mode; $g(x_{Si})$ represents the program operation data x, and the system program risk severity function of data node i under the s-type network management mode. ω_2 represents the management system, the financial data of the trust-breaking risk indicators; μ represents the throughput of untrusted data; q_{Si} represents the risk formation probability of the trust-breaking index under s management model; m represents the total amount of data; $x \subseteq (-\infty, \infty)$, which represents massive data. By integrating the calculation results of Formula (2), the calculation formula of comprehensive risk index in the context of big data is obtained:

$$\omega = \sum\nolimits_{i=1}^{n} \frac{\gamma_n \times [\omega_1 + \omega_2]}{E(D_i)} \tag{3}$$

Where: ω is the comprehensive risk index of the management system; $E(D_i)$ represents the correlation function of node degree value D under the node of class i data; γ_n is the importance of the management system node whose data amount is n. By combining the two types of risk indicators, a more complete risk index function formula is obtained.

3.3 Assess the System Level of Risk

After determining the system risk index, estimate the risk level of the financial information management system at this time. In practice, it is not rigorous enough to judge system risk only according to the size of risk indicators, because some risks can be ignored. Meanwhile, risk residual value should also be considered in the system risk level. Assume that the adjusted failure probability of the system is P0, the default function value of the system is J, and calculate the risk residual value R. At this time, the necessary and sufficient conditions to be considered include: the functional risk of a certain function J in each system level and module, the functional risk of a certain function J in each system sub-module and sub-unit, as well as the weight of system risk transmission and reference index.

The risk grade estimation formula is defined by using the exponential function to calculate the risk residual value, and the risk grade categories of the financial system are divided according to the calculation results, as shown in Table 1. According to the calculated results, the management personnel compared the risk level in Table 1 to timely maintain the system with security threats, so as to realize the financial information management system risk estimation in the context of big data.

Table 1. Financial information management system risk level definition

Level	Comment
A	No loopholes in the test results and no risks in the system
B	Some general information such as leaking server version information, which does not affect the safety of the system
C	General hazards, such as data storage order is out of order, the saved file name is changed
D	Data uploading fails, storage fails, and system modules do not execute control commands
E	Very serious risks, such as distortion of data after upload and artificial changes in the calculation formula of report data

4 Construction Strategy of Financial Management Informatization in the Era of Big Data

4.1 Strengthen Financial Supervision

In the construction of financial management informatization, supervision and management are very important. With the rapid development of financial industry, increasing financial supervision is the basic prerequisite for ensuring the healthy and sustainable development of financial industry. In order to realize the informatization construction of financial management, supervision should be strengthened first. In particular, the global mobile financial industry has achieved rapid development, and it is necessary to strengthen financial supervision. In the era of big data, it is necessary to strengthen financial supervision, so as to keep pace with the development of the times, restrain and supervise internet finance under the macro-economic environment, and constantly optimize the corresponding management work. The model structure of enterprise financial management informatization construction is shown in Fig. 3.

In the construction of financial management informatization, the volume of financial market is increasing. Although it is more open and convenient with the development of technology, it is precisely because of its openness that it will face great problems in the operation of relevant financial management mechanisms. Because information technology itself is highly interactive, it will also make the traditional supervision methods unable to meet the development needs of contemporary Internet financial services. Therefore, we should do a good job of keeping pace with the times in time, and be able to combine the macro-economic and financial needs in the process of integration, so as to continuously improve the management.

4.2 Improve the Internet Financial Credit System

In the process of financial risk control, enterprises should establish a corresponding risk early warning mechanism, which can also help enterprises find out the problems in the process of financial management in time and take corresponding measures to solve them.

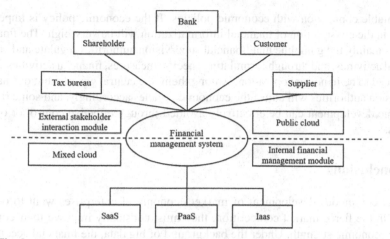

Fig. 3. The construction model of enterprise financial management informatization

At present, there will be a series of problems in the construction of financial informatization, which will bring great influence to the macro economy. The related problems are also closely related to the imperfect credit system. Therefore, it is necessary to improve the credit system and formulate an effective network financial credit system, so as to lay the foundation for its future development. For listed or large-scale enterprises, due to the development needs, many sets of financial management information systems have been built one after another, and the main system is the main system, and many sets of financial management subsystems coexist. At present, the problems encountered in the construction of financial informatization are characterized by diversification, which will hinder the development of macro-economy, among which the imperfection of financial credit information system is one of the important problems. Perfecting the internet financial credit system can not only improve the efficiency of management, but also reduce the probability of some violations, thus effectively reducing risks.

4.3 Sound Economic Policies

For the information construction of financial management in the era of big data, it needs to be connected with the current economic policies. Without the support of a stable economic environment, the probability of the risk of financial informatization construction is also very high. The construction of enterprise financial management informatization is a comprehensive systematic work, which not only involves the financial management informatization project, but also includes the corresponding supporting system construction. Through the information-based performance evaluation system, enterprises can effectively investigate the key factors in the process of building financial management information, improve the efficiency of problem solving, and show the work of participating employees more intuitively in the form of performance rating. This will help to find out the problems existing in employees' working process in time, and encourage employees to improve their abilities independently through performance appraisal. Under the background of big data, the construction of financial management informatization has an inevitable connection with economic policies. If the economic policy is imperfect, the risk in the construction of financial informatization will be very high. The financial policy is mainly the guideline that financial supervision authorities regulate and control financial activities, and through formulating specific measures, financial activities can be guaranteed to be in normal operation. Among them, the central government or financial supervision authorities will adjust the economic policies accordingly, and some risks in economic development can be effectively avoided through effective control or overall policies.

5 Conclusions

With the continuous development of market economy, if enterprises want to occupy a place in the fierce market competition, they must constantly improve their comprehensive economic strength. Under the background of big data, the financial accounting management of enterprises should also change the original development direction, which can not only input new blood for financial management, but also promote the reform of financial accounting. The main purpose of strengthening big data management is to realize the utilization of big data analysis results, continuously tap the potential value of big data, help to use data more effectively, and provide scientific decision-making basis for financial industry management. In the era of big data, financial information security needs our constant integration and improvement. By establishing a careful security mechanism, we can lay a solid foundation for financial institutions to develop big data strategies. Information can be innovated with the continuous development of massive data and Internet technology, and gradually move towards online platform, e-commerce and online payment, so as to promote the development, marketing and service of online financial products. In order to promote the sustainable development of enterprises and prepare for economic strategy, it is necessary to formulate scientific and reasonable management measures for future development, and construct a reasonable construction scheme for financial accounting operation mode, so as to combine enterprise business with financial management.

References

1. Qiu, M., Khisamutdinov, E., et al.: RNA nanotechnology for computer design and in vivo computation. Philos. Trans. Roy. Soc. A **371**, 20120310 (2013)
2. Qiu, M., Xue, C., Shao, Z., Sha, E.: Energy minimization with soft real-time and DVS for uniprocessor and multiprocessor embedded systems. In: IEEE DATE Conference, pp. 1–6 (2007)
3. Guo, Y., Zhuge, Q., Hu, J., et al.: Optimal data allocation for scratch-pad memory on embedded multi-core systems. In: IEEE ICPP Conference, pp. 464–471 (2011)
4. Qiu, M., Chen, Z., Liu, M.: Low-power low-latency data allocation for hybrid scratch-pad memory. IEEE Embed. Syst. Lett. **6**(4), 69–72 (2014)
5. Zhang, L., Qiu, M., Tseng, W., Sha, E.: Variable partitioning and scheduling for MPSoC with virtually shared scratch pad memory. J. Signal Process. Syst. **58**(2), 247–265 (2010)
6. Liu, M., Zhang, S., et al.: H infinite state estimation for discrete-time chaotic systems based on a unified model. IEEE Trans. Syst. Man Cybern. (B) (2012)

7. Qiu, H., Qiu, M., Lu, Z.: Selective encryption on ECG data in body sensor network based on supervised machine learning. Inf. Fusion **55**, 59–67 (2020)

8. Zhao, H., Chen, M., et al.: A novel pre-cache schema for high performance Android system. Futur. Gener. Comput. Syst. **56**, 766–772 (2016)

9. Gai, K., Qiu, M., Elnagdy, S.: A novel secure big data cyber incident analytics framework for cloud-based cybersecurity insurance. In: IEEE BigDataSecurity (2016)

10. Qiu, H., Qiu, M., Memmi, G., Ming, Z., Liu, M.: A dynamic scalable blockchain based communication architecture for IoT. In: International Conference on Smart Blockchain, pp. 159–166 (2018)

11. Lu, Z., Wang, N., Wu, J., Qiu, M.: IoTDeM: an IoT big data-oriented MapReduce performance prediction extended model in multiple edge clouds. J. Parallel Distrib. Comput. **118**, 316–327 (2018)

12. Lu, R., Jin, X., Zhang, S., Qiu, M., Wu, X.: A study on big knowledge and its engineering issues. IEEE Trans. Knowl. Data Eng. **31**(9), 1630–1644 (2018)

13. Qiu, L., Gai, K., Qiu, M.: Optimal big data sharing approach for tele-health in cloud computing. In: IEEE International Conference on Smart Cloud (SmartCloud), pp. 184–189 (2016)

14. Qiu, M., Cao, D., Su, H., Gai, K.: Data transfer minimization for financial derivative pricing using Monte Carlo simulation with GPU in 5G. Int J. Commun. Syst. **29**(16), 2364–2374 (2016)

15. Gai, K., Qiu, M., Sun, X., Zhao, H.: Security and privacy issues: a survey on FinTech. In: Qiu, M. (ed.) SmartCom 2016. LNCS, vol. 10135, pp. 236–247. Springer, Cham (2017). https://doi.org/10.1007/978-3-319-52015-5_24

16. Chen, G.: Application of big data in internet financial risk prevention and control. China Manag. Inf. Technol. **20**(016), 98–100 (2017)

17. Bi, H.: Research on the application of big data in the financial field. Sci. Technol. Innov. **143**(23), 160–161+163 (2019)

18. Zhang, Q.: Big data application model and value analysis based on internet finance. Netw. Secur. Technol. Appl. **232**(04), 152–153 (2020)

19. Cui, L.: Research on big data credit investigation application based on internet financial platform. Times Financ. **694**(12), 21 (2018)

20. Chen, R.: Analysis on the risk factors and preventive measures of accounting informatization in the era of big data. Times Financ. **687**(05), 192–193 (2018)

21. Sun, R.: Application of big data technology in internet finance. Electron. Technol. Softw. Eng. **132**(10), 198–199 (2018)

22. Li, Y.: Analysis and research on the prospects of internet finance under the background of big data. Bus. Observ. **66**(02), 100–102 (2020)

23. Xu, C.: Opportunities and challenges of internet finance development in the big data era. Public Invest. Guide **329**(09), 11–12 (2019)

24. Zhang, Z.: Discussion on the opportunities and risk response measures for the development of Internet finance in the era of big data. Mod. Bus. Trade Ind. **40**(13), 112–113 (2019)

AreaTransfer: A Cross-City Crowd Flow Prediction Framework Based on Transfer Learning

Xiaohui Wei, Tao Guo, Hongmei Yu, Zijian Li, Hao Guo, and Xiang Li[✉]

College of Computer Science and Technology, Jilin University, Changchun, China
{weixh,hmyu,lixiang_ccst}@jlu.edu.cn,
{taoguo19,lizj19,guohao17}@mails.jlu.edu.cn

Abstract. Urban transfer learning transfers knowledge from the data-rich city to the data-scarce city, effectively solving the cold-start crowd flow prediction problem. In urban transfer learning, the selection of source cities mainly focuses on the experimental evaluation, which lacks methods for assessing the transferability of source cities. Besides, the complex regional matching relationships between source-target cities have not been fully addressed. To resolve these challenges, we propose a cross-city crowd flow prediction framework based on transfer learning, called AreaTransfer. AreaTransfer aims to select the appropriate source city from multi-source candidate cities and establish effective area matching relationships to improve crowd flow prediction accuracy. First, we design a source city selection algorithm based on the city's layout characteristics to select the final source city. Then, we propose a modified deep residual neural network to allow area-level prediction. Finally, we optimize the pre-trained model by integrating the area matching results during the city selection process. Experimental results exhibit that AreaTransfer can improve the prediction accuracy by 15%–17% compared with other state-of-the-art models.

Keywords: Urban transfer learning · Cold-start problem · Crowd flow prediction · Source city selection

1 Introduction

Big Data transferring and processing [1,2] had become a critical research area in many applications, following the break through in computer hardware [3,4], software [5,6], networks [7,8], and algorithm design [9,10]. With the development

This work is supported by the National Natural Science Foundation of China (NSFC) (Grants No. U19A2061, No. 61772228), National key research and development program of China under Grant No. 2017YFC1502306.

Original data are retrieved from Didi Chuxing, https://gaia.didichuxing.com, under the Creative Commons Attribution-NonCommercial-NoDerivatives 4.0 International license. All data are fully anonymized.

M. Qiu et al. (Eds.): SmartCom 2021, LNCS 13202, pp. 238–253, 2022.
https://doi.org/10.1007/978-3-030-97774-0_22

of big data techniques, it has become popular to solve problems in smart cities by using urban data [11]. One of the critical issues in the smart city is crowd flow prediction, which is helpful for improving urban planning, ensuring public safety, and relieving traffic congestion by exploring the movement patterns of crowds in cities [12,13]. However, due to the unbalance of urban development, many cities cannot benefit from their scarce urban data. Thus, existing studies [14,15] attempted to leverage knowledge extracted in data-rich source cities to help the learning tasks of the data-scarce target cities, called urban transfer learning.

Nowadays, the works on urban transfer learning [16,17] mainly focus on two aspects: 1) designing a reasonable and efficient method to extract the knowledge of source cities and 2) establishing the knowledge transfer relationship of source-target cities. In the case of the number of source cities and each of which source data is sufficient, domain generalization technology can transfer the common knowledge from the source city data set and then achieve the goal of crowd flow prediction for the target (i.e., data-scarce) cities [18,19]. However, acquiring the mentioned abundant data requires enormous resources and is also prone to the problem of missing data, thus lacking feasibility in practice. Under the limited number of source cities, some studies [20] select source cities based on the level of urban development. For example, the experimental results show that New York and Washington have a more significant development gap than New York and Chicago. However, the crowd flow data of New York is more similar to Washington than Chicago. *Therefore, it is necessary to evaluate the transferability of source cities.*

Suitable source cities can improve the prediction quality of target cities. In addition, establishing appropriate knowledge transfer relationships can also effectively guide the transfer process. Most existing works [17,20,21] use auxiliary data to establish knowledge transfer relationships. Auxiliary data have a certain degree of correlation with the target data and can be used to infer the patterns of the target data. For example, social check-in data from source-target cities are regarded as auxiliary data to predict crowd flow patterns. The method can guide the transfer of crowd flow patterns across cities. However, auxiliary data are correlated but not identical to the target data. Taking social check-in data as an example [22], its only covers a small number of locations visited by users and is closely related to users and locations in terms of check-in frequency. The above auxiliary data reflects limitations in the actual patterns, which may eventually lead to negative transfer. *Therefore, more rational use of cross-modality data is needed to establish reliable transfer relationships between cities.*

To solve the above challenges, we propose a cross-city crowd flow prediction framework based on transfer learning called AreaTransfer. It can select the suitable city from multiple source cities as the final source city and construct reliable knowledge transfer relationships of source-target cities to improve the target city's prediction accuracy. The main novelties of AreaTransfer are as follows: (1) To find the overall best matching relationship at the area-level of source-target cities based on the layout characteristics of cities and leverage the match results to guide the final source city selection. (2) To capture the spatial dependencies in urban problems, existing studies [23-25] design the deep residual structure as the base model for urban prediction. However, the deep residual structure focuses on the city as a whole, and thus it isn't easy to enable area-level knowledge transfer. Therefore, we designed a new deep neural network based on residual units to achieve area-level prediction. In our designed network structure, we first stack ResUnit to fully capture the transfer knowledge in the target data. Then, to achieve area-level prediction, we add Conv unit with 1×1 filter kernels. Finally, during the training process, we not only consider the prediction errors but also the reduction of the representation difference between source-target cities areas to optimize the model.

In brief, the main contributions of this paper lies in three folds:

1. We design a new deep transfer learning framework for cross-city crowd flow prediction, AreaTransfer, which focuses on the selection of source cities and utilizes city overall layout characteristics to establish regional matching relationships for source-target cities. Leveraging the established regional matching relationship, we can calculate city similarity to guide the final source city selection.
2. We propose a new model parameter optimization algorithm based on area matching and area classification results. We add the 1×1 filter to the deep residual network, using its feature of fusing different dimensional features at the same location to help the residual network to be able to focus on area-level features.
3. Using the real-world dataset for evaluation, AreaTransfer improves the prediction performance by 15%-17% compared with the state-of-the-art methods.

The remainder of the paper is organized as follows. We first discuss related works in Sect. 2, and then formally define the studied problem in Sect. 3. Section 4 introduces the proposed framework AreaTransfer. In Sect. 5, we evaluate our method and report the results. Finally, we conclude the work in Sect. 6.

2   Related Work

2.1   Crowd Flow Prediction

In urban computing, crowd flow prediction is a significant issue. Existing work mainly focused on the same city prediction. M. Qiu's group [26] had proposed a novel *Topological Graph Convolutional Network* (TGCN) to predict urban traffic flow and density. Tan et al. [27] proposed a hybrid method based on ARIMA model for short-term traffic prediction. However, ARIMA is a linear model, which is not applicable to medium and long-term prediction. To capture the non-linear relationship in crowd flow data, researchers incorporated RNN, CNN and other structures into the prediction model. Kang et al. [28] proposed LSTM Recurrent Neural Network, which can accomplish the learning of time series features under long time dependence. As the research progressed, the spatial features of crowd flow data attracted attention. Zhang et al. [29] proposed DeepST based on CNN structure, which is able to extract spatial features effectively while focusing on temporal features in crowd flow data. In addition to spatio-temporal factors, ST_ResNet [23] considered external factors such as weather, weekday and incorporated a residual structure with stronger prediction capability. Different from the above work, our work focuses on cross-city crowd flow prediction.

2.2 Urban Transfer Learning

To address the data scarcity problem faced by cross-city studies, researchers have introduced transfer learning into the domain of urban computing to form urban transfer learning. Guo et al. [30] considered dual inter- and intra-city knowledge transfer for the address recommendation problem of cross-city chain stores. Ding et al. [31] used data on users' visiting behaviors in the city of residence to predict users' points of interest in a new city. He et al. [18] used trajectory data from multiple source cities to find users' travel patterns and predict travel intentions in the target cities. Wang et al. [20] proposed the use of social media check-in data as auxiliary data to establish inter-city transfer relationships for crowd flow prediction in the cross-city problem. At this stage, [18] is impractical for crowd flow prediction. While the problem scenario of [20] is similar to our work, the assessment of source city transferability and the establishment of knowledge transfer relationships are still lack.

3   Problem Formulation

Definition 1. Source-Target City: In the cross-city study, the studied cities R are divided into source cities and target cities. The data-rich cities are called source cities and represented by S and the data-scarce cities are called target cities and represented by T.

Definition 2. Area: Depending on different segmentation methods, urban areas have different results. In our work, cities are divided into $I \times J$ equal-size grids based on the longitudes and latitude, where each grid represents an area. $S_{i,j}$ and $T_{i,j}$ respectively denote the area in source city S and target city T.

Definition 3. Crowd Flow Data: The crowd flow data is a set of sample in a continuous spatio-temporal range. We divide time into K timestamps of equal-length as in the previous work. Here, we specify the earliest timestamp as t_c. Therefore, the area set of the city can be denoted as:

$$D_{s,t} = [D_{s,t_c}, D_{s,t_{c+K}}] \tag{1}$$

And we define the final representation of the whole city as follows:

$$D_{S,t} = \{D_{S_{i,j},t_{c+k}} | i \in [1,I], j \in [1,J], k \in [1,K]\} \in \mathbb{R}^{I \times J \times K} \tag{2}$$

Problem. Given a collection of source cities $D = \{D_{S_1,t}, D_{S_2,t}, ..., D_{S_n,t}\}$ with rich crowd flow data and the scarce data in target city $D_{T,t'}$ ($|t'| \ll |t|$), our goal is to select the final source city to help the target city complete the prediction $\tilde{D}_{T,t'_{c+K+1}}$.

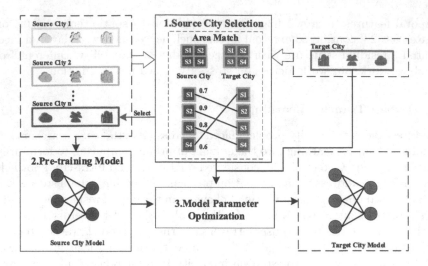

Fig. 1. Overview of AreaTransfer

$$\min_f \text{error} \left(\widetilde{D}_{T,t_c+K+1}, D_{T,t_c+K+1} \right)$$

$$\text{where } \widetilde{D}_{T,t_c+K+1} = f(D_{S,t}, D_{T,t'}), D_{S,t} \in D \qquad (3)$$

4   AreaTransfer

4.1   Overview

Figure 1 gives an overview of the AreaTransfer framework, which mainly consists of three steps:

1) Source city selection: Based on city layout features, we employ a critical mechanism to assess the transferability of source cities. Crowd flow patterns are influenced by urban spatial patterns. Meanwhile batches of stable and easy-to-collect city layout data reflect potential patterns, which guide the learning of crowd flow patterns effectively. We first remodel the city layout features to construct a new representation for each area of the source-target city. Then we find similar area pairs based on the feature differences among areas. Finally we utilize the KM algorithm to analyze the similarity between cities and select the final source city.

2) Pre-trained prediction model: In the crowd flow prediction, deep residual neural networks can capture the spatial relationships according to the data effectively. However, previous work mainly focused on city-level and could hardly achieve cross-city prediction at the area-level. In view of the advantages of merging information about the same location features, Mlpconv layer was added into the network structure as an improvement to focus on area-level prediction. In this part, we will pre-train the model using data of selected source city.

3) Model parameter optimization: Based on the source city selection algorithm and the improved deep residual neural network mentioned above, we propose a network parameter optimization strategy. The strategy takes the area matching results into consideration to further optimize the pre-trained model parameters by reducing the difference in feature representation of the source-target city matching area during training process.

4.2   Source City Selection

AreaTransfer needs to select appropriate city as final source city and it's worth mentioning that selection is based on the target city. In brief, the objective is to assess the transferability and analyze the similarity between source-target cities.

Layout Feature Modeling. The study of urban spatial structure is based on the rational analysis and utilization of POI data. According to the mobility characteristics of crowd flow, urban mobility is influenced by the functional differences of various regions [32], and mobility intention is also limited by the travel distance. POI (Point of Interest) is a concept in field of GIS (Geographic Information System). It refers to geographical objects that can be abstracted as points, such as schools, shopping malls, and other geographical entities that are closely related to people's live. By collecting POI information in a certain spatial area, we can understand the number of various functional points of interest, which can be utilized to represent various city areas as priori knowledge.

At present, most of the studies [33] on POI are limited to the statistics on the number of single types of POI alone, and these methods mostly ignore the original differences in the number of different functional POIs, which cannot truly reflect the function types of the area. For example, in a scenic area, the POI number of the restaurant category is much larger than that of the scenic category. But within the very area, the main function is essentially tourist landscape, and the catering points are all dependent on the construction of the scenic area. Hence the function of the area cannot be measured simply by the POI number. Considering following two factors: 1) the importance of a specific function in different regions. 2) the importance of different functions under the same area, this paper improves the way of characterizing the urban spatial structure with POI data, which can more realistically reflect the actual influence of each area within the city. Meanwhile it can define the specific functional structure of the area and reduce the influence brought by the discrepancies of POI quantity. We express the regional characteristics as Frequency Density (FD) and Category Ratio (CR), where r represent an area of the city R. In addition, n_r^k denotes the number of k-th POI in area r.

$$n_{max}^k = max\{n_r^k | r \in R\} \tag{4}$$

$$n_{min}^k = min\{n_r^k | r \in R\} \tag{5}$$

$$FD_r^k = \frac{n_r^k - n_{min}^k}{n_{max}^k - n_{min}^k}(k = 1, 2, ..., K) \tag{6}$$

The Frequency Density (FD) indicates the importance of the specific function in different regions, n represents the specific value of the POI with the k-th function in r area, and n_{max}^k and n_{min}^k represents the maximum and minimum values of the k-th POI under the city.

$$CR_r^k = \frac{FD_r^k}{\sum_{i=1}^K FD_r^k}(k = 1, 2, ..., K) \tag{7}$$

The Category Ratio (CR) indicates the importance of different functions under the selected area. The function proportion of different typies of POI under an area is counted according to the FD. Based on the explicit area features, the corresponding Area Feature (AF) can be constructed, and then the area can be compared numerically. Here we denote the identified area as r.

$$AF_r = \{FD_r^0, FD_r^1, ..., FD_r^k, CR_r^0, CR_r^1, ..., CR_r^k\}, r \in R \tag{8}$$

Similarity Measure of Source-Target Cities. The area similarity between source and target cities mainly contains two aspects: characteristics of regional function and traffic situation. AF can describe the characteristics from both global and local area. The Pearson coefficient is used to calculate the similarity between source and target cities as follows,

$$\text{Similarity}(AF_s, AF_t) =$$

$$\frac{n\sum AF_{s_i}AF_{t_i} - \sum AF_{s_i}\sum AF_{t_i}}{\sqrt{n\sum AF_{s_i}^2 - (\sum AF_{s_i})^2} \cdot \sqrt{n\sum AF_{t_i}^2 - (\sum AF_{t_i})^2}} \tag{9}$$

where s and t represent an area in the source and target city, respectively, and s_i and t_i represent a feature of the area.

In our framework, it is unnecessary to calculate similarity for every two regions. For example, a commercial street located in the center of a city is usually different from an industrial area at the edge of the city. The relative locations and the density of land POI in the areas they are located varies greatly due to land cost issues. Based on a priori knowledge, regions with excessive differences are not necessary for similarity comparison. Since the POI density of cities conforms to the heavy-tailed distribution, we classify urban areas into six categories (C1–C6) based on this method [34] with C1 being the highest POI density while C6 the lowest. When researching a city, the areas arc always classified into six categories. Each category is complicated in terms of realistic functions, thus we provide some typical instances, where a representation in C1 may be a specific commercial street, and a representation in C6 could be an industrial district. The heavy-tailed interrupted classification method firstly tries to divide all data into two parts based on the arithmetic mean, then select the head (the part above the mean) and continue the iterative process until the data in the head is no longer in the heavy-tailed distribution. Table 1 shows the classification in Chengdu as an example. The purpose of the classification is to reduce the computational cost for subsequent area matching.

Table 1. Area classification of Chengdu city

Area number	POI density average	Head number	Tail number	Ratio of head	Ratio of tail
256	517.75	104	152	0.594	0.406
104	971.39	41	63	0.605	0.395
41	1548.90	16	25	0.609	0.391
16	2358.89	6	10	0.625	0.375
6	3072.00	2	4	0.667	0.333

Optimal Area Matching. The optimal match is to find best source city that most similar to the target city in terms of population mobility patterns among the existing set of source cities. We focus on the optimal match in the overall area, rather than the optimal match in a single area. Focusing only on the optimal matching of a single area will, to a large extent, result in multiple target city regions with high similarity to an area of the source city, leading to the transfer of knowledge being influenced by only a few regions, and thus the final extracted pattern is flawed. To avoid the phenomenon, after obtaining the similarity results of the source-target city areas, we implement the KM algorithm [35] in order to achieve the overall optimal matching. The KM algorithm is used to address the matching problem of bipartite graphs, which can solve the maximum weights under complete matching, fitting the city area matching problem based on the characteristics.

The specific process is shown in Algorithm 1. We use two kinds of nodes to represent regions in the source and target cities, and the similarity of the corresponding two areas is the weights of the edges between the two kinds of nodes. Moreover, according to the pre-classification results mentioned above, there are differences in the number of regions after city classification, and different cities have different number of areas in the same class. In order to reduce the errors caused by the classification process, we stipulate that the matching process between regions only occurs in the regions of adjacent classes. The overall optimal regional matching across cities can be obtained after KM matching, and the overall similarity between the target city and the final source city can be obtained from the regional similarity. The time complexity of the algorithm is $O(n^3)$ and n is the number of urban areas. Eventually, the source city that best matches the target city can be selected based on the comparison of the overall similarity among source cities.

4.3 Pre-trained Prediction Model

We design a novel network of crowd flow prediction with area representation capability, divided into three parts to integrate the effects of spatial, temporal and external factors, as shown in Fig. 2. The crowd flow in a single area of a city needs to consider the influence of all areas within the whole city, not only the adjacent areas, but also the more distant edge areas. However, the convolutional neural network (CNN) is limited by the size of the convolutional kernel and can

---

Algorithm 1. Calculate city similarity based on KM algorithm

Input: Source city area S, Target City area T, Area total number N,
Current matching city area C_s, C_t, Match result R,
Area similarity $List(T_n) = \{(s, sim\,(AF_s, AF_t))|s \in S, t \in T\}, n \in N$
Output: Source-target City Similarity Sim

1: Initialize the top similarity values for all areas of the target city
   $A(T_n) = MAX(List(T_n)), B(S_n) = 0$
2: **for** n $\in$ N **do**
3:     $C_t \vee \{T_n\}$
4:     **if** findCrossPath$(T_n, S_m) = true$ **then**
5:         $C_s \vee \{B_m\}$
6:         $R \vee \{A(T_n) + B(S_n)\}$
7:     **else**
8:         $d = calMinDrop(A(T_n)), T_n \in C_t$
9:         $A(T_n) = A(T_n) - d, T_n \in C_t$
10:        $B(S_m) = B(S_m) + d, S_m \in C_s$
11:    **end if**
12: **end for**
13: $Sim = SUM(R)$
14: **return** Sim

---

capture a limited spatial range [29], but the setting of continuously increasing the number of layers tends to lead to the gradient problem. In order to consider the spatial factor comprehensively, residual structure was selected as the basic unit of feature extraction. It effectively alleviate the degradation problem existing in deep neural networks. In terms of time factor, we selected the time-stamp sampling method to extract time features into three cycles, with sampling intervals in hours, days and weeks respectively.

First, Fig. 2 depicts the overall flow of our proposed network:

$K \in \mathbb{N}$: K is the number of Input time-stamps
$X_t = \{D_{s,t}|t \in [t_c, t_{c+K}]\}$: All crowd flow data input
X_h, X_d, X_w: Input for different time periods
$X_{res} = f(X_h, X_d, X_w)$: Intermediate features of the fusion after the ResUnit
X_{ext}: External factor input
X_{reg}: Area factor input
$y = \{D_{s,t}|t = t_{c+K+1}\}$: Ground-truth result at timestamp t_{c+K+1}
$\tilde{y}$: Prediction at timestamp t_{c+K+1}

The input data of the model consists of three parts, the first part is the input of the historical data of crowd flow X_h, X_d, X_w, which denote the data sampled at different times mentioned above, respectively, and denoted as X_{res} after fusion. The second part is the features of weather and other data, which are extracted by two fully connected layers, denoted as X_{ext}. The third part is the area features of the city, which are processed by One-hot, denoted as X_{reg}. These features are collectively denoted as X_{merge} after concentrate operation. After concatenating X_{res}, X_{ext} and X_{reg} to X_{merge}, we add a two-layer Mlpconv

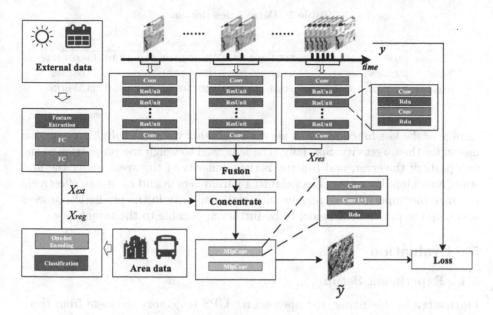

Fig. 2. Network structure

structure to get the prediction $\tilde{y}_t$, where the main structure 1×1 filter is able to extract only the features of different channels of the same position. This feature makes it possible to focus on area-level prediction.

4.4 Model Parameter Optimization

The pre-training model is for the crowd flow patterns of the source city, and its parameters imply shared characteristics across cities as well as proprietary characteristics of the source city. In order that the model can better learn the patterns of the target city, we propose to use the inter-city area matching results to achieve parameter optimization of the network model. In optimizing the model parameters, in order to allow areas with a high degree of cross-city similarity to occupy a higher proportion, we not only consider the minimization of the prediction error part, but also include the area matching error optimization part to achieve a comprehensive optimization combining the two parts.

$$\theta_{tar} \leftarrow \arg\min_{\theta}(1-w)\sum_{r \in R}\|\tilde{y}_r - y_r\|^2 +$$
$$w\sum_{r \in R}\sum_{t \in T}c_r \cdot \text{sim}\left(AF_r, AF_{r'}\right)\cdot\left\|X_{res,r,t} - X_{res,r',t}\right\|^2 \tag{10}$$

The above θ_{tar} represents the parameters of the prediction network model. r is an area of the target city and the corresponding one in the final source city is r'. The area importance denotes as c_r and we use the network parameter learning method *Adam* to record the update of its parameters according to the

Table 2. Dataset description.

City	Location	Time span	Total
Chengdu	[30.65580, 104.04214] [30.72775, 104.12584]	[2016-10-01, 2016-11-31]	138,007,474
Xi'an	[34.20829, 108.91118] [34.28024, 108.99825]	[2016-10-01, 2016-11-31]	74,065,585
Haikou	[19.96121, 110.20930] [20.03316, 110.29241]	[2017-09-01, 2017-10-31]	49,330,413

change of the loss function of the network to obtain the most suitable prediction model for the target city. Specially, The w is used to weigh the proportion of the two parts of the error, and pearson is the similarity of the areas under the first stage matching. By setting the weighting parameters w and c_r, it can effectively enhance the importance of regions with high similarity in the prediction process and help the pre-trained model to be further applicable to the target city.

5   Evaluation

5.1   Experiment Setup

Datasets. In this paper, the open-source GPS trajectory datasets from three cities, Chengdu, Haikou and Xi'an are used for experimental validation. The trajectory data are further processed into the crowd flow data for the research according to the data open-source plan is processed. The details of each dataset are shown in Table 2. In addition, considering that urban issues are influenced by multiple sources of data, the experiments combine data on urban weather conditions, holidays and other information. We also use urban POI data obtained from the map development platform as the basic information of each functional unit of the city in order to find the correlation between crowd flow patterns and urban layout features. In the experiment, this paper integrates the crowd flow data, external data and area data of three cities to verify the effectiveness of the proposed cross-city crowd flow prediction framework. Each city is divided into 16×16 areas of the same size (each area is approximately $500\,\mathrm{m} \times 500\,\mathrm{m}$ in size). For the experiment on cross-city transfer, we choose the one city as the target city and the other two cities as the set of source cities. It is assumed that the source city has rich historical crowd flow data, but only very little data exists for the target city. For the measurement of the experimental results, we choose the same evaluation method as previous work, and both reflect the effect of the prediction model by the square root error RMSE of the final predicted value and the true value.

Evaluation Metric. We measure our method by Root Mean Square Error (RMSE) as:

$$RMSE = \sqrt{\frac{1}{n} \sum_r (y_r - \tilde{y}_r)^2} \tag{11}$$

where $\tilde{y}_r$ and y_r are the predicted value and ground truth, respectively. n is the number of all regions.

Table 3. Urban similarity.

Source city	Target city		
	Chengdu	Haikou	Xi'an
Chengdu	–	0.64543	0.87703
Haikou	0.62043	–	0.57141
Xi'an	0.87703	0.62006	–

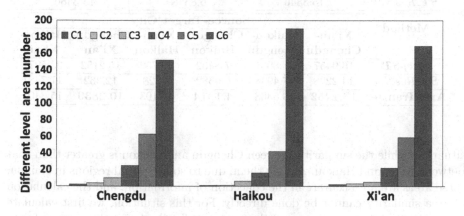

Fig. 3. Area classification in cities

Baseline Method. We choose the classical prediction models HM, HMM, $ARIMA$, $DeepST$ and ST_ResNet as the comparison methods, and all of the above network models we set the network parameters as recommended in the paper.

- HM: the common historical mean statistics method, which returns the mean prediction based on the input historical data series.
- HMM: the Hidden Markov Model used to describe a Markov process with implicit unknown parameters, and is the classical statistical model to describe the unknown case.
- $ARIMA$: a classical statistical model for time series forecasting that widely used in statistics for short-term smooth data series.
- $DeepST$ [29]: a deep spatio-temporal prediction network based on convolutional neural network, for modeling the temporal features, manually selecting the timestamps with high correlation to form a new time feature series.
- ST_ResNet [23]: a deep spatio-temporal prediction framework based on residual structure, which achieves end-to-end prediction on the city as a whole and can effectively model the spatial features of the city.

5.2 Evaluation Results

Table 3 shows the results of similarity calculation between cities, in which it can be seen that Chengdu and Xi'an possess higher similarity in terms of city layout

Table 4. Experimental results.

Method	Only Target City		
	Chengdu	Haikou	Xi'an
HM	14.2695	5.0924	13.4509
HMM	14.4000	5.5529	12.7962
ARIMA	14.8745	5.0729	13.8619
DeepST	14.9548	7.1388	14.0296
ST_ResNet	15.3846	6.8348	13.3480

Method	Source-Target City					
	Xi'an-Chengdu	Haikou-Chengdu	Chengdu-Haikou	Xi'an-Haikou	Chengdu-Xi'an	Haikou-Xi'an
DeepST	16.9457	31.8981	7.8462	8.8752	15.2152	23.5971
ST_ResNet	14.2228	27.4948	6.0582	7.828	12.362	17.7481
AreaTransfer	**12.1452**	19.5368	**4.1914**	4.2193	**10.2839**	15.3401

situation, while the similarity between Chengdu and Haikou is greater than that between Xi'an and Haikou. Among them, due to some special regions in Haikou, these areas are not accurate in the collection of information, and the calculation of area similarity cannot be done directly. For this situation, we first calculate the similarity information around the area, and finally derive the mean value of similarity given to the area, so that when Haikou is used as the target city and the source city, its similarity situation all has a certain float. Figure 3 shows the different levels of regional classification for the three cities. The overall number of regional levels between different cities is close on C1–C2, C3–C6, but there are differences in the proportion of each part. This is because the development of cities follows a certain pattern, and there is a pattern in the composition of regions in cities. For example, each city has its own central area (C1–C2) and edge area (C3–C6), which account for roughly the same proportion, but can differ in their specific allocation. In terms of the area composition of different cities, the closer the proportion of areas in each part of two cities, the higher the degree of similarity the cities may have.

Top half of Table 4 shows the results obtained by using short-term data of the target city and making predictions directly with the baselines. We assume that the target city has only one week of crowd traffic data, so as to simulate the situation of data scarcity in the city. The final results of the direct prediction using the short-term data of the target city as training data show that the statistical models HM, HMM and ARIMA outperform the deep spatio-temporal prediction models in most cases, and it can be seen that the prediction results of the latter are not stable in the case of insufficient data. In the case that we increase the historical crowd flow data in the target cities, we find that the degree of variation of HM, HMM, and ARIMA is small, but the effect of the deep spatio-temporal prediction model gradually increases, and finally reaches 8.3989, 3.1742, and 6.7509 in Chengdu, Haikou, and Xi'an, respectively. Meanwhile, we regard these three values as the upper limit of the model prediction performance in this experiment.

The second half is a comparison of the prediction performance of AreaTransfer with the previous advanced models after adding the transfer learning factor. It is clear that AreaTransfer outperforms the other models in all cases. Secondly, we found that the results of direct training using source city data are unsatisfactory, and therefore, the direct transfer method may exist inferior to the direct prediction method for short-term data. This may be due to the lack of reasonable guidance on the knowledge transfer relationship during the direct transfer, thus leading to poor results. In addition, when we used two cities with low city similarity for transfer, even negative transfer was observed. This is in line with our previous description and proves the importance of assessing the transferability of cities. Ultimately, from an overall perspective, our model has a 15%, 17%, and 17% improvement in prediction for each city, respectively.

6 Conclusion

To address the problem of cross-city crowd flow prediction, we have proposed a novel framework based on transfer learning, called AreaTransfer. In this work, we focused on the selection of source cities and the establishment of knowledge transfer relationships to improve the ability of prediction in target city. Eventually, its effectiveness was verified by experiments on three real-world datasets. In future work, the exploration of crowd flow prediction will require confronting challenges at different city scales. We will incorporate the above challenges in AreaTransfer to make up for deficiencies in cross-city prediction problems.

References

1. Gai, K., Qiu, M., Chen, L., Liu, M.: Electronic health record error prevention approach using ontology in big data. In: IEEE 17th HPCC Conference (2015)
2. Lu, R., Jin, X., Zhang, S., Qiu, M., Wu, X.: A study on big knowledge and its engineering issues. IEEE Trans. Knowl. Data Eng. **31**(9), 1630–1644 (2018)
3. Qiu, M., Ming, Z., Li, J., Liu, S., Wang, B., Lu, Z.: Three-phase time-aware energy minimization with DVFS and unrolling for chip multiprocessors. J. Syst. Archit. **58**(10), 439–445 (2012)
4. Niu, J., Liu, C., et al.: Energy efficient task assignment with guaranteed probability satisfying timing constraints for embedded systems. IEEE Trans. Parallel Distrib. Syst. **25**(8), 2043–2052 (2013)
5. Zhang, K., Kong, J., Qiu, M., Song, G.L.: Multimedia layout adaptation through grammatical specifications. Multimed. Syst. **10**(3), 245–260 (2005)
6. Tao, L., Golikov, S., et al.: A reusable software component for integrated syntax and semantic validation for services computing. In: IEEE Symposium on Service-Oriented System Engineering (SOSE), pp. 127–132 (2015)
7. Gai, K., Qiu, M., Zhao, H., Xiong, J.: Privacy-aware adaptive data encryption strategy of big data in cloud computing. In: IEEE 3rd CSCloud Conference (2016)
8. Su, H., Qiu, M., Wang, H.: Secure wireless communication system for smart grid with rechargeable electric vehicles. IEEE Commun. Mag. **50**(8), 62–68 (2012)

9. Guo, Y., Zhuge, Q., Hu, J., et al.: Data placement and duplication for embedded multicore systems with scratch pad memory. IEEE Trans. CAD **32**, 809–817 (2013)

10. Qiu, H., Qiu, M., Memmi, G., Ming, Z., Liu, M.: A dynamic scalable blockchain based communication architecture for IoT. In: Qiu, M. (ed.) SmartBlock 2018. LNCS, vol. 11373, pp. 159–166. Springer, Cham (2018). https://doi.org/10.1007/978-3-030-05764-0_17

11. Zheng, Y., Capra, L., Wolfson, O., Yang, H.: Urban computing: concepts, methodologies, and applications. ACM Trans. Intell. Syst. Technol. (TIST) **5**(3), 1–55 (2014)

12. Zhou, Q., Gu, J.J., Ling, C., Li, W.-B., Yi, Z., Wang, J.: Exploiting multiple correlations among urban regions for crowd flow prediction. J. Comput. Sci. Technol. **35**, 338–352 (2020)

13. Yu, X., Sun, L., Yan, Y., Liu, G.: A short-term traffic flow prediction method based on spatial-temporal correlation using edge computing. Comput. Electr. Eng. **93**, 107219 (2021)

14. Wang, L., Guo, B., Yang, Q.: Smart city development with urban transfer learning. Computer **51**(12), 32–41 (2018)

15. Li, D., Gong, Z., Zhang, D.: A common topic transfer learning model for crossing city poi recommendations. IEEE Trans. Cybern. **49**(12), 4282–4295 (2018)

16. Chen, L., Wang, L.: Exploring context modeling techniques on the spatiotemporal crowd flow prediction. arXiv preprint arXiv:2106.16046 (2021)

17. Liu, Y., et al.: MetaStore: a task-adaptative meta-learning model for optimal store placement with multi-city knowledge transfer. ACM Trans. Intell. Syst. Technol. (TIST) **12**(3), 1–23 (2021)

18. He, T., et al.: What is the human mobility in a new city: transfer mobility knowledge across cities. In: Proceedings of the Web Conference 2020, pp. 1355–1365 (2020)

19. Fan, Z., Song, X., Shibasaki, R., Li, T., Kaneda, H.: CityCoupling: bridging intercity human mobility. In: Proceedings of the 2016 ACM International Joint Conference on Pervasive and Ubiquitous Computing, pp. 718–728 (2016)

20. Wang, L., Geng, X., Ma, X., Liu, F., Yang, Q.: Cross-city transfer learning for deep spatio-temporal prediction. In: IJCAI International Joint Conference on Artificial Intelligence, p. 1893 (2019)

21. Wang, L., et al.: SPACE-TA: cost-effective task allocation exploiting intradata and interdata correlations in sparse crowdsensing. ACM Trans. Intell. Syst. Technol. (TIST) **9**(2), 1–28 (2017)

22. Wang, X., Ding, J., Uhlig, S., Li, Y., Jin, D.: Deviations of check-ins and human mobility trajectory. In: 2019 5th International Conference on Big Data Computing and Communications (BIGCOM), pp. 115–123. IEEE (2019)

23. Zhang, J., Zheng, Y., Qi, D.: Deep spatio-temporal residual networks for citywide crowd flows prediction. In: Thirty-First AAAI Conference on Artificial Intelligence (2017)

24. Guo, G., Zhang, T.: A residual spatio-temporal architecture for travel demand forecasting. Trans. Res. Part C: Emerg. Technol. **115**, 102639 (2020)

25. Dai, G., Hu, X., Ge, Y., Ning, Z., Liu, Y.: Attention based simplified deep residual network for citywide crowd flows prediction. Front. Comput. Sci. **15**(2), 1–12 (2020). https://doi.org/10.1007/s11704-020-9194-x

26. Qiu, H., Zheng, Q., et al.: Topological graph convolutional network-based urban traffic flow and density prediction. IEEE Trans. ITS **22**(7), 4560–4569 (2020)

27. Tan, M.-C., Wong, S.C., Xu, J.-M., Guan, Z.-R., Zhang, P.: An aggregation app-roach to short-term traffic flow prediction. IEEE Trans. Intell. Transp. Syst. **10**(1), 60–69 (2009)
28. Kang, D., Lv, Y., Chen, Y.: Short-term traffic flow prediction with LSTM recur-rent neural network. In: 2017 IEEE 20th International Conference on Intelligent Transportation Systems (ITSC), pp. 1–6. IEEE (2017)
29. Zhang, J., Zheng, Y., Qi, D., Li, R., Yi, X.: DNN-based prediction model for spatio-temporal data. In: Proceedings of the 24th ACM SIGSPATIAL International Conference on Advances in Geographic Information Systems, pp. 1–4 (2016)
30. Guo, B., Li, J., Zheng, V.W., Wang, Z., Yu, Z.: CityTransfer: transferring inter- and intra-city knowledge for chain store site recommendation based on multi-source urban data. Proc. ACM Interact. Mob. Wearable Ubiqui. Technol. **1**(4), 1–23 (2018)
31. Ding, J., Yu, G., Li, Y., Jin, D., Gao, H.: Learning from hometown and current city: cross-city poi recommendation via interest drift and transfer learning. Proc. ACM Interact. Mob. Wearable Ubiquit. Technol. **3**(4), 1–28 (2019)
32. Fistola, R., Raimondo, M., La Rocca, R.A.: The smart city and mobility: the functional polarization of urban flow. In: 2017 5th IEEE International Conference on Models and Technologies for Intelligent Transportation Systems (MT-ITS), pp. 532–537. IEEE (2017)
33. Chen, Z., Gong, Z., Yang, S., Ma, Q., Kan, C.: Impact of extreme weather events on urban human flow: a perspective from location-based service data. Comput. Environ. Urban Syst. **83**, 101520 (2020)
34. Jiang, B.: Head/tail breaks: a new classification scheme for data with a heavy-tailed distribution. Prof. Geogr. **65**(3), 482–494 (2013)
35. Zhu, H., Zhou, M.C.: Efficient role transfer based on Kuhn-Munkres algorithm. IEEE Trans. Syst. Man Cybern.-Part A: Syst. Hum. **42**(2), 491–496 (2011)

Parallel Improved Quantum Evolutionary Algorithm for Complex Optimization Problems

Yapeng Sun[1,2](✉) 🆔

[1] School of Automation, Central South University, Changsha 410083, Hunan, China
yapengsun@csu.edu.cn
[2] School of Computer Science and Engineer, Hunan University of Science and Technology, Xiangtan 411201, Hunan, China

Abstract. As for the problems of premature convergence, slow convergence and long computing time in solving complex continuous function optimization by traditional quantum evolutionary algorithm, a dynamic parallel quantum evolutionary algorithm for solving complex continuous function optimization problem is proposed in this paper. Multi population co-evolution is adopted, and each sub-population evolves in different search areas according to their own evolution objectives to form a parallel search mode, which can speed up the algorithm convergence and avoid premature convergence; Quantum computation is introduced into the differential evolution algorithm. In this method, the probability amplitude representation of qubits is applied to the real number coding of chromosomes, the chromosome position is updated by quantum mutation, quantum crossover and quantum selecting operations, the two probability amplitudes of qubits are exchanged by quantum non-gate, and an adaptive operator is introduced to improve the population diversity, It can not only prevent the premature convergence of the algorithm, but also make the algorithm converge faster and improve the problem-solving ability of the optimization algorithm. Taking the function extreme value problem as an example, the effectiveness of the algorithm is verified by this algorithm.

Keywords: Parallel computing · Message passing interface · Quantum evolutionary algorithm

1 Introduction

Evolutionary algorithm [1, 2] is an effective tool for solving theoretical calculation and engineering optimization problems, such as memory [3–5] and data allocations [6, 7]. However, for some multi-variable optimization problems, although evolutionary algorithm can obtain the global optimal solution in theory, it slowly converges application in practical because of the huge search space [8], so it cannot get effective results in the allowable time range [9]. This can be solved in two ways: one is parallelization to speed up the evolutionary algorithm solutions [10, 11], another is to improve the efficiency of search space [12]. This paper mainly studies the acceleration method of

M. Qiu et al. (Eds.): SmartCom 2021, LNCS 13202, pp. 254–264, 2022.
https://doi.org/10.1007/978-3-030-97774-0_23

using evolutionary algorithms to solve large search space problems. The main work is as follows:

As for the problem of improving search efficiency [13], an improved quantum evolutionary algorithm is proposed. The quantum evolutionary algorithm introduces quantum computing into the differential evolutionary algorithm. In this method, the probability amplitude representation of qubits is applied to the real number coding of chromosome, and the chromosome position is updated by quantum mutation, quantum crossover and quantum selection operations, The quantum non-gate is used to exchange the two probability amplitudes of qubits, and the adaptive operator is introduced to improve the population diversity, which can prevent the premature convergence of the algorithm, and improve the problem-solving ability of the optimization algorithm [14]. Through theoretical analysis and experimental verification, it is proved that this method can improve the search ability of evolutionary algorithm for large search space problems.

Based on *Message Passing Interface* (MPI) mechanism [15, 16], the parallel computing of the improved quantum evolutionary algorithm is analyzed [17]. The coarse-grained mode of parallel quantum evolutionary algorithm is discussed, and the parallel improved quantum evolutionary algorithm of coarse-grained mode is realized. The effectiveness of the program is verified by using the standard test function.

2 Improved Quantum Evolutionary Algorithm

Quantum evolutionary algorithm, which was proposed by the Korean scholar Han, K. H. at the end of the 20th century [8, 18], is an evolutionary algorithm based on probability. It is the product of the combination of quantum theory and evolutionary algorithm. Compared with classical evolutionary algorithm, it has many performance advantages: better population diversity and global optimization ability; small population size but not affecting the search performance; speeding up the search in the process of evolution by using the historical information of individual evolution.

By investigating various quantum evolutionary algorithms and their applications at home and abroad, we find that the low efficiency in the coding of chromosome gene digit and the calculation of the rotation angle of quantum revolving gate is one of the main factors limiting the improvement of the performance of quantum evolutionary algorithms.

For the above reasons, it is meaningful to explore a new quantum evolutionary algorithm with high efficiency and global optimization. Based on the existing research on quantum mechanism and differential evolution mechanism, this paper proposes a more practical and improved adaptive quantum differential evolution algorithm, which uses quantum bits to form chromosomes, encodes quantum bits with real numbers, updates operation of quantum chromosome by using quantum revolving gate and performs chromosomes mutation with quantum non-gates, finally the optimization of complex problems is realized.

2.1 Self-adaptive Quantum Differential Evolution Algorithm

Self-Adaptive Quantum Differential Evolution Algorithm (SAQDEA) is a search optimization algorithm combining quantum computing theory and differential evolution algorithm. In SAQDEA, the chromosome is composed of qubits, the qubits are encoded by the real numbers, the updating operation of quantum chromatin is realized by quantum revolving gate, and the chromosome is mutated by quantum non-gate, so that it can achieve the optimization of the goal Solution.

The composition and coding of quantum chromosome, quantum chromosome is composed of qubits which meet the requirements of normalizing condition. A qubit consists of a pair of corresponding states $|0>$ and the probability amplitudes of $|1>$ that are defined in a unit space, defining: $|\varphi>= \alpha|0 > +\beta|1 >$, among them, α and β are a pair of complex numbers, called the probability amplitude of the qubit's corresponding state [19]. $|\alpha|_2$ is the probability of quantum state collapsing to $|0>$, $|\beta|_2$ is the probability of quantum state collapsing to $|1>$, and satisfies the normalization condition, $|\alpha|_2 + |\beta|_2 = 1$. Therefore, qubit can also be described as $\left[cos(q), sin(q)\right]^T$.

In quantum difference evolution algorithm, the real number code is used for quantum chromosomes, and the coding method is as follows:

$$Q_{i,j} = \left[\left| \begin{matrix} cos(\theta_{i,1}) \\ sin(\theta_{i,1}) \end{matrix} \right| \left| \begin{matrix} cos(\theta_{i,2}) \\ sin(\theta_{i,2}) \end{matrix} \right| \Lambda \left| \begin{matrix} cos(\theta_{i,D}) \\ sin(\theta_{i,D}) \end{matrix} \right| \right] \tag{1}$$

Among them, $\theta = 2\pi\, rand$, rand $\in$ [0, 1], i $\in$ {1, 2, ..., N}, j $\in$ {1, 2, ..., D}, D is the problem's dimension and N represents the population scale.

In the solution space transformation method of optimization problem and quantum differential evolution algorithm [20], the ergodic space of quantum is unit space I = [−1, 1] in order to analyze the performance of quantum chromosome, it is necessary to map the variable of quantum chromosome from unit space to the solution space of optimization problem. Each quantum chromosome variable corresponds to an optimization variable of the optimization problem. Let's define the domain of the solution space variable $X_{i,j}$ of the optimization problem as $[a_j, b_j]$ and the qubit code as $\left[cos(\theta_{i,j}), sin(\theta_{i,j})\right]^T$. Then the corresponding solution space variables are:

$$\begin{bmatrix} X_{i,j}^0 \\ X_{i,j}^1 \end{bmatrix} = \begin{bmatrix} \frac{b_j-a_j}{2} & 0 \\ 0 & \frac{b_j-a_j}{2} \end{bmatrix} \begin{bmatrix} cos(\theta_{i,j}) \\ sin(\theta_{i,j}) \end{bmatrix} + \begin{bmatrix} \frac{b_j+a_j}{2} \\ \frac{b_j+a_j}{2} \end{bmatrix} \tag{2}$$

By simplifying the above formula, we can get the following results

$$\begin{bmatrix} X_{i,j}^0 \\ X_{i,j}^1 \end{bmatrix} = \frac{1}{2} \begin{bmatrix} 1 + cos(\theta_{i,j}) & 1 - cos(\theta_{i,j}) \\ 1 + sin(\theta_{i,j}) & 1 - sin(\theta_{i,j}) \end{bmatrix} \begin{bmatrix} b_j \\ a_j \end{bmatrix} \tag{3}$$

Among them, the quantum chromosome represented by cosine probability amplitude corresponds to $X_{i,j}^0$, and the quantum chromosome represented by sine probability amplitude corresponds to $X_{i,j}^1$.

When the quantum state is updating, the rotation angle of the quantum position is also adjusted, and the formula is as follows:

$$\Delta\theta_{ij}^g = \theta_{min} + fit \cdot (\theta_{max} - \theta_{min})rand_j\, exp(\frac{gen}{maxgen}) \tag{4}$$

$$fit = \frac{fit_{gBest} - fit_i}{fit_{gBest}} \tag{5}$$

Among them, θ_{min} is the minimum value $0.001\,\pi$ of $\Delta\theta$ interval, θ_{max} is the maximum value $0.05\,\pi$ of $\Delta\theta$ interval, fit_{gBest} is the adaptability of the whole optimal individual searched, fit_i shows adaptability of the present individual, $rand_{ij}$ is the random number between $[0, 1]$; gen is the current iteration times of population, and maxgen represents max iteration times of the limited population.

Quantum mutation's operation: corresponding to the standard differential evolution algorithm, a quantum's chromosome is chosen at random from quantum's population through this method. It takes the quantum bit phase as a basis vector and quantum bit phase of the other two different quantum chromosomes as the difference vector. The generation method is as follows:

$$v_{i,j}^{g+1} = \theta_{r1,j}^g + F \cdot rand \cdot (\theta_{r2,j}^g - \theta_{r3,j}^g) \tag{6}$$

Among them, $r1, r2, r3 \in \{1, 2..., N\}$, and $r1 \neq r2 \neq r3$, $F \in [0, 1]$ is a contraction factor, rand represents a random number between interval $[0, 1]$, g represents the current population, and $g + 1$ represents the next generation population.

If the mutation rate is too large, the global optimal solution is low. If the mutation rate is small, the population diversity will decrease, and the phenomenon of "early maturity" is easy to appear. In this paper, a self-adaptive mutation operator is introduced. In this way, the mutation operator is $2F_0$ at the beginning, and the diversity can be maintained at the initial stage to prevent premature maturity. With the progress, the mutation operator decreases and finally changes to F_0 to avoid the destruction of the optimal solution. The calculation method is as follows:

$$\varphi = e^{1 - \frac{G_m}{G_m + 1 - G}}, F = F_0 \times 2^\varphi \tag{7}$$

Among them, G_m is the maximum algebra, G is the current algebra, and e is the natural constant. In this way, the population can have better diversity in the early stage of evolution, and it is beneficial to local fine search in the later stage of evolution, which can bring better results.

Quantum crossover operation: producing a new individual by combined the quantum mutation individual and the predetermined parent individual according to certain rules.

$$u_{i,j}^{g+1} = \begin{cases} v_{i,j}^{g+1}, & if \ (rand_j \leq c_r \ or \ j = j_{rand}) \\ x_{i,j}^g, & otherwise \end{cases} \tag{8}$$

Among them, $j \in \{1,2..., D\}$, D is the dimension of the problem, $rand_j$ is a random number between $[0, 1]$, j_{rand} is $\{1,2..., D\}$. C_r is a quantum crossover factor and is generally a random number in the interval $[0, 1]$. In this paper, a crossover operator of random range is designed as follows:

$$C_r = 0.5 \times [1 + rand(0, 1)] \tag{9}$$

In this way, the mean value of the crossover operator is 0.75, which can better maintain the diversity of the population.

Quantum selection operation: selection operation adopts one-to-one greedy selection. The principle of selection is that individuals with better fitness enter the next generation. It can be expressed as follows:

$$\theta_{i,j}^{g+1} = \begin{cases} u_{i,j}^{g+1}, & if \quad f(u_{i,j}^{g+1}) \leq f(\theta_{i,j}^{g}) \\ \theta_{i,j}^{gt}, & otherwise \end{cases} \tag{10}$$

$$\theta_{i,j}^{gt} = \theta_{i,j}^{g} + \Delta\theta_{ij}^{g} \tag{11}$$

Among them, f is the fitness function, the two new bits after the updating are:

$$Q_{i,j}^{g+1} = \left[\left| \begin{matrix} cos(\theta_{i,1}^{g+1}) \\ sin(\theta_{i,1}^{g+1}) \end{matrix} \right| \left| \begin{matrix} cos(\theta_{i,2}^{g+1}) \\ sin(\theta_{i,2}^{g+1}) \end{matrix} \right| \Lambda \left| \begin{matrix} cos(\theta_{i,D}^{g+1}) \\ sin(\theta_{i,D}^{g+1}) \end{matrix} \right| \right] \tag{12}$$

It can be seen that by rotating the quantum phase angle, the position of two quantum chromosomes can be moved at the same time, which can speed up the convergence of the algorithm.

Mutation processing of quantum non-gate: make the mutation probability be P_m, if *rand* < P_m, randomly select several qubits in the quantum chromosome, and use the quantum non-gate to mutate the qubits, and the optimal position of its memory remains unchanged.

$$\begin{bmatrix} 0 & 1 \\ 1 & 0 \end{bmatrix} \begin{bmatrix} cos(\theta_{ij}) \\ sin(\theta_{ij}) \end{bmatrix} = \begin{bmatrix} sin(\theta_{ij}) \\ cos(\theta_{ij}) \end{bmatrix} = \begin{bmatrix} cos(\pi/2 - \theta_{ij}) \\ sin(\pi/2 - \theta_{ij}) \end{bmatrix} \tag{13}$$

2.2 Coarse Grained Parallel Algorithm Based on MPI

If the master-slave parallel evolutionary algorithm can only speed up the evolutionary algorithm solution, then the coarse-grained parallel evolutionary algorithm improves the solution quality of evolutionary algorithm [21]. The coarse-grained model is composed of multiple populations, and each population or sub-population evolves independently on different processors. After a certain evolutionary generation, each sub-population will migrate several individuals to introduce excellent genes of other populations. It can be said that migration operator is the core of coarse-grained parallel evolutionary algorithm. Due to the addition of migration, a new operator, and the introduction of many new parameters, the complexity of the algorithm increases [15].

The new evolutionary algorithm parameters introduced by migration are briefly described below.

Migration topology: Migration topology determines the path of individual migration between various groups. Migration topology mostly depends on the architecture of parallel computer system. Software method can also be used for simulation. Common migration topology includes no migration, unidirectional ring, bidirectional ring, hypercube, grid, full interconnection and so on [17].

Migration cycle: The migration cycle determines the time interval of individual migration, generally once every several generations. Experiments show that if the interval period is too long, various groups will not make full use of the excellent solutions of other groups, so the convergence of the algorithm will be slow, and if the interval period is too short, the diversity among sub-groups will be destroyed. Although the convergence is fast, the quality of the solution is not high. Therefore, the choice of migration cycle depends on the specific problems.

Migration scale mobility: In each migration, several individuals can be migrated. Migration scale refers to the number of individuals migrated each time or the migration rate of the migrated individuals in the population size.

Migration selection strategy: The migration selection strategy is used to specify how to select the removed individuals in each migration. The usual strategies include selecting the best individual, random selection and selection according to fitness ratio. Migration replacement strategy: Migration replacement strategy is used to select the replaced individuals in the population when individuals migrate in. The usual strategies include selecting the worst individual, random selection and selection according to fitness ratio.

Immigration selection strategy: When the number of immigrants moving in is more than the number of individuals moving out, such as full interconnection topology, immigration selection strategy is needed to determine the number of immigrants moving in. The usual strategies are the same as the migration selection strategy, including selecting the best individual, random selection and selection according to fitness ratio.

Program implementation: Coarse grained parallel evolutionary algorithm adds migration operation on the basis of serial evolutionary algorithm. In order to increase the flexibility of the program, the migration related parameters are designed in a configurable form, That is, it can be read from the configuration file.

2.3   Parallel Quantum Differential Evolution Algorithm Steps

In a word, the implementation steps of the Parallel Self-Adaptive Quantum Differential Evolution Algorithm (PSAQDEA) proposed in this paper are as follows:

Step 1. Each node initializes the population separately: the initial population Q composed of N quantum chromosomes is generated according to formula (1); Take the mutation probability as PM and contraction factor as F.
Step 2. Each node carries out solution space transformation and fitness ratio calculation separately: according to formula (3), every quantum's chromosome Q is corresponding to a solution X in optimization problem, the fitness degree f (x) of each solution is calculated, and the global optimal solution is updated according to the greedy principle.
Step 3. Each node performs quantum differential operation separately: For every quantum's chromosome in population, the rotating angle of its position is calculated according to (4) and (5), the quantum mutation operation is performed according to (6) and (7), the quantum crossover operation is performed according to (8) and (9), and the quantum selection operation is performed according to (10) and (11).
Step 4. Each node performs quantum non-gate mutation on each quantum chromosome according to formula (13).

Step 5. Each node communicates with each other, migrates and replaces individuals in the cross node population according to the fitness value and the set parameters and migration strategy, and generates the offspring population.

Step 6. Compare the calculation results of fitness: if the convergence conditions are met, the results are output and the program ends; If not, return to step 2.

In the parameter optimization test of some common complex functions, good test results are obtained.

3   Comparison and Analysis of Simulation Results

Take function extreme value as an example, simulation comparison and analysis are carried out to verify the performance of the algorithm.

In the experiment, 12 basic test functions listed in Table 1 are used to verify the performance of the algorithm. The table lists the function abbreviation, function name, dimension, value range, optimal value and threshold. The Performance Experiments study on *Common Ant Colony Algorithm* (CACA) [22], *Common Differential Evolution Algorithm* (CDEA) [23], *Common Genetic Algorithm* (CGA) [24], *implement Quantum Genetic Algorithm* (QGA) [25] and the *Parallel Self-Adaptive Quantum Differential Evolution Algorithm* (PSAQDEA) proposed in this paper and the results are compared.

The five algorithms are programmed with visual studio 2010 and MPICH, and the test results are run on a personal computer with Intel (R) core (TM) i7-6700 3.41 GHz CPU and 8 GB memory. Each algorithm runs 30 times independently, and the iterations' max number is 10000. When the algorithm reaches the specified accuracy or the maximum number of iterations, it is terminated. The average and variance of 30 experiments are recorded, and the number of successful runs of the algorithm is recorded according to the experimental outcome. The experimental outcome of the five algorithms are listed in Table 2. M is the mean and V is the variance.

Table 1. Basic information of related function adopted in the test experiment

Function	name	Dimension	Value range	Optimal value	Solution Accuracy
$f1$	Sphere	30	[−100,100]	0	1.00E−006
$f2$	Rosenbrock	30	[−30,30]	0	1.00E−001
$f3$	Ackley	30	[−32,32]	0	1.00E−006
$f4$	Griewank	30	[−600,600]	0	1.00E−006
$f5$	Rastrigin	30	[−5.12,5.12]	0	1.00E−006
$f6$	Dixon-price	30	[−10,10]	0	1.00E−006
$f7$	Zakharov	10	[−5,10]	0	1.00E−006
$f8$	Michalewicz $_{10}$	10	[0,pi]	−9.6602	−

(*continued*)

Table 1. (*continued*)

Function	name	Dimension	Value range	Optimal value	Solution Accuracy
f_9	Peaks	2	[−3,3]	8.1062	–
f_{10}	Schaffers f_6	2	[−5,5]	0	1.00E-006
f_{11}	Schaffers f_7	2	[−100,100]	0	1.00E-006
f_{12}	Shubert	2	[−10,10]	−186.7309	–

From the Table 2, it can be seen that the algorithm in this paper performs best among the five algorithms. It obtains the global optimal solution of seven test functions and the global optimal solution of 11 test functions. QGA algorithm only obtains the global optimal solution of three test functions and the global optimal solution of 6 test functions. Moreover, the performance of PSAQDEA in this paper is better than QGA algorithm on twelve test functions. Except that the optimization effect on optimizing F6 function is slightly worse than CDEA, it is generally superior to other algorithms, thus it proved the effectiveness of the rules.

Table 2. Comparison of simulation results between the proposed algorithm in the paper and other four algorithms

F	CACA M ± V	CDEA M ± V	CGA M ± V	QGA M ± V	PSAQDEA M ± V
$f1$	6.49E−22 ± 1.64E−36	2.90E−00 ± 4.03E−00	1.31E−19 ± 3.02E−32	3.02E−30 3.4 ± E−32	5.35E−41 ± 0.84E−40
$f2$	2.51E + 01 ± 1.48E−01	3.24E + 02 ± 1.14E + 04	7.70E−00 ± 1.41E−01	2.62E + 01 ± 1.46E−00	1.12E−5 ± 4.72E−06
$f3$	1.81E−14 ± 1.21E−25	1.99E + 01 ± 0.00E−00	3.71E−10 ± 2.71E−20	9.01E−16 + 3.92E−26	9.46E−20 + 3.4E−28
$f4$	3.09E−02 ± 4.28E−04	5.77E−01 ± 8.80E−02	1.12E−12 ± 6.36E−22	0.00 ± 0.00E−00	0.00 ± 0.00E−00
$f5$	2.19E + 01 ± 5.01E + 01	9.96E−02 ± 8.01E−02	1.05E−01 ± 9.18E−02	9.948E−02 ± 8.94E−02	0.00 ± 0.00E−00
$f6$	4.02E−00 ± 1.57E−00	0.00 ± 0.00E−00	7.92E−03 ± 6.50E−04	3.958E−00 ± 1.62E−00	6.87E−06 ± 8.83E−07
$f7$	3.41E−40 ± 8.8 E−42	1.21E + 01 ± 1.28E + 03	4.66E−40 ± 2.69E−40	4.269 E−290 ± 00E−00	0.00 ± 0.00E−00
$f8$	− 6.901 ± 4.18E + 01	− 9.5976E ± 1.18E−03	− 9.6262 ± 4.02E−05	−9.625 ± 8.6E−04	− 9.6601 ± 1.27E−08
$f9$	5.1469 ± 5.01E−01	8.1069 ± 4.13E−30	8.0915 ± 8.67E−25	8.1062 ± 3.16E−30	8.1062 ± 0.00E−00
$f10$	0.00 ± 0.00E−00	2.98E−02 ± 0.00E−00	0.00 ± 0.00E−00	0.00 ± 0.00E−00	0.00 ± 0.00E−00
$f11$	0.00 ± 0.00E−00	0.00 ± 0.00E−00	0.00 ± 0.00E−00	0.00 ± 0.00E−00	0.00 ± 0.00E−00
$f12$	−186.7290 ± 4.96E−04	−186.731 ± 9.04E−09	−186.7309 ± 0.0E−00	− 186.7309 ± 0.00E−00	− 186.7309 ± 0.00E−00

Table 3 shows the success rate of execution of the five algorithms on different test functions. We can say that CGA, QGA and PSAQDEA are better than CDEA and CACA in the success rate of execution, and the PSAQDEA algorithm has the highest success rate. It indicates that the quantum evolutionary algorithm has the advantages of strong exploration ability and good robustness. It also further explains that the algorithm in this paper maintains the advantages of the quantum evolutionary algorithm and overcomes the disadvantages that it is easy to fall into precocity, so that it can achieve better optimization effect.

Table 3. Comparison of execution success rates of the five algorithms

Function	CACA	CDEA	CGA	QGA	PSAQDEA
	SR%				
f1	20	100	100	100	100
f2	0	0	40	15	93
f3	0	100	100	100	100
f4	42	19	100	100	100
f5	25	16	90	100	100
f6	0	100	93	21	100
f7	92	100	100	100	100
f8	37	8	69	38	87
f9	100	0	100	100	100
f10	91	100	100	100	100
f11	74	100	100	100	100
f12	83	47	100	100	100

It can be seen from the above that different algorithms show different performance in different function optimization problems, and the algorithms in this paper all have high convergence ability and strong exploration ability. The reason why PSAQDEA can produce excellent solutions and has better convergence ability is that it adopts learning mode and mutation mode. The learning mode accelerates the development of the population towards the optimal solution, while the mutation mode maintains the diversity of the population. Therefore, the algorithm in this paper can balance the reconnaissance ability and convergence ability.It can control the population diversity in a certain range while keeping good convergence, which further proves the effectiveness of the algorithm.

4   Conclusion

Combined with quantum mechanism and evolutionary algorithm, this paper puts forward a self-adaptive real-coded quantum evolutionary algorithm. It introduces self-adaptive mutation operator and crossover random operator under the framework of two strategies of quantum and differential evolution, so that in the early stages of evolution it makes the population have a better diversity, and in the later stages of the evolution it is advantageous to the local fine search. The algorithm searches the optimal solution quickly and carefully in the solution space. Moreover, due to the introduction of parallel computing based on MPI, the computing power is strengthened. The comparative analysis of the numerical optimization of the test function proves its effectiveness.

Acknowledgments. This research was supported by general scientific research project of education department of Hunan Province in China (21C0338).

References

1. Narayanan, A., Moore, M.: Quantum-inspired genetic algorithms. In: Proceedings of IEEE International Conference on Evolutionary Computation (2002)
2. Abbass, H.A.: The self-adaptive Pareto differential evolution algorithm. In: Evolutionary Computation, 2002. CEC 2002. Proceedings of the 2002 Congress on (2002)
3. Gao, Y., et al.: Performance and power analysis of high-density multi-GPGPU architectures: a preliminary case study. In: IEEE 17th HPCC (2015)
4. Zhao, H., Chen, M., et al.: A novel pre-cache schema for high performance android system. Future Gener. Comput. Syst. **56**, 766–772 (2016)
5. Guo, Y., et al.: Optimal data allocation for scratch-pad memory on embedded multi-core systems. In: IEEE ICPP Conference, pp. 464–471 (2011)
6. Qiu, M., Chen, Z., Liu, M.: Low-power low-latency data allocation for hybrid scratch-pad memory. IEEE Embed. Syst. Lett. **6**(4), 69–72
7. Zhang, L., Qiu, M., Tseng, W., Sha, E.: Variable partitioning and scheduling for MPSoC with virtually shared scratch pad memory. J. Signal Process. Syst. **58**(2), 247–265 (2010)
8. Han, K.H., Kim, J.H.: Quantum-inspired evolutionary algorithm for a class of combinatorial optimization. IEEE Trans. Evolut. Comput. **6**(6), 580–593 (2002)
9. Alba, E., Dorronsoro, B.: The exploration/exploitation tradeoff in dynamic cellular genetic algorithms. IEEE Trans. Evolut. Comput **9**(2), 126–142 (2005)
10. Gropp, W.D., Lusk, E.L., Skjellum, A.: Using MPI–portable parallel programming with the message-parsing interface (1994)
11. Pacheco, P.S.: Parallel Programming with MPI. Argonne National Laboratory, Lemont (1997)
12. You, X., Sheng, L., Shuai, D.: You, X., Liu, S., Shuai, D.: On parallel immune quantum evolutionary algorithm based on learning mechanism and its convergence. In: Jiao, L., Wang, L., Gao, X., Liu, J., Wu, F. (eds.) Advances in Natural Computation. ICNC 2006. LNCS, vol. 4221, pp. 908–913. Springer, Berlin, Heidelberg (2006). https://doi.org/10.1007/118810 70_119
13. Mikki, S.M., Kishk, A.A.: Quantum particle swarm optimization for electromagnetics. IEEE Trans. Antennas Propag. **54**(10), 2764–2775 (2006)
14. Nodehi, A., Tayarani, M., Mahmoudi, F.: A novel functional sized population quantum evolutionary algorithm for fractal image compression. In: Computer Conference (2009)
15. Neto, O., Pacheco, M.: A parallel evolutionary algorithm to search for global minima geometries of heterogeneous ab initio atomic clusters. In: Proceedings of the IEEE Congress on Evolutionary Computation, CEC 2011, New Orleans, LA, USA, 5–8 June 2011
16. Xin, W., Fujimura, S.: Parallel quantum evolutionary algorithms with client-server model for multi-objective optimization on discrete problems. In 2012 IEEE Congress on Evolutionary Computation (2012)

17. Patvardhan, C., Bansal, S., Srivastav, A.: Parallel improved quantum inspired evolutionary algorithm to solve large size quadratic knapsack problems. Swarm Evol. Comput. **26**, 175–190 (2016)
18. Li, J., Li, W.: A new quantum evolutionary algorithm in 0-1 knapsack problem. In: Peng, Hu., Deng, C., Wu, Z., Liu, Y. (eds.) ISICA 2018. CCIS, vol. 986, pp. 142–151. Springer, Singapore (2019). https://doi.org/10.1007/978-981-13-6473-0_13
19. Zheng, Y., et al.: A variable-angle-distance quantum evolutionary algorithm for 2D HP model. In: Sun, X., Pan, Z., Bertino, E. (eds.) Cloud Computing and Security. ICCCS 2018. LNCS, vol. 11068. Springer, Cham (2018). https://doi.org/10.1007/978-3-030-00021-9_30
20. Jiang, J., Guan, S., Mu, X.: Dynamic assignment model of terminal distribution task based on improved quantum evolution algorithm. In: Atiquzzaman, M., Yen, N., Xu, Z. (eds.) Big Data Analytics for Cyber-Physical System in Smart City. BDCPS 2019. AISC, vol. 1117. Springer, Singapore (2020). https://doi.org/10.1007/978-981-15-2568-1_50
21. Atayan, A.M.: Solving the diffusion-convection problem using MPI parallel computing technology. J. Phys. Conf. Ser. **1902**(1), 012098 (2021)
22. Dorigo, M., Maniezzo, V., Colorni, A.: Ant system: optimization by a colony of cooperating agents. IEEE Trans. Syst. Man Cybern. Part B **26**(1), 29–41 (1996)
23. Dong, W.: Research and application based on differential evolution algorithm. Sci. Technol Eng. (2009)
24. Liu, H.: Genetic algorithm based on function optimization. In: Software Guide (2009)
25. Zhang, Z.: Novel improved quantum genetic algorithm. Comput. Eng. **36**(6), 181–183 (2010)

A Privacy-Preserving Auditable Approach Using Threshold Tag-Based Encryption in Consortium Blockchain

Yunwei Guo[1,2], Haokun Tang[1], Aidi Tan[3], Lei Xu[4], Keke Gai[2,4(✉)], and Xiongwei Jia[5]

[1] School of Computer Science and Technology, Beijing Institute of Technology, Beijing 100081, China
{3220211008,3220211194}@bit.edu.cn
[2] Yangtze Delta Region Academy of Beijing Institute of Technology, Jiaxing 314019, Zhejiang, China
gaikeke@bit.edu.cn
[3] China Institute of Marine Technology and Economy, Beijing 100081, China
tanaidi@cimtec.net.cn
[4] School of Cyberspace Science and Technology, Beijing Institute of Technology, Beijing 100081, China
6120180029@bit.edu.cn
[5] China Unicom Research Institute, Beijing 100032, China
jiaxw9@chinaunicom.cn

Abstract. The rising attention of deploying consortium blockchain in the industry has facilitated a wide scope of enterprise-level applications. In consortium blockchain, each participant's identity needs to be verified before it joins the blockchain network, which implies both identity leakage and the linkability between entites are targets for privacy attackers. In this paper, we propose a novel approach to hide both identity and linking relations between participants. An auditor role is developed in our solution to trace down suspicious transactions to identify malicious participants in a decentralized manner. Security analysis and experiment evaluations are given for evidencing the effectiveness of our approach in this work.

Keywords: Consortium blockchain · Threshold tag-based encryption · Privacy-preserving · Auditable blockchain

1 Introduction

Blockchain technology has attracted increasing interests of worldwide researchers in recent years because of its potential benefits to commerce and authoritative administration. As a type of permissioned blockchain, consortium blockchain only allows authorized participants to join the network. The identifiable entities/ members in a consortium blockchain have different accessability and authorities

M. Qiu et al. (Eds.): SmartCom 2021, LNCS 13202, pp. 265–275, 2022.
https://doi.org/10.1007/978-3-030-97774-0_24

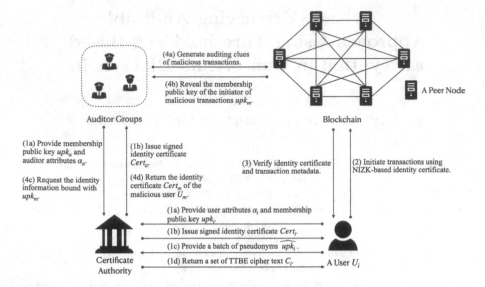

Fig. 1. The major workflow of the proposed scheme *i.e.* (1) Identity Preparation, (2) Transaction Initiation, (3) Transaction Validation, and (4) Transaction Auditing.

by their attributes. Therefore, a member must prove that it has the right authority that satisfies the predetermined access control policies whenever interacting with the blockchain.

Blockchain privacy has become the focus of research along with its growth [1–3]. An anonymous blockchain network generally is required to achieve both *identity privacy*, and *transaction unlinkability* [4]. The identity privacy emphasizes screening the real identity of the participant. Many current blockchain systems use pseudonym-based solutions to hide identities, e.g., bitcoin. However, true anonymity cannot be achieved by this type of solutions, as it can hardly hide linkage relations of different users. The transactional behavior of an bitcoin user can be analyzed under deanonymization attacks [5–7]. So far, many cryptographic mechanisms such as mixing services, ring signature scheme, zero-knowledge proof *etc.*, have been leveraged in order to enhance the privacy in permissionless blockchains [8–10]. As for consortium blockchains, anonymity is relatively hard to realize since it relies on the user identities to realize access control. Whereas anonymity property is necessary in many business scenarios, a number of related works has been done recently [11–13].

While anonymity is important in blockchain, the demand for accountability is also a major concern. Perfect anonymity in blockchain could abet malicious transactions, which compromises the security of a blockchain network. Malicious users abuse the anonymity of cryptocurrencies (public blockchains) to conduct blackmailing, money laundering, ransomware dissemination, *etc.*, which seriously harms the social security. The contradiction between the anonymity and accountability makes them difficult to coexist in a blockchain network, This dilemma urges researchers to come up with better solutions to achieve both anonymity and accountability simultaneously in blockchain.

In this paper, we propose ATChain—a privacy preserving threshold auditable consortium blockchain framework. To be more specific, ATChain allows its users to interact with the blockchain without revealing its real-world identity information while the users can still prove the authorization legitimacy. We also introduce *auditors* to ATChain, who are empowered to collaboratively trace down questionable transactions. When encounter a problematic transaction, each auditor publishes its own auditing clue, and subsequently combine the collected clues to disclose the real-world identity of the initiator of this transaction. The high level workflow is depicted by Fig. 1.

In summary, the main contributions of our work are twofold:

- We propose ATChain, which is a scheme that allows users to transact anonymously in a consortium blockchain, and transactions are auditable by auditors in a distributed manner. We modified the blockchain transaction validation process to comply with our scheme.
- We design smart contracts that ensures the transaction auditing process is executed automatically under regulation.

The remainder of the paper is organized as follows: Next, we present the modeling and detailed workflow of ATChain in Sect. 2. In Sect. 3, we analyze the security of ATChain, and conducted experiments to evaluate the performance of ATChain. Finally, we draw a conclusion of our work in Sect. 4.

2   Proposed Model

2.1   System Objectives

The proposed scheme is designed to fulfill the following system objectives:

- **Identity Privacy:** The users in the consortium blockchain network transact anonymously without revealing the identity information. However, users can still prove the identity legitimacy to the peer nodes.
- **Transactions Unlinkability:** The unlinkability feature of our scheme is reflected in two aspects: (1) The linkage between the blockchain transactions of a user's real identity cannot be detected by the public. That is, it cannot be detected that a certain number of transactions are initiated by the same user; (2) The linkage between the blockchain transaction identity and the real-world identity of a user is shielded.
- **Transactions Threshold Accountability:** The auditors in the blockchain network are empowered to trace down suspicious and problematic transactions in a decentralized manner. When encounter a questionable transaction, the auditors can collaboratively trace down the real identity of the user who proposed the transaction. Also, malicious users cannot forge malicious transactions that ends up tracing to honest users.

We apply the following security assumptions for each entity to our scheme:

1. **Certificate Authority (CA):** We assume that the certificate authority is honest who issues correct identity certificates to other entities and will not deviate from the proposed scheme. The CA will leak a certificate only if the corresponding user is malicious and has been traced down.
2. **Users:** The users acts arbitrarily for the best of their benefits. Therefore, they can be malicious and attempt to compromise the security of our system. They may forge identities and initiates malicious transactions using identities of honest users.
3. **Peers and Blockchain:** We assume the given consensus algorithm is secure enough to tolerate the dishonesty of peer nodes. The peers obeys the proposed scheme to validate the blockchain transactions.
4. **Auditors:** We assume the honest auditors can rightfully judge the legitimacy of a transaction. Auditors can be compromised by adversaries and thereby behave maliciously. The number of malicious auditors is under the predetermined threshold value.

2.2 Main Components

As depicted by Fig. 1, there are mainly four kinds of entities in our system.

1. **Certificate Authority (CA):** A certificate authority (CA) is utilized to manage the identities of the entities in the consortium blockchain network. An consortium blockchain entity such as an user must possesses an identity certificate issued by the CA. The CA receives the attributes and the public key from a user, and issues an identity certificates signed by the secret key of the CA in exchange. In addition to the user public key and user attributes, the certificate contains the signature of the CA. The copies of signed identity certificates of the blockchain entities are stored locally by the CA.
2. **Users:** An user makes interactions with the consortium blockchain network by initiating transactions. An user in the system model possesses attributes (hereinafter denoted as α) which reflect its real-world identity information such as email address, department etc. In the proposed system, users transact anonymously without revealing their real-word identity information.
3. **Peer Nodes:** Peer nodes (hereinafter referred to peers) are entities that process and verify transactions initiated by blockchain users by leveraging a consensus algorithm. Peers are responsible to ensure that the transactions are from legitimate users according to the access control policy of the consortium blockchain network. Transactions that are verified by the peers can be recorded on the blockchain ledger.
4. **Auditors:** The group of auditors is a predetermined quorum to monitor and administrate the transactions in the consortium blockchain network in a distributed way. A leader is selected among the auditors to initialize ATChain. The auditors spot questionable transactions in the blockchain and collaboratively track down the identity information of a malicious user. When carrying out their duties, auditors should present their legitimate identity certificates issued by the certificate authority.

2.3   Workflow Design

Initialization. The initialization of the ATChain consists of the setup of the blockchain network and the cryptographic parameters. The leader of the auditors A^* brings up the consortium blockchain network according to the network configuration NetConf, and set the access control policy Φ. The notation Φ defines an attribute-based access control policy for the consortium blockchain. Then, A^* obtains the TTBE public keys tpk, a list of TTBE verification keys $tvk = \{tvk_1, \ldots, tvk_n\}$, and a list of TTBE private keys $tsk = \{tsk_1, \ldots, tsk_n\}$ by invoking $\Pi_{\text{TKPE}}.\text{Setup}(1^\lambda, t, n)$. The leading auditor A^* disseminates tvk and tsk to n auditors respectively. Also, A^* invokes $\Pi_{\text{NIZK}}.\text{SetUp}(1^\lambda, \mathcal{R})$, where $\mathcal{R}$ is an NIZK relation, to get the common reference string (pk, vk) for NIZK. Finally, the blockchain ledger records the initialization parameters $(A^*, \text{NetConf}, t, n, \Phi, tpk, tvk)$, and hence the initialization completes.

User Identity Preparation. For each user U_i in the ATChain, a pair of asymmetric key $uk_i = (upk_i, usk_i)$ is generated. The user U_i uses upk_i to obtain an identity certificate from the certificate authority CA. From the perspective of CA, upon receiving the input (upk_i, α_i), the CA invokes $\Pi_{\text{SIG}}.\text{Sign}(csk, (upk_i, \alpha_i))$ to generate a signature σ_{U_i} using the private key csk of CA. With the signature σ_{U_i}, an identity certification $Cert_i = \{uk_i, \alpha_i, \sigma_{U_i}\}$ issued by CA is returned to U_i. The CA stores $Cert_i$ to its local database $\mathcal{B}$. Also, a list of m pseudonymous asymmetric keys $\widehat{uk_i} = \{(\widehat{upk_{i1}}, \widehat{usk_{i1}}), \ldots, (\widehat{upk_{im}}, \widehat{usk_{im}})\}$ is generated for subsequent blockchain transactions. The user U_i can generate as many pseudonymous keys as it wants at any time. However, before a pair of pseudonymous keys $\widehat{uk_{ij}} = (\widehat{upk_{ij}}, \widehat{usk_{ij}})$ can be used for transactions, a tag-based cipher text of $\widehat{uk_{ij}}$ generated by CA is needed. Therefore, the user U_i sends a portion of its pseudonymous public keys $\widehat{upk_i}' = \{\widehat{upk_{i1}}, \ldots, \widehat{upk_{im'}}\}$, where $\widehat{upk_i}' \subseteq \widehat{upk_i}$, to CA. For each public key in $\widehat{upk_i}'$, a corresponding TTBE cipher text c_{ij} is generated by CA using the algorithm $\Pi_{\text{TTBE}}.\text{Encrypt}$. With inputting the TTBE public key tpk, the public key of U_i i.e. upk_i, and $\widehat{upk_{ij}} \in \widehat{upk_i}'$ as a tag, $\Pi_{\text{TTBE}}.\text{Encrypt}$ outputs TTBE cipher text c_{ij}. In addition, a signature for c_{ij} is generated by invoking $\Pi_{\text{SIG}}.\text{Sign}(csk, c_{ij})$, which returns $\sigma_{c_{ij}}$ Finally, the CA returns a list C_i consists of $\{(c_{i1}, \sigma_{c_{i1}}), \ldots (c_{im'}, \sigma_{c_{im'}})\}$ to U_i. The user U_i pushes the elements of TTBE cipher text list C_i into the locally maintained stack Θ_i. For clarity, the above procedure can be concluded into Algorithm 1.

Transaction Initiation. A user U_i utilizes its various pseudonymous asymmetric key pairs to transact in the ATChain in order to preserve unlinkability. Also, ATChain leverages non-interactive zero-knowledge (NIZK) proof technique to hide the identity information of U_i. The anonymous transaction procedure is conducted as the following steps:

Algorithm 1. Identity Preparation Algorithm

Require: $upk_i, \alpha_i, \widehat{uk_{ij}}, csk, tpk, \mathcal{B}$.
Ensure: $Cert_i, C_i$.
1: **for all** certification $Cert_k$ in $\mathcal{B}$ **do**
2:    **if** $Cert_k == Cert_i$ **then**
3:       **return** $\perp$.
4:    **end if**
5: **end for**
6: $\sigma_{U_i} \leftarrow \Pi_{\mathrm{SIG}}.\mathsf{Sign}(csk, (upk_i, \alpha_i))$.
7: Set $Cert_i \leftarrow \{uk_i, \alpha_i, \sigma_{U_i}\}$.
8: Set $C_i \leftarrow \emptyset$.
9: **for all** pseudonymous public key $\widehat{upk_{ij}} \in \widehat{upk_i}'$ **do**
10:    $c_{ij} \leftarrow \Pi_{\mathrm{TTBE}}.\mathsf{Encrypt}(tpk, upk_i, \widehat{upk_{ij}})$.
11:    $\sigma_{c_{ij}} \leftarrow \Pi_{\mathrm{SIG}}.\mathsf{Sign}(csk, c_{ij})$.
12:    Append $(c_{ij}, \sigma_{c_{ij}})$ to C_i.
13: **end for**
14: Store $Cert_i$ to local database $\mathcal{B}$ of CA.
15: **return** C_i and $Cert_i$ to user U_i.

---

1. U_i checks its stack Θ_i, if $\Theta = \emptyset$, the anonymous transaction procedure is aborted. Else, U_i pops an element $\theta_i = (c_{ij}, \sigma_{c_{ij}})$ from the stack Θ_i. The $\widehat{uk_{ij}} = \{\widehat{upk_{ij}}, \widehat{usk_{ij}}\}$ corresponding to θ_i will be used as the current transaction key pair.
2. U_i invokes $\Pi_{\mathrm{SIG}}.\mathsf{Sign}(usk_i, \widehat{upk_{ij}})$ to get a signature $\widehat{\sigma_{upk_{ij}}}$ on $\widehat{upk_{ij}}$ signed by its secret key usk_i.
3. U_i generates an NIZK proof $\pi_{ij} = \Pi_{\mathrm{NIZK}}.\mathsf{Prove}(pk, x, w)$, where $x = (c_{ij}, \sigma_{c_{ij}}, \Phi, tpk, cpk)$, and $w = (upk_i, \alpha_i, \widehat{\sigma_{upk_{ij}}})$.
4. U_i computes a signature σ_Γ on $(\pi_{ij}, c_{ij}, \sigma_{c_{ij}}, \widehat{upk_{ij}})$ using current pseudonymous private key $\widehat{usk_{ij}}$ by invoking $\Pi_{\mathrm{SIG}}.\mathsf{Sign}$. Henceforth, the $\Gamma = (\pi_{ij}, c_{ij}, \sigma_{c_{ij}}, \widehat{upk_{ij}}, \sigma_\Gamma)$ is appended to every blockchain transaction initiated by the U_i in the future.

Transaction Validation. The peer nodes in ATChain maintains the blockchain ledger via a given consensus algorithm. Additional to the original consensus algorithm, an extra validation step is required as a part of the consensus procedure. The peers should verify that the transactions are signed correctly and initiated by users that has certified attributes satisfying the access control policies.

From the perspective of a peer node P_k, the following procedure is conducted for every received transaction tx:

1. P_k extracts Γ from the transaction tx, where $\Gamma = (\pi, c, \sigma_c, \widehat{upk}, \sigma_\Gamma)$. Run $\Pi_{\mathrm{SIG}}.\mathsf{Verify}(\widehat{upk_{ij}}, \sigma_\Gamma, (\pi, c, \sigma_c, \widehat{upk}))$ and get the result r_1. If $r_1 = 0$, P_k rejects the transaction tx. Else, if $r_1 = 1$, which implies that σ_Γ is valid, proceed on to the next step.

Algorithm 2. Smart Contract - Audit

Require: $tpk, tvk_j, \mu_j, \Gamma_j$
Ensure: Update the auditing record AR_j of Γ_j on the blockchain ledger.

1: **if** $\Pi_{\mathrm{TTBE}}.\mathsf{ShareVer}(tpk, tvk_j, \Gamma_j.fpk, \Gamma_j.c, \mu_j) = 0$ **then**
2:     return Failed.
3: **end if**
4: Set $AR_j \leftarrow \emptyset$.
5: Fetch all auditing records AR from ledger $\mathcal{L}$.
6: **for all** Auditing records $AR_k \in AR$ **do**
7:     **if** $AR_k.\Gamma_k = \Gamma_j$ **then**
8:       Set $AR_j \leftarrow AR_k$.
9:     **end if**
10: **end for**
11: **if** $AR_j = \emptyset$ **then**
12:     Set $st_j \leftarrow$ collecting.
13:     Set $AC_j \leftarrow \{\mu_j\}$.
14:     Set $TVK_j = \{tvk_j\}$.
15:     Set $AR_j \leftarrow (\Gamma_j, AC_j, TVK_j, st_j)$.
16:     Publish AR_j to $\mathcal{L}$.
17: **end if**
18: Append μ_j to $AR_j.AC_j$.
19: Append tvk_j to $AR_j.TVK_j$.
20: **if** $|AR_j.AC_j| = t$ **then**
21:     Set $r \leftarrow \Pi_{\mathrm{TTBE}}.\mathsf{Combine}(tpk, AR_j.TVK_j, \Gamma_j.fpk, \Gamma_j.c, AR_j.AC_j)$.
22:     **if** $r \neq \perp$ **then**
23:       Append r to AR_j.
24:       Publish AR_j to $\mathcal{L}$.
25:       return Success.
26:     **else**
27:       return Failed.
28:     **end if**
29: **end if**

---

2. P_k runs $\Pi_{\mathrm{SIG}}.\mathsf{Verify}(cpk, \sigma_c, c)$ to check whether the TTBE cipher text c is generated by the CA rather than a forge one generated by blockchain users. If the algorithm $\Pi_{\mathrm{SIG}}.\mathsf{Verify}$ returns a $r_2 = 0$, P_k rejects tx. Else, if $r_2 = 1$, P_k proceeds on thr following step.

3. P_k runs algorithm $\Pi_{\mathrm{NIZK}}.\mathsf{Verify}(vk, \pi, x)$, where $x = (c, \sigma_c, \Phi, tpk, cpk)$, to get the result r_3. If $r_3 = 0$, reject the transaction tx. Else, if $r_3 = 1$, which implies that the initiator of tx genuinely possesses attributes α and a legal signature σ_U.

The tx is valid if $r_1 \wedge r_2 \wedge r_3 = 1$ or tx is rejected otherwise.

Transaction Auditing. When transaction disputes occurs, the group of auditors can collaboratively track down the malicious user by finding its public key. A transaction audition procedure can be concluded into the following steps:

Table 1. The performance evaluation of smart contract Audit.

Threshold	Time cost (s)
8	14.21
9	17.28
10	20.11
11	21.18
12	23.62
13	24.19
14	25.43
15	27.76

Table 2. The performance of *User Identity Preparation* procedure.

Batch size	Time cost (ms)
5	205
10	401
15	653
20	842
25	1001
30	1242

1. When an auditor A_k finds a transaction $\Gamma_j = (\pi_i, c_i, \sigma_{c_i}, \widehat{upk_i}, \sigma_{\Gamma_j})$ is possibly been compromised, A_k queries the blockchain ledger to check whether this transaction Γ_j has already been issued. If Γ_j has already been recorded on the blockchain ledger as a questionable transaction, A_k goes on to the next step. Else, A_k initializes a triple $AR_j = (\Gamma_j, AC_j, TV_j, st_j)$, where AC_j is an array of auditing clues whose initial value is $\emptyset$, $st_j \in \{\texttt{collecting}, \texttt{combined}\}$ is the status of auditing record AR_j.

2. A_k computes an auditing clue μ_k by invoking $\Pi_{\text{TTBE}}.\mathsf{ShareDec}(tpk, tsk_k, \widehat{upk_i}, c_i)$. By invoking smart contract, A_k appends the auditing clue μ_k to array AC_j of the AR_j.

3. After t auditing clues has been collected with respect to the auditing record AR_j, the smart contract will automatically combines them using $\Pi_{\text{TTBE}}.\mathsf{Combine}(tpk, tvk, c_i, \widehat{upk_i}, \mu)$, which outputs the decryption of c_i *i.e.* upk_i.

4. With the public key of U_i, auditors are able to query the CA and get the identity information of U_i stored in the database $\mathcal{B}$ of CA.

The smart contract that is used in the transaction audition process is illustrated in Algorithm 2.

3 Experiment Evaluations

To examine the practicality and adoptability, we simulated ATChain based on Hyperledger Fabric[1] which is an infrastructural framework of consortium blockchain. To be fully compatible with ATChain, we made some modifications towards the original Fabric source code. We modified the validation system chaincode (VSCC) and endorsement system chaincode (ESCC) of Fabric by making it supportive towards NIZK proof validation. We also developed a certificate authority service that functions as the CA in ATChain. The smart contracts

---

[1] https://github.com/hyperledger/fabric.

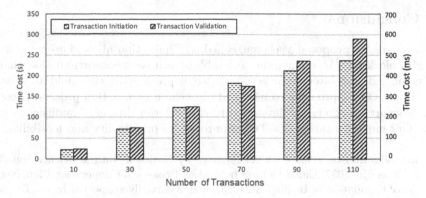

Fig. 2. The performance of *transaction initiation* and *transaction validation* procedures.

and off-chain operations in ATChain were developed in Golang. We used go-snark which is a Golang open source library to realize NIZK proof in ATChain. The digital signature scheme we used in the implementation is based on the RSA signature scheme. For the instantiation of threshold tag-based encryption scheme, we implemented the scheme proposed by Ghadafi [14] using the Type-III BN256 elliptic curve Golang library[2]. The following evaluations were conducted on a Lenovo laptop equipped with an 8-core CPU AMD Ryzen 7800H 3.2 GHz, 16 GB RAM, running the Windows 11 64-bit operating system.

First of all, we tested the performance of smart contract Audit of Algorithm 2 among 15 auditors. The threshold value t of TTBE scheme was set to a range from 8 to 15. We developed automatic testing scripts to make auditors invoke the smart contract respectively on 300 ms time interval. The Table 1 displays the time cost of the smart contract Audit with different TTBE threshold value. We observe that the time cost has a linear relationship with the threshold value. In addition, we tested the performance of initiating transactions in ATChain, which includes the *transaction initiation* and *transaction validation* procedures mentioned in Sect. 2.3. The initiation was measured in seconds while the validation was measured in milliseconds. To conduct this experiment, we created a dummy smart contract where no operations is done since the execution time of the smart contract is irrelevant to this experiment. The Fig. 2 shows the time consumption of running transactions from 10 to 110 times. Finally, we tested the performance of the *User Identity Preparation* procedure. We set the batch size of the pseudonymous public keys from 5 to 30. The time consumption is illustrated in Table 2. The time cost increases linearly as the batch size grows bigger.

---

[2] https://cs.opensource.google/go/x/crypto.

4   Conclusions

In this paper, we proposed a scheme, called ATChain, that allowed users to interact with blockchain by anonymous auditable identities in consortium blockchain. We combined non-interactive zero-knowledge proof with threshold tag-based encryption. Our approach also modified blockchain transaction process. A compatible smart contract was developed to support the threshold auditing procedure. Our implementation of ATChain proved its practicality and feasibility.

Acknowledgements. This work is supported by National Natural Science Foundation of China 61871037, China Unicom Innovation Ecological Cooperation Plan, Natural Science Foundation of Beijing (M21035), and is partially supported by the Defense Industrial Technology Development Program (Grant No. JCKY2020206C058).

References

1. Gai, K., et al.: Differential privacy-based blockchain for industrial Internet-of-Things. IEEE Trans. Ind. Inform. **16**(6), 4156–4165 (2019)
2. Gai, K., et al.: Permissioned blockchain and edge computing empowered privacy-preserving smart grid networks. IEEE Internet Things J. **6**(5), 7992–8004 (2019)
3. Gai, K., et al.: Privacy-preserving energy trading using consortium blockchain in smart grid. IEEE Trans. Ind. Inform. **15**(6), 3548–3558 (2019)
4. Feng, Q., et al.: A survey on privacy protection in blockchain system. J. Netw. Comput. Appl. **126**, 45–58 (2019)
5. Ron, D., Shamir, A.: Quantitative analysis of the full bitcoin transaction graph. In: Sadeghi, A.-R. (ed.) FC 2013. LNCS, vol. 7859, pp. 6–24. Springer, Heidelberg (2013). https://doi.org/10.1007/978-3-642-39884-1_2
6. Androulaki, E., Karame, G.O., Roeschlin, M., Scherer, T., Capkun, S.: Evaluating user privacy in bitcoin. In: Sadeghi, A.-R. (ed.) FC 2013. LNCS, vol. 7859, pp. 34–51. Springer, Heidelberg (2013). https://doi.org/10.1007/978-3-642-39884-1_4
7. Fleder, M., Kester, M., Pillai, S.: Bitcoin transaction graph analysis. arXiv preprint arXiv:1502.01657 (2015)
8. Ben-Sasson, E., et al.: Zerocash: decentralized anonymous payments from bitcoin. In: IEEE Symposium on Security and Privacy, pp. 459–474. IEEE (2014)
9. Monero project. https://www.getmonero.org
10. Bonneau, J., Narayanan, A., Miller, A., Clark, J., Kroll, J.A., Felten, E.W.: Mixcoin: anonymity for bitcoin with accountable mixes. In: Christin, N., Safavi-Naini, R. (eds.) FC 2014. LNCS, vol. 8437, pp. 486–504. Springer, Heidelberg (2014). https://doi.org/10.1007/978-3-662-45472-5_31
11. Androulaki, E., et al.: Privacy-preserving auditable token payments in a permissioned blockchain system. In: 2nd ACM Conference on Advances in Financial Technologies, pp. 255–267 (2020)
12. Shao, W., et al.: AttriChain: decentralized traceable anonymous identities in privacy-preserving permissioned blockchain. Comput. Secur. **99**, 102069 (2020)
13. Hardjono, T., et al.: Anonymous identities for permissioned blockchains (2014)
14. Ghadafi, E.: Efficient distributed tag-based encryption and its application to group signatures with efficient distributed traceability. In: Aranha, D.F., Menezes, A. (eds.) LATINCRYPT 2014. LNCS, vol. 8895, pp. 327–347. Springer, Cham (2015). https://doi.org/10.1007/978-3-319-16295-9_18

15. Nakamoto, S.: Bitcoin: a peer-to-peer electronic cash system. Decentralized Business Review, p. 21260 (2008)
16. Miers, I., Garman, C., Green, M., Rubin, A.: Zerocoin: anonymous distributed e-cash from bitcoin. In: IEEE Symposium on S & P, pp. 397–411. IEEE (2013)

A Hop-Parity-Involved Task Schedule for Lightweight Racetrack-Buffer in Energy-Efficient NoCs

Wanhao Cao[1], Jihe Wang[2(✉)], Danghui Wang[3], and Kuizhi Mei[4]

[1] School of Computer Science, Northwestern Polytechnical University, Xi'an, China
caowh@mail.nwpu.edu.cn
[2] School of Computer Science, Northwestern Polytechnical University and National
Engineering Laboratory for Integrated Aero-Space-Ground-Ocean Big Data
Application Technology, Xi'an, China
wangjihe@nwpu.edu.cn
[3] School of Computer Science, Northwestern Polytechnical University
and Engineering Research Center of Embedded System Integration,
Ministry of Education, Xi'an, China
wangdh@nwpu.edu.cn
[4] Institute of Artificial Intelligence and Robotics, Xi'an Jiaotong University,
Xi'an, China
meikuizhi@mail.xjtu.edu.cn

Abstract. Traditional NoC's buffer design mainly bases on SRAM that could not break through the high static power consumption characteristics by itself, which could be solved by emerging NVMs, such as energy-efficient RTM (Racetrack Memory). Using RTM instead of SRAM for NoC buffer design can directly reduce the static energy to near-zero level. However, RTM is not friendly to random access due to its port alignment operation, called *invalid shift*. This paper proposes to replace random FIFO-buffer with sequential LIFO-buffer for lightweight transmission in NoC, which can overcome the expense of *invalid shift*. However, the LIFO design incurs flits flipping during transmission and leads to extra endianess-correction cost in odd-path. Therefore, this paper designs a hop-parity-involved task schedule that avoids those odd-path during the communications among tasks, by which the extra endianess-correction can be totally removed. Our experiments show that RTM-LIFO buffer design can achieve over 50% energy saving than SRAM-FIFO buffer.

Keywords: Racetrack memory · Network on chip · Scheduling algorithm · Shift

1 Introduction

NoC (Network-on-Chip) is the main communication architecture for on-chip interconnection of multi-core processors [1], as NoC has fast speed and good

M. Qiu et al. (Eds.): SmartCom 2021, LNCS 13202, pp. 276–285, 2022.
https://doi.org/10.1007/978-3-030-97774-0_25

Table 1. Characteristics of Different Memory Technologies (R/W = read/write) [11]

Feature	SRAM	EDRAM	STT-RAM	PCM	RTM
Cell size (F^2)	120–200	60–100	6–50	4–12	≥ 2
Write Endurance	10^{16}	10^{16}	$4*10^{12}$	$10^8 - 10^9$	10^{16}
Speed (R/W)	Very fast	Fast	Fast/slow	Very slow	Fast/slow
Leakage Power	High	Medium	Low	Low	Low
Dynamic Energy (R/W)	Low	Medium	Low/high	Medium/high	Low/high

scalability which is particularly suitable for large-scale complex networks. But every node in the NoC contains buffer called virtual channel which mainly use SRAM as a storage medium to ensure nanosecond-level read and write speeds. However, a single SRAM-Cell contains six transistors, resulting in extremely low energy efficiency of NoC [2–4]. Especially due to the dark silicon effect, a large number of unused SRAMs also generate great static power consumption. Therefore, SRAM-based NoC-buffer become the main reason for NoC's energy efficiency bottleneck [5]. The use of new storage materials with lower power consumption and smaller size to build buffers is a trend in on-chip interconnect research.

Since the traditional SRAM technology has been unable to adapt to NoC's low-power, high-density on-chip storage requirements, researchers try to use a variety of NVM to build NoC-buffer, such as PCM [6], ReRAM [7], STT-RAM [8], Racetrack Memory [9], etc. Among them, RTM has the smallest cell size under the same process, and is faster than other magnetic storage media in terms of read and write latency, and also has extremely low static power consumption characteristics. Compared with SRAM, the storage density of RTM can be increased by 32.4 times [10]. At the same time, RTM has a feature of almost zero static power consumption as a magnetic memory, which meets the design requirements of an ideal NoC-buffer (Table 1).

RTM is a kind of sequential access-friendly memory. A large number of cells are divided by using magnetic domain walls on the ferromagnetic nanowire. It represents 0 and 1 according to the rotation direction of the electrons in the cell. One or more access ports can be set on a nanowire according to requirements. When the RTM performs a read or write operation, the magnetic domain wall is first moved by current to align the corresponding cell with the port, and then the memory access operation is performed through the port. This shift operation bring additional energy and delay overhead, and it is necessary to adapt the design according to the memory access characteristics of the memory to reduce the shift operation as much as possible to achieve the excellent characteristics of RTM with low power consumption and high integration.

NoC buffer is designed based on the random access characteristics, which cause much shift operations in RTM to cause performance degradation [12]. The solution is to design a reasonable memory access order according to data transmission. The unit processed by NoC buffer is flits whose length is determined according to the network protocol, and is processed in the rule of FIFO. By using flit as a minimum processing object, each flit is assigned on a ferromagnetic nanowire and read-write port, and the flit is processed according to the LIFO method. In each flit transmission process, the access port first move from the initial position to the end to realize the writing process, and then move back to read data. The process of LIFO can eliminate the existence of invalid shift operations. However, an odd number of read-write operations cause the endianness of the data to be inverted. Recovering the endianness cause a large delay. The original task scheduling scheme needs to be adjusted to avoid the performance degradation caused by the odd number of read-write operation in a single transmission.

The traditional scheduling algorithm is based on task characteristics and network characteristics, and reasonably matches each task with the processor [15]. However, it not consider the delay overhead caused by the additional endianness recovering operation at the end of the transmission caused by the data transmission path that requires an odd number of read-write. Gradually improving scheduling performance through multiple scheduling is a common processing method [16–18]. This paper proposes a scheduling correction algorithm. First, based on the original scheduling, find out the matching relationships that cause an odd number of read-write paths, and store the nodes in these relationships in a priority queue for sequential processing. Afterwards, in the process of rescheduling each node, avoid the generation of odd-numbered read-write paths and Reschedule according to the earliest completion priority criterion. This can ensure that all the elements in the queue can be processed after a limited number of iterations, and finally achieve unending adjustment through task scheduling.

The rest of the paper is organized as follows. The second section is background, introducing the characteristics of Racetrack Memory. The third section is the RTM-LIFO buffer design, and the fourth section is the scheduling correction algorithm. Section 5 shows the experiments and results of this article. The sixth section is conclusion.

2   Background

RTM is a magnetic tape-like memory that stores one bit of data by splitting ferromagnetic nanowires into a large number of domains with domain wall. The direction of electronic rotation in the domain can represent 0 and 1. When the RTM accesses memory, the domain wall is first driven by current to move to align the domain with the memory access port, and then read or write operations are implemented through the port. A nanowire can store hundreds of bits but its area is insignificant compared to a transistor. Because a memory cell can store multiple bits, RTM has an advantage in integration compared to other NVMs.

But the RTM's tape-based memory access characters brings additional challenges. When performing random storage on the RTM, each data access need to be shifted for alignment operations. Irregular storage bring a large number of invalid shifts, causing a sharp drop in performance. RTM can be applied to all levels of storage structures with its large capacity, fast speed, and nearly zero static power consumption features, but it must be designed to reduce or eliminate invalid shifts to ensure performance [22] (Fig. 1).

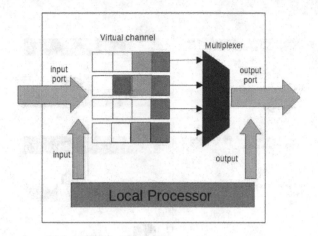

Fig. 1. Schematic diagram of NoC node

3   Method

NoC is the main communication method of the multi-core system, replacing the bus connection with the advantages of high speed and high scalability. Each NoC node is composed of processing units, routers, communication ports, etc. The data enters the buffer called the virtual channel inside the router through the port, and then flows to the output port or the local processing unit through the multiplexer. When sending data locally, it is also written into the buffer first, and then routed to the next node. Buffer plays an important role in the process of data transmission.

The traditional buffer processing method is FIFO, with a clear sequence, which has no effect on the SRAM that is stored at random, and can process data simply and effectively. But for RTM, it naturally cause huge shift overhead. Take Fig. 2 as an example. When the data stream abc is written into the RTM, the write port moves three units to the right from a and stays at the data c. When the data should be read for routing, the port must first return to data a, so that two invalid shifts be generated, and then read to the position of data c in turn, and finally restored. In this way, half shift operations are invalid, which cause higher energy consumption and delay losses. By increasing the port and adjusting the position of the port, the effect of changing space for time can be achieved, but for FIFO-based buffers, the shift operation can only be reduced to a certain extent, which still constitutes a performance bottleneck.

The LIFO buffer design proposed in this article can completely eliminate invalid shifts. First of all, each RTM memory cell (containing a nanowire) is used as a minimum storage unit, and the bits in a flit be completely stored on one nanowire, and the memory cell be exclusively used during storage. As shown in Fig. 3, when an arbitrary fixed-length data stream (take abc as an example) is written, the read-write port sequentially writes data from the initial position to the last bit. When it is the turn of the data to be read and routed, the read-write

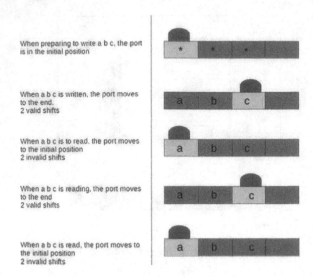

Fig. 2. Memory access process based on FIFO buffer

port directly reads the data from the position where it stayed before, until the reading is completed. This scheme has no invalid shifts at all, which guarantees the performance of RTM. The length of the flit is generally several or dozens of bits, which is less than the design length of the nanowire to ensure that the data does not overflow.

But after a read-write operation, the endianness of the data is reversed, which cause the data that needs an odd number of read-write operations to reach the sink node require an additional reversal operation. If a data reversal device is added to each node, each flit arriving at the target node may cause additional waiting time and greater time overhead. The current NoC network is highly robust, and there are usually multiple paths to choose from between nodes. By adjusting the task scheduling scheme, it is possible to avoid paths through odd-numbered nodes, thereby avoiding additional performance overhead caused by inconsistent endianness.

4   Scheduling Algorithm

Task scheduling algorithm is an important tool to improve the efficiency of multi-core systems [19–21]. Its task model is a DAG (Directed Acyclic Graph) model. In this model, DAG $= (V, E, t, w)$, $V = \{v_1, v_2, v_3, ...v_i\}$ is the set of the tasks. $E \subset V * V$ is the relationship between tasks and represented by the direction of edges, and the communication between task i and task j is represented by the w_{ij}. Time needed by task i is t_i. For NoC, it is formed by N*N homogeneous tile which have a processor and a router. The ultimate goal is to match the task with each processing unit in the multi-core system to increase the processing speed as high as possible. This scheduling algorithm is an NP-hard problem, and

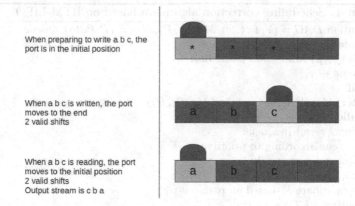

When preparing to write a b c, the
port is in the initial position

When a b c is written, the port
moves to the end
2 valid shifts

When a b c is reading, the port
moves to the initial position
2 valid shifts
Output stream is c b a

Fig. 3. Memory access process based on LIFO buffer

it cannot guarantee an optimal solution. It can only approximate the optimal situation based on known information. The traditional scheduling algorithm only performs task scheduling when the processing unit's processing capacity and mutual communication overhead are known, and cannot count the number of nodes passed by the path, so it cannot solve the problem of inconsistency in the endianness appeared here, so it needs to be adjusted. Therefore, it is necessary to modify the original scheduling result to adapt it to the new buffer design scheme.

This paper proposes a parity correction scheduling algorithm to improve on the original scheduling, so that it can completely realize the communication path from odd to even. Based on the initial pre-scheduling, the second round of scheduling based on more information is an effective scheduling strategy [23]. The goal of this algorithm is to reschedule all previously existing odd-numbered paths into even-numbered paths based on the least possible impact on the original scheduling algorithm. The algorithm is divided into two steps.

First, according to the original scheduling results, the transmission path is searched with breadth first search from the initial node. If an odd-numbered transmission path is found, it is judged whether its start node has been marked, and if not, its end node is marked. After the search is completed, at least one node is marked for every odd-numbered transmission path. Then calculate the priority of all marked nodes, the priority is expressed as follows:

$$Pri(v_k) = \sum_{i,j \in v_{link}} w_{i,j} \tag{1}$$

The priority of a node is determined by the sum of the communication values of subsequent connected nodes in the same set. The goal is to ensure that the priority of each node that executes first must be higher than the node that executes later. At the same time, for nodes that do not interfere with each other, the priority is determined based on the total communication volume of

---

Algorithm 1. Scheduling correction algorithm based on RTM-LIFO

1: Initialization:$DAG = (V, E, t, w), Map(V, P), Net = (P, Path), Queue$
2: **while** $number(Map(V, P))! = 0$ **do**
3:    **if** $Map(v_i, p)$ brings odd path **then**
4:       $Queue \leftarrow v_i$
5:    **end if**
6:    $number(Map(V, P)) = number(Map(V, P)) - 1$
7: **end while**
8: computing $Pri(v_i)$ in Queue
9: sorting Queue according to priority
10: **while** Queue != empty **do**
11:    pull v_{first}
12:    judge candidate P_i based on path
13:    computing $EFT(v_{first}, P_i)$
14:    Scheduling v_{first}
15: **end while**
Output: Map(V,P)

---

each node. It is generally believed that nodes with more communication volume should be more Priority treatment. After that, all the nodes are sorted according to the priority to generate a priority queue.

The second step is to process the elements in the queue in turn, taking out an element from the queue with the highest priority each time, and then reschedule it. The criteria for rescheduling are still commonly used $EFT(v_i, p_k)$ method. It represents the earliest completion time when task v_i is scheduled to the processing unit p_k. Then, according to the sequence relationship between the node and the scheduled node, all possible scheduling paths are searched out, and the task is scheduled according to the shortest completion principle. If the task does not have such a path, it is still scheduled according to the shortest completion length, but after the scheduling is completed, the priority of the end node of the newly formed odd transmission path is calculated, and then stored in the priority queue, and the priority queue Make dynamic adjustments. The pseudo code is as follows:

5   Experimental Result

We evaluated the performance of RTM-LIFO buffer through a NoC network based on 4×4 mesh using XY routing, and by default all nodes are homogeneous. For simulation, we use a modified flit-level cycle-accurate NoC simulator BookSim to realize the evaluation [14]. At the same time, using NVsim based on a modified version [13] simulate the RTM reading and writing overhead, shift overhead and power consumption area. NVsim can also evaluate the performance of SRAM.

5.1 Power consumption

LIFO's data transmission method can completely overcome the performance degradation caused by invalid shift operation. Based on the extremely low static power consumption characteristics of RTM, the solution of using RTM instead of SRAM can greatly liberate the power consumption bottleneck of NoC itself and further improve performance (Figs. 4 and 5).

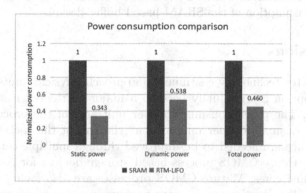

Fig. 4. Power consumption comparison of SRAM buffer and RTM-LIFO buffer

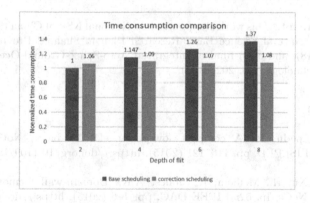

Fig. 5. Time consumption comparison of base scheduling and correction scheduling

5.2 Comparison of Scheduling

In order to evaluate the performance of the corrective scheduling algorithm, this paper adopts the DAG data set randomly generated by the algorithm proposed by [15], and uses the classic HEFT scheduling algorithm as the performance benchmark [15]. Because the depth of flit determines the waiting delay when reversing the endianness, this article tests the delay difference between the two algorithms when the depth of flit is different.

The main drawback of RTM-LIFO-based buffer design is the potential endianness correction problem. As the depth of flit stored in the buffer increases, the waiting time due to endianness flipping continue to increase each time. The correction scheduling algorithm can avoid this increase in communication overhead and maintain the communication overhead at a stable level, as close as possible to the time consumption of the SRAM-based buffer design.

6   Conclusions

As semiconductor technology continues to approach physical limits, the cost of power consumption has gradually become a major bottleneck restricting computer systems. The power consumption per unit area of the processor is close to the power consumption per unit area at the end of the rocket jet. Therefore, performance are needed to be improved through multiple cores. However, it is inevitable to use CMOS process-based storage devices for communication between multiple cores. Mature CMOS processes are also facing the dilemma that it is difficult to continue to improve performance due to approaching physical limits. New storage devices will eventually replace CMOS process storage elements (SRAM, DRAM) Although NVM has excellent performance, but it is not mature in itself. If it can overcome its shortcomings, for example, RTM's shift operation, huge performance improvements can be bring.

Acknowledgement. This work is supported by National NSF of China (No. 61802312 and 61472322), Natural Science Basic Research Plan in Shaanxi Province of China (No. 2019JQ-618), and open fund of Integrated Aero-Space-Ground-Ocean Big Data Application Technology (No. 20200105).

References

1. Li, C., Ampadu, P.: A compact low-power eDRAM-based NoC buffer. In: IEEE/ACM ISLPED, pp. 116–121 (2015). https://doi.org/10.1109/ISLPED.2015.7273500
2. Kline, D., Xu, H., Melhem, R., Jones, A.K.: Domain-wall memory buffer for low-energy NoCs. In: 52nd IEEE DAC, pp. 1–6 (2015). https://doi.org/10.1145/2744769.2744826
3. Qiu, M., Xue, C., et al.: Energy minimization with soft real-time and DVS for uniprocessor and multiprocessor embedded systems. IEEE DATE, pp. 1–6 (2007)
4. Gao, Y., Iqbal, S., et al.: Performance and power analysis of high-density multi-GPGPU architectures: a preliminary case study. In: IEEE 17th HPCC (2015)
5. Rani, K., Kapoor, H.K.: Investigating frequency scaling, nonvolatile, and hybrid memory technologies for on-chip routers to support the era of dark silicon. IEEE TCAD 40(4), 633–645 (2021). https://doi.org/10.1109/TCAD.2020.3007555
6. Joo, Y., et al.: Energy-and endurance-aware design of phase change memory caches. In: DATE, pp. 136–141 (2010)

7. Wang, J., et al.: i2WAP: improving non-volatile cache lifetime by reducing inter- and intra-set write variations. In: HPCA, pp. 234–245 (2013)
8. Li, Y., et al.: A software approach for combating asymmetries of non-volatile memories. In: ISLPED, pp. 191–196 (2012)
9. Venkatesan, R., et al.: TapeCache: a high density, energy efficient cache based on domain wall memory. In: ISLPED, pp. 185–190 (2012)
10. Gu, S., Sha, E., Zhuge, Q., Chen, Y., Hu, J.: Area and performance co-optimization for domain wall memory in application-specific embedded systems. In: 52nd DAC, p. 20 (2015)
11. Mittal, S., Vetter, J.S., Li, D.: A survey of architectural approaches for managing embedded DRAM and non-volatile on-chip caches. IEEE TPDS **26**(6), 1524–1537 (2015). https://doi.org/10.1109/TPDS.2014.2324563
12. Kline, D., Xu, H., Melhem, R., Jones, A.K.: Racetrack queues for extremely low-energy FIFOs. IEEE TVLSI **26**(8), 1531–1544 (2018). https://doi.org/10.1109/TVLSI.2018.2819945
13. Dong, X., Xu, C., Xie, Y., Jouppi, N.P.: NVSim: a circuit-level performance, energy, and area model for emerging nonvolatile memory. IEEE TCAD **31**(7), 994–1007 (2012). https://doi.org/10.1109/TCAD.2012.2185930
14. Jiang, N., et al.: A detailed and flexible cycle-accurate network-onchip simulator. In: IEEE ISPASS, Austin, USA, pp. 86–96 (2013)
15. Topcuoglu, H., Hariri, S., Wu, M.-Y.: Performance-effective and low-complexity task scheduling for heterogeneous computing. IEEE TPDS **13**(3), 260–274 (2002). https://doi.org/10.1109/71.993206
16. Qiu, M., Chen, Z., Liu, M.: Low-power low-latency data allocation for hybrid scratch-pad memory. IEEE Embedd. Syst. Lett. **6**(4), 69–72
17. Zhang, L., Qiu, M., Tseng, W., Sha, E.: Variable partitioning and scheduling for MPSoC with virtually shared scratch pad memory. J. Signal Process. Syst. **58**(2), 247–265 (2010)
18. Zhao, H., Chen, M., et al.: A novel pre-cache schema for high performance Android system. FGCS **56**, 766–772 (2016)
19. Guo, Y., Zhuge, Q., Hu, J., et al.: Optimal data allocation for scratch-pad memory on embedded multi-core systems. In: IEEE ICPP Conference, pp 464–471 (2011)
20. Qiu, L., Gai, K., Qiu, M.: Optimal big data sharing approach for tele-health in cloud computing. In: IEEE SmartCloud, pp. 184–189 (2016)
21. Qiu, M., Liu, J., et al.: A novel energy-aware fault tolerance mechanism for wireless sensor networks. In: IEEE/ACM Conference on Green Computing and Communications (2011)
22. Xu, R., Sha, E.H.M., Zhuge, Q., Shi, L., Gu, S.: Architectural exploration on racetrack memories. In: IEEE SOCC, pp. 31–36 (2020). https://doi.org/10.1109/SOCC49529.2020.9524792
23. Zhao, Y., Cao, S., Yan, L.: List scheduling algorithm based on pre-scheduling for heterogeneous computing. In: IEEE International Conference on Parallel & Distributed Processing with Applications, pp. 588–595 (2019)

Analysis and Discussion on Standard Cost Allocation Model in State Grid

Shaojun Jin[✉], Jun Pan, Qian Chen, and Bo Li

State Grid Zhejiang Electric Power Company Jinhua Power Supply Company, Zhengjiang, Jinhua 321000, China
{panjun,chenqian}@sgcc.com.cn

Abstract. With the rapid development of smart grid, the traditional financial system gradually does not meet the needs of the current power grid financial decision-making. As a new data processing means, data analysis and statistical regression can make up for some shortcomings of the traditional financial system. This paper discusses the application of big data analysis and artificial intelligence theory in the activity-based transformation of power grid standard cost, in order to provide new ideas for power grid cost management. Firstly, the stepwise regression analysis and forward driver selection method are used to select the most significant driver variables from many driver variables, and then on this basis, the selected variables are visually analyzed to further eliminate the high correlation between variables. Finally, the machine learning model in artificial intelligence and lifting algorithm are used to optimize and discuss the cost allocation model. The experimental results show that the average absolute error of the total cost calculated by the model is 6% lower than the actual total cost. Big data analysis and AI can more efficiently process power grid financial data, which is of great help to improve the accuracy of calculation.

Keywords: Cost allocation · Standard cost · Artificial intelligence · Stepwise regression · Decision tree

1 Introduction

The supply demand of electric energy is gradually improving with the continuous progress of industry and people's life. The word "smart grid" comes into the public's sight. Electric energy, as a sustainable and pollution-free energy, fits the contemporary green and low-carbon atmosphere very well [1, 2]. At the same time, big data analysis technology [3–5] has begun to develop rapidly in the last half century. Both traditional machine learning and current deep learning have made significant progress [6–8], and the era of *artificial intelligence* (AI) is approaching quietly. Under the two backgrounds, the organic combination of smart power grid and artificial intelligence has become an emerging research hotspot. How to use artificial intelligence in smart power grid system to solve practical problems is worth further research.

The financial system of smart grid mainly studies the financial problems related to smart grid system, including electricity consumption analysis, electricity price decision, standard cost formulation, etc. However, the traditional standard cost formulation process of the existing power grid has a large amount of manual data processing, data processing efficiency is not high, timeliness is not strong. At the same time, errors caused by subjective experience and averaging may lead to imbalanced budget arrangement and too low or too high allocation of resources in some units. In addition, the agent of each item of expenditure is different, and the relationship with actual expenditure cost is not obvious, which is more unfavorable to cost control.

As for the historical disbursement data of power grid, namely time series, the theories and methods in the field of artificial intelligence can be used to analyze the hidden features behind the figures and explore the law of the development and change of phenomena, which is helpful to provide new ideas and help for the calculation of power grid cost system. This paper adopts the historical cost data of Jinhua Power Supply Company in Zhejiang province, and proposes a new cost calculation method based on data analysis and artificial intelligence.

2 Related Work

As for the financial system of smart grid, a lot of research has been done at home and abroad, mainly including cost allocation, electricity consumption analysis and cost analysis. Huiping Yu [9] fully considers the effect of power supply reliability on consumers, and gives a new method of power network cost analysis and the corresponding mathematical evaluation model. Based on the activity-based costing method, Yutong Fang [10] proposed that the standard should be established on the basis of the time-driven activity, and the standard cost of activity should be established according to the time. Zhaoxun Chen [11] uses neural network algorithm, which has the advantage of making more rational use of intelligent network technology to study activity-based costing. He uses LCNN and RULEX network algorithm, which can allocate product costs scientifically and determine activity drivers and resource drivers reasonably. Qian Peng [12] proposed a cost allocation method based on participants' contribution to the power grid system, namely efficiency. Lishun Wei [13] designed and implemented a decision support system, which can predict and analyze electricity consumption and maintain electricity consumption data. Xiaobing Liu [14] proposed a method based on neighborhood rough set, random distribution theory and support vector machine to predict standard cost, and verified its validity through an example.

Beliaeva [15] worked out some cyclical and seasonal patterns by going back over four years of data on a household's electricity use, This allows people to predict future electricity demand. Based on ar-DEA and cooperative game theory, Xufei Meng [16] proposed a method of transmission fixed cost allocation. Yehao Ding [17] uses several common electricity consumption forecasting methods, such as electric elasticity coefficient method, to model the electricity consumption of Guangdong Province, and gives the corresponding forecasting process and prediction results. Zheng Chen [18] applies the step allocation method in accounting to the transmission cost allocation, and gives the allocation scheme according to different voltage levels, and verifies it with calculation examples. Pendharkar [19] uses genetic algorithm and *data envelopment analysis* (DEA) techniques to come up with fixed cost allocation schemes. Dan Li [20] proposed that time-driven activity-based costing could be applied to traditional activity-based costing, which proved that it could simplify the model construction, directly show the resource utilization and economic benefits of a certain activity link, and conducted feasibility analysis on time-driven activity-based costing.

According to the seasonal and weekend effects of daily cash flow data of electric power, Richeng Hu [21] uses multi-order difference time series to study and analyze the non-stationarity of such data. Based on the cost-sharing method of efficiency, Yongli Wang [22] uses Lasso regression method to give the cost-sharing scheme of single project of power grid engineering. Sanyal [23] analyzed the cost of hybrid system reliability and unreliable power grids for electrified villages in India. Fenghua Wu [24] used 18 years of power generation and consumption data of Guizhou province to establish a differential autoregression model to predict power supply and demand, and found that ARIMA prediction model is more accurate and reliable, which largely reflects the successful application of artificial intelligence in the power field.

This paper proposes a standard cost allocation model and method based on big data analysis and artificial intelligence to provide accurate help for intelligent financial system. Power grid has the characteristics of large scale, many equipment, wide coverage area, long operation time and complex operation conditions, which determine that the formulation of product operation standard cost is affected by many attributes. Therefore, in this paper, the forward selection factor method is adopted from a factor-free model, attribute reduction is carried out according to the importance of features, so as to achieve the same effect by replacing all features with fewer features, then stepwise regression was used to calculate AIC values of all models with one factor added or one factor reduced, get the final subset of quality drivers. Finally, machine learning algorithm is used to improve the performance of the model, and release the cost calculation results.

3   Stepwise Regression Method and Chooses Agent Method

3.1   Stepwise Regression Method

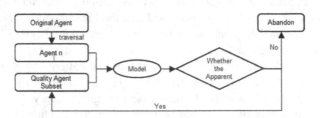

Fig. 1. Standard cost stepwise regression analysis process

Stepwise regression method reduces the degree of multicollinearity by eliminating the variables that are not very important and highly correlated with other drivers. Factor the agent variables into the model one by one, F test should be carried out after each substitution, and T test should be carried out one by one for the selected dynamic variables.

If a new agent variable is introduced and the previous one is no longer significant, the old variable is deleted to ensure that only significant variables are included in the equation before each new variable is introduced. This cycle is iterated until no new significant agent variables are added and no insignificant agent variables are deleted. In this way, the final agent variables are of the best quality, The standard cost step-by-step analysis process in this paper is shown in Fig. 1.

3.2 Forward Selection Agent Method

For n agent variables $x_1, x_2, \cdots, x_n$, each agent and the target variable y respectively builds a regression model $y = a_0 + \sum_{i=1}^{n} a_i x_i + \varepsilon$, $i = 1, 2, \cdots n$, Calculate the value of the f-test statistic of the variable x_i and the corresponding regression coefficient, remember to $F_1^{(1)}, \cdots, F_n^{(1)}$, take the maximum $F_{i1}^{(1)}$, namely $F_{i1}^{(1)} = max\{F_1^{(1)}, \cdots, F_n^{(1)}\}$, for a given level of significance α, write the corresponding critical value as F^2, $F_{i1}^{(1)} \geq F^1$, then x_{i1} is introduced into the regression model, Write I_1 as the set of selected agent indicators.

The binary regression model of target variable y and subset $\{x_{i1}, x_1\}, \cdots, \{x_{i1}, x_{i1-1}\}, \{x_{i1}, x_{i1+1}\}, \cdots, \{x_{i1}, x_n\}$ of agent variable is established, a total of $n - 1$. Calculate the statistical value of regression coefficient F test of the agent variable, namely $F_k^{(2)}(k \neq I_1)$, choose the largest one, remember to $F_{i2}^{(2)}$, namely $F_{i2}^{(2)} = max\{F_1^{(2)}, \cdots, F_{i1-1}^{(2)}, F_{i1+1}^{(2)}, \cdots, F_n^{(2)}\}$, for a given level of significance α, write the corresponding critical value as F^2, $F_{i1}^{(2)} \geq F^2$, then x_{i2} is introduced into the regression model, otherwise, the process of agent variable introduction is terminated.

Iterate over the above process, pick one agent variable at a time that has never been brought into the model, until no new agent variable is introduced through the test, only then can the optimal agent subset be determined.

4 Quantification and Visualization of Cost Agent Data

This paper uses the data of various prefecture-level cities and county-level cities in Zhejiang province from 2014 to 2018, 5 years of data from 75 districts to establish cost regression models. Due to the variety of transmit electricity and power distribution costs, this paper takes travel expenses as an example to show the process of data mining, model building and model optimization, and finally gives the calculation results of other types of costs.

4.1 Data Structure

Through stepwise regression analysis, six factors have been found to influence the cost category of travel expenses, Including the number of management staff (company leaders), management staff (middle-level cadres, and the full staff of some functional departments), technical (transportation and inspection Department, construction Department, part of the full-time), skills (front-line production personnel), service, region. So the input data has seven dimensions, the specific data description and structure are shown in the Table 1, the total number of rows is 375, namely 375 pieces of data. The area is text-type data and one-HOT encoding is adopted, create a binary attribute for each category, the calculated output is a SciPy sparse matrix, this matrix only has one 1 in each row, and all the rest are zeros. To save memory, use the Label Binarizer class, which returns a dense NumPy array. Each of the five types of staff and travel expenses accounted for one dimension, and the regional attribute accounted for 75 dimensions, The first 80 dimensions are the features of the data to be learned by machine learning, The last dimension is labels and supervised learning.

Table 1. Data structure and types

Agent	Economics Management	Management	Technology	Technical Ability	Serve	Area	Travel cost
Amount	375	375	375	375	375	375	375
Type	Int					Text	Float
Dimension	1	2	3	4	5	6–80	81

4.2 Visual Data

(1) The statistical characteristics of each agent are shown in Table 2, you can clearly see the mean, standard deviation, minimum, maximum and three quantiles for each category, view the center, fluctuation, relative position, dispersion, and correlation of the data.

Table 2. Statistical characteristics of each dimension (Unit: Ten thousand yuan)

Agent	Economics Management	Management	Technology	Technical Ability	Serve	Area
Mean	6.4	73.0	36.8	297.0	26.7	295.2
Standard deviation	1.1	65.7	59.0	281.7	31.6	405.7
Minimum	3.0	23.0	0.0	75.0	0.0	29.8
1/4points digits	6.0	41.0	9.0	154.0	7.0	103.2
1/2points digits	6.0	50.0	16.0	185.0	13.0	141.2

(continued)

Table 2. (*continued*)

Agent	Economics Management	Management	Technology	Technical Ability	Serve	Area
3/4points digits	7.0	61.0	24.0	279.0	44.0	200.4
Maximum	16.0	381.0	345.0	1385.0	213.0	2236.1

(2) Correlation analysis was conducted on all motivation variables [25], and the correlation coefficients were shown in Fig. 2. The correlation coefficient is a parameter used to represent 2 variables, For example, The index of the closeness of the relationship between (x, y), which is denoted here by r, its definition as:

$$r = \frac{\sum_{t=1}^{n}(x_t - \bar{x}_t)(y_t - \bar{y}_t)}{\sqrt{\sum_{i=t}^{n}(x_t - \bar{x}_t)^2}\sqrt{\sum_{i=t}^{n}(y_t - \bar{y}_t)^2}}$$

Where x_t, y_t represents the value of the agent variable, and $\bar{x}_t, \bar{y}_t$ represents the average value of x_t and y_t respectively. Therefore, when the absolute value of r is closer to 1, it indicates that the correlation between them is more significant and the degree of linear correlation is stronger. The one shown in Fig. 2 is even more yellow. Strongly correlated variables can remove these characteristic attributes in subsequent processing to improve the accuracy of the algorithm.

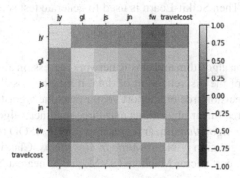

Fig. 2. Correlation coefficient diagram between variables

(3) As we can see from Fig. 2, travel cost have the greatest correlation with technical personnel, in order to clearly show the relationship between them, another scatter diagram of travel cost and technical personnel is made as shown in Fig. 3. You can clearly see that the data points are clustered in the lower left corner, namely, technician data between 0 and 50 is a lot. And you can see a piece of data, Personnel

in 10 or so technical personnel scattered dots connected into a short line. Corresponding data were removed in subsequent processing to prevent the algorithm from repeating these coincidences.

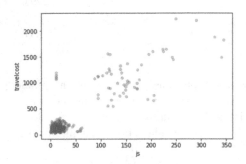

Fig. 3. Scatter diagram of travel cost and technical personnel

5   Cost Allocation Model Based on Artificial Intelligence

The method of stratified sampling is used to extract training set and verification set. Based on the previous analysis, technical staff is an important attribute of travel cost, so it is important to ensure that the test set represents multiple categories of the overall data set. The number of technicians is divided into five categories: 0–10, 0–20, 20–30, 30–40, 40 and above, Then Scikit-Learn is used to generate test sets.

5.1   Model Selection

Firstly, linear regression algorithm and elastic network regression algorithm are adopted. The second, because of the discretization of data, it may be possible to generate high accuracy models by decision tree or support vector machine algorithms. In order to get the optimal model, three linear algorithms and three nonlinear algorithms are selected for comparison. *Linear algorithm*: linear regression (LR), LASOO regression (LASOO) and elastic network regression (EN); *Nonlinear algorithms*: Classification and regression Tree (CART), Support vector Machine (SVM) and K-nearest Neighbor Algorithm (KNN).

5.2   Empirical Analysis

Use default parameters for all algorithms, 10 fold cross validation was used to separate the data and compare the accuracy of the algorithm, Here we are comparing the mean of the mean absolute error with the standard variance. The training data set is transformed here, normalize all the data. During data normalization, in order to prevent data leakage, Pipeline is used to normalize data and evaluate the model. The evaluation results are shown in Table 3. From the execution result, linear regression has the best MSE, followed by classification and regression tree algorithm.

Table 3. Preliminary model mean and standard deviation

	LR	LASSO	EN	KNN	CART	SVM
Mean	49.16	62.65	99.80	70.04	61.97	198.67
Std	12.45	11.43	18.90	21.94	15.63	79.82

5.3 Optimization Model

In order to improve the accuracy of the model, the integrated algorithm can be used to test the algorithm. The following is the integration of linear, regression, KNN, classification and regression tree algorithms with better performance.

Bagging algorithm: *random forest* (RF) and *extreme random tree* (ET);

Lifting algorithms: *AdaBoost* (AB) and *Stochastic gradient ascent* (GBN).

Table 4. Mean and standard deviation of the promoted model

	AB	AB-KNN	AB-LR	RBF	ETR	GBR
Mean	60.83	50.62	50.23	57.15	48.38	52.22
Std	10.44	17.44	12.80	15.20	9.06	10.70

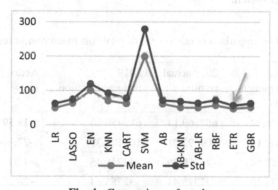

Fig. 4. Comparison of results

The previous evaluation framework and normalized data are still used to analyze the relevant algorithms. Compared with the previous algorithm, the accuracy of this time has been improved. The results are shown in Table 4, it can be seen that extreme random tree (ETR) has smaller error and more compact distribution. The results of the model before and after were drawn as a line graph, as shown in Fig. 4, It can be seen from the figure that the overall effect of the optimized model is better than that of the model initially selected, and the overall effect of the extreme random tree is the best.

5.4 Model Analysis

The extreme random tree algorithm consists of many decision trees, and there is no correlation between each decision tree. The main process is two random samples, which ensures the randomness of data training and greatly reduces the over-fitting. First of all, the input data has been put back to the line sampling method, so there are repetitions. Assuming we input M samples, we take M samples, in this case, the input of each decision tree is not all the samples, therefore, over-fitting phenomenon is reduced. The next step is column sampling, pick out n (n < < N) of N features, choose the completely split method to construct the decision tree. Doing so will cause the leaves to fail to continue splitting or give the same classification result.

Based on the model experiments we did earlier, the *extreme random tree* (ET) algorithm is slightly better than other algorithms and features of extreme random trees, so extreme random tree algorithm is used to train the final model. And evaluate the accuracy of the algorithm by evaluating the data set. The cost of power grid mainly includes main distribution network, marketing operation and inspection, labor cost and other expenses, here, we consider the total cost of other types of expenses in each region, use the method proposed in this paper to calculate and compare with the actual subordinate cost. The results are shown in Table 5.

It can be seen from the table that although the effect of the method in this paper is not ideal in some regions, the error is reduced in most regions, and the absolute error for the total cost of the province is reduced by 6%. It can be seen that the combination of big data analysis and artificial intelligence is of substantial help to the expansion of power grid financial system.

Table 5. Comparison of other types of total cost measurement results

	2019 measurement results	2018 actual results	2019 budget allocation	Actual rate%	Predicting rate %
ZheJiang	543526.53	667669.14	619450.00	**−18.59**	**−12.25**
HangZhou	79609.15	109597.01	102102.37	−27.36	−22.03
JiaXing	45122.54	45750.19	43258.45	−1.37	4.31
HuZhou	26774.12	37325.41	32785.34	−28.27	−18.33
JinHua	49440.45	58691.25	60640.10	−15.76	−18.47
QuZhou	25076.34	32760.48	31854.00	−23.46	−21.28
NingBo	68020.04	85153.95	78331.02	−20.12	−13.16
ShaoXing	42511.10	45120.37	45932.22	−5.78	−7.45
LiShui	31470.93	60805.45	51628.53	−48.24	−39.04
TaiZhou	50399.42	79614.49	74769.40	−36.69	−32.59
WenZhou	60613.31	85866.35	66375.90	−29.41	−8.68
ZhouShan	23420.67	26984.18	31772.67	−13.21	−26.29

6 Conclusion

In this paper, the statistical characteristics of the original data were analyzed for data cleaning, and stepwise regression was used to select significant motivation variables. Based on this, six commonly used machine learning algorithms were selected for comparison. In order to improve the accuracy and precision of algorithm fitting, six kinds of integration algorithms are used to carry out experiments. The results show that the extreme random tree algorithm has the best fitting effect and high accuracy, which is suitable for standard cost estimation.

Acknowledgements. This paper was funded by State Grid Zhejiang Electric Power Co., LTD. This paper is also supported by the Science and technology project of State Grid Zhejiang Electric Power Co., LTD. The project name: Research and application of standard cost activity-based transformation based on machine learning (Project No.: 5211JH1900LZ).

References

1. Qiu, M., Chen, Z., Liu, M.: Low-power low-latency data allocation for hybrid scratch-pad memory. IEEE Embed. Syst. Lett. **6**(4), 69–72
2. Guo, Y., et al.: Optimal data allocation for scratch-pad memory on embedded multi-core systems. In: IEEE ICPP Conference, pp. 464–471 (2011)
3. Qiu, L., Gai, K., Qiu, M.: Optimal big data sharing approach for tele-health in cloud computing. In: IEEE SmartCloud, pp. 184–189 (2016)
4. Qiu, M., Cao, D., et al.: Data transfer minimization for financial derivative pricing using Monte Carlo simulation with GPU in 5G. J. Commun. Syst. **29**(16), 2364–2374 (2016)
5. Lu, R., Jin, X., Zhang, S., Qiu, M., Wu, X.: A study on big knowledge and its engineering issues. IEEE Trans. Knowl. Data Eng. **31**(9), 1630–1644 (2018)
6. Qiu, H., Qiu, M., Lu, Z.: Selective encryption on ECG data in body sensor network based on supervised machine learning. Inf. Fusion **55**, 59–67 (2020)
7. Lu, Z., Wang, N., Wu, J., Qiu, M.: IoTDeM: an IoT Big Data-oriented MapReduce performance prediction extended model in multiple edge clouds. JPDC **118**, 316–327 (2018)
8. Liu, M., et al.: H infinite state estimation for discrete-time chaotic systems based on a unified model. IEEE Trans. Syst. Man Cybern. (B) (2012)
9. Yu, H., Liu, J., Cheng, H., Chen, Z., Ma, Z.: Research on cost-benefit analysis and evaluation of power grid planning scheme. Power Grid Technol. **07**, 32–35 (2001)
10. Fang, Y.: Construction of time-driven standard activity-based costing system. Mon. J. Financ. Account. (002), 81–82 (2009)
11. Chen, Z.: Research on Product Allocation Based on Intelligent Technology and Activity-based Costing. Shanghai Jiaotong University (2009)
12. Peng, Q., Ma, C., Yang, X., Fan, Y.: Power Grid Technol. **34**(02), 92–96 (2010)
13. Wei, L., Pan, R., Ding, S.: J. Hefei Univ. Technol. (Nat. Sci.) **34**(12), 1836–1840 (2011)
14. Liu, X., et al.: Comput. Integr. Manuf. Syst. **18**(10), 2287–2296 (2012)
15. Beliaeva, N., Petrochenkov, A., Bade, K.: Data set analysis of electric power consumption. Eur. Res. **61**(10–2), 2482–2487 (2013)
16. Xufei, M.: Research on Transmission Fixed Cost Allocation Based on AR-DEA and Kernel Solution of Cooperative Game. Zheng Zhou University (2016)
17. Ding, Y.: Maggie. Electr. Meas. Instrum. **54**(14), 14–23 (2017)

18. Chen, Z., Xiao, J., Jing, Z., Zhang, X., Zhang, H., Leng, Y.: Power Grid Technol. **41**(07), 2124–2130 (2017)
19. Pendharkar, P.C.: A hybrid genetic algorithm and DEA approach for multi-criteria fixed cost allocation. Soft Comput. **22**(22), 7315–7324 (2018)
20. Li, D., Liu, Z., Zhang, Z.: Feasibility Analysis of time-driven activity-based costing. Chin. Foreign Entrep. (32) (2019)
21. Richeng, H., Jin, X., Wang, D., et al.: Daily cash flow prediction based on non-stationary time series. J. Appl. Math. Chin. Univ. **34**(3), 253–263 (2019)
22. Wang, Y., Wang, X., Wang, S., Haiyang, Y., Zhang, F., Li, R.: Power grid Technol. **44**(01), 332–339 (2020). (in Chinese)
23. Sanyal, A., Upadhaya, A., Das, P.: Cost analysis of a reliable versus unreliable grid associated with a hybrid system for the electrified villages of Arunachal Pradesh India. J. Inst. Eng. (India) Ser. B **101**(6), 2250–2114 (2020)
24. Fenghua, W., Cheng, H., Jiang, Z., et al.: Application of ARIMA model in power supply and demand forecast. Energy Eng. **4**, 82–87 (2020)
25. Lin, Z., Huang, Y., Zhang, Y., et al.: Power load prediction for wave power generation based on correlation analysis of support vector machine. J. Nanchang Univ. (Sci. Edit.) **43**(5), 504–510 (2019)

A Novel Deception Defense-Based Honeypot System for Power Grid Network

Mingjun Feng[1]([envelope]), Buqiong Xiao[1], Bo Yu[1], Jianguo Qian[2], Xinxin Zhang[1], Peidong Chen[1], and Bo Li[3]

[1] State Grid Tibet Electric Power Co., Ltd., Chengdu, China
[2] State Grid Zhejiang Electric Power Co., Ltd., Quzhou, China
[3] Beihang University, Beijing 100191, China

Abstract. In recent years, as cyber-attacks have become more and more rampant, power grid networks are also facing more and more security threats, which have gradually become the focus attention of attackers. Traditional defense methods are represented by intrusion detection systems and firewalls, whose main purpose is to keep attackers out. However, with the diversification, concealment and complexity of attack methods, traditional defense methods are usually difficult to cope with the endless attack methods. To this end, this paper proposes a new type of honeypot system based on deception defense technology. While retaining the nature of the honeypot, it adopts dynamic deception approach to actively collect unused IP addresses in the power grid networks. Then, these unused IP addresses are used to construct dynamic virtual hosts. When an attacker initiates network access to these dynamic virtual hosts, they will proactively respond to the attacker or redirect the attack traffic to the honeypot in the background, thereby deceiving and trapping the attacker. The experimental results show that the proposed honeypot system can effectively expands the monitoring range of traditional honeypots and has a good defense effect against unknown attacks, thus effectively making up for the shortcomings of traditional defense methods.

Keywords: Honeypot · Deception defense · Power grid network · Virtual hosts

1 Introduction

Power grid networks becomes an important part of the industrial Internet with the development of computer [1, 2] and big data technologies [4, 5]. Due to the increasing number of hacker attacks on power grid networks, it is urgent to build a security protection ecosystem for smart power grid networks [6]. On the one hand, the power network infrastructure has become a key target of hackers, and the pressure on protection has increased unprecedentedly. On the other hand, compared with traditional network security, power grid network security presents new characteristics, which further increases the difficulty of security protection. Currently, power grid networks mainly have the following security risks: (1) Vulnerabilities are frequently discovered in power grid equipment with high availability [7, 8]. (2) A large amount of power grid equipment is exposed to the

M. Qiu et al. (Eds.): SmartCom 2021, LNCS 13202, pp. 297–307, 2022.
https://doi.org/10.1007/978-3-030-97774-0_27

Internet [9]. (3) The security of the enterprise intranet is low, and it is easy to be used as a springboard to penetrate the control layer of the production network of the power grid systems [10].

Lockheed Martin proposed an intrusion attack chain to describe network intrusion activities. In this model, intrusion activities are divided into seven stages, including network reconnaissance, weaponization, delivery, vulnerability exploitation, installation, command and control, and action. Bou-harb et al. [11] pointed out that up to 70% of attacks are targeted scanning activities before they are launched. Advanced attackers use advanced attack methods to conduct long-term and persistent network reconnaissance on specific targets to obtain useful information about the target network [12].

The network security protection products commonly used in the existing network defense system at the network level are mainly various software/hardware products such as firewalls, intrusion detection, isolation gateways, traffic detection, etc. [13, 14], achieving network attack detection and network attack protection for the network that needs to be protected [15, 16]. However, due to the static nature of the network architecture and the continuous evolution of attack methods, network security technologies are often inadequate in the face of constantly evolving attack technologies [17, 18]. Attackers often have enough time to analyze the internal network architecture, host system, and security technology through network reconnaissance, thus finding out the vulnerabilities and gradually penetrate the network to reach the target of the attack.

Deception defense is a defense mechanism evolved from honeypots. In a network attack, the attack generally needs to determine the next action based on the information obtained by network reconnaissance. Deception defense uses this feature to induce the attacker to take actions that are beneficial to the defender by interfering with the attacker's cognition [19]. Machine learning and blockchain can also be used for this purpose [20, 21].

In view of the shortcomings of the existing protection methods of power grid networks, this paper proposes a new type of honeypot system based on deception defense technology. While retaining the nature of the honeypot itself, it adopts a dynamic deception method to actively collect the unused IP addresses in the power grid network needed to be protected, these unused IP addresses are used to construct dynamic virtual hosts. When an attacker initiates network access to a dynamic virtual host, it will redirect the attack traffic to the honeypot in the background, thereby deceiving and trapping the attacker. The basic principle of the system is that most of the traffic accessing unused IP addresses is suspicious. We collect this part of the traffic and redirect it to the honeypot, thus solving the shortcomings of traditional honeypots that can only be sniffed passively, and making the effectiveness of the traditional honeypot being greatly enhanced. At the same time, the corresponding change strategy is adopted to make the IP addresses of virtual hosts continuously changing, so that the virtual hosts are not easy to be marked by the attacker and the risk of the honeypot system is reduced.

The follow-up work of this article is as follows. Section 2 introduces the research foundation and related work, Sect. 3 introduces the detailed design of the proposed honeypot system based on deception defense technology, Sect. 4 conducts experimental tests, and Sect. 5 summarizes the paper.

2 Related Work

2.1 Honeypot Technology

Honeypot is a kind of active defense technology. To change the situation of information asymmetry between offense and defense in the network, the defender proposes such an active defense technology, which induces attackers by deploying hosts without real business requirements [22, 23]. Attacking the host deployed by the defending party enables the defending party to capture and analyze the attacking behavior of the attacker through the honeypot, and then understand the attacker's attack method and purpose, and even have the effect of traceability and deterrence. Since the release of honeypot technology, it has won the great attention of security personnel and organizations. The ecology is well-established, and it has become an indispensable technical means for Internet security detection. Honeypot technology is a means to deceive the attacker. By arranging some virtual nodes and network services like the real host, the attacker can be induced to attack it, so that the defender can strengthen the network security deployment based on the attacker's behavior. Honeypots are like traps in the network. At the beginning of their birth, they were designed to allow attackers to attack them to analyze the purpose and methods of attackers.

Therefore, the purpose of deploying honeypots in the system is to hope that the honeypots will be detected, to be discovered by the attacker, or even be occupied. In addition, honeypots do not have services that actively provide functions to the outside world. Therefore, if it is a request to try a honeypot, we think it is suspicious and malicious, and needs to be recorded and analyzed [24]. At the same time, the honeypot has its own protocol stack, so the honeypot can delay the attacker's behavior, which greatly delays the attacker's attack on the real target and plays a role in protecting the system. In addition, currently widely used honeypots and honey farms such as T-pot, in addition to the characteristics of the honeypot itself, can also record the behavior of attackers, to analyze and understand their attack methods and behaviors through data analysis.

The existing honeypot defense system has its shortcomings [25]. It is well known that after a honeypot is deployed artificially, it adopts passive sniffing, like a trap waiting for the attacker to set foot. Therefore, honeypots cannot completely replace all security protection mechanisms [26]. Although the effect of honeypots is very good, honeypots mainly have the following shortcomings. In specific application scenarios, they often need to be combined with other security mechanisms to learn from each other and better protect the network.

3 The Proposed Honeypot System

The new honeypot system based on deception defense technology proposed in this paper is mainly aimed at the defense of the network reconnaissance targeting power grid networks. The system is based on a new type of cyber defense concept of *Moving Target Defense* (MTD), and uses cyber deception technology to build a dynamic environment. MTD is different from previous network security technologies. It aims to deploy and operate uncertain, random and dynamic networks and systems, making it difficult for attackers to find real targets, greatly reducing the probability of system weaknesses being exposed, and changing the passiveness of network defense. The system is based on the idea of MTD. Based on maintaining the integrity of the original network configuration, the user's normal network applications are not affected, and the network topology is complicated and dynamically adjusted, Turn the network into a labyrinth that cannot be detected and predicted, greatly improving the detection and trapping capabilities of reconnaissance attacks on power grid networks.

3.1 Basic Principles of the System

The basic principle of the system is shown in Fig. 1. The basic technical idea is to use the active detection method to learn network nodes according to the network segment configured by the user, intelligently and automatically learn the unused IP addresses in the user's network and build virtual hosts. These virtual hosts are invisible to normal users, but for an attacker, no matter how the attacker scans and reconnaissance the target network in any form (including known and unknown network reconnaissance tools), he will have a high probability to encounter a virtual host automatically generated by the system. Optionally, the virtual hosts can automatically respond to the attacker with false information based on the attacker's access data, or automatically redirect the attack traffic to one or more honeypots, thereby expanding the protection of the honeypot Scope. The system can intelligently sense the IP address changes in the network (such as host online and offline, new host access, etc.), and automatically dynamically transform the constructed virtual hosts, so that the target network becomes an undetectable "network labyrinth". Introducing the attacker into the false environment is not to block the intrusion attack chain, but to let the attacker complete the attack chain in the deception environment, so that the defender can conduct an in-depth and complete analysis of the attack behavior in the deception environment. The system can detect and trap attackers automatically in real time, accurately identify reconnaissance attacks against the target network, break the accumulation of attacks, and make it impossible to accurately obtain the topology and host information of the target network, thereby losing the opportunity to carry out the next attacks.

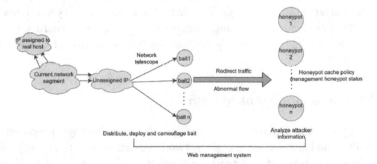

Fig. 1. Basic principle diagram of the system

3.2 Detailed Module Design

The detailed modular design of the system is shown in Fig. 2. It includes a management module, a virtual host module, a traffic processing module, a network node learning module, an attack detection module, a dynamic response module and a dynamic transformation module. Each module will be introduced in detail below.

The management module is used to manage the configuration of information, and configure the basic network element information for the virtual host module, including the virtual IP address range, the virtual MAC address range, the virtual operating system type and version, and the virtual open port range, the OPTION field and TTL field in the IP header of the response data packet, the window size of the TCP header in the response data packet and the type and arrangement order of the option fields, etc.. At the same time, the management module issues attack processing strategies for the virtual hosts, including the system's automatic false responses and redirection to honeypots. The management module also configures the network node learpning module with an IP address range and port range for active detection and passive learning (user network segment). Finally, the management module configures the dynamic conversion time interval and other information for the dynamic transformation module.

The virtual host module randomly selects a part of the unused IP addresses to construct virtual hosts based on the unused IP address and port distribution in the network provided by the network node learning module, and configures each virtual host with a virtual IP address, a virtual MAC address, a virtual operating system type and version, several open ports, etc. When an IP address changes from an unused state to a used state, it needs to be removed from the generated virtual host list. In addition, the virtual host module periodically regenerates a new virtual host according to the conversion information sent by the dynamic transformation module, thereby realizing a dynamic network environment.

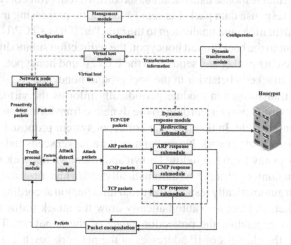

Fig. 2. System detailed module design

The flow processing module processes the two-way network communication data packet, matching the destination IP of the data packet, if the destination IP address is the IP address used by the network node learning module, the data packet is judged as an active detection response data packet and sent to the network node learning module to learn the IP address and port distribution currently in use in the target network, otherwise the data packet is sent to the attack detection module. The traffic processing module uses DPDK technology to improve the processing performance of data packets. The DPDK technology provides a set of API interfaces for fast processing of data packets. The network card driver can run in the user space without modifying the kernel, thereby eliminating the data copies between the kernel and the user space and reducing the number of shared bus operations, thus effectively reducing communication delays, increasing network throughput, and greatly improving packet processing performance.

The network node learning module includes the active detection sub-module and the traffic learning sub-module. According to the configuration information issued by the management module, it periodically sends detection data packets such as ARP, ICMP, TCP, and UDP to detect the target network; The learning sub-module receives the detection response data packets sent by the traffic processing module, extracts the MAC address, IP, port and other data in the response data packets, constructs an online list of network nodes and sends it to the virtual host module.

The attack detection module detects the data packets sent by the traffic processing module in real time, queries the virtual host list generated by the virtual host module, and if the access target is a virtual host, it will be sent to the dynamic response module or redirects to the honeypot, Otherwise, it is regarded as a normal data packet and returned to the traffic processing module for release.

The dynamic response module includes an ARP response submodule, an ICMP response submodule, a TCP response submodule, and a redirection submodule. The dynamic response module queries the virtual host generated by the virtual host module, and constructs a virtual response data packet based on different protocol types to conduct attack traffic. The response data packet is sent to the traffic processing module after the second layer encapsulation, and finally sent to the attacker. If it is a TCP/UDP data packet that needs to be sent to the background honeypot, the redirection submodule modifies the IP and MAC of the data packet and sends it to the background honeypot, thus observing and recording the attacker's behavior in the background honeypot.

The dynamic transformation module periodically informs the virtual host module to regenerate new virtual hosts according to the dynamic transformation interval issued by the management module. In this way, the honeypot system proposed in this paper is arranged on the power grid network. No matter how the attacker scans and reconnaissance the target network in any form (including known and unknown network reconnaissance tools), they will encounter a virtual host automatically with a high probability. Optionally, the virtual host can automatically respond to virtual information according to the different visits of the attacker, and can also automatically draw the attack traffic to one or more honeypots, thereby expanding the protection range of the honeypot. The system can intelligently sense the changes of IP addresses in the network (such as host online and offline, new host access, etc.), and automatically dynamically transform the constructed virtual host nodes, so that the target network becomes a "network maze" that is difficult to detect. And without manual intervention, it can automatically adapt to various network environments, greatly reducing network operation, maintenance and management costs. By introducing the attacker into the virtual environment, instead of blocking the intrusion attack chain, the attacker can complete the attack chain in the deception environment, so that the defender can conduct an in-depth and complete analysis of the attack behavior in the deception environment.

3.3 The System Workflow

The workflow of the system includes the following five steps:

(1) Configure user network segment, port range, dynamic change interval and other information;
(2) Set the active detection timer. According to the user network segment and port range configured in step (1), the system periodically sends ARP, ICMP, TCP, UDP and other detection data packets to detect the target network. After receiving the detection response data packets, it extracts the MAC address, IP, port and other data in the response data packets to construct an online list of network nodes;
(3) The system randomly selects a part of unused IP addresses to construct virtual hosts, and configure each virtual host including a virtual IP address, a virtual MAC address, a virtual operating system type and version, several virtual open ports, etc. If an address appears in the online list of real network nodes, and it is removed from the generated virtual host list;
(4) The system processes the two-way network communication data packet and queries the generated virtual host list. If the access target is not a virtual host, then it is considered as a normal data packet and let go, otherwise the data packet is redirected to the honeypot or changed into a response packet.
(5) The system periodically performs dynamic transformation operations to regenerate new virtual hosts.

4 Experimental Evaluation

The schematic diagram of the experimental test environment is shown in Fig. 3. We dynamically generate multiple virtual hosts in the test network, thereby effectively expanding the monitoring range of the honeypot. The background honeypot uses T-pot to simulate. T-Pot honeypot is a community honeypot project under Deutsche Telekom. The Linux-based network installer is a Docker container-based system that integrates many honeypot programs for different applications. A system uses multiple honeypots, which is easy to update while simplifying research and data capture. The honeypot daemon and other supporting components in use have been containerized using Docker, which allows users to run multiple honeypot daemons on the same network interface while keeping a small footprint and restricting each honeypot to its own environment.

The test environment is a small local area network environment. The network segment of the local area network is 172.16.1.0/128. There are 30 real hosts connected to the network. The probability of an unused IP being selected as a virtual host in the network

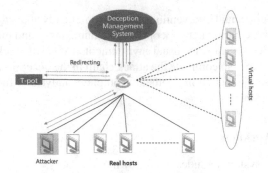

Fig. 3. Schematic diagram of the experimental test environment

is set to 0.5. The experiment lasted for 6 h, during which some real hosts were randomly brought online or offline. Figure 4 shows the trend of the number of real and virtual hosts over time. We can see that the number of virtual hosts is negatively correlated with the number of real hosts. When the number of real hosts increases, the number of virtual hosts decreases, and vice versa. The reason for this is that the virtual hosts are generated by using unused IP addresses in the network. The virtual hosts cannot occupy the IP addresses of the online real hosts, otherwise they will affect the normal business of users. When the number of real hosts increases, the number of unused IP addresses decreases, so as the number of virtual hosts.

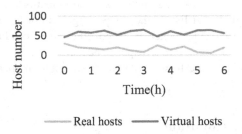

Fig. 4. The trend of the number of real and virtual hosts over time

In addition, we also counted the number of online hosts and corresponding open TCP ports in the network with and without virtual hosts. The statistical results are shown in Table 1. It can be seen that when the virtual hosts are enabled, the number of online hosts and open TCP ports in the network has increased significantly, thereby greatly increasing the monitoring range of attack deception and trapping.

Finally, we conducted an attack comparison experiment. We selected a real host in the network as the attack target, and simulated the attacker to scan the network randomly. If the attacker touches the T-pot or a virtual host before the attack target is discovered, the attack failed. Otherwise, the attack is considered successful. Experiments were carried out with and without virtual hosts. When virtual hosts were enabled, we further carried

Table 1. The trend of the number of online hosts and open TCP ports over time

Time (h)	With T-pot only		With T-pot and virtual hosts	
	Number of online hosts	Number of open TCP ports	Number of online hosts	Number of open TCP ports
0	30	15	46	278
0.5	20	15	60	300
1	18	20	58	290
1.5	15	17	63	315
2	20	24	52	282
2.5	12	8	62	310
3	8	5	65	333
3.5	25	30	48	270
4	14	15	61	292
4.5	22	26	52	278
5	7	7	63	299
5.5	5	6	64	340
6	19	22	56	304

out experiments under the conditions of enabling different numbers of virtual hosts. Each experiment environment was carried out 50 experiments, and the average value of the successes number is used as the probability of a successful attack. The experimental results are shown in Fig. 5. It can be seen that as the number of virtual hosts in the network increases, the probability of an attacker's successful attack gradually decreases. When the number of virtual hosts enabled in the network reaches 60, the probability of successful attack drops by about 40%, which fully proves the effectiveness of the honeypot system based on deception defense proposed in this paper.

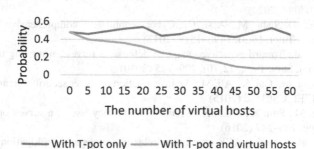

Fig. 5. The trend in the probability of successful attacks

5 Conclusion

This paper proposes a new honeypot system based on deception defense technology, which collects unused IP addresses in the power grid network through active detection, and then randomly selects a part of the IP addresses to generate virtual hosts. The honeypot system proposed in this paper aims to expand the monitoring range of traditional honeypots, so that it can deceive and trap attackers more effectively. In addition, through the introduction of a dynamic defense mechanism, the implementation of regular dynamic changes to the virtual hosts furtherly confuses the attacker, breaks the attacker's information collection and attack accumulation, and effectively improves the protection level of the honeypot and its own security.

References

1. Qiu, M.: Low-power low-latency data allocation for hybrid scratch-pad memory. IEEE Embed. Syst. Lett. **6**(4), 69–72
2. Qiu, M., et al.: RNA nanotechnology for computer design and in vivo computation. Philos. Trans. R. Soc. A (2013)
3. Guo, Y., et al.: Optimal data allocation for scratch-pad memory on embedded multi-core systems. In: IEEE ICPP Conference, pp. 464–471 (2011)
4. Zhang, L., Qiu, M., Tseng, W., Sha, E.: Variable partitioning and scheduling for MPSoC with virtually shared scratch pad memory. J. Signal Process. Syst. **58**(2), 247–265 (2010)
5. Lu, R., Jin, X., Zhang, S., Qiu, M., Wu, X.: A study on big knowledge and its engineering issues. IEEE Trans. Knowl. Data Eng. **31**(9), 1630–1644 (2018)
6. Guo, Q., et al.: A remote test method for power grid security and stability control system and its engineering application. In: E3S Web of Conference. EDP Science, p. 260 (2021)
7. Eskandarpour, R., Gokhale, P., Khodaei, A., et al.: Quantum computing for enhancing grid security. IEEE Trans. Power Syst. **35**(5), 4135–4137 (2020)
8. Aoufi, S., et al.: Survey of false data injection in smart power grid: attacks, countermeasures and challenges. J. Inform. Secur. Appl. **54**, 102518 (2020)
9. Butt, O.M., Zulqarnain, M., Butt, T.M.: Recent advancement in smart grid technology: future prospects in the electrical power network. Ain Shams Eng. J. **12**(1), 687–695 (2021)
10. Gunduz, M.Z., Das, R.: Cyber-security on smart grid: threats and potential solutions. Comput. Netw. **169**, 107094 (2020)
11. Bou-Harb, E., Debbabi, M., Assi, C.: Cyber scanning: a comprehensive survey. IEEE Commun. Surv. Tutor. **16**(3), 1496–1519 (2013)
12. Cho, J.-H., et al.: Toward proactive, adaptive defense: a survey on moving target defense. IEEE Commun. Surv. Tutor. **22**(10), 709–745 (2020)
13. Thakur, K., Qiu, M., Gai, K., Ali, M.: An investigation on cyber security threats and security models. In: IEEE CSCloud (2015)
14. Gai, K., Qiu, M., Sun, X., Zhao, H.: Security and privacy issues: a survey on FinTech. In: SmartCom, pp. 236–247 (2016)
15. Zhang, Z., et al.: Jamming ACK attack to wireless networks and a mitigation approach. In: IEEE GLOBECOM Conference, pp. 1–5 (2008)
16. Qiu, M., et al.: A novel energy-aware fault tolerance mechanism for wireless sensor networks. In: IEEE/ACM Conference on Green Computing and Communications (2011)
17. Antonatos, S., Akritidis, P., Markatos, E.P., et al.: Defending against hitlist worms using network address space randomization. Comput. Netw. **51**(12), 3471–3490 (2007)

18. Jafarian, J.H., Al-Shaer, E., Duan, Q.: An effective address mutation approach for disrupting reconnaissance attacks. IEEE TIFS **10**(12), 2562–2577 (2015)
19. Jajodia, S., et al.: Cyber Deception. Springer, Heidelberg (2016)
20. Qiu, H., Qiu, M., Lu, Z.: Selective encryption on ECG data in body sensor network based on supervised machine learning. Inf. Fusion **55**, 59–67 (2020)
21. Qiu, H., Qiu, M., Memmi, G., Ming, Z., Liu, M.: A dynamic scalable blockchain based communication architecture for IoT. In: SmartBlock, 159–166 (2018)
22. Naik, N., Jenkins, P., Savage, N., et al.: A computational intelligence enabled honeypot for chasing ghosts in the wires. Complex Intell. Syst. **7**(1), 477–494 (2021)
23. Sun, Y., Tian, Z., Li, M., et al.: Honeypot identification in softwarized industrial cyber-physical systems. IEEE Trans. Ind. Inf. **17**(8), 5542–5551 (2020)
24. Mondal, A., Goswami, T.: Enhanced Honeypot cryptographic scheme and privacy preservation for an effective prediction in cloud security. Microprocess. Microsyst. **81**, 103719 (2021)
25. Ziaie Tabari, A., Ou, X.: A multi-phased multi-faceted iot honeypot ecosystem. In: ACM SIGSAC Conference on Computer and Communications Security, pp. 2121–2123 (2020)
26. Naik, N., et al.: D-FRI-Honeypot: a secure sting operation for hacking the hackers using dynamic fuzzy rule interpolation. IEEE Trans. Emerg. Top. Comput. Intell. (2020)

Seamless Group Pre-handover Authentication Scheme for 5G High-Speed Rail Network

Zongxiao Li[1], Di Liu[1], Peiran Li[1], Dawei Li[1], Yu Sun[1(✉)], Zhenyu Guan[1],
Jianwei Liu[1], and Jie Gao[2]

[1] School of Cyber Science and Technology, Beihang University, Beijing 100191, China
{lizongxiao,liudi2020,lipeiran,lidawei,sunyv,guanzhenyu,
liujianwei}@buaa.edu.cn
[2] Infosky Technology Co., Ltd., Beijing 100020, China
gaojie@infosky.com.cn

Abstract. The rapid development of global wireless networks has promoted the innovation of 5G network application scenarios and the improvement of infrastructure. The deployment of 5G network in high-speed railway network system has important practical application prospects. Data security and user experience are significant factors to consider for 5G high-speed rail network. However, existing 5G network handover authentication mechanisms still have challenging issues in terms of security and efficiency. Considering the complexity and diversity of the future 5G high-speed rail network, this paper proposes a secure and efficient group pre-handover authentication scheme based on *Mobile Relay Node* (MRN). MRN with trusted execution environment assists 5G *User Equipment* (UE) on high-speed rail to complete the handover process before reaching the next 5G base station in the authentication and handover execution phase, so as to improve the security and handover efficiency of UE in the authentication and handover process. Therefore, this scheme can reduce handover delay and realize fast and secure group handover of high-speed UEs under the dense-deployed 5G base station. After comprehensive performance evaluation, security and communication efficiency are superior to other schemes.

Keywords: 5G · Authentication · Group handover · Trusted execution environment · Mobile relay node

1 Introduction

The rapid development of 5G networks has promoted the landing of new services and new scenarios. The *International Telecommunication Union* (ITU) defines three typical 5G application scenarios: *Enhanced Mobile Broadband* (eMBB), *Massive Machine-Type Communications* (mMTC), and Ultra-reliable and Low Latency Communications (uRLLC) [1]. Among them, mMTC supports the connection of a large number of terminal devices, allowing base stations to have greater ability to manage a large number of network interruptions. uRLLc focuses on providing services for industrial Internet, automatic driving and other scenarios with stricter delay and reliability. One of the features of the 5G high-speed rail network is the dense deployment of base stations. During high-speed train travel, the 5G *User Equipment* (UE) on the train will frequently switch to another target 5G gNB, which poses a challenge for the 5G network to provide a smooth communication experience.

The emergence of *Mobile Relay Node* (MRN) provides the possibility for efficient authentication of high-speed rail networks. 3GPP introduced MRN as a relay device that aggregates a large number of UEs, and provides a stable service for a large number of users to access the 5G network [2]. However, the introduction of traditional MRN into the 5G network will bring new security problems. Therefore, in order to protect the security of users, MRN must be authenticated by Home Network. In the moving process of high-speed trains, due to the fast moving speed, MRN must leave the signal range of the source base station before establishing a connection with the target base station to complete the handover process [3], so traditional MRN cannot provide users with a smoother user experience.

Our Contributions. Based on the above mentioned problems and solutions, this paper proposes a secure and efficient group pre-handover authentication scheme based on the MRN, taking advantage of MRN's ability to aggregate messages, we improve the authentication and handover process in the 5G high-speed rail network scenario, and give a unified authentication handover scheme under the high-speed rail network. After analysis, it is proved that the scheme is secure and can reduce communication overhead. The specific contributions of this paper are as follows:

- We investigate the 5G network authentication and handover process, and propose the handover efficiency and security issues faced by the high-speed rail 5G network handover and the introduction of MRN in the early stage.
- We design a trusted MRN with trusted execution module and trajectory prediction module to process and train the path information data. We provide UE with smooth user communication experience.
- We propose a secure and seamless group pre-handover authentication scheme based on trusted MRN, improve the security and efficiency of 5G UEs in the authentication and handover process, and achieve UEs' seamless group handover in a dense deployment environment of gNB under 5G high-speed rail networks.

2 Related Work

With the development of computer hardware [4, 5], networks [6, 7], and algorithm design [8, 9], big data transferring and processing [10, 11] had become the central theme of current era. Due to the diversification of 5G network scenarios [12], 5G network handover scenarios can be divided into two categories according to the technology and type of the access network [13]: vertical handover and horizontal handover. Vertical handover refers to the handover of many different networks involved in the access process, such as the handover between 5G network and 4G network, and the handover between 5G network and WiFi. The type of handover in which the type of access network does not change during the handover process is called horizontal handover. Horizontal handover can also be further divided according to the *Mobile Service Controller* (MSC) participating in the handover [14]. If the two base stations involved in a handover are controlled by the same MSC, then the intra-MSC handover is called Xn-based inter-NG-RAN handover [15]. If the base station for a handover belongs to two different MSCs, then the inter-MSC handover is called N2 based inter-NG- RAN handover. In the 5G high-speed rail network scenario, due to the dense deployment of 5G base stations and our paper focuses on solving the problem of fast and secure pre-handover under 5G networks [16], we assume that the handover scenario belongs to Xn-based handover.

In recent years, researchers have done substantial research on 5G network handover and authentication in different wireless access scenarios. Mishra et al. [17] proposed a mobile topology that can dynamically capture the wireless network, and can perform fast authentication during the handover process. However, in order to ensure physical security, it is necessary to add servers to the network structure to ensure security, which greatly increases the complexity of the network system. Kim et al. [18] proposed an identity authentication scheme based on ID encryption, which is used for identity verification in the handover authentication process. However, due to the implementation of bilinear pairing operations, which brings huge system computing overhead. Sharma and Vishal, et al. [19] proposed a secure and relatively efficient handover authentication protocol, which can solve the security problems in WIFI, WiMAX and LTE networks, but the key escrow problem has not been solved.

At present, there are few handover authentication schemes for MRN, and the existing schemes have different degrees of defects in security and performance. Pan et al. [20] proposed a handover scheme under the LTE high-speed rail network, which improves network service quality by deploying multiple MRNs. However, in this scheme, the MRN needs to run the handover process first, which will increase the delay in handover authentication. And this scheme also has certain security vulnerabilities. Ma et al. [21] proposed a secure and efficient handover authentication protocol suitable for multiple MRNs, which can reduce handover delay, but MRN needs to store a large amount of base station node information for fast handover, so this scheme is not flexible.

3   System Model

3.1   System Architecture

Figure 1 shows the handover model of the 5G high-speed rail network, which includes 5G gNBs, UEs, and 5G trusted relay (MRN). MRN is a group authentication and handover relay running in a high-speed rail carriage, including a prediction module and a trusted computing module.

3.2   Security Model

The goals of the system security model mentioned in this paper are as follows.

(1) We assume that the MRN broadcasts the random number r_1 of the handover request during handover phase. UE and MRN are connected through a wireless channel.

Any UE within the coverage of the relay can obtain r_1. Before the handover phase, UEs complete the 5G group *Authentication and Key Agreement* (AKA) protocol with the assistance of MRN and accesses the 5G network.

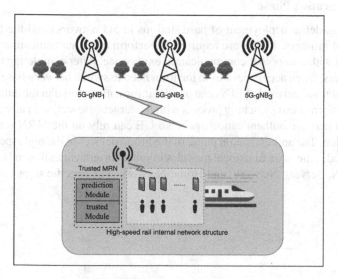

Fig. 1. System architecture.

(2) A trusted execution environment runs in each MRN, and the MRN is trusted for the UE.

(3) The network connection between the Home Network and the 5G gNB is trusted.

4 Proposed Scheme

In this section, we introduce a seamless group pre-handover authentication scheme based on trusted MRN under 5G high-speed rail networks, including group authentication phase and handover phase for 5G UEs.

In the authentication phase, MRN acts as the authenticated group master relay to assist user devices in the high-speed railway that want to access the 5G network through the high-speed railway to perform improved 5G-AKA authentication and complete the authentication process. After the authentication is completed, MRN and UE can obtain a *Globally Unique Temporary Identification* (GUTI) for the 5G network. Meanwhile, a white list of devices' users who have passed the 5G-AKA authentication is stored in the MRN.

In the handover phase, since the group master MRN has already saved the valid temporary identifiers of the certified devices when the MRN detects that the group is far away from the signal coverage of the source base station gNode1 during the operation of the high-speed railway, the MRN will send a handover request to the certified group members, triggering the group switching protocol and assisting the group members to complete the pre-handover at the same time.

4.1 Authentication Phase

Because of the dense deployment of base stations in 5G networks and the high speed of high-speed railways, MRNs are required to perform a pre-authentication process to provide users with a smoother communication experience. After completing the authentication process, when access devices in the train need to switch between base stations in the same attribution network, MRNs can use the information stored in the authentication process to perform a fast switching process with the target base station in advance. There is no need to perform authentication again, so UE can rely on the MRN for smoother communication. The authentication phase of the group devices in the high-speed railway network includes the main functional modules involved in authentication in User Device, Trusted MRN, Serving Network, and Home Network. The specific steps are shown in Fig. 2.

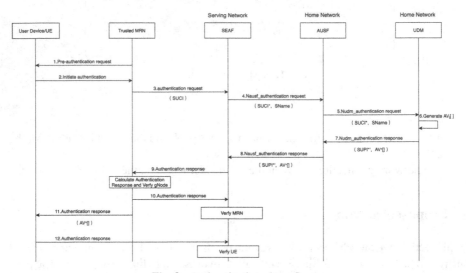

Fig. 2. Authentication phase flow.

Step 1: MRN generates authentication requests regularly during operation and broadcasts them to users in range, asking for UEs that want to access the 5G high-speed rail networks and join the group.

Step 2: UE_i that receives the pre-handover request makes an authentication response to MRN and encrypts its $SUPI_i$ to $SUCI_i$ according to the public key of Home Network and sends it to MRN as the initial authentication response.

Step 3: After calculating $SUCI_0$ and $SUCI = SUCI_1||SUCI_2||SUCI_3 \ldots ||SUCI_i$, MRN sends the authentication response message with shared packet header including SUCI to

Serving Network, where $SUCI_i$ represents the user's permanent identity corresponding to $SUPI_i$.

Step 4: After receiving the authentication request from MRN, Serving Network forwards the group authentication request ($SUCI$, $SName$, other) to Home Network.

Step 5: The AUSF in the Serving Network processes the message and also forwards the $SUCI$, $SName$ request to the UDM module of the Home Network for authentication.

Step 6: UDM recovers $SUCI_0, SUCI_1, SUCI_2 \ldots$ from the SUCI and uses the authentication vector of the 5G-AKA protocol for bulk authentication of UE, and sets MRN as "group master", and calculates the authentication vector 5G-$AV_i[RAND, AUTN, HRES^*, K_{SEAF}]$. $RAND$ is shared by the group users, and $AUTN$ is generated by Home Network using $AUTN = AUTN_0 || AUTN_1 || AUTN_2 || AUTN_3 \ldots || AUTN_i$.

Step 7: After that, Home Network will package the generated 5G-$AV_i[]$ and the authenticated $SUCI^*$ and prepare to send them to Serving Network ($SUCI^* = SUCI_0 || SUCI_1 || SUCI_2 || SUCI_3 \ldots || SUCI_k$, $SUCI_k$ means the temporary identifier of the UE user authenticated by the core network).

Step 8: After receiving the authentication response message, the AUSF extracts and returns the 5G-$AV_i[]$ and the authenticated $SUCI^*$ to the Serving Network.

Step 9: The AUSF in Serving Network extracts the $RAND$ and $AUTN$ from the response message and sends them to MRN.

Step 10: MRN sends the $AUTN$ and $RAND$ received from AUSF to the trusted module to verify the validity of 5G-$AV_i[]$. If the verification passes, the trusted module calculates the response RES^* and sends SHA256 ($< RAND, RES^* >$) to the Serving Network. After the base station authenticates the MRN pass, Serving Network calculates the session key K_{SEAF} through CK and IK.

Step 11: MRN forwards $AUTN_i$ and $RAND$ of other authenticated members through UDM to other UEs in the group.

Step 12: MRN assists group users to complete authentication and generates a "whitelist" of authenticated users for subsequent handover phase.

4.2 Handover Phase

After the UEs in the group have completed authentication under the leadership of MRN, the derived key K_s is generated between the UEs and the accessed Home Network to ensure the channel security. k_i is the session key between Home Network and the base station $gNode_i$ to ensure the confidentiality of the communication data between Home Network and the base station. When the Home Network is about to leave the signal coverage of the base station $gNode_1$, the MRN detects the change of signal and starts the pre-switching process. In the pre-handover process, MRN predicts the base station to be accessed by the prediction module and also accepts the valid temporary identifiers sent by the group members to prepare the handover service of the 5G network in advance, and the specific handover process will be carried out according to Fig. 3.

Step 1: First, MRN uses the prediction module to predict and generate the $XnapID$ of the target base station $gNode_2$ based on the $XnapID$ of $gNode_1$, which is used for the subsequent handover. Because the handover and prediction process of MRN group is carried out within the signal range of $gNode_1$, the UEs in MRN group can get stable 5G network service while completing pre-hadnover within $gNode_1$.

Step 2: MRN broadcasts the handover request and passes the generated random number r_1 to the members of the group to prepare for the handover.

Step 3: After UE_i in the group receives the handover request, it sends the identifier $GUTI_i$ of UE_i and the r_1 to MRN as the switch accordingly, where $GUTI_i$ is the temporary identifier corresponding to UE_i during the switch phase.

Step 4: MRN generates HANDOVER ACCEPT $HA = \{t, GUTI, SC, SP\}$, where $GUTI = GUTI_0 || GUTI_1 || GUTI_2 || GUTI_3 \dots || GUTI_i$, t represents the valid time of handover credentials, and SC represents the security capability identifier of encryption and integrity algorithms supported by the UE, and SP represents the security policy of the UE at the network side. After generating HA, MRN calculates $MAC_i = h(GUTI_i, XnapID)$, and $h()$ is a secure one way hash function.

After MRN calculates MAC_i of each group member, it calculates $MAC = MAC_0 \oplus MAC_1 \oplus MAC_2 \oplus MAC_3 \dots \oplus MAC_i$, and the MAC is sent to the Software Guard Extensions (SGX) Quoting Enclave in the Trusted Module for signing. The Quoting Enclave first verifies the report, and then uses the private key in the EPID for signing to generate a locally verifiable report quote for the platform Quoting Enclave, and then returns the *quote* to the MRN for verification by Home Network.

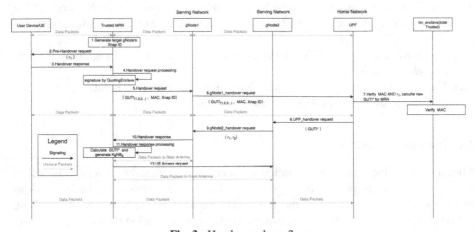

Fig. 3. Handover phase flow.

Step 5: After MRN finishes the request preparation for pre-handover, it sends the information including $GUTI$, MAC, r_1, $XnapID$, group user common message (including GUAMI), AMF interface and security capability of MRN, PDU List, QosFlow, etc. to $gNode_1$.

Step 6: $gNode_1$ forwards the handover request to the UPF function module in Home Network, and Home Network prepares for the handover coordination of the base station.

Step 7: After receiving the handover request, UPF first verifies whether the r_1 from MRN is fresh, and then looks for the corresponding SUPI according to GUTI and verifies the *MAC* correctness. If the verification passes, the MAC is verified using the Intel SGX global online verification facility called Intel Attestation Server (IAS). The remote authentication is required because UPF and MRN are in two different enclaves. Because *quote* can only be verified by Intel, UPF forwards *quote* to IAS. After completing the validity check of the platform, IAS creates a new proof verification report combining the EPID public key and Attestation Verification Service to certify *quoto* to complete the trusted authentication. If the verification is successful, it generates a positive report. After completing the SGX-based trusted authentication, the UPF generates a new $GUTI^* = h(r_1, K_s) \oplus SUPI$ (at this point, the downlink data on the user side has been got through).

Step 8: Home Network sends a handover request to $gNode_2$ and informs $gNode_2$ as the target handover base station of MRN to prepare for the data link of MRN to be got through. After receiving the handover request from Home Network, $gNode_2$ calculates the session key $K_{gNB_2} = KDF(GUTI^*, XnapID)$ between $gNode_2$ and MRN.

Step 9: After completing the preparation for the pre-handover, $gNode_2$ sends a handover request to $gNode_1$. The handover request includes $\{r_1, r_2\}$ information and requests to guide MRN to shift the data channel to $gNode_2$.

Step 10: After receiving the handover request from $gNode_2$, $gNode_1$ sends the handover response to MRN, and guides MRN to complete the handover of base station, and guides MRN to forward the users' uplink data to $gNode_2$.

Step 11: After receiving the handover response, MRN calculates the updated $GUTI^*$ and the session key K_{gNB_2} between MRN and $gNode_2$, using the calculation method mentioned above, and sends $\{r_2 - 1\}$ to $gNode_2$ to deliver the handover success message.

Step 12: The uplink data channel is got through and the pre-handover is completed. As long as the high-speed railway enters the signal range of $gNode_2$, MRN can use the session key K_{gNB_2} generated in the pre-handover process to communicate with the target base station and ensure the communication security.

5   Security Analysis

This section analyzes the 5G high-speed railway network seamless group pre-handover scheme proposed by this paper from the aspects of theory, feasibility, and security.

– **Mutual Authentication.** In the process of authentication, UE completes group authentication based on 5G-AKA protocol with the help of MRN, so only legitimate UE have *SUPI* and *GUTI*. In the process of handover, each UE uses *GUTI* to generate *MAC* for identity verification, and the MRN group owner aggregates all the *MACs*, and UPF verifies MAC validity. If one of the *MAC* of a UE is invalid, the authentication will fail. Moreover, using a lightweight authentication scheme to perform handover protocols does not introduce significant communication overhead for frequent handover in the dense deployment environment of 5G base stations, and achieves security and privacy protection requirements, which is conducive to the sustainable development of the 5G high-speed railway network ecosystem.

- **Key Agreement.** The session key K_{gNB} is generated between MRN and the base station, and the session key will derive a new session key using $GUTI^*$ and $XnapID$ when the high-speed railway travels to the next new base station. Attackers cannot compute the session key without access to $GUTI^*$.
- **Resistance Memory Access Attacks.** Thanks to the trusted execution module in MRN, the SGX trusted execution session needs to place integrated code in a separate area, and checks the read and write access and computation of variables in that area. Only after passing the checking, can the users actually access the users' data and protect the UEs' memory.
- **Computational Integrity Protection.** The MRN equipped with a trusted execution module can generate a secure summary message for the running protocol process in the internal SGX container during the computation. Then, it collects and integrates these summaries and uploads them to the ISA. UPF can check whether the intermediate structure interferes with the execution of the computation like the ISA application after receiving a pre-handover request.
- **Resistance Sybil Attack.** Because MRN goes through the unified authentication of the UEs during the pre-handover process, the generation of authentication and handover messages afterward are performed in a trusted execution environment, ensuring the trustworthiness of the information sent by the device from the source. After the handover protocol applies SGX remote authentication mode, it generates the unique authentication key signature of the platform, and the anonymous attacker cannot pass the authentication.
- **Resistance against Replay Attacks.** This scheme can effectively resist against replay attacks as the handover protocol generates new random numbers r_1 and r_2 each time when the scheme executed the handover process.
- **Resistance against Impersonation Attacks.** With the help of MRN, the UE uses private $SUPI$ to calculate the hash value and generate the session key for each handover. Adversaries can't generate a valid hash and then forge a legitimate MRN or base station. Therefore, this scheme can resist against impersonation attacks.

6   Conclusion

In this paper, we presented a secure and efficient group handover authentication scheme for 5G high-speed railway network. Our scheme used pre-handover and trusted execution modules to realize a fast and secure group handover and ensured users have smooth and secure communication experience while the high-speed railway is in motion. Our scheme solves the switching problem of the massive UEs in the 5G network while the high-speed railway is in motion. After the security analysis, our group handover authentication scheme is applicable and secure, and the handover consumption is reasonable.

Acknowledgement. This work was supported by the National Key R&D Program of China through project 2020YFB10056, the Natural Science Foundation of China through projects 62002006, 62172025, U21B2021, 61932011, 61932014, 61972018, 61972019, 61772538, 32071775 and 91646203.

References

1. Series, M.: IMT vision–framework and overall objectives of the future development of IMT for 2020 and beyond. Recomm. ITU **2083** (2015)
2. 3rd Generation Partnership Project: Technical Specification Group Radio Access Network; NR; NR and NG-RAN Overall Description; Stage 2 (Release 15): 38.300. Global: 3GPP (2018)
3. 3rd Generation Partnership Project: Technical Specification Group Radio Access Network Evolved Universal Terrestrial Radio Access (E-UTRA); Study on mobile relay (Release 12): 36.836. Global: 3GPP (2014)
4. Qiu, M., Ming, Z., Li, J., Liu, S., Wang, B., Lu, Z.: Three-phase time-aware energy minimization with DVFS and unrolling for chip multiprocessors. J. Syst. Archit. **58**(10), 439–445 (2012)
5. Zhao, H., Chen, M., et al.: A novel pre-cache schema for high performance android system. Future Gener. Comput. Syst. **56**, 766–772 (2016)
6. Su, H., Qiu, M., Wang, H.: Secure wireless communication system for smart grid with rechargeable electric vehicles. IEEE Commun. Mag. **50**(8), 62–68 (2012)
7. Qiu, M., Ming, Z., Li, J., Liu, J., Quan, G., Zhu, Y.: Informer homed routing fault tolerance mechanism for wireless sensor networks. J. Syst. Archit. **59**(4–5), 260–270 (2013)
8. Tang, X., Li, K., et al.: A hierarchical reliability-driven scheduling algorithm in grid systems. J. Parallel Distrib. Comput. **72**(4), 525–535 (2012)
9. Li, J., et al.: Feedback dynamic algorithms for preemptable job scheduling in cloud systems. In: IEEE/WIC/ACM Conference on Web Intelligence (2010)
10. Gai, K., Qiu, M., Thuraisingham, B., Tao, L.: Proactive attribute-based secure data schema for mobile cloud in financial industry. In: IEEE 17th HPCC (2015)
11. Zhang, K., Kong, J., Qiu, M., Song, G.: Multimedia layout adaptation through grammatical specifications. Multimed. Syst. **10**(3), 245–260 (2005)
12. Tayyab, M., Gelabert, X., Jäntti, R.: A survey on handover management: from LTE to NR. IEEE Access **7**, 118907–118930 (2019)
13. Ahmed, A., Boulahia, L.M., Gaiti, D.: Enabling vertical handover decisions in heterogeneous wireless networks: a state-of-the-art and a classification. IEEE Commun. Surv. Tutor. **16**(2), 776–811 (2013)
14. Zhao, D., et al.: Is 5G handover secure and private? A survey. IEEE Internet Things J. (2021)
15. 3rd Generation Partnership Project: Technical Specification group Services and System Aspects; Security Architecture and Procedures for 5G System (Rel 15), 3GPP TS, Technical report 33.501 V15.4.0 (March 2019)
16. Cao, Jin, et al.: A survey on security aspects for 3GPP 5G networks. IEEE Commun. Surv. Tutor. **22**(1), 170–195 (2019)
17. Mishra, A., et al.: Proactive key distribution using neighbor graphs. IEEE Wirel. Commun. **11**(1), 26–36 (2004)
18. Kim, Y., et al.: SFRIC: a secure fast roaming scheme in wireless LAN using ID-based cryptography. In: 2007 IEEE International Conference on Communications (2007)
19. Sharma, V., et al.: Secure and efficient protocol for fast handover in 5G mobile Xhaul networks. J. Netw. Comput. Appl. **102**, 38–57 (2018)
20. Pan, M.-S., Lin, T.-M., Chen, W.-T.: An enhanced handover scheme for mobile relays in LTE-A high-speed rail networks. IEEE Trans. Veh. Technol. **64**(2), 743–756 (2014)
21. Ma, R., et al.: FTGPHA: fixed-trajectory group pre-handover authentication mechanism for mobile relays in 5G high-speed rail networks. IEEE Trans. Veh. Technol. **69**(2), 2126–2140 (2019)

Anomaly Detection System of Controller Area Network (CAN) Bus Based on Time Series Prediction

Xiangtian Tan[1], Chen Zhang[2], Bo Li[1(✉)], Binbin Ge[1], and Chen Liu[1]

[1] Beihang University, Beijing 100191, China
{tanxt,libo,gebinbin,liuchen}@act.buaa.edu.cn
[2] Information and Telecommunication Branch, State Grid Zhejiang Electric Power Co., Beijing 310007, China

Abstract. With the development of intelligent networked vehicles, the research on the safety of in-vehicle networks has gradually become a hot spot. CAN (controller area network) is the most widely used in-vehicle network bus, and its safety problem has become the most critical problem to be solved in the development process of intelligent networked vehicles. This paper aims at the in-vehicle can be used in intelligent networked vehicles Bus network, its communication characteristics and security problems are analyzed and dissected. Meanwhile, with the increase in demand for in-vehicle network communication applications, the corresponding attacks have also increased year by year. Therefore, this paper only increases the anomaly detection of in-vehicle application log in the anomaly detection of CAN bus, aiming to detect the abnormal behavior of vehicles in an all-around way. To solve the field data lacking's problem, we collect a data set containing several types of data from multiple channels, including different types of attack can bus messages. Due to the different elements in the message having different effects on the classification results, the attention mechanism is introduced to give different weights to different messages and log data segments, which increases the effect of classification detection.

Keywords: CAN bus · Anomaly detection · Time series prediction · Vehicle safety

1 Introduction

With the increasing complexity of electronic systems [1–3] and the increasing requirements for the communication capabilities [4–6] between the electronic units of the internal control functions of the car, the large-scale use of point-to-point links has also rapidly increased the number of wiring harnesses in the car. This brought great troubles to design and manufacturing of the car for reliability, safety, and weight when considering the internal communication [7–9]. Therefore, in order to reduce in-vehicle connections to achieve data sharing and rapid exchange, as well as improve reliability [10–12], more and more companies implement the vehicle electronic network system with basic structures on fast-developing computer networks, i.e., vehicle-mounted network, including CAN, LAN, LIN, MOST [13–17].

In recent years, with the frequent occurrence of Internet of Vehicles security incidents, many domestic and foreign researchers aim to explore security vulnerabilities and detection technologies [18–21]. In 2010, researchers from the University of South Carolina and Rutgers University implemented an attack on the electronic tire pressure monitoring system of automobiles. They have realized the remote control of turning on and off the tire pressure warning light, which will enable the driver to judge the tire pressure status of the vehicle, thereby achieving certain illegal purposes. In 2011, Subaru used verification text messages to attack vulnerabilities on the Internet of Vehicles services on cars. At the DEFCON conference, technicians used intercepted verification text messages sent by car owners to unlock the vehicle.

Later, at the 2013 DEFCON conference, hackers used the Ford Escape and Toyota Prius software vulnerabilities to intervene in the vehicle network to control the vehicle's key systems such as accelerator and brake. In 2014, 360 company used the process design loopholes in the Tesla car application to realize a series of operations such as remote unlocking and turning on and off the lights. In 2015, the Jeep Grand Cherokee's brakes and steering systems were remotely controlled due to loopholes in the in-vehicle entertainment system, which eventually led to the recall of 1.4 million problematic cars by Chrysler, causing huge economic losses. In 2016, Tencent's Keen Lab realized a remote invasion of Tesla. They replaced Tesla's main screen with the logo of Keen Lab, making it impossible for the car owner to operate. What's more, they also realized the remote unlocking of the vehicle and the control of some functions of the vehicle during the journey, such as brakes, rearview mirrors, and trunk lights. After 2017, the security vane of the Internet of Vehicles has rapidly shifted to the issues of customer data security and privacy security. For example, in June of that year, the database of a dealer group in the United States was attacked, involving the leakage of sales data of more than 10 million vehicles from multiple brands [22–24].

This paper is organized according to the following parts. The first part is the source of data set and the generation method of attack data. The second part is the design of anomaly detection system based on LSTM. The third part is a specific experiment, including the statistics of data distribution, the determination of loss function and the training results of some ID data.

2   CAN Bus Dataset

2.1 Disadvantages of CAN Bus Dataset

1. Broadcast transmission. CAN bus is a single common channel, and the protocol stipulates that all nodes can monitor bus messages, so malicious nodes can easily obtain all messages on the bus.

2. There is no authentication mechanism. The message on the CAN bus does not have fields indicating the source of the information and the purpose of the message, which means that the sender of the message cannot be distinguished, and the source of the message cannot be distinguished from a normal node or a malicious node.

3. The message is unencrypted. Almost all of the CAN bus is transmitted in plain text, and the message content is only 64 bits at most, which is easy to be cracked by an attacker.

4. Information arbitration based on ID number. The message priority on the CAN bus is indicated by the ID number of each message, the smaller the ID number, the higher the priority. Therefore, if a node keeps sending the message with the lowest priority, other messages cannot be sent normally, which will affect the normal use of the CAN bus. Obviously, this is a Dos attack [16] (Fig. 1)

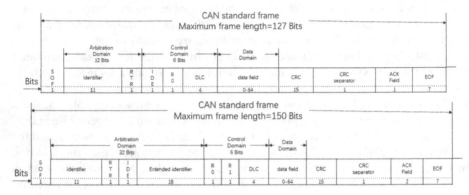

Fig. 1. CAN protocol format

The message transmission process of CAN protocol includes data frame, remote frame, error frame, overload frame, and frame interval.

- Data frame: A frame used by the sending node to transmit data to the receiving node.
- Remote frame: A frame used by the receiving node to transmit data to the sending node with the same ID.
- Error frame: A frame used to notify other nodes of the error when an error is detected.
- Overload frame: A frame used to notify the receiving node that it is not ready.
- Frame interval: Used to separate data frames and remote frames from previous frames.

CAN is a message-oriented transmission protocol originally designed for the automotive industry in an attempt to reduce the wiring complexity of automobiles [22]. An *Electronic Control Unit* (ECU) uses CAN to broadcast its frames onto a bus [26]. There is no addressing scheme. Instead each frame is assigned an 11 bit unique identifier, known as the "arbitration ID" or "CAN ID", which defines both the function and the priority of the frame where 0x000 has highest priority and 0x7FF lowest. The priority resolves conflict when two or more nodes try to send a frame at the same time. A frame may also contains up to 8 bytes of data. While an ECU may broadcast multiple CAN IDs, each CAN ID is bound to a single ECU; two ECUs cannot send data frames with the same CAN ID. Every time a frame is transmitted, all ECUs on the bus will receive it, and will determine, based on the CAN ID whether they should accept and further process the message [24, 27].

2.2 Abnormal Data Generation Algorithm

As demonstrated in previous research [14, 15, 17, 25, 27]. Since there is no publicly available attack traffic repository, and the actual attack effect on the car is time-consuming and dangerous. Since there is no publicly available attack traffic repository, and the actual attack effect on the car is very time-consuming and dangerous. Therefore, we consider synthesizing abnormal data by modifying the captured data. For example, switch the message id to simulate a fake transmitter, or insert harmless random packets into the real-time bus.

Considering that the high-speed CAN messages are very regular, which only contains three basic ways to manifest the attack: adding a data packet, the expected data packet does not appear, or the data content of the data packet is unusual. Since we did not use any time information in the attack scenario, we can create an attack signature just by changing the sequence of data packets obtained from the data capture. Moreover, we can ensure that each data packet is valid, and in order to achieve the expected detection effect, each packet must contain legal information. As far as we know, abnormal data is abnormal only in the context of adjacent data packets. The only exception is to invert unused bits to simulate hidden commands and control methods.

In summary, five kinds of abnormal phenomena can be produced:

1. Abnormal message attack (diagnostic attack): CAN bus is an unauthenticated and unencrypted broadcast bus, anyone can read and send any message. The ECU may have a message conflict resolution mechanism. When receiving conflicting values, the ECU will react differently according to the implemented mechanism. Thus, the ECU has a "diagnostic mode" that allows maintenance operations. Car manufacturers design their cars in their own specific ways, making the car's ECU and canID mapping very diverse. Moreover, the mapping from canID to their respective ECUs differs for different models. Therefore, in order to achieve the target of the attack, the attacker may need to know the architecture of the vehicle and which canID is linked to the specific ECU. We have seen that when the CAN bus is accessed for the first time, it is quite difficult to achieve a purposeful attack without prior knowledge. Therefore, during the reconnaissance phase, an attacker can perform a diagnostic attack by sending a message with a random CANID and payload value and observing the response. This attack allows the attacker to understand the architecture and behavior of the vehicle.
2. Suspend attack: We can delete some messages in the middle of a normal subsequence to simulate an attack that suppresses the ECU.
3. Obfuscation attack: One is to inject 20 unknown data packets, there is no CANID in the training data set, and it is lower than CANID0x700. Another obscure attack is to replace the 10-frame payload that belongs to the legal CANID without injecting

new data packets. Among them, the bytes of the payload are set to values that are not used for this CANID in the training data set.

4. Replay attack: Replicate by injecting any packet 30 times the data set in the data set. In particular, we simulated a data packet that was sent to the bus 10 times faster than usual by adjusting the timestamp. Since we do not know the function of this CANID and the semantics of its payload, we directly inject it without modification.
5. DOS attack: We will replace all messages within 10 s with CANID 0x000 and process it at a rate of 4 data packets per millisecond. This simulates a 500 Kbps CAN bus [28].

3   Anomaly Detection of Lstm Model

3.1   Feature Selection

The sorting table of the collected messages indicates that the field of the message was a hexadecimal value. The data field of each message consists of 8 bytes, and each byte represents a different functional instruction. To obtain a uniform data field length, two zero digits were used to represent a null value in each column. The CAN bus messages are sent from different CAN IDs and carry the data information for some particular functions or control commands. Although the inherent changes in the normal internal operation of the vehicle and abnormal tampering attacks will affect the data field of the message. The data bit changes caused by the normal operation of the vehicle will remain or change regularly during a certain period, therefore a time series data anomaly detector can be used to detect whether the message has been tampered with. According to the detector requirements of the experiment, anomaly detection in the message stream of the CAN bus was performed for each ID separately.

3.2   LSTM-Based detector

The basic structure of our proposed detector is similar to the previous LSTM anomaly detector. However, since the input of the CAN message is a high-dimensional binary vector, we add a linear embedding layer to project the binary input into a real-valued state space [22]. Therefore, the final network structure contains a linear segment, a recursive segment, and a linear output segment. Given the input sequence, $x_1, x_2, x_3, \ldots, x_n$, where x_i is a 64-bit vector, the network trains a subsequent target y_i for each i, such that $y_i = x_i + 1$. Specifically, The 64-bit vector of input xi is converted by two acyclic hidden layers, and each hidden layer has 128 units and employs tanh activation function. The output of the linear layer is input to two cyclic LSTM layers, each layer has 512 units and employs the tanh activation function. The last layer is a fully-connected layer containing 64 units, which can output detection values between 0 and 1 using the s-type activation function. It is worth noting that we train a separate network for each CAN bus ID [28].

Different from traditional feature selection, there are changes between the values in two formats of the data field for each message. It can be found that a constant bit in the hexadecimal format of different IDs is also a constant bit in the corresponding binary format, but a constant bit in the binary form does not guarantee that the data are unchanged in the hexadecimal form; that is, the two data forms have a relationship but differ. These differences affect the performance of the detection algorithm, which will be examined later work (Fig. 2).

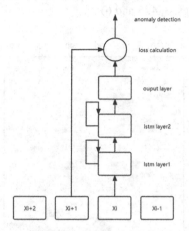

Fig. 2. Lstm-based detector

Existing researches usually calculate the loss between the predicted data, and the actual data in the final detection phase, instead of calculating the priority of the caID, the time interval and other variables in a unified way. This paper considers that before training the model, the Messages are divided into different types according to the probability of each byte changing, the average value of each person, and other characteristics. For example, if the basic data segment of a type of canID is the same, the time interval is the priority of the difference, then the canID has a greater impact on the value of the loss, and the difference between the two data has a smaller impact on the final judgment result.

4 Experiment

4.1 Data Distribution Analysis

Since the implementation of the can bus on different vehicles is very different, in order to ensure the reliability of the anomaly detection system, it is more important to collect data from different vehicles. The existing data comes from three systems, Opel Astra, Renault Clio, and a build Prototype.

The following are statistics on the data distribution of the three systems. Each system contains two distribution diagrams, which respectively represent the average value of each bit of all messages of each canID in the system, and the relative value of each byte relative to the message. Probability of 8 bytes change. The calculation method is that the former counts the sum of the number of 1s divided by the total number of messages, and the latter corresponds to a set per byte. The probability of change is obtained by calculating the set size divided by the sum of the 8 sets size.

The darker the color, indicating that the probability value approaches 1, on the contrary, it is close to 0 (Figs. 3, 4, 5 and 6).

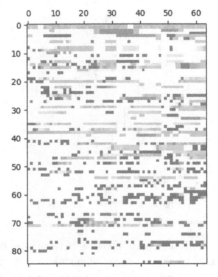

Fig. 3. In Opel Astra each average for 64 bits in 85 canIDs

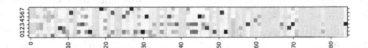

Fig. 4. In Opel Astra each average for 8 bits in 85 canIDs

4.2   Metric of Detection Abnormality

The error of the LSTM network depends on the logarithmic loss of binary data between the output and the next data segment, where the logarithmic loss between binary data is defined as:

$$L\left(\hat{b}_k, b_k\right) = -(b_k \log\left(\hat{b}_k + \epsilon\right) + (1 - b_k)\log(1 - \hat{b}_k + \epsilon))$$

Where b_k is the $k - th$ bit in the target Y_i, $\hat{b}_k$ is the predicted value of the $k - th$ network in step I, ϵ is a fixed value used to limit the maximum loss. As shown in

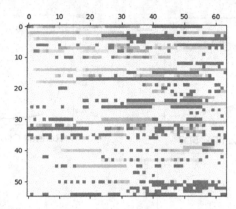

Fig. 5. In Renault Clio each average for 64 bits in 55 canIDs

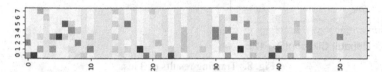

Fig. 6. In Renault Clio each average for 8 bits in 55 canIDs

Figure x, the logarithmic loss function is relatively low for the incorrect but intermediate prediction, but very high for the confident but incorrect prediction. For a completely incorrect prediction, there is a loss approaching infinity; In practice, its upper limit is $-\log(\epsilon)$. Currently, temporarily ϵ is set to $10 - 15th$ power, which indicates that the maximum logarithmic loss of binary data is about 35 (Fig. 7).

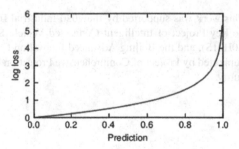

Fig. 7. Metric of detection abnormality

4.3 Some Representative ID Training Results

See Fig. 8.

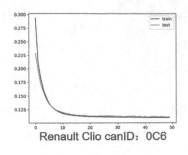

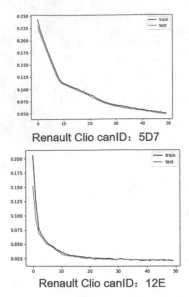

Renault Clio canID: 12E

Fig. 8. Training results of 3 ids.

5 Conclusion

Under the condition of ensuring the abnormal detection effect, at present, the false positive rate is about 0.02%–0.008%, but it will still produce false positive false positives every minute. False positives always exist, and it is hard to complete the detection of all messages with a unified detection model. In this paper, the false positive rate of some ID was already reduced to 0.002%.

Acknowledgements. This work was supported by the 2020 Industrial Internet Innovation and Development Project-the Key Project of Intelligent Connected Vehicle Safety Inspection Platform (Tender No. TC200H01S), and the Beijing Advanced Innovation Center for Big Data and Brain Computing, and supported by Project of Comprehensive Protection Platform for Industrial Enterprise Network Security.

References

1. Gao, Y., Iqbal, S., et al.: Performance and power analysis of high-density multi-GPGPU architectures: a preliminary case study. In: IEEE 17th HPCC (2015)
2. Zhao, H., Chen, M., et al.: A novel pre-cache schema for high performance android system. Futur. Gener. Comput. Syst. **56**, 766–772 (2016)
3. Qiu, M., Xue, C., Shao, Z., Sha, E.: Energy minimization with soft real-time and DVS for uniprocessor and multiprocessor embedded systems. In: IEEE DATE Conference, pp. 1–6 (2007)
4. Qiu, L., Gai, K., Qiu, M.: Optimal big data sharing approach for tele-health in cloud computing. In: IEEE SmartCloud, pp. 184–189 (2016)

5. Qiu, H., Qiu, M., Memmi, G., Ming, Z., Liu, M.: A dynamic scalable blockchain based communication architecture for IoT. In: Qiu, M. (ed.) Smart Blockchain, vol. 11373, pp. 159–166. Springer, Cham (2018). https://doi.org/10.1007/978-3-030-05764-0_17
6. Qiu, H., Qiu, M., Lu, Z.: Selective encryption on ECG data in body sensor network based on supervised machine learning. Inf. Fusion **55**, 59–67 (2020)
7. Checkoway, S., et al.: Comprehensive experimental analyses of automotive attack surfaces. In: USENIX Security Symposium (2011)
8. Miller, C., Valasek, C.: Remote exploitation of an unaltered passenger vehicle. Black Hat USA, vol. 2015 (2015)
9. Woo, S., Jo, H.J., Lee, D.H.: A practical wireless attack on the connected car and security protocol for in-vehicle can. IEEE Trans. Intell. Transp. Syst. **16**(2), 993–1006 (2015)
10. Szilagyi, C., Koopman, P.: Low cost multicast authentication via validity voting in time-triggered embedded control networks. In: Proceedings of 5th Workshop on Embedded Systems Security, p. 10. ACM (2010)
11. Lin, C.-W., Sangiovanni-Vincentelli, A.: Cyber-security for the controller area network (CAN) communication protocol. In: Proceedings International Conference on Cyber Security. IEEE (2012)
12. Groza, B., Murvay, S.: Efficient protocols for secure broad cast in controller area networks. IEEE Trans. Ind. Inform. **9**(4), 2034–2042 (2013)
13. Jaynes, M., Dantu, R., Varriale, R., Evans, N.: Automating ecu identififcation for vehicle security. In: 15th IEEE International Conference on Machine Learning and Applications (ICMLA), pp. 632–635 (2016)
14. Moore, M.R., Bridges, R.A., Combs, F.L., Starr, M.S., Prowell, S.J.: Modeling inter-signal arrival times for accurate detection of can bus signal injection attacks: a data-driven approach to in-vehicle intrusion detection. In: ACM Proceedings of CISRC, p. 11 (2017)
15. Moore, M.R., Bridges, R.A., Combs, F.L., Ander son, A.L.: Data-driven extraction of vehicle states from CAN bus traffic for cyber protection and safety. Consumer Electronics Magazine (to appear). https://goo.gl/8LUvNH
16. Miller, C., Valasek, C.: Adventures in automotive networks and control units. Def Con **21**, 260–264 (2013)
17. Cho, K.-T., Shin, K.G.: Error handling of in-vehicle networks makes them vulnerable. In: Proceedings of the 2016 ACM SIGSAC Conference on Computer and Communications Security, pp. 1044–1055. ACM (2016)
18. Zhang, Z., Wu, J., et al.: Jamming ACK attack to wireless networks and a mitigation approach. IEEE GLOBECOM Conference, pp. 1–5 (2008)
19. Thakur, K., Qiu, M., Gai, K., Ali, M.: An investigation on cyber security threats and security models. In: IEEE CSCloud (2015)
20. Gai, K., Qiu, M., Sun, X., Zhao, H.: Security and privacy issues: a survey on FinTech. In: Qiu, M. (ed.) Smart Computing and Communication, pp. 236–247. Springer, Cham (2017). https://doi.org/10.1007/978-3-319-52015-5_24
21. Gai, K., Qiu, M., Elnagdy, S.: A novel secure big data cyber incident analytics framework for cloud-based cybersecurity insurance. In: IEEE BigDataSecurity (2016)
22. Hoppe, T., Kiltz, S., Dittmann, J.: Security threats to automotive CAN networks – practical examples and selected short-term countermeasures. In: Harrison, M.D., Sujan, M.-A. (eds.) Computer Safety, Reliability, and Security, pp. 235–248. Springer, Heidelberg (2008). https://doi.org/10.1007/978-3-540-87698-4_21
23. Hoppe, T., Kiltz, S., Dittmann, J.: Applying intrusion detection to automotive it-early in sights and remaining challenges. J. Inf. Assur. Secur. (JIAS) **4**(6), 226–235 (2009)
24. Gmiden, M., Gmiden, M.H., Trabelsi, H.: An intrusion detection method for securing in-vehicle CAN bus. In: Proceedings of Sciences and Techniques of Automatic Control and Computer Engineering. IEEE (2016)

25. Song, H.M., Kim, H.R., Kim, H.K.: Intrusion detection system based on the analysis of time intervals of can messages for in-vehicle network. In: 2016 International Conference on Information Networking (ICOIN), pp. 63–68. IEEE (2016)
26. Cho, K.-T., Shin, K.G.: Fingerprinting electronic control units for vehicle intrusion detection. In: USENIX Security Symposium, pp. 911–927 (2016)
27. Taylor, A., Leblanc, S., Japkowicz, N.: Anomaly detection in automobile control network data with long short-term memory networks. In: Proceedings of Sciences and Techniques of Automatic Control and Computer Engineering. IEEE (2016)
28. Dupont, G., Hartog, J.D., Etalle, S., Lekidis, A.: Evaluation framework for network intrusion detection systems for in-vehicle CAN

High-Performance and Customizable Vector Retrieval Service Based on Faiss in Power Grid Scenarios

Pengyu Zhang[✉]

Big Data Center of State Grid Corporation of China, Beijing 100000, China

Abstract. With the rapid development of machine learning and deep learning, more and more services in the power grid have introduced machine learning and deep learning technologies, and related application scenarios and services have become more and more, especially vector retrieval services. With the increase of the amount of data and the increase of the demand, higher requirements are put forward for the vector retrieval service performance and service management. In order to solve this problem, this paper designs a high-performance and customizable vector retrieval service, referred to as HCFRS. The HCVRS service uses Fiass as the underlying framework of the vector retrieval service, supporting functions such as service registration, service unloading, resource allocation, load balancing, and data management. This paper verifies whether the HVCRS service meets the service design requirements from the three aspects of functional testing, accuracy testing and performance testing. The experimental results show that the HVCRS service has complete functions and good performance, which basically solves the difficulties encountered by the State Grid in vector retrieval services.

Keywords: Faiss · Vector retrieval · Service registration · Service unloading · Resource allocation · Load balancing

1 Introduction

With the rapid development of the Internet and computer fields, the development of machine learning [1–3] and deep learning [4, 5] has also entered the fast lane. More and more industries have begun to embrace the Internet, including power companies, transportation Industry, petroleum industry, etc. Therefore, a huge amount of data is generated every day.

In the power grid field, as more and more services introduce intelligent application software [6–8], more and more unstructured data are generated every day [9, 10]. In the business of the power grid, pictures, texts, and languages are the most frequently encountered data types in the business. Other more complex data types can also be converted into basic data types for processing. In the actual business of the power grid, massive amounts of data are generated every day, and there is a growing trend. Then, data mining [1, 11, 12] and recommendation [13–17] in such a large amount of data will become very difficult. Without special data processing, the recommendation business of the grid will become very difficult. In the business of the power grid, the recommendation task still adopts a more traditional way. As the amount of data increases, recommendations become more and more difficult. On the one hand, time-consuming increases. Another aspect is that the recommendation is imprecise.

2 Related Work

With the rapid development of the networks [18–20] and the informatization and tech-nicalization of various traditional industries [21–23], various informatization services will generate a large amount of data [24–26]. In the actual business of the power grid, technicians often face the application requirements of retrieval. However, it is very difficult to retrieve from the massive data of the power grid. With the rapid development of machine learning and deep learning, all kinds of pictures, text, voice, etc., can be used, and data can be processed into feature vectors through Embedding [27–29] technology and various deep learning technologies [30, 31]. The vector contains the characteristics of multiple latitudes of the data [32–34]. Through this series of processing, the service retrieval problem is transformed into a vector retrieval problem [35–38]. Vector retrieval is a very important research direction in the industry and has attracted great attention from the academic and industrial circles. Many Internet companies have developed and open-sourced vector retrieval frameworks, such as FaceBook, Google, and Microsoft.

Faiss (Facebook AI Similarity Search) [39] is a framework open sourced by Face-Book in 2017 to provide efficient similarity retrieval for dense vectors, with fast retrieval speed and support for GPU calls. Faiss supports precision search and ANN [40–42]. ANN uses technologies such as PCA [34, 35] and PQ [45, 46] to compress the data set, which greatly improves the retrieval speed with a certain loss of accuracy. SPTAG is Microsoft's open source retrieval framework, providing retrieval methods such as kd tree [47, 48] and relative neighborhood graph [49, 50] and balanced k-means tree & relative neighborhood graph [51–53]. Milvus is a domestic open source retrieval framework with features such as convenient invocation and depression expansion, and has been favored by many domestic Internet companies. Milvu's high-performance solutions rely on high-performance Mysql and high-performance GPU resources. Elasticsearch is also a common technical solution for vector retrieval. ES provides some search plug-ins, such as BM52 Similarity, DFR Similarity, DFI Similarity, etc.

3 EOSP Service

3.1 HCVRS Service Operation Framework

In the context of the rapid development of machine learning and deep learning, there are more and more scenarios where technology in the recommended field is applied to the power grid. In Taichung, the service center of the power grid, more and more services are beginning to use recommendation technology, such as text recommendation and smart search. However, when the amount of data is large, it becomes difficult to recommend services. Therefore, this article introduces Faiss to specifically solve this problem. Triggered from the business perspective of the power grid, this article is designed to serve

HVCRS. HCVRS mainly includes 3 main modules, namely ServerModel, FaissIndexN-ode, and service configuration module. The overall architecture diagram of the HCVRS service is shown below. HVCRS mainly contains 3 main modules, namely ServerModel, FaissIndexNode and service configuration module. The following is a brief overview of these three modules (Fig. 1).

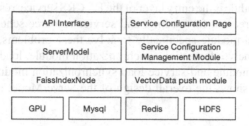

Fig. 1. HCVRS overall architecture diagram

ServerModel. The service management module is the basic module of HCFRS for service management and scheduling. All the parts about service configuration, service scheduling and execution will depend on this module. ServerModel contains 4 sub-modules, namely configuration information synchronization module, load balancing module, resource allocation module and service load synchronization module. The timing task in ServerModel will periodically obtain the configuration information of the service from Redis and analyze it. ServerModel will use the parsed data for service management and resource allocation. In addition, ServerMode also includes the implementation of load balancing, which can improve the efficiency of service access.

FaissIndexNode Model. FaissIndexNode is the core module of HCFRS, using Faiss framework as the underlying retrieval technology. The service loads the vector file into the memory and uses Faiss to build it as a Faiss index. FaissIndexNode contains 4 modules, which are service status information synchronization module, data download module, Faiss index building module and search engine.

Service Configuration Module. The service configuration module is one of the more basic modules of HVCRS. Both online and offline services need to be operated on the service configuration module. The service configuration module is mainly divided into two parts, namely the front-end page of the service configuration and the service information synchronization module. When the service is online, the user configures the service on the configuration page. The timing task in the service information synchronization module will load the service configuration information into Redis.

Service Configuration Module. The service data management module is a data service in HVCRS. The vector data push module is mainly responsible for the data management and version control of the service. This module provides two methods: data download and data push. The user can control the version of the service data through the web page. The data loading module of the service will synchronize the data information to the

Redis cluster. When the index is built, the system will select the corresponding version to build (Fig. 2).

3.2 Design of ServerModel Module

The ServerModel module is the entry layer of the HVCRS service, responsible for service application, service request forwarding, and service resource scheduling. This article designs ServerModel module specifically to solve these problems. ServerModel contains 4 modules, namely information synchronization module, load balancing module, resource allocation module and service load synchronization module. After the above analysis, this article shows the overall design of the ServerModel module as shown in Fig. 3.

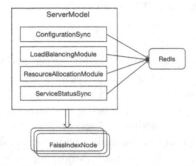

Fig. 2. The overall architecture of ServerModel.

Design of Configuration Information Synchronization Module. The configuration synchronization module is responsible for synchronizing configuration information to the Redis cluster. The configuration information mainly includes information such as the service name, the model and version number of the processing service data set, the version number of the data set, and the version number of the valid data set. The Syn_Model module is mainly responsible for the synchronization of information, and is responsible for synchronizing the Json data of the configuration information to the Redis cluster.

Fig. 3. Configuration information synchronization module.

Load Balancing Module. In ServerModel, functions such as service registration and service request are included. When a new service is registered in the ServerModel, the service will not be registered on all FaissIndexNodes under the ServerModel, but select some machines with less load pressure. Therefore, a list of nodes included in the service and their IP information will be recorded in the service memory. In order to ensure the stable access of the service, this paper designs a load balancing module to solve the data forwarding function of ServerModel. In this paper, the design of load balancer is relatively simple to proceed according to the probability model. First, ServerModel will sort the service nodes into a doubly linked list according to the load pressure of the service. When requesting forwarding, the service will give priority to requesting nodes with lower load pressure. If you request the node with the least service pressure, it is bound to happen that the request will hit the same node in a short time. The strategy adopted in this article is to split the linked list of services into two parts. One part is the first third of the linked list, and the other part is the remaining two thirds of the linked list. Service requests will be evenly forwarded to the top third of the linked list with a probability of 75% according to the probability model. For the remaining part, the request will be randomly forwarded to the nodes on the last two-thirds of the linked list (Fig. 4).

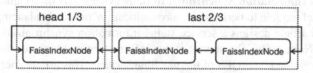

Fig. 4. Load balancing module.

Resource Allocation Module. ServerModel contains multiple FaissIndexNodes. When a new service is connected to the system, ServerModel will choose a node with a smaller load to register. The resource allocation of a service is restricted by two parameters, which are the number of services on the node and the load of the services. Each node contains a threshold for the number of services and a threshold for CPU load, beyond which no new services will be allocated.

Service Load Synchronization Module. The function of this module is relatively simple, mainly responsible for synchronizing FaissIndexNode node status information. This module contains a timed task. The timing task will synchronize the status information of the FaissIndexNode node in Redis to the memory of the ServerModel. Other modules will use the information in the memory for resource scheduling and request information forwarding.

3.3   Design of FaissIndexNode Module

The FaissIndexNode module is the execution module of the vector retrieval in the entire HVCRS, which is very important for the entire service. In this paper, the FaissIndxN-ode module is designed to solve the vector retrieval problem. FaissIndexNode contains four modules, namely the service status information synchronization module, the data download module, the Faiss index building module and the search engine.

After the above analysis, this article shows the overall design of the FaissIndexNode module as shown in the figure below (Fig. 5).

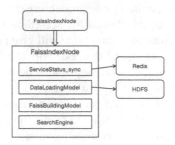

Fig. 5. The overall architecture of FaissIndexNode

Service Status Information Synchronization. Service status information is the basis for ServerModel module to perform resource allocation and load balancing scheduling. Therefore, this article designs a service status information synchronization module in the FaissIndexNode node. The service status information includes information such as cpu_util, network load, and QPS of the machine service. This article encapsulates it as ServerStation. This information will be synchronized to the Redis cluster through the synchronization module (Fig. 6).

Fig. 6. Service status information synchronization module.

Data Download Module. Data is the basis of vector retrieval services. When the service is registered, the related information of the service will be stored in the memory of the FaissIndexNode node. In this paper, the data download module is designed as a timed task. The scheduled task will obtain information about the services in the memory, and will detect whether there is the latest version of the data file in the HDFS cluster. After the scheduled task detects the vector data, if the load of the service is lower than the threshold, the service will download the vector data to the specified folder of the node.

Service Status Information Synchronization. Faiss index construction is the most basic module for HVCRS service. In this paper, the Faiss index building module is designed as a timed task. The timed task will detect whether there is the latest vector file in the file path specified by the node. The service information in the memory and the file name of the vector file will contain the information for the construction of the index.

The timing task will determine whether the two information is consistent, and if they are inconsistent, an exception will be returned. When constructing the index, the service will choose the time when the service load is low. After the Faiss index is constructed, the index information will be stored in memory.

Service Status Information Synchronization. The search engine is the docking interface layer of FaissIndexNode, responsible for request parsing, vector retrieval, and encapsulation of returned results. When the service receives a request for vector retrieval, the service parses the request parameters into a package class of request parameters. The search engine will use the request parameters to get the Faiss index in memory, and then get the request vector from Redis. The request vector will be passed into the search method of the Faiss index, and the service will encapsulate the search result and return the final result.

Service Configuration Management Module. The service configuration management module is a vital module in the HVCRS service, responsible for the online configuration of the service, the control of the effective data version, and the service uninstallation. The design of the service is relatively simple, including a front-end page for service configuration and a configuration information synchronization module for data synchronization. When a new task is launched, the user needs to configure the service on the configuration page, such as the service name, the data storage address of the service, and the effective data version of the service (the latest version by default) and other information. After configuring the information, the data will be stored in Mysql and will be synchronized to the Redis cluster. The diagram of the service configuration management module is shown in the figure below (Fig. 7).

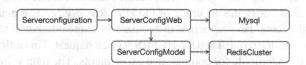

Fig. 7. Service configuration management module.

4   Experiment

The following three experiments are mainly used to verify the effect of the HVCRS service. Experiment 1. Functional test of HVCRS. Experiment two, service accuracy test. Experiment three, service performance test. In the experiment, the service was built using Django, and the versions of python and Faiss were 3.6.7 and 1.5.3 respectively. The service is deployed on a Kubernetes cluster built on three 128G physical machines. HCVRS contains 10 FaissIndexNode nodes and 2 ServerModel nodes.

Experiment One. In order to verify whether the function of the HVCRS service meets the design requirements, this article mainly conducts functional tests from four aspects.

First, the function test of the service configuration module mainly includes the synchronization of service configuration and service configuration information on the web. Second, the functional test of SeverModel mainly includes functions such as service registration, service unloading, load balancing, and request forwarding. Third, the function test of FaissIndexNode mainly includes functions such as index construction, vector retrieval, and data download. In addition, HVCRS services need to be unit tested. If the test passes, it means that the HVCRS service is operating normally and meets the design requirements (Table 1).

Table 1. Results of experiment one.

Function	Result	Function	Result
Web configuration function for service configuration function	Fit	ServerModel request forwardingfunctions	Fit
Synchronization module for service configuration function	Fit	Faiss index building function	Fit
Service registration function	Fit	Data download function	Fit
Service uninstall function	Fit	Unit test	Fit

It can be seen from the above table that all aspects of the functions of the HVCRS service have passed the functional test, so it can be considered that the HVCRS meets the design requirements of the service.

Experiment Two. Using Faiss to construct vector retrieval services is a new technical solution. In order to verify the accuracy of the HVCRS service. The main verification method used in the second experiment is to compare the same number of results returned by the traditional service request and the HCFRS service request. This article uses data of different orders of magnitude for comparative experiments. The data volume of 20,000, 50,000, and 80,000 are used respectively (Table 2).

Table 2. Results of experiment two.

Data set size	Accuracy
20000	83%
50000	82%
80000	86%

It can be seen from the above table that compared with the traditional vector retrieval method in the power grid, the accuracy of the HVCRS service is as high as 82%. This effect is already very good and basically meets the expectations of the service design.

Experiment Three. The performance test of HCVRS service is mainly measured by QPS and average time-consuming. To test the performance of the HVCRS service. This article mainly uses three different magnitude data sets for testing, namely 50,000, 100,000 and 150,000. The data will be downloaded by the service and built into a Faiss index in memory. This article conducts a stress test on HVCRS. The stress test is carried out at 99%. The test results are shown in the table below (Table 3).

Table 3. Results of experiment three.

Data set size	QPS	Cost
50000	180	10.9 ms
100000	178	11.3 ms
150000	160	12.6 ms

5 Conclusion

In order to solve the difficulty of increasing pressure on the recommended services of the State Grid, this paper proposed a vector retrieval service based on Faiss-HCVRS service. It includes modules such as service vector retrieval, resource allocation, and load balancing. On the one hand, it improves the performance of vector retrieval services. On the other hand, it improves the utilization of resources. All in all, it not only solves the difficulty of recommending services under the large amount of data in the power grid, but also provides an effective solution to this problem.

References

1. Witten, I.H., et al.: Data Mining: Practical Machine Learning Tools and Techniques, 4th edn. Morgan Kaufmann, Cambridge (2017)
2. Marsland, S.: Machine Learning: An Algorithmic Perspective, 2 edn. CRC Press, Boca Raton (2014, 2015)
3. Kang, M., Choi, E.: Machine Learning: Concepts, Tools and Data Visualization. World Scientific Publishing Co., Pte. Ltd., Singapore (2021)
4. Bhattacharyya, S., et al.: Deep Learning: Research and Applications. De Gruyter, Berlin (2020)
5. Ramsundar, B., et al.: Deep Learning for the Life Sciences: Applying Deep Learning to Genomics, Microscopy, Drug Discovery and More, 1st edn. O'Reilly Media, Sebastopol (2019)
6. Silhavy, P., Silhavy, R., Prokopova, Z.: Intelligent Systems Applications in Software Engineering. In: Proceedings of 3rd Computational Methods in Systems and Software, 20191046 (2019)
7. Hörmann, B.O., Bizubac, D., Popa, M.S.: Industrial intelligent software applications of the overall equipment effectiveness in manufacturing. In: MATEC Web of Conference, vol. 299, p. 5011 (2019)

8. Qiuyi, L.: Intelligent terminal multi-application software control method (2020)
9. Kim, N., et al.: Dynamic patterns of industry convergence: evidence from a large amount of unstructured data. Res. Policy **44**(9), 1734–1748 (2015)
10. Baars, H., Kemper, H.: Management support with structured and unstructured data-an integrated business intelligence framework. Inf. Syst. Manag. **25**(2), 132–148 (2008)
11. Han, J., Kamber, M., Pei, J.: Data Mining: Concepts and Techniques, 3rd edn. Elsevier, Burlington (2012)
12. Torgo, L.: Data Mining with R: Learning with Case Studies, 2nd edn. CRC Press, Taylor & Francis Group, Boca Raton (2017)
13. Li, G., et al.: Recommendation system based on users preference mining generative adversarial networks. Jisuanji Kexue Yu Tansuo **14**(5), 803–814 (2020)
14. Chen, R., Hendry, Liu, L.: Enhancing personal recommendation system using familiarity factor on social network (2017)
15. Wu, S.Y.J.: Recommendation system for medical consultation integrating knowledge graph and deep learning methods. Jisuanji Kexue Yu Tansuo, 15(8), 1432–1440 (2021)
16. Yunfei, Z., Yeli, L., Huayan, S.: Research of personalized recommendation system based on deep neural network. Diànzǐ Jìshù Yīngyòng **45**(1), 14–18 (2019)
17. Wang, S., Lo, D., Vasilescu, B., Serebrenik, A.: EnTagRec ++: an enhanced tag recommendation system for software information sites. Empirical Softw. Eng. **23**(2), 800–832 (2017). https://doi.org/10.1007/s10664-017-9533-1
18. Qiu, H., Qiu, M., Lu, Z.: Selective encryption on ECG data in body sensor network based on supervised machine learning. Inf. Fus. **55**, 59–67 (2020)
19. Qiu, L., Gai, K., Qiu, M.: Optimal big data sharing approach for tele-health in cloud computing. In: IEEE SmartCloud, pp. 184–189 (2016)
20. Lu, Z., Wang, N., Wu, J., Qiu, M.: IoTDeM: an IoT big data-oriented MapReduce performance prediction extended model in multiple edge clouds. J. Parallel Distrib. Comput. **118**, 316–327 (2018)
21. Qiu, M., Chen, Z., Liu, M.: Low-power low-latency data allocation for hybrid scratch-pad memory. IEEE Embedd. Syst. Lett. **6**(4), 69–72 (2014)
22. Zhang, L., Qiu, M., Tseng, W., Sha, E.: Variable partitioning and scheduling for MPSoC with virtually shared scratch pad memory. J. Signal Process. Syst. **58**(2), 247–265 (2010). https://doi.org/10.1007/s11265-009-0362-3
23. Qiu, M., Xue, C., Shao, Z., Sha, E.: Energy minimization with soft real-time and DVS for uniprocessor and multiprocessor embedded systems. In: IEEE DATE Conference, pp. 1–6 (2007)
24. Lu, R., Jin, X., Zhang, S., Qiu, M., Wu, X.: A study on big knowledge and its engineering issues. IEEE Trans. Knowl. Data Eng. **31**(9), 1630–1644 (2018)
25. Qiu, M., Cao, D., Su, H., Gai, K.: Data transfer minimization for financial derivative pricing using Monte Carlo simulation with GPU in 5G. Int'l J. Comm. Sys. **29**(16), 2364–2374 (2016)
26. Liu, M., Zhang, S., et al.: H infinite state estimation for discrete-time chaotic systems based on a unified model. IEEE Trans. Syst. Man Cybern. (B) (2012)
27. Mikolov, T., et al.: Efficient estimation of word representations in vector space (2013)
28. Barkan, O., Koenigstein, N.: ITEM2VEC: neural item embedding for collaborative filtering. (2016). https://doi.org/10.1109/MLSP.2016.7738886
29. Perozzi, B., Al-Rfou, R., Skiena, S.: DeepWalk: online learning of social representations (2014). https://doi.org/10.1145/2623330.2623732
30. Huifu, Z., Kazhong, D., Hongdong, F.: SAR images unsupervised change detection based on combination of texture feature vector with maximum entropy principle. Ce Hui Xue Bao **45**(3), 339–346 (2016)
31. Lakshmi Priya, G.G., Domnic, S.: Walsh-Hadamard Transform Kernel-Based Feature Vector for Shot Boundary Detection. IEEE Trans. Image Process. **23**(12), 5187–5197 (2014)

32. Hu, S., et al.: Multi-dimensional big data feature attribute processing method and device, terminal and storage medium (2020)
33. Ahmadi, N., Akbarizadeh, G.: Hybrid robust iris recognition approach using iris image pre-processing, two-dimensional gabor features and multi-layer perceptron neural network/PSO. IET Biometrics **7**(2), 153–162 (2018)
34. Heimrath, K., et al.: Modulation of pre-attentive spectro-temporal feature processing in the human auditory system by HD-tDCS. Eur. J. Neurosci. **41**(12), 1580–1586 (2015)
35. Zhichang, Y., Xu, Z., Yingfeng, Z.: Distributed vector retrieval engine (2019)
36. Shishi, W., Xi, Z., Zhiqiang, Y.: Vector retrieval method, system, device and medium (2020)
37. Bettenhausen, M.H., et al.: A nonlinear optimization algorithm for WindSat wind vector retrievals. IEEE Trans. Geosci. Remote Sens. **44**(3), 597–610 (2006)
38. Zhimin, L., Gang, T.: Conversation response method, device and system based on vector retrieval (2020)
39. Johnson, J., Douze, M., Jégou, H.: Billion-scale similarity search with GPUs (2017)
40. Liu, Y., et al.: SK-LSH: an efficient index structure for approximate nearest neighbor search. Proc. VLDB Endow. **7**(9), 745–756 (2014)
41. Dingcheng, M., Xiaoliang, X., Yuxiang. W.: Approximate nearest neighbor search method combining VP tree and guide nearest neighbor graph (2021)
42. Komorowski, M., Trzciński, T.: Random binary search trees for approximate nearest neighbour search in binary spaces. Appl. Soft Comput. **79**, 87–93 (2019)
43. Friston, K.J., et al.: Functional connectivity: the principal-component analysis of large (PET) data sets. J. Cereb. Blood Flow Metab. **13**(1), 5–14 (1993, 2016)
44. Abdi, H., Williams, L.J.: Principal component analysis. Wiley Interdisc. Rev. Comput. Stat. **2**(4), 433–459 (2010)
45. Jégou, H., Douze, M., Schmid, C.: Product quantization for nearest neighbor search. IEEE Trans. Pattern Anal. Mach. Intell. **33**(1), 117–128 (2011)
46. André, F., Kermarrec, A., Le Scouarnec, N.: Cache locality is not enough: high-performance nearest neighbor search with product quantization fast scan. Proc. VLDB **9**(4), 288–299 (2015)
47. Goswami, P., et al.: An efficient multi-resolution framework for high quality interactive rendering of massive point clouds using multi-way KD-trees. Vis. Comput. **29**(1), 69–83 (2013). https://doi.org/10.1007/s00371-012-0675-2
48. Adams, A., et al.: Gaussian KD-trees for fast high-dimensional filtering. ACM Trans. Graph. **28**(3), 1–12 (2009)
49. Keil, J.M., Vassilev, T.S.: The relative neighbourhood graph is a part of every 30° -triangulation. Inf. Process. Lett. **109**(2), 93–97 (2008)
50. Kleindessner, M., Von Luxburg, U.: Lens depth function and k-relative neighborhood graph: versatile tools for ordinal data analysis. J. Mach. Learn. Res. **18**, 1–52 (2017)
51. Melchert, O.: Percolation thresholds on planar Euclidean relative-neighborhood graphs. Phys. Rev. E, Stat. Nonlinear Soft Matter Phys. **87**(4), 042106 (2013)
52. Keil, J.M., Vassilev, T.S.: The relative neighbourhood graph is a part of every 30°-triangulation. Inf. Process. Lett. **109**(2), 93–97 (2008)
53. Kunz, P., et al.: Most classic problems remain np-hard on relative neighborhood graphs and their relatives (2021)

APT Attack Heuristic Induction Honeypot Platform Based on Snort and OpenFlow

Bo Dai[1], Zhenhai Zhang[1], Ling Wang[1], and Yuan Liu[2(✉)]

[1] State Grid Zhejiang Electric Power Corporation Information and Telecommunication Branch, Zhejiang, China
daobo@zj.sgcc.com.cn, atakawl@vip.sina.com
[2] Beijing Inshine Technology Co., Ltd., Beijing, China

Abstract. The honeypot can record attacker's aggressive behavior and analyze methods of attack in order to develop more intelligent protection policies in the system. While traditional honeypot technology has evolved from static configuration over to the dynamic deployment and greatly reduces the possibility of an attacker identifying a honeypot. But most of the prior technology, there are passive listening, high maintenance costs, controllable weak, low monitoring coverage, easy to identify and other issues. In this paper, T-Pot Multi-platform honeypot based Snort and OpenFlow technology, we proposed the attack traffic into the Multi-platform honeypot to prevent further harm to the system. In order to reduce system load and improve system performance, perform feature extraction and modeling analysis on the attack data set, and Based on the ATT&CK model, a multi-honeypot platform for APT attack recognition is implemented.

Keywords: Honeypot technology · APT · Active defense · Snort · OpenFlow control · Multi-platform honeypot

1 Introduction

With the fast advance of Internet and smart grid technology [1, 2], security and privacy protection [3–5] become a critical issue. Among the various attacks, APT (*Advanced Persistent Threat*) attack is especially harmful [6–8]. It persistently invades a specific target through specific means and maintains high concealment in a long period of time. The 2010 Stuxnet virus, the world's first state-level weapon, led to the failure of Iran's nuclear program. The Google Aurora attack of the same year, in which a Google employee clicked on a malicious link in an instant message [9], resulted in the search engine being infiltrated for months and data being stolen from various systems. In order to timely block APT attacks and reduce harm, honeypot technology [10] is undoubtedly a better choice.

This paper aims to summarize and analyze the development and advantages of honeypots, propose solutions according to the problems that honeypots are easy to identify, combine honeypot recognition technology, and put forward T-POT multi-honeypot system to solve the problems related to traditional honeypots by considering the construction cost, controllability, maintenance cost and other factors.

© The Author(s), under exclusive license to Springer Nature Switzerland AG 2022
M. Qiu et al. (Eds.): SmartCom 2021, LNCS 13202, pp. 340–351, 2022.
https://doi.org/10.1007/978-3-030-97774-0_31

The main contributions are as follows: 1) the advantages and disadvantages of existing honeypot technology were analyzed and summarized, and the method of OpenFlow technical drainage was proposed to solve the passive monitoring problem of traditional honeypot; Aiming at the problems of weak controllability and high maintenance cost of traditional honeypot, a unified management method using T-POT multi-honeypot platform was proposed.

2) According to the existing identification means of anti-honeypot technology, a series of countermeasures such as hiding honeypot and disguising honeypot are put forward. Aiming at the problem of high overhead of traditional honeypot, tF-IDF algorithm is used to extract feature and model analysis of attack data in advance when entering honeypot stage, so as to filter out trusted data at the beginning stage and reduce the load of honeypot system.

3) The initial access and execution stage attack means of APT attack are analyzed and summarized, and a series of methods are formulated to optimize Snort's rule base.

2 OpenFlow and the Multi-honeypot Platform

2.1 OpenFlow Overview

OpenFlow [11, 12] originated from the Clean Slate project of Stanford University. The original intention of the project is to enable network administrators to easily customize security control policies based on network flows. The data forwarding and routing control modules of traditional network devices are layered, and the centralized controller manages and configures various network devices with standardized interfaces, so that security policies can be applied to each security device to achieve security control over the entire network.

2.2 T-pot Multi-honey Pot Platform

With the development of virtualization technology, a variety of virtual honeypots have also developed, and a lot of high-interaction honeypots have emerged. Unlike in the past, expensive hardware equipment is required to support honeypots, which greatly reduces the cost of deploying honeypots. MHN (Modern Honeypot) is a very good open source honeypot product. MHN simplifies the deployment of honeypots and integrates a variety of honeypots, which can achieve rapid deployment. However, multiple system sensors need to be manually installed to realize different honeypots. Version T-POT19.03 [13] runs on Debian (Sid), a multi-honeypot platform based on Docker and Docker-compose technology.

T-pot Multi-honeypot platform mainly includes 16 kinds of honeypots and 6 kinds of tools. Honeypot platform based on T-pot is enough for unified management through analyzing the log improve controllability and T - pot of honeypot system is based on the Docker containers, capture all kinds of attacks can well simulate the system environment as well as visual according to need to open and close the honeypot container, custom out conforms to the honeypot platform of this system to reduce deployment and maintenance costs.

3 Design of Multi-honeypot Platform Based on Snort and OpenFlow

3.1 The Overall Design

In order to solve the problems of passive monitoring, weak controllability and high deployment and maintenance cost of traditional honeypots, the combination of Open-Flow and T-POT multi-honeypot platform is proposed. Based on the characteristics of OpenFlow, the passive monitoring mode of traditional honeypots can be changed, and active capture attack can be introduced into honeypots for further analysis.

When users or attackers send requests or attacks to the network, Snort analyzes the traffic and delivers the flow table to the OpenFlow switch. According to the OpenFlow protocol, the controller introduces the normal traffic to the real host and returns the real information. Meanwhile, the attack traffic is introduced into the pre-designed honeypot. Returns a default message to the attacker. In the system design, methods such as avoiding cloud server to deploy honeypot on the exnet, deploying an operating system that matches the real environment in front of honeypot, and setting the port that matches the real environment in honeypot system are adopted to avoid single information returned by honeypot, and regularly changing message information returned by honeypot. The system structure is shown in Fig. 1.

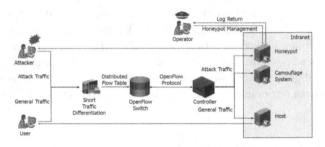

Fig. 1. System structure.

When a large amount of attack traffic floods in, the system performance will be greatly reduced, and honeypot identification and bypass will make honeypot passive. Meanwhile, due to the characteristics of APT attacks that are difficult to identify, the following methods are added according to the existing honeypot identification technology to improve the availability of the system. 1) Honeypot attack detection: after the honeypot is placed, only the ports matching the real environment should be opened as far as possible to avoid too many open ports being quickly identified. The Snort rule base is matched and improved based on the ATT&CK model. 2) Use OpenFlow technology for drainage, so as to introduce attack flow into honeypot; Aiming at the problems of weak controllability and high maintenance cost of traditional honeypot, a unified management method using T-POT multi-honeypot platform is proposed. In the Intranet, an operating system matching with the real environment is deployed in front of honeypot as far as possible, so that the attacker will mistake the scanned system as the real system.

TF-IDF algorithm is used for feature extraction of traffic data, modeling and analysis, and filtering out normal traffic information. Attack capture is mainly based on the Snort device identification of attacks. Due to the particularity of APT attacks, a large amount of traffic will cause heavy load to Snort, so the traffic should be de-weighted before traffic identification.

3.2 Improve the Snort Rule Library Based on the ATT&CK Model

There are endless attack methods of APT attack, and the rule base of Snort is not enough to completely detect the attack behavior. By referring to the attack methods of initial access and execution in ATT&CK model [15], features in the attack are extracted and a series of rules are given to reduce such attacks. The ATT&CK model framework is shown in Table 1.

Table 1. Initial access and execution of the framework table

Initial Access (9 techniques)	Execution (10 techniques)
Drive-by Compromise	Command and Scripting Interpreter
Exploit Public-Facing Application	Exploitation for Client Execution
Extremal Remote Services	Inter-Process Communication
Hardware Additions	Native API
Phishing	Scheduled Task/Job
Replication Through Removable Media	Shared Modules
Supply Chain Compromise	Software Deployment Tools
Trusted Relationship	System Services
Valid Accounts	User Execution
	Windows Management Instrumentation

3.2.1 Initial Access and Execution Phases

During the initial access phase, the attacker has nine methods: one is the "sneak compromise": the victim visits the controlled site by injecting malicious code into the victim's browser. Public-facing applications: Attackers use software, data, and commands to exploit vulnerabilities in Internet-facing computers or programs such as websites, databases, standard services, and Web servers. External remote services: Attackers use VPN, Citrix and other external remote services to establish connections from external to internal network resources to obtain sensitive information and leave a back door. Hardware addition: An attacker introduces computer attachments, or network hardware, into a system or network that can be used as a vehicle to gain access. Phishing: An attacker sends phishing messages electronically in combination with social engineering to obtain sensitive information or gain access to a victim's system. Removable media replication: Attackers copy malware to removable media and execute code when the media is inserted into the system. Supply chain compromise: An attacker manipulates a product or product delivery mechanism before it reaches the consumer. Trusted relationships: Attackers exploit existing connections through trusted third party relationships by disrupting or exploiting organizations that have access to the intended victim. Valid account: An attacker gains initial access by obtaining and exploiting the credentials of an existing account.

In the execution stage, attackers have 10 methods respectively command and script interpreter: attackers use to execute commands, scripts, binary files to control and exploit the computer system. Exploit client execution: Attackers build on vulnerabilities in browsers and office software in order to be able to execute code on remote systems. Interprocess communication: attackers use the implementation to share data, interwork and synchronize execution. Native API: Attackers exploit the ability to interact directly with native application programming interfaces to execute commands. For example, the Windows API CreateProcess() or fork() will allow programs and scripts to start other processes. Scheduled task jobs: Attackers use scheduled task capabilities to initialize or repeat malicious code. Shared modules: By executing malicious payloads, an attacker can instruct the Windows module loader to load DDL from any local path and any common naming convention network path. Software deployment tool: An attacker accesses and uses third-party software installed on an enterprise network, such as management software, to move the network horizontally. System services: Attackers execute malicious content by interacting with system services, daemons, or by creating services. User execution: An attacker exploits a social worker's user, for example by opening a malicious document or link, to enable them to execute malicious code through improper actions. Windows Management specifications: Attackers use *Windows Management Instrumentation* (WMI) to implement execution, WMI for Windows system components to provide a unified environment for local and remote access.

3.2.2   Snort Rule Description Based on Initial Access and Execution Phases

Table 2. Snort mapping table during initial access

Attack methods	Snort rules
Drive-by Compromise	This section describes how to detect abnormal browser behaviors on the endpoint system, such as suspicious file writing to disk, process hiding, and abnormal traffic
Exploit Public-Facing Application	Detect for abnormal behavior in the application logs, such as injecting packet characteristics based on SQL
Extremal Remote Services	Collect authentication logs and analyze abnormal access patterns, active Windows, and access outside normal working hours

(continued)

Table 2. (*continued*)

Attack methods	Snort rules
Hardware Additions	The asset management system detects computer systems or network devices that should not exist on the network, and establishes network access control policies to restrict network access and hardware installation
Phishing	Checking URL in E-mail messages, including extended shortened links, helps detect links to known malicious endpoints
Replication Through Removable Media	Monitor file access on removable media and detect processes that are executed on removable media after installation or after user startup
Valid Accounts	Manage the accounts and permissions used by all parties in the trusted relationship, and find the behaviors of the accounts in the system. For example, unauthorized user rights assignment operations

According to the characteristics of initial access attacks, a series of Snort rules are formulated to detect the initial access phase. The Snort comparison table is shown in Table 2.

According to the attack characteristics in the execution phase, a series of Snort rules are formulated to detect the attack characteristics in the execution phase, as shown in Table 3.

Table 3. Execution phase Snort mapping table

Attack methods	Snort rules
Command and Scripting Interpreter	Capture illegal command line and script activity by filtering illegal command line arguments
Exploitation for Client Execution	Intercept abnormal behaviors of the browser or Office processes, including suspicious files written to disks, hidden evidence of process injection, and abnormal network traffic
Inter-Process Communication	Abuse generated processes by monitoring strings in files and commands, DLL libraries loaded, and IPC mechanisms
Native API	By monitoring DLL load, especially for abnormal or potentially malicious processes

(*continued*)

Table 3. (*continued*)

Attack methods	Snort rules
Shared Modules	Limit DLL module loading to %SystemRoot% and %ProgramFiles% to detect module loading from unsafe paths
System Services	Changes to Windows services are reflected from the registry, monitoring modified command line calls that are inconsistent with normal software usage, patch cycles, and so on
User Execution	Captures application execution and command-line arguments that an attacker uses to gain access to user interactions
Windows Management Instrumentation	Monitoring network traffic for WMI connections, execution process monitor 1 captures command line arguments for "WMIC" and detects commands for remote behavior

3.2.3 APT Attack Detection Instance

Take "China Chopper" for example, "China Chopper" is a backdoor with Web Shell command and control (CnC) client binaries and text-based Web Shell payloads, its text-based payloads can be so short that an attacker simply has to enter them manually on the target server.

After analyzing the traffic of China Chopper and viewing the typical traffic content, the client initiates the connection through TCP port 80 using HTTP POST method. When Wireshark is used to "follow TCP" traffic, it is found that most of the attacker traffic is Base64 encoded. After decoding, two key codes are found.

```
GetString ( System.Convert.FromBase64String ( Request. Item["z1"] ) ) ) );
GetString ( System.Convert.FromBase64String ( Request. Item["z2"] ) ) ) );
```

Try to Base64 decode the content stored as Z1 and Z2. Check that the parameter after decoding z1 and Z2 is.

```
z1 = cmd
z2 = cd / d" c:\inetpub\wwwroot\"&whoami&echo[S]&cd&echo[E]
```

When it comes to understanding the content of China Chopper and its traffic, use standard Snort rules, which were provided early on for China Chopper.

```
alert tcp any any ->any 80 ( sid:900001; content:"base64_decode";
http_client_body;fiow:to_server,established;content:"POST";nocase;http_metho
d;;msg:"Websheel Detected Apache";)
```

To reduce false positives, strengthen Snort's detection rules by looking for any combination of "FromBase64String" and "Z".

```
alert tcp $EXTERNAL_NET any ->$HTTP_SERVERS $HTTP_PROTS(msg:
"China Chopper with all Commands Detected"; flow:to_server,established;
content:"FromBase64String";content:"z";pcre:"/Z\d{1,3}/i";content:"POST";
nocase:http_method;classtype:web-application-attack;)
```

3.3 TF-IDF Algorithm Traffic Feature Extraction and Modeling

When a large amount of attack traffic enters the system, it will have a large load, which has a great impact on the efficiency of the whole system. Therefore, it is necessary to optimize data and extract traffic characteristics to improve the system efficiency. As the attack traffic has obvious characteristics, TF-IDF algorithm [14] has an important application in text classification. Next, the HTTP CSIC 2010 data set is used to simulate attack traffic and normal traffic, and then the TF-IDF algorithm is used for feature extraction. The HTTP CSIC 2010 dataset contains the attack dataset, which contains 36,000 normal requests and more than 250,000 attack requests. The sample format is shown in Table 4.

It can be seen that there is no attack Payload except HTTP method, path and parameter in the data set, so there is a lot of redundant information. When classifying data, the efficiency of TF-IDF algorithm will be reduced. Therefore, the data set needs to be formatted and only HTTP method, path and parameter should be retained. The data after processing is shown in Table 5.

Table 4. HTTP CSIC 2010 dataset

At-tack data set	GET http://localhost:8080/tienda1/publico/anadir.jsp?id=2&nombre=Jam%F3n+I b%E9rico&precio=85&cantidad=%27%3B+DROP+TABLE+usuarios%3B+SELEC T+*+FROM+datos+WHERE+nombre+LIKE+%27%25&B1=A%F1adir+al+carrito HTTP/1.1 User-Agent: Mozilla/5.0 (compatible; Konqueror/3.5; Linux) KHTML/3.5.8 (like Gecko) Pragma: no-cache Cache-control: no-cache Accept: text/xml,application/xml,application/xhtml+xml,text/html;q=0.9,text/plain;q =0.8,image/png,*/*;q=0.5 Accept-Encoding: x-gzip, x-deflate, gzip, deflate Accept-Charset: utf-8, utf-8;q=0.5, *;q=0.5 Accept-Language: en Host: localhost:8080 Cookie: JSESSIONID=B92A8B48B9008CD29F622A994E0F650D Connection: close
Nor mal data set	GET http://localhost:8080/tienda1/index.jsp HTTP/1.1 User-Agent: Mozilla/5.0 (compatible; Konqueror/3.5; Linux) KHTML/3.5.8 (like Gecko) Pragma: no-cache Cache-control: no-cache Accept: text/xml,application/xml,application/xhtml+xml,text/html;q=0.9,text/plain;q =0.8,image/png,*/*;q=0.5 Accept-Encoding: x-gzip, x-deflate, gzip, deflate Accept-Charset: utf-8, utf-8;q=0.5, *;q=0.5 Accept-Language: en Host: localhost:8080 Cookie: JSESSIONID=EA414B3E327DED6875848530C864BD8F Connection: close

Table 5. Post-processing data table

Pro cess ed	get http://localhost:8080/tienda1/publico/anadir.jsp? id=2&nombre=Jam%F3n+Ib%E9rico&precio=85&cantidad=%27%3B+DROP+T ABLE+usuarios%3B+SELECT+*+FROM+datos+WHERE+nombre+LIKE+%27%25 &B1=A%F1adir+al+carrito
da-ta	post http://localhost:8080/tienda1/publico/anadir.jsp?id=2/&nombre=jamn+ibric o&precio=85&cantidad=49&b1=aadir+al+carrito

Because the components of Web attacks have good structural characteristics, Web attacks can be classified, and TF-IDF algorithm is used to classify data. Data need to be integrated, labeled and divided into test sets and training sets before tF-IDF algorithm classifies the data. After that, tF-IDF algorithm is used for feature extraction. Due to the large dimension of extracted features, only part of extracted feature vectors are listed here as shown in Table 6.

Table 6. Comparison table of feature vector and frequency of occurrence

Characteristic	Number of occurrences	Characteristic	Number of Occurrences
get	19606	nombre	25744
http	20938	vino	32658
localhost	23232	rioja	28665
8080	8750	precio	27578
tiendal	31274	100	1079
index	21282	cantidad	14443
jsp	21914	55	6608
publico	27735	b1	12410
anadir	11513	aadir	10396
id	21106	al	10904

Before the model training, Sklaern's StandardScaler method was used to normalize the data and cross_val_score method was used to divide the data set into 5 different training sets and test sets for cross-validation to improve the accuracy of model training. Since it is the distinction between normal traffic and attack traffic, logistic regression algorithm is easy to understand in dealing with dichotomy problems, so the logistic regression algorithm is selected for model training. During model training, the grid search method is adopted, and the grid search parameters are set as follows: reciprocal 'C' of policy intensity is [0.1, 1, 3, 5, 7], and penalty is set to ['11', '12']. The cross-validation training results are shown in Table 7.

Table 7. Training results table

Training time	3'32s
Best Results	'C':7'penalty':'12'
gird_search.best_score_	0.9690464440657187
Test Set Score	0.97972643136278666
Accurate Rate	0.9972253738033524
Recall Rate	0.940990623085181
F1-Score	0.9694921669341241

From the table of training results, it can be seen intuitively that the training accuracy of TF-IDF feature extraction algorithm combined with logistic regression algorithm is quite considerable, which can optimize the flow and reduce the data load, and improve the Snort system performance.

3.3.1 System Performance Test and Analysis

In this paper, DVWA vulnerability platform was selected as the experimental object, and penetration test was carried out by automatic and manual methods. By analogy with Snort before and after updating rules and modeling after removing redundancy honeypot platform, the efficiency results are shown in Table 8.

Table 8. Snort and honeypot performance results table

State	Snort efficiency (detection rate)	Honeypot efficiency (memory ratio)
No update, no redundancy	97%	60%
Update, no redundancy	98%	65%
Update, eliminate redundancy	98%	52%

As can be seen from Table 8, Snort detection efficiency is improved after the Snort rules are updated, but the honeypot memory consumption is increased due to the data redundancy processing is not removed. After data redundancy is removed, honeypot memory ratio is lower than the initial state. It can be seen that the method proposed in this paper can improve the attack detection rate, reduce the system load, and meet the requirements of HIGH accuracy and low load of APT detection.

Acknowledgement. This paper analyzes the development of honeypot and the advantages and disadvantages of the current honeypot technology, and proposes a multi-honeypot platform based on Snort and OpenFlow as a general host intrusion method. In combination with the ATT&CK model in the initial access and execution stage, the response scheme is proposed. In order to reduce the system load, tF-IDF algorithm is used to extract the characteristics of the traffic and conduct modeling analysis.

References

1. Gao, Y., Iqbal, S., et al.: Performance and power analysis of high-density multi-GPGPU architectures: a preliminary case study. In: IEEE 17th HPCC (2015)
2. Qiu, H., Qiu, M., Memmi, G., Ming, Z., Liu, M.: A dynamic scalable blockchain based communication architecture for IoT. In: Qiu, M. (ed.) SmartBlock 2018. LNCS, vol. 11373, pp. 159–166. Springer, Cham (2018). https://doi.org/10.1007/978-3-030-05764-0_17
3. Thakur, K., Qiu, M., Gai, K., Ali, M.: An investigation on cyber security threats and security models. In: IEEE CSCloud (2015)
4. Gai, K., Qiu, M., Sun, X., Zhao, H.: Security and privacy issues: a survey on FinTech. In: Qiu, M. (ed.) SmartCom 2016. LNCS, vol. 10135, pp. 236–247. Springer, Cham (2017). https://doi.org/10.1007/978-3-319-52015-5_24
5. Zhang, Z., Wu, J., et al.: Jamming ACK attack to wireless networks and a mitigation approach. In: IEEE GLOBECOM Conference, pp. 1–5 (2008)
6. Stojanović, B., Hofer-Schmitz, K., Kleb, U.: APT datasets and attack modeling for automated detection methods: a review. Comput. Secur. **92**, 101734 (2020)

7. Chen, R., Zhang, X., Niu, W., et al.: Research on APT attack detection and countermeasure technology system. J. Univ. Elec. Sci. Tech. China **48**(06), 870–879 (2019)
8. Hai-Bo, L.I.U., Tian-Bo, W.U., Jing, S.H.E.N., et al.: APT attack detection based on GAN-LSTM. Comput. Sci. **47**(01), 281–286 (2020)
9. Qin, Y., Liu, S., Liu, L.: Analysis of telecommunications fraud technique such as forged web pages and malicious links. J. Jiangxi Police Inst. **04**, 29–33 (2018)
10. Shi, L.-Y., Li, Y., Ma, M.-F.: New development of honeypot technology research. J. Electron. Inf. Technol. **41**(02), 498–508 (2019)
11. Song, C.-Y., Han, X.-H., Ye, Z.-Y.: Attack scene capture and reconstruction method based on honeynet technology. Netinfo Secur. **10**, 41–43 (2009)
12. Jia, Z.-P., Fang, B.-X., Liu, C.-G., et al.: Overview of network deception technology. J. Commun. **38**(12), 128–143 (2017)
13. Cicioğlu, M., Çalhan, A.: Energy-efficient and SDN-enabled routing algorithm for wireless body area networks. Comput. Commun. **160**, 228–239 (2020)
14. Zuo, Q.-Y., Chen, M., Zhao, G.-S., et al.: Research on SDN technology based on OpenFlow. J. Softw. **24**(05), 1078–1097 (2013)
15. T-Pot documentation. https://dtag-dev-sec.github.io/mediator/feature/2019/04/01/tpot

An Automatic Design Method of Similarity Fusion Neural Network Based on SG-CIM Model

Xiaoqi Liao[1], Xinliang Ge[1], Yufei Li[1], Wenhui Hu[2(✉)], Xin He[3], Shijie Gao[3], Xiaoming Chen[3], and Xueyang Liu[2]

[1] Big Data Center of State Grid Corporation of China, Beijing, China
[2] National Engineering Research Center for Software Engineering, Peking University, Beijing, China
{huwenhui,liuxueyang}@pku.edu.cn
[3] Beijing China-Power Information Technology Co., Ltd., Beijing, China

Abstract. The State Grid Enterprise Public Data Model (SG-CIM 4.0) is a semantically unified data model that can be provided for smart grid business applications. The model is based on a standard table to find similar entities in the physical model for consistency checking. The standard table entities and physical model entities contain both continuous attributes and discrete attributes. How to accurately calculate the similarity of these different attributes and fuse them into a unique similarity, which can be used to efficiently and accurately mine the entity pairs with the highest similarity, are problems to be solved. In order to solve the above problems and make this similarity calculation and fusion method scalable, this paper calculates the syntactic similarity of continuous attributes, semantic similarity, and discrete attribute similarity to the content of different attributes in the entity and introduces a NAS (Neural Architecture Search) based on these similarities Similarity Fusion Neural Network automatically designed a method to achieve the fusion of similarity, which will be called SFNAS (Similarity Fusion NAS). The neural network fusion similarity calculated using SFNAS is better than the traditional linear weighted average similarity in terms of entity pair matching hit rate. This paper can provide useful references for subsequent research on SG-CIM models.

Keywords: Knowledge graph · Natural language processing · Language identification · Similarity fusion · Neural Architecture Search

1 Introduction

Big data research [1–3] had become a hot research area due to the fast advance in computer and network technologies [4–6]. SG-CIM 4.0 data model [7] specifies the management requirements of the data standard, data quality, data sharing, and data demand, which are related to many aspects such as model design and control, model standard application and management, data application, and quality governance [8].

However, the SG-CIM 4.0 data model, as a comprehensive abstraction of the company's enterprise-level data, contains physical model tables and data standard tables that are not fully aligned with each other. Therefore, to realize the unification and practical application of the SG-CIM data model, the alignment matching task between physical table entities and standard table entities needs to be completed efficiently.

In order to achieve entity alignment and unification between physical and standard tables, multiple similarity calculation methods are used to calculate multiple different similarities. Based on multiple similarity values from different sources, the following problem arises:

(1) The difficulty of fusion between similarities from multiple different sources makes it difficult to effectively use multiple similarity values to accurately determine consistency between physical table entities and standard table entities.
(2) There are still limitations in using the linear weighting method to integrate multiple similarities.

To address the above two problems, this paper proposes an automatic design method of Similarity Fusion Neural Network based on SG-CIM model, which can solve the above problems from the following two aspects:

(1) Effectively fuse multiple similarity values and obtain accurate matching of physical table entities and standard table entities.
(2) The design and training of neural networks capture the deep nonlinear, and logical relationships between multiple similarities, breaking through the limitations of linear methods.

In the first part of this paper, the background and the problem is introduced and a Similarity Fusion Neural Network automatic design method is proposed. The second part introduces the relevant domain technologies used in this Similarity Fusion Neural Network automatic design method. The third part describes the architecture and implementation process of the Similarity Fusion Neural Network automatic design method in detail. In the fourth part, experiments are designed and conducted to compare the performance of the linear method and the fusion neural network automatic design method; in the fifth part, based on the description of the fusion neural network automatic design method and the results of the experiments in the previous section, a conclusion is drawn.

2 Related Work

2.1 SG-CIM Public Data Model

The SG-CIM Public Data Model is an enterprise public data model built by State Grid with reference to international standards (IEC 61970/61968/62325) [9, 10] and industry best practices (SAP/ERP) [11], combined with the company's core business requirements, data dictionaries of in-operation systems, etc.

2.2 Similarity Related Technologies

2.2.1 Levenshtein Distance

The Levenshtein distance, is also known as the Minimum Edit Distance (MED) [12, 13]. Specifically, the Minimum Edit Distance refers to the minimum number of single-character edit operations required to convert from one word to another between two words. There are only three single-character editing operations defined here: Insertion, Deletion, and Substitution.

2.2.2 BERT Similarity

In 2018, Google proposed the BERT model, fully known as Bidirectional Encoder Representation from Transformer [14]. Its architecture is mainly based on the Encoder part of the Transformer [15]. BERT can solve the sentence-level modeling problem well. This class of problems belongs to Sentence Pair Classification Task, and BERT gives Fine-tuning scheme to handle sentence pair classification and similarity calculation problems.

2.2.3 Jaccard Index

Jaccard Index [16], also known as Intersection over Union and Jaccard similarity coefficient, is a statistical measure used to compare the similarity and diversity of sample sets. The Jaccard coefficient measures the similarity of a finite set of samples and is defined as the ratio between the size of the intersection of two sets and the size of the concurrent set.

2.3 Neural Architecture Search

Neural Architecture Search (NAS for short) [17] is a technique for automatically designing neural networks, allowing algorithms to automatically design high-performance network structures based on sample sets.

The principle of NAS is that given a set of candidate neural network structures called search space, the optimal network structure is searched from it using some strategy. The merit of the neural network structure, i.e., the performance, is measured by certain metrics such as accuracy and speed, called performance evaluation.

2.3.1 Search Space

Search Space defines the types of neural networks that can be searched by the NAS algorithm and also defines how to describe the neural network structure. The computation implemented by a neural network can be abstracted as a *directed acyclic graph* (DAG) with no isolated nodes.

2.3.2 Search Strategy

The search strategy defines how to find the optimal network structure, which is usually an iterative optimization process and is essentially a hyperparameter optimization problem.

Currently, the known search methods are random search, Bayesian optimization, genetic algorithms, reinforcement learning, and gradient-based algorithms. The main search algorithms used today are reinforcement learning, genetic learning, and gradient-based optimization [18–20].

2.3.3 Performance Evaluation

The goal of the search strategy is to find a neural network structure that maximizes some performance metrics, such as accuracy on previously unseen datasets. To guide the search process, the NAS algorithm needs to estimate the performance of a given neural network structure, which is called a performance evaluation strategy.

3 Solution Exploration and Implementation of Similarity Fusion Neural Network Automatic Design Based on SG-CIM Model

3.1 Similarity Matrix Acquisition Between Physical and Standard Tables

In order to solve the problem of incomplete alignment between the physical model table and data standard table in the SG-CIM4.0 data model, alignment matching between physical table entities and standard table entities is needed, which is mainly based on similarity. In this paper, we use the method of multiple similarity calculation to calculate and obtain four similarity matrices [21–23]. These include the English name similarity matrix, Chinese name similarity matrix, Description information similarity matrix, Fields similarity matrix. The process of obtaining the above four similarity matrices is shown in Fig. 1.

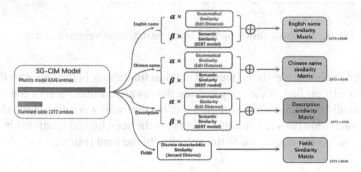

Fig. 1. The process of obtaining the four similarity matrices

3.2 Find the Corresponding Entities in the Standard Table and Physical Table Based on the Fused Similarity Matrix

The four similarity fusions of English name similarity, Chinese name similarity, description similarity, and fields similarity are combined into a unified fusion similarity matrix.

Based on this similarity, we can quickly find which entity is the same entity in the standard table model entity and the physical model entity. In this way, we are able to fully combine the continuity features and discrete features in the entities for the similarity calculation. As shown in Fig. 2, the method of finding the corresponding entities in the standard table and the physical table is based on the fused similarity matrix.

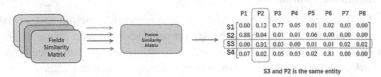

Fig. 2. The method of finding the corresponding entities in the standard table and physical table based on the fused similarity matrix

3.3 Similarity Fusion Method Based on the Linear Weighted Average

The next problem we need to face is how to fuse the four similarities - English name similarity, Chinese name similarity, description similarity, and fields similarity - into a unified similarity. Based on the existing integrated learning knowledge and intuition, we first think of the similarity fusion method based on the linear weighted average [24]. As shown in Fig. 3.

Fig. 3. Similarity fusion method based on the linear weighted average

However, the linear weighting method still has limitations in dealing with the above multiple similarities: first, it can only capture the linear relationship between variables, but not the nonlinear relationship structure; second, the linear weighting method can only obtain the correlation between variables, ignoring the deep logical relationship between variables, which is not conducive to the accuracy of the final results.

3.4 NAS-Based Similarity Fusion Neural Network Automatic Design Framework

We introduced a neural network approach to achieve similarity fusion to address the limitations imposed by linear weighted averaging methods. The deep learning model can automatically learn useful features, moving away from the reliance on feature engineering. It achieves results beyond other algorithms on tasks such as images and speech [25]. Its effectiveness is due in large part to the emergence of new neural network structures.

In this paper, we design a NAS framework that can achieve similarity fusion and name it SF-NAS (Similarity Fusion NAS) framework. The network generated based on this framework is SF-NAS Net, which is able to unify English name similarity, Chinese name similarity, description similarity, and fields similarity fusion into a unified similarity matrix. We name it SF-NAS Net similarity matrix. As Fig. 4 shows the calculation process of similarity fusion by the SF-NAS framework. The specific design of the SF-NAS framework is described in detail next.

Fig. 4. Calculation flow of similarity fusion by SF-NAS framework

3.4.1 Search Space Design of SF-NAS Frame

Similarity Fusion Neural Network mainly consists of three parts: layer neural network, activation function, and Dropout layer. Meanwhile, in order to achieve the function of weight sharing, we design each part of the search unit to correspond to a dictionary to store the parameters obtained so far by its training after selection by the controller. All cells in the search space form a supernet, which we can view as a *directed acyclic graph* (DAG), where nodes can be viewed as pre-set search cells and edges can be viewed as the flow of information predicted by the controller.

3.4.2 Search Controller Design for SF-NAS Frame

In order to realize the automated design and construction of the Similarity Fusion Neural Network, the design of the controller is particularly important. In the SF-NAS frame, the search controller is designed based on a recurrent neural network, where we use the LSTM algorithm [26] for the recurrent neural network. As shown in Fig. 5, the search controller design for the NAS frame is shown.

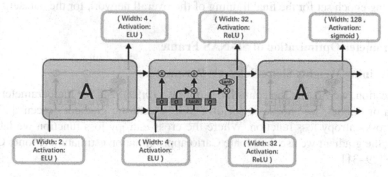

Fig. 5. Search controller design for SF-NAS frame

3.4.3 Training and Network Generation Steps of SF-NAS Frame

Next, the training and network generation steps about the SF-NAS frame will be introduced. For the overall SF-NAS frame, the overall module composition and training steps
are shown in Fig. 6:

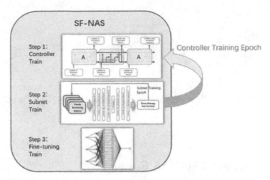

Fig. 6. Module composition and training steps of the overall SF-NAS frame

In the first step, a sequence of modules of sub-networks is predicted based on the
LSTM recurrent neural network. In the early stage of network generation, the prediction
results of each module are randomly initialized, and a Sequential neural network of
length 8 is generated based on this setting.

In the second step, the neural network is trained for this through-order generation,
the training data are four similarity matrices, and the output is the fused similarity
matrix. Also, the training is based on a binary cross-entropy loss function for gradient
descent backpropagation, which predicts that each position of the fused matrix can be
considered as a binary classification problem. Then the first step is repeated according
to the Controller Training Epoch Numbers set in advance. Repeatedly train Subnet and
controller until convergence.

In the third step, after completing the Controller Train step, the final network is
called SF-NAS Net [26]. We need to perform the final Fine-tuning according to the final
Fine-tuning epoch set for the final training of the overall network for the dataset.

3.5 Parameter Optimization of SF-NAS Frame

3.5.1 Training Weights Share Subnet's Parameters

In this section, we first fix the controller's policy $\pi(m; \theta)$, and for the parameter optimization of Subnet, we choose to perform SGD stochastic gradient descent [27, 28]
on the cross-entropy loss function. Where the cross-entropy loss function we label as
$L(m; \omega)$, the gradient we use the Monte Carlo approximation estimation (Monte Carlo)
estimate [29–31].

$$\nabla_\omega \mathbb{E}_{m \sim \pi(m;\theta)}[\mathcal{L}(m;\omega)] \approx \frac{1}{M} \sum_{i=1}^{M} \nabla_\omega \mathcal{L}(m_i, \omega) \tag{1}$$

Where M represents the number of subnetworks sampled at one time and $m_i = \pi(m; \theta)$ represents the number of subnetworks sampled by m_i. Finally, we save the trained ω as values in the subnetwork dictionary.

3.5.2 Training Controller Policy Parameters

In this section, we fix the Subnet parameter ω and update the policy parameter θ at the same time to maximize the desired reward.

$$\mathbb{E}_{m \sim \pi(m; \theta)}[\mathcal{R}(m, \omega)] \qquad (2)$$

Adam optimizer, for which the gradient is computed using REINFORCE, with a moving average baseline to reduce variance.

We need to note that the reward function $\mathcal{R}(m, \omega)$ is computed on the validation set, allowing the SF-NAS frame to choose the parameters that best fit the validation set rather than overfitting on the training set.

4 Experiments

4.1 Experimental Results of Similarity Fusion Based on the Linear Weighted Average

This part of the experiment focuses on the four similarities of English name similarity, Chinese name similarity, description similarity, and fields similarity, which are fused into a unified similarity matrix by using a linear weighted average method. The hit accuracy is calculated based on this fused similarity matrix. The parameter matrix with the highest accuracy in the mission is finally found as the final parameter.

(1) **Experimental results of rough tuning stage:**

Images are plotted for the accuracy of the different parameter matrices during the fixed step descent. As can be seen from the images, the parameter matrix interval that makes the highest model accuracy lies around [0.05, 0.2, 0.25, 0.5]. The highest standard table entity matching hit accuracy with the physical model entity is 83.89% (Fig. 7).

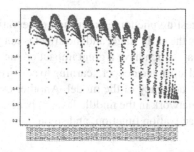

Fig. 7. Schematic diagram of the experimental results of the rough tuning stage

(2) **Fine-tuning stage experimental results:**
   Reinitialize the parameter matrix to [0.05, 0.2, 0.25, 0.5]. Adjust the learning rate to 0.01 to continue the fine-tuning phase of training (Fig. 8).

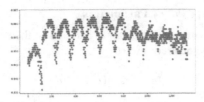

Fig. 8. Schematic diagram of the experimental results of the fine-tuning stage

   The accuracy of different parameter matrices for the fine-tuning step descent process is plotted. The images show that the parameter matrices that make the highest model accuracy are [0.05, 0.20, 0.24, 0.51]. The highest standard table entity matching hit accuracy with the physical model entity is 86.35%.

4.2 Experimental Results of Similarity Fusion Based on SF-NAS Net

This part of the experiment focuses on four similarities, namely English name similarity, Chinese name similarity, description similarity, and fields similarity, which are fused into a unified similarity matrix using SF-NAS Net. The hit accuracy is calculated based on this fused similarity matrix (Tables 1 and 2).

Table 1. Subnet module setting specific type and content

Module type	Specific values
Layer neural network	Number of layer neurons: [2, 4, 8, 16, 32, 64, 128]
Activation function	Activation function type: [sigmoid, tanh, ReLU, ELU]
Dropout layer	Dropout rate: [0.2]

   We can find some interesting phenomena through observation. The Subnet module predicts almost randomly in the early stage, and the effect is not very good. For example, two random dropouts appear, which have a great impact on the similarity. As the neural network continues to train deeper and deeper, learning to add dropout after more neurons can effectively improve the accuracy of the model. Another example is learning to get tend to add a wider neural network in the middle layer is beneficial to the training of the model, a lot of use of relu activation function, and so on.

Table 2. Experimental results of similarity fusion based on SF-NAS Net

Controller epoch	Neural network structure	Accuracy on SG-CIM
1	(128, 'sigmoid'), (4, 'sigmoid'), (dropout), (128, 'relu'), (8, 'tanh'), (16, 'sigmoid'), (dropout), (1, 'sigmoid')	45.41%
2	(32, 'sigmoid'), (4, 'relu'), (32, 'elu'), (128, 'relu'), (dropout), (8, 'sigmoid'), (16, 'elu'), (1, 'sigmoid')	65.32%
5	(4, 'elu'), (16, 'relu'), (32, 'elu'), (64, 'relu'), (128, 'sigmoid'), (dropout), (64, 'elu'), (1, 'sigmoid')	81.67%
10	(2, 'elu'), (16, 'relu'), (32, 'relu'), (128, 'sigmoid'), (dropout), (64, 'relu'), (8, 'elu'), (1, 'sigmoid')	**90.41%**

5 Conclusion

In order to accomplish the task of alignment matching between physical model tables and standard tables in SG-CIM 4.0, this paper proposed a new method to compute multiple similarity matrices between physical tables and standard tables in an impermissible manner and provides an automated fusion neural network based on Neural Architecture Search design scheme based on Neural Architecture Search. An automatically designed fusion neural network achieves the effective fusion between several different similarity matrices mentioned above. The scheme substantially improves the alignment effect and matching accuracy between physical and standard table entities based on this similarity fusion matrix. The solution improves the alignment matching process between physical and standard tables and introduces an automatic design fusion neural network method based on multiple similarity matrix. It helps to improve the intelligence of State Grid and realize the unification of physical model tables and data standard tables in SG-CIM4.0.

Acknowledgment. This work financially supported by Science and Technology Program of State Grid Corporation of China under Grant No.: 5211DS21000T.

References

1. Lu, R., Jin, X., Zhang, S., Qiu, M., Wu, X.: A study on big knowledge and its engineering issues. IEEE Trans. Knowl. Data Eng. **31**(9), 1630–1644 (2018)
2. Qiu, M., Cao, D., et al.: Data transfer minimization for financial derivative pricing using Monte Carlo simulation with GPU in 5G. J. Commun. Syst. **29**(16), 2364–2374 (2016)
3. Qiu, H., Qiu, M., Lu, Z.: Selective encryption on ECG data in body sensor network based on supervised machine learning. Inf. Fusion **55**, 59–67 (2020)
4. Qiu, M., Khisamutdinov, E., et al.: RNA nanotechnology for computer design and in vivo computation. Philos. Trans. R. Soc. A (2013)

5. Qiu, M., Xue, C., Shao, Z., Sha, E.: Energy minimization with soft real-time and DVS for uniprocessor and multiprocessor embedded systems. In: IEEE DATE Conference, pp. 1–6 (2007)

6. Qiu, L., Gai, K., Qiu, M.: Optimal big data sharing approach for tele-health in cloud computing. In: IEEE SmartCloud, pp. 184–189 (2016)

7. Wan, Q., Wang, S., He, X.: Application method of Taiwan SG-CIM model in data. Telecommun. Sci. **36**(03), 140–147 (2020)

8. Wang, J., Wang, J.: Design and implementation of public data model for electric power enterprises based on IEC standard. China Electr. Power **44**(2), 87–90 (2011)

9. Shenming, Z., Guoding, L.: Introduction of standard IEC 61970. Autom. Electr. Power Syst. **14**, 1–6 (2002)

10. Uslar, M., Specht, M., Rohjans, S., Trefke, J., González, J.M.: The Common Information Model CIM: IEC 61968/61970 and 62325-A Practical Introduction to the CIM. Springer, Heidelberg (2012)

11. Rolia, J., Casale, G., Krishnamurthy, D., Dawson, S., Kraft, S.: Predictive modelling of SAP ERP applications: challenges and solutions. In: ICST Conference on Performance Evaluation Methodologies and Tools, pp. 1–9, October 2009

12. Gomaa, W.H., Fahmy, A.A.: A survey of text similarity approaches. Int. J. Comput. Appl. **68**(13), 13–18 (2013). https://doi.org/10.5120/11638-7118

13. Yujian, L., Bo, L.: A normalized Levenshtein distance metric. IEEE Trans. Pattern Anal. Mach. Intell. **29**(6), 1091–1095 (2007)

14. Devlin, J., Chang, M.W., Lee, K., Toutanova, K.: BERT: pre-training of deep bidirectional transformers for language understanding. arXiv preprint arXiv:1810.04805 (2018)

15. Vaswani, A., et al.: Attention is all you need. In: Advances in Neural Information Processing Systems, pp. 5998–6008 (2017)

16. Hamers, L.: Similarity measures in scientometric research: the Jaccard index versus Salton's cosine formula. Inf. Process. Manag. **25**(3), 315–318 (1989)

17. Elsken, T., Metzen, J.H., Hutter, F.: Neural architecture search: a survey. J. Mach. Learn. Res. **20**(1), 1997–2017 (2019)

18. Zoph, B., Le, Q.V.: Neural architecture search with reinforcement learning. arXiv preprint arXiv:1611.01578 (2016)

19. Kramer, O.: Genetic algorithms. In: Kramer, O. (ed.) Genetic Algorithm Essentials, vol. 679, pp. 11–19. Springer, Cham (2017). https://doi.org/10.1007/978-3-319-52156-5_2

20. Liu, H., Simonyan, K., Yang, Y.: DARTS: differentiable architecture search. arXiv preprint arXiv:1806.09055 (2018)

21. Marzal, A., Vidal, E.: Computation of normalized edit distance and applications. IEEE Trans. Pattern Anal. Mach. Intell. **15**(9), 926–932 (1993)

22. Reimers, N., Gurevych, I.: Sentence-BERT: sentence embeddings using siamese BERT-networks. arXiv preprint arXiv:1908.10084 (2019)

23. Niwattanakul, S., Singthongchai, J., Naenudorn, E., Wanapu, S.: Using of Jaccard coefficient for keywords similarity. In: International Multiconference of Engineers and Computer Scientists, vol. 1, no. 6, pp. 380–384, March 2013

24. Stanimirovic, I.P., Zlatanovic, M.L., Petkovic, M.D.: On the linear weighted sum method for multi-objective optimization. Facta Acta Univ. **26**(4), 49–63 (2011)

25. Wistuba, M., Rawat, A., Pedapati, T.: A survey on neural architecture search. arXiv preprint arXiv:1905.01392 (2019)

26. Graves, A.: Long short-term memory. In: Graves, A. (ed.) Supervised Sequence Labelling with Recurrent Neural Networks, pp. 37–45. Springer, Heidelberg (2012). https://doi.org/10.1007/978-3-642-24797-2_4

27. Bottou, L.: Stochastic gradient descent tricks. In: Montavon, G., Orr, G.B., Müller, K.-R. (eds.) Neural Networks: Tricks of the Trade. LNCS, vol. 7700, pp. 421–436. Springer, Heidelberg (2012). https://doi.org/10.1007/978-3-642-35289-8_25
28. Bottou, L.: Large-scale machine learning with stochastic gradient descent. In: Proceedings of COMPSTAT'2010, pp. 177–186. Physica-Verlag HD (2010)
29. Karp, R.M., Luby, M., Madras, N.: Monte-Carlo approximation algorithms for enumeration problems. J. Algorithms 10(3), 429–448 (1989)
30. Veness, J., Ng, K.S., Hutter, M., Uther, W., Silver, D.: A Monte-Carlo AIXI approximation. J. Artif. Intell. Res. 40, 95–142 (2011)
31. Wong, C., Houlsby, N., Lu, Y., Gesmundo, A.: Transfer learning with neural automl. arXiv preprint arXiv:1803.02780 (2018)

A Detection Method for I-CIFA Attack in NDN Network

Meng Yue[1]($\boxtimes$), Han Zheng[2], Wenzhi Feng[2], and Zhijun Wu[1]

[1] The College of Safety Science and Engineering, Civil Aviation University of China,
Tianjin 300300, China
myue_23@163.com, zjwu@cauc.edu.cn
[2] The College of Electronic Information and Automation, Civil Aviation University of China,
Tianjin 300300, China
myth96ers@163.com, 2020071044@cauc.edu.cn

Abstract. In recent years, *Named Data Networking* (NDN) has become a hot topic of research as an emerging network architecture. In particular, the security of NDN has received widespread attention, because NDN networks could resist most of the denial-of-service attacks under the current TCP/IP architecture. However, with the continuous evolution of attack models, the security of NDN networks has been greatly threatened. At present, a new type of attack I-CIFA poses a threat to NDN network. This paper proposes new detection features and sets up sample sets with different detection granularity to improve detection accuracy. And combine Random Forest algorithm for real-time detection of I-CIFA attacks. Experiments show that the scheme could detect I-CIFA attacks more rapidly and has a higher detection rate than other detection schemes. The experiment result show that the detection performance of this scheme is better than other schemes. The detection probability is 97.5%, false negative probability is 1.2% and the error rate is 3.0%.

Keywords: Named Data Networking · Collusive interest flooding attack · Random Forest algorithm

1 Introduction

With the development of computer and networks, security and privacy [1–3] protection become a critical issue in various applications [4, 5]. *Named data networking* (NDN) [6] is an *Information Centric Networking* (ICN) implementation scheme, which retains the thin waist architecture of TCP/IP and ensures that each routing node can transmit information securely and efficiently with diverse and flexible routing strategies. Each NDN routing node includes three modules: *Content Store* (CS), *Pending Interest Table* (PIT) and *Forwarding Information Base* (FIB). This data structure, combined with the unique "flow balancing" mechanism of the NDN network, is resistant to most of the *Distributed Denial of Service* (DDoS) attacks that occur under the current TCP/IP architecture.

In recent years, with the continuous optimization of attack forms against NDN network, the security of NDN environment has been greatly threatened. *Flood of Interest Attack* (IFA) [7] has the most serious impact on the network environment due to its high packet transmission rate, but it is easy to be detected. CIFA [8] attack is based on the *Low-rate Denial of Service* (LDoS) in the traditional TCP/IP network structure [9, 10]. Its low rate and high concealment make it difficult to detect hidden malicious traffic among a large number of legitimate traffic. As the initiator of CIFA attack does not know the actual PIT capacity of downstream routing node Ra, the size of attack traffic cannot be determined, which reduces the effectiveness of the attack.

By analyzing the shortcomings of existing CIFA attacks, an improved CIFA (I-CIFA) attack method was proposed [11]. The added detection method can better detect the PIT capacity of downstream bottleneck routing nodes and reduce the attack cost of attackers. By improving the packet sending mode of an attacker, the cooperation between attackers can be improved, thus increasing the impact range and effectiveness of attacks on the network topology.

Based on the traffic impact of I-CIFA attacks on the network, this paper proposes two new features to improve the detection of such attacks and combines Random Forest algorithm to determine the security state of the network by real-time detection of various detection indicators of routing nodes through machine learning. The experiment results show that the scheme has a high detection rate against I-CIFA attack.

The remaining part of the paper is organized as follows. The current research status of NDN network security is summarized. Then, the scheme based on random forest algorithm for detecting I-CIFA is proposed in Sect. 3. In Sect. 4, the experiments verify that the scheme has the better detection effect than other existing schemes. In the end, this article discusses and summarizes the detection schemes such attacks in the future.

2 Related Works

To further the development of new network architectures, many researchers have shown great interest in the security of NDN networks. To reduce the impact of DDoS on NDN, researchers have proposed many feasible detection and mitigation schemes.

Gasti et al. [12] proposed Interest Flooding Attacks against PIT and proposed corresponding countermeasure strategies but did not provide a corresponding assessment of its performance. Alexander et al. [7] proposed satisfaction-based defense scheme for resisting IFA attacks. Experimental simulations showed that this scheme has the ability to mitigate the impact of CIFA attacks. Dai et al. [13] evaluated the danger of IFA and proposed the interest packet backtracking method. This scheme determines whether the network is under attack by detecting the number of PIT entries. The drawback to this method is that it might misconstrue a sudden increase in legitimate interest packets in a short period of time as an attack, and cause damage to legitimate users. Xin et al. [14] proposed a detection scheme based on accumulated entropy for interest flooding packets and proposed a method for identifying malicious prefixes through the theory of relative entropy. The idea of this method is novel, but the detection is time-consuming, which affects the detection performance. Lou et al. [15] proposed a detection and defense mechanism for IFA based on the Gini coefficient, which used Gini impurity to measure the dispersion of the interest packets' names requested in NDN routers. Hani et al. [16] proposed a central control framework called Common that exploits the topology feature. The Common framework designates certain nodes in the topology as routing nodes for content monitoring and forces most traffic to pass through these nodes. However, the location of a particular router usually cannot be changed. In the real world, the status of the network is constantly changing, which exposes the limitations of the framework. Jing et al. [17] proposed an *isolation forest* (iForest) based IFA detection mechanism and provided a countermeasure. Simulation results show that the proposed mechanism can effectively increase the number of data packets received by consumers, thus mitigating IFA attack.

Alberto et al. [18] proposed a mitigation strategy called Poseidon, whose goal is to identify anomalous traffic due to IFA attacks on a specific interface and mitigate their impact. However, this method relies on mutual collaboration among routing nodes, which may lead to complete failure if an attacker maliciously coerces a routing node. Guang et al. [19] proposed a mechanism to detect the sophisticated IFA from the network-wide view. The experimental results validated that our mechanism can timely detect and mitigate the sophisticated IFA without throttling requests from legitimate consumers. We have studied the detection method in the early stage. By analyzing the impact of CIFA attacks on network traffic and related attributes of PIT entries, the detection scheme based on combination of rolling time window algorithm and confidence interval was proposed [20].

Most existing detection schemes in the NDN network have one or all of the following three drawbacks.

(1) In the specific detection algorithm, the importance of the selected features is not verified.
(2) Existing detection schemes, due to their own limitations, mostly judge the status of the network by a small number of detection features, which causes high misjudgment rate and omission rate in the face of complex network attacks.

To solve the abovementioned problems, this paper proposes a detection scheme for I-CIFA attacks based on deep learning. We establish a sample set by extracting detection features of different granularity on key routing nodes and finally incorporate a Random Forest algorithm to detect I-CIFA attacks in real time. This paper clarifies the nodes of feature extraction, demonstrates the reliability of the proposed method through experiments. Finally, experiments demonstrate that the scheme has a precision and a low error rate. By classify a large amount of network traffic in the NDN network using deep learning, the status of the network can be detected in time.

3 Proposed Method

3.1 New Network Features

The method of network feature extraction is often used for network anomaly detection. It can reflect the network behavior by extracting the dynamic characteristics of the features and enhances network security in attack detection and access control. Additional periodic malicious traffic could severely impact network performance and significantly destabilize the network. This suggests that network traffic is a good indicator for assessing the state of the network. For example, throughput, satisfaction of interest packets and other indicators have been used as important network indicators to judge the state of the network [7, 8]. When malicious network traffic is injected into an NDN network, these network indicators will change to different degrees. In this paper, we analyze the characteristics of network traffic in the normal network status and use detection features with different detection granularities for more accurate detection of CIFA-type attacks. The network features selected in this paper are shown in Table 1.

Table 1. The extracted detection features and their meanings

Detect feature	Character description
T_j^i LifeTime	In each sampling period τ, the average existence time of the PIT entries generated from the incoming interest packets from ith interfaces of the jth routing node is recorded
CS_j^i the numbers of entry	In each sampling period τ, the number of items in CS increases when the incoming interest packets from the ith interface of the jth routing node pass through the routing node in real time
Num_j^i in-interest	In each sampling period τ, the number of interest packets incoming from ith interfaces of the jth routing node is recorded
Num_j^i out-interest	In each sampling period τ, the number of interest packets outgoing from ith interfaces of the jth routing node is recorded
Num_j^i in-data	In each sampling period τ, the number of incoming packets from ith interfaces of the jth routing node is recorded
Num_j^i out-data	In each sampling period τ, the number of packets outgoing from ith interfaces of the jth routing node is recorded

We extract the above network features according to the negative effects of CIFA-type attacks on the network, where T_j^i LifeTime, CS_j^i the numbers of entry are feature extraction for different functions of different modules within the routing nodes, which are coarse-grained detection features. The calculation method is:

$$T_j^i \ LifeTime = \frac{\text{Existence time of each PIT entry during the sampling cycle}}{\text{Number of PIT entries generated by route node } j \text{ during the sampling cycle}} \quad (1)$$

$$CS_j^i \ the \ number \ of \ entry = \text{Number of CS entries generated during the } (i+1)\text{th sampling cycle}$$
$$- \text{number of CS entries generated during the } i\text{th sampling cycle} \quad (2)$$

Num_j^i in-interest, Num_j^i out-interest, Num_j^i in-data, Num_j^i out-data are the statistics of the forwarding of interest packets and data packets for different interfaces of the routing nodes in the sampling interval. They are a type of fine-grained detection feature. Such detection features are collected through the tracer file designed in the ndnSIM experimental platform, and the collection module is ndn::L3RaterTracer. This module counts the data of InInterests, OutInterests, InData, and OutData of each interface on the routing nodes in the network topology in real time.

3.2 Detection Model

The *Random Forests* (RF) algorithm is a classification and prediction algorithm proposed by Breiman [21], which improves the prediction accuracy without significantly increasing the amount of computation. This section selects network characteristics based on the adverse impact of I-CIFA attacks on the network. The random forest model is established by establishing sample training set for anomaly detection.

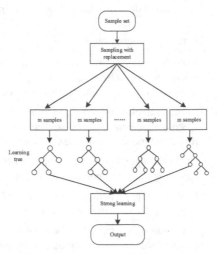

Fig. 1. Flowchart for random forest establishment process

The flowchart for its process is shown in Fig. 1, in which m samples are randomly selected from the sample set. Then a randomly selected indefinite number of detection features from multiple detection features are used to build independent decision trees.

The pseudocode of the random forest algorithm training process on a training set is shown in Table 2.

3.3 Evaluation Indicators

We evaluate the detection model of random forest through confusion matrix, also known as error matrix, which is a standard format for precision evaluation and mainly includes four cases: true positive case, false positive case, true negative case and false negative case. Let *TP*, *FP*, *TN* and *FN* respectively denote the number of corresponding samples. *TP* represents the rational behavior marked correctly, *FP* represents the rational behavior marked incorrectly, *TN* represents the irrational behavior marked correctly, and *FN* represents the irrational behavior marked incorrectly. The evaluation indicators we choose is detection probability, false negative probability and false positive probability.

Table 2. The process of random forest algorithm

Algorithm: Random forest algorithm

Input: Training set D: a set of d training tuples;
   k ←The number of models of classification decision tree;
   G←Gini coefficient or information entropy algorithm;
   X ← test set sample;
   N ← leaf node contained amount of data;
   n_{min}←Minimum amount of data contained in a leaf node

Output: Random forest model constituted by classification decision tree $\{T_b\}_1^k$
       The B classification decision tree is $C_b(x)$

Process:
  1. For i=1 to k
  2.   The sample size of Bootstrap sample Z* obtained from the random repeated sampling
      of the original training data D is d;
  3.   Parameter optimization;
  4.   While n != n_{min} *do*
  5.   Repeat the following steps recursively for each end node of the decision tree with
        sample Z*;
  6.   Randomly select m features from Z features;
  7.   Select the optimal feature from m according to G;
  8.   Divide the node into two child nodes;
  9.   End While;
 10. End For
 11. Generate random forest $\{T_b\}_1^k$;
 12. Test set sample x as input value;
 13. Determine the network status as $C_{rf}^k(x) = majority\ vote\{C_b(x)\}_1^k$;

---

4 Experiment and Verification

4.1 Experimental Environment

The ndnSIM 1.0 platform implements the NDN protocol stack of the NS-3 network (http://www.nsnam.org/) [9], which can simulate and run various network topologies and scenarios. The large-scale network topology is more in line with the actual network environment, so we conduct an experimental simulation under an internet service provider (ISP)-like topology. Spring et al. [22] used Rocketfuel to collect maps from 10 ISPs and published them to the community. These 10 ISPs were implemented by NDN developers in ndnSIM.

Due to the different locations of each routing node, the selected network parameters have different ranges of values, which can simulate the network environment more realistically. The experimental parameters of the specific network topology are shown in Table 3.

The other important experiment parament we set include Packet size (1100 Bytes), the lifetime of the PIT entry (5 s), package rate for legitimate users (20/s), the simulation

Table 3. Network parameter

Link type	Network delay	Bandwidth
Backbone node - Backbone node	5–10 ms	40–100 Mbps
Gateway Node - Backbone node Gateway Node - Gateway node	5–10 ms	10–20 Mbps
User node - Gateway node	10–70 ms	1–3 Mbps

time CS capacity (300000), the size of attack samples (400), the size of legal samples (800), etc.

4.2 Performance Evaluation

In this paper, when an attack occurs, routing nodes at different locations in the network topology are classified considering the degree of influence of attack on different nodes and the importance of detection. Finally, the changes of detection features on different nodes are verified. The classification standard is that routing nodes with 1-hop distance from the producer are classified as type A; routing nodes with 2-hop distance are classified as type B and the rest are classified into class C. When an I-CIFA attack occurs, the collusive interest packets are injected into the network. The features selected in this paper (existence time of PIT entries, cache changes of CS table) will significantly change. The variation in the existence time of PIT entries is shown in Fig. 2.

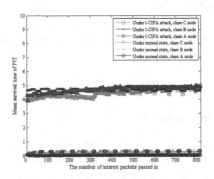

Fig. 2. Average existence time of PIT entries of routing nodes

The existence times of PIT entries in the three types of network nodes are counted separately in this paper. Under normal circumstances, legitimate interest packets could be replied to quickly by legitimate producers, and the PIT in the three types of routing nodes would have a shorter existence time. When an I-CIFA attack occurs, the existence time of the PIT entries in the routing nodes is prolonged because the PIT entries generated by collusive interest packets experience a delay in the replies by the collusive producers. Under normal circumstances, the network traffic tends to have a stable value. However, when a I-CIFA attack occurs, the subsequent packet cache is further unbalanced because the PIT entries corresponding to the collusive interest packets intermittently stay among the bottleneck routing nodes. The results are shown in Fig. 3.

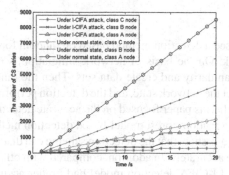

Fig. 3. Changes in CS cache entries of routing nodes

In the normal network states, the variation in the growth of the cache of the routing nodes at each level tends to have a stable value. Since the downstream bottleneck routing node will receive interest packets sent by multiple users from upstream. We assume that the cache of the CS table is large enough, the closer the downstream routing node, the faster the growth rate of the local cache. When the I-CIFA attack occurs, the network traffic balance is broken. This further results in the CS table not caching the data packet, that is, the number of CS entries does not grow from 0 to 6 s, as shown in Fig. 3.

Table 4. Comparison of detection schemes

Detection algorithm	Detection probability	False negative probability	False positive probability
Detection scheme in this paper	97.5%	1.2%	3.0%
Detection scheme based on rolling time window and confidence interval [20]	91.9%	4.0%	9.0%
Detection scheme based on wavelet analysis [8]	82.6%	9.3%	12%

Finally, the detection model was compared with the existing detection scheme. The comparison results are shown in Table 4. In large network topologies, the detection scheme proposed in this paper outperforms existing detection schemes against CIFA attacks. It has a higher precision rate and a lower error rate, mainly because this scheme solves the problem of detection scheme based on wavelet analysis having fewer nodes. Different from detection scheme based on rolling time window and confidence interval, this scheme extracts detection features of different granularity and combines machine learning algorithm, which saves time and improves the detection performance.

5 Conclusion

In this paper, we proposed a detection method based on random forest model for I-CIFA attack in NDN network. On the basis of network simulation, we extracted detection features of different granularity and create data sets. Then the random forest detection model was used to detect the network state, and the detection performance is improved by machine learning model. This paper focused on the accurate detection of I-CIFA attacks in NDN, and proposed a random forest model-based detection method of DDoS attacks in NDN. Simulation results show that the detection scheme can distinguish normal traffic from attack traffic more accurately. In addition, compared with other detection schemes, the random forest-based I-CIFA detection model had higher accuracy and lower error rate.

Acknowledgment. This work was supported in part by the National Natural Science Foundation of China (No. 62172418, No. U1933108, No. 61802276), the Scientific Research Project of Tianjin Municipal Education Commission (No. 2019KJ117) and the Fundamental Research Funds for the Central Universities of CAUC (No. 3122020076).

References

1. Zhang, Z., Wu, J., et al.: Jamming ACK attack to wireless networks and a mitigation approach. In: IEEE GLOBECOM Conference, pp. 1–5 (2008)
2. Thakur, K., Qiu, M., Gai, K., Ali, M.: An investigation on cyber security threats and security models. In: IEEE CSCloud (2015)
3. Qiu, H., Qiu, M., Memmi, G., Ming, Z., Liu, M.: A dynamic scalable blockchain based communication architecture for IoT. In: Qiu, M. (ed.) SmartBlock 2018. LNCS, vol. 11373, pp. 159–166. Springer, Cham (2018). https://doi.org/10.1007/978-3-030-05764-0_17
4. Gai, K., Qiu, M., Sun, X., Zhao, H.: Security and privacy issues: a survey on FinTech. In: Qiu, M. (ed.) Smart Computing and Communication, pp. 236–247. Springer, Cham (2017). https://doi.org/10.1007/978-3-319-52015-5_24
5. Gai, K., Qiu, M., Elnagdy, S.: A novel secure big data cyber incident analytics framework for cloud-based cybersecurity insurance. In: IEEE BigDataSecurity (2016)
6. Matthew, S., et al.: Named data networking. Int. J. Eng. Res **6**(7), 371–372 (2017)
7. Alexander, A., et al.: Interest flooding attack and countermeasures in named data networking. In: IFIP Networking Conference, pp. 1–9. IEEE (2013)
8. Xin, Y., et al.: Detection of collusive interest flooding attacks in named data networking using wavelet analysis. In: 2017 IEEE Military Communications Conference (MILCOM), pp. 557–562. IEEE (2017)
9. Dan, T., et al.: MF-Adaboost: LDoS attack detection based on multi-features and improved Adaboost. Futur. Gener. Comput. Syst. **106**, 347–359 (2020)
10. Ye, F., et al.: FR-RED: fractal residual based real-time detection of the LDoS attack. IEEE Trans. Reliab. **70**, 1–15 (2020)
11. Wu, Z., et al.: I-CIFA: an improved collusive interest flooding attack in named data networking. J. Inf. Secur. Appl. **61**, 102912 (2021)

12. Gasti, P., et al.: DoS & DDoS in named-data networking. In: 2013 IEEE Conference on Computer Communication and Networks (ICCCN), pp. 1–7. IEEE (2013)
13. Dai, H., et al.: Mitigate DDoS attacks in NDN by interest traceback. In: 2013 IEEE Conference on Computer Communications Workshops (INFOCOM WKSHPS), pp. 381–386. IEEE (2013)
14. Xin, Y., et al.: A novel interest flooding attacks detection and countermeasure scheme in NDN. In: 2016 IEEE Global Communications Conference, pp. 1–7. IEEE (2016)
15. Zhi, T., Luo, H., Liu, Y.: A Gini impurity-based interest flooding attack defence mechanism in NDN. IEEE Commun. Lett. **22**(3), 538–541 (2018). https://doi.org/10.1109/LCOMM.2018.2789896
16. Hani, S., et al.: Lightweight coordinated defence against interest flooding attacks in NDN. In: 2015 IEEE Conference on Computer Communications Workshops (INFOCOM Workshops), pp. 103–104. IEEE (2015)
17. Jing, C., et al.: Isolation forest based interest flooding at-tack detection mechanism in NDN. In: 2019 2nd International Conference on Hot Information-Centric Networking (HotICN), pp. 58–62 (2019)
18. Alberto, C., et al.: Poseidon: mitigating interest flooding DDoS attacks in named data networking. In: 38th Annual IEEE Conference on Local Computer Networks, Sydney, Australia, October 2013, pp. 630–638. IEEE (2013)
19. Guang, C., et al.: Detecting and mitigating a sophisticated interest flooding attack in NDN from the network-wide view. In: 2019 IEEE First International Workshop on Network Meets Intelligent Computations (NMIC), pp. 7–9. IEEE (2019)
20. Wu, Z., et al.: Mitigation measures of collusive interest flooding attacks in named data networking. Comput. Secur. **97**, 101971 (2020)
21. Leo, B.: Random Forests. Mach. Learn. **45**(1), 5–32 (2001)
22. Neil, S., et al.: Measuring ISP Topologies with Rocketfuel. CCR (2002)

InterGridSim: A Broker-Overlay Based Inter-Grid Simulator

Abdulrahman Azab[✉]

Division of Research Computing, University Center for Information Technology,
University of Oslo, Oslo, Norway
azab@uio.no

Abstract. Large scale Grid computing systems are often organized as
an inter-Grid architecture, where multiple Grid domains are interconnected through their local broker. In this context, the main challenge is
to devise appropriate job scheduling policies that can satisfy goals such
as global load balancing together with maintaining the local policies of
the different Grids. This paper presents INTERGRIDSIM, a simulator for
scalable resource discovery and job scheduling technique in broker based
interconnected Grid domains. Inter-Grid scheduling decisions are handled jointly by brokers in a broker overlay network. A Broker periodically
exchanges its local domain's resource information with its neighboring
brokers. INTERGRIDSIM offers several network structures and workload
allocation techniques for Tier-1 and Tier-0 networks and large workload
capacity. The paper presents sample simulations for throughput, utilisation, and load balancing in a network of 512 brokers and 50k nodes.

1 Introduction

Grid computing is based on coordinated resource sharing in a dynamic environment of multi-institutional virtual organizations, VOs [1]. The target of computational Grid, which is our main focus, is to aggregate many Grid compute
resources as one powerful unit on which computational intensive applications
can run and produce results with low latency. Computational Grid Model is
mainly composed of three components: (i) worker/ executor, to which computational jobs are submitted and where they are executed, (ii) client/ user, from
which jobs are submitted and by which the Grid is consumed, and (iii) broker/
scheduler, which is responsible of allocating submitted jobs by clients to suitable
workers [2]. The InterGrid concept [3] has been evolved due to the dramatic
increase in the resource demands of Grid application together with the submission rate. The idea of resource sharing between different domains is already in
use in the network level and known as peering [4–6]. The interconnection of Grid
domains may be implemented in one of three levels:

Client level where the client/user machine can have access to multiple Grid
domains using associated access rights [7,8]. This can be implemented either by
granting multiple access rights to each Grid client [7], or by installing multiple
Grid clients on the same user machine to access multiple domains with different

M. Qiu et al. (Eds.): SmartCom 2021, LNCS 13202, pp. 374–383, 2022.
https://doi.org/10.1007/978-3-030-97774-0_34

architectures [8]. This alternative is not scalable, since it is not applicable to grant access to hundreds of domains to thousands of clients which may result in a massive number of contentions.

Worker level where worker/executer nodes could have the task executors of multiple Grid domains installed so that it become available for submission requests from either of those domains [9]. Based on our experience [10], this alternative would negatively influence the capacity of the worker machine which would in turn have a negative result on the resource capacity in each of the interconnected domains.

Broker level where the interconnection is to be carried out through *Local Resource Brokers*, LRB. Two methodologies have been implemented in this direction: (i) *Central meta-scheduler*, and (ii) *Grid federation*. The role of a central meta-scheduler [11] to manage and control the interGrid submission requests allocating each to a LRB with matching resource requirements on its domain. This methodology is implemented by Condor-G [12] where the Condor-G meta-scheduler can exchange submission requests between Condor pools and Globus VOs. A similar mechanism is implemented by Nimrod-G [13]. This methodology suffers from the centralization problem where the meta-scheduler may be overloaded with inter-Grid requests, in addition to single point of failure. Grid federation is to establish the interconnection between LRBs in an overlay, giving equal rights to all connected brokers to participate in the interconnection task allocation decision. Such a federation of Grid domains [3] would avoid the limitations of the central meta-scheduler methodology. This methodology is implemented in condor-flock-p2p [14] through the establishment of a pastry [15] based p2p overlay between brokers. A little different mechanism is adopted by the InterGrid project [3,16] where LRBs are responsible only for local brokering while the interconnection and management of interGrid submission requests are carried out by fixing a dedicated gateway in each domain.

This paper presents INTERGRIDSIM [17], a simulator for Inter-Grid resource management. Different techniques can be implemented in INTERGRIDSIM from fully centralised to peer-to-peer. The main technique promoted in INTERGRIDSIM is SLICK [18–20] which is built on a hybrid peer-to-peer overlay network [21]. SLICK aims at reducing the overall complexity of the system, enabling transparent access to regular participants, while ensuring efficient resource utilization, load balancing and failure handling. The underlying idea of the architecture is that each participating node may offer or claim computational resources as necessary for their application. This technique is suitable for interconnected domains, each with one broker node responsible for local resource management within its virtual organization. The broker receives requests for resources from participating nodes, compare the requirements in each request with available resources at nodes in the network, and forwards the requests to suitable nodes. Each node interacts only with its attached broker, and both regular node and broker failures are handled. Brokers associated with the different domains take part in an overlay network of brokers that are responsible for global resource management and task deployment throughout the network.

INTERGRIDSIM has been implemented in the PeerSim simulation environment [22], and has been evaluated experimentally for various load conditions, network sizes, and topologies. The results show that the architecture is able to allocate compute tasks quickly and efficiently for different broker overlay topologies.

2   The Inter-grid Architecture

The Inter-Grid architecture in INTERGRIDSIM is based on global resource sharing and collaboration of Grid domains. Each domain consists of one domain controller (i.e. Broker), and a collection of regular nodes. Components of the grid system are:

Job in INTERGRIDSIM refers to a computational job. It has five execution parameters: 1) Required CPU, the computational power required for running the job. 2) Required Memory, the memory size required for running the job. 3) Expiration Time, the amount of time to wait for allocation. 4) Creation Time, the time at which the job is created for allocation. 5) Allocation attempts, the maximum number of attempts to deploy the job before it is expired.

Regular node refers to each non-broker node in the Grid. Each regular node can be a member of one domain, and can submit and/or run a job. A regular node is also responsible for periodically sending information about the current available resource state of the node to its broker. Each regular node has two resource parameters: 1) Available CPU, which refers to the available computational power in the node, and 2) Available Memory space. Regular is equivalent to Peer in HIMAN, which contains two components: Worker (W), which is responsible for task execution, and Client (C), which is responsible for task submission [23, 24].

Broker is a node which works as a domain controller, can also work as a regular node in case of lack of available regular nodes. It is responsible for: 1) Allocating jobs to suitable nodes. A suitable node for a job is elected by performing a matchmaking process between the job requirements and the available resources of attached Grid nodes [2]. 2) Storing the current resource state for local nodes (i.e. in the same domain) as well as global nodes (i.e. in other domains).

Grid Domain (Virtual Organization) is an overlay of nodes, which can be allocated in different regions and be members of several organizations. Each domain is composed of one broker and regular nodes and is structured as a star logical topology, so that; communication is between the broker and regular nodes. There is no direct communication between regular nodes within the same domain.

Broker overlay is a network of brokers through which communication and data exchange between different Grid domains is performed.

INTERGRIDSIM simulates resource discovery and global job scheduling for interconnected Grid domains. INTERGRIDSIM supports several architecture of the broker overlay. One is structured-p2p [15] that each broker has a `nodeID` and a routing table, and the routing table of each broker is filled with `nodeID`s of brokers which share different prefixes with the current broker's `nodeID`. Another example is gossip [25] where each broker has a set of neighbors, and resource information is distributed through periodically exchanging data with a neighbor broker. SLICK, implements the first architecture where each broker must be holding a routing table in which the addresses of its neighboring brokers are stored. INTERGRIDSIM gateway broker is designed to work on the top of the local broker of the Grid domain as three layers architecture. The different layers and components of SLICK are described in the main SLICK paper [18].

Fault Tolerance: INTERGRIDSIM mainly manages Broker failures, where worker and client failures are managed internally by the broker in each Grid domain. Each regular node has direct communication with its broker. Periodically, each node sends its resource information to the broker to update its associated resource-information record to the current state. Each node holds a list of information about all existing brokers in the broker overlay. This information is retrieved and updated periodically from its local broker. A regular detects its local broker failure when it attempts to send its resource information to the broker. In case of broker failure, all regular nodes in the domain are detached from the Grid, and each node sends a membership request to the first broker in the list. If the request is granted, the regular node sets the new broker as the attached broker; otherwise the request is repeated to the next broker in the list.

3   Simulation Model

INTERGRIDSIM is designed using PeerSim [22]; a Java-based simulation-engine designed to help protocol designers in simulating their P2P protocols. The simulation model is based on cycle-based simulation. Input parameters for the simulation engine are read from a configuration text file. In cycle-based simulation, each simulation cycle is considered as one time unit. Four main Interfaces are used: Node, Linkable, CDProtocol, and Control. The overlay network is a collection of Node objects. Before starting simulation, a collection of Initializer objects, specified in the configuration file, are created and execute initialization functions. All Initializer objects must implement Control Interface This initialization process includes constructing the network by connecting Node objects together based on the specified topology. Pointers to all neighboring nodes are stored in a Linkable Protocol object attached to each Node object. Any other initializations can be included. The default Linkable Protocol is the IdleProtocol. Each node object is attached to a collection of CDProtocol (i.e. cycle driven protocol) objects. Each CDProtocol object is responsible for simulating one communication protocol in the attached node with identical objects in other nodes. This is carried out by calling a nextCycle() method in each CDProtocol object by the simulation engine each simulation cycle. Each simulation cycle, the simulation engine calls a collection of execute() methods in Control objects. Control objects are created to carry out all control operations needed for the simulation, including modification of simulation parameters. Another role of Control objects is the observation and recording of data related to simulation environment state each simulation cycle. All Control objects must implement `Control` Interface.

In this model, a `GridNode` class implements the `Node` Interface is built. `GridDeployer`, and `GridFailureControl` class objects are included as a `Control` object for performing job deployment and failure handling. Three CD Protocols as `CDProtocol` classes are built:

Grid CD Protocol. This protocol is included in each regular node and responsible for communicating with the attached broker and sends the resource information each simulation cycle.

Deployment Protocol. This protocol is included in each regular node. It is responsible for responding to the deployment requests from the broker by one of two responses: *Deployed*, if the job deployment is successful, and *Failed*, if the local resources are not enough for deploying the job.

Grid Broker Protocol. This protocol is included in broker nodes and responsible for: 1) Receiving jobs from the job deployer and append them to the job queue. 2) Receiving resource information from attached regular nodes and replaces the current stored blocks in the resource information data set with the new ones. 3) Picking one job each cycle from the job queue and invoking the job deployment algorithm. 4) Exchanging resource information with one neighbor broker each cycle by invoking the resource information exchange algorithm.

Figure 1 describes the Grid simulation model and the communication between different protocols. `GridNode` class is a reference for node objects. `GridAllocator` and `GridFailureControl` classes are included as references for `Control` objects which simulate job allocation and failure handling. Three cycle-driven `Protocol` classes are also built: 1) `Grid CD Protocol`, included in each

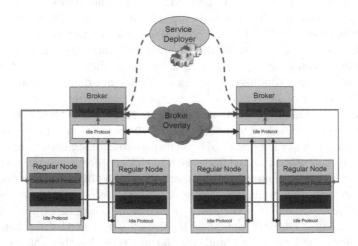

Fig. 1. Simulation model

regular node and is responsible for communicating with the attached broker and sends the resource information in each simulation cycle. 2) `Allocation Protocol`, included in each regular node and is responsible for responding to the Allocation requests from the broker. 3) `Grid Broker Protocol`, included in each broker node for performing the tasks associated with the broker (described in the previous sections). The `Idle Protocol` is in the main `PeerSim` package and is included in each node to be responsible for establishing communication with neighboring nodes.

4   Simulation Results

We present the results of simulating a large number of domains with INTER-GRIDSIM inter-Grid simulator using SLICK workload management technique. We simulate a system of 50,000 nodes in 512 interconnected domains. The domains are connected through local brokers in a HyperCube logical topology, i.e. in case of a network size of N, each broker will have k neighbours in its routing table where $k = \frac{\ln N}{\ln 2}$. In case of 512 brokers, each broker will have 9 neighbors. SLICK is tested against the centralised meta-scheduling technique where we implement logical star topology between an orchestrator and the brokers in the broker overlay. Compute node specifications are of two groups which are different in four static attributes: [group1: 2 CPU slots, 4 GB Memory, Windows OS, No java support] and [group2: 4 CPU slots, 8 GB Memory, Linux OS, Java support] Nodes are divided equally between the two groups, 25,000 each, but scattered among the domains. We create a load of total 80,000 synthetic jobs divided into 100 sequences. Each sequence is assigned to one broker. Using a random frequency $50 < f < 100$ time instance, a random number of jobs $50 < j < 100$ is submitted periodically by each sequence. Job resource requirements are randomly set. The process continues until all the 80,000 jobs are submitted. The total simulation time of the experiment is set to 2000 time instances. Each time instance, the local scheduler processes one job from the local queue, and the gateway scheduler processes one job from the gateway queue. Each time instance each broker synchronizes the resource information database with one neighbor broker.

We use three benchmarks: *Job allocation throughput, resource utilisation,* and *Load balancing.* Job allocation throughput is measured by reading the total number of waiting jobs in the system/time, Fig. 2(a), and number of job allocations/time Fig. 2(b). It is clear that SLICK is achieving higher throughput. SLICK manages to reach a steady state were all jobs are allocated, within 1344 time instances, while in other systems, a bottleneck case happens. This can be described that in case of centralized allocation, there is only the central meta-scheduler to carryout the interconnections, which in case of cross-domain submissions allocates only one job per time instance. The breakdown both cases is after ≈ 800 time instances is because all job sequences complete their submissions by that time. We made this in purpose in order to validate the system performance when job allocation is carried out only inter-domain and not intra-domain. Resource utilisation is measured by reading the number of saturated

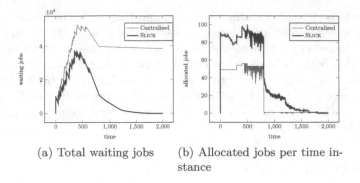

(a) Total waiting jobs   (b) Allocated jobs per time instance

Fig. 2. System throughput: overall job allocation ratio

domains/time, e.g. those domains which workers are fully saturated with jobs. Figure 3(a) shows that SLICK in the time of high load ≈ 500 time instances, is achieving larger utilisation. Load balancing is measured by calculating for brokers, throughout the simulation: How long did it take to allocate all jobs owned by the domain of each broker, and what is the average waiting time. In Fig. 3(b), it is clear that for SLICK, the total allocation time never exceeded 1500 time instances and the maximum average waiting time is below 800. For centralized allocation, none of the domains got all of its jobs allocated during the 2000 time. The value of 2000 for both total allocation time and average waiting time indicates that this broker's jobs were not totally allocated.

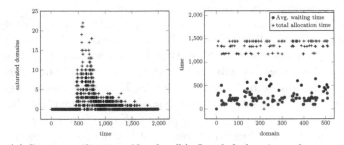

(a) System utilisation: Number of saturated domains per unit time

(b) Load balancing: Average waiting time and total allocation time of jobs submitted to each of 100 domains

Fig. 3. Broker overlay coordination with 100 domains

Fault Tolerance: This experiment demonstrates how the broker overlay based architecture is tolerant to broker failures. Broker failures are injected during the simulation. With the existence of broker failures, it is expected that the deviation of the reading time values of the stored resource information from the current cycle will increase due to failure. The reason is that resource information of the regular nodes which have been attached to the failed broker, will remain old and not updated until they are attached to other brokers and start sending resource information blocks. In the following experiments, a new parameter is taken into account: *Data Age*, which is the maximum age in cycles of resource information in a broker resource data set. In each simulation cycle, the broker protocol checks the reading time of each block in the resource information data set. If the reading time of a block is $\leq (Currenttime - DataAge)$, then, this block is removed from the data set. If a new block for the same node is received later, in an exchange operation, it is added to the data set. The following experiments are performed by varying the value of Data Age.

Four topologies are used: ring, fully connected, and Wire-k-Out ($k = 60$), and hyper-cube. The network size is fixed to N = 500, and M = 100. The number of simulation cycles is 300. The experiment is performed with varying the number of broker failures: The data age is fixed to 10 cycles with 4 and 8 injected broker failures, depicted in Fig. 4.

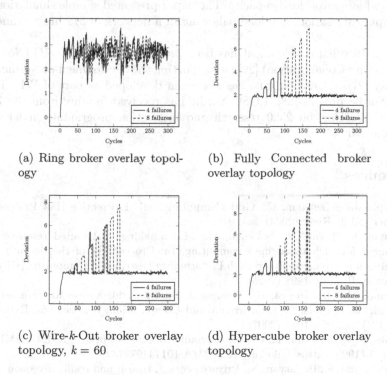

(a) Ring broker overlay topology

(b) Fully Connected broker overlay topology

(c) Wire-k-Out broker overlay topology, $k = 60$

(d) Hyper-cube broker overlay topology

Fig. 4. Impact of failures on the deviation of the resource information for: data age of 10 cycles with 4 and 8 injected broker failures

In Fig. 4, it is clear that for fully connected, wire-k-out, and hyper-cube topologies, the system can recover from failures and return to stable state. But When Data Age = 30, the system stability is not settled because of the existence of old data. In case of ring topology, the deviation has terrible and unstable variation with failures. This can be described that, because of the lack of possible direct communications between brokers, it takes time for a broker to reach data stored in non-neighbor brokers.

5   Conclusions and Acknowledgments

This paper presented INTERGRIDSIM, a simulator for interconnected Grid domains. The key feature of INTERGRIDSIM is that both resource state and hardware specifications of each domain are stored in small datasets which enables the exchange of resource information among brokers. Using this information in matchmaking, cross-scheduling decisions are made accurate in most cases. INTERGRIDSIM offers several network structures and workload allocation techniques and large workload capacity. The paper presented sample simulations for throughput, utilisation, and load balancing in a network of 512 brokers and 50k nodes.

INTERGRIDSIM development has been partially funded by NeIC (Nordic e-Infrastructure Collaboration) [26] for supporting the development of Nordic Tier-1 activity [27]. INTERGRIDSIM has also been developed as part of WP5 in the EOSC-Nordic project [28]. EOSC-Nordic has received funding from the European Union's Horizon 2020 research and innovation programme under grant agreement No 857652.

References

1. Joseph, J., Fellenstein, C.: Grid Computing, vol. 1. Prentice Hall Professional, Upper saddle River (2004)
2. Raman, R., Livny, M., Solomon, M.: Matchmaking: distributed resource management for high throughput computing. In: Proceedings of the Seventh IEEE International Symposium on High Performance Distributed Computing (HPDC7), Chicago, IL, July 1998 (1998)
3. Assuno, M.D.D., Buyya, R., Venugopal, S.: Intergrid: a case for internetworking islands of grids. In: Concurrency and Computation: Practice and Experience (CCPE), pp. 997–1024 (2007)
4. Baake, P., Wichmann, T.: On the economics of internet peering. NETNOMICS 1, 89–105 (1999). https://doi.org/10.1023/A:1011449721395
5. Chakrabarti, S., Badasyan, N.: Private peering, transit and traffic diversion. NETNOMICS 7(2), 115–124 (2005). https://doi.org/10.1007/s11066-006-9007-x
6. Huston, G.: Interconnection, peering and settlements-part I. Internet Protocol. 2(1) (1999)
7. Evers, X., de Jongh, J.F.C.M., Boontje, R., Epema, D.H.J., van Dantzig, R.: Condor flocking: load sharing between pools of workstations. Technical report, Delft, The Netherlands (1993)

8. Aiftimiei, C., et al.: Design and implementation of the gLite CREAM job management service. Future Gener. Comput. Syst. **26**(4), 654–667 (2010)
9. NorduGrid: Nordic Testbed for Wide Area Computing and Data Handling. http://www.nordugrid.org/
10. Azab, A., Meling, H.: Stroll: a universal filesystem-based interface for seamless task deployment in grid computing. In: Göschka, K.M., Haridi, S. (eds.) DAIS 2012. LNCS, vol. 7272, pp. 162–176. Springer, Heidelberg (2012). https://doi.org/10.1007/978-3-642-30823-9_14
11. Schopf, J.: Ten actions when superscheduling. In: Global Grid Forum (2001)
12. Frey, J., Tannenbaum, T., Livny, M., Foster, I., Tuecke, S.: Condor-G: a computation management agent for multi-institutional grids. Clust. Comput. **5**(3), 237–246 (2002). https://doi.org/10.1023/A:1015617019423
13. Buyya, R., Abramson, D., Giddy, J.: Nimrod/G: an architecture for a resource management and scheduling system in a global computational grid. In: Proceedings of HPC ASIA 2000, pp. 283–289 (2000)
14. Butt, A.R., Zhang, R., Hu, Y.C.: A self-organizing flock of condors. J. Parallel Distrib. Comput. **66**(1), 145–161 (2006)
15. Rowstron, A., Druschel, P.: Pastry: scalable, decentralized object location, and routing for large-scale peer-to-peer systems. In: Guerraoui, R. (ed.) Middleware 2001. LNCS, vol. 2218, pp. 329–350. Springer, Heidelberg (2001). https://doi.org/10.1007/3-540-45518-3_18
16. Assuncao, M.: Provisioning techniques and policies for resource sharing between grids. Ph.D. dissertation, The University of Melbourne, Australia (2009)
17. Azab, A.: Intergridsim: inter-grid simulator based on peersim. https://github.com/abdulrahmanazab/intergridsim
18. Azab, A., Meling, H.: Slick: a coordinated job allocation technique for inter-grid architectures. In: 7th European Modelling Symposium (EMS) (2013)
19. Azab, A., Meling, H., Davidrajuh, R.: A fuzzy-logic based coordinated scheduling technique for inter-grid architectures. In: Magoutis, K., Pietzuch, P. (eds.) DAIS 2014. LNCS, vol. 8460, pp. 171–185. Springer, Heidelberg (2014). https://doi.org/10.1007/978-3-662-43352-2_14
20. Azab, A.: Binary matchmaking for inter-grid job scheduling. In: Silhavy, R., Senkerik, R., Oplatkova, Z.K., Silhavy, P., Prokopova, Z. (eds.) Modern Trends and Techniques in Computer Science. AISC, vol. 285, pp. 433–443. Springer, Cham (2014). https://doi.org/10.1007/978-3-319-06740-7_36
21. Androutsellis-Theotokis, S., Spinellis, D.: A survey of peer-to-peer content distribution technologies. ACM Comput. Surv. **36**(4), 335–371 (2004)
22. Montresor, A., Jelasity, M.: PeerSim: a scalable P2P simulator. In: Proceedings of the 9th International Conference on Peer-to-Peer (P2P'09), Seattle, WA, Sep 2009, pp. 99–100 (2009)
23. Condor project. http://www.cs.wisc.edu/condor/
24. El-Desoky, A.E., Ali, H.A., Azab, A.A.: A pure peer-to-peer desktop grid framework with efficient fault tolerance. In: ICCES'07, Cairo, Egypt, pp. 346–352 (2007)
25. Allavena, A., Demers, A., Hopcroft, J.E.: Correctness of a gossip based membership protocol. In: Aguilera, M.K., Aspnes, J. (eds.) PODC, ACM, pp. 292–301 (2005)
26. Neic: Nordic e-infrastructure collaboration. https://neic.no/
27. Nordic wlcg tier-1 facility. https://neic.no/nt1/
28. Eosc-nordic project. https://eosc-nordic.eu/

Vertical Handover of Satellite-Ground Fusion Network Based on Time and Location Under Early Access Strategy

Yun Liu[1], Shenghao Ding[2(✉)], Jiaxin Huang[2], Hao Jiang[2], Jing Wu[2], Ruiliang Song[1], Ningning Lu[1], and Zhiqun Song[1]

[1] The 54th Research Institute of China Electronics Technology Group Corporation, Beijing, China

[2] Wuhan University, Wuhan, China

{jh,wujing}@whu.edu.cn

Abstract. Satellites have been integrated into the terrestrial mobile network to meet the 5G requirements of providing connectivity regardless of time and location. The user terminal needs to switch between the satellite and base station, known as vertical handover, to achieve continuous and high-quality communication. The credit method avoids frequent network state measurement. However, it requires the status of all networks for credit calculation, which may lead to incomplete and delayed data acquisition. Therefore, a handover decision method based on time-space attribute reputation is proposed in this study. The proposed method takes the user's location and time factors into account. Considering the changes of the network topology caused by satellite and user mobility, the target network is selected according to the overall reputation of candidates and the user's current location. The early untrusted network information is eliminated in time to obtain an effective and accurate result. Moreover, since uplink vertical handover has an undesirably high propagation delay during protocol implementation, this study optimizes the existing execution process and proposes an early access strategy to reduce the handover delay. Both designs have been tested and are proved to be effective.

Keywords: Vertical handover · Decision-making · Spacio-temporal Factor · Protocol process · Random access · Delay

1 Introduction

Internet assess [1, 2] becomes an essential need for human society due to the fast advance in computer [3, 4], software [5, 6], and communication techniques [7–9]. Like electricity and water, to access information freely turns out to be a fundamental need. However, it is difficult to construct terrestrial networks that rely on base stations in harsh regions and are vulnerable to damage in natural disasters. There has been an upsurge in efforts to achieve global coverage through a low earth orbit constellation. However, high maintenance overhead [10], high latency [11], low capacity [12], and low security [13–15], are problems that need to be overcome. Accordingly, integrating terrestrial network and satellite network is an inevitable trend [16]. Vertical handover technology is required when the user terminal switches between the two networks. However, the communication latency and inconsistent mobility are likely to present difficulties. This study focuses on the handover decision and execution stages that directly determine the communication experience of the user. This will also provide the potential to improve network security [17, 18] and big data processing capabilities [19, 20].

During the handover decision stage, the commonly adopted traditional credit algorithm [21] can store the service conditions of each network in a previous time period as the reference for the current handover. However, the network with the highest credit may not be available to the user, and the early network states become increasingly unreliable over time. Therefore, considering the spatio-temporal factors is indispensable. The handover execution stage refers to the disconnection from the original network and connection to the target. The long-distance satellite-ground link is likely to further increase the signaling transmission delay, resulting in poor handover experience. This problem can only be solved by adjusting the ordinary protocol process.

In this study, Sect. 2 primarily introduces some common methods in vertical handover and analyzes their defects. Section 3 introduces the proposed decision and execution methods in detail. Section 4 presents the results of testing both designs, which are proved to be effective. Lastly, a conclusion summarizes the study.

2 Related Work

The *Third Generation Partnership Project* (3GPP) has considered multiple application scenarios with satellites in "5G New Gaps for Non-Terrestrial Networks" [22]. Scholars have proposed a variety of decision methods for the vertical handover in the satellite-ground fusion network. The decision algorithm based on *received signal strength* (RSS) always selects the network with the highest signal strength as the target access [23, 24] while neglecting other states, such as delay and jitter. The multi-attribute decision-making (MADM) method and game theory algorithm need to acquire large amounts of real-time network information [25, 26] for comprehensive results. In addition, both methods occupy significant satellite bandwidth resources and are too time-consuming to be applied in practice.

The reputation-based algorithm can reduce the overhead and delay caused by repeated calculation and make a fast and appropriate network selection by selecting the network with the highest credit based on the historical service information. T. Bi et al. applied the reputation-based network selection algorithm to maintain the best video transmission by considering the movement of users [27]. S. Radouche et al. adopted the utility function and credits to achieve better network indicators than those obtained using the original MADM method [28]. C. Desogus et al. proposed a reputation algorithm based on business types, which significantly improved the network access performance of different services. However, all the above methods ignored the effect of time lapse and user's location on the reputation. Therefore, this study proposes a *handover decision* method based on *time-space attribute reputation* (HD-TSR) to eliminate the earliest data promptly and make decisions based on the position of the user.

The handover process can be executed after calculating the reputation and selecting the target satellite. Upon receiving the reconfiguration command, the terminal must disconnect the current channel and initiate a random access request. Consequently, there is a service outage time. Therefore, it is critical to design a suitable switching scheme to reduce the interval time, particularly when a satellite-ground link exists.

The advanced synchronization strategy is suitable for scenarios involving satellites. It can reduce the overall interruption time by ensuring synchronization before the random access process. The advanced synchronization strategy can be easily applied if the base station is in sync with the satellite. This study proposes an early access strategy by optimizing the current execution process. The proposed strategy is applied when the base station is out of sync with the satellite. Since the handover target is predictable, the terminal is designed to request the random access process in advance, parallel with the handover request step executed by the base station.

3   Handover Decision and Execution Design

Based on the description in Sect. 2, the implementation of the vertical switching method involves two fundamental steps: handover decision and handover execution. Compared with the original reputation algorithm, the first section illustrates the proposed HD-TSR method in detail and shows its advantages. Subsequently, the second section introduces the protocol process of the early access strategy.

3.1   Handover Decision Based on Time-Space Attribute Reputation

In the satellite-ground fusion network discussed in this study, the user is within the coverage of the ground base station and simultaneously available to multiple satellites. Based on the historical evaluation of communication services by other terminals of the same type, the access expectation of the entire candidate networks can be evaluated. However, the fluctuation of the network reduces the credibility of the user's evaluation over time, and the user's specific service report is related to the location. Therefore, the study adopts an evaluation mechanism with time and space attributes to enhance the timeliness and efficacy of credit to improve the traditional credit algorithm.

Users, multiple access networks, and the core network are the basic components of the vertical handover scenario. The decision based on the credit algorithm is directly related to the network reputation, including delay, jitter, and other *Quality of Service* (QoS) indicators, and an attribute weight is set for each using the *analytic hierarchy process* [29] (AHP). The user terminal can evaluate the states of the network it is connecting with and adopt the sigmoid function to normalize the attributes before sending out the report [30, 31]. Once the access network receives the evaluation report, it calculates the credit and sends the result to the core network. The core network collects and distributes the credit records to all the access networks periodically. As a result, all the access networks can have the credit information of others. After receiving the measurement report from the user again, the access network screens the candidate networks according to the credit and selects the one with the maximum credit as the handover target.

In the proposed method, the access network records the time to prioritize the receival of measurement reports. The network selects the reports in the latest L time points for credit calculation. Subsequently, a vector V is defined to store all the time weights. The time degree [32] λ is used to control the increase or decrease in the weight of the early data, and the entropy of the time weight vector can be calculated. While the entropy refers to the ability to absorb objective information, the relative proximity degree between the time weight vector V and ideal series considers the preferences of the decision-maker. The parameters mentioned above can be combined with the single-objective optimization model as follows. If the parameter α is small, the decider determines the weight based more on objective information. If the parameter α is large, the decider's subjective judgement is more significant.

$$
\begin{cases}
g = \alpha \dfrac{\sqrt{\sum\limits_{l=2}^{L} v_l^2 + (1 - v_1)^2}}{\sqrt{\sum\limits_{l=1}^{L-1} v_l^2 + (1 - v_L)^2} + \sqrt{\sum\limits_{l=2}^{L} v_l^2 + (1 - v_1)^2}} + (1 - \alpha)\left(-\sum\limits_{l=1}^{L} v_l \ln v_l\right) \\
\sum\limits_{l=1}^{L} \dfrac{L - l}{L - 1} v_l = \lambda, \ \sum\limits_{l=1}^{L} v_l = 1, v_l \in [0, 1], l = 1, 2, ..., L
\end{cases}
$$

(1)

In the following expression, Q_i represents all the existing measurements and M_i represents the user aggregation served by the network i. The reputation of the network E_i is calculated by the temporary credit value e_i.

$$
E_i(t) = \sum_{l=0}^{L} v(l) e_i(t - l), \ e_i(t) = \frac{Q_i(t)}{M_i(t)} = \frac{\sum\limits_{m \in M_i(t)} Q_{m,i}(t)}{M_i(t)}
$$

(2)

The distance of the user from the satellite and base station has a significant effect on the communication quality. The coverage of the network can be classified into a few regions with different radii. Each region has an Id and users are required to send their Id with the reports. Although the number of available networks remains the same, the evaluation reports needed for credit calculation is declined for a specific user. The complete expression of credit calculation is obtained by incorporating the space factor into Eq. 2.

$$
E_i^d(t) = \sum_{l=0}^{L} v(l) e_i^d(t - l) = \sum_{l=0}^{L} \frac{\sum\limits_{m \in M_i^d(t-l)} Q_{m,i}^d(t - l) v(l)}{M_i^d(t - l)}
$$

(3)

In summary, the time weight only serves as the weighting coefficient of the evaluation report, and has no effect on the calculation method of the report. Moreover, the location of the user can be sent along with the measurement report without affecting each other. In addition to retaining the superiority of the traditional credit method, the HD-TSR algorithm also enhances the computational efficiency and accuracy. Considering that all networks are respectively separated into R regions, each user's report eventually influences the handover results of the other users in the same region. As a result, the time complexity tc of the scale of n users can be expressed as follows.

$$tc = n * \frac{n}{R} = o(n^2) \tag{4}$$

3.2 Early Access Strategy and Handover Scheme Design

Vertical handover can be classified into two types: downlink and uplink. In downlink handover, the random access process causes a low transmission delay. Thus, retaining the original handover implementation mechanism is acceptable. In uplink handover, satellites exhibit high transmission delay. Therefore, it is necessary to adopt a corresponding strategy to shorten the interruption time. If the satellite and ground network are synchronous, the terminal can get synchronized with the satellite before the access process by calculating the time difference between the two networks relative to its own location [33]. However, if the ground network and satellite are asynchronous, the early access strategy to optimize the uplink vertical switching procedure is proposed, as shown in Fig. 1.

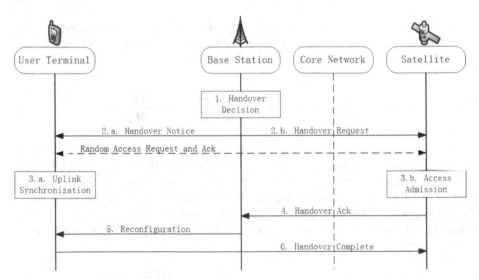

Fig. 1. Protocol process of the uplink vertical handover based on the early access strategy.

Based on the credits received by the base station, it triggers the vertical handover process when better choices are available for the user. Subsequently, the user terminal uses up an idle time slot to make a random access request to its target in advance. Because the random access process is initiated before the redistribution command, it is conducted concurrently with steps 2 and 3. After synchronizing to the target network, the terminal waits for a random access response message within a specific time window. After receiving the message or at the end of the time window, the terminal resumes the connection with the original base station, waiting for reconfiguration instructions. If the random access process is completed in advance, the target network is directly connected after the arrival of the reconfiguration command. If the redistribution command arrives first, the user needs to wait for the random access acknowledgement, and then connects to the target network to complete the process.

4   Simulation and Analysis

Although all users have the ability to send measurement reports, only the target user is focused on while switching. The network parameters listed in Table 1 were used in the Starlink [34] satellite model to perform the simulation.

Table 1. Simulation parameters.

Parameter	Value
User uplink and downlink band (GHz)	2.3–2.35
Antenna power (dBm)	32
Channel bandwidth (MHz)	20
Antenna height (m)	1–50

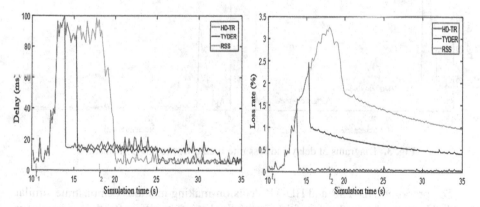

Fig. 2. Diagrams of delay and loss rate.

Initially, the target user connects with the ground base station and moves randomly under its coverage. The coverage of the satellite is divided into three areas based on the distance to the sub-satellite point. In this study, the classic RSS handover algorithm and traffic type-based differentiated reputation (TYDER) method were used as the contrast object. When compared with the HD-TSR decision method that ignores the space attribute (HD-TR), the simulation results are as follows, as shown in Fig. 2. The delay and loss rate are determined to represent the states of the network that the target user accesses.

At time point $t1$, there is an increase in the number of users and services connected to the ground network. Because the classic RSS algorithm only considers the signal strength, it does not trigger the vertical handover. Consequently, several business indicators worsen and an increasing amount of data is lost due to congestion. The TYDER method considers the business indicator. Therefore, the ground network credit gradually reduces and becomes lower than that of a satellite until the simulation time of 15.5 s. The HD-TR method considers the instantaneity of user evaluations. Consequently, the ground network reputation significantly declines with the update of the time-weighted credit. Then the target user switches to a satellite at 13.5 s and the QoS indicators recover. At point $t2$, there exists a decrease in the user scale and business volume. In the RSS algorithm, the business indicators immediately rise and return to normal at 20 s, primarily owing to the continuous connection with the base station. Meanwhile, the TYDER method accumulates a large amount of historical data and becomes insensitive to new information. Until the simulation time of 32 s, the credit of the base station eventually exceeds that of a satellite. However, the HD-TR decision method achieves a rapid reputation update. It switches back to the base station at 25 s and the states return to the initial level. The simulation results after considering the space factor are as follows, as shown in Fig. 3.

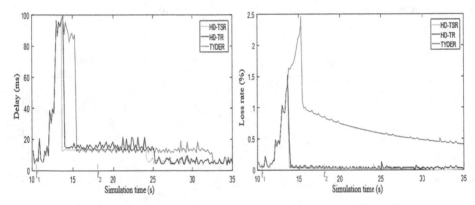

Fig. 3. Diagrams of delay and loss rate including the HD-TSR method.

The proposed HD-TSR and HD-TR decision-making methods demonstrate similar trends. However, the amplitudes of the longitudinal axis data differ after the key handover time point. The HD-TSR method improves the precision of credit calculation. Thus, the user may choose another satellite with the highest credit relative to its location. It is evident that the delay and packet loss rate are lowest when the HD-TSR method is adopted.

In another scenario, the regions of satellite coverage are named as the center, transition, and edge. In each region, the target user initiates uplink vertical handover at random positions. The simulation results are shown below, as shown in Fig. 4.

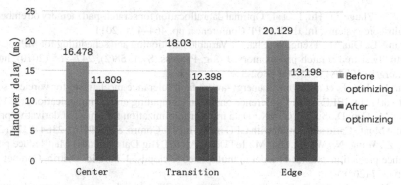

Fig. 4. Statistics of the handover delay in different regions.

As shown in Fig. 4, the interruption time of the switching is significantly different when the target user is in different regions of satellite coverage. As the distance from the sub-satellite point increases, the handover delay also increases, which is caused by the increase in propagation delay. When the target user adopts the optimized upstream vertical switching strategy, the synchronization process is completed in advance, which avoids transmission in user links. As a result, the service interruption time can be reduced. The further away the user is from the sub-satellite point, the more obvious the optimization effect of the handover delay is, with a maximum reduction of more than 34%.

5 Conclusion

This study proposed a handover decision method based on space and time factors and optimized the uplink vertical handover scheme for a specific satellite-ground fusion network architecture. The simulation results indicated that the proposed HD-TSR decision method exhibited the best response to network states and had the best QoS indicators. Moreover, the early access strategy significantly shortened the service handover delay by 34%.

Acknowledgement. This work was funded by the 54th Research Institute of China Electronics Technology Group Corporation in "The Manned Space Advanced Research Project under Grant [060501]" and "The Civil Aerospace Technology Advance Research Project under Grant [B0105]."

References

1. Zhao, H., Chen, M., et al.: A novel pre-cache schema for high performance Android system. Futur. Gener. Comput. Syst. **56**, 766–772 (2016)
2. Qiu, L., Gai, K., Qiu, M.: Optimal big data sharing approach for tele-health in cloud computing. In: IEEE SmartCloud, pp. 184–189 (2016)
3. Qiu, M., Khisamutdinov, E., et al.: RNA nanotechnology for computer design and in vivo computation. Philos. Trans. R. Soc. A **371**, 20120310 (2013)

4. Guo, Y., Zhuge, Q., Hu, J., et al.: Optimal data allocation for scratch-pad memory on embedded multi-core systems. In: IEEE ICPP Conference, pp. 464–471 (2011)
5. Zhang, L., Qiu, M., Tseng, W., Sha, E.: Variable partitioning and scheduling for MPSoC with virtually shared scratch pad memory. J. Sig. Process. Syst. **58**(2), 247–265 (2010). https://doi.org/10.1007/s11265-009-0362-3
6. Qiu, M., Liu, J., et al.: A novel energy-aware fault tolerance mechanism for wireless sensor networks. In: IEEE/ACM Conference on Green Computing and Communications (2011)
7. Qiu, M., Cao, D., Su, H., Gai, K.: Data transfer minimization for financial derivative pricing using Monte Carlo simulation with GPU in 5G. Int'l J. Comm. Sys. **29**(16), 2364–2374 (2016)
8. Lu, Z., Wang, N., Wu, J., Qiu, M.: IoTDeM: An IoT Big Data-oriented MapReduce performance prediction extended model in multiple edge clouds. J. Parallel Distrib. Comput. **118**, 316–327 (2018)
9. Qiu, H., Qiu, M., Lu, Z.: Selective encryption on ECG data in body sensor network based on supervised machine learning. Inf. Fusion **55**, 59–67 (2020)
10. Qiu, M., Chen, Z., Liu, M.: Low-power low-latency data allocation for hybrid scratch-pad memory. IEEE Embed. Syst. Lett. **6**(4), 69–72 (2014)
11. Gao, Y., Iqbal, S., et al.: Performance and power analysis of high-density multi-GPGPU architectures: a preliminary case study. In: IEEE 17th HPCC (2015)
12. Qiu, M., Xue, C., Shao, Z., Sha, E.: Energy minimization with soft real-time and DVS for uniprocessor and multiprocessor embedded systems. In: IEEE DATE Conference, pp. 1–6 (2007)
13. Gai, K., Qiu, M., Elnagdy, S.: A novel secure big data cyber incident analytics framework for cloud-based cybersecurity insurance. In: IEEE BigDataSecurity (2016)
14. Thakur, K., Qiu, M., Gai, K., Ali, M.: An investigation on cyber security threats and security models. In: IEEE CSCloud (2015)
15. Gai, K., Qiu, M., Sun, X., Zhao, H.: Security and privacy issues: a survey on FinTech. In: Qiu, M. (ed.) SmartCom 2016. LNCS, vol. 10135, pp. 236–247. Springer, Cham (2017). https://doi.org/10.1007/978-3-319-52015-5_24
16. Giambene, G., Kota, S., Pillai, P.: Satellite-5G integration: a network perspective. IEEE Network **32**(5), 25–31 (2018)
17. Zhang, Z., Wu, J., et al.: Jamming ACK attack to wireless networks and a mitigation approach. In: IEEE GLOBECOM Conference, pp. 1–5 (2008)
18. Qiu, H., Qiu, M., Memmi, G., Ming, Z., Liu, M.: A dynamic scalable blockchain based communication architecture for IoT. In: SmartBlock, pp. 159–166 (2018)
19. Lu, R., Jin, X., Zhang, S., Qiu, M., Wu, X.: A study on big knowledge and its engineering issues. IEEE Trans. Knowl. Data Eng. **31**(9), 1630–1644 (2018)
20. Liu, M., Zhang, S., et al.: H infinite state estimation for discrete-time chaotic systems based on a unified model. IEEE Trans. Syst. Man, Cybern. (B) (2012)
21. Desogus, C., Anedda, M., Murroni, M., et al.: A traffic type-based differentiated reputation algorithm for radio resource allocation during multi-service content delivery in 5G heterogeneous scenarios. IEEE Access **7**, 27720–27735 (2019)
22. 3GPP. Study on New Radio (NR) to support non-terrestrial networks[S]. 2019
23. Ahuja, K., Singh, B., Khanna, R.: Network selection algorithm based on link quality parameters for heterogeneous wireless networks. Optik **125**(14), 3657–3662 (2014)
24. Rahman, M.A., Salih, Q.M., Asyhari, A.T., et al.: Traveling distance estimation to mitigate unnecessary handoff in mobile wireless networks. Ann. Telecommun. **74**(11), 717–726 (2019)
25. Lahby, M., Attioui, A., Sekkaki, A.: An improved policy for network selection decision based on enhanced-topsis and utility function. In: 2017 13th International Wireless Communications and Mobile Computing Conference (IWCMC), pp. 2175–2180. IEEE (2017)
26. Zhu, Y., Li, J., Huang, Q., et al.: Game theoretic approach for network access control in heterogeneous networks. IEEE Trans. Veh. Technol. **67**(10), 9856–9866 (2018)

27. Bi, T., Zou, L., Chen, S., et al.: RA3D: reputation-based adaptive 3D video delivery in heterogeneous wireless networks. In: 2019 International Conference on High Performance Computing and Simulation (HPCS), pp. 48–54. IEEE (2019)
28. Radouche, S., Leghris, C., Adib, A.: MADM methods based on utility function and reputation for access network selection in a multi-access mobile network environment. In: 2017 International Conference on Wireless Networks and Mobile Communications (WINCOM), pp. 1–6. IEEE (2017)
29. Goyal, R.K., Kaushal, S.: Network selection using AHP for fast moving vehicles in heterogeneous networks. In: Chaki, R., Cortesi, A., Saeed, K., Chaki, N. (eds.) Advanced Computing and Systems for Security. AISC, vol. 395, pp. 235–243. Springer, New Delhi (2016). https://doi.org/10.1007/978-81-322-2650-5_15
30. Goutam, S., Unnikrishnan, S., Karandikar, A.: Algorithm for handover decision based on TOPSIS. In: 2020 International Conference on UK-China Emerging Technologies (UCET), pp. 1–4. IEEE (2020)
31. Jiang, D., Huo, L., Lv, Z., et al.: A joint multi-criteria utility-based network selection approach for vehicle-to-infrastructure networking. IEEE Trans. Intell. Transp. Syst. **19**(10), 3305–3319 (2018)
32. Yang, Z., Li, J., Huang, L., et al.: Developing dynamic intuitionistic normal fuzzy aggregation operators for multi-attribute decision-making with time sequence preference. Ex-pert Syst. Appl. **82**, 344–356 (2017)
33. Li, K., Li, Y., Qiu, Z., et al.: Handover procedure design and performance optimization strategy in leo-hap system. In: 2019 11th International Conference on Wireless Communications and Signal Processing (WCSP), pp. 1–7. IEEE (2019)
34. Cakaj, S.: The parameters comparison of the "Starlink" LEO satellites constellation for different orbital shells. Front. Commun. Networks (2021)

Research on Graph Structure Data Adversarial Examples Based on Graph Theory Metrics

Wenyong He[1], Mingming Lu[1(✉)], Yiji Zheng[1], and Neal N. Xiong[2]

[1] School of Computer Science and Engineering, Central South University,
Changsha 410083, Hunan, China
mingminglu@csu.edu.cn
[2] Department of Computer Science and Mathematics, Sul Ross State University,
Alpine, USA

Abstract. Graph neural networks can learn graph structure data directly and mine its information, which can be used in drug research and development, financial fraud prevention, and other fields. The existing research shows that the graph neural network is lacking robustness and is vulnerable to attack by adversarial examples. At present, there are two problems in the generation of confrontation examples for graph neural networks. One is that the properties of graph structure are not fully used to describe the antagonistic examples, the other is that the gradient calculation is linked with the loss function and not directly linked with the properties of graph structure, which leads to excessive search space. To solve these two problems, this paper proposes a graph structure data confrontation example generation scheme based on graph theory measurement. In this paper, the average distance and clustering coefficient is used as the basis for each step of disturbance, and the counterexamples are generated under the premise of keeping the data characteristics. Experimental results on small-world networks and random graphs show that, compared with the previous methods, the proposed method makes full use of the nature of graph structure, does not need complex derivation, and takes less time to generate confrontation examples, which can meet the needs of iterative development.

Keywords: Adversarial examples · Graph convolutional network · Graph theory metrics

1 Introduction

The graph structure data is filled of our life, such as citation network data, autonomous systems structure data, road networks data, and so on. Especially, the wireless network is a natural graph structure data, While classical deep learning models (e.g., Convolutional Neural Networks(CNN) [1] and Recurrent Neural Networks(RNN) [2]) cannot directly use the graph structure data as

M. Qiu et al. (Eds.): SmartCom 2021, LNCS 13202, pp. 394–403, 2022.
https://doi.org/10.1007/978-3-030-97774-0_36

input. However, Graph Neural Networks(GNN) [3] can take graph structure data as input and can efficiently extract their features. In addition, GNN have been widely used in areas such as traffic flow prediction [4,5], recommender systems [6], and financial fraud prevention [7].

Recent studies have shown that deep learning models are extremely vulnerable to attacks. The attacker misclassifies the model by making small changes to the data, and the misclassified data are called adversarial samples. Through generating the adversarial samples to find model weaknesses, and further improving model robustness has become an important- research direction. The study of adversarial samples originated in the field of computer vision. In generally, it is easy to obtain an adversarial sample by updating each pixel in the input image with the opposite direction. The adversarial samples can be used as the training set to continue training the CNN, so that the classification accuracy of the model for the adversarial samples is improved, i.e., adversarial training. Adversarial training improves the robustness of the neural network and is equivalent to performing regularization [8]. In the image domain, it is common practice to use matrix parametrization to measure the perturbation size.

However, compared to regularized image data, the more general graph structure data is non-Euclidean data. It contains extremely rich information, and using only matrix parametric as a measure of perturbation size is not sufficient. Besides, Node degree distribution, inter-node accessibility, and clustering are three typical geometric properties of graph-structured data [9], which are three fundamental properties and properties of the structural statistical properties of graph data [10,11]. It is not sufficient to consider only the node degree distribution as a judgment of the perturbation size generated by adversarial samples to graph-structured data. Therefore, in this paper, we propose to use the mean distance and clustering coefficient, which are well established in graph theory, to measure the perturbation size and generate adversarial samples based on these two metrics.

2   Related Work

A lot of works [12–23] in wireless Network does not consider this feature, thus it limits the overall performance. Goodfellow et al. [24] proposed a gradient-based adversarial sample generation method Fast Gradient Sign Method (abbreviated as FGSM uses an infinite number of parameters to measure the size of the perturbation, while Papernot et al. [25] use 0-parameters to measure the size of the perturbation instead. Baluja [26] introduces the idea of adversarial learning to design a feedforward neural network to generate adversarial samples. Moosavi-Dezfooli [27] finds that adversarial samples are constructed specifically for a particular model (e.g., deep residual networks) and that specially constructed adversarial samples are portable and can work by attacking other models.

Compared with image data, the adversarial samples for generating graph-structured data have special characteristics, namely, how to reasonably measure the size of the applied perturbation and the structure of the graph is discrete. To address these two difficulties, Zugner [28] proposed that the adversarial samples obtained by adding/removing a small number of edges to the original data should have a nodal degree distribution close to that of the original data. The likelihood function is used as the basis to generate the adversarial samples, and the operation of adding/removing edges is discrete. To mine deeper information in the data, Bojchevski [29] uses DeepWalk [30] to select nodes and edges, and the selection process yields an approximate solution by singular value decomposition, which is equivalent to limiting the Frobenius norm value of the perturbation. Gaitonde [31] and Tran [32] argue that the perturbation changes the spectrum corresponding to the graph structure data, so the spectrum The inter-spectral difference value can be used to measure the magnitude of the perturbation.

Dai [33] treated the applied perturbation as a Markov Decision Process (MDP) and used reinforcement learning to learn the process and stop when the number of added and deleted edges reached a threshold. Tang et al. [34] used the attention coefficient to calculate the contribution of edges to the classification performance of the model. Related schemes also include self-coding graph structures [35] and doing graph embedding based on genetic algorithms [36]. However, the above-mentioned works do not fully utilize the graph structure-property, and the use of gradient methods cannot be directly linked to the graph property, which is prone to the problem of excessive search space.

In order to solve the above problems, this paper starts from the inherent nature of graphs, and in each step of applying perturbation, nodes and edges are first selected based on the average distance and clustering coefficients, and perturbation is applied on this basis until the changes of the two measures reach a threshold value, and then the perturbed data are taken out to verify whether they are adversarial samples. Therefore, the scheme in this paper is more relevant in the graph structure data scenario and makes full use of the nature of the graph structure data itself, which is conducive to the fast convergence of the training process.

3   Method

3.1   Adversarial Sample Generation Scheme

Overall Process. This paper uses two basic graph-theoretic measures, namely, clustering coefficient and mean distance, instead of gradient information as the basis for applying perturbation. Thus, the applied perturbation can be linked to the properties of the graph structure data and the graph structure properties can be fully utilized. The adversarial sample generation scheme can be the following:

(1) Pre-training GCN models to a high level of accuracy, which can ensure that the attack is meaningful.
(2) Calculating two graph-theoretic measures of the original data: the values of the average distance and the clustering coefficients, which are utilized to determine the perturbation threshold.

(3) Inputting the perturbed data into the pre-trained model to perform node-classification test. If the model is incorrect, the attack is successful and the perturbed data is a qualified adversarial sample.

3.2 The Calculation of Graph Theory Metrics

This paper calculates the average distance and the clustering coefficient to determine the threshold of perturbation.

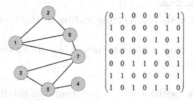

Fig. 1. The graph structure data (left) and the corresponding adjacency matrix (right).

Firstly, We can calculate the average distance by finding the shortest distance value between pairs of nodes in the graph using Dijkstra's algorithm. Figure 1 shows the diagram of graph structure data, and the corresponding adjacency matrix. Dijkstra's algorithm starts from any node i and searches for the value of row i of the adjacency matrix. Thus it stores the position of the element with value 1 in the dictionary, Dic, and marking node i as searched. Then we iterate the dictionary Dic and search for the new directly reachable node. If the new reachable node has already been searched and the path is shorter, update the position in the dictionary Dic. This iterates until all nodes in the graph are labeled.

3.3 Impose Disturbance

Again, the graph structure data in the left panel of Fig. 1 is used as an example to illustrate the calculation of clustering coefficients. The neighboring nodes of node 1 are node 2/node 6/node 7, and there are 2 edges inside the set of nodes composed of these three nodes: 2–6, 6–7. The total number of possible edges of these three nodes is $C(3,2) = 3$, so the clustering coefficient of node 1 is 2/3. Obviously, the clustering coefficient is less than or equal to 1, and the closer a node is to 1, the stronger the clustering of nodes around that node. The clustering coefficient of the graph is the average of the clustering coefficients of all nodes, and the closer it is to 1, the stronger the mutual clustering of the nodes in the graph structure.

The formal formulation of the perturbation that makes the average distance smaller is shown in Algorithm 1, and the perturbation that makes the average

---

Algorithm 1. Average distance perturbation

1: Input: the range of perturbation G_s, Adjacency matrix $A_S \in \{0,1\}^{n*n}$, n is the number of nodes in the perturbation range, m is the number of nodes in the rest of the original map.

2: Input: G_s shortest distance matrix M_s, its constituent elements are the shortest distance between node pairs Shortest distance matrix, $\bar{L}_s$ is the average distance of G_s, $\overline{L'_s}$ is the average distance of G_s after each round of perturbation, the initial value $\bar{L}_s{}' = \bar{L}_s$.

3: Input: threshold Δ, the number of edges added per perturbation ζ, Average distance from the original map $\bar{L}$.

4: **while** $\frac{n^2-n}{(m+n)(m+n-1)} \frac{\overline{L_s}-\overline{L_s}'}{L} < \Delta$ **do**

5:    Find and record the node pair corresponding to the first ζ large elements of M_s.

6:    Set the corresponding position elements of the above node pairs to 1 collectively in A_S, update $G_s, M_s, \bar{L}_s{}'$.

7: **end while**

8: Collectively set 0 in the position of the last round of setting 1 in step 6 in A_S, and update G_s, M_s, $\bar{L}_s{}'$.

9: Output: A_S, M_S, $\bar{L}_S{}'$.

---

distance larger can be followed in this way. The perturbation that makes the clustering coefficient smaller can be formally formulated as Algorithm 2, while the perturbation that makes the clustering coefficient larger can be formulated in the same way.

Algorithm 2. Clustering coefficient perturbation

1: Input: the range of perturbation G_s, Adjacency matrix $A_S \in \{0,1\}^{n*n}$, n is the number of nodes, m is the number of nodes in the rest of the original map.

2: Input: G_S Clustering coefficient vector $C_s \in R^{n*1}$, its component elements are the clustering coefficients of the nodes, G_S Clustering coefficient $\bar{C}_s$, $\bar{C}'_s$ is the clustering coefficient of G_s after each round of perturbation, the initial value $\bar{C}_s{}' = \bar{C}_s$.

3: Input: threshold Δ, the number of points deleted per perturbation ζ, the clustering coefficient of original map $\bar{L}$.

4: **while** $\frac{n}{n+m} \frac{\overline{C_s}-\overline{C_s}'}{\bar{c}} < \Delta$ **do**

5:    sorting the nodes corresponding to G_s, finding and recording the nodes corresponding to the top ζ large clustering coefficients.

6:    delete the above node from the row in A_s, update $G_s, C_s, \bar{C}'_s$.

7: **end while**

8: Restoring the last deleted row in step 6 in A_S, update $G_s, C_s, \bar{C}'_s$.

9: Output: A_S, C_S, $\bar{C}_S{}'$.

---

4 Result

4.1 The Overview of Experimental Data

We conduct experiments with five datasets, which are named Cora, Citeseer, Polblogs, Synthie, and Synthetic. This paper limits the disturbance range to the node-set composed of neighbor nodes within 3 hops of each node. To ensure that the disturbance space is large enough, the number of nodes included in the disturbance range accounts for more than 1% of the total number of nodes in the original graph. At the same time, to eliminate the error interference of the dataset itself, this paper randomly selects 500 different nodes in the same dataset as the nodes to be attacked. On this basis, using them as the central node to delimit the perturbation range and then impose perturbation, 500 pieces of perturbed data can be obtained. Among them, the data that makes the GCN node classification model misjudge is a qualified adversarial sample. Table 1 is an overview of some randomly selected node information in different datasets.

Table 1. The examples of node information for each dataset

Dataset	Sequence number	Perturbation node counts	Perturbation proportion	Category
Cora	88	231	8.5%	Rule Learning
Citeseer	37	380	8.0%	AI
Polblogs	39	275	1.4%	Liberal
Synthie	176	1698	1.1%	Class 2
Synthetic	701	1403	1.2%	Class 3

4.2 The Analysis of Attack Effect

The Effectiveness of Analysis of Small Datasets. Node 88 in the Cora dataset, which was selected as the attacked node, is used as an example for the illustration of perturbation. This node belongs to Class 2 (Rule Learning). As shown in the left panel of Fig. 2, the probability of classifying this node to the correct class using the pre-trained GCN (shown in the yellow column) is 93%. Since this value is already greater than the probability value that the GCN considers the node to belong to other classes, the GCN classification result is correct. Figure 2 on the right shows the result of using GCN to classify this node after getting the data after applying a mean distance perturbation with a threshold Δ of 2%. The probability of deciding that this node belongs to the correct Class 2 is 20%, which is less than the probability of being classified as Class 4, 38%, so the GCN produces a misclassification and the data is an adversarial sample, and the method of this paper is successfully attacked.

The left panel of Fig. 3 is consistent with the left panel of Fig. 2, it also shows the probability value of the pre-trained model to classify this node. The right panel of Fig. 3 represents the results of the data obtained after applying

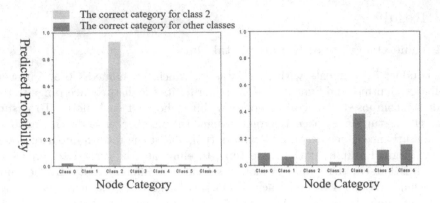

Fig. 2. Node classification average distance results in Cora dataset.

a perturbation of the clustering coefficient with a threshold Δ of 2% to classify this node using GCN. The probability of determining that the node belongs to the correct Class 2 is 10%, which is less than the probability of classifying it as Class 1, 43%. Therefore, the GCN determines that the node belongs to Class 1, the model produces a misjudgment, the data is an adversarial sample, and the attack of this paper's method is successful.

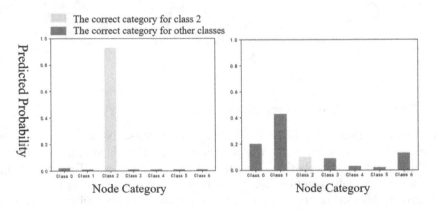

Fig. 3. Node classification clustering coefficient results in Cora dataset.

The time spent on generating adversarial samples includes the sum of the time spent on calculating the graph theory metric, applying perturbations, and testing the data to make the model misspecify respectively, and the less time spent, the less computational cost required. Therefore, this paper counts the average time spent on generating adversarial samples as an important index to consider the adversarial sample generation scheme. For the small-world network dataset, this paper uses them as the original data to generate perturbation samples, and summarizes the relevant parameter settings and experimental results as shown in Tables 2. The scale of the perturbation range of the Polblogs dataset is small in the original graph, so only two graph-theoretic metric perturbations with a threshold of 1% are imposed.

Table 2. The result of adversarial samples attack in three datasets.

Dataset	Configurations	Adversarial sample proportion	Average generation time
Cora	Average distance perturbation $\Delta = 1\%/2\%$	41.2%/79.0%	20.2 s/42.0 s
	Clustering coefficient perturbation $\Delta = 1\%/2\%$	40.8%/80.8%	27.1 s/43.1 s
	Power-law distribution perturbation $\epsilon = 0.04$	79.4%	45.3 s
	RL-S2V	82.6%	51.2 s
Citeseer	Average distance perturbation $\Delta = 1\%/2\%$	35.2%/75.0%	24.8 s/41.3 s
	Clustering coefficient perturbation $\Delta = 1\%/2\%$	36.8%/77.2%	23.4 s/41.4 s
	Power-law distribution perturbation $\epsilon = 0.04$	75.6%	50.3 s
	RL-S2V	79.2%	55.0 s
Polblogs	Average distance perturbation $\Delta = 1\%$	41.0%	53.5 s
	Clustering coefficient perturbation $\Delta = 1\%$	40.4%	50.4 s
	Power-law distribution perturbation $\epsilon = 0.04$	60.8%	70.5 s
	RL-S2V	63.2%	60.2 s

Cora et al.'s three citation network datasets belong to small-world networks [37], for which the adversarial sample scheme proposed in this paper attacks the GCN model successfully. Except for the Polblogs dataset, this paper obtains an approximate attack effect with less time cost than previous methods. With the same threshold value, the clustering coefficient perturbation generates a larger proportion of adversarial samples and takes a long time on average than the average distance perturbation on the Cora dataset. Therefore, the adversarial sample generation method proposed in this paper has advantages in practical attack and defense scenarios, such as face recognition and biometric fingerprint generation, and can quickly obtain adversarial samples to advance subsequent research work.

5   Conclusion

In this paper, we use the average distance and the clustering coefficient as the basis for selecting perturbation locations to generate adversarial samples. (2) The time consumption of this paper's scheme to generate adversarial samples in those datasets are less than previous methods. On the premise of guaranteeing the success of the attack model, the adversarial sample generation scheme in this paper takes less time and shows its advantages in fast attack and defense scenarios, which has better prospects for promotion.

References

1. O'Shea, K., Nash, R.: An introduction to convolutional neural networks. arXiv preprint arXiv:1511.08458 (2015)
2. Lipton, Z.C., Berkowitz, J., Elkan, C.: A critical review of recurrent neural networks for sequence learning. arXiv preprint arXiv:1506.00019 (2015)
3. Wu, Z., Pan, S., Chen, F., Long, G., Zhang, C., Philip, S.Y.: A comprehensive survey on graph neural networks. IEEE Trans. Neural Netw. Learn. Syst. **32**(1), 4–24 (2020)
4. Yu, B., Yin, H., Zhu, Z.: Spatio-temporal graph convolutional networks: a deep learning framework for traffic forecasting. arXiv preprint arXiv:1709.04875 (2017)
5. Li, H., Liu, J., Wu, K., Yang, Z., Liu, R.W., Xiong, N.: Spatio-temporal vessel trajectory clustering based on data mapping and density. IEEE Access **6**, 58939–58954 (2018)
6. He, R., Xiong, N., Yang, L.T., Park, J.H.: Using multi-modal semantic association rules to fuse keywords and visual features automatically for web image retrieval. Inf. Fusion **12**(3), 223–230 (2011)
7. Weber, M., et al.: Anti-money laundering in bitcoin: Experimenting with graph convolutional networks for financial forensics. arXiv preprint arXiv:1908.02591 (2019)
8. Shaham, U., Yamada, Y., Negahban, S.: Understanding adversarial training: Increasing local stability of neural nets through robust optimization. arXiv preprint arXiv:1511.05432 (2015)
9. Di, Z., Wu, J.: Complex network research from statistical physics. PhD thesis (2004)
10. Wang, G.C.X., Li, X.: Complex Network Theory and Its Applications. Tsinghua University Press Co., Ltd., Beijing (2006)
11. Guangrong, C., Xiaofan, W., Li, X.: Introduction to Network Science, vol. 6. Higher Education Press, Beijing (2012)
12. Wang, Z., Li, T., Xiong, N., Pan, Y.: A novel dynamic network data replication scheme based on historical access record and proactive deletion. J. Supercomput. **62**(1), 227–250 (2012)
13. Guo, W., Xiong, N., Vasilakos, A.V., Chen, G., Cheng, H.: Multi-source temporal data aggregation in wireless sensor networks. Wirel. Pers. Commun. **56**(3), 359–370 (2011)
14. Yao, Y., Xiong, N., Park, J.H., Ma, L., Liu, J.: Privacy-preserving max/min query in two-tiered wireless sensor networks. Comput. Math. Appl. **65**(9), 1318–1325 (2013)
15. Zhang, Q., Zhou, C., Tian, Y.-C., Xiong, N., Qin, Y., Bowen, H.: A fuzzy probability bayesian network approach for dynamic cybersecurity risk assessment in industrial control systems. IEEE Trans. Ind. Inf. **14**(6), 2497–2506 (2017)
16. Mou, W., Tan, L., Xiong, N.: A structure fidelity approach for big data collection in wireless sensor networks. Sensors **15**(1), 248–273 (2015)
17. Huang, S., Liu, A., Zhang, S., Wang, T., Xiong, N.N.: BD-VTE: a novel baseline data based verifiable trust evaluation scheme for smart network systems. IEEE Trans. Netw. Sci. Eng. (2020)
18. Yin, J., Lo, W., Deng, S., Li, Y., Zhaohui, W., Xiong, N.: Colbar: a collaborative location-based regularization framework for qos prediction. Inf. Sci. **265**, 68–84 (2014)

19. Wan, Z., Xiong, N., Ghani, N., Vasilakos, A.V., Zhou, L.: Adaptive unequal protection for wireless video transmission over ieee 802.11 e networks. Multimed. Tools Appl. **72**(1), 541–571 (2014)
20. Qu, Y., Xiong, N.: RFH: a resilient, fault-tolerant and high-efficient replication algorithm for distributed cloud storage. In: 2012 41st International Conference on Parallel Processing, pp. 520–529. IEEE (2012)
21. Gai, K., Qiu, M.: Reinforcement learning-based content-centric services in mobile sensing. IEEE Netw. **32**(4), 34–39 (2018)
22. Gai, K., Qiu, M.: Optimal resource allocation using reinforcement learning for iot content-centric services. Appl. Soft Comput. **70**, 12–21 (2018)
23. Gai, K., Qiu, M., Zhao, H., Sun, X.: Resource management in sustainable cyber-physical systems using heterogeneous cloud computing. IEEE Trans. Sustain. Comput. **3**(2), 60–72 (2017)
24. Goodfellow, I.J., Shlens, J., Szegedy, C.: Explaining and harnessing adversarial examples. arXiv preprint arXiv:1412.6572 (2014)
25. Papernot, N., McDaniel, P., Jha, S., Fredrikson, M., Celik, Z.B., Swami, A.: The limitations of deep learning in adversarial settings. In: 2016 IEEE European Symposium on Security and Privacy (EuroS&P), pp. 372–387. IEEE (2016)
26. Baluja, S., Fischer, I.: Adversarial transformation networks: Learning to generate adversarial examples. arXiv preprint arXiv:1703.09387 (2017)
27. Moosavi-Dezfooli, S.M., Fawzi, A., Frossard, P.: Deepfool: a simple and accurate method to fool deep neural networks. In: Proceedings of the IEEE Conference on Computer Vision and Pattern Recognition, pp. 2574–2582 (2016)
28. Zügner, D., Akbarnejad, A., Günnemann, S.: Adversarial attacks on neural networks for graph data. In: Proceedings of the 24th ACM SIGKDD International Conference on Knowledge Discovery & Data Mining, pp. 2847–2856 (2018)
29. Bojchevski, A., Günnemann, S.: Adversarial attacks on node embeddings via graph poisoning. In: International Conference on Machine Learning, pp. 695–704. PMLR (2019)
30. Perozzi, B., Al-Rfou, R., Skiena, S.: Deepwalk: online learning of social representations. In: Proceedings of the 20th ACM SIGKDD International Conference on Knowledge Discovery and Data Mining, pp. 701–710 (2014)
31. Gaitonde, J., Kleinberg, J., Tardos, E.: Adversarial perturbations of opinion dynamics in networks. In: Proceedings of the 21st ACM Conference on Economics and Computation, pp. 471–472 (2020)
32. Dai, H., et al.: Adversarial attack on graph structured data. In: International Conference on Machine Learning, pp. 1115–1124. PMLR (2018)
33. Sun, M., et al.: Data poisoning attack against unsupervised node embedding methods. arXiv preprint arXiv:1810.12881 (2018)
34. Chen, J., Shi, Z., Wu, Y., Xu, X., Zheng, H.: Link prediction adversarial attack. arXiv preprint arXiv:1810.01110 (2018)
35. Yu, S., Zheng, J., Chen, J., Xuan, Q., Zhang, Q.: Unsupervised euclidean distance attack on network embedding. In: 2020 IEEE Fifth International Conference on Data Science in Cyberspace (DSC), pp. 71–77. IEEE (2020)
36. Hamilton, W., Ying, Z., Leskovec, J.: Inductive representation learning on large graphs. Adv. Neural Inf. Process. Syst. **30** (2017)
37. Kleinberg, J.: The small-world phenomenon: an algorithmic perspective. In: Proceedings of the Thirty-Second Annual ACM Symposium on Theory of Computing, pp. 163–170 (2000)

Computation Offloading and Resource Allocation Based on Multi-agent Federated Learning

Yiming Yao[1], Tao Ren[1(⊠)], Yuan Qiu[2], Zheyuan Hu[2], and Yanqi Li[1]

[1] Hangzhou Innovation Institute, Beihang University, Hangzhou 310051, China
taotao_1982@126.com
[2] Beihang University, Beijing 110191, China
huzheyuan18@buaa.edu.cn

Abstract. Mobile edge computing has been provisioned as a promising paradigm to provide *User Equipment* (UE) with powerful computing capabilities while maintaining low task latency, by offloading computing tasks from UE to the *Edge Server* (ES) deployed in the edge of networks. Due to ESs' limited computing resources, dynamic network conditions and various UEs task requirements, computation offloading should be carefully designed, so that satisfactory task performances and low UE energy consumption can both be achieved. Since the scheduling objective function and constraints are typically non-linear, the scheduling of computation offloading is generally NP-hard and difficult to obtain optimal solutions. To address the issue, this paper combines deep learning and reinforcement learning, namely deep reinforcement learning, to approximate the computation offloading policy using neural networks and without the need of labeling data. In addition, we integrate *Multi-agent Deep Deterministic Policy Gradient* (MADDPG) with the federated learning algorithm to improve the generalization performance of the trained neural network model. According to our simulation results, the proposed approach can converge within 10 thousand steps, which is equivalent to the method based on MADDPG. In addition, the proposed approach can obtain lower cost and better QoS performance than the approach based only on MADDPG.

Keywords: Deep reinforcement learning · Multi-agent deep deterministic policy gradient · Federated learning · Mobile edge computing

1 Introduction

Mobile Edge Computing (MEC) [1,2] already showed great potential in future development due to the fast advance in computer [3,4] and network technologies [5,6]. It can greatly improve QoS and reducing latency by offloading some computation-intensive jobs to a nearby *Access Point* (AP) integrated with a

M. Qiu et al. (Eds.): SmartCom 2021, LNCS 13202, pp. 404–415, 2022.
https://doi.org/10.1007/978-3-030-97774-0_37

MEC server (MES) [7]. How to optimize the two key technologies–computation offloading and wireless resource allocations–has draw extensive interests of researchers [8].

Reinforcement Learning (RL) is concerned with how agents ought to take certain actions in an environment to maximize reward. The agents gets either rewards or penalties for the actions it performs. It selects the next action according to the feedbacks to increase the probability of receiving a positive reward [9]. *Markov Decision Processes* (MDP) decision making in discrete, stochastic situations, which involves actions [10]. It serves as a basic theoretical tool for reinforcement learning.

Researchers have proposed plenty of approaches about computational offloading and resource allocation in recent years. Someone designed a DQN algorithm for multiple base stations [11]. This paper proposed an optimization framework for offloading from a single mobile device to multiple edge devices. [12] Unfortunately, these approaches are poorly suited to multi-agent domains.

There are other studies that have focused on dynamic downlink power control for maximum rate sum in multi-user wireless cellular networks. A multi-agent DRL framework is proposed. [13] Wireless channels have been proposed for multiple user equipment (UE) to transfer the computation tasks to the MEC servers [14]. Qiu and Gai [15] proposed a novel wireless reinforcement learning approach. Also, MEC resource allocation optimization framework was proposed in [16]. These studies are helpful for computation offloading decision making in multi-user environments.

Multi-agent Deep Deterministic Policy Gradient (MADDPG) has been recognized as an effective solution in better offloading computation tasks and allocating resources in dynamic system. The MADDPG algorithm, an improvement of a *Deep Deterministic Policy Gradient* (DDPG), enables all agents to maximize the performance of a collaborative planning task. In MADDPG, each agent has a DDPG network, and each agent's critic network is given access to the observations and actions of all the agents. That is to say, we propose centralized training with *Distributed Execution* (CTDE). MADDPG optimize the set of strategies trained by each agent's DDPG network to improve the algorithm's stability.

Federated learning is a machine learning technique that trains an algorithm across multiple decentralized edge devices or servers. It enables multiple actors to build a common, robust machine learning model which can be updated in servers [17,18]. Since each agent has its reward function in MADDPG, we merged the reward functions.

In this paper, we aimed to explore the minimum cost of the computation offloading and resource allocation in the multi-agent MEC environment. Inspired by existing researches, we use MADDPG algorithm to achieve the goal. To avoid the possible over-fitting of the reward functions, we adopted the model merging mechanism of federated learning to improve the model performance. The main contributions of this work are as follows:

- By using model fusion of the federated learning, the trained models on each agent generate a new model, which is optimized via DDPG algorithm with experiment data from the experience pool.
- The proposed distributed algorithm is based on MADDPG, which optimizes the overall effect of strategies on all agents during evolution, improving the stability and robustness of the algorithm to fit the non-stationarity of the wireless environment.

The rest of this paper is organized as follows. Section 2 presents system models, which include models of MEC, task and computing. Section 3 presents the needs to optimize the computation offloading and resources allocation. In Sect. 4, we developed a MADDPG and federated learning algorithm to solve the issues related to Sect. 3. In Sect. 5, we obtained simulation results to evaluate the performance of the proposed algorithm. Section 6 serves as the conclusion part of the paper.

2   System Model

In this section, we first introduce the MEC network structure diagram and build the multi-agent deep deterministic policy gradient model and computing model.

2.1   Network Model

We first create a MEC domain with multi-agent cellular network randomly distributed by UEs, as shown in Fig. 1. Each agent generates computation tasks with different latency tolerance and computation resource requirements. Their individual conditions determine whether the tasks are allowed to be offloaded to the MEC server.

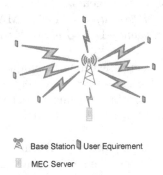

🗠 Base Station 📱 User Equirement
▦ MEC Server

Fig. 1. An illustration of the multi-agent model

2.2 Task Model

We consider a MADDPG model for multi-agent environment training. Each UE n has its task $B_n \triangleq (D_n, M_n, \sigma_n)$. These tasks can be executed either with the MEC or locally. D_n is the size of the data for each task. M_n is the number of CPU cycles, or computing resources, required to complete a task. Maximum tolerance delay of task B_n is expressed as σ_n. It means that the delay of each user cannot exceed σ_n. Maximum tolerance delay is a constraint of optimization. These three parameters are closely related to the application and can be randomly set in task configuration.

2.3 Computation Model

When UE n tasks are executed locally, we set UE transmitting power and BS computing ability to 0. If UE n tasks are executed by offloading on MEC server. we set UE transmitting power and BS computational capacity to the values of transmitting power and BS computational capacity contained in the action in the environment. When UE n tasks are executed locally, that is, when offloading is not selected, we define f_n as the computational capacity assigned to task B_n, then the delay T_n required for tasks B_n to execute locally is:

$$T_n^l = \frac{M_n}{f_n} . \tag{1}$$

The energy consumption corresponding to task B_n is G_n, which is expressed as:

$$G_n^l = 10^{-27} \times f_n{}^2 \times M_n \tag{2}$$

According to the practical measurement, we set $10^{-27} f_n^2$ as the amount of energy consumed in one CPU cycle to complete a task B_n .

We define H_n^l as the cost of our local computation, that is, local cost, which is expressed as:

$$H_n^l = L_n^t \times T_n^l + L_n^g \times G_n^l . \tag{3}$$

Here L_n^t and L_n^g represent energy cost weight and time cost weight respectively, which of the two optimization objectives is more important, Their range is (0, 1), and add up to 1. We set them to stay at 0.5 this paper.

If UE n tasks are executed by offloading on MEC server, we should calculate the offloading uplink time first, and define it as U_n:

$$U_n^o = \frac{M_n}{r_n} ; \tag{4}$$

where r_n indicates the data transmission rate of UE n on the network.

According to the above calculation results, we can get offloading uplink energy, which is defined as:

$$G_{n,u}^o = P_n \times U_n^o ; \tag{5}$$

where P_n is the transmission power of UE n transmits data to MEC server.

Then we need to calculate the MEC server processing time for incoming data, which can defined as:

$$R_n^o = \frac{M_n}{f_n} \; ; \tag{6}$$

where f_n is defined as the CPU cycles per second by the MEC server to complete task B_n, which is the allocated computational resource.

Since the resources of the entire MEC server are limited, the total amount of resources that can be allocated cannot exceed the resources of the entire MEC server. As a result, some UEs are idle. The power in the idle state is defined as P_n^i, and the power consumption in the idle state is:

$$G_{n,c}^o = P_n^i \times R_n^o \; . \tag{7}$$

According to (4) and (6), the overall time delay of UE n can be expressed as follows:

$$T_n^o = U_n^o + R_n^o \; . \tag{8}$$

According to (5) and (7), the overall energy consumption of offloading of UE n can be expressed as follows:

$$G_n^o = G_{n,u}^o + G_{n,c}^o \; . \tag{9}$$

According to (8) and (9), we can obtain the cost of computation offloading in the same way as the cost obtained when the task is executed locally. H_n^o is defined as the total cost of computation offloading, which is expressed as:

$$H_n^o = L_n^t \times T_n^o + L_n^g \times E_n^o \; . \tag{10}$$

According to the cost obtained in the local and MEC server above, we can calculate the cost value of all UE, defined as H_{all} :

$$H_{all} = \sum_{n=1}^{N} \alpha_n \times H_n^o + (1 - \alpha_n) \times H_n^l \; ; \tag{11}$$

where α_n is the offloading decision of UE n, it$\in \{0, 1\}$, if UE n tasks are offloaded on the MEC server, $\alpha_n = 1$, otherwise, $\alpha_n = 0$.

3   Problem Formulation

In this section, our goal is to optimize the computational offloading and resource allocation of the MEC system. That is to say, we need to minimize the weighted sum of execution delay and energy consumption of all users in the MEC system. The problem is described under the following constraints:

$$\min_{A,f} \sum_{n=1}^{N} \alpha_n H_n^o + (1 - \alpha_n)H_n^l \ ;$$

$$C1 : \alpha_n \in \{0,1\}, \forall n \in N \ ;$$

$$C2 : (1 - \alpha_n)H_n^l + \alpha_n H_n^o <= \sigma_n, \forall n \in N \ ; \tag{12}$$

$$C3 : \sum_{n=1}^{N} \alpha_n f_n <= F, \forall n \in N \ .$$

In the formula above, A represents the set of decisions about whether to offload the task to the MEC server, $A = [\alpha_1, \alpha_2, ..., \alpha_n]$. f is the set of allocation of computing resources, $f = [f_1, f_2, ..., f_n]$. Here are a few constraints:

C1: It expresses UE n selects whether to offload the task to the MEC server or to execute the task locally.

C2: Delay cannot exceed preset maximum tolerance delay, whether the task is offloaded to the MEC server executed locally.

C3: The sum of the number of computing resources allocated to all tasks cannot exceed available sum of the entire system.

As the environment become increasingly complex with more active agents, the problem becomes more challenging. Instead of the NP, reinforcement learning is an effective way to optimize A and f. Here in this multi-agent environment, we use MADDPG instead of traditional reinforcement learning methods learn methods to solve the problem.

4 Problem Solution

In this section, we first introduce the three key elements of RL in detail: state, action, and reward, then MADDPG in detail. In order to reduce cost, we propose to integrate MADDPG and federated learning, which will result in a new model by merging the policy network of each agent in MADDPG.

4.1 Three Key Elements of RL

- **state**: State consists of five parts: $s = (D_n, M_n, \sigma_n, e, c)$, D_n represents the size of the data for each task, M_n represents computing resources, σ_n represents the maximum tolerance delay, e represents residual energy, and c represents the channel gain to the base station.
- **action**: Action consists of two parts, namely the set of computation offloading decision A and the set of resource allocation f for each UE.
- **reward**: Every step an agent executes an action in a state, it will get a reward. Because the purpose of RL is to maximize reward, while the objective function proposed, and our purpose is to minimize cost in this paper. So reward is negatively correlated with the objective function.

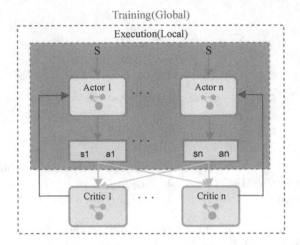

Fig. 2. An illustration of MADDPG

It's challenging for traditional RL to apply to the multi-agent environment. The main reason is the strategies of all agent are continuously changing in the training process, resulting in the environment being very unstable from the perspective of each agent. After denying of other unfitting methods, we chose MADDPG to solve the problem.

4.2 MADDPG Method

MADDPG as a whole is basically similar to DDPG that still adopts the structure of actor-critic, but adds information of other agents in the critic part. A total of four networks are used, actor, target actor, critic, target critic. For a deterministic policy, its gradient can be expressed as:

$$\nabla_{\theta_i} J \approx \frac{1}{S} \sum_j \nabla_{\theta_i} \pi_i(s_i^j) \nabla_{a_i} Q_i^\pi(u^j, a_1^j, ..., a_i^j, \ a_N^j)|_{a_i = \pi_i(u_i^j)}; \quad (13)$$

where $J(\theta)$ is the cumulative expected reward of the ith agent, s_i is the observation of the ith agent and $X = [s_1, s_2, ..., s_i]$ express state. Q_i^π is critic network. We use this gradient to update the actor network.

$$\mathcal{L}(\theta_i) = \frac{1}{S} \sum_j (q^j - Q_i^\pi(u^j, a_1^j, ..., a_N^j))^2. \quad (14)$$

For critic network, we need to calculate its mean square error with the target network as loss to update the parameter.

$$q^j = r_i^j + \gamma Q_i^{\pi'}(1 - d^j)(u'^j, a_1', ..., a_N')|_{a_k' = \pi_k'(u_k^j)}. \quad (15)$$

Algorithm 1 Multi-Agent Deep Deterministic Policy Gradient for N agents

1: **for** *episode* $= 1$ to T **do**

2:    Initialize process N to explore action;

3:    Receive initial state x;

4:    **for** $t = 1$ to *maxepisode* **do**

5:       Each agent i needs to choose action $a_i = \pi_{\theta_i}(u_i) + \mathcal{N}_t$ write the current strategy and exploration;

6:       Execute set of actions a=$(a_1,...a_N)$and get new state u$'$ and reward r;

7:       Store(u, a, r, u', d)in experience replay buffer $\mathcal{D}$;

8:       u $\leftarrow$ u$'$;

9:       **for** $agent_i$ to N **do**

10:          A minibatch of S samples are randomly from the experience replay buffer;

11:          $(u^j, a^j, r^j, u'^j, d^j)$from $\mathcal{D}$;

12:          $q^j = r_i^j + \gamma Q_i^{\pi'}(1 - d^j)(u'^j, a_1', ..., a_N')|_{a_k' = \pi_k'(u_k^j)}$;

13:          Critic is updated by minibatch the loss :

14:          $\mathcal{L}(\theta_i) = \frac{1}{S}\sum_j(q^j - Q_i^\pi(u^j, a_1^j, ..., a_N^j))^2$;

15:          Actor is updated using the sampled policy gradient:

16:          $\nabla_{\theta_i}J \approx \frac{1}{S}\sum_j \nabla_{\theta_i}\pi_i(s_i^j)\nabla_{a_i}Q_i^\pi(u^j, a_1^j, ..., a_i^j, \ a_N^j)|_{a_i = \pi_i(u_i^j)}$;

17:       **end for**

18:       For each agent i, target network parameters are updated:

19:       $\theta_i' \leftarrow \tau\theta_i + (1 - \tau)\theta_i'$;

20:       For each agent i, critic network parameters are updated:

21:       $\pi_i' \leftarrow \tau\pi_i + (1 - \tau)\pi_i'$;

22:    **end for**

23: **end for**

In order to adapt to multi-agent environment, DDPG algorithm is improved. The most important part is that the critic part of each agent can access to the actions of all other agents for realizing centralized training and decentralized execution.

4.3   Model Fusion Method

According to MADDPG, we get a target policy for each agent. As shown in Fig. 3, by using the method of weighted model fusion, we fuse the target policy of each agent into a final target policy. In this paper, we set the weight to 0.008; that is, the weight of each new model, when fused into the final target policy, is 0.008, and the weight of the final target policy is 0.992. After obtaining the final Target policy, we trained the final target policy to get a better model.

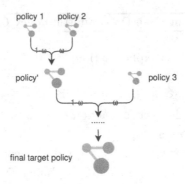

Fig. 3. An illustration of model fusion

We define the final target policy is ρ_{final} after model fusion, which is expressed as:

$$\rho_{final} = (1 - \omega)\rho_{final-1} + \omega\rho_n;$$
$$\rho_{final-1} = (1 - \omega)\rho_{final-2} + \omega\rho_{n-1}. \tag{16}$$

Table 1. Configurations

Config number	Five Configurations		
	Number of UEs	bs computational capacity	Bandwidth
1	10	10000000000.0	10000000.0
2	20	20000000000.0	20000000.0
3	30	30000000000.0	30000000.0
4	40	40000000000.0	40000000.0
5	50	50000000000.0	50000000.0

5   Simulation Result

In this section, the results of simulation experiments are presented to assess the performance of the proposed method. In the simulation experiments, we consider using a hexagon network with a base station that contains the server in the center and UE randomly distributed within 2 km from the base station in the center. Assuming the computational capacity of each UE is 1 GHz, the data size of offloaded $D_n(kbits)$ is distributed between $(400, 500)$, and the number of CPU cycles $M_n(megacycles)$ is distributed between $(800, 900)$. The transmission power is $P_n = 500\,mW$ and idle power is $P_n^i = 100\,mW$. For simplicity, we set the decision weight to 0.5, that is, $L_n^t = L_n^g = 0.5$. We set up five different configurations as shown in Table 1.

Figure 4 shows that the total cost of the MEC system changes with configurations. In general, when the three configuration resources are too small or too large, the model fusion algorithm performs better than the MADDPG. And, when the number of user equipment increase with the growth of base station computational capacity and bandwidth, the cost will decrease continuously. When the number of user equipment is $\{30, 40\}$, The model fusion algorithm perform similarly as the MADDPG algorithm.

In Fig. 5, We compare the cost values of MADDPG and model fusion algorithms in the same configuration. The value is config No. 5, which is number of user equipment = 50, Base station computational capacity = 50 GHz, and bandwidth = 50 Mbps. As shown in Fig. 5, the proposed model fusion method has a better effect, faster convergence speed, and smaller cost.

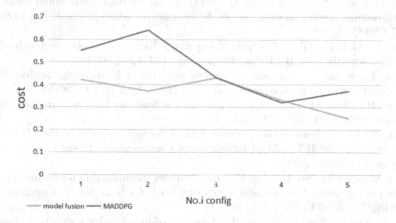

Fig. 4. Cost of MADDPG and model fusion algorithm in different configurations

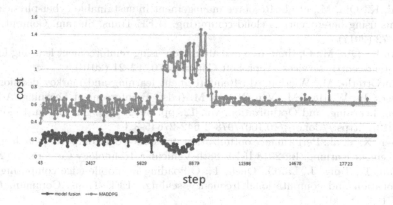

Fig. 5. Cost of MADDPG and model fusion algorithm in No. 5 configuration

6   Conclusion

This paper proposed a model fusion algorithm based MADDPG and federated learning. It's used to solve computation offloading decision and resource allocation problems in a multi-agent environment. First, we compared the proposed algorithm with the classic MADDPG under different configuration. Then, we compared the two algorithms' convergence speed and objective function value under the same configuration condition. Simulation results showed that compared with traditional MADDPG, under different configuration the scheme has better performance, faster convergence speed, stronger stability and robustness in a complex environment.

References

1. Lu, Z., Wang, N., Wu, J., Qiu, M.: IoTDeM: an iot big data-oriented mapreduce performance prediction extended model in multiple edge clouds. JPDC **118**, 316–327 (2018)
2. Qiu, L., Gai, K., Qiu, M.: Optimal big data sharing approach for tele-health in cloud computing. In: IEEE SmartCloud, pp. 184–189 (2016)
3. Gao, Y., et al.: Performance and power analysis of high-density multi-GPGPU architectures: a preliminary case study. In: IEEE 17th HPCC (2015)
4. Zhao, H., Chen, M., et al.: A novel pre-cache schema for high performance android system. FGCS **56**, 766–772 (2016)
5. Qiu, M., et al.: A novel energy-aware fault tolerance mechanism for wireless sensor networks. In: IEEE/ACM International Conference on Green Computing and Communications (2011)
6. Qiu, M., Cao, D., Su, H., Gai, K.: Data transfer minimization for financial derivative pricing using Monte Carlo simulation with GPU in 5G. J. Commun. Syst. **29**(16), 2364–2374 (2016)
7. Li, Z., Xie, R., Sun, L., Huang, T.: A survey of mobile edge computing. Telecommun. Sci. **34**(1), 87–101 (2018)
8. Gai, K., Qiu, M., et al.: Resource management in sustainable cyber-physical systems using heterogeneous cloud computing. IEEE Trans. Sustain. Comput. **3**(2), 60–72 (2017)
9. Gai, K., Qiu, M.: Optimal resource allocation using reinforcement learning for IoT content-centric services. Appl. Soft Comput. **70**, 12–21 (2018)
10. Van Otterlo, M., Wiering, M.: Reinforcement learning and markov decision processes. In: Wiering, M., Van Otterlo, M. (eds.) Reinforcement Learning. Adaptation, Learning, and Optimization, vol. 12, pp. 3–42. Springer, Berlin, Heidelberg (2012). https://doi.org/10.1007/978-3-642-27645-3_1
11. Chen, X., et al.: Performance optimization in mobile-edge computing via deep reinforcement learning. In: 2018 IEEE 88th Vehicular Technology Conference (2018)
12. Dinh, T., Tang, J., La, Q., Quek, T.: Offloading in mobile edge computing: task allocation and computational frequency scaling. IEEE Trans. Commun. **65**(8), 3571–3584 (2017)
13. Meng, F., Chen, P., Wu, L., Cheng, J.: Power allocation in multi-user cellular networks: deep reinforcement learning approaches. IEEE Trans. Wirel. Commun. **19**(10), 6255–6267 (2020)

14. Li, J., Gao, H., Lv, T., Lu, Y.: Deep reinforcement learning based computation offloading and resource allocation for MEC. In: 2018 IEEE Wireless Communications and Networking Conference (2018)
15. Gai, K., Qiu, M.: Reinforcement learning-based content-centric services in mobile sensing. IEEE Netw. **32**(4), 34–39 (2018)
16. Wang, J., Zhao, L., Liu, J., Kato, N.: Smart resource allocation for mobile edge computing: a deep reinforcement learning approach. IEEE Trans. Emerg. Top. Comput. **9**(3), 1529–1541 (2021)
17. Konečný, J., McMahan, H.B., Yu, F.X., Richtárik, P., Suresh, A.T., Bacon, D.: Federated learning: strategies for improving communication efficiency. arXiv:1610.05492 (2016)
18. Li, L., Fan, Y., Lin, M.: A review of applications in federated learning. Comput. Ind. Eng. **149**, 106854 (2020)

Multi-agent Computation Offloading in UAV Assisted MEC via Deep Reinforcement Learning

Hang He[1], Tao Ren[1(✉)], Yuan Qiu[2], Zheyuan Hu[2], and Yanqi Li[1]

[1] Hangzhou Innovation Institute, Beihang University, Hangzhou 310051, China
taotao_1982@126.com
[2] Beihang University, Beijing 100191, China
huzheyuan18@buaa.edu.cn

Abstract. Due to its high maneuverability and flexibility, there have been a growing popularity to adopt *Unmanned Aerial Vehicles* (UAVs) on *Mobile Edge Computing* (MEC), serving as edge platforms in infrastructure- unavailable scenarios, e.g., disaster rescue, field operation. Owing to the weak workload, UAVs are typically equipped with limited computing and energy resources. Hence, it is crucial to design efficient edge computation offloading algorithms which could achieve high edge computing performance while keeping low energy consumption. A variety of UAV assisted computation offloading algorithms have been proposed, most of which focus on the scheduling of computation offloading in a centralized way and could become infeasible when the network size increases greatly. To address the issue, we propose a semi-distributed computation offloading framework based on *Multi-Agent Twin Delayed* (MATD3) deep deterministic policy gradient to minimize the average system cost of the MEC network. We adopt the actor-critic reinforcement learning framework to learn an offloading decision model for each *User Equipment* (UE), so that each UE could make near-optimal computation offloading decisions by its own and does not suffer from the booming of the network size. Extensive experiments are carried out via numerical simulation and the experimental results verify the effectiveness of the proposed algorithm.

Keywords: Mobile edge computing · Deep reinforcement learning · Unmanned aerial vehicle · Computation offloading · Resource allocation

1 Introduction

With high maneuverability and flexibility, *unmanned aerial vehicles* (UAVs) [1] can serve as communication reply stations to improve communication and network [2,3] performance in specific scenarios, such as disaster rescue and field operation, where network infrastructures are unavailable or limited. Meanwhile, *mobile edge computing* (MEC) [4–6] is a promising paradigm in *cloud radio access network* (CRAN), which can improve the computation performance of

M. Qiu et al. (Eds.): SmartCom 2021, LNCS 13202, pp. 416–426, 2022.
https://doi.org/10.1007/978-3-030-97774-0_38

mobile networks by deploying high-performance edge servers in proximity to end users. UAV-assisted MEC has drawn extensive attention from both academia and industries. As a result, UAV can now be used as an edge computing platform with higher computing and energy [7-9] resources than the resource-constraint *user equipment* (UE) and support to execute the computation-intensive and latency-sensitive tasks offloaded by the UE.

Recent researches have focused on UAV serving as aerial base stations to enhance communication and computing services [10,11] for the ground users to reduce latency [12], enhance computation ability [13], improve efficiency [14] and maximize confidentiality [15]. In the researches aimed to maximize the energy efficiency of ground user equipment, [16] proposed to achieve the goal by planning UAV trajectory and allocating task data and computing resources. In the researches aimed to minimize UAV energy consumption, [17] designed a scheme synthesizing computation offloading, resource allocation, and UAV trajectory to minimize UAV energy and time consumption. Meanwhile, a Pareto's optimal solution for the tradeoff between UAV energy and time consumption is also presented. In the researches aimed to minimize the total energy consumption of UAVs and ground equipment, [18] studied the UAV-assisted MEC system based on *non-orthogonal Multiple Access* (NOMA), and reviewed the weighted energy consumption of UAVs and ground equipments. However, paper [18] did not consider the delay constraint to deal with offloaded data by UAV, thus the energy consumption model cannot be applied extensively.

This paper investigates the computation offloading in UAV-assisted MEC, which includes one drone with high computing capacity and multiple user equipments. In particular, we design a computation offloading framework supported by multi-agent twin-delayed deep deterministic policy gradient(MATD3) [19] algorithm. To start with, we establish the system model, communication model and calculation model of the MEC network. Then we propose to minimize the average cost of the system through joint optimization of computing resources and transmission power. We further formulate the joint optimization problem as a Markov decision process [20] and apply the deep reinforcement learning algorithm to optimize the offloading policy. Finally, simulation results verify the performance of the MATD3 algorithm.

2   System Model

2.1   UAV Assisted MEC System Model

In this paper, we design a UAV-assisted MEC system model, which consists of multiple user equipment and one drone carrying a *Micro Base Station* (MBS), as shown in Fig. 1. MBS is deployed with an edge server, whose computing capacity and energy budget are represented as F^{mbs} and E^{mbs}. Let $\mathbb{U} = \{1, 2, \ldots, U\}$ denote the set of UEs, where U is the number of UEs. The system time is evenly divided into T intervals and denoted by the set $\mathbb{T} = \{1, 2, \ldots, T\}$. Besides, the region of space is described by tree-dimensional coordinates, with which the positions of the UE u at time slot t and MBS are denoted by $P_u^t = (x_u^t, y_u^t, z_u^t)$ and $P^{mbs} = (x^{mbs}, y^{mbs}, z^{mbs})$.

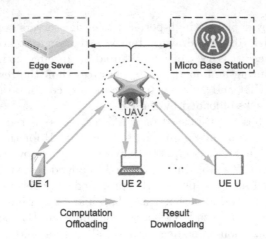

Fig. 1. UAV assisted MEC system model.

In the begining of each interval t, one task arrives UE u is denoted by $J_u^t = (B_u^t, F_u^t, D_u^t)$, where B_u^t is the task data size (measured in bits), F_u^t is the required number of CPU frequency to complete a bit the task data, and D_u^t is the maximum tolerance task delay. In this paper, we adopt a binary offloading decision strategy, where each task is executed either locally or remotely. The offloading decision of each task J_u^t is represented by a offloading variable $o_u^t = \{0, 1\}$.

2.2 Communication Model

This paper adopts a wireless interference model and the offloading transmission rate is calculated as

$$r_u^t = W\log_2\left(1 + \frac{p_u^t g_u^t}{\sigma^2 + \sum_{k\neq u, o(k)=1}^{U} p_k^t g_k^t}\right) \tag{1}$$

where W represents the transmitting bandwidth, p_u^t represents the transmitting power of UE u at time slot t, σ^2 represents the background noise power (without loss of generality, we assumed the same value for all UEs), and g_u^t represents the channel gain between the MBS and UE u at time slot t.

Following the LTE standard [21], the path-loss is modeled by

$$g_u^t = 128.1 + 37.6 * log_{10}(d_u^t), u \in \mathbb{U}, t \in \mathbb{T} \tag{2}$$

where $d_u^t = \left\|P_u^t - P^{mbs}\right\|$ is the Euclidean distance (measured in km) between the MBS and UE u at time slot t.

Supposing the maximum transmitting power of UEs is p^{max}, the allocated transmitting power should not exceed the maximum, as follow

$$p_u^t \le p^{max}, u \in \mathbb{U}, t \in \mathbb{T} \tag{3}$$

Given the above, we can calculate the time and energy cost to offload the task J_u^t from UE u to the MBS by

$$\tilde{t}_u^t = \frac{B_u^t}{r_u^t} \tag{4}$$

and

$$\tilde{e}_u^t = p_u^t \tilde{t}_u^t = \frac{B_u^t p_u^t}{r_u^t} \tag{5}$$

Due to the results of most tasks being smaller than the uploaded task size, the time and energy to download the edge computing result from the MBS are ignored.

2.3   Computation Model

When the offloading variable $o_u^t = 0$, i.e., the task J_u^t is executed locally on the arrived UE u, the task execution latency of J_u^t can be given by

$$\hat{t}_u^t = \frac{B_u^t F_u^t}{f_u^t}, u \in \mathbb{U}, t \in \mathbb{T} \tag{6}$$

where f_u^t represents the allocated computing capacity by UE u at t time slot and should satisfies

$$f_u^t \le f_{max}^u, \forall u \in \mathbb{U}, t \in \mathbb{T} \tag{7}$$

where f_{max}^u represents the maximal available computing capacity of UE u. the consumed energy can be given by

$$\check{e}_u^t = \kappa^u \left(f_u^t\right)^{v_u} \frac{B_u^t F_u^t}{f_u^t}, u \in \mathbb{U}, t \in \mathbb{T} \tag{8}$$

where κ^u and v^u are the energy consumption cofficients [22] that are related to the chip architecture of UE u.

When the offloading variable $o_u^t = 0$, i.e., the task J_u^t is offloaded and executed on the MBS, the task execution latency of J_u^t can be given by

$$\hat{t}_u^t = \frac{B_u^t F_u^t}{f_{mbs,u}^t}, u \in \mathbb{U}, t \in \mathbb{T} \tag{9}$$

where $f_{mbs,u}^t$ represents the allocated computing capacity from the MBS to UE u at t time slot and should satisfies

$$\sum_{u=1}^{\mathbb{U}} f_{mbs,u}^t \le F^{mbs}, \forall t \in \mathbb{T} \tag{10}$$

The consumed energy can be given by

$$\check{e}_u^t = \hat{p}^{mbs}\hat{t}_u^t = \frac{\hat{p}^{mbs}B_u^t F_u^t}{f_{mbs,u}^t} \tag{11}$$

where $\hat{p}^{mbs}$ is the power of MBS when it works.

3   Problem Formulation

At each time slot t, the system costs of the task latency and the energy consumption of J_u^t of UE u can be given by

$$\check{C}_u^t = \left(1 - o_u^t\right)\check{t}_u^t + o_u^t\left(\tilde{t}_u^t + \hat{t}_u^t\right) \tag{12}$$

and

$$\hat{C}_u^t = \left(1 - o_u^t\right)\check{e}_u^t + o_u^t\left(\tilde{e}_u^t + \hat{e}_u^t\right) \tag{13}$$

respectively. Therefore, under the goal of minimizing both taks execution latency and enery consumption of UE, the weighted cost of UE u at t can be defined as

$$C_u^t = \mu \check{C}_u^t + (1 - \mu)\hat{C}_u^t \tag{14}$$

where μ is the weigth of execution latency. The average system cost for all UEs during T is defined as

$$C^{sys} = \frac{1}{T}\sum_{t=1}^{T}\sum_{u=1}^{U}C_u^t \tag{15}$$

Our aim to reduce both task execution latency and energy consumption of all UEs can be formulated to minimizing the average system cost C^{sys} by jointly optimizing the variables under certain constraints:

$$P : \min_{\left(o_u^t, f_u^t, f_{mbs,u}^t, p_u^t\right)} C^{sys} \tag{16}$$

$$st.\forall u \in \mathbb{U}, t \in \mathbb{T}, C1 : o_u^t = \{0,1\}, C2 : p_u^t \le p^{max}, C3 : f_u^t \le f_{max}^u,$$

$$C4 : \sum_{u=1}^{U} f_{mbs,u}^t \le F^{mbs}, C5 : \left(1 - o_u^t\right)\check{t}_u^t + o_u^t\left(\tilde{t}_u^t + \hat{t}_u^t\right) \le D_u^t,$$

$$C6 : \sum_{t=1}^{\dot{t}}\left(1 - o_u^t\right)\check{e}_u^t + o_u^t\tilde{e}_u^t \le E^u, \forall \dot{t} \in \mathbb{T}, C7 : \sum_{t=1}^{\dot{t}}o_u^t\hat{e}_u^t \le E^{mbs}, \forall \dot{t} \in \mathbb{T}.$$

4   MATD3-Based Computation Offloading Framework

This section first briefly introduces the essential elements of our DRL-based offloading optimization framework, then describes the structure and the execution process of the MATD3 algorithm.

4.1   Essential Elements of DRL

In deep reinforcement learning, the agent (i.e., the UE) interacts with the environment (i.e., the UAV-assisted MEC network) by generating actions and receiving rewards from the environment under the current state, and observing next states. Here, the essential elements–state, action, and reward adopted in this paper for MATD3 offloading optimization framework are defined as follows:

1) **State.** Owing to the need of decentralized offloading for the UAV assisted MEC network, the UE only observe limited state information from environment, which includes its current position, lastest arrived task, current battery capacity. Therefore, the state s_u^t of UE u at time slot t is denoted by $s_u^t = (g_u^t, J_u^t, E_u^t)$, where channel gain g_u^t is calculated by its current position P_u^t, E_u^t can be computed as $E_u^t = E^u - \sum_{i=1}^{t-1} \left((1 - o_u^t) \check{e}_u^t + o_u^t \tilde{e}_u^t \right)$.

2) **Action.** Similarly, the UE could only make its own offloading decision since the decentralized offloading constraint. According to the offloading optimization problem formulation, the action a_u^t of the UE u at time slot t is denoted by $a_u^t = \left(o_u^t, \hat{f}_u^t, p_u^t \right)$. we combine f_u^t and $f_{mbs,u}^t$ into one new variable $\hat{f}_u^t$ for simplify, which can be given by

$$\hat{f}_u^t = \begin{cases} f_u^t & o_u^t = 0, \\ f_{mbs,u}^t & o_u^t = 1. \end{cases} \tag{17}$$

3) **Reward.** Since we hope to minimize the average system cost in terms of the offloading problem P, the reward R_u^t of UE u at time slot t and the UE current cost should be inversely correlated. Therefore, we define reward as $r_u^t = -C_u^t$. According to the Bellman Equation, Q value Q_u^t can be denoted by

$$Q_u^t - r_u^t + \delta r_u^{t+1} = r_u^t + \delta^1 r_u^{t+1} + \delta^2 r_u^{t+2} + \cdots \tag{18}$$

where δ represents the discount factor of future reward, and it should satisfy

$$0 \le \delta \le 1 \tag{19}$$

owing to the definitions of the three essential elements, the optimization problem P can be transformed into a new problem $\hat{P}$, which is denoted by

$$\hat{P} : \max_{\pi} Q_u^t \tag{20}$$

where π is the neural network, input is state r_u^t, output is the action a_u^t. Our target is to attain the optimal network parameters to maximize Q value.

4.2   Network Structure of MATD3

As shown in Fig. 2, the MATD3 network structure mainly includes execution and training. During the execution phrase, each UE has an individual actor network π^u built using deep neural network with parameters ω^u, which interacts with the UAV assisted MEC network relying on its own current state. Specially, the UE u observes the own current state s_u^t at time slot t, makes its own offloading decision variable a_u^t obtained by the its actor network $a_u^t = \pi^u(s_u^t)$, and receives the immediate reward r_u^t from environment and own next state s_u^{t+1}. Then the all UEs generated experience tuple (S_t, A_t, S_{t+1}, R_t) is put into reply buffer at time slot t, where $S_t = \{s_1^t, s_2^t, \cdots, s_U^t\}$, $A_t = \{a_1^t, a_2^t, \cdots, a_U^t\}$, $S_{t+1} = \{s_1^{t+1}, s_2^{t+1}, \cdots, s_U^{t+1}\}$, $R_t = \{r_1^t, r_2^t, \cdots, r_U^t\}$. When the reply buffer is full, the algorithm starts the train part.

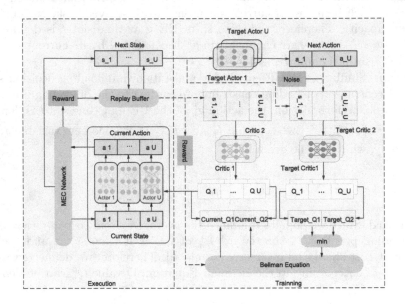

Fig. 2. MATD3 network structure.

During training phrase, we firstly random sample a mini-batch experience tuple from $(\mathbf{S}, \mathbf{A}, \hat{\mathbf{S}}, \mathbf{R})$ from replay buffer M. Then, We take the next state s_u^{t+1} of the corresponding UE u in the tuple and feed it to the respective target network $\hat{\pi}^u$ to get the next action a_u^{t+1}. We next feed the next state $\hat{s}_u^{t+1}$ and the next action a_u^{t+1} to target critic1 and target critic2 to get Target $\hat{Q}1$ and Target $\hat{Q}2$, respectively. We take the smaller of $\hat{Q}1$ and $\hat{Q}2$ as y. Meanwhile, we feed the current state s_u^t and the current action a_u^t to critic1 and critic2 to get current $Q1$ and current $Q2$, respectively. Afterward, We calculate the loss function and backpropagation update critic1 and critic2 network parameters θ^1 and θ^2. Finally, we update the actor network of each UE at *delay_update_frequency*. At the same time, we also soft update the target actor network of each UE and two target critic network parameters. The detailed execution process of the MATD3 algorithm, as shown in Algorithm 1.

Algorithm 1. Multi-Agent Twin Delayed Deep Deterministic Policy Gradient Algorithm

---

1: Create actor neural network π^u for each UE u by using random parameters ω^u.
2: Create two critic networks Q^1, Q^2 by using random parameters θ^1 and θ^2.
3: Initialize target actor network for each UE u, $\hat{\omega}^u \longleftarrow \omega^u$.
4: Initialize two target critic networks $\hat{Q}^1, \hat{Q}^2$, $\hat{\theta}^1 \longleftarrow \theta^1, \hat{\theta}^2 \longleftarrow \theta^2$.
5: Initialize replay buffer M, $replay\_buffer\_sizes = 0$.
6: **for** $episode\ i = 1$ to $episodes\_max$ **do**
7:     Generate randomly noise for finding actions, and acquire original state S^0, attain each UEs's observations through state $S^0 = \{s_1^0, s_2^0, \cdots, s_U^0\}$.
8:     **for** $step\ t = 1$ to max_steps **do**
9:         **for** each UE $u = 1$ to U **do**
10:             Select actions a_u^{t-1} from own observation s_u^{t-1} and deterministic policy by adding noise ε_a, $a_u^{t-1} = clip\left(\pi^u\left(s_u^{t-1}\right) + N\left(\varepsilon_a\right), a_{min}, a_{max}\right)$.
11:         **end for**
12:         Excute action A_{t-1} and obtain new state S_t and reward R_{t-1}.
13:         Store exprience tuple $(S_{t-1}, A_{t-1}, S_t, R_{t-1})$ into replay buffer M, $replay\_buffer\_sizes+ = 1$.
14:     **end for**
15: **end for**
16: **if** $replay\_buffer\_sizes > max\_buffer\_sizes$ **then**
17:     Random sample a mini-batch experience tuple $\left(\mathbf{S}, \mathbf{A}, \hat{\mathbf{S}}, \mathbf{R}\right)$ from replay buffer.
18:     Calculate target critic Q value:
19:     $y = R + \min \hat{Q}^{1,2}\left(\left(\hat{S}^1, \hat{A}^1\right), \ldots, \left(\hat{S}^U, \hat{A}^U\right)\right)$
20:
21:     $\theta^{1,2} \longleftarrow \mathrm{argmin}_{\theta^{1,2}} \sum_{u=1}^{U} \left(Q^{1,2}\left(S, A\right) - y\right)^2$
22:     **if** $i\ mod\ delay\_update\_frequency$ **then**
23:         Update all the policies
24:         $\nabla_{\omega^u} J\left(\pi^u\right) =$
25:         $EO_{,\mathbf{A} \sim D}\left[\nabla_{\omega^u}\pi^u\left(A^u \mid S^u\right)\nabla_{A^u}Q_\pi\left(\mathbf{S}^1, \mathbf{A}^1\right)\right]$
26:         Soft update target networks' parameters:
27:         $\hat{\pi}^u \longleftarrow \lambda\pi^u + (1-\lambda)\hat{\pi}^u$
28:         $\hat{\theta}^{1,2} \longleftarrow \lambda\theta^{1,2} + (1-\lambda)\hat{\theta}^{1,2}$
29:     **end if**
30: **end if**

---

5   Simulation Results

In this section, the performance of the MATD3 algorithm is evaluated via numerical simulation with the following settings. A MBS with the position $\mathrm{P}^{mbs} = (0, 0, 20\,\mathrm{m})$ and coverage $1000 \times 1000\ m^2$ is considered, where the deploying edge server is equipped with 1×10^4 MHz computation capacity. The channel bandwidth and the noise power δ^2 is set 10 MHz and -100 dBm, respectively.

The task size B_u^t and F_u^t are sampled from $[400000, 500000]$ bit and $[800, 900]$ cycles, respectively. The CPU frequency of each UE is 1×10^3 MHz computation capacity. Moreover, the critic networks are composed of four hidden layers $1024 \times 512 \times 256 \times 128$, and the actor networks are composed of two hidden layers 128×128. The activation function of actor and critic networks is ReLU, and the learning rates of the actor and critic are 10^{-3} and 10^{-4}, respectively. The mini-batch size is 64, the discount factor for future reward is 0.98. the action noise is normal distribution, which mean is 0 and variance is 1.

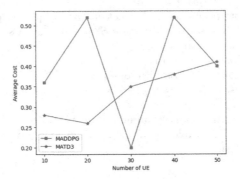

Fig. 3. Average cost comparison between MADDPG and MATD3 w.r.t. different UE numbers

We evaluate the performance of MADDPG and MATD3 with different numbers of UE, as shown in Fig. 3. It can be noticed that the MADDPG algorithm is unstable and has significant fluctuations, which could result formulate the reason that It is easier for the MADDPG to dramatically overestimate Q values, which leads to policy breaking because it exploits the errors in the Q-function. In contrast, the MATD3 algorithm is more robust. As the number of UE increases, so does the cost of the system.

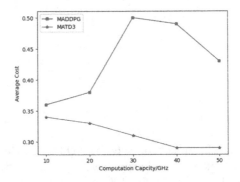

Fig. 4. Average cost comparison between MADDPG and MATD3 w.r.t. different MBS computation capacity

We evaluate the performance of MADDPG and MATD3 with different MBS computation capacities, as shown in Fig. 4. It can be noticed that the MADDPG algorithm curve firstly rise and then fall, which could result formulate the reason that multiple agents compete with each other when the MBS computation capacity increases. In contrast, the MATD3 algorithm is more robust. As the MBS computation capacity MBS increases, the cost of the system reduces.

6   Conclusion

This paper concentrates on studying a MATD3 computation offloading algorithm for UAV-assisted MEC networks. Given the high complexity of solving multiply closely coupled offloading decision variables for the MEC using conventional numerical optimization methods, The old optimization problem was firstly formulated into an MDP problem which can be handled via deep reinforcement learning. Three essential elements of deep reinforcement learning were defined: state, action, and reward. Then, the network structure and execution process of the MATD3 algorithm were illustrated in detail. Next, we adopt the actor-critic reinforcement learning framework to generate the offloading decision model and implement the framework in an uncentralized way, where each UE has an individual actor. Finally, we train the model by using the collected experience and update the model cyclically to all UE. In this way, we can effectively relieve the overestimation of the Q value. Simulation results have demonstrated performance experienced notable improvements compared with other distributed offloading approaches.

References

1. Zeng, Y., Zhang, R., Lim, T.J.: Wireless communications with unmanned aerial vehicles: opportunities and challenges. IEEE Commun. Mag. **54**(5), 36–42 (2016)
2. Qiu, H., Qiu, M., Memmi, G., Ming, Z., Liu, M.: A dynamic scalable blockchain based communication architecture for IoT. In: SmartBlock, pp. 159–166 (2018)
3. Qiu, H., Qiu, M., Lu, Z.: Selective encryption on ECG data in body sensor network based on supervised machine learning. Inf. Fusion **55**, 59–67 (2020)
4. Li, J., Gao, H., Lv, T., Lu, Y.: Deep reinforcement learning based computation offloading and resource allocation for MEC. In: IEEE Conference (WCNC), pp. 1–6 (2018)
5. Qiu, L., Gai, K., Qiu, M.: Optimal big data sharing approach for tele-health in cloud computing. In: IEEE SmartCloud, pp. 184–189 (2016)
6. Lu, Z., Wang, N., et al.: IoTDeM: an IoT big data-oriented MapReduce performance prediction extended model in multiple edge clouds. JPDC **118**, 316–327 (2018)
7. Qiu, M., et al.: Energy minimization with soft real-time and DVS for uniprocessor and multiprocessor embedded systems. In: IEEE DATE Conference, pp. 1–6 (2007)
8. Liu, M., et al.: H infinite state estimation for discrete-time chaotic systems based on a unified model. IEEE Trans. Syst. Man Cybern. (B). **42**(4), 1053–1063 (2012)

9. Qiu, M., et al.: A novel energy-aware fault tolerance mechanism for wireless sensor networks. In: ACM International Conference on Green Computing and Communications (2011)

10. Zhang, Z., et al.: Jamming ACK attack to wireless networks and a mitigation approach. In: IEEE GLOBECOM Conference, pp. 1–5 (2008)

11. Qiu, M., Cao, D., et al.: Data transfer minimization for financial derivative pricing using Monte Carlo simulation with GPU in 5G. J. Commun. Syst. 29(16), 2364–2374 (2016)

12. Kaleem, Z., Yousaf, M., Qamar, A., et al.: UAV-empowered disaster-resilient edge architecture for delay-sensitive communication. IEEE Netw. 33(6), 124–132 (2019)

13. Zhou, F., Wu, Y., Hu, R.Q., Qian, Y.: Computation rate maximization in UAV-enabled wireless powered mobile-edge computing systems. IEEE J. Sel. Areas Commun. 36(9), 1927–1941 (2018)

14. Zeng, Y., Zhang, R.: Energy-efficient UAV communication with trajectory optimization. IEEE Trans. Wirel. Commun. 16(6), 3747–3760 (2017)

15. Zhou, X., Wu, Q., Yan, S., Shu, F., Li, J.: UAV-enabled secure communications: Joint trajectory and transmit power optimization. IEEE Trans. Veh. Technol. 68(4), 4069–4073 (2019)

16. Li, M., Cheng, N., et al.: Energy-efficient UAV-assisted mobile edge computing: resource allocation and trajectory optimization. IEEE Trans. Veh. Technol. 69(3), 3424–3438 (2020)

17. Zeng, Y., Xu, X., Zhang, R.: Trajectory design for completion time minimization in UAV-enabled multicasting. IEEE Trans. Wirel. Commun. 17(4), 2233–2246 (2018)

18. ANasir, A.A., Tuan, H.D., Duong, T.Q., Poor, H.V.: UAV-enabled communication using NOMA in arXiv preprint arXiv:1806.03604 (2018)

19. Ackermann, J., Gabler, V., Osa, T., Sugiyama, M.: Reducing overestimation bias in multi-agent domains using double centralized critics (2019)

20. Puterman, M.L.: Markov Decision Processes: Discrete Stochastic Dynamic Programming. Wiley, NY, USA (2014)

21. Mir, Z.H., Filali, F.: LTE and IEEE 802.11p for vehicular networking: a performance evaluation. EURASIP J. Wirel. Commun. Netw. 2014(1), 1–15 (2014)

22. Kwak, J., Kim, Y., Lee, J., Chong, S.: DREAM: dynamic resource and task allocation for energy minimization in mobile cloud systems. IEEE J. Sel. Areas Commun. 33(12), 2510–2523 (2015)

OPN-DTSP: Optimized Pointer Networks for Approximate Solution of Dynamic Traveling Salesman Problem

Zhixiang Xiao[1], Mingming Lu[1(✉)], Wenyong He[1], Jiawen Cai[1], and Neal N. Xiong[2]

[1] School of Computer Science and Engineering, Central South University, Changsha, China
mingminglu@csu.edu.cn
[2] Department of Computer Science and Mathematics, Sul Ross State University, Alpine, USA

Abstract. The Traveling Salesman Problem (TSP), a classic problem in combinatorial optimization, is a well-known NP-hard problem with a wide range of real-world applications. Dynamic TSP is a further upgrade of TSP. Its dynamic change information leads to the greater complexity of the problem. Over the years, numerous excellent algorithms have been proposed by researchers to solve this problem, from the early exact algorithms to approximate algorithms, heuristics, and more recently, machine learning algorithms. However, these algorithms either only work with static TSP or have an unacceptable time consumption. To this end, we propose an optimized pointer network for approximate solution of dynamic TSP, which guarantees a high-quality approximate solution with very low time consumption. We introduce an attention mechanism in our model to fuse the dynamically changing edge information and the statically invariant node coordinate information and use reinforcement learning to enhance the decision-making of the model. Finally, the superior performance for dynamic TSP with low time-cost is verified on comparison experiments.

Keywords: Dynamic TSP · Pointer networks · Attention · Reinforcement learning

1 Introduction

The Traveling Salesman Problem (TSP) problem is a classic problem in the combinatorial optimization domain [1, 2]. In graph theory, the TSP problem can be defined as that, in an undirected weighted complete graph, we randomly choose a node as the starting point, then visit all other nodes in turn once, and finally return to the starting point. The goal is to find the traversal path with a minimum weight sum of edges on the path. Many problems in real life can be regarded as TSP problems or their variants, such as electrical wiring, vehicle routing planning, logistics planning, pipeline laying and processing schedules and other issues [3]. Therefore, solving the TSP problem effectively is of great practical significance in real life.

Since the feasible solution of TSP which is an NP-hard problem [4, 5] is the complete arrangement of all vertices, the possible combinations grow explosively with the

© The Author(s), under exclusive license to Springer Nature Switzerland AG 2022
M. Qiu et al. (Eds.): SmartCom 2021, LNCS 13202, pp. 427–437, 2022.
https://doi.org/10.1007/978-3-030-97774-0_39

increasing of vertices number. Early researchers used precise algorithms to solve the problem, including [6–10]. Precise algorithms can obtain the exact optimal solution, but it is accompanied by a high time complexity, making it suitable only for very small-scale cases. Therefore, in subsequent research, researchers focus on approximation algorithms and heuristic algorithms for TSP, which have faster-running speed with ensuring the solution quality, including [11–20]. In addition to the above traditional methods, scholars have also introduced deep learning to solve the TSP problem in recent years, such as [21–24].

The number and weight of the vertices and edges of the graph in the above TSP will not change, so it is also called the static TSP. However, in real life, the problems we may encounter are more likely to be dynamic TSP [25], that is, changes in the weight of edges between nodes or in the number of nodes in the graph, and so on. Many practical problems such as real-time vehicle deployment and resource dynamic dispatch can be approximated as dynamic TSP. Compared with static TSP, dynamic TSP has dynamically changing information, which increases the difficulty of solving the problem, but at the same time, it has greater practical application value. Therefore, an effective solution for dynamic TSP in a short time has more important practical value. The time consumption for finding an accurate solution of dynamic TSP is unbearable. Therefore, it is necessary to find an approximate algorithm with lower complexity but still meets the requirements in the case that finding an accurate solution in a limited time is not feasible. In the solution based on traditional methods, [29] combined several traditional methods into a method that can solve the dynamic TSP problem. The heuristic-based methods include [26–30]. Although the dynamic TSP problem can be approximated by these methods, it takes a lot of time.

To address the limitations of the above methods, we consider the quality of the approximate solution as well as to ensure that the computation time is not too long. Therefore, we adopt a deep learning approach in an approximate solution to the dynamic TSP problem. More specifically, we propose to use the pointer network model to find an approximate solution to the dynamic TSP problem. We have improved the architecture of the pointer network and introduced an attention mechanism to fuse the dynamically changing edges information and the static node coordinate information in the dynamic TSP problem. We also use reinforcement learning to enhance the decision-making ability of our model. We summarized our main contributions as follows:

1. We first apply the pointer network model to the dynamic TSP problem.
2. We introduce attention to analyzing dynamic edge weights in dynamic TSP to improve the pointer network, which improves the model's decision-making ability.
3. We use reinforcement learning methods to improve the accuracy of the approximate solution of the model.
4. We have conducted extensive experiments comparing multiple baseline methods to demonstrate the effectiveness and low time consumption of our model.

The rest of this paper is organized as follows. First, we discuss related works in Sect. 2. We then describe the dynamic TSP problem and the methodologies implementation in Sect. 3. Next, we present experimental settings and evaluation results in Sect. 4. Finally, we make conclusions for ours work in Sect. 5.

2 Related Works

2.1 RNN

In the last decade, the application of Recurrent Neural Network (RNN) has become more and more extensive, and it has become one of the most classic time series models [31], because of its memory function to remember distant information. Although RNN can process part of the historical information, when the time series is too long, the problem of "long-term dependence" occurs. To solve this problem, researchers have proposed many improvements on the basis of the RNN model. The most widely used variants are the long short-term memory model (LSTM) [32] and GRU model [33], both of which can well alleviate the long-term dependency limitation.

The Seq2Seq [34] model is based on the Encoder-Decoder framework, which can handle the problem of unequal length of input and output sequences. It can be used to assist RNN. [35] propose an attention mechanism to further optimize Seq2Seq model. The output length of the Seq2Seq model is fixed, which makes it impossible to use it in dynamic TSP. To solve the problem of "heavy dependence of output on input", researchers have proposed a pointer network [21] based on the attention mechanism.

2.2 Reinforcement Learning

Reinforcement learning [36], also known as evaluation learning or augmented learning. It is widely used in various interaction scenarios in which an intelligence agent with a transformed environment to learn a learning strategy that maximizes the total reward or achieves a particular goal through single interaction rewards [37, 38]. Reinforcement learning can be divided into Value-Based algorithms [39] and Policy-Based algorithms [40]. The famous DQN [41] algorithm is one of the Value-Based algorithms, which uses CNN [42] to approximate the value function.

3 PN-DTSP Model

3.1 Definition

In a graph $G = (V, E)$, there are $|V|$ nodes and $|E|$ edges, where $V = \{v_1, v_2 \ldots v_n\}$ is the set of nodes and $E = \{e_1, e_2 \ldots e_{n \times (n-1)}\}$ is the set of edges. The attributes of each node in graph G consist of horizontal coordinate x and vertical coordinate y. For any two nodes v_a and v_b distance $l(v_a, v_b)$ in the graph, the distance can be calculated according to Eq. (1)

$$l(v_a, v_b)(t) = \sqrt{\left(x_{v_a} - x_{v_b}\right)^2 + \left(y_{v_a} - y_{v_b}\right)^2} + d_{ab}(t), \tag{1}$$

where $\sqrt{\left(x_{v_a} - x_{v_b}\right)^2 + \left(y_{v_a} - y_{v_b}\right)^2}$ is the Euclidean distance, $d_{ab}(t)$ is a function of time t, which represents the changes of edge weights in dynamic TSP. The problem is suitably simplified in our study. The edge distance matrix of the graph corresponding to the dynamic TSP problem changes over time, but the number of nodes in the graph does not change, and the distance of the edges in the graph only changes with each new node reached during the traversal. Thus, in a dynamic TSP problem with n nodes, the full graph changes n times.

The dynamic TSP can be described as that we choose any node in the graph as the starting point. Then, we traverse each other nodes in turn and finally return to the starting point with the goal to minimize the sum of edge weights on the traversed paths. The optimization objective of dynamic TSP can be described as Eq. (2)

$$Min(d(T(t))) = \min\left(\sum_{i=1}^{n(t)} d_{T_i, T_{i+1}}(t)\right),$$

(2)

where $D = \{d_{ij}(t)\}$ denotes the edge weight matrix of the corresponding graph and $d_{ij}(t)$ denotes the weights of nodes v_i and v_j at the edge at time t.

3.2 OPN-STSP

In a graph $G = (V, E, D)$, we first construct the input $\{x^i = (s^i, d^i)\}$ for the pointer network, where s^i is the two-dimensional coordinate of node i, which belongs to the static part, not changing with moments. d^i is the dynamic part, which represents the change value of the edges from node i to other nodes at all moments. The expression of d^i is given in Eq. (3)

$$d^i = \left[d_0^i; d_1^i; \ldots; d_{T-1}^i\right],$$

(3)

where the symbol ; represents the splicing operation of vectors, and T represents the number of times, which is the same as the number of nodes.

Our optimized pointer network (OPN-DTSP) has two modules: Encoder and Decoder. Different from Encoder in the original pointer network [21] by using RNN, the Encoder module encodes the input $\{x^i = (s^i, d^i)\}$ as a multidimensional vector by using one-dimensional convolution with 1×1 kernel size. We calculate the static part and the dynamic part separately with different parameters. The Encoder module uses GRU [33] at each decoding step to point to input. We provide the static information as input to the decoder network. For each input, the decoder network will output the probability of each node being selected as the next hop, and select the node with the highest probability, and so on until all the nodes are traversed and returned to the starting point. Then the solution of the dynamic TSP problem is completed.

The architecture of OPN-DTSP is shown in Fig. 1, the dynamic information is a stitching of the amount of edge changes at each moment of the node and we use the attention for the processing of dynamic elements. In step i of the decoder, we use the context-based attention to extract relevant information by vector a_t, where the role of attention is to determine the input in the next moment t. The attention vector a_t can be calculated according to Eq. (2) and Eq. (3)

$$a_t = a_t\left(x_t^i, h_t\right) = softmax(u_t),$$

(4)

$$u_t^i = v_a^T \tanh\left(W_a\left[x_t^i; h_t\right]\right),$$

(5)

where $h_t \in R^D$ is the memory unit of GRU at moment t, ; represents the splicing of two vectors. Then the obtained attention is added to the input to obtain the vector with attention c_t

$$c_t = \sum_{i=1}^{M} a_t^i x_t^i \qquad (6)$$

After obtaining the attention vector, the values are normalized by the decoding part and using the softmax function according to Eq. (7)

$$P(y_{t+1}|Y_t, X_t) = softmax\left(v_c^T \tanh\left(W_c\left[x_t^i; c_t\right]\right)\right) \qquad (7)$$

The v_a, v_c, W_a, W_c in Eq. (9) and (10) are hyperparameters for learning.

In decoding, assuming that, in moment t, when making decisions, the information of edge weight changes before moment t already has an impact on the encoding vectors, so it is only necessary to consider the information of edge weight changes afterward. At the moment of decoding moment t, the dynamic part information of node i is updated in this paper as shown in Eq. (8)

$$d^i = \left[0; 0; \ldots, d_t^i \ldots; d_{T-1}^i\right] \qquad (8)$$

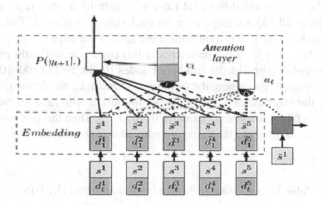

Fig. 1. The architecture of OPN

The detailed algorithm is shown in Algorithm 1. Since the dynamic TSP problem is more complex than the static TSP problem, it is difficult to obtain the exact solution of the problem in a short period of time, and therefore it is more difficult to obtain labeling information for training in a supervised manner. For this reason, we use the reinforcement learning approach Actor-Critic to learn the dynamic TSP problem.

Algorithm 1. Pointer Networks for Approximate Solution of dynamic TSP

```
Input: Node coordinates S、Dynamic edge weight matrix D
S← norm(S)
ENCODER: static_encoder ← Conv1d(S)
ENCODER: dynamic_encoder ← Conv1d(D)
xⁱ=[static_encoder ; dynamic_encoder]
DECODER in time t : dynamic_hidden ← Conv1d(Sₜ)
GRU hidden: hₜ = GRU(dynamic_hidden)
Attention: aₜ = soft max (vₐᵀtanhWₐ[xₜⁱ, hₜ]))
While terminating condition!=True
Encoder With Attention cₜ = Σᵢ₌₁ᴹ aₜⁱxₜⁱ
The Probability of Each Node at t+1
            p(t + 1) = soft max (vᶜᵀ tanh (Wᶜ[xₜⁱ; cₜ]))
Pred=max(p(t+1))
Return Pred
```

4 Experiment

4.1 Dataset and Experiment Settings

In this paper, we consider the case where the change weights of edges are discrete. Specifically, the time required to travel from any node to another is a one-time unit, and the weights of all edges change once for each time unit elapsed. The optimization objective of the dynamic TSP is to minimize the sum of the edge weights on the path.

The graph data used for the experiments in this paper are randomly generated. We define four types of graphs with the number of nodes 10, 20, 50 and 100. 100000 graphs are generated for each type, where the *training set : test set : validation set* $= 7 : 2 : 1$. In each graph, the coordinates of the nodes are initialized with random values, and the node coordinates take values range from $(0, 0)$ to $(1, 1)$. Then the side weight variable $d_{ij}(t)$ is a function of time, and the range of variation is set between $(-0.1, +0.1)$ (Table 1).

Table 1. Description of the data in the dataset for OPN-DTSP

Variable	Type	Description
x	Float	Horizontal coordinate of node
y	Float	Vertical coordinate of node
id	Int	Node ID
$d_{ij}(t)$	Float	weights of edge e_{ij} at t time

We mainly compared the approximate solutions of the traditional methods in our experiments. We also compare the exact solution based on dynamic programming, but the complexity of the dynamic programming method is high and cannot be computed when the number of nodes is too large. We set the learning rate to 0.1.

We conduct experiments to investigate the appropriate number of hidden layers in the dataset with 20 nodes. The number of hidden layers is set to 32, 64, 128, 256, 512 and 1024, respectively. We select the parameter with the smallest loss value as the best parameter. The experimental results are shown in Fig. 2(a). It can be seen that the best hidden layers are around 256 and 512. Although the 512 layers is slightly better than 256, but the decline is smaller. In order to reduce the time cost, we finally choose the 256 hidden layers. To explore the appropriate dropout values, we conducted experiments in a data set with 20 nodes. The dropout values were set to 0.0, 0.1, 0.2, 0.3, 0.4 and 0.5, respectively. The parameter with the smallest loss value was selected as the best parameter. The experimental results are shown in Fig. 2(b). It can be seen that the loss value is the smallest when the dropout value is 0.1.

4.2 Performance on Static Graph

To verify that OPN-DTSP model can effectively utilize the dynamic edge weight information of the dynamic graph, we compare the original pointer network model on the static graph. We visualize several solutions from the test results of the static model and the dynamic model, respectively. Figure 3 presents the partial solution of the static graph in the static model, as well as the partial solution of our model. The same node coordinate data is used for both parts, and the difference is that the graph edge weights used in Fig. 2(a) are statically invariant. It is observed that the two partial decompositions are generally similar, but in terms of details, there are still differences, which indicates that the dynamic model makes different decisions from the static model after considering the dynamically changing edge weights.

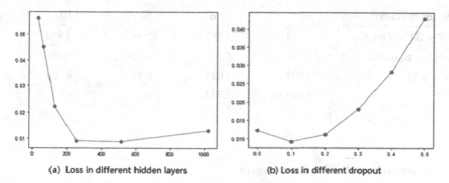

(a) Loss in different hidden layers   (b) Loss in different dropout

Fig. 2. The impact of the number of hidden layers and dropout

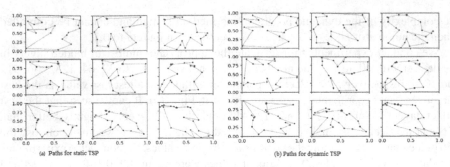

Fig. 3. Paths for TSP

4.3 Performance Comparison on Dynamic TSP

To verify OPN-DTSP performance of the dynamic TSP problem approximation solution, we compared with other traditional approximation algorithms, including genetic algorithm [25], NS-ACO [26] and dynamic programming violence methods (DP), respectively. A comparison experiment was made on four types of graphs with the number of nodes 10,20,50,100 respectively. Because of the unbearable time consumption on 50 and 100 nodes, we did not calculate these graphs by DP.

From the experimental results in Table 2, we know that the effect of OPN-DTSP is optimal relative to other approximation algorithms in all three data sets of 20, 50 and 100 nodes. It is only slightly inferior to the NS-ACO method in the data set with 10 nodes, but the difference is very small.

Table 2. Sum of solution paths of different methods on datasets

Nodes in graph	10	20	50	100
OPN-DTSP(Ours)	2.623	3.882	5.997	8.890
Genetic algorithm	2.756	4.125	6.224	9.250
NS-ACO	2.603	4.021	6.125	8.993
DP	2.493	3.773	~	~

4.4 Comparison of Time Consumption

To verify the time-consuming performance of the OPN-DTSP, we compared it with other traditional approximation algorithms, which are the same as Sect. 4.3. The time-consuming comparison experiment is the total time in seconds to compute 256 test cases. For the deep learning-based approach proposed in this paper, only the training phase takes a long time, and once the model is trained, the testing phase does not take very long, and, since it can be accelerated with the GPU, it takes less and less time. The results are shown in Table 3 and Fig. 4.

Table 3. Time consumption of baseline methods

Nodes in graph	10	20	50	100
OPN-DTSP (Ours)	0.026	0.126	1.569	8.265
Genetic algorithm	0.089	1.658	17.326	235.326
NS-ACO	0.076	1.459	16.592	210.469
DP	0.189	268.326	~	~

From the results, it can be seen that the time consumption of our OPN-DTSP is much shorter than the enumeration-based DP method and the approximate solution of the dynamic TSP problem based on traditional methods. The time consumption of our model grows flatter as the size of the graph becomes larger.

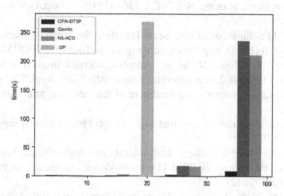

Fig. 4. Comparison of time consumption in different models

5 Conclusion

The main purpose of our work is to solve the problem that the dynamic TSP is unsolvable in polynomial time, and the brute force search and traditional approximation methods take too long. Our solution is OPN-DTSP model, which fuse the dynamically changing edge information and the static node coordinate information, to handle the dynamic TSP. Our work is based on the following two premises: (1) deep learning has a strong fitting ability for dynamic TSP, a relatively satisfactory approximate solution can be obtained within an affordable time; (2) when looking for a path in a dynamic TSP, we need to consider the edge weight changes of the unselected nodes to achieve good results. Finally, we verify that our model is better than traditional algorithms based on comparative experiments. With the increasing of nodes, the time consumption of traditional algorithms becomes unbearable. In contrast, the computational time consumption of OPN-DTSP increases at a slower rate.

References

1. Jünger, M., Reinelt, G., Rinaldi, G.: The traveling salesman problem. Math. Teach. **65.7**, 601–601 (1994)
2. Wang, Z., Li, T., Xiong, N., et al.: A novel dynamic network data replication scheme based on historical access record and proactive deletion. J. Supercomput. **62**(1), 227–250 (2012). https://doi.org/10.1007/s11227-011-0708-z
3. Reinelt, G.: The traveling salesman problem: computational solutions for TSP applications, Lecture Notes Computer Science **840** (1994)
4. Guo, W., Xiong, N., Vasilakos, A.V., et al.: Multi-source temporal data aggregation in wireless sensor networks. Wireless Pers. Commun. **56**(3), 359–370 (2011)
5. Gusfield, D., Karp, R., Wang, L., et al.: Graph traversals, genes, and matroids: an efficient case of the travelling salesman problem. In: Proceedings of CPM, 167–180 (2006)
6. Yin, J., Lo, W., Deng, S., et al.: Colbar: a collaborative location-based regularization framework for QoS prediction. Inf. Sci. **265**, 68–84 (2014)
7. Carpeneto, G., Toth, P.: Some new branching and bounding criteria for the asymmetric travelling salesman problem. Manage. Sci. **26**(7), 736–43 (1980). http://www.jstor.org/stable/263 0706, INFORMS
8. Dantzig, G., et al.: Solution of a Large-Scale Traveling-Salesman Problem. J. Oper. Res. Soc. Am. **2**(4), 393–410 (1954). http://www.jstor.org/stable/166695, INFORMS
9. Wan, Z., Xiong, N., Ghani, N., et al.: Adaptive unequal protection for wireless video transmission over IEEE 802.11 e networks. Multimedia Tools Appl. **72**(1), 541–571 (2014)
10. Bellman, R.: Dynamic programming treatment of the travelling salesman problem. J. ACM **9**, 61–63 (1962)
11. Meng, F.: Genetic algorithm of traveling salesman problem. Systems Engineering—Theory and Practice (1997)
12. Qu, Y., Xiong, N.: RFH: a resilient, fault-tolerant and high-efficient replication algorithm for distributed cloud storage. In: 2012 41st International Conference on Parallel Processing, pp. 520–529. IEEE (2012)
13. He, R., Xiong, N., Yang, L.T., et al.: Using multi-modal semantic association rules to fuse keywords and visual features automatically for web image retrieval. Inf. Fusion **12**(3), 223–230 (2011)
14. Zhang, Q., Zhou, C., Tian, Y.C., et al.: A fuzzy probability Bayesian network approach for dynamic cybersecurity risk assessment in industrial control systems. IEEE Trans. Industr. Inf. **14**(6), 2497–2506 (2017)
15. Tsai, C.F., Tsai, C.W., Tseng, C.C.: A new hybrid heuristic approach for solving large traveling salesman problem. Inf. Sci. **166**(1–4), 67–81 (2004)
16. Liu, Y.J.: An algorithms with taboo search in traveling salesman problem. J. Jiangxi Univ. Sci. Technol. (2006)
17. Wu, M., Tan, L., Xiong, N.: A structure fidelity approach for big data collection in wireless sensor networks. Sensors **15**(1), 248–273 (2015)
18. Huang, S., Liu, A., Zhang, S., et al.: BD-VTE: A novel baseline data based verifiable trust evaluation scheme for smart network systems. IEEE Trans. Network Sci. Eng. **8**, 2087–2105 (2020)
19. Li, H., Liu, J., Wu, K., et al.: Spatio-temporal vessel trajectory clustering based on data mapping and density. IEEE Access **6**, 58939–58954 (2018)
20. Yeo, G.A.: Polynomial approximation algorithms for the TSP and the QAP with a factorial domination number. Discrete Appl. Math. **119**, 107–116 (2002)
21. Vinyals, O., Fortunato, M., Jaitly, N.: Pointer networks. Comput. Sci. **28** (2015)

22. Dai, H., Khalil, E.B., Zhang, Y., et al.: Learning combinatorial optimization algorithms over graphs. In: Proceedings of NeurIPS, pp. 6351–6361 (2017)
23. Nazari, M., et al.: Reinforcement learning for solving the vehicle routing problem (2018)
24. Kool, W., Van Hoof, H., Welling, M., et al.: Attention, learn to solve routing problems! In: International Conference on Learning Representations (2019)
25. Zhou, A., Kang, L., Yan, Z.: Solving dynamic TSP with evolutionary approach in real time. In: Congress on Evolutionary Computation IEEE (2003)
26. Wang, Y., Zhe, X., Sun, J., Han, F., Todo, Y., Gao, S.: Ant colony optimization with neighborhood search for dynamic TSP. In: Tan, Y., Shi, Y., Niu, B. (eds.) Advances in Swarm Intelligence, pp. 434–442. Springer International Publishing, Cham (2016). https://doi.org/10.1007/978-3-319-41000-5_43
27. Gharehchopogh, F.: A new approach in dynamic traveling salesman problem: a hybrid of ant colony optimization and descending gradient. Int. J. Managing Public Sect. Inf. Commun. Technol. 3(2), 1–9 (2012)
28. Yao, Y., Xiong, N., Park, J.H., et al.: Privacy-preserving max/min query in two-tiered wireless sensor networks. Comput. Math. Appl. 65(9), 1318–1325 (2013)
29. Mavrovouniotis, M., Van, M., Yang, S.: Pheromone modification strategy for the dynamic travelling salesman problem with weight changes. IEEE, pp. 1–8 (2017)
30. Gai, K., Qiu, M.: Reinforcement learning-based content-centric services in mobile sensing. IEEE Network 32(4), 34–39 (2018). https://doi.org/10.1109/MNET.2018.1700407
31. Hochreiter, S.: Untersuchungen zu Dynamischen Neuronalen Netzen[D]. Technische Universität München, Diploma (1991)
32. Hochreiter, et al.: Long short-term memory. Neural Comput. (1997)
33. Cho, K., et al.: Learning phrase representations using RNN encoder-decoder for statistical machine translation. Comput. Sci. (2014)
34. Sutskever, I., Vinyals, O., Le, Q.V.: Sequence to sequence learning with neural networks. In: Proceedings of NeurIPS, pp. 3104–3112 (2014)
35. Bahdanau, D., Cho, K., Bengio, Y.: Neural machine translation by jointly learning to align and translate. Comput. Sci. (2014)
36. Littman, M.L.: Reinforcement learning : a survey. J. Artif. Intell. Res. 4, 237–285 (1996)
37. Gai, K., Qiu, M.: Optimal resource allocation using reinforcement learning for IoT content-centric services. Appl. Soft Comput. 70, 12–21 (2018)
38. Gai, K., Qiu, M., Zhao, H., Sun, X.: Resource management in sustainable cyber-physical systems using heterogeneous cloud computing. IEEE Trans. Sustain. Comput. 3(2), 60–72 (2018). https://doi.org/10.1109/TSUSC.2017.2723954
39. Watkins, C.J.C.H.: Learning from delayed rewards. Ph.D. thesis Kings College University of Cambridge (1989)
40. Sutton, R.S.: Policy gradient methods for reinforcement learning with function approximation. In: Proceedings of NIPS, pp. 1057–1063 (2000)
41. Mnih, V., Kavukcuoglu, K., Silver, D., et al.: Human-level control through deep reinforcement learning. Nature 518(7540), 529–533 (2015)
42. Krizhevsky, A., Sutskever, I., Hinton, G.E.: Imagenet classification with deep convolutional neural networks. In: Proceedings of NeurIPS, pp. 1097–1105 (2012)

A Novel Client Sampling Scheme for Unbalanced Data Distribution Under Federated Learning

Bo Chen[1,2], Xiaoying Zheng[1,2], Yongxin Zhu[1,2(✉)], and Meikang Qiu[3]

[1] Shanghai Advanced Research Institute, Chinese Academy of Sciences, Shanghai, China
zhuyongxin@sari.ac.cn
[2] University of Chinese Academy of Sciences, Beijing, China
[3] Computer Science Department, Texas A&M University Commerce, Commerce, USA

Abstract. Federated learning is one computation paradigm used to address privacy preservation and efficient collaboration computing nowadays. Especially, in the environment where edge devices are facing different data scenarios, it is a challenge to enhance the prediction model accuracy. Since the data distributions on different edge devices might not be independent identical distributions, and also due to the communication obstacles existing in the modern complicated wireless world, it is an essential problem to sample which client devices to contribute to the server learning model. In this paper, instead of making the assumption on uniform distributed data sources, we assume the agnostic data distribution presumption. One indicator called client reward is defined applicable on the proposed client sampling algorithm. Combing with the redefined loss functions on the agnostic data distribution, a novel client sampling scheme is proposed and tested on real world datasets. The experiment results show that the client sampling scheme improves prediction accuracy on unbalanced data sources from different edge devices and achieves reasonable computing efficiency.

Keywords: Edge computing · Internet of Things · Machine learning · Supervised learning

1 Introduction

The federated learning is suitable for addressing learning problems faced in a distributed system. It is natural and common to see that over billions wired and wireless devices are connected sharing some categorical features, which produce data from different sources in real world. For the devices on the edge, there is not enough computing facilities [1] and power [2] to support a sophisticated enough learning model. Think about the sensors attached to solar panels across remote rural areas, where the power supply and wireless connections are not as good as in the cities [3, 3]. On the contrary, the central devices, which might be located in a computing center or servers supported with continuous and stable power supply and with state-of-the-art computing facilities, may not have rich enough data sources to train the prediction model [5, 5].

There are many challenges in federated learning, such as how to determine which data sources are selected in participating in the model training, how to sample client

© The Author(s), under exclusive license to Springer Nature Switzerland AG 2022
M. Qiu et al. (Eds.): SmartCom 2021, LNCS 13202, pp. 438–449, 2022.
https://doi.org/10.1007/978-3-030-97774-0_40

devices to have fairly good representations of different data sources and how to design the orchestration of server and client devices to mitigate the negative impact caused by unstable communication channels.

A lot of interests have been inspired recently, whose sampling schemes are usually unfit for non-independent identical distributed training data. To improve communication efficiency, the data transferred are compressed through the channels between server and client devices. The lossy compression [7], the structured and sketched updates [8], and FEDBOOST [9] were proposed. Their work is primarily focused on the communication efficiency and try to reduce data transferred under limited bandwidth. FedAvg [10] was proposed to select clients randomly and average the model parameters on server. FedPAQ [11] adapted quantizer operator to compress the model parameters. However, these proposals have not addressed the problem that how to sample client devices to contribute to the model training when the underlying data distributions are not independent identical distributed.

In this paper, we handle the tough condition that the underlying distributions are not independent identical distributed and the target whole distribution is not simple uniform union of all the client distributions. Instead, the proposed client sampling scheme is able to work with the condition that the target distribution is unknown. In order to evaluate which clients to be selected, one metric called client reward is defined as the indicator. Furthermore, after defining loss functions by setting up updated weighted factors, the scheme tries to find alignment between the client rewards with the weighted factors to determine which devices to be sampled on the run.

The contributions of the paper can be summarized as follows:

(1) A novel client sampling scheme is proposed to handle the tough condition that the underlying distributions are not independent identical distributed.
(2) The sampling scheme is improved by incorporating the condition that the target whole distribution is not simple uniform union of all the client distributions.
(3) Extensive experiments are conducted to validate the scheme we proposed.

This paper is organized as follows. The Sect. 2 is the brief introduction on related work and discussion on the contributions. The Sect. 3 is the client sampling scheme description and explanations on what is going on under the hood. The Sect. 4 is the experiment part, where EMNIST dataset is used to show the scheme testing accuracy results and the comparisons with the baselines. The Sect. 5 is the conclusion which talks about the application areas and possible further work.

2 Related Work

The related work on addressing challenges under federated learning can be grouped as two sets. One is improving the communication efficiency, and the other is improving the model prediction accuracy and learning fairness.

With the advance of computing software [12, 12], networks [14, 14], and algorithm design [16], lager amounts of data [17] need to be transferred and processed efficiently and securely [18, 19]. Communication efficiency can be improved by reducing the communication frequency between clients and server. Qiu et al. proposed an optimal resource allocation using reinforcement learning for IoT content-centric services and communication [20]. One way to reduce the communication frequency is to arrange more model training on the client devices. Federated Proximal [21] suggests that during one communication round, only part of the clients would be sampled and updated. The calculation epochs on client devices can be adjusted dynamically, and it is not required that all clients have the same calculation epochs. Federated Proximal is more suitable for non-independent identical distributions compared with FedAvg. Overlap Federated Averaging [22] is trying to utilize client cluster computing power to expedite the federated learning process, which is a trade-off between the number of clients participating in each round and the communication frequency. Another way to improve the communication efficiency is compressing the updated model being transferred between clients and server. One example is random sparsification, which is using sparse matrices to describe the updated local model and for each client, the sparse matrix is generated independently. Flexible Sparsification [23] allows only part of the gradients with significance to be uploaded to the server. Another example is quantification, which may use weight factors assigned to the local model parameters and lower the precision of gradients in order to reduce the communication cost. Multiple Access Channel based gradient sensing quantification [24] suggests that parameters optimization could be based on both the client gradients and the underlying channel conditions. Multiple Access Channel based quantification could take more advantage of the communication channels than uniform quantification.

Besides communication frequency reduction and model compression, client sampling is a popular technique for improving communication efficiency and model prediction accuracy. Federated Client Selection [25] selected the clients to participate in the update based on Cumulative Effective Participation. Yet Federated Client Selection performs not well under complicated network structure and non-independent identical distributions. To handle non-independent identical distribution situation, Hybrid Federated Learning [26] makes the server to sample clients in order to build a dataset locally with quasi-independent identical distribution for training. However, compared with FedAvg and Federated Client Selection, Hybrid Federated Learning achieves better accuracy at the cost of the communication efficiency.

The client sampling related work barely considered what the true target distribution is. Normally one combined uniform distribution is assumed across all clients in these proposals. In this paper, the sampling client scheme is proposed with unknown target distribution, which is natural and reasonable in real world. Since not all clients are sampled during each round, the scheme improves communication efficiency and suitable for some cases when local power supply is limited and sometimes not possible for the server to talk to all the clients.

3   Sampling Scheme

There are two major reasons to sample clients instead of poll all clients. One is that not all clients are available at all times. For instance, when the server is polling, some clients might be short of power or shut down. Another reason is that not all clients have access to the data distribution similar with the underlying global data distribution. The lack of similarity between distributions of some clients and the global one would cause the learning process converge slowly or even diverge at some point. Let's imagine that the underlying global distributions is D_g, and the data on some of the clients are with distributions similar to D_g. However, some of the other clients may have access to the data with distributions very distant from the D_g. If the client device k is polled, whose data distribution D_k shares little commonness with the global distribution D_g, the contributed model parameters by device k might cause the global model to underperform. Since the local parameters trained by the client device k may overfit to the local biased data source or data set.

Practically, the underlying global distribution is not the simple uniform union of distributions from all client, and it should be unknown. This gives inspiration that it would be helpful to first find out one global distribution which could make the total loss maximize and then find out the model wights W_g which could make the total loss minimize [27]. Once the global distribution with maximum loss being found out, the clients with the closest data distribution compared with the global one can be sampled to be contributing to the model updating. There are several steps in the whole process, which would be outlined below. Before that, let's define the data distribution which would be used in the following.

The data distribution is defined as the data class distribution, which means that two client devices are said to have the same data distribution if they have access to the same data classes with equal data samples for each class. Assume there are totally p classes.

3.1 Initialization

At time t, each client receives the global model weights W_g^t to assign to its own model weights, for client k, there is

$$W_k^t = W_g^t. \tag{1}$$

Each client computes the loss and the gradients with the newly assigned model weights. Especially, the gradients corresponding with every class is computed as follows, which is named as G_k^t,

$$G_k^t = \left[\Delta L_1^k(W^t), \Delta L_2^k(W^t), \cdots, \Delta L_p^k(W^t) \right]. \tag{2}$$

In (2), L is the loss function and each element of G_k^t is the gradient for the corresponding class. For instance, $\Delta L_p^k(W^t)$ is the gradient for class p on client k at time t.

3.2 Estimate the Class Distributions for Clients

What being transferred from clients to the server are the model weights, loss and gradients. Due to the privacy and communication concerns, the raw data are not known to the server. To estimate the class distributions, the gradients for different classes can be harnessed [28]. Let's define the expectations of gradients squared norms for class 1 and class 2 as $E\|\Delta L_1^k(W^t)\|^2$ and $E\|\Delta L_2^k(W^t)\|^2$ at time t for client k. The class distributions of data accessed by client k can be obtained by the following, where n_1^2 and n_2^2 are the squared of the quantities of samples for class 1 and class 2,

$$\frac{E\|\Delta L_1^k(W^t)\|^2}{E\|\Delta L_2^k(W^t)\|^2} \approx \frac{n_1^2}{n_2^2}. \tag{3}$$

By (3), the class distribution D_k^t on client k at time t can be estimated as,

$$D_k^t = \left[\frac{E\|\Delta L_1^k(W^t)\|^2}{\sum_{i=1}^p E\|\Delta L_i^k(W^t)\|^2}, \cdots, \frac{E\|\Delta L_p^k(W^t)\|^2}{\sum_{i=1}^p E\|\Delta L_i^k(W^t)\|^2}\right]. \tag{4}$$

3.3 Estimate the Global Class Distribution by Maximizing Loss

Since the underlying global class distribution is unknown, it is shown to model the minimizing loss process by quasi two-party game theory [27]. To model the estimation of the global class distribution, it can be constructed by first retrieving the unknow global distribution which makes the global loss max, and then using the weighted factors realized for each client to estimate the global distribution. Assume the class distribution for client k at time t is D_k^t, and global class distribution D_g^t is $\sum_{j=1}^K \beta_j D_j^t$ for totally K clients, where β_j's are the weighted factors. The pseudocode for computing β_j's is shown in Fig. 1. The global class distribution can be estimated as,

$$D_g^t = \left[\sum_{j=1}^K \beta_j \frac{E\|\Delta L_1^j(W^t)\|^2}{\sum_{i=1}^p E\|\Delta L_i^j(W^t)\|^2}, \cdots, \sum_{j=1}^K \beta_j \frac{E\|\Delta L_p^j(W^t)\|^2}{\sum_{i=1}^p E\|\Delta L_i^j(W^t)\|^2}\right]. \tag{5}$$

3.4 Define the Rewards for Client Selection

Now the individual class distribution and global distribution are estimated. The rewards for selection can be defined to rank the clients, the top ones of which would be sampled to take part in the model updating. Let's define the primary reward R_k^t for client k at time t as Cosine-based Similarity between client and global distribution as follows,

$$R_k^t = \frac{D_k^t \cdot D_g^t}{\|D_k^t\|\|D_g^t\|}. \tag{6}$$

After the primary rewards R_k^t's being obtained, the clients can be ranked from top to bottom. The clients ranked top would be likely to have the most similar class distributions as the estimated global distribution. It is reasonable to say that if the model updates are applied to the clients with the similar distribution with the global one, the learning process might improve on convergency and the accuracy would improve on average, especially on the worst cases under traditional uniform distribution assumption. However, since the distributions are made by estimators, it would be helpful to add one adjusted term to the primary rewards generated. This term would be related to the reward itself and can have counter effect on the ranking, which we define as follows,

$$Radj_k^t = \gamma \log \|R_k^t\|^{-1}. \tag{7}$$

In (7), $\gamma \in (0, 1)$ and can be tuned in runtime. Furthermore, to prevent the situation that the same set of clients are selected over and over again, one regulation term related how many times one client being selected should be included. First, define the times client k has been selected as T_k at time t. The regulation term for client balancing is defined as below,

$$Rreg_k^t = \eta \frac{t}{T_k}. \tag{8}$$

In (8), $\eta \in (0, 1)$ and can be tuned in the sampling process. Now let's put (6), (7) and (8) together, the reward is as below,

$$Rclient_k^t = \frac{D_k^t \cdot D_g^t}{\|D_k^t\| \|D_g^t\|} + \gamma \log \|R_k^t\|^{-1} + \eta \frac{t}{T_k}. \tag{9}$$

3.5   Update the Model with Sampled Clients

The updated model from the server can be retrieved as shown in the pseudocode in Fig. 1. Since the weighted factors β_j's are computed by the assumption that the global loss $L_g = \sum_j^K \beta_j L_j$ can be maximized under this set of β_j's, the combined maximum loss can be used to get the model parameters W on the server by $\underset{W}{\arg\min} L_g$ [26]. After the sampled clients receive the updated model parameters, they would train the model locally and get the new gradients, which can be uploaded to the server for the next round. However, even though every client receives the updated model parameters every round, not all clients participate in the local model training except for the sampled ones. At first glance, one would like to make all client devices compute the model parameter gradients and upload them to the server every round.

However, there is a trade-off to do so. Local client devices are usually facing power supply and computing resource challenges. The communication environment may also not allow too much data transfer for many clients. It is not practical to poll every client and make everyone compute the gradients each round. Therefore, one hyper-parameter M can be set to determine after how many rounds the server would poll all clients and make them upload the gradients computed locally. It should be pointed out that for each round the server still would broadcast the updated model parameters to every client device. The pseudocode of updating process is shown in Fig. 2.

Algorithm to Find the Client Rewards

Initialization:
Client weighted factors $\boldsymbol{\beta}^0$,
Model parameters W^0

Hyper-parameters:
$\gamma \in (0,1), \eta \in (0,1), \xi > 0, \rho > 0$

For $n = 1\ to\ N$:
Uniform randomly select J from K, K is the total number of clients
Uniform randomly select q from Q, Q is the total number of data samples on client j
$\Delta \beta_j^{n-1} = K L_q^J$ for $j = J$, else $\Delta \beta_j^{n-1} = 0$, where L_q^J is the loss corresponding to sample q on client J
$\Delta W^{n-1} = \boldsymbol{\beta}^{n-1} \cdot \Delta \boldsymbol{L}_q$, where $\Delta \boldsymbol{L}_q$ is the gradient vector whose element is the single data gradient uniform randomly sampled from the dataset on all clients K
$\boldsymbol{\beta}^n = argmin_{\beta^n} \|\boldsymbol{\beta}^n - \boldsymbol{\beta}^{n-1} - \xi \Delta \boldsymbol{\beta}^{n-1}\|_2$, such that $\beta_j^n \geq 0$ and $\sum_{j=1}^K \beta_j^n = 1$
$W^n = argmin_{W^n} \|W^n - W^{n-1} + \rho \Delta W^{n-1}\|_2$

Update weighted factors: $\boldsymbol{\beta}^{updated} = \frac{1}{N} \sum_{n=1}^N \boldsymbol{\beta}^n$

Update model parameters: $W^{updated} = \frac{1}{N} \sum_{n=1}^N W^n$

Calculate D_g based on $\boldsymbol{\beta}^{updated}$ by (5)
Calculate reward R_k for client k based on (9)
Rank R_k's for $k = 1\ to\ K$

Fig. 1. Pseudocode for Client Rewards.

Algorithm to Update the Model and Client Sampling

Initialization:
Client weighted factors $\boldsymbol{\beta}^0$,
Model parameters W^0

Hyper-parameters:
$M > 1$,
$S > 1$, which is the Number of Clients Sampled
While True:
Broadcast model parameters
Poll all clients and update model
Rank all clients by the algorithm as in Fig. 1
Sample top S clients ranked by rewards
For $m = 1\ to\ M$ rounds:
Broadcast model parameters
Update model by S clients sampled

Fig. 2. Pseudocode for Updating Process.

4 Experiments

The experiments to be shown are focused on the feasibility of the proposed scheme. Two aspects of the scheme were inspected, the accuracy of the predictions and the communication efficiency. One natural thought for the general learning experiments is to seek prediction accuracy as good as possible. However, there are some details under the accuracy achievement which might be worth looking into further. Assume there are some cases where the underlying distributions are similar on most of the edge or client devices. The uniform aggregated global model would be similar with the local client models trained on individual data sources. Compared with local models' prediction accuracy, the client sampling effect would be relatively not that significant. Therefore, if the local models are set with intensively training, the global model would converge to the best fit eventually [29]. Even though the client sampling could have contributed a lot under other cases, it would show little effect here. Considering the problem mentioned above, the experiments are designed to include comparatively intensive local training and light training for imbalanced data sources.

The data set used for the experiments is CIFAR-10. The data set contains 10 classes and 6 thousand images per class. There are 50 thousand training images and 10 thousand test images.

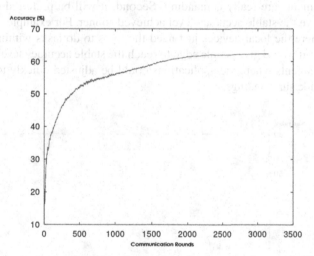

Fig. 3. Accuracy curve by baseline. (X axis: number of communication rounds, Y axis: accuracy in percentage).

The baseline adopted intensive local computing on client devices. The experiments showed that it took about 30 rounds to get 30% accuracy, and more than 2200 rounds to make the accuracy behave stably as shown in Fig. 3.

The experiments with batch size of 20 in Fig. 4 showed that the convergency looks better compared with baseline curve. There was 30% accuracy achieved less than 10 rounds. On top of the curve where it showed that within 400 rounds the accuracy reached the stable status. There are several good points to have these features. First of all, it will

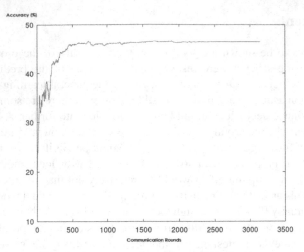

Fig. 4. Accuracy curve with small batch size.

be helpful to achieve a reasonable accuracy level soon, which would make the local applications suitable for certain scenarios, such as environment in which communication requirements are really demanding. Second, it will be preferred over absolute accuracy to have the stable accuracy level achieved sooner. For example, for some outdoor cases where the local devices just need the tools to do tasks within limited time frame. Thirdly, it would give people edge to reach the stable accuracy level under power critical environments where the applications could be adjusted quickly to adapt to the changing outside surroundings.

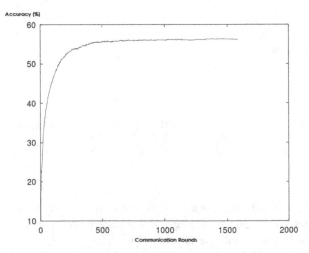

Fig. 5. Accuracy curve with medium batch size.

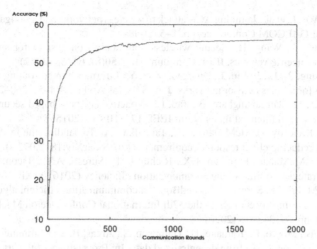

Fig. 6. Accuracy curve with large batch size.

To compare the results with different training batch sizes, the experiments with batch size 50 and 150 were introduced in Fig. 5 and Fig. 6. It can be concluded that with more batch sizes, the overall accuracy improved over 10%, and the convergency advantage was still kept. It took less than 150 rounds to get 50% accuracy compared with more than 400 rounds from the baseline. However, there was not much change with larger batch size loaded. It can be seen that there were some jitters.

5 Conclusions

In this paper, we designed a client sampling scheme for federated learning scenario. It is assumed that the unknown global distribution fits the real world. Based on the modeling of the underlying distributions, the important or available client devices are selected by corresponding rewards. The experiment results showed that the proposed scheme performs well on imbalanced client data sources. The communication efficiency and model prediction accuracy can be balanced on the number of clients being selected each round. The convergency of global model training can be balanced with local devices training and the aggregations on server. Furthermore, there are interesting topics to be covered next step, such as applying the global distributions to various domains other than different single client device.

References

1. Gao, Y., Iqbal, S., et al.: Performance and power analysis of high-density multi-GPGPU architectures: a preliminary case study. In: IEEE 17th HPCC (2015)
2. Qiu, M., Ming, Z., Li, J., Liu, S., Wang, B., Lu, Z.: Three-phase time-aware energy minimization with DVFS and unrolling for chip multiprocessors. J. Syst. Architect. **58**(10), 439–445 (2012)

3. Zhang, Z., Wu, J., et al.: Jamming ACK attack to wireless networks and a mitigation approach. In: IEEE GLOBECOM Conference, pp. 1–5 (2008)
4. Su, H., Qiu, M., Wang, H.: Secure wireless communication system for smart grid with rechargeable electric vehicles. IEEE Commun. Mag. **50**(8), 62–68 (2012)
5. Qiu, M., Ming, Z., Li, J., Liu, J., Quan, G., Zhu, Y.: Informer homed routing fault tolerance mechanism for wireless sensor networks. J. of Systems Archi. **59**(4–5), 260–270 (2013)
6. Gai, K., Qiu, M., Thuraisingham, B., Tao, L.: Proactive attribute-based secure data schema for mobile cloud in financial industry. In: IEEE 17th HPCC (2015)
7. Caldas, S., Konečny, J., McMahan, H.B., Talwalkar, A.: Expanding the reach of federated learning by reducing client resource requirements (2018). arXiv:1812.07210
8. Konečný, J., McMahan, H.B., Yu, F.X., Richtárik, P., Suresh, A.T., Bacon, D.: Federated learning: strategies for improving communication efficiency (2016). arXiv:1610.05492
9. Hamer, J., Mohri, M., Suresh, A.T.: FedBoost: a communication-efficient algorithm for federated learning. In: Proceedings of the 37th International Conference on Machine Learning, PMLR 119, pp. 3973–3983 (2020)
10. McMahan, B., Moore, E., Ramage, D., Hampson, S., Arcas, B.A.: Communication-efficient learning of deep networks from decentralized data. In: Proceedings of the 20th International Conference on Artificial Intelligence and Statistics, PMLR 54:1273–1282 (2017)
11. Reisizadeh, A., Mokhtari, A., Hassani, H., Jadbabaie, A., Pedarsani, R.: FedPAQ: a communication-efficient federated learning method with periodic averaging and quantization. In: Proceedings of the 23rd International Conference on Artificial Intelligence and Statistics, PMLR 108:2021–2031 (2020)
12. Tao, L., Golikov, S., et al.: A reusable software component for integrated syntax and semantic validation for services computing. In: IEEE Symposium on Service-Oriented System Engineering, pp. 127–132 (2015)
13. Zhao, H., Chen, M., et al.: A novel pre-cache schema for high performance Android system. Futur. Gener. Comput. Syst. **56**, 766–772 (2016)
14. Li, J., Qiu, M., Niu, J., et al.: Feedback dynamic algorithms for preemptable job scheduling in cloud systems. In: IEEE/WIC/ACM Conference on Web Intelligence (2010)
15. Tang, X., Li, K., et al.: A hierarchical reliability-driven scheduling algorithm in grid systems. J. Parallel Distrib. Comput. **72**(4), 525–535 (2012)
16. Qiu, H., Qiu, M., Memmi, G., Ming, Z., Liu, M.: A dynamic scalable blockchain based communication architecture for IoT. In: Qiu, M. (ed.) SmartBlock 2018. LNCS, vol. 11373, pp. 159–166. Springer, Cham (2018). https://doi.org/10.1007/978-3-030-05764-0_17
17. Zhang, K., Kong, J., Qiu, M., Song, G.: Multimedia layout adaptation through grammatical specifications. Multimedia Syst. **10**(3), 245–260 (2005). https://doi.org/10.1007/s00530-004-0155-2
18. Thakur, K., Qiu, M., Gai, K., Ali, M.: An investigation on cyber security threats and security models. In: IEEE CSCloud (2015)
19. Gai, K., Qiu, M., Sun, X., Zhao, H.: Security and privacy issues: a survey on FinTech. In: Qiu, M. (ed.) SmartCom 2016. LNCS, vol. 10135, pp. 236–247. Springer, Cham (2017). https://doi.org/10.1007/978-3-319-52015-5_24
20. Gai, K., Qiu, M.: Optimal resource allocation using reinforcement learning for IoT content-centric services. Appl. Soft Comput. **70**, 12–21 (2018)
21. Sahu, A.K., Li, T., Sanjabi, M.: Federated optimization for heterogeneous networks (2021). arXiv:1812.06127
22. Zhou, Y., Qing, Y., Lv, J.: Communication-efficient federated learning with compensated overlap-FedAvg (2021). arXiv:2012.06706
23. Shi, W., Zhou, S., Niu, Z.: Joint device scheduling and resource allocation for latency constrained wireless federated learning. IEEE Trans. Wireless Communications **20**(1), 453–467 (2020)

24. Chang, W.T., Tandon, R.: Communication efficient federated learning over multiple access channels (2021). arXiv:2001.08737
25. Nishio, T., Yonetani, R.: Client selection for federated learning with heterogeneous resources in mobile edge. In: Proceedings of the 2019 IEEE International Conference on Communications (ICC). Piscataway, pp. 1–7. IEEE (2019)
26. Yoshida, N., Nishio, T., Morikura, M.: Hybrid-FL for wireless networks: cooperative learning mechanism using non-IID data. In: Proceedings of the 2020 IEEE International Conference on Communications (ICC). Piscataway, pp. 1–7. IEEE (2020)
27. Mohri, M., Sivek, G., Suresh, A.T.: Agnostic federated learning. In: Proceedings of the 36th International Conference on Machine Learning, PMLR 97, pp. 4615–4625 (2019)
28. Anand, R., Mehrotra, K.G., Mohan, C.K., Ranka, S.: An improved algorithm for neural network classification of imbalanced training sets. IEEE Trans. on Neural Networks **4**(6), 962–969 (1993)
29. Yang, M., Wong, A., Zhu, H., Wang, H., Qian, H.: Federated learning with class imbalance reduction (2020) *arXiv: 2011.11266*

A Novel Secure Speech Biometric Protection Method

Lan Yang[1,2(✉)], Zongbo Wu[1,2], and Jun Guo[1,2]

[1] Software College, Quan Zhou University of Information Engineering, Quan Zhou 362000, China
[2] Key Laboratory of Cloud Computing and Internet-of-Thing Technology, Quan Zhou University of Information Engineering, Quan Zhou 362000, China

Abstract. In recent years, *automatic speaker verification* (ASV) has been widely used in speech biometrics. The ASV systems are vulnerable to various spoofing attacks, such as *synthesized speech* (SS), *voice conversion* (VC), replay attacks, twin attacks, and simulation attacks. The research to ensure the application of voice biometric systems in various security fields has attracted more and more researchers' interest. The combination of credibility and voice is particularly important in this period when biometric systems are widely used. We propose a novel secure speech biometric protection method. This article also summarizes previous research on spoofing attacks, focusing on SS, VC, and replay, as well as recent efforts to improve security and develop countermeasures for *spoofing speech detection* (SSD) tasks. At the same time, it pointed out the limitations and challenges of SSD tasks.

Keywords: Automatic speaker verification · Voice deception · Synthesized voice · Voice conversion · Spoofing detection · Deep learning

1 Introduction

With the development of information technology [1–3] and network technology [4–6], big data processing and transferring [7, 8] become a common way for various applications. However, how to protect the security and privacy [9, 10] of various applications emerges as a critical problem [11, 12]. For example, speech-based biometrics is already a mature technology that has been commercially applied and promoted. This technology is used in fields that are closely related to information, such as acccss control, application monitoring, and forensics. However, the unprotected ASV system is extremely vulnerable to various spoofing attacks [13]. Using voice spoofing technology, an attacker can easily and illegally enter the relevant system to steal information or perform various damages, which is extremely harmful.

Speaker recognition usually refers to speaker recognition and speaker verification. The speaker recognition system recognizes who is the speaker, and the *automatic speaker verification* (ASV) system determines whether the identity statement is true or false. The former is a multi-class classification problem, and the latter is a hypothesis test.

A general ASV system is robust to common imitation substitution attacks, but it is somewhat powerless against more complex attacks. This kind of vulnerability is one of the security issues of the ASV system.

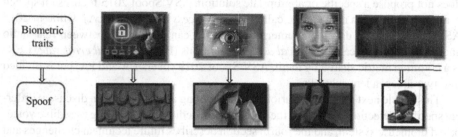

Fig. 1. Biometric recognition and spoofing technology for fingerprints, iris, face, and voice

Since a person's biological characteristics are easily obtained, deception attacks using related technologies are always unavoidable. Figure 1 shows some examples of how different techniques can be used to deceive the original biometric pattern. In this article, we only focus on voice-based deception and anti-spoofing technologies for ASV systems. Spoofed speech samples can be obtained through speech synthesis, speech conversion, or replay of recorded speech. According to how the spoofed samples are presented to the ASV system, attacks are roughly divided into two categories, namely direct attacks and indirect attacks. In a direct attack, the sample is applied to the ASV system through the sensor as an input, that is, the attack is carried out at the microphone and transmission level. In indirect attacks, samples involve attacks through sensors, namely the ASV system software process, access during feature extraction, interference models, and decision-making or score calculations [14], as shown in Fig. 2.

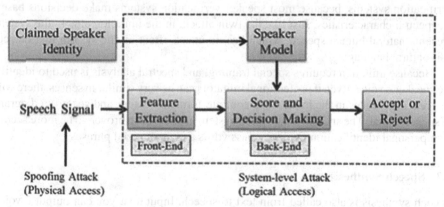

Fig. 2. Brief description of the *automatic speaker verification* (ASV) system

In the initial stage of the rise of this research field, many scholars used many different data sets and different indicators for research work, which made the relevant results impossible to compare horizontally. In order to gather a community with a standard database and performance indicators, a series of anti-spoofing competitions were born, for example, the *Automated Speaker Verification Spoof and Countermeasures* (ASV Spoof) challenge, as the challenge of the INTERSPEECH special conferences in 2013, 2015, 2017 and 2019. ASV Spoof 2013 aims to raise this serious deception problem, but does not propose a specific or appropriate solution. ASV Spoof 2015 focuses on speech synthesis and speech conversion, called *logical access conditions* (LA), while in 2017 ASV Spoof aims to develop countermeasures that can distinguish between real audio and replayed audio, called *physical access* conditions (PA). The *equal error rate* (EER) is a common metric shared by them. ASV Spoof 2019 covers LA and PA, but is divided into two independent subtasks.

This article next introduces various voice spoofing attacks, and then discusses different spoofing detection methods in the third section, dedicated to building a credible voice-based biometric system, and the fourth section describes future technical challenges and research prospects.

2 Voice Spoofing

In many research documents, voice spoofing attacks can be roughly divided into four types: Impersonation, Synthetic speech, Voice conversion, and Replay.

2.1 Imitate

Although human voice is independent, it can also be imitated. Professional imitators or some special twins can imitate part of the target's biological characteristics without any technical background or machinery. However, some studies have found that professional voice imitators intend to imitate the prosody, accent, pronunciation, vocabulary, and other advanced speaker characteristics of the claimed speaker. This imitation may mislead human perception, however, it is less efficient when attacking speaker verification systems, because most speaker verification systems make decisions based on spectral characteristics. Just like the twin attack, in the imitation attack, the system presents natural human speech, which has no attack effect on the system that detects non-natural language.

Because imitation requires special training, and spectral analysis is used to identify the speaker's voice. Even if professional imitators can be very similar in senses, there will be great differences in the mode, tone contour, formant contour and spectrum diagram of speech signal. The speaker verification system has also been proven to be more secure than personal identification numbers, passwords and memorized phrases.

2.2 Speech Synthesis

Speech synthesis is also called from text to speech. Input text, you can output a voice signal. It uses a variety of methods to imitate the human voice system, which is a highly threatening deception method. In recent years, considerable progress has been made in unit selection [15], statistical parameters [16], hybrid [17] and DNN-based TTS methods. Speech synthesis technology can now produce high-quality speech. Recently, technologies based on deep learning, such as *Generative Adversarial Networks* (GAN) [18], Tacotron [19], Wavenet [20], etc. It can produce a very natural sound and rhythm on the timbre. Speech synthesis technology uses the attributes of the speaker's voice characteristics and the frequency spectrum of natural speech as clues, which is a very effective speech deception technology.

2.3 Voice Conversion

Voice conversion is the process of converting the voice of the source speaker into a voice similar to the voice of the target speaker. The evaluation criteria of voice conversion mainly focus on the converted voice quality and the similarity with the target speaker. Early research mainly used statistical methods, such as *Gaussian Mixture* Model (GMM) [21], *Hidden Markov Model* (HMM) [22], *Unit Selection* [23], *Principal Component Analysis* (PCA) [24], VC task *Non-negative matrix factorization* (NMF) [25]. These methods usually require fixed identities of the source and target speakers, the algorithm has poor versatility, and requires frame-level aligned training data.

In recent years, there have been many new methods that go beyond the limitations of traditional technologies, such as DNN [26], WaveNet [20], etc. in addition to surpassing the traditional methods in terms of sound quality and similarity, the more important achievement of these methods is to break the limitation that training data needs frame level alignment, and some of them also break the limitation of fixed speaker identity. Figure 3 shows the general process of voice conversion:

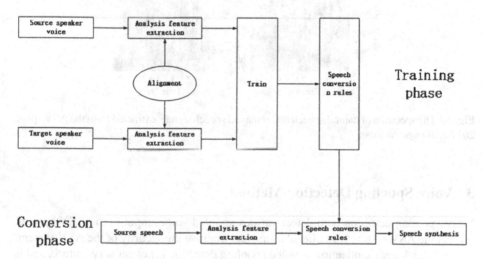

Fig. 3. The general flow of the voice conversion spoofing method

2.4 Replay Attack

The replay attack is one of the easiest ways to implement voice deception. The attacker replays the pre-recorded voice from the target speaker to the system to gain access. This attack is only meaningful for speaker verification systems that rely on text. Use high-quality recording and playback audio equipment, the replayed voice is highly similar to the original voice, and the spectrum content will slightly change due to the impulse response of the device. Therefore, replay is a serious threat to text-dependent speaker verification systems.

An important part of replay attack detection is the feature representation process. In order to obtain the distinguishing information between the natural speech signal and the reproduced speech signal, people should pay attention to the spectral characteristics of the information representing the intermediate device. Figure 4 shows the spectrum analysis of natural speech and replayed speech signals extracted from the ASV spoof 2017 challenge database. It can be seen that there is a slight difference in time and frequency spectrum between the natural voice signal and the reproduced voice signal.

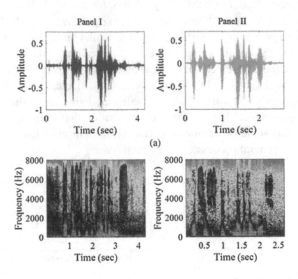

Fig. 4. The spectrum of natural speech and replayed speech signals extracted from the ASV spoof 2017 challenge database

3   Voice Spoofing Detection Method

Voice spoofing detection is to detect various spoofed voices input to the ASV system, protect the ASV system from illegal users, and improve the security of the ASV system. Since the technical application of voice spoofing detection is not yet very mature, and is limited by the data set of voice spoofing detection, there is no more universal spoofing detection technology. Most voice spoofing detection methods only detect specific types of spoofing methods. These methods can be roughly divided into speech deception detection based on traditional acoustic features and speech deception detection based on deep neural networks.

3.1   Voice Deception Detection Based on Traditional Acoustic Features

In the research based on traditional acoustic characteristics, Md Sahidulla has made a lot of achievements [27]. He based on the ASVspoofing2015 dataset, compared the MEL frequency inverted spectrum coefficient, linear frequency inverted spectrum coefficient, inverted MEL frequency inverted spectrum coefficient, rectangular filter inverted spectrum coefficient, linear prediction inverted spectrum coefficient, correction group and the delay. The discovery of the difference between natural speech and attacking speech in the above-mentioned traditional acoustic characteristics is of great significance to the detection of deceptive speech.

The field of traditional acoustic characteristic collar research is derived from signal processing methods, and many researchers have proposed effective detection methods and systems in this regard. Massimilliano Todisco transplanted the method in the field of vocal music, and proposed the constant Q cepstral coefficient feature [28], Suthokumar proposed a feature based on the centroid frequency of the modulation spectrum [29], and Gunendradasan proposed a frequency modulation feature based on *Linear Predictive Coefficients* (LPC).

3.2   Speech Deception Detection Based on Deep Learning

With the rapid development of deep learning, researchers combine research methods in the fields of speech recognition and voiceprint recognition to apply it to speech deception detection.

The advantage of being able to distinguish between nonlinear features gives deep neural networks impressive results in speech deception detection. The application of deep learning in speech deception detection can be roughly divided into three categories: the speech deception detection algorithm based on feedforward fully connected neural network [30], the speech deception detection algorithm based on convolutional neural network [31] and the speech deception detection algorithm based on recurrent neural network [32]. Soni et al. proposed the sub-band autoencoder feature, using the amplitude spectrum as the input and training label of the autoencoder, and finally output the features of the bottleneck layer. Hardik proposed a convolutional RBM to learn the parameters of the filter set and then extract the amplitude and frequency modulation information of the sound signal. Francis Tom built two neural networks based on residual networks, using the input of the first network as the group delay feature, and outputting two labels corresponding to real speech and fake speech, and taking the output of the last hidden layer of the first network as input to the second network. They both finished well at the ASV Spoof Challenge.

In general, most researches are still biased towards feature extraction and detection. The speech deception detection method and its improvement based on *Generative Adversarial Neural Network* (GAN) is a hot research direction recently.

3.3   Comparison of Results of Various Methods

To effectively compare the algorithms, we need standard databases and general evaluation metrics. The following method uses the ASV Spoof2017 dataset, and the performance of the relevant system is described by the *equal error rate* (EER), which is the Eval item in Table 1.

Table 1. Comparison of the results of the ASV spoof 2017 Challenge (in terms of EER)

Feature Set	Classifier	Dev	Eval
CQCC (BL) [24]	GMM	10.35	28.48
ESA-IFCC [122]	GMM	4.12	12.79
VESA-IACC [121]	GMM	6.12	11.94
AWFCC [143]	GMM	6.37	11.72
LFCC [116]	GMM	10.31	16.54
SCFC [116]	GMM	24.51	24.83
SSFC [116]	GMM	12.81	22.38
SCMC [116]	GMM	9.32	11.49
RFCC [116]	GMM	6.91	11.90
VESA-IFCC [120]	GMM	4.61	14.06
CFCCIF [120]	GMM	6.80	34.49
CQCC (6–8 kHz) [117]	GMM	5.13	17.31
HFCC [136]	GMM	5.9	23.90
SFCC [119]	GMM	2.35	20.20
SCC [129]	GMM	3.16	19.79
qDFTspec [144]	GMM	–	11.43
qPspec [144]	GMM	–	11.85
EOC$_m$ [140]	–	–	18.2
ConvRBM-CC [139]	GMM	0.82	8.89
LFMGDCC [130]	GMM	20.70	20.84
ESA-IFCC [147]	GMM+CNN	1.90	10.42
LPCC [138]	SVM *i-vector*	9.80	12.54
CQCC [137]	DNN	5.18	19.41
CQCC [137]	ResNet	5.05	18.79
MFCC [137]	ResNet	10.95	16.26
GD Spectrum [141]	ResNet	0.0	0.0
CQCC [135]	ResNet	6.32	23.14
AF-DRN [142]	ResNet	6.55	8.99
SFCC [119]	BLSTM	3.66	22.40
FFT features [138]	LCNN	4.53	7.37
CQT features [138]	LCNN	4.80	16.54
AFCC [133]	–	4.01	27.80
ARP [133]	–	9.11	12.65

BL, baseline

4 Discussion

The paper discussed some research results and methods in the field of voice deception detection This is an area to be studied, from the creation of the ASV Spoof Challenge in 2015 to the present, Voice spoofing detection has achieved significant results.

In terms of establishing a standard voice spoofing detection data set and attracting many research institutions and giant technology companies to participate in the competition, ASV Spoof is of great significance to the development of voice spoofing detection. Today's speech deception detection algorithms have been able to achieve very high accuracy, but they still need further development and research in terms of versatility and practicability.

In terms of multi-data source speech spoofing detection, the current database still does not support the research and application of this aspect. In the future, the construction of a full-covered spoofing speech database is an urgent problem to be solved. In addition, in the detection of various types of spoofed voices, there is still no algorithm that can detect and recognize most types of fake voices. The mainstream method is to build a process-based framework, and the implementation of each method is formed into a streaming voice. Fraud detection framework. The signal mixed with the deceptive voice will enter from the input terminal, and will be identified and filtered by various detection algorithms, and finally a credible voice will be output to the target position we want.

While the deceptive speech detection algorithm based on deep learning has achieved good results, it will also bring about interpretability problems. The signal processing method of speech is not easy to understand. The application of deep learning is more like a black box. It is difficult for humans to understand the meaning of the nonlinear model composed of hundreds of parameters. This is also based on depth at this stage. The problem that the learned speech deception detection algorithm needs to solve.

5 Conclusion

This paper first introduced the background of voice spoofing and explains the importance of research on voice spoofing detection and explained why we need to build a trusted voice detection and recognition system. Then it introduced four different voice deception methods and their implementation principles in detail. Finally, the paper sorted out some research results and methods in the field of voice deception detection.

Acknowledgments. This work was supported by the 2020 Education Research Programs for Young Scholars in Fujian Province (JAT200815).

References

1. Gao, Y., Iqbal, S., et al.: Performance and power analysis of high-density multi-GPGPU architectures: a preliminary case study. In: IEEE 17th HPCC (2015)
2. Qiu, M., Khisamutdinov, E., et al.: RNA nanotechnology for computer design and in vivo computation. Philos. Trans. R. Soc. A **371**, 20120310 (2013)

3. Qiu, M., Cao, D., et al.: Data transfer minimization for financial derivative pricing using Monte Carlo simulation with GPU in 5G. J. Commun. Sys. **29**(16), 2364–2374 (2016)
4. Zhao, H., Chen, M., et al.: A novel pre-cache schema for high performance Android system. Futur. Gener. Comput. Syst. **56**, 766–772 (2016)
5. Zhang, Z., Wu, J., et al.: Jamming ACK attack to wireless networks and a mitigation approach. In: IEEE GLOBECOM Conference, pp. 1–5 (2008)
6. Qiu, M., Chen, Z., Liu, M.: Low-power low-latency data allocation for hybrid scratch-pad memory. IEEE Embed. Syst. Lett. **6**(4), 69–72 (2014)
7. Lu, R., Jin, X., Zhang, S., Qiu, M., Wu, X.: A study on big knowledge and its engineering issues. IEEE Trans. Knowl. Data Eng. **31**(9), 1630–1644 (2018)
8. Lu, Z., Wang, N., et al.: IoTDeM: An IoT Big Data-oriented MapReduce performance prediction extended model in multiple edge clouds. JPDC **118**, 316–327 (2018)
9. Thakur, K., Qiu, M., Gai, K., Ali, M.: An investigation on cyber security threats and security models. In: IEEE CSCloud (2015)
10. Gai, K., Qiu, M., Sun, X., Zhao, H.: Security and privacy issues: a survey on FinTech. SmartCom, pp. 236–247 (2016)
11. Gai, K., Qiu, M., Elnagdy, S.: A novel secure big data cyber incident analytics framework for cloud-based cybersecurity insurance. IEEE BigDataSecurity (2016)
12. Qiu, H., Qiu, M., Memmi, G., Ming, Z., Liu, M.: A dynamic scalable blockchain based communication architecture for IoT. SmartBlock, pp. 159–166 (2018)
13. ISO/IEC 30107–1: Information technology-Biometric presentation attack detection-part1: framework (2016). https://www.iso.org/obp/ui/#iso:std:iso-iec:30107:-1:ed-1:v1:en
14. Muckenhirn, H., Magimai-Doss, M., Marcel, S.: Presentation attack detection using long-term spectral statistics for trustworthy speaker verification. In: IEEE International Conference of the Biometrics Special Interest Group (BIOSIG), Darmstadt, Germany, pp. 1–6 (2016)
15. Hunt, A.J., Black, A.W.: Unit selection in a concatenative speech synthesis system using a large speech database. In: IEEE International Conference on Acoustics, Speech, and Signal Processing, Atlanta, Georgia, USA, pp. 373–376 (1996)
16. Zen, H., Tokuda, K., Black, A.W.: Statistical parametric speech synthesis. Speech Commun. **51**(11), 1039–1064 (2009)
17. Qian, Y., Soong, F.K., Yan, Z.J.: A unified trajectory tiling approach to high quality speech rendering. IEEE Trans. Audio Speech Lang. Proc.**21**(2), 280–290 (2013)
18. Saito, Y., Takamichi, S., Saruwatari, H.: Statistical parametric speech synthesis incorporating generative adversarial networks. IEEE/ACM Trans. Audio Speech Lang. Process. **26**(1), 84–96 (2018)
19. Wang, Y., Skerry-Ryan, R.J., Stanton, D., Wu, Y., Saurous, R.A.: Tacotron: towards end-to-end speech synthesis. arXiv preprint. arXiv 1703.10135 (2017). https://arxiv.org/abs/1703.10135. Accessed 17 Oct 2018
20. van den Oord, A., et al.: WaveNet: a generative model for raw audio. In: ISCA Speech Synthesis Workshop (SSW), Sunnyvale, California, USA, pp. 1–15 (2016)
21. Stylianou, Y., Cappé, O., Moulines, E.: Continuous probabilistic transform for voice conversion. IEEE Trans. Audio Speech Lang. Process. **6**(2), 131–142 (1998)
22. Eun-Kyoung, Kim, Yung-Hwan, Oh: Hidden Markov model based voice conversion system using dynamic characteristics of speaker. European Conference on Speech Communication and Technology, Rhodes, Greece, 1–4, 1997
23. Sundermann D., Hoge H., Bonafonte A., Ney H., Black A., Narayanan S.: Text-independent voice conversion based on unit selection. In: IEEE International Conference on Acoustics, Speech and Signal Processing (ICASSP), Toulouse, France, pp. I–81–I–84 (2006)
24. Wilde, M., Martinez, A.: Probabilistic principal component analysis applied to voice conversion. In: IEEE Asilomar Conference on Signals, Systems and Computers, Pacific Grove, California, vol. 2, pp. 2255–2259 (2004)

25. Zhang, S., Huang, D., Lei, X., Chng, E.S., Li, H., Dong, M.: Non-negative matrix factorization using stable alternating direction method of multipliers for source separation. In: IEEE APSIPA, pp. 222–228 (2015)
26. Desai, S., Raghavendra, E.V., Yegnanarayana, B., Black, A.W., Prahallad, K.: Voice conversion using artificial neural networks. In: IEEE International Conference on Acoustics, Speech and Signal Processing (ICASSP), Taipei, Taiwan, pp. 3893–3896 (2009)
27. Sahidullah Md, Kinnunen, T., Hanilçi, C.: A comparison of features for synthetic speech detection. In: Interspeech (2015)
28. Todisco M, Héctor Delgado, Evans N.: A new feature for automatic speaker verification antispoofing: constant Q Cepstral coefficients. In: Odyssey 2016 - The Speaker and Language Recognition Workshop (2016)
29. Suthokumar, G., Sethu, V., Wijenayake, C.: Modulation dynamic features for the detection of replay attacks. In: Interspeech 2018 (2018)
30. Shim, H., Jung, J., Heo, H., Yoon, S., Yu, H.: Replay attack spoofing detection system using replay noise by multi-task learning (2018)
31. Gaina, L., Sergey, N., Egor, M., Alexander, K., Shchemelinin, V.: Audio replay attack detection with deep learning frameworks. Interspeech 2017 (2017)
32. Chen, Z., Zhang, W., Xie, Z., Xu, X., Chen, D.: Recurrent neural networks for automatic replay spoofing attack detection. In: 2018 IEEE International Conference on Acoustics, Speech and Signal Processing (ICASSP), pp. 2052–2056 (2018)

Thunderstorm Recognition Based on Neural Network PRDsNET Models

ShengChun Wang[1], DanYi Hu[1(✉)], ChangQing Zhou[2,3], and JingYu Xu[2,3]

[1] School of Information Science and Engineering, Hunan Normal University, Changsha, China
scwang@hunnu.edu.cn

[2] Hunan Meteorological Observatory, Changsha 410118, China
evereen@live.cn

[3] Hunan Provincial Key Lab of Meteorological Disaster Prevention and Reduction, Changsha, China

Abstract. Thunderstorm is a kind of severe weather with strong sudden and destructive ability. It is still difficult to warn and forecast accurately in the meteorological industry. In this paper, a neural network model of encoder decoding structure -- PRDsNET is constructed, which includes a LSTM variant structure Causal LSTM unit, high-speed characteristic channel GHU (Gradient Highway Units) and DenseBlock module in dense connection. 11 SA/SB Doppler radars and lightning data from 2017 to 2020 in Hunan province were used to verify the effect of thunderstorm recognition. In addition, multiple groups of network architectures with different encoding and decoding and multiple loss functions and optimizers were selected for cross-comparison experiments. Experimental results show that the model has an average hit rate of 95% and an average false alarm rate of 5%. The results are satisfactory and have broad application scenarios in the future meteorological automation work.

Keywords: Thunderstorm · Doppler Radar · Neural Network · DenseBlock

1 Introduction

Thunderstorms are generally strong convective weather systems generated by strong convective cumulonimbus clouds, often accompanied by strong turbulence, ice accumulation, lightning and strong winds, and sometimes hail, tornado and downburst and other dangerous weather phenomena, with characteristics of small horizontal scale and short life cycle [1]. At present, the near forecast and early warning technologies of severe convective weather mainly focus on extrapolation forecast, empirical forecast and statistical forecast [2], probability prediction [3] and other traditional methods, the proximity technology for severe convective weather identification still has many deficiencies [4]. The accuracy of operational forecasting services is also low. Therefore, it is of great significance to use the new method to carry out the research on severe convective weather prediction and early warning, and to enhance the service effect of disaster prevention and mitigation.

M. Qiu et al. (Eds.): SmartCom 2021, LNCS 13202, pp. 460–469, 2022.
https://doi.org/10.1007/978-3-030-97774-0_42

In recent years, there are many researches on severe convective weather identification and prediction based on machine learning/deep learning [5, 18–20]. Authors of [5–7] developed automatic recognition algorithms for thunderstorm gale and hail respectively by using fuzzy logic method. Recently, Liu Xinwei classified and identified three types of severe convective weather, including hail, thunderstorm gale and short-time heavy precipitation, based on LightGBM (Light Gradient Boosting Machine) algorithm [18–20]. Although this kind of algorithm has high efficiency and low memory consumption, the calculation is relatively rough, and the feature rules need to be formulated manually. The performance of the algorithm depends on the accuracy of the extracted feature [8, 21–23].

Deep learning is a method based on data representation learning in machine learning [33–35]. Its advantage is to replace manual feature acquisition with unsupervised or semi-supervised feature learning and hierarchical feature extraction algorithms [24–26]. Meikang Qiu et al. proposed a novel selective encryption method on ECG data in body sensor network based on supervised machine learning [36]. Zheng Yue used two convolutional neural network models, Faster R-CNN and SSD, to identify precipitation, regions generated by thunderstorm weather and precipitation intensity in radar images, and verified the applicability and feasibility of using convolutional neural network to identify weather radar image products [9, 27–30]. [10] applied the lightning proximity prediction method based on convolutional neural network structure in combination with radar products and lightning data of multiple time series. Lstm-rnn(Long short-term memory-Recurrent neural network) has the characteristics of long-term information dependence in learning [11, 31]. Shi et al. defined precipitation near prediction as a spatio-temporal series prediction problem, and proposed ConvLSTM model, which had convolution structure in input and state transition, and extended LSTM to realize synchronous feature extraction in space and time [12]. The forecast accuracy has been improved significantly [13–15].

In this paper, the cyclic neural network with Causal LSTM (cascade operation of temporal and spatial memory units) was used as the encoder [16], and the temporal and spatial low-dimensional mapping information was taken as intermediate features. Dimensionality reduction was performed twice after feature fusion and the dense connection network with DenseBlock module was input for decoding and classification [17], i.e. PRDsNET model. Then, 11 SA/SB Doppler radar and lightning data modeling training in Hunan province from 2017 to 2020 were selected. Finally, the model is compared with other network structure algorithms, and then evaluated according to meteorological indicators to comprehensively evaluate whether the model can be used to judge whether there are thunderstorms in a certain area and whether it is reasonable and feasible.

2 Materials and Methods

2.1 Information Description

In this experiment, the problem of thunderstorm identification and tracking is transformed into the main idea of judging whether there are thunderstorms in the surrounding area centered on the site, and the radar sample data set centered on the site is established. The data used were 11 SA/SB Doppler radar and lightning location data from 2017 to

2020 in Hunan Province. Doppler radar data used VCP21 mode, 6 min per individual sweep, reflectivity range library length of 1000 m, maximum range database number of 460. The speed and spectral width range library is 250 m long, and the maximum range library number is 920. Lightning location data is obtained at an interval of 1 h. The lightning location data is used to determine the reflectance data of the nearest radar with the detection range of 50–200 km from the automatic station in 3400+ area of Hunan as the center. If the station is not within the detection range of 50–200 km from the nearest radar, the radar data with the second closest distance is selected, and so on. If all radars do not meet the requirements, the sample will be removed.

Six elevation angles, such as 0.5°, 1.45°, 2.40°, 3.35°, 4.30° and 6.00°, were selected for the radar reflectivity of each sample. The range of interception was centered on the site (θ, j), and 48 libraries (J $\pm$ 48) were selected from the radial upward to the inward and outward, and 16° ($\theta \pm 16°$) were selected from the left and right azimuths (Fig. 1). After data interception, data of each elevation layer is formed into a data matrix with azimuth Angle as abscis and radial distance library number as ordinate. Then 6 elevation data matrices at the same time are stacked, and finally a 6 * 32 * 96 sample data is built and saved as a.npy file. Since the timing network is used for training in this experiment, the data input into the network should be a continuous timing data. The experiment takes 06 min, 12 min, 18 min, 24 min, 30 min, 36 min, 42 min, 48 min, 54 min,00 min within 1 h. A total of 10 landmine radar data were used as a sample of the dataset.

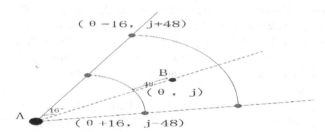

Fig. 1. Interception range of echo data of single-layer elevation radar. Point a is the radar station and point B is the observation station, θ Is the azimuth of the observation point relative to the radar station, and j is the radial library length from the observation station to the radar station. The cut area is exactly the area contained by the four small gray dots.

2.2 PRDsNET Model

Because a thunderstorm is a convective cell that is constantly moving and evolving, the identification and tracking of a thunderstorm cell should be based on the spatio-temporal variation of radar echo intensity and characteristics in a certain area. The neural network needs to judge whether there is thunderstorm in the time series according to the distribution law of radar reflectance factor in different time periods. The key point is not only to record the spatial distribution of the current radar reflectivity factors but also to obtain the memory of part of the preorder neural network. Causal LSTM structure will have the ability to obtain spatial correlation and short-term dynamic modeling, both the time memory module, also has a spatial memory module transmission route, strengthen the spatial information at different levels and different time of neurons in the spread, and on the basis of the level, add more nonlinear operation, makes the characteristics of the amplifier, Suitable for dealing with short-term dynamic changes and emergencies. At the same time, in order to solve the problem of Gradient disappearance caused by too long network transmission, that is, strong echo features may be lost, GHU (Gradient Highway Units) is built, which is similar to a Highway in time. It directly connects the history and the future without going through the time memory unit and zigzag spatial memory transmission route. Ensure the transmission of radar echo characteristics of the time series. The feature information of radar echoes in different time series can be extracted effectively, and then selected and fused into the decoder.

And decoder, namely reduction figure characteristics of the task, select the populated with DenseBlock module to connect to the Internet, in the network, has a direct connection between any two layers, namely the network input of each layer are all previous output layer, and set the layer directly to study the characteristics of the figure will be passed on to the behind all layers as input, However, the network channel is relatively large, so the number of output feature map of each convolutional layer of DenseBlock is set to be relatively small. This method can not only reduce the dimension and computation, but also integrate the radar echo distribution characteristics of each channel, which further improves the classification effect. This paper designs this group of encoding and decoding network (Fig. 2) - PRDsNET model. Through iterative training of a large number of radar sample data sets, the model learns the characteristics of radar reflectivity factors at different scales and their evolution rules on the time line.

Causal LSTM Unit Calculation: The Causal LSTM unit is actually an extension of THE LSTM unit. In the warning and prediction based on radar data, the advantage of the Causal LSTM unit compared with LSTM is reflected in the addition of convolution operation, which can obtain the radar echo distribution characteristics of different time series. As well as its added spatial memory module, it contributes to the deep propagation of radar echo value information between different dimensions in the network. The time memory of k layer of Causal LSTM is C_t^k and the spatial memory is M_t^k, the two memory modules have three gate structures respectively, the forgetting gate f_t, the f_t' controls the memory content to be forgotten in the module, the input gate i_t, i_t' determines the content to be remembered by the module at the current time and the output gate g_t, g_t' determines the output of the hidden layer, and each gate is determined by X and H and C. H_t^k is the output result of layer K. The operation formula of the cell block is as follows.

Here * is the convolution operation, $\otimes$ is the multiplication of elements, σ is the Sigmoid function, square brackets denote series of tensors, parentheses denote systems of equations. W1–5 are convolution filters, among which W3 and W5 are 1×1 convolution filters used to change the number of filters. The final output H is determined by the dual memory states M and C.

$$\begin{pmatrix} g_t \\ i_t \\ f_t \end{pmatrix} = \begin{pmatrix} tanh \\ \sigma \\ \sigma \end{pmatrix}_1 \left[X_t, H_{t-1}^k, C_{t-1}^k \right] \tag{1}$$

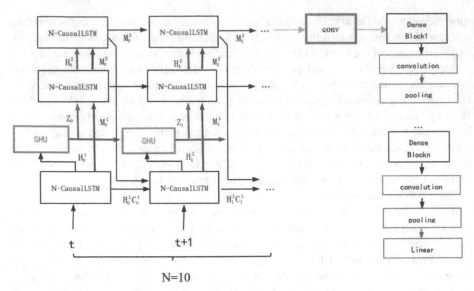

Fig. 2. PRDsNET model.input ten consecutive radar data sets, enter the three-layer causal LSTM network on the left, then extract and fuse the features, input one-layer convolution network, and enter the dense connection network for decoding and classification.

$$c_t^k = f_t \otimes c_{t-1}^k + i_t \otimes g_t \tag{2}$$

$$\begin{pmatrix} g_t' \\ i_t' \\ f_t' \end{pmatrix} = \begin{pmatrix} tanh \\ \sigma \\ \sigma \end{pmatrix}_2 \left[X_t, C_t^k, M_t^{k-1} \right] \tag{3}$$

$$M_t^k = f_t' \otimes \tanh \left(W_3 * M_t^{k-1} \right) + i_t' \otimes g_t' \tag{4}$$

$$o_t = \tanh \left(W_4 * \left[X_t, C_t^k, M_t^k \right] \right) \tag{5}$$

$$H_t^k = o_t \otimes \tanh \left(W_5 * \left[C_t^k, M_t^k \right] \right) \tag{6}$$

3   Experimental Results and Analysis

3.1   Experimental

The experimental training in this paper uses the sample radar data set processed in Section 0. In order to improve the quality of the dataset, the dataset is further screened and filtered. If the maximum value of radar echo in the non-thunderstorm data is less than 35 dbz, the data will be retained. On the contrary, the data with the highest radar echo value greater than or equal to 35 dbZ should be retained for the data with thunderstorms.

The data are labeled as lightning strikes within a radius of 30 km from the center of the site in the first hour. According to the analysis of visual echo value distribution of clipped data (Fig. 3), the echo intensity of non-lightning is generally lower than 35 dbZ, the radar echo intensity of lightning less than 10 times is mostly concentrated in 30–45 dbz, and the radar echo intensity of lightning more than 10 times is concentrated in 50–65 dbz.

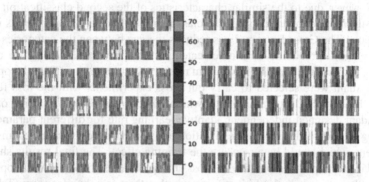

Fig. 3. Shows the distribution of visual radar reflectance values of elevation clipping data of each layer with a 6-min interval of body scanning within one hour. The left one shows the distribution of echo data without lightning, and the right figure shows the distribution of echo data with lightning. The color bar in the middle represents the radar echo value, in DBZ (Color figure online).

On this basis, this experiment tested two groups of classification experiments with the model: the first group was a binary classification experiment, that is, according to the number of lightning to determine whether there is a thunderstorm; The second group was a three-classification experiment. No lightning was judged as no thunderstorm according to the number of lightning. The number of lightning less than 10 times was considered as weak thunderstorm, and the number of lightning more than 10 times was considered as strong thunderstorm. Ten input data are labeled and then put into PRDsNET network model training. At the same time, in order to verify the feasibility of the technical route of determining the occurrence of thunderstorms according to the radar emissibility value of the model in this paper, several groups of comparison experiments of different model architectures are added, as well as the combined cross experiments of PRDsNET network, multiple loss functions and optimizers. Then POD and FAR were used to evaluate the identification results.

3.2 Test Results

As can be seen from Table 2, POD and FAR results of binary classification and triple classification experiments of PRDsNET model are better than those of other network models. This indicates that simultaneously obtaining radar echo distribution characteristics of different time series and radar echo value information of different dimensions can greatly improve the identification effect of thunderstorm occurrence, that is, the importance of the combination of time series and space. It also reflects the good encoding and decoding model collocation architecture, which can better retain the main features with and without thunderstorms to the maximum and reduce the value of FAR. 2 results show that the model and table after fine-tuning, can further enhance the network model generalization ability, first adjust the loss function, Yao et al. (2019) based on multi-source windy weather convolution neural network used in Centerloss loss function (center) [32], experimental think between the kinds of clustering effect is very good, can not only narrow the differences inside the class. And it can amplify differences between classes. However, due to the similar characteristics of the second classification and the third classification of thunderstorms, the classification effect of thunderstorms identification is poor. The Cross Entropy Loss reduces the gap between the categories of total probability and 0 probability and other categories, improves the confidence of other categories, and thus reduces the false alarm rate of other categories. Then the optimizer SGD and Adam were selected to carry out cross experiments with the loss function. SGD was difficult to select learning rate, which was easy to cause over-fitting of experiments. Adam designed independent adaptive learning rate for different parameters by calculating the first-order moment estimation and second-order moment estimation of the gradient, which could better ensure the training effect. The final results show that the model in this paper, combined with cross entropy loss function and Adam optimizer, can obtain the optimal result of identifying whether there is a thunderstorm (Table 1).

Fig. 4. 0.5° elevation radar echo of Changsha station (left: 01:00, middle: 01:29, right: 01:58)

In terms of individual cases, taking a thunderstorm and strong wind in Yueyang city on the night of May 4, 2020 as an example, from the actual weather records, there were 479 records of thunder and lightning from 01st to 02nd on The 5th at Pingjiang Station (Station No. 57682), and a maximum wind of 20.1m/s appeared at 02nd. According to the radar chart, the strong echo was still on the left of Pingjiang station (marked by black box in Fig. 4) at 1:30, and moved above Pingjiang station at 1:30, and moved out of Pingjiang station after 2:00. PRDsNET model algorithm was used to identify radar echoes of Pingjiang station from 0:00 to 0200 on 5th, and the results showed that there were thunderstorms, and the thunderstorms were strong. It was confirmed that PRDsNET model algorithm could correctly classify and identify thunderstorms by comparing the elevation echo intensity of each layer.

Table 1. The hit rate and false alarm rate of two classification and three classification experiments of each network model are compared

Category\Network		lstm	Predrnn++	Predrnn++ resnet18	Predrnn++ resnet50	PRDsNET
Three way classification	No thundestorm	0.44/0.61	0.62/0.44	0.64/0.43	0.62/0.40	0.65/0.35
	Weak thundestorm	0/0	0.50/0.50	0.48/0.50	0.17/0.65	0.60/0.40
	Strong thudestorms	0/0	0.70/0.36	0.55/0.35	0.49/0.50	0.75/0.33
Dichotomy	No thundestorm	0.51/0.55	0.89/0.10	0.89/0.08	0.97/0.08	0.98/0.06
	Thundestorm	0.78/0.32	0.88/0.10	0.92/0.08	0.83/0.10	0.95/0.05

Table 2. Cross experimental results of prdsnet model with loss function and optimizer

Category\loss function + optimizer		CrossEntropyLoss + Adam	CrossEntropyLoss + SGD	Centerloss + Adam	Centerloss + SGD
Three way classification	No thundestorm	0.65/0.35	0.60/0.38	0.58/0.44	0.54/0.64
	Weak thundestorm	0.60/0.40	0.58/0.50	0.40/0.70	0.38/0.20
	Strong thunderstorms	0.75/0.33	0.68/0.40	0.49/0.48	0.45/0.57
Dichotomy	No thundestorm	0.98/0.06	0.97/0.06	0.87/0.12	0.85/0.12
	Thunderstorm	0.95/0.05	0.92/0.05	0.89/0.12	0.89/0.12

4 Conclusion

In this paper, the neural network model -- PRDsNET is introduced in detail, and the effect of thunderstorm identification is tested by using 11 SA/SB Doppler radar and lightning data from 2017 to 2020 in Hunan Province, and compared with other network structure algorithm models. A thunderstorm windy weather in Yueyang City is taken as an example to verify. The main conclusions are as follows: (1) The PRDsNET model architecture is composed of the Causal LSTM. (2) Evaluation of model identification results shows that the average hit rate of determining whether there are thunderstorms or not. (3) The case test shows that PRDsNET model has an accurate ability to identify thunderstorms.

References

1. Hui, Y.W., You, H.X., Jin, Z.Y., et al.: Introduction of 3d structure recognition technology of thunderstorm cells based on improved DBSCAN clustering algorithm. J. Trop. Meteorol. **36**(4), 542–551 (2020). (in Chinese)
2. Seed, A.W.: A dynamic and spatial scaling approach to advection forecasting. J. Appl. Meteorol. Climatol. **42**, 381–388 (2003)
3. Fox, N.I., Wikle, C.K.: A Bayesian quantitative precipitation now- cast scheme. Weather Forecast. **20**(3), 264–275 (2005)
4. Gung, Z.Y., Hui, Z.K., Jie, S., et al.: Advances in severe convective weather monitoring and forecasting. J. Appl. Meteorol. **26**(6), 641–657 (2015). https://doi.org/10.11898/1001-713. 20150601. (in Chinese)
5. Mecikalski, J.R., Williams, J.K., Jewett, C.P., et al.: Probabilistic 0–1-h convective initiation nowcasts that combine geostationary satellite observations and numerical weather prediction model data. J. Appl. Meteorol. Climatol. **54**, 1039–1059 (2015)
6. Xiang, Z.B., Cui, L.G., Ping, L.L., et al.: Hail weather radar recognition algorithm based on fuzzy logic. J. Appl. Meteorol. **25**(4), 414–426 (2014)
7. Hui, Z.K., Guang, Z.Y., Bo, W.T., et al.: Classification method of thunderstorm gale and non-thunderstorm gale based on fuzzy logic. Meteorol. Monthly **43**(7), 781–791 (2017). https://doi.org/10.7519/J.issn.1000-0526. (in Chinese)
8. Liu, X., et al.: Classification and recognition of severe convective weather based on Light GBM algorithm. Plateau Meteorology (2020)
9. Zheng, Y.: Research on precipitation and thunderstorm identification in Civil Aviation Weather Radar Image based on CNN, Master degree thesis of Yunnan University (2019)
10. Yifang, Z., Zhenzhen, F., Bing, L.: Lightning near warning model based on convolutional neural network. Meteorological Monthly **47**(3), 373–380 (2021). (in Chinese)
11. Hochreiter, S., Schmidhuber, J.: Long short-term memory. Neural Comput. **9**(8), 1735–1780 (1997)
12. Shi, X., Chen, Z., Wang, H., Yeung, D.-Y., Wong, W., Woo, W.: Convolutional LSTM network: A machine learning approach for precipitation nowcasting. In: NIPS (2015)
13. Jianfeng, G., Guobing, Z., Bojun, L., et al.: Preliminary research and application of artificial intelligence technology in Chongqing near forecast business. Meteorol. Monthly **46**(10), 1286–1296 (2020). (in Chinese)
14. Shi, X., Gao, Z., Lausen, L., Wang, H., Yeung, D.-Y.: Deep learning for precipitation nowcasting: a benchmark and a new model. In: NIPS (2017)
15. Ronneberger, O., Fischer, P., Brox, T.: U-Net: convolutional networks for biomedical image segmentation. In: International Conference on Medical Image Computing and Computer-Assisted Intervention (2015)
16. Wang, Y., Gao, Z., Long, M., et al.: PredRNN++: towards a resolution of the deep-in-time dilemma in spatiotemporal predictive learning (2018)
17. Huang, G., Liu, Z., Laurens, V., et al.: Densely Connected Convolutional Networks. IEEE Computer Society (2016)
18. Wang, Z., Li, T., Xiong, N., Pan, Y.: A novel dynamic network data replication scheme based on historical access record and proactive deletion. J. Supercomput. **62**(1), 227–250 (2012)
19. Guo, W., Xiong, N., Vasilakos, A.V., Chen, G., Cheng, H.: Multi-source temporal data aggregation in wireless sensor networks. Wireless Pers. Commun. **56**(3), 359–370 (2011)
20. Yin, J., Lo, W., Deng, S., Li, Y., Wu, Z., Xiong, N.: Colbar: a collaborative location-based regularization framework for QoS prediction. Inf. Sci. **265**, 68–84 (2014)
21. Wan, Z., Xiong, N., Ghani, N., Vasilakos, A.V., Zhou, L.: Adaptive unequal protection for wireless video transmission over IEEE 802.11 e networks. Multimedia Tools Appl. **72** (1), 541–571

22. Qu, Y., Xiong, N.: RFH: A resilient, fault-tolerant and high-efficient replication algorithm for distributed cloud storage. In: The 41st International Conference on Parallel Processing, pp. 520–529 (2012)
23. He, R., Xiong, N., Yang, L.T., Park, J.H.: Using multi-modal semantic association rules to fuse keywords and visual features automatically for web image retrieval. Inf. Fusion **12**(3), 223–230 (2011)
24. Zhang, Q., Zhou, C., Tian, Y.C., Xiong, N., Qin, Y., Hu, B.: A fuzzy probability Bayesian network approach for dynamic cybersecurity risk assessment in industrial control systems. IEEE Trans. Industr. Inf. **14**(6), 2497–2506 (2017)
25. Wu, M., Tan, L., Xiong, N.: A structure fidelity approach for big data collection in wireless sensor networks. Sensors **15**(1), 248–273 (2015)
26. Huang, S., Liu, A., Zhang, S., Wang, T., Xiong, N.: BD-VTE: A novel baseline data based verifiable trust evaluation scheme for smart network systems. IEEE Trans. Netw. Sci. Eng. (2020). https://doi.org/10.1109/TNSE.2020.3014455
27. Li, H., Liu, J., Wu, K., Yang, Z., Liu, R.W., Xiong, N.: Spatio-temporal vessel trajectory clustering based on data mapping and density. IEEE Access **6**, 58939–58954 (2018)
28. Yao, Y., Xiong, N., Park, J.H., Ma, L., Liu, J.: Privacy-preserving max/min query in two-tiered wireless sensor networks. Comput. Math. Appl. **65**(9), 1318–1325 (2013)
29. Xia, F., Hao, R., Li, J., Xiong, N., Yang, L.T., Zhang, Y.: Adaptive GTS allocation in IEEE 802.15. 4 for real-time wireless sensor networks. J. Syst. Arch. **59**(10), 1231–1242 (2013)
30. Gao, K., Han, F., Dong, P., Xiong, N., Du, R.: Connected vehicle as a mobile sensor for real time queue length at signalized intersections. Sensors **19**(9), 2059 (2019)
31. Lu, Y., Wu, S., Fang, Z., Xiong, N., Yoon, S., Park, D.S.: Exploring finger vein based personal authentication for secure IoT. Future Gener. Comput. Syst. **77**, 149–160 (2017)
32. Jiang, Y., Yao, J., Qian, Z.: A method of forecasting thunderstorms and gale weather based on multisource convolution neural network. IEEE Access 7, 107695–107698 (2019)
33. Guo, Y., Zhuge, Q., Hu, J., et al.: Optimal data allocation for scratch-pad memory on embedded multi-core systems. In: IEEE ICPP Conference, pp. 464–471 (2011)
34. Wu, G., Zhang, H., et al.: A decentralized approach for mining event correlations in distributed system monitoring. JPDC **73**(3), 330–340 (2013)
35. Zhao, H., Chen, M., et al.: A novel pre-cache schema for high performance Android system. Future Gener. Comput. Syst. **56**, 766–772 (2016)
36. Qiu, H., Qiu, M., Lu, Z.: Selective encryption on ECG data in body sensor network based on supervised machine learning. Inf. Fusion **55**, 59–67 (2020)

The Development and Trend of Vehicle Functional Safety

Jun Guo[1,2(✉)], Gejing Xu[1,2], Junjie Wu[1,2], Lan Yang[1,2], and Han Deng[3]

[1] Software College, Quan Zhou University of Information Engineering, Quan Zhou 362000, China
[2] Key Laboratory of Cloud Computing and Internet-of-Thing Technology, Quan Zhou University of Information Engineering, Quan Zhou 362000, China
[3] Big Data Development and Research Center, Guangzhou College of Technology and Business, Guangzhou 528138, China

Abstract. In the development stage of vehicle applications, ensuring the safety of the vehicle is always a key condition. However, the current automotive functional safety design is challenged by a variety of factors, such as the complexity of the new generation of automotive *electrical and electronic* (E/E) architecture, the continuous update of the automotive functional safety standard ISO26262, and the new AUTOSAR adaptive platform standard. The release of different types of cost increases. This paper summarizes the latest developments of vehicle functional safety design methods through analysis, design, optimization and operation stages: 1) functional safety analysis; 2) functional safety assurance; 3) safety perception cost optimization; 4) safety-critical multi-functional dispatch. It then provides the future trend of functional safety design methods, which will be directly oriented to automatic vehicles.

Keywords: Vehicle · Design · Functional safety · Cost optimization · Analysis

1 Introduction

1.1 Background

At present, people generally tend to buy cars with stronger applicability, lower fuel consumption and better driving experience [1]. However, in the process of achieving the above goals, ensuring safety is always a prerequisite [2, 3]. From the earliest seat belts to later airbags and anti-lock braking systems, various safety measures have greatly improved the safety performance of the car Even so, in the United States alone, about 40,000 people die in car accidents and 3 million are injured every year.

In order to enable different automotive software/hardware developers to follow the same safety development principles, the *International Organization for Standardization* (ISO) officially released the road vehicle functional safety standard ISO26262 in 2011. In order to further strengthen the development of security, a compressed version was released in December 2018. In addition to ISO26262, the Japanese Automotive Software Platform and Architecture Company was established in September 2004, aimed to standardizing the electronic control systems and software of automotive networks, so as to jointly realize the efficient development of the entire automotive industry and improve reliability.

1.2 Purpose

In order to meet the functional safety requirements of safe automotive applications, such as brake-by-wire, electronic stability control, emergency brake assist, adaptive cruise control, airbags, etc. It is necessary to reduce the risks caused by potential safety hazards at the beginning of the development life cycle, so as to further avoid hazards or accidents.

Paper [4] has already discussed the latest developments and future trends of automotive embedded systems. Nardi and Armato [5] briefly introduced the functional safety design methods of automotive applications, including functional safety basics, functional safety analysis, functional safety requirements and design procedures, and briefly discussed the functional safety assessment and design of reliable automotive applications. However, the vehicle functional safety design method still faces the following severe challenges.

1) The architecture of the vehicle has evolved into an integrated architecture. In the past, the automotive industry used experimental measurement methods to obtain response times. Due to the inconsistent results under various measurement conditions, the experimental measurement method is not suitable for the real-time communication of the electrical and electronic structure of the new generation of automobiles. Recent developments have begun to perform real-time analysis of central gateway and cross-gateway messages to obtain consistent response times.

2) The trend of cost growth is one of the important indicators of the design quality of automotive embedded systems. In view of the cost sensitivity of the automotive industry, it is necessary to optimize costs to improve design quality while meeting functional safety requirements. However, the cost of automotive embedded systems is affected by various complex factors.

3) The first version of the AUTOSAR adaptive platform standard released in 2017 provides a foundation for the dynamic and flexible operation of automotive embedded systems. The AUTOSAR adaptive platform standard requires automotive embedded systems to execute adaptively at runtime. Therefore, it is necessary to propose an adaptive dynamic scheduling algorithm suitable for automotive embedded systems.

In view of the above challenges, vehicle functional safety design has been challenged by many factors. These challenges show that although ISO26262 provides many safety design specifications to guide the design and development of automotive embedded systems, it is not enough to design and develop systems in accordance with ISO26262 standards.

1.3 Contributions and Summary

In order to meet the above challenges, this paper proposes the latest developments in vehicle functional safety design methods, which are described through analysis, design, optimization and operation phases: 1) functional safety analysis; 2) functional safety assurance; 3) safety perception cost optimization; 4) Safety-critical multi-function scheduling.

Both recent developments and future trends involve the actual automotive industry, as well as scientific and engineering literature. However, functional safety design methods are extensive and go far beyond the scope outlined above in this article. For example, design processes, design patterns, product and service processes, and manufacturing processes all affect functional safety.

2 Functional Safety Summary

2.1 Fault Classification

In ISO26262, failure behavior may be caused by system failures or random hardware failures. System failures are related to a cause in a deterministic way. Therefore, system failures can be eliminated by changing the design or changing the manufacturing process, operating procedures, documents or other related factors. For real-time system design, missing the real-time requirements of safety-critical automotive applications, namely deadlines, response time requirements or delays, and waiting time requirements, are typical system failures; random hardware failures are caused by embedded radiation and flash memory characteristics, etc. Caused by hardware (such as ECU) bit flip. This failure occurs unpredictably during the life of the hardware component, but the failure rate can be predicted with reasonable accuracy because random hardware failures obey a probability distribution. Through Table 1, the differences and relationships between these terms are easy to understand.

Table. 1. ISO 26262's terms such as failure, failure, failure behavior, hazard, dangerous event, damage and risk

Term	Definition	Supplementary explanation
Fault	Abnormal condition that can cause an element or an item to fail	Permanent, intermittent, and transient faults (especially soft errors) are considered
Failure	Termination of an intended behaviour of an element or an item due to a fault manifestation	Termination can be permanent or transient
Malfunctioning behavior	Failure or unintended behavior of an item with respect to the design intent	Malfunctioning behavior results from random hardware failures and systematic failures
Hazard	The potential source of harm	A hazard is an agent which has the potential probability to cause harm to a vulnerable target; hazard is caused by malfunctioning behavior
Hazardous event	Combination of a hazard and an operational situation	Such as the brake suddenly fails and the door was suddenly opened
Harm	Physical injury or damage to the health of people	Such as death, injury, and damage
Risk	Combination of the probability of occurrence of harm and the severity of that harm	Harm is associated with severity and a probability of occurrence

2.2 Determination of Automotive Safety Integrity Level (ASIL)

In ISO26262, Automotive Safety Integrity Level (ASIL) is a risk classification scheme that helps define functional safety requirements. ISO26262 has determined four levels of ASIL: ASIL A, ASIL B, ASIL C and ASIL D, where ASIL A and ASIL D represent the lowest and highest levels respectively. ASIL reflects the degree of risk. The higher the ASIL, the greater the risk and the more effort required to reduce the risk. In addition to these four basic factors, classified quality management (QM) is used, which shows that the quality process is sufficient to manage the identified risks without having to consider safety-related design.

ASIL integrates severity, exposure and controllability. Exposure represents the probability of causing injury; severity represents the degree of injury; controllability represents the ability to avoid injury through the driver's timely response. Table 2 shows the ASIL formed by the combination of severity, exposure and controllability in ISO26262.

Table. 2. ASIL combines the severity, exposure and controllability of ISO26262

Severity	Exposure	Controllability		
		C1	C2	C3
S1	E1	QM	QM	QM
	E2	QM	QM	QM
	E3	QM	QM	A
	E4	QM	A	B
S2	E1	QM	QM	QM
	E2	QM	QM	A
	E3	QM	A	B
	E4	A	B	C
S3	E1	QM	QM	A/QM
	E2	QM	A	B
	E3	A	B	C
	E4	B	C	D

3 Functional Safety Analysis

The lack of real-time requirements is a typical system failure, which is related to the severity of the risk classification, while low reliability is caused by high random hardware failures and is related to the exposure of the risk classification. Therefore, functional safety analysis is an important measure before functional safety assurance. Its purpose is to ensure safety at the beginning of the development life cycle, avoid injuries or accidents, and avoid design defects.

3.1 Real-Time Analysis of In-Vehicle Network

Compared with the United Automobile system structure, the biggest feature of the integrated system structure is the introduction of a central gateway, through which multiple subsystems can be integrated and connected. In addition, gateway delay has become a bottleneck in system communication, and real-time analysis has also become a necessary process for the central gateway.

In recent years, references [6–8] have studied the time analysis of the multi-domain CAN system integrated by the central gateway and its worst response time. In recent years, some important progress has been made in the real-time analysis of the CAN bus. The first type is used for end-to-end messages in the CAN bus, and the second type is used for message processing tasks in the central gateway.

For end-to-end messages on the CAN bus, Azketa et al. [9] first considered the streamlining of information packets in the gateway and studied real-time analysis methods. Different from the traditional real-time analysis of CAN messages, the difficulty of real-time analysis of end-to-end CAN messages lies in the interaction between source-end messages and destination-end messages. Xie et al. [10] proposed a busy sequence to help analyze the real-time nature of end-to-end CAN messages. In order to reduce the pessimism of the real-time analysis method in paper [10], Xie et al. proposed an exploratory real-time analysis method to obtain a stricter WCRT by checking the actual arrival sequence of the gateway messages. If the message encounters WCRT on the source side, the probability of encountering WCRT on the target side is extremely low. The reason is that the information of different terminals interferes and affects each other. Develop a holistic method that combines source and target messages, which essentially reduces the pessimism of real-time analysis, but there is no significant progress on this issue.

3.2 System Theory Analysis

There are many types of faults, including safety faults, single-point faults, residual faults, multiple-point faults, delayed faults, detectable faults, etc. The combination of these failures increases the difficulty of reliability analysis. ISO26262 proposes the two most common reliability analysis techniques: *Fault Tree Analysis* (FTA) and *Failure Mode and Effect Analysis* (FMEA).

FTA and FMEA are only applicable to the safety analysis of random hardware failures. However, in potential scenarios without random hardware failures, hazards will still occur due to unsafe and accidental interactions between components (including humans, hardware, and software). In order to analyze the hazards caused by the interaction between components, a new hazard analysis method based on system theory rather than reliability theory called *System Theory Process Analysis* (STPA) appeared.

4   Functional Safety Guarantee

One of the purposes of functional safety standards is to ensure that the risks of developed automotive applications are within acceptable limits. After a car manufacturer takes a series of measures for an automotive application, the application will be certified by a third-party functional safety certification agency.

4.1 Functional Safety Verification

After analyzing the real-time and reliability of automotive applications, functional safety verification can be carried out. Functional safety verification is to determine whether an application program meets its functional safety requirements.

Real-time and reliability are two important functional safety features in automotive applications. However, for distributed applications, this is a conflict process between maximizing reliability (that is, minimizing exposure) and minimizing response time. Real-time and reliability coverage is a two-criteria optimization problem, as shown in Fig. 1. Each point is the dual-criteria minimization solution in Fig. 1. Among them, x1, x2, x3, x4, x5 represent Pareto optimal solutions, and a Pareto curve is constructed: 1) x1, x5 represent weak optimal solutions; and 2) x2, x3, x4 represent strong optimal solutions untie. Paper [11] proposed a two-criteria *scheduling heuristic* algorithm (BSH) to obtain an approximate Pareto curve. Considering that each point has a response value (y coordinate in Fig. 1) and a reliability value (x coordinate in Fig. 1), the carrying value of each point can be used as a verification input to verify functional safety; The point can meet the reliability and real-time requirements at the same time, and the functional safety verification is passed. However, BSH has a high time complexity. In addition, the number of ECUs in automobiles will further increase in the future. Due to the cost sensitivity of the automotive industry, shortening the verification time during the development life cycle is critical.

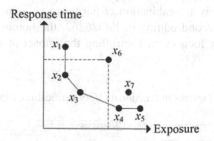

Fig. 1. Two-criteria optimization problem between minimizing response time and maximizing reliability.

4.2 Functional Safety Enhancement

Safety issues run through the entire life cycle of vehicle development, so the maximum possible safety value should be known in the early design stage to help control the risks in the actual development process. Increasing the safety value, for example, reducing the exposure level by increasing the reliability value, is required for risk control. Considering that real-time requirements cannot be changed, improving reliability is a common practice to improve security.

ISO2626 provides a variety of security enhancement technologies, including anti-jamming, static recovery mechanism, fault weakening, homogeneous redundancy, diversified redundancy, data error correction code, access authority management, etc. Among these technologies, static recovery mechanisms have recently been used to enhance the security of distributed automotive applications.

4.3 Functional Safety Guarantee

Functional safety assurance means that the safety requirements are sufficient and a sufficient level of integrity has been reached on the basis of inspection and testing.

In recent years, through the introduction of reliability pre-allocation strategies, in-depth research has been carried out on vehicle functional safety verification methods. In reference [12], a reliability target-based resource minimization algorithm called MRCRG is proposed, and a reliability requirement verification method that assigns the maximum reliability value to unallocated tasks in advance is proposed. However, MRCRG is a pessimistic reliability pre-allocation, which leads to an imbalance in the use of reliability among tasks. In order to make the distribution of reliability requirements more uniform, Xie et al. [13] introduced geometric mean and proposed a non-fault-tolerant reliability pre-allocation method called GMNRP based on geometric mean. The above two methods are non-fault-tolerant methods. Due to the lack of replication, it is difficult to verify their high reliability requirements. Therefore, for high reliability requirements, fault tolerance methods are required.

There are two types of fault-tolerant redundancy in ISO26262: homogeneous and heterogeneous. Homogeneous redundancy is the duplication of elements, while heterogeneous redundancy is a combination of hardware equipment and software tasks. As pointed out in the second edition of ISO26262, the homogeneous redundancy in the design phase mainly focuses on controlling the impact of random failures on the hardware (Table 3).

Table. 3. The latest developments in functional safety verification, enhancement and assurance.

Algorithm	Verification/Enhancement/Validation	Use replication	Feature comparison and analysis
Formal methods [51]–[53]	Verification	No	Formal methods focus on the design of hybrid systems.
RLC [54]	Verification	No	RLC focuses on the design of CPS to reduce the verification conservation.
UFSV [55]	Verification	No	RLC uses Markov analysis and model checking together to improve the accuracy in estimating quantified risk.
FFSV1 [56]	Verification	No	FFSV1 aims to minimize response time while meeting the reliability requirement.
FFSV2 [56]	Verification	No	FFSV2 aims to maximize reliability while meeting the real-time requirement.
RET [57]	Enhancement	No	RET is a backward recovery because the exploration process is from exit to entry tasks.
SFSV [58]	Validation	No	SFSV is oriented to automotive battery management systems.
VFSV [59]	Validation	No	VFSV is oriented to autonomous vehicles by using extreme value theory.
MRCRG [60]	Validation	No	MRCRG pre-assigns maximum reliability values to unassigned tasks.
GMNRP [61]	Validation	No	GMNRP pre-assigns geometric mean-based reliability values to unassigned tasks
GMFRP [61]	Validation	Yes	GMFRP pre-assigns geometric mean-based reliability values to unassigned tasks.

5   Security Perception Cost Optimization

In the fierce market competition, automakers and component suppliers must pursue high profits, and rising costs are an urgent problem to be solved. After achieving the safety guarantee for automotive applications, it is necessary to optimize costs and improve design quality while ensuring functional safety requirements. However, the cost types of automotive embedded systems are more complex and can be roughly divided into two categories: hardware cost and development cost (software cost): 1) hardware cost refers to the price of ECU and other hardware equipment such as wiring harness; 2) development cost Refers to the programmer's labor when developing applications.

5.1 Hardware Cost Optimization

In order to optimize hardware costs, as long as the correct execution of the application is not affected, some additional ECUs can be deleted. In recent years, significant progress has been made in hardware cost optimization methods. Gu et al. studied the *Mixed Integer Linear Programming* (MILP) method and a heuristic algorithm based on the divide-and-conquer method to optimize the hardware cost of distributed automotive applications while meeting real-time and safety requirements. However, focus on safety requirements from the perspective of functional safety, while ignoring reliability requirements. While meeting functional safety requirements, Xie proposes *exploratory hardware cost optimization* (EHCO) for distributed applications, gradually *enhances EHCO* (EEHCO), and simplifies the EEHCO algorithm. In addition to the above hardware cost optimization methods, part of the hardware can be replaced with software through ASIL-certified virtualization technology to optimize hardware costs.

5.2 Development Cost Optimization

Due to the use of the ISO26262 standard, the development process of safety-critical automotive applications is a highly structured and systematic process. This standard increases development costs because of the additional process and complexity in the development and testing of automotive applications, as well as software and hardware redundancy solutions. When decomposing a high ASIL task into a low ASIL task, the development cost can be reduced by 25–100%. Therefore, ASIL decomposition is usually used for development cost optimization.

Xie proposed a reliability target development cost minimization (MDCRG) algorithm based on ASIL decomposition to optimize the development cost of distributed automotive applications while meeting its reliability requirements. In addition to development cost optimization, ASIL decomposition is also used for safety-critical GPU design. Table 4 lists the latest developments in cost optimization for security awareness.

Table. 4. The latest progress in cost optimization of automotive embedded systems.

Algorithm	Cost type	Requirement assurance	Feature comparison and analysis
MILP [64]	hardware cost	real-time requirement, security requirement	MILP focuses on security requirement and does not considers reliability requirement from a functional safety perspective.
EHCO [65]	hardware cost	functional safety requirement	EHCO iteratively removes the ECUs until the functional safety requirement is not met (i.e., open-to-close).
PPHCO [66]	hardware cost	functional safety requirement	PPHCO is the combination of PPHCO1 (close-to-open) and PPHCO2 (open-to-close).
HV [67]	hardware cost	-	The hardware virtualization technology is adopted to address the task allocation problem.
RSV [68]	hardware cost	-	The shared resources virtualization is adopted to address the hardware/software trade-off problem.
GA [69]	development cost	real-time requirement	SIL decomposition for development cost optimization.
Tabu search [70], [71]	development cost	real-time requirement	SIL decomposition for development cost optimization.
MDCRG [17]	development cost	reliability requirement	Five ASIL decomposition schemes for ASIL D are obtained.

6 Safety-Critical Multi-function Dispatch

In automotive embedded systems, multiple application programs are executed on one ECU, and one application program is distributed on multiple ECUs. Currently, more than 800 functions have been implemented in high-end cars, and this scenario requires an efficient scheduling strategy.

6.1 Safety-Critical Multi-function Static Dispatch

Multifunctional static scheduling means the release of multiple applications at the same time. Papers [14] and [15] study the scheduling problem of multi-cycle applications, while [14] is for *time-triggered* (TT) automotive embedded systems, and [15] is for TT avionics application systems. Generally speaking, there are three types of applications in automotive embedded systems: active safety, passive safety and non-safety applications. This application classification has produced the concept of mixed criticality. Active safety applications are usually high-critical applications, and passive safety applications are usually low-critical applications. In ISO26262, high-critical (such as ASIL D) applications have a higher risk than low-critical (such as ASIL A) applications, and greater efforts are required to reduce the risk.

6.2 Safety-Critical Multi-function Dynamic Scheduling

In order to allow the same software or applications to be executed in different hardware devices developed by component manufacturers, the first version of the AUTOSAR classic platform standard was released in 2003. The runtime environment introduced by the AUTOSAR classic platform shields the internal details related to hardware devices, thereby improving the efficiency of automotive software development. At present, the AUTOSAR classic platform is usually used to deploy functional safety solutions, especially those in the automotive industry that have obtained ASIL C/D certification. Research work in recent years has made some important attempts and explorations on multi-functional dynamic scheduling. Xie et al. developed a multifunctional dynamic scheduling algorithm for scheduling trade-offs between high performance and low DMR. They further developed an adaptive dynamic scheduling algorithm to solve some of the problems in the AUTOSAR adaptive platform.

7 Summarize

This article introduces the latest developments and future trends of vehicle functional safety design, including automotive E/E architecture, standards, cost and AUTOSAR, and summarizes the research progress in recent years from four aspects: 1) Functional safety analysis, including real-time analysis and Reliability analysis method; 2) Functional safety assurance, including functional safety verification, enhancement and verification; 3) Safety perception cost optimization, including optimization of hardware cost and development cost; 4) Safety-critical multi-function scheduling, including multi-function static scheduling And multifunctional dynamic scheduling. Finally, the future trend of functional safety design methods directly oriented to autonomous vehicles is discussed. As the source of design methodology, functional safety analysis lays the foundation for building a functional safety-driven design paradigm; functional safety assurance is a timely remedy for failed functional safety analysis results. Safety perception cost optimization is a useful supplement to improve system design. Safety-critical multi-function dispatching is the guarantee of functional safety during the operation phase. The above four aspects support each other and jointly build the latest development of the automotive embedded system functional safety design methodology.

Acknowledgments. This work was supported by the Educational Research Project of Young and Middle-aged Teachers of Fujian Provincial Department of Education (JAT200801), 2021 Quanzhou Institute of Information Engineering Education and Teaching Reform Research Project (2021JXGG006), the scientific research project of Guangzhou College of Technology and Business (No. KA202108), and the higher education reform project of Guangzhou College of Technology and Business (No. ZL20201223).

References

1. Qiu, M., Chen, Z., Liu, M.: Low-power low-latency data allocation for hybrid scratch-pad memory. IEEE Embed. Syst. Lett. **6**(4), 69–72 (2014)
2. Thakur, K., Qiu, M., Gai, K., Ali, M.: An investigation on cyber security threats and security models. In: IEEE CSCloud (2015)
3. Zhang, Z., Wu, J., et al.: Jamming ACK attack to wireless networks and a mitigation approach. In: IEEE GLOBECOM Conference, pp. 1–5 (2008)
4. Lo Bello, L., Mariani, R., Mubeen, S., Saponara, S.: Recent advances and trends in on-board embedded and networked automotive systems. IEEE Trans. Ind. Inform. **15**(2), 1038–1051 (2019)
5. Nardi, A., Armato, A.: Functional safety methodologies for automotive applications. In: 2017 IEEE/ACM ICCAD, pp. 970–975 (2017)
6. Liang, W., Zhang, D., Lei, X., Tang, M., Li, K., Zomaya, A.: Circuit copyright blockchain: blockchain-based homomorphic encryption for IP circuit protection. IEEE Trans. Emerg. Top. Comput. (2020)
7. Ding, H., Liang, Y., Mitra, T.: Shared cache aware task mapping for WCRT minimization. In: 2013 18th Asia and South Pacific Design Automation Conference (ASP-DAC), pp. 735–740 (2013)
8. Xie, G., Zeng, G., Kurachi, R., Takada, H., Li, Z., et al.: WCRT analysis and evaluation for sporadic message-processing tasks in multicore automotive gateways. IEEE TCAD **38**(2), 281–294 (2019)
9. Azketa, E., Gutiérrez, J.J., Palencia, J.C., Harbour, M.G., Almeida, L., et al.: Schedulability analysis of multi-packet messages in segmented CAN. In: IEEE 17th ETFA Conference, pp. 1–8 (2012)
10. Xie, Y., Zeng, G., Chen, Y., Kurachi, R., Takada, H., Li, R.: Worst case response time analysis for messages in controller area network with gateway. IEICE Trans. Inf. Syst. **96**(7), 1467–1477 (2013)
11. Girault, A., Kalla, H.: A novel bicriteria scheduling heuristics providing a guaranteed global system failure rate. IEEE Trans. Depend. Secure Comput. **6**(4), 241–254 (2009)
12. Liang, W., Xiao, L., Zhang, K., Tang, M., He, D., Li, K.C.: Data fusion approach for collaborative anomaly intrusion detection in blockchain-based systems. IEEE Internet Things J. (2021)
13. Liang, Y., Li, Z., et al. Nbnrp1 mediates Verticillium dahliae effector PevD1-triggered defense responses by regulating sesquiterpenoid phytoalexins biosynthesis pathway in Nicotiana benthamiana. Gene **768** (2021)

14. Menglan, H., Luo, J., Wang, Y., Lukasiewycz, M., Zeng, Z.: Holistic scheduling of real-time applications in time-triggered in-vehicle networks. IEEE Trans. Ind. Inf. **10**(3), 1817–1828 (2014)
15. Liang, W., Xie, S., Cai, J., et al.: Deep neural network security collaborative filtering scheme for service recommendation in intelligent cyber-physical systems. IEEE Internet Things J. (2021)

Design and Development of Simulation Software Based on AR-Based Torricelli Experiment

Yan Hui[1], Jie Zhan[1(✉)], Libin Jiao[2], and Xiu Liang[1]

[1] Hunan University of Science and Technology, Xiangtan 411201, China
[2] Science and Technology on Communication Networks Laboratory, Shijiazhuang, People's Republic of China

Abstract. This paper proposes to use AR technology to design and develop simulation software based on the Torricelli experiment of AR. In the physics experiment teaching, Torricelli experiment clearly confirmed the existence of atmospheric pressure with simple devices and easy-to-understand principles and measured that the size of a standard atmospheric pressure is about 760 mm Hg. However, due to the possibility of causing mercury hazards and other problems during the experiment, it is not recommended to demonstrate the actual operation of the Torricelli experiment. This paper first uses smartphones to scan device pictures to obtain virtual three-dimensional models, and to conduct interactive learning on the screen of the mobile phone, so as to ensure the personal safety of teachers and students and the premise of environmental safety. Next, we improve students' learning motivation and mastery of physics knowledge. In the development process of this system, Unity3d software is used as the main development tool, Vuforia is used technically to realize AR recognition, and the current mainstream development language C# is selected for programming.

Keywords: AR · Torricelli experiment · Simulation software · Software design and development

1 Introduction

AR (Augmented Reality) is one of the virtual and real fusion modes, based on the real world, on which three-dimensional virtual objects are presented [1]. In recent years, with the improvement of mobile phone CPU performance [2–4] and big data processing and transferring capability [5–7], the popularization of high-definition dual-camera cameras have created a foundation for the realization of AR technology on the mobile terminal. Compared with traditional virtual experiments, AR-based virtual experiments have obvious advantages in terms of interactivity, realism, and immersion [8]. The focus of virtual experiments based on AR is to show the experimental principles that are not easy to describe in traditional real physics experiments, or unobvious and invisible experimental phenomena, through AR technology, simplify the experimental operating environment, improve student participation, and help students have good grasp of the physical principles [9].

M. Qiu et al. (Eds.): SmartCom 2021, LNCS 13202, pp. 481–490, 2022.
https://doi.org/10.1007/978-3-030-97774-0_44

This subject is based on the.NET Framework and built the physical model required for the "Torricelli experiment" on Unity3D. Using the idea of equivalent substitution, a standard atmospheric pressure was calculated by the height of the mercury column under the action of the external atmospheric pressure, and a comparative experiment was designed., Proved that the experimental results have nothing to do with the thickness of the glass tube, and completed the exploration of a standard atmospheric pressure and the design and development of simulation software [10].

The organization of this paper is as follows. Section 2 focuses on the traditional Torricelli experiment and its existing hazards and problems, thus proving the significance of the realization of the subject. Then, the design process and operation process of the simulation software based on the Torricelli experiment of AR are mainly described in Sect. 3. Section 4 shows the realization results of the system. Finally, the conclusions are drawn in Sect. 5.

2   Requirements Elaboration

2.1   Traditional Torricelli Experiment

The Torricelli experiment clearly confirmed the existence of atmospheric pressure with simple devices and easy-to-understand principles and measured a standard atmospheric pressure of about 760 mm mercury column or 10.3 m water column, which can be described as an outstanding classic experiment in the history of physics [11].

2.2   The Harm and Existing Problems of Traditional Torricelli Experiment

Hazard of Mercury. Mercury is the only metal that exists in liquid form under normal atmospheric pressure and room temperature. The liquid characteristics of mercury determine its not easy to store characteristics. Mercury is easy to evaporate into the air and cause harm. Scientific research shows that after 1 g of mercury is completely evaporated, it can make a 15 square meter large and 3 m high indoor mercury concentration reach 22.2 mg/cubic meter. In a room with a mercury concentration of 1–3 mg/m^3, ordinary people can cause headache, fever, abdominal cramps, dyspnea and other symptoms in just two hours. Not only that, the respiratory tract and lung tissue of the poisoned person may be affected. In severe cases, it may even die of respiratory failure. So far, scientists have not found an effective remedy for mercury pollution.

In summary, mercury is volatile, and mercury vapor is toxic. Once a house, such as a classroom, is contaminated by mercury vapor, it is difficult to treat and the treatment takes a long time. The Torricelli experiment uses hundreds of grams of mercury at a time, and the laboratory area is only one hundred and eighty square meters. In the face of dozens of students, once a spillage accident causes mercury pollution, the adverse effects are difficult to save.

Existing Problems of Traditional Torricelli Experiment. It is difficult for one person to operate during the experiment, and untrained students cannot assist in completing it; Slender glass tube is easy to break; Although some improved experimental devices do not need to be filled with mercury, they are complicated in structure, which affects the understanding of physical concepts, and are costly. They are difficult to operate and inconvenient to carry; For a long time, the Torricelli experimental device has been lacking a better solution, which makes it difficult to conduct experiments in the classroom.

3 Software Design

The main goal of this system is to design and develop an AR-based Torricelli experiment. The entire program needs to use Unity3D software and Vuforia toolkit. First, analyze the physics experiment to understand the principles and operation steps of the physics experiment. On this basis, outline the functions that the software needs to achieve [12]; second, design the data organization structure of the program; finally, set up the experimental scene in Unity3D and realize augmented reality effects through Vuforia [13].

3.1 Feature Design

In Terms of Service Objects. This project will design and develop AR-based Torricelli experimental simulation software based on physics experiment courses, mainly for students studying physics experiments.

In Terms of Learners' Starting Level. Considering the rapid popularization of informatization in today's society, most students already have a certain understanding of information technology equipment (especially household digital equipment), and have the basis for innovative experimental teaching based on new technologies.

In Terms of Operating Interaction. Due to the widespread popularity of smart phones in recent years, most students are already familiar with the techniques of scanning QR code images with cameras and conventional touch operations. Therefore, this software introduces AR technology, scans and recognizes the designated floor plan, zooms and conventionally touches the acquired 3D model, and clicks to switch between the 3D model and the experimental scene.

In Terms of Functional Design. It specifically includes:
Realize the function of pouring the mercury in the beaker into the glass tube. In the process of pouring the mercury, it is necessary to consider the situation of fullness, underfilling, overflow, etc.; 1). To realize the function of blocking the glass tube nozzle by hand, consider blocking the glass tube opening and not blocking the glass tube opening; Note: collision detection is required; in 3D mode, a plug can be used instead of hand; 2). Realize the function of inverting the glass tube and inserting it into the mercury tank; 3). Realize the function that mercury in the glass tube drops to a certain height after releasing the finger; 4). Realize the function of measuring the height difference between the mercury surface in the mercury tank and the mercury in the glass tube; 5). Realize the function of tilting left and right and moving the glass tube up and down without changing the height of mercury; 6). Realize the function of using glass tubes of different thicknesses and lengths to complete the comparative test.

3.2 Data Structure Design

The overall program framework [14] is shown in Fig. 1:

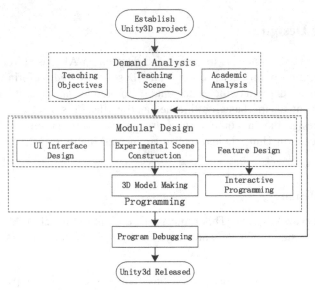

Fig. 1. Overall framework diagram

When the function of pouring the mercury in the beaker into the glass tube is realized, the data structure diagram when considering the situation of full, under-filled, overflow, etc. in the process of pouring mercury is as follows: (Fig. 2)

3.3 Interface Design

For the setting of the experimental interface, plug-in UGUI is mainly used. Because it is directly integrated in the Unity editor, it has the advantages of high efficiency, easy use and expansion. Under Canvas, directly click GameObject→UI→Button→Text, where Button and Text are the parent-child relationship, and then edit the buttons and text in the Inspector view. After the interface is generated, if you want to implement some functions, you also need code assistance.

Inject Mercury. By clicking this button, you can inject mercury into the test tube; **Test tube inversion.** To achieve inverted glass tube; **Pull out the cork.** When the inverted glass tube is immersed in the mercury tank, the cork is pulled out so that the mercury in the test tube can flow out.

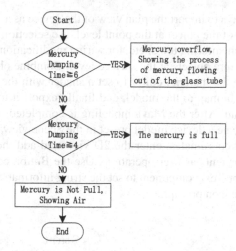

Fig. 2. The data structure diagram of pouring mercury

3.4 Software Operation Process

The structure of the software is mainly divided into two parts: AR image recognition and Unity response operation. The operation process is shown in Fig. 3, where the image acquisition of the camera will be the first step of the software. The user opens the software to automatically start the camera, and the AR camera automatically runs and recognizes the plane image within the lens range. When it meets the matching characteristics, it will display a specific 3D model at the specified location. This part of the work is mainly undertaken by AR technology.

The trigger display of the 3D model and the browsing of the associated media are the next steps in the process. After the AR camera recognizes the image, the user can zoom in on the 3D model that appears on the screen, adjust the visual effect of the model according to the real environment, and make it at a better viewing angle to enhance the experience.

The three-dimensional models in the program are modeled and designed in accordance with real equipment to complement the teaching content of the physics experiment course. The plan view and the three-dimensional model used in the recognition are also matched, and the selection is based on the popular digital equipment data from the current society.

3.5 Software Development Process

Software development is mainly divided into three-dimensional modeling and program development. The former is based on the modeling software Maya, and the latter is based on the Unity engine.

3D Modeling. Use Maya to import the plan view of the device as a modeling reference, set the surface features of the object at the point level, use selection tools, multi-cutting tools, extrusion tools, chamfering tools, etc. for wiring modification, and use geometric tools to draw linear feature objects at the surface level, Combine objects with different physical signs, and use the material editor to set a shader with the characteristics of a digital device, apply a bitmap to the model, and finally export it to an Fbx format file through the export menu. After the Maya modeling is completed, use Unity to import the created Fbx file, create a device model preset in the Scene view, use the editing tool to adjust the scale and coordinates, enter the 2D view and add the necessary Button, Image and other components as user operations Use the Button component to set the click monitoring, use the Text component to set the string information of the device, and use the Image to set the icon prompt.

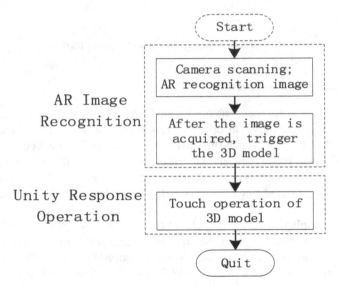

Fig. 3. Software operation flow chart

4 Achieved Results

4.1 3D Scene Realization Results

Step 1. Fill the glass tube with mercury, as follows:

Take out the glass tube;

Take out the measuring cup with mercury (be careful not to touch the ruler or the mercury trough, the measuring cup will fly);

Click the right mouse button on the measuring cup to inject mercury into the glass tube (there will be a prompt, "full", "not full" and "overflow") (Fig. 4).

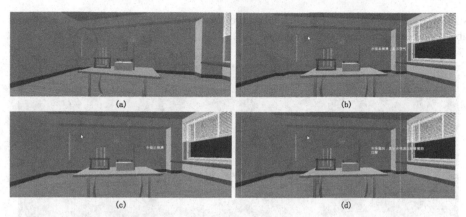

Fig. 4. (a) glass tube and measuring cup filled with mercury; (b) prompt "full"; (c) prompt "not full"; (d) prompt "overflow"

Step 2. Drag the mouse to place the measuring cup on the table (Fig. 5);

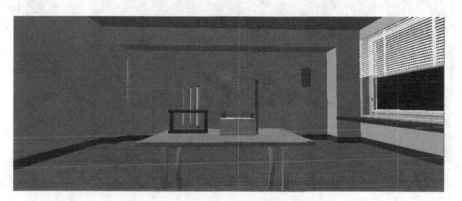

Fig. 5. Put the measuring cup back on the table

Step 3. Drag the mouse to place the glass tube filled with mercury into the mercury tank (note: the current test tube is upright);

Step 4. Click the right mouse button on the glass tube and turn the glass tube upside down. Click the middle button of the mouse on the inverted glass tube to remove the stopper on the test tube, so as to realize the downward flow of mercury:

Step 5. View the results, the specific operations are as follows:

Adjust the position of the magnifying glass to see that the height of mercury in the glass tube is 13.6 cm;

Adjust the position of the magnifying glass to see that the height of the mercury in the mercury tank is 6 cm;

The vertical height difference between the height of mercury in the glass tube and the height of mercury in the mercury tank is 7.6 cm, that is, the experimental result: the size of 1 standard atmosphere is equal to the pressure produced by a mercury column about 760 mm high (Figs. 6, 7 and 8).

Fig. 6. Put the glass tube into the mercury tank

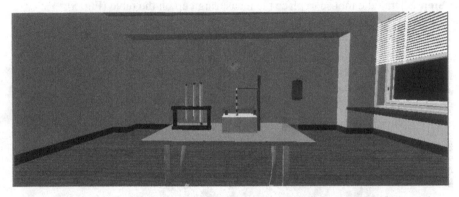

Fig. 7. The glass tube is upside down, mercury flows down

Fig. 8. (a) The height of mercury in the glass tube; (b) The height of mercury in the mercury tank

4.2 AR Scene Display

As shown in Fig. 9, after the user uses the camera of the Android phone to recognize a specific floor plan [15], a virtual test tube can appear on the screen, and the test tube can be operated virtual by touch to adjust its proportion, and click the test tube to switch to Experimental scene (Fig. 10).

Fig. 9. The rendering after scanning the floor plan

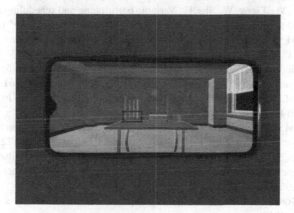

Fig. 10. Experimental scene

5 Conclusions

In this paper, aiming at the problems of low safety and difficulty of operation in traditional Torricelli experiment, we designed and developed an AR-based Torricelli experiment simulation software. This article first analyzes and designs the system in detail, then explains the feasible implementation process, and demonstrates the results of the implementation. It is foreseeable that with the development of technology, AR will become more and more perfect, providing a new way and concept for teaching.

Acknowledgments. This work was supported by the National Natural Science Foundation of China (Grant No. 61875054), Complex System Simulation Key Laboratory Fund (Grant No. XM2020XT1004), Communication Network Information Transmission and Distribution Technology Key Laboratory Fund (Grant No. 6142104190315).

References

1. Garzón, J., Acevedo, J.: Meta-analysis of the impact of Augmented Reality on students' learning gains. Educ. Re. Rev. **27**, 244–260 (2019)
2. Qiu, M., Chen, Z., Liu, M.: Low-power low-latency data allocation for hybrid scratch-pad memory. IEEE Embed. Syst. Lett. **6**(4), 69–72 (2014)
3. Qiu, M., Zhang, L., Ming, Z., et al.: Security-aware optimization for ubiquitous computing systems with SEAT graph approach. J. Comput. Syst. Sci. **79**(5), 518–529 (2013)
4. Gao, Y., Iqbal, S., et al.: Performance and power analysis of high-density multi-GPGPU architectures: a preliminary case study. In: IEEE 17th HPCC (2015)
5. Qiu, M., Chen, Z., Niu, J., et al.: Data allocation for hybrid memory with genetic algorithm. IEEE Trans. Emerg. Top. Comput. **3**(4), 544–555 (2015)
6. Lu, R., Jin, X., Zhang, S., Qiu, M., Wu, X.: A study on big knowledge and its engineering issues. IEEE Trans. Knowl. Data Eng. **31**(9), 1630–1644 (2018)
7. Zhang, L., Qiu, M., Tseng, W., Sha, E.: Variable partitioning and scheduling for MPSoC with virtually shared scratch pad memory. J. Sig. Process. Syst. **58**(2), 247–265 (2010)
8. Gai, K., Qiu, M.: Optimal resource allocation using reinforcement learning for IoT content-centric services. Appl. Soft Comput. **70**, 12–21 (2018)
9. Lindner, C., Rienow, A., Jürgens, C.: Augmented Reality applications as digital experiments for education - an example in the Earth-Moon System. Acta Astronaut. **161**, 66–74 (2019)
10. Gai, K., Qiu, M.: Reinforcement learning-based content-centric services in mobile sensing. IEEE Netw. **32**(4), 34–39 (2018)
11. Gai, K., Qiu, M., et al.: Resource management in sustainable cyber-physical systems using heterogeneous cloud computing. IEEE Trans. Sustain. Comput. **3**(2), 60–72 (2018)
12. Liang, W., Xie, S., Cai, J.: Deep neural network security collaborative filtering scheme for service recommendation in intelligent cyber-physical systems. IEEE Internet Things J. https://doi.org/10.1109/ЛОТ.2021.3086845
13. Burns & McDonnell and Manitoba hydro partner on augmented reality software. Transm. Distrib. World (2019)
14. Liang, W., Xiao, L., Zhang, K., Tang, M., He, D., Li, K.C.: Data fusion approach for collaborative anomaly intrusion detection in blockchain-based systems. IEEE Internet Things J. 1 (2021). https://doi.org/10.1109/JIOT.2021.3053842
15. Liang, W., Long, J., Li, K.-C., Xu, J., Ma, N., Lei, X.: A fast defogging image recognition algorithm based on bilateral hybrid filtering. ACM Trans. Multimed. Comput. Commun. Appl. **17**(2) (2021). Article 42. https://doi.org/10.1145/3391297

Short Papers

Study on the Organization and Governance of Bigdata for Lifelong Education

Li Ma[1](✉), Zexian Yang[2] (iD), Wenyin Yang[1] (iD), Huihong Yang[2] (iD), and Qidi Lao[2] (iD)

[1] Electronic and Information Engineering School, Foshan University, Foshan, China
molly_917@fosu.edu.cn
[2] Mechatronics Engineering and Automation School, Foshan University, Foshan, China
2112052024@stu.fosu.edu.cn

Abstract. The open university is carrying out various types of academic and non-academic education to serve the city's citizens and usually has gained a good reputation in the local area. However, previously, due to its inadequate hardware system, fragmented information system, and incomplete data collection, it carried out various operations more by empirical judgment and lacked objective data support, thus making it impossible to promote the development of a lifelong education system accurately. By collecting, integrating, and analyzing these lifelong education projects, converting them into lifelong education big data, and establishing various lifelong education data visualization and analysis models, we can promote the transformation of life-long education from discrete demand to education big data precision-driven development mode, provide support for the supply-side structural reform of lifelong education, and at the same time improve the leading role of the open university in the construction of lifelong education system, thus promoting the high-quality development of lifelong education for citizens.

Keywords: Lifelong education · Analysis model · Big data

1 Background and Significance

How to play the leading role of grass-roots open universities in building a lifelong education system [1] is an important research topic nowadays. By collecting, integrating, and analyzing education projects, converging into lifelong education big data, and establishing various lifelong education data visualization and analysis models, it is important to promote the high-quality development of regional lifelong education.

(1) Big Data Research on Lifelong Education Can Improve the Quality of Grass-roots Open Universities and Accelerate Their Transformation and Development. As an important support for building a lifelong education system and forming a learning society, the Open University (Liu Yandong, a member of the Political Bureau of the CPC Central Committee and State Councilor, inaugurated the National Open University and delivered a speech entitled "Striving to Run an Open University with Chinese Characteristics") has served local economic development for many

years and accumulated a large amount of lifelong education data, which can be integrated and analyzed to more clearly identify the problems in the process of running schools and explore better solutions. After integration and analysis, we can identify problems in the process of education and find better solutions, and finally realize the cycle of "discovering problems -> improving problems -> improving quality -> discovering problems again" through the support of big data, and accelerate the transformation and development of the grass-roots open university.

(2) The Organization and Governance of Lifelong Education Big Data Can Promote the Transformation of Lifelong Education to Big Data Development Mode and Provide New Support for Promoting the Supply-side Structural Reform of Lifelong Education. With the advent of the big data era for various applications [16–18], big data in education [2, 3] is innovating the model of education in an unprecedented way. In the field of lifelong education, how to solve the following urgent problems through the organization and governance of big data: firstly, to help establish a lifelong education visualization model and application path; secondly, to innovate lifelong learning public services and talent training models; thirdly, to promote the transformation of lifelong education into a big data development model; fourthly, to enhance the service capacity and supply level of lifelong education; fifthly, to provide a scientific basis for promoting scientific management of lifelong education Sixth, to provide new support for promoting the supply-side structural reform of lifelong education; Seventh, to achieve large-scale applicable education and thus continuously innovate the talent cultivation mode.

(3) Through the Construction of Foshan Lifelong Education Digital Service Center and the Integration of Foshan, Lifelong Education Big Data Can Provide the Experience that Can be Learned from the Construction of Lifelong Education System for Open Universities around the World. According to the "Foshan Open University Construction Program (2019–2021)" approved by Foshan Office Letter [2019] 229, Foshan Government agrees to Foshan Open University to build a lifelong education digital service center. By means of collecting, converging, integrating, mining, and analyzing the data related to lifelong education in Foshan, it will establish a lifelong education visualization data analysis model, explore the promotion and application path, innovate public services for lifelong learning for all people, and promote the transformation of lifelong education from discrete demand to an accurate development mode driven by education big data, while providing solid and powerful support for enhancing the local lifelong education capacity and improving the development level of lifelong education. The construction of this project has important theoretical research significance and practical value.

This paper proposes a lifelong education big data, and then compares it with the current situation at home and abroad, and then studies the content of the lifelong education data governance framework, and then studies a lifelong education data governance framework.

2 Related Work

Lifelong education has been developed in foreign countries, especially in the United States, Japan, and South Korea, where it has made great progress. The experiences and practices of developed countries and regions have important significance for promoting the legislation and development of lifelong education in China. Chinese scholars have analyzed the legislation and implementation aspects of lifelong education in foreign countries, thus making reliable suggestions for the development of lifelong education in China. Scholar Sun Yi analyzed the reasons for and implementation process of foreign legislation on lifelong education and proposed specific measures for implementation and inspiration from foreign legislation on lifelong education in China. Huang Fusheng and Wu Zunming analyzed the characteristics, advantages, and shortcomings of lifelong education laws in foreign developed countries and regions, as well as the inspiration from them.

In the study of data governance, most foreign scholars have proposed a framework for data governance to ensure the operability, logicality, and stringency of the data governance process and enhance the value of data. The definitions proposed by foreign authorities such as DAMA (The Data Management Association) and DGI (The Data Governance Institute) are the most representative and authoritative. These governance frameworks have their scope of application. Since there is no national-level specification for the qualifications framework that the lifelong education system currently relies on, and its data governance has needs and characteristics such as gradualness, complexity, and scalability, this project proposes a set of data governance frameworks suitable for the current lifelong education.

In 2014, Tsinghua University established the "Research Centre for Massive Online Education." The Centre used big data technology to analyze data on the learning behaviors left by many learners on the platform to discover which knowledge points were of interest to learners and which learning tools and learning materials were used most frequently so as to create a more adaptive and intelligent learning platform. In the same year, Peking University joined the MOOC platform created by Edx, a U.S. company, which provides free, independent and open access to courses from top universities around the world for students [4]. In 2015, Fudan University also joined the US-based Coursera platform to build a global online course network with Coursera, Inc. On this network, learning services such as course selection, online videos, and online tests are provided to learners around the world [5–9].

The advent of the big data era has provided an unprecedented and great opportunity for theoretical innovation in lifelong education. In lifelong education, big data promotes the development of education platforms from teaching and teaching management information systems to big data applications. Undoubtedly, in the field of lifelong learning [10], big data provides technical support for quantifiable learning outcomes of learners.

3 Research Content and Objective

3.1 Research Content

Construction of Data Governance Framework for Lifelong Education. Building a data governance framework for lifelong education can provide theoretical guidance for specific practices and ensure the standardization, scalability, and security of lifelong education data. Lifelong education data governance framework usually needs to consider the following aspects: first, logical relationships and functions of components; second, guidelines and objectives of data governance [11]; third, organizational structure and division of responsibilities of data governance; fourth, data governance domain; fifth, establishment of data governance evaluation mechanism and implementation methods [12]. Through in-depth analysis and scientific refinement of the operational mechanism and data characteristics of lifelong education, the data governance framework of lifelong education is innovatively proposed.

Study on Data Specification of Lifelong Education Development. Lifelong education data standardization is achieved, and data standards, code standards, interface specifications, and information standard specifications for platform access were developed. Data integration for non-academic education such as academic education, vocational education, and socialized training is realized. Lifelong education digital file bag management, lifelong education growth diagnosis report, display and analysis statistics of lifelong education data, etc., are realized.

Study on Evaluation Indicators for Lifelong Education Growth. The lifelong education growth evaluation indicators and personal learning portraits of citizens are proposed. The main functions of the lifelong education growth evaluation indicators include development evaluation analysis, development data and statistics, development graphs, and other personal growth evaluation management; the main functions of the personal learning portrait include career development roadmap, independent career development planning, professional learning community, benchmark model learning, career development process management, and other citizen career development maps.

Evaluation and Analysis of Learning City. The learning city evaluation index is proposed, and its main functions include learning city development evaluation management, visual model analysis and large screen display of the city's lifelong education status, and citizen education quality evaluation.

3.2 Research Objectives

Establish a Framework for Lifelong Education Data Governance. In order to achieve the overall strategy and goals of data governance, we need to develop a data governance framework for lifelong education that describes the basic components (e.g., principles, organizational structures, processes, and rules) and the logical relationships between components (concepts) in the field of lifelong education data governance.

Develop a Set of Data Specification Standards for Lifelong Education. In order to realize the standardized processing of lifelong education data, we need to develop a set of data specification standards [13], so as to achieve the goal of ensuring the usability and effectiveness of data management and guaranteeing stability and high value of the data itself.

Propose a Lifelong Education Growth Evaluation Model. In order to realize real-time monitoring and dynamic analysis of lifelong education data, as well as to provide a decision-making basis for lifelong education supervision and evaluation and building learning cities, we need to establish a lifelong education visual data analysis display and evaluation model by means of collecting, aggregating, integrating, mining and analyzing lifelong education-related data.

4 Lifelong Education Data Governance Framework

The construction of a data governance framework for lifelong education (Fig. 1) can provide theoretical guidance for specific practices and ensure the standardization, scalability, and security of lifelong education data. The lifelong education data governance framework usually requires the following considerations: first, the logical relationships and the functions of components; second, the guidelines and the objectives of data governance; third, the organizational structure and the division of responsibilities of data governance; fourth, the data governance domain; and fifth, the establishment of data governance evaluation mechanism and the implementation methods.

In terms of building smart learning communities, building a prior learning certification database, and credit system that are currently popular on the market, the lifelong education data governance framework proposed in this paper includes the content it proposes, not just conducting research from one side, but research and design from a multi-level, multi-dimensional, and rational perspective. Further promote the co-construction, sharing, and public use of data, provide support for the supply-side structural reform of lifelong education, realize large-scale applicability education, continue to innovate talent training models, and ultimately promote the high-quality development of lifelong education for citizens.

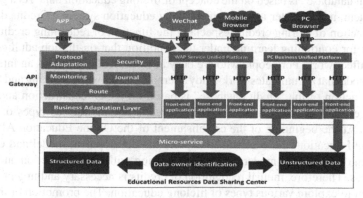

Fig. 1. Lifelong education data governance framework

5   Lifelong Education Data Resource Sharing Mechanism

By integrating the lifelong education data resources of Foshan City, we build a data resource sharing center [14] based on the data owner as of the core and the data owner's identification as the key value as well as the sharing of data in the form of microservices to provide common sharing. We can realize the separation organization of application system and data, structured + unstructured data storage model [15], and establish the visual data analysis display and evaluation model of basic education. The lifelong education data sharing mechanism is shown in Fig. 2.

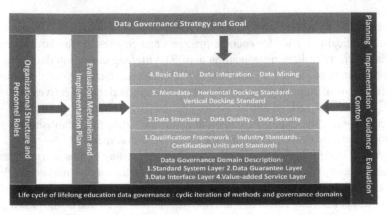

Fig. 2. Data Sharing mechanism for lifelong education data

6   "Credit Database" in Lifelong Education Data Governance

The "credit database" is based on the concept of lifelong education data. As a guarantee of the system, it will better improve the lifelong education system. "Credits database" has the function of storing credits, especially the function of redeeming credits, which is suitable for continuing learning under the condition that on-the-job adult education does not affect work. For people who are busy at work, it also provides an intermittent learning mode that accumulates work-study alternate credits while working and learning. The construction of the "credit database" is based on the co-construction and sharing of resources, and the mutual recognition of credits among various types of lifelong education. At the beginning of the establishment of the Online Education Alliance of Continuing Education, the goal was to explore the development model and operating mechanism of innovative modern distance education with co-construction and sharing of resources. Therefore, mutual recognition of credits is necessary and urgent, and it is very urgent to explore various types of lifelong education. The promotion of the online education alliance requires the active participation of the continuing education colleges of various universities to take the lead. The practice objects will take the students of the school as examples, further strengthen the joint construction and sharing of resources, and implement the mutual recognition of various types of lifelong education credits. Finally, promote the construction of the "credit database".

7 Summary

This paper detailed the research proposal and functions of lifelong education data organization and governance, which included lifelong education data governance framework and lifelong education data resource sharing mechanism research, in order to promote lifelong education from discrete demand to education big data precision-driven development model and improve the leading role of the open university in the construction of lifelong education system, and then promoted the high-quality development of lifelong education in Foshan.

Acknowledgments. This work was supported by grants from the Natural Science Foundation of Guangdong Province No. 2018A0303130082, The Features Innovation Program of the Department of Education of Foshan No. 2019QKL01, Basic and Applied Basic Research Fund of Guangdong Province No. 2019A1515111080.

References

1. Taşçı, G., Titrek, O.: Evaluation of lifelong learning centers in higher education: a sustainable leadership perspective. Sustainability **12**(1), 22 (2020)
2. Luan, H., Geczy, P., Lai, H., et al.: Challenges and future directions of big data and artificial intelligence in education. Front. Psychol. **11**, 580820 (2020)
3. Ang, K.L.M., Ge, F.L., et al.: Big educational data & analytics: survey, architecture and challenges. IEEE Access **8**, 116392–116414 (2020)
4. Hu, H., Zhang, G., Gao, W., Wang, M.: Big data analytics for MOOC video watching behavior based on Spark. Neural Comput. Appl. **32**(11), 6481–6489 (2019). https://doi.org/10.1007/s00521-018-03983-z
5. Baturay, M.H.: An overview of the world of MOOCs. Proc. Soc. Behav. Sci. **174**, 427–433 (2015)
6. Dai, H.M., Teo, T., Rappa, N.A., et al.: Explaining Chinese university students' continuance learning intention in the MOOC setting: a modified expectation confirmation model perspective. Comput. Educ. **150**, 103850 (2020)
7. Jung, E., Kim, D., Yoon, M., et al.: The influence of instructional design on learner control, sense of achievement, and perceived effectiveness in a supersize MOOC course. Comput. Educ. **128**, 377–388 (2019)
8. Son, N.T., Jaafar, J., Aziz, I.A., et al.: Meta-heuristic algorithms for learning path recommender at MOOC. IEEE Access **9**, 59093–59107 (2021)
9. Ruipérez-Valiente, J.A., Halawa, S., Slama, R., et al.: Using multi-platform learning analytics to compare regional and global MOOC learning in the Arab world. Comput. Educ. **146**, 103776 (2020)
10. Farr, A., Aliberti, S., Loukides, S., et al.: A pathway to keep all lifelong learners up to date: the ERS continuing professional development programme. Eur. Respir. J. **55**(2), 1902425 (2020)
11. Castro, A., Villagrá, V.A., García, P., et al.: An ontological-based model to data governance for big data. IEEE Access **9**, 109943–109959 (2021)
12. Zhou, X.: The establishment of education quality evaluation system and standards of open universities. Agro Food Ind. Hi Tech **28**(1), 3061–3063 (2017)
13. Mandinach, E.B., Schildkamp, K.: Misconceptions about data-based decision making in education: an exploration of the literature. Stud. Educ. Eval. **69**, 100842 (2021)

14. Xu, H., He, Q., Li, X., et al.: BDSS-FA: a blockchain-based data security sharing platform with fine-grained access control. IEEE Access **8**, 87552–87561 (2020)
15. Zhang, D., Wang, Y., Liu, Z., et al.: Improving NoSQL storage schema based on Z-curve for spatial vector data. IEEE Access **7**, 78817–78829 (2019)
16. Qiu, M., Cao, D., Su, H., Gai, K.: Data transfer minimization for financial derivative pricing using Monte Carlo simulation with GPU in 5G. Int. J. Commun. Syst. **29**(16), 2364–2374 (2016)
17. Lu, R., Jin, X., Zhang, S., Qiu, M., Wu, X.: A study on big knowledge and its engineering issues. IEEE Trans. Knowl. Data Eng. **31**(9), 1630–1644 (2018)
18. Qiu, H., Qiu, M., Lu, Z.: Selective encryption on ECG data in body sensor network based on supervised machine learning. Inf. Fusion **55**, 59–67 (2020)

Fault Location Technique of Distribution Power Network Based on Traveling Wave Measurement

Chunyi Lu[1](✉), Kaili Yan[2], and Mi Zhou[3]

[1] State Grid Zhejiang Electric Power Co., LTD., Lanxi Power Supply Company, Hangzhou, China
luchunyi@sohu.com
[2] State Grid Zhoushan Power Supply Company, Zhejiang, China
yan_kaili@zj.sgcc.com.cn
[3] State Grid Hangzhou Power Supply Company, Zhejiang, China
zhou_mi@zj.sgcc.com.cn

Abstract. Distribution network is the most important part of power system, distribution network fault location technology can help power companies to find and eliminate faults quickly, can provide reliable and continuous power supply plays a very important role. Based on traveling wave detection principle, this paper puts forward the corresponding solution of distribution network fault location system, and gives different types of traveling wave fault location methods.

Keywords: Distribution network · Traveling wave · Fault location

1 Introduction

The purpose of the distribution system is to provide continuous quality power supply to all end users. However, the failure of the distribution line due to the influence of environment, external force or aging can lead to permanent power outage [1]. The existing fault location methods in power distribution system can be divided into two types: impedance method and traveling wave method [2, 3]. The fault location method based on impedance has been proved to be unable to be used in the distribution network through research and practice [2].

With the development of computer capability [4–6], networks [7, 8], and big data processing techniques [9–11], the traveling wave method becomes the most important research direction for finding distribution network fault locations [12]. Traveling wave method can be divided into single-terminal method and double-terminal method. The two-terminal method requires the installation of signal detection devices and GPS (Global positioning system) time synchronization devices at both ends of the line. The single-end system only needs to install signal detection device at one end of the line, and does not need to install GPS clock synchronization device. Therefore, compared with the two-ended system, the single-ended system has lower cost and simpler structure, but its positioning accuracy is less affected by signal attenuation and distortion than that of the two-ended system [13].

M. Qiu et al. (Eds.): SmartCom 2021, LNCS 13202, pp. 501–507, 2022.
https://doi.org/10.1007/978-3-030-97774-0_46

In the existing fault location techniques based on travelling wave, the transient wave at fault elimination is used to replace the transient wave at fault occurrence. Moreover, the single-terminal method based on the transient waveform of fault elimination is more suitable for distribution system [14, 15].

2 Basic Principle of Traveling Wave Method

Traveling wave is the transient wave generated on transmission line or distribution line. Most of the transient waves generated on transmission and distribution line are caused by phase short circuit, single phase grounding and other faults. Once a fault occurs on a line, the voltage and current transients it generates, known as transient waves, propagate from the point of failure down the line in both directions [16, 17] (Fig. 1).

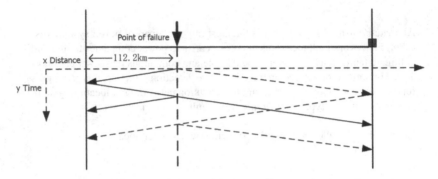

Fig. 1. Schematic diagram of fault traveling wave propagation

The accuracy of fault location method based on traveling wave in distribution system depends on the correct calculation of wave velocity which is related to distribution line parameters [18–20].

1) Type A traveling wave signal detection device: The detection device is installed at one end of the line, and the fault location is carried out by single-end method.
2) B-type traveling wave signal detection device: The detection device is installed at both ends of the line, and the double-end method is used to locate faults.
3) E-type traveling wave type detection device: The detection device is installed at one end of the circuit and locates faults by detecting the transient waves generated by the action of the circuit breaker, rather than the transient waves generated by the fault [21–23].

3 Fault Location Method

3.1 System Architecture

In this paper, the recommended method is to replace the fault transient wave generated by the fault with the single terminal short fault elimination transient wave (E type), and to apply the Clark transform to the three-phase voltage of the system. The three-phase line contains electromagnetic signals coupled in each phase of the wire. The three-phase voltage can be decomposed into a modal transformation [24].

$$U_m = T^{-1} \times U_p$$

$$I_m = T^{-1} \times I_p$$

Here, U is the voltage, I is the current, M is the number of modes, P is the number of phases and T is the transformation matrix.

In this paper, Clark transform is used to transfer the three - phase parameters into the mode transform.

$$\begin{bmatrix} U_0 \\ U_\alpha \\ U_\beta \end{bmatrix} = \frac{1}{\sqrt{3}} \begin{bmatrix} 1 & 1 & 1 \\ \sqrt{2} & -1/\sqrt{2} & -1/\sqrt{2} \\ 0 & \sqrt{3}/2 & -\sqrt{3}/2 \end{bmatrix} \begin{bmatrix} U_a \\ U_b \\ U_c \end{bmatrix}$$

After the phase component is transferred to the modal number, wavelet transform is used to calculate the first, second and third received transient wave. The received transient wave is used to find the fault section of cable or overhead line in the distribution system. Since the α mode can simplify the analysis of the three-phase circuit, the α mode component is used among the three modal components: 0, α and β. Figure 2 shows the peak voltage transient wave generated by the breaker. In α mode, in order to calculate the peak value, you need to calculate the threshold value, and then calculate the start and end elements of the peak value. When the starting and ending elements are calculated, the following formula can be used to calculate the maximum peak value [25]:

$$\text{peak} \approx (\text{start} + \text{end})/2$$

X axis: Time (ms) Y axis: voltage (p.u)

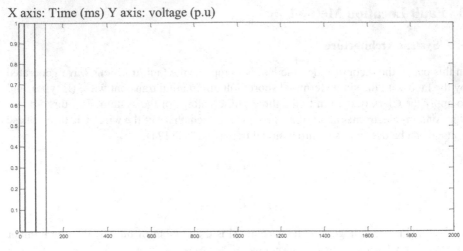

Fig. 2. Peak of α mode

The starting element is the first peak value of the initial waveform, and the terminating element is the last peak value of the initial waveform. After calculating the peak value, use the following formula to calculate the distance between the two initial waveforms (Distance) [25].

$$\text{Distance} \approx (\text{peaks}(3) + \text{peaks}(2))/2$$

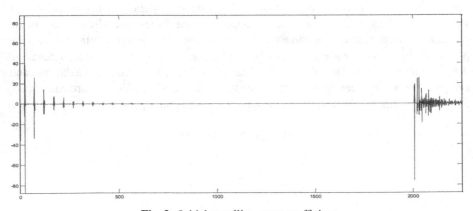

Fig. 3. Initial travelling wave coefficient

The above formula can be used to calculate the distance between the two initial waveforms (as shown in Fig. 3), and then the single-ended method can be used to calculate the position of the fault point relative to the signal detection device.

As the line lengthens, the peak amplitude decreases correspondingly. For the overhead and ground cable mixed line, the first, second and third initial traveling waves (as shown in Fig. 2) are used to calculate the fault section, and the first, second and third initial waves generated are shown in Fig. 4.

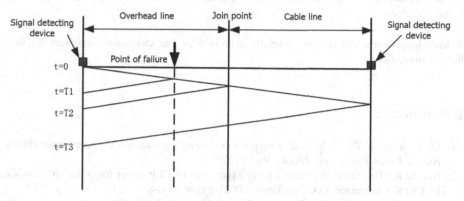

Fig. 4. Mixed line fault waveform propagation diagram

In Fig. 4, the first initial wave is transmitted from the signal detection device to the point of failure and then back to the signal detection device from the point of failure. The second initial wave is from the signal detection device to the overhead line and cable line join point and back to the signal detection device. The third initial wave travels from the signal detection device to the remote end and back to the signal detection device.

The wave velocity is calculated by the following formula [26]:

$$V = \frac{L}{t}$$

Where, V is the wave speed, L is the length of the distribution line, and T is the waveform propagation time from the signal detection device to the far end of the line. When the wave velocity is calculated, the exact location of the fault point relative to the signal detection device can be calculated by using the following:

$$X \approx V * \frac{T}{2}$$

Where X is the distance between the measuring end and the fault point, V is the wave speed, and T is the total time for the transient wave to travel from the circuit breaker to the fault point and then back to the circuit breaker.

Traveling wave method can be applied to different types of faults and various types of power lines [27, 28], including AC or DC transmission lines; Distribution line; Hybrid overhead and underground cable lines. The single-ended method proposed in this paper uses the transient waves generated by the circuit breaker rather than the transient waves where the fault occurs. Compared with the two-terminal method and impedance method, this method is simpler, cheaper and easier to implement. Since the length of distribution lines is much smaller than transmission lines, this single-end method is more suitable for distribution lines.

4   Conclusion

This paper presented a traveling wave fault location method based on single end measurement for distribution network. The paper also introduced the basic principle of traveling wave measurement and different kinds of signal detection devices based on traveling wave principle.

Acknowledgement. The authors gratefully acknowledge the anonymous reviewers for their helpful suggestions.

References

1. Li, Y., Wang, J., Zheng, Y., et al.: Comparison of several traveling wave ranging algorithms. Autom. Electr. Power Syst. **25**(14), 36–39 (2001)
2. Hoi, M.K.: Travelling wave fault locator experience on CLP power transmission net-work. In: CEPSI Conference, Fukuoka, Japan (2002). Paper T2-B-8
3. Huang, X., Wang, Z., Yin, X., et al.: Traveling wave velocity determination method for traveling wave location of high voltage transmission line. Power Syst. Technol. **28**(19), 4 (2004)
4. Gao, Y., Iqbal, S., et al.: Performance and power analysis of high-density multi-GPGPU architectures: a preliminary case study. In: IEEE 17th HPCC (2015)
5. Zhao, H., Chen, M., et al.: A novel pre-cache schema for high performance Android system. Future Gener. Comput. Syst. **56**, 766–772 (2016)
6. Zhang, L., Qiu, M., Tseng, W., Sha, E.: Variable partitioning and scheduling for MPSoC with virtually shared scratch pad memory. J. Sig. Process. Syst. **58**(2), 247–265 (2010)
7. Wu, G., Zhang, H., Qiu, M., et al.: A decentralized approach for mining event correlations in distributed system monitoring. JPDC **73**(3), 330–340 (2013)
8. Qiu, H., Qiu, M., Memmi, G., Ming, Z., Liu, M.: A dynamic scalable blockchain based communication architecture for IoT. In: Qiu, M. (ed.) SmartBlock 2018. LNCS, vol. 11373, pp. 159–166. Springer, Cham (2018). https://doi.org/10.1007/978-3-030-05764-0_17
9. Lu, R., Jin, X., Zhang, S., Qiu, M., Wu, X.: A study on big knowledge and its engineering issues. IEEE Trans. Knowl. Data Eng. **31**(9), 1630–1644 (2018)
10. Qiu, M., Chen, Z., Liu, M.: Low-power low-latency data allocation for hybrid scratch-pad memory. IEEE Embed. Syst. Lett. **6**(4), 69–72 (2014)
11. Guo, Y., Zhuge, Q., Hu, J., et al.: Optimal data allocation for scratch-pad memory on embedded multi-core systems. In: IEEE ICPP Conference, pp. 464–471 (2011)
12. Thomas, D.W.P., Christopoulos, C., Tang, Y., Gale, P., Stokoe, J.: Single-ended travelling wave fault location scheme based on wavelet analysis. In: Eighth IEE International Conference on Developments in Power System Protection, 5–8 April 2004, vol. 1, pp. 196–199 (2004)
13. Shu, H., Tian, X., Dong, J., et al.: Single end traveling wave location of cable based on fault characteristic frequency band and TT transform. Proc. CSEE **36**(22), 103–112 (2013)
14. Wilson, R.E.: Uses of precise time and frequency in power systems. Department of Engineering, Idaho University, Moscow, ID. Proceedings of the IEEE Publication, vol. 79, 7, July 1991
15. Wang, Y.: Study on electromagnetic Transient Analysis of Transmission Line Fault Model and Application of traveling wave Ranging. Kunming University of Science and Technology (2008)

16. Zhao, W., Song, Y.H., Chen, W.R.: Improved GPS travelling wave fault locator for power cables by using wavelet analysis. Int. J. Electr. Power Energy Syst. 23(5), 403–411 (2001)
17. Huang, J., Zhi, X.: Single terminal traveling wave ranging method for mixed lines in distribution network. Autom. Electr. Power Syst. (2009)
18. Xiangjun, K., Liu, Z., Yin, X.: Fault location using traveling wave for power networks. In: 39th IEEE IAS Annual Meeting, vol. 4, pp. 2426–2429 (2004)
19. Maesong, Gao, H., Xu, B., et al.: Power System Protection and Control (11), 6 (2009)
20. Rajendra, S., McLaren, P.G.: Traveling-wave techniques applied to protection of teed circuits: principle of traveling wave techniques. IEEE Trans PAS 104, 3544–3550 (1985)
21. Yang, Y.: Research on Fault Location of Distribution Network. South China University of Technology (2013)
22. da Silva, M., Oleskovicz, M., Coury, D.V.: A fault locator for three-terminal lines based on wavelet transform applied to synchronized current and voltage signals. In: Transmission and Distribution Conference and Exposition: TDC 2006, pp.1–6. IEEE/PES August 2006
23. Liu, J., Zhang, Z., Huang, W., et al.: Electr. Power Constr. 36(1), 115–121 (2015). (in Chinese)
24. Niazy, I., Sadeh, J.: A new single ended fault location algorithm for combined transmission line considering fault clearing transients without using line parameters. Electr. Power Energy Syst. 44 (2013)
25. Li, X.: Research and realization of fault location of 10 kV distribution network. Chenghua (12), 1 (2020)
26. Alanzi, E.A., Younis, M.A.: A new faulted phase identification technique for overhead distribution system. Comput. Eng. Intell. Syst. 3 (2012)
27. Ji, T., Sun, T., Xue, Y., et al.: Current situation and prospect of distribution network fault location technology. Relay 33(024), 32–37 (2005)
28. Elhaffar, A.M.: Power transmission line fault location based on current traveling waves. In: ESPOO (2008)

Unikernel and Advanced Container Support in the Socker Tool

Abdulrahman Azab[(⊠)]

Division of Research Computing, University Center for Information Technology,
University of Oslo, Oslo, Norway
azab@uio.no

Abstract. Linux containers, with the build-once-run-anywhere approach, are becoming popular among scientific communities for software
packaging and sharing. Docker is the most popular and user friendly platform for running and managing Linux containers. Unikernels are single-
application fully virtualised lightweight packages designed to run as virtual machines. For some applications, unikernels can be alternative to
containers due to the benefits they provide in terms of performance and
security. presents an update for SOCKER, a wrapper for running Docker
containers on Slurm that enforces running unpriviliges containers within
Slurm jobs. The update to SOCKER includes: Improved security, MPI
support, and support for OSv unikernels.

1 Introduction

Sharing of software tools is an essential demand among scientists and researchers
in order to reproduce results. Virtual machines (VMs) are widely adopted as a
software packaging method for sharing collections of tools, e.g. BioLinux [1].
Each VM contains its own operating system. A VM monitor, also known as
hypervisor, is the platform for managing and monitoring VMs. VM technology
is suitable for packaging collections of tools that run independently or depen-
dently on the top of a specific OS platform, e.g. a GUI that runs python and
R tools on the top of Ubuntu Linux. VMs are also effective in cases where a
specific Linux kernel or Windows OS is needed, the cases in which, Linux containers cannot be used as a solution. Linux containerisation is an operating
system level virtualisation technology that offers lightweight virtualisation. An
application that runs as a container has its own root filesystem, but shares the
kernel with the host operating system. This has many advantages over virtual
machines. First, containers are much less resource consuming since there are no
guest OS. Second, a container process is visible on the host operating system,
which gives the opportunity to system administrators for monitoring and controlling the behaviour of container processes. Linux containers are monitored
and managed by a container engine which is responsible for initiating, managing, and allocating containers. Docker [2] is the most popular platform among
users and IT centres for Linux containerisation. A software tool can be packaged

M. Qiu et al. (Eds.): SmartCom 2021, LNCS 13202, pp. 508–512, 2022.
https://doi.org/10.1007/978-3-030-97774-0_47

as a Docker image and pushed to the Docker public repository, Docker hub, for sharing. A Docker image can run as a container on any system that has a valid Linux kernel. HPC targeted platforms, e.g. Singularity [3] and Sarus [4], make it possible to use Docker containers in production for HPC systems. Unikernels are lightweight single application operating systems developed for the cloud, edge computing, Internet of Things, etc. They fit into small images, have low memory foot-print, and boot in less than one second. They are known for accelerating the execution of programs and improving throughput of network applications. This technology has proven its qualities for these domains with numerous platforms and publications [5–8]. Figure 1 describes an architectural comparison between containers, traditional VMs and unikernels.

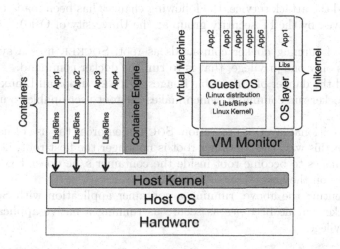

Fig. 1. Architectural view: containers vs traditionals VMs vs unikernels

This paper presents an update of SOCKER [9], a wrapper for running lightweight virtualised workload on Slurm [10]. SOCKER has been initially developed as a secure wrapper for the Docker engine [2]. The new update resolves security issues and enables running containerised workload as well as Unikernels.

2 Architecture

SOCKER is a wrapper that uses the underlying runtime to manage and run lightweight virtualtised workloads on Slurm. It enforces running OCI [11] containers through the docker engine but as the actual user in addition to enforcing the membership of a running container inside a SLURM job in the cgroups assigned by SLURM to the job. Primary testing has been performed as a proof of concept [9], and SOCKER introduces almost no additional overhead to containerised workloads.

2.1   Security Improvements

During security evaluation of, the following attack surface has been found:

- SOCKER is a wrapper which runs with SUID privilege. Bugs in the code might give root privileges to the user.
- SOCKER forces the container to run as the user, by enforcing the `--user` option of the docker run command. This option will not prevent a vulnerable image from attacking the system. A typical use case is a Docker image with a section in the sudoers file to grant sudo rights to a specific UID
- On the other hand, SOCKER does its job well forcing the container to consume only the CPU and memory resources assigned by Slurm to the container job.

To avoid the attack service, the following changes has been made to SOCKER (and approved by the IT security group at the University of Oslo):

- Instead of running docker commands as root, SOCKER uses a system user that has only one privilege, that is to run the docker command.
- To avoid the danger of vulnerable images, SOCKER drops all Linux privileges in the docker run command, which makes the root user unable to use all root privileges.
- As an additional layer of protection, SOCKER enforces the use of user namespaces. In this way, the container root is no longer the host root, i.e. even if a user manages to become root inside the container s/he doesn't get any root privileges on the host
- Implementing the above, running a container application with SOCKER on the Docker engine becomes as secure as running a native application with user privileges.

The new SOCKER architecture, depicted in Fig. 2, describe the support for OCI containers as well as Osv unikernel applications.

2.2   MPI Support

SOCKER doesn't offer implicit MPI support so far. It can be used with MPI by doing the following:

- Install MPI (and IB drivers if any) on the host
- Use a Docker container with MPI supporting application (and the IB driver installed if any)
- Run SOCKER with MPI as:
  ```
  mpiexec -np <N> socker run -e LD_LIBRARY_PATH=/usr/lib <app>
  <args>
  ```

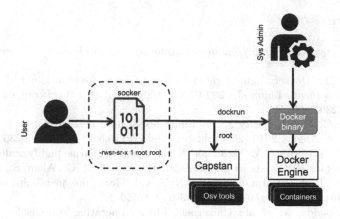

Fig. 2. SOCKER architecture

2.3 Unikernels Support

Similar to containers unikernels offer lightweight virtualization. In addition, they offer advantages over containers:

- *Reduced system-calls:* Containers share the kernel with the host. In recent Linux versions, There are more than 400 system calls [12], which respresent a huge attack serface. System calls in unikernels become common function calls. Unikernels reduces system call latency of two to three orders of magnitude [13].
- *Reduced kernel noise:* Since unikernels include only the necessary software in addition to the application itself, i.e. no background software included, Kernel noise is kept minimum [14].

As shown in Fig. 1 SOCKER supports running OSv [6] unikernel images via the Capstan tool [15]. OSv is the versatile modular unikernel, developed from scratch by Cloudius, and designed to run Linux applications on lightweight VMs. is a libc-level binary-compatible unikernel that interfaces with the application at runtime using the standard libc API level.

3 Conclusions

SOCKER is a wrapper that uses the underlying runtime to manage and run lightweight virtualtised workloads on Slurm. It consumes the Docker engine to enforce running unprivileged OCI containers. The paper presents several improvements to SOCKER, including: security improvements reducing the attack surface for running containers, support for MPI containers, and support for OSv based unikernels.

Acknowledgements. This work was financially supported by the PRACE-6IP project [16] funded in part by the EU's Horizon 2020 Research and Innovation programme (2014–2020) under grant agreement 823767.

References

1. bio-linux overview. http://environmentalomics.org/bio-linux/. Accessed 21 May 2016
2. Merkel, D.: Docker: lightweight Linux containers for consistent development and deployment. Linux J. **2014**(239) (2014). http://dl.acm.org/citation.cfm?id=2600239.2600241
3. Kurtzer, G.M.: Singularity 2.1.2 - Linux application and environment containers for science, August 2016 (2016). https://doi.org/10.5281/zenodo.60736
4. Benedicic, L., Cruz, F.A., Madonna, A., Mariotti, K.: Sarus: highly scalable docker containers for HPC systems. In: Weiland, M., Juckeland, G., Alam, S., Jagode, H. (eds.) ISC High Performance 2019. LNCS, vol. 11887, pp. 46–60. Springer, Cham (2019). https://doi.org/10.1007/978-3-030-34356-9_5
5. Madhavapeddy, A., et al.: Unikernels: library operating systems for the cloud. SIGARCH Comput. Archit. News **41**(1), 461–472 (2013). https://doi.org/10.1145/2490301.2451167
6. Kivity, A., et al.: OSv–optimizing the operating system for virtual machines. In: USENIX Annual Technical Conference (USENIX ATC 14), pp. 61–72. USENIX Association, Philadelphia, PA (2014)
7. Kuo, H.-C., Williams, D., Koller, R., Mohan, S.: A Linux in unikernel clothing. In: Proceedings of the Fifteenth European Conference on Computer Systems, pp. 1–15. ACM (2020). https://dl.acm.org/doi/10.1145/3342195.3387526
8. Kuenzer, S., et al.: Unikraft: fast, specialized unikernels the easy way. In: Proceedings of the Sixteenth European Conference on Computer Systems, pp. 376–394. ACM (2021). https://dl.acm.org/doi/10.1145/3447786.3456248
9. Azab, A.: Socker: a wrapper for secure running of docker containers on slurm. https://github.com/unioslo/socker. Accessed 01 Dec 2016
10. Yoo, A.B., Jette, M.A., Grondona, M.: SLURM: simple Linux utility for resource management. In: Feitelson, D., Rudolph, L., Schwiegelshohn, U. (eds.) JSSPP 2003. LNCS, vol. 2862, pp. 44–60. Springer, Heidelberg (2003). https://doi.org/10.1007/10968987_3
11. Open Container Initiative. https://opencontainers.org/. Accessed 24 Dec 2021
12. Tsai, C.-C., Jain, B., Abdul, N.A., Porter, D.E.: A study of modern Linux API usage and compatibility: what to support when you're supporting. In: Proceedings of the Eleventh European Conference on Computer Systems, pp. 1–16 (2016)
13. Olivier, P., Chiba, D., Lankes, S., Min, C., Ravindran, B.: A binary-compatible unikernel. In: Proceedings of the 15th ACM SIGPLAN/SIGOPS International Conference on Virtual Execution Environments - VEE 2019, pp. 59–73. ACM Press (2019). http://dl.acm.org/citation.cfm?doid=3313808.3313817
14. Lankes, S., Pickartz, S., Breitbart, J.: HermitCore: a unikernel for extreme scale computing. In: Proceedings of the 6th International Workshop on Runtime and Operating Systems for Supercomputers, pp. 1–8. ACM (2016). https://dl.acm.org/doi/10.1145/2931088.2931093
15. Capstan: a command-line tool for rapidly running application on OSv unikernel. https://github.com/cloudius-systems/capstan. Accessed 24 Dec 2021
16. Partnership for advanced computing in Europe. http://www.prace-project.eu. Accessed 16 Oct 2019

Author Index

Printed in the United States
by Baker & Taylor Publisher Services

Printed in the United States
by Baker & Taylor Publisher Services